A VOYAGE AROUND
THE QUEEN

A VOYAGE AROUND THE QUEEN

CRAIG BROWN

4th ESTATE • *London*

4th Estate
An imprint of HarperCollins*Publishers*
1 London Bridge Street
London SE1 9GF

www.4thestate.co.uk

HarperCollins*Publishers*
Macken House, 39/40 Mayor Street Upper
Dublin 1, D01 C9W8, Ireland

First published in Great Britain in 2024 by 4th Estate

2

A catalogue record for this book is
available from the British Library

ISBN 978-0-00-855749-2 (hardback)
ISBN 978-0-00-855750-8 (trade paperback)

Set in Minion Pro
Printed and bound in the UK using 100%
renewable electricity at CPI Group (UK) Ltd

'One does what one is; one becomes what one does.'

Robert Musil

'It's you they want to meet. But it's themselves
they want to talk about.'

Cyril Connolly

'Without their crowns and coronets, how could the English
be distinguished from Icelanders?'

John Updike

1

The *London Gazette*
21 April 1926

Her Royal Highness The Duchess of York was safely delivered of a Princess at 17, Bruton Street, Mayfair.

His Royal Highness The Duke of York and the Countess of Strathmore were present. Secretary William Joynson-Hicks was also present. Her Royal Highness and the Infant Princess are doing perfectly well.

The happy event was made known by the firing of the Park and Tower guns.

2

Also born in April 1926 were Hugh Hefner, J. P. Donleavy, Harper Lee and Ian Paisley; and, that same year, Miles Davis, Fidel Castro, Michel Foucault, Chuck Berry, Marilyn Monroe and David Attenborough.

Claude Monet died in 1926, and so did Harry Houdini, Rudolph Valentino, Rainer Maria Rilke and Annie Oakley.

New songs that year included 'Are You Lonesome Tonight?', 'Bye Bye Blackbird', 'Tiptoe Through the Tulips' and 'Someone to Watch Over Me'.

The television was invented in 1926, and so were the aerosol can, the electric lawn mower, the bulldozer, the combine harvester, cellophane and traffic lights.

Among the words and expressions first chronicled in 1926 were 'Bible belt', 'business lunch', 'car park', 'kitsch', 'market research', 'pop song', 'publicity stunt', 'recycle', 'sugar daddy' and 'totalitarian'.

3

A few days after my mother's death in the spring of 2023, I was sorting through cupboards when I came across a navy-blue leather photograph album, filled with old black-and-white photographs of soldiers marching, crowds waving, dignitaries standing in line, and the 25-year-old Princess Elizabeth smiling and shaking hands. What was it doing there?

On the first page, handwritten in navy-blue ink, italic script, with the capital letters finished off in red and gold, was this:

On Thursday 21 June 1951 the Old Colours
of the Third Battalion Grenadier Guards were laid
up in Manchester Cathedral in the presence of
Her Royal Highness The Princess Elizabeth –
Duchess of Edinburgh – Colonel of the Regiment.

This pictorial record is sent to Mrs Moncrieff Brown
by the President of the Manchester Branch
Grenadier Guards Comrades Association
as a happy reminder of a memorable occasion.

Mrs Moncrieff Brown was my grandmother. Thirteen full-page photographs charted the young Princess's progress through Manchester on that day, three-quarters of a century ago: her arrival at London Road station; the parade of Grenadier Guards leaving the police headquarters en route to the Cathedral, via Albert Square, Piccadilly and Market Street; the arrival of Her Royal Highness at the Cathedral; the lord mayor in all his finery presenting her to the sub-dean, the bishop of Middleton and the lord bishop of Manchester; the March Past at Albert Square; and the Salute outside the Town Hall, through to the Presentations.

Under the heading 'Presentations', a photograph shows the Princess passing along a line of men and women. Those she has just spoken to look a good deal more relaxed than those she is about to speak to.

And there, two along from Mr C. G. S. Pigott, Hon. Sec. Manchester Branch Comrades Association, whom the Princess seems to be addressing, and his wife, named sparely as Mrs Pigott, is my grandmother, 'Mrs G. Moncrieff Brown'.

I remember her as an old lady, sharp and delightful, always at hand with treats, like Crunchie bars and Kit-Kats. She could play the ukulele, and was skilled with her hands, sewing fancy little toy mice dressed in their Sunday best, which, in the early 1970s, were on display in a glass

cabinet in the Imperial Hotel Torquay, and for sale in a gift shop on a cobbled street opposite Windsor Castle.

What was she doing there in Manchester, being presented to Princess Elizabeth on Thursday, 21 June 1951? In the photograph, she is looking down the line towards Mr C. G. S. Pigott, with a smile. She was born in 1892, so back then she would have been 59 years old, but compared to most of the dumpy, severe women in the surrounding photographs, she looks to me much younger, dainty and elegant in her exotic headdress.

I never knew her husband, my grandfather Andrew Moncrieff Brown. He killed himself in 1940, when he was barely fifty. His two sons, my father Peter and his brother Ian, were away at the war. My father told me that my grandfather was a demanding man, unforgiving towards waiters, often drunk and prone to great rages. Over dinner, he would regularly pick a fight with my grandmother before storming off, slamming the door behind him. On the night of 1 September 1940, he embarked on another of his perennial tantrums and stormed off, slamming the door, leaving my grandmother alone at the table. The silence was broken by a gunshot. Seconds later, my grandfather staggered back into the dining room, blood gushing from his stomach. He managed to splutter, 'Now look what you've made me do.' They were his last words. When my father was given the news by his commanding officer, he collapsed.

In the First World War, Andrew Moncrieff Brown had been a cavalry officer in the Grenadier Guards, riding a horse into battle while brandishing a sword. In the 1990s, my father gave my little son that sword. It still sits on a shelf in its battered leather sheath.

My father's elder brother Ian had followed his father into the Grenadier Guards. Three years after my grandfather's suicide, on 10 September 1943, I. A. Moncrieff Brown, Second Lieutenant, 6th Battalion, Grenadier Guards, service number 130875, son of Andrew Moncrieff Brown and Gwendoline Mary Brown, was killed in combat at Salerno at the age of 26. He is buried in the war cemetery at Salerno. Within the space of three years, my father had lost both his father and his brother. He was still only 23.

No one in human history lived a more chronicled life than the Queen.* We can chart her movements, on an almost daily basis, from the moment she was born to the moment she died. There was barely a week in her ninety-six years when she was not photographed, often by hundreds or even thousands of people. In no time at all we can find out where she was and what she was doing on just about any day in her long, long life. We know who her great-great-great-great-great-great-grandparents were, their characters and habits, their successes and failures, their likes and dislikes, the rumours surrounding them. We know her cousins and her sister and her uncles and her aunts. We know her children, and their children, and their children, and many of us hold strong opinions about this one or that. Like it or not – like them or not – the Royal Family are under our skin.

Much of the late Queen's life was filmed for public consumption. With my grandmother's photo album in front of me, all I have to do is tap a few words on a keyboard and up pops a Pathé News Special on Princess Elizabeth's visit to Manchester on 21 June 1951.

Princess Elizabeth alights from her train, smiling, her hand already outstretched, ready for the shaking.

'Greeted by the Lord Lieutenant, Lord Derby, Princess Elizabeth arrives in Manchester for one of the most colourful spectacles seen in the city for years!' exclaims the Pathé commentator in his clipped

---

* Just to warn you: from now on, I will usually refer to her as the Queen, rather than Princess Elizabeth, or Queen Elizabeth II, or Elizabeth, or Her Majesty. The names of the Royal Family chop and change, making things particularly hazardous for biographers, especially those, like me, who are not doggedly chronological. They sometimes take over each other's names, too. For example, the Queen's youngest child was born Prince Edward in 1964, and subsequently became the Earl of Wessex (1999–2019) and the Earl of Wessex and Forfar (2019–23). In 2023 he transformed into the Duke of Edinburgh, the name of his late father. At this point, his son James, previously known as Viscount Severn, became the Earl of Wessex and Forfar. I realise that this footnote is beginning to read like the instructions to an impossible boardgame. Up to her accession in 1952, the Queen was Princess Elizabeth, and her mother was Queen Elizabeth; after it, Princess Elizabeth became Queen Elizabeth and her mother became Queen Elizabeth the Queen Mother, or the Queen Mother for short. As no narrative can withstand such a muddle of toing and froing, for simplicity's sake I plan to stick with their most familiar names: the Queen, the Queen Mother, Prince Philip, Prince Charles, Prince Edward and so forth. If ever I break my own rules, it will be only for simplicity's sake.

voice. 'With the Lord Mayor, she leaves for Manchester Cathedral, where the 3rd Battalion, the Grenadier Guards are to lay out their old colours!'

We watch her walk along the platform accompanied by a man in tails, holding his top hat behind him. Grandees follow them at a discreet distance, medals pinned to their lapels. They pass slightly tattered Union Jacks, draped here and there along the platform, possibly covering up something unsightly.

The film cuts to a marching band in their uniforms and busbies parading through the city centre, followed by more soldiers with raised bayonets. Jubilant crowds cheer.

'The detachment is accompanied by the Manchester branch of the Grenadier Guards Old Comrades Association!' explains the commentator. He speaks in a series of exclamations. 'The Princess, who is a Colonel of the Grenadiers, recently presented new colours to the 3rd Battalion on behalf of the King!'

We are now outside Manchester Cathedral. The Princess is shaking hands with senior clerics, including the Lord Bishop of Manchester and the Bishop of Middleton. A man with a chain of office, in a big fluffy hat and a coat fringed with ermine, glances at his little notepad, taking care to get their names and titles right before presenting them.

'And now, before the town hall, their old colours safely laid up, the Grenadiers march past their Colonel!'

The marching band plays 'The British Grenadiers'. Like many schoolboys of the 1960s, I still have the words in my head:

> Some talk of Alexander, and some of Hercules
> Of Hector and Lysander, and such great names as these.
> But of all the world's brave heroes, there's none that can compare.
> With a tow, row, row, row, row, row, to the British Grenadiers!

Men in flat caps and suits and ties gaze at the Princess; stocky old women with floral hats wave hankies and cheer. When did crowds stop waving their handkerchiefs? It was a strange tradition, when you come to think of it – though altogether friendlier than our contemporary practice of shielding our faces with iPhones.*

'By entrusting their old colours to the safekeeping of Manchester Cathedral, the 3rd Grenadiers mark their close association between the Regiment and the city!'

Men in suits and trilbies march proudly in serried columns behind the soldiers, their chests stacked with medals.

'From this area, it draws more recruits than from any other outside London! The Grenadiers know where to look for good men when they want them!'

The Pathé News report on YouTube finishes there, but the last photograph in my grandmother's album takes the story a little further: 'Lord and Lady Derby Say Farewell to Her Royal Highness at London Road Station'.

The Princess stands at the open window of a railway carriage, ready to depart. Perhaps she looks a little too happy.

I assume that my grandmother was invited to join the group of bigwigs presented to Her Royal Highness because she was the widow of one Grenadier officer and the bereaved mother of another. Perhaps she was on some committee or other. I should know, just as I should know a hundred other things about her. Where was she living at the time? Eleven years after her husband's suicide, had she married again? We always knew her as Granny Lane, because she had at some point married a man called Lane, whose Christian name none of us can remember. What happened to Lane? As children, we never saw him. Perhaps he was already dead by the time we came along, in the late 1950s. I remember my mother telling me that he was a wanderer, and that, one day, he just wandered off, leaving my grandmother alone.

I know that my grandmother's maiden name was Sidebotham: it's a name we always found funny. She once joked with us – at least I think

---

* The Queen told the US ambassador, Matthew Barzun, in 2013, 'There have always been tourists and they always used to have regular cameras. They'd put them up, take a picture, and then put them down. Now they put these things up and they never take them down. And I miss seeing their eyes.'

it was a joke – that her parents pronounced it 'Sidday-b'tome'. Ancestry. com informs me that she was born on 1 March 1892 in Bowdon, Cheshire, that her father was Edward John Sidebotham, also born in Bowdon, Cheshire, 1860–1929, and that her mother was Benedicta Mary Adams, born in Bodmin, Cornwall, 1869–1956. But that's as far as it goes. I don't know what my great-grandparents did, or what they looked like, or how they managed to meet, given that one was from Cornwall and the other from Cheshire. In fact, I know nothing of them but their names.

Of Queen Elizabeth II's great-grandparents, on the other hand, I know plenty. Her great-grandfather was King Edward VII, the rakish son of Queen Victoria, who found him irritating ('Alas! I feel very sad and anxious about him: he is so idle and weak,' she wrote in her journal in 1858, when he was seventeen). For one reason or another, I have read two biographies of Edward VII over the years: one, by Giles St Aubyn, of 555 pages, and the other, by Jane Ridley, of 608 pages. Edward VII married the steadfast Princess Alexandra of Denmark,* subject of at least three biographies.† I have also read three biographies of his son, the Queen's grandfather, King George V, by Harold Nicolson, Kenneth Rose and Jane Ridley, and they are all well written, but a total of 1,643 pages serves only to make it clear that he was one of the stuffiest men who ever lived. Harold Nicolson was his authorised biographer and tackled the task with great skill, but even he found him dreary. 'For seventeen years he did nothing at all but kill animals and stick in stamps,' he complained to his diary. George V was singularly lacking in curiosity and empathy. His life was full of drama, but it left no emotional mark. For instance, in 1898, his wife, Queen Mary,

---

* For whom the Poet Laureate, Alfred, Lord Tennyson, wrote this welcoming ode, perhaps not his finest:

> Sea King's daughter from over the sea,
> Alexandra!
> Saxon and Norman and Dane are we,
> But all of us Danes in our welcome of thee,
> Alexandra!

† None of which I have read, unfortunately.

launched a battleship on the Thames at Blackwall, and it all went horribly wrong: a platform collapsed, and 200 spectators were swept into the river. Writing up his diary that evening, King George V mentioned the incident, but only as an afterthought. 'I am afraid over 30 were drowned. Got home at 4.15.'

King George V was born in 1865, twenty-five years before my grandfather, and died in 1936, just four years before him. It seems shameful that I should know so much about King George V and so little about my own grandfather. The same goes for my mother. She was born a fortnight after Princess Margaret, but I know much more about Princess Margaret's childhood and youth – her nannies, her pets, her boyfriends, her relationship with her parents – than I do about my mother's. And I know more about the Queen's children than I do about my own siblings, though we are roughly their ages: in fact my two younger brothers are exactly the same ages as Prince Andrew and Prince Edward. I know, for instance, how the Windsor children got on at their various schools, and the exams they took, and their favourite books and television programmes, and what makes them laugh, and their various girlfriends and boyfriends and their opinions on everything from architecture to sex. I have watched them losing their tempers and listened in on their sexually explicit phone calls. Thanks to reading a biography by Gyles Brandreth, I can even tell you whether Prince Charles was breast-fed (yes) and whether he was circumcised (yes, on 20 December 1948, by a Dr Snowman).

But in few of these areas could I answer questions about my own siblings. There are even times when I wonder if I know more about the Queen and her family than I do about myself. What was I doing on a given day in, say, 1968 or 1979 or 1994? What did I do last year, or last month? I can easily find out what the Queen or Prince Charles or Meghan Markle got up to, but my own activities have left scarcely a trace. And I know their faces better than my own, as I see them more often. If I glimpsed myself in profile across a crowded room would I recognise who it was? Possibly not. But I would certainly recognise, say, Princess Anne, or Princess Anne's daughter, or Princess Anne's daughter's husband.

This distribution of attention is absurd, but it is something we must learn to live with. Henry 'Chips' Channon* noted our national obsession with royalty when he was watching the unveiling of a statue of King George V. Though the ceremony was over in twenty minutes, it was followed by 'that interminable pause whilst the Royalties greeted each other, interkissed and chatted. It is only in England that a crowd of several thousands can stand happily in the rain and watch one family gossip.'

When King George V died at the start of 1936, the left-wing editor of the *New Statesman*, Kingsley Martin, was struck by the ubiquity of grief. 'No one who talked to his neighbour on a bus, to the charwoman washing the steps or to a sightseer standing at the street corner, could doubt the almost universal feeling of loss, nor could any perceptive observer fail to notice the peculiarly personal character of this emotion,' he wrote. 'People who had never seen the king and only heard his voice on the wireless talked about him as if he were a personal friend or a near relative cut off in his prime.' And this grief extended across the world. Virginia Woolf noted in her diary, with a touch of hyperbole: 'The people of America are in mourning as if for their own King, and the Japanese are in tears.'

In the same way, many people around the world who never met Princess Diana shed tears at her death. Some of them had been dry-eyed at deaths in their own families. I remember meeting friends in a pub the evening after that fatal crash. Though the pub was full, I was struck by its whispery, funereal atmosphere. At one point, my group was laughing about something else entirely and a voice from another table barked, 'Have you NO RESPECT?!'

When the Queen died, a quarter of a century later, even some committed anti-monarchists found themselves moved. Their tears seemed to contradict their beliefs, and they were baffled by this contradiction. But others remained defiantly unmoved. The protesters at the ceremonies in the days after the Queen's death would probably have

---

* Henry 'Chips' Channon (1897–1958), gossipy Chicago-born politician, diarist and socialite, heir to a shipping fortune.

agreed with Engels, who regarded monarchism as a 'loathsome cult'; he deplored the psychological confusion that transforms ubiquity into devotion.

'Is monarchy a suitable institution for a grown-up nation?' asked Hilary Mantel, chronicler of the Tudors, before replying to her own question: 'I don't know.'

4

Anne Frank was born in 1929. She was a year older than Princess Margaret and three years younger than Princess Elizabeth, who was the same age as Anne's sister Margot.

For her thirteenth birthday, on 12 June 1942, Anne's father, Otto Frank, gave her a red-and-white chequered autograph book, which she immediately used as a diary. She hoped this diary would one day act as a testament to the privations families like hers had endured through the days of Nazism. She was ambitious: she wrote in her diary that she dreamt of becoming a journalist, 'and later on a famous writer'.

Five days before Anne was given this birthday present, Princess Elizabeth had confided her own hopes and fears to her friend Alathea Fitzalan Howard, who jotted them down in her own diary: 'She said she wondered if she'd ever marry, and I assured her she would, and she said if she really wanted to marry someone she'd run away, but I know she wouldn't really – her sense of duty's too strong, though she's suited to a simpler life.' Alathea then added, 'But tonight I learned to know a new Lilibet: I saw behind the outward calm and matter of factness into something lovable and sincere.'

A month after Anne began writing her diary, on 6 July 1942, the Frank family – Anne and her elder sister Margot, together with their mother and father – went into hiding from the Nazis. For the next two years and thirty days, they were to remain in the small attic annexe of Prinsengracht 263, in central Amsterdam, unable to venture outside, or even to look out of a window, for fear of being seen.

Anne immediately set to work decorating the bedroom she shared with Margot. 'Thanks to Father – who brought my entire post-card and movie-star collection here beforehand – and to a brush and a pot of glue, I was able to plaster the walls with pictures. It looks much more cheerful.' Among these pictures were two little black-and-white photographs: one of Princess Elizabeth and the other of Princess Margaret. They were symbols of hope: Britain was free, and so were the little Princesses.

'Yesterday, as you've probably already discovered, was our Führer's fifty-fifth birthday. Today is the eighteenth birthday of Her Royal Highness Princess Elizabeth of York,' Anne wrote in her diary on 21 April 1944, nearly two years into her time in the annexe. 'The BBC reported that she hasn't yet been declared of age, though royal children usually are. We've been wondering which prince they'll marry this beauty off to, but can't think of a suitable candidate; perhaps her sister, Princess Margaret Rose, can have Crown Prince Baudouin of Belgium!'

In the rest of her entry for that day, Anne chronicled the progress of her sore throat, her boredom, the theft of some of the family's flour provision and her hope of selling one of her fairy tales to a magazine, 'under a pseudonym, of course'.

She pinned an old school map to the wall. Things were looking up: listening each night to the BBC on her wireless, she charted the line of the Allied advance. The war might be over in months, even weeks. On 21 July 1944, she wrote in her diary: 'Now I am getting really hopeful. Now things are going well at last – yes, really, they're going very well.'

Two weeks later, on the morning of 4 August 1944, the Franks' hiding place was raided by the police. The Franks were led away at gunpoint. Picking up Otto Frank's briefcase, the chief policeman saw a book inside it and threw it to the floor, so as to make room for the small quantity of valuables and money he had found. This was the diary of Anne Frank.

As they were all marched down the stairs, Otto Frank harboured the hope that they might be saved by providence. But it was not to be. The family were transported in freight cars to Auschwitz on the very last train. In November, Anne and her sister Margot were transferred from Auschwitz to Bergen-Belsen. At some time in February or early March 1945, Margot died, followed, the next day, by Anne. A fellow victim witnessed Anne's pitiful end. She had thrown off her clothes, because she could no longer tolerate the lice, and was standing naked but for a blanket. By then, she knew her mother and sister had both perished, and she imagined her father had, too. She just stood there, delirious with typhus. 'It wasn't the same Anne. She was a broken girl.'

Thirty years later, in 1974, Queen Elizabeth II learned that Anne Frank had stuck pictures of her and her sister to her bedroom wall. She wrote to Otto Frank, the sole survivor of the family, expressing the hope that 'perhaps this photograph gave your daughter a moment's pleasure during that dreadful time'.

On 26 June 2015, at the age of 89, the Queen visited Bergen-Belsen concentration camp in northern Germany to commemorate the seventieth anniversary of its liberation by British soldiers. First, she met a small group of survivors and their liberators. Then she walked to the memorial gravestone to Margot Frank, 1926–45, and Anne Frank, 1929–45, and bowed her head in homage.

5

When people looked at the Queen, what did they see?

On one level, the answer is obvious: they saw a living representation of the face they had absorbed, often without noticing, almost every day of their lives: on television, on coins and postcards, in newspapers and books and magazines, online, on walls, in galleries and on stamps.

Those presented to the Queen found the experience discombobulating. Though it may have been the first time they had ever set eyes on her, they were often more familiar with her face than with their own. They knew it in profile; they knew it head-on; they knew it from above and below; they had seen it refracted through the visions of countless artists and photographers. Their memories carried the imprint of what it had been like ten, twenty, forty, eighty years, ninety years before; they could picture her as a child and a baby. Hers was the most familiar, most photographed face in human history. A few tyrants or celebrities – Chairman Mao, the Beatles, Princess Diana, Donald Trump – may have been snapped as often over a given period, but none of them as frequently throughout their lives: in her case, just short of a century. Adolf Hitler, for instance, became a familiar face only in middle age, from his early forties until his death at the age of 56. The Beatles had to wait until they were in their late teens or early twenties. Princess Diana was famous for seventeen of her thirty-six years, from halfway through 1980 to her death in 1997; Gandhi was in his late forties before his face became familiar to the world.

So to meet the Queen face to face was apt to make you feel giddy or woozy, as though a well-loved family portrait, familiar since childhood, handed down from generation to generation, had suddenly sprung to life. For most, the experience was unnerving, even terrifying. In 2005, the Queen visited the opening of the Stubbs exhibition at the National Gallery.* 'Some clever person had reckoned this would be our best shot of getting the Queen into the gallery,' recalls Nicola Shulman, who was a Trustee, 'and they were right, she came. It was a limited affair and we all had to assemble beforehand. I suppose one awkwardness that has been spared her is being the first at a party. While she and Prince Philip went around the show unmolested, we were made to wait outside, in that bit where they sell postcards. Someone came along and divided us into groups of four or five, separated by a few paces: an archipelago of embarrassment. You can imagine what types of people were there: not exactly stammering apprentices. They were Captains of Industry, senior diplomats, heads of FTSE 100 companies, leading architects and so on. And yet as she came towards us you could feel the swell of fear. We were silent with terror, like people on an aeroplane with an engine on fire. And as she left the circle to our right and began to approach, every manjack of my group stepped smartly backwards and stared inquisitively at the floor; leaving me, who had stayed where I was, as the only person who could talk to her. Because they had all scurried away, it left me looking as if I had deliberately thrust myself forward to talk to her.'

She was what we made of her. The First Lady, Michelle Obama, first met the Queen at Buckingham Palace in 2009. 'Sitting with the Queen, I had to will myself out of my own head – to stop processing the splendour of the setting and the paralysis I felt coming face-to-face with an honest-to-goodness icon. I'd seen Her Majesty's face dozens of times before, in history books, on television, and on currency, but here she was in the flesh, looking at me intently and asking questions.'

A friend of mine, a magazine editor, was asked to one of the Queen's regular 'informal' lunches for distinguished people from different walks of life. As he was ushered in, a senior courtier suggested that he

---

* George Stubbs (1724–1826) is widely regarded as the greatest painter of horses, though it would irk him to read this. ''Tis said that nought so much the temper rubs / Of that ingenious artist, Mr Stubbs / As calling him a horse-painter,' wrote his contemporary, the satirist Peter Pindar.

might care to spend a penny. When he said he didn't think it necessary, the courtier advised him it was best to be on the safe side: one or two previous guests had 'had an accident' upon being presented.

The comic novelist Kingsley Amis was invited to one such lunch in 1975. 'He had been terrified for days about the unpremeditated fart or belch and was on a strict non-bean-and-onion diet,' one of his oldest friends, Robert Conquest, gossiped sneakily to another, Philip Larkin. His fear reignited itself fifteen years later. Before going to Buckingham Palace to receive a knighthood, Amis grew so frightened of defecating in front of the Queen that, in the words of his son Martin, he 'had his doctor lay down a firewall of Omidium,* and there was some doubt, afterwards, whether he would ever again go to the toilet'.

---

* Amis must surely have meant Imodium, taken to prevent diarrhoea.

Another eminent man of letters – sophisticated, posh, loosely republican – accepted an invitation to one of the Queen's informal lunches with his usual worldly mix of curiosity and condescension. Over the course of his life, he had met Marlene Dietrich, Jackie Kennedy, Dame Rebecca West ... why on earth should he feel any different about meeting Her Majesty? But the moment the Queen arrived he turned to jelly. 'Suddenly I felt physically ill. My legs felt weak, my head swam and my mind went totally blank. "So you're writing about such-and-such?" said the Queen. I had no idea what I was writing about, or even if I was writing a book at all. All I could think of to say was, "What a pretty brooch you're wearing, ma'am." So far as I can recall she was not wearing a brooch at all. Presumably she was used to such imbecility; anyway, she paid no attention to my babbling ... I have never felt like that before. I hope that I never do again. I would not have believed that I could have reacted in such a way.'

Perhaps she was less a painting, more a mirror. With her interior world screened from public view, and her conversation restricted by protocol to questions not answers, she became a human looking-glass: the light cast by fame bounced off her, and back on to those she faced. To the optimist, she seemed an optimist; to the pessimist, a pessimist. To the insider, she appeared intimate, to the outsider, distant; to the cynic, prosaic, and to the awestruck, charismatic. Having sat next to her at a banquet in Buckingham Palace in 1956, the Soviet general secretary Nikita Khrushchev came away with the impression that she was 'the sort of young woman you'd be likely to meet walking along Gorky Street on a balmy summer afternoon'.

Sometimes, people would recognise in her not themselves but a close relation: a mother, sister, aunt or grandmother. Reading a newspaper story about the Queen's humdrum daily habits, the forthright Australian republican Germaine Greer immediately thought of her own mother, and the two became melded in her mind. 'Her Majesty watches telly while she eats, and she eats, apparently, five times a day, just like an old lady in a care home. Like an old lady in a care home, although she is given food at prescribed hours, she often doesn't eat it ... The Queen watches *EastEnders* and *The Bill*, when she could watch absolutely anything she chose, but she does not choose. Just like my mother in her aged care facility.'*

When people spoke of her, they spoke of themselves, and when they dreamt of her, they dreamt of themselves. She was a window into their hopes and anxieties. 'Princess Elizabeth and Philip are back in town, and across the street tonight,' wrote the troubled young suspense writer Patricia Highsmith, staying in Rome on the night of 19 April 1951. 'Traffic bottlenecked & everyone angry & bewildered.'

The words the Queen spoke often seemed, as if by magic, to vanish into the air. Afterwards, those she encountered could remember only what they had said, and how they had behaved: the Queen's words would evaporate, leaving her subjects with memories only of themselves. A member of the Palace staff used to enjoy eavesdropping on those who had just received honours. 'They would be properly attired in morning dress, with wives or close relations waiting for them. The first question always would be: "What did she say to you?" and the answer generally: "I can't remember." It fascinated me how people are struck dumb in her presence ... The person meeting her is generally so busy taking in her appearance and being mesmerised by her quite beautiful eyes that every other thought flies from his or her head.' In their memoirs, successive prime ministers have written about their weekly meetings with her, but, even allowing for the demands of discretion, most have only the haziest recollection of anything she ever said. It is almost as though she were a mirage.

'She's the only person in this country who I can talk to about anything, because she's not after my job,' the ever-wary prime minister Harold Wilson said of her. His wife Mary, quieter and more private, once wrote a poem about the quietness and the privacy:

> Walking free upon her own estate,
> Still in her solitude, she is the Queen.

---

* Greer has portrayed her mother, Peggy, as an unstable, impatient woman who once, in a fit of rage, pulled the cord of a toaster out of its socket and whipped her daughter with it. Yet toasters in all the Royal residences remain intact.

After the US president Ronald Reagan and his wife had enjoyed dinner and an overnight stay on the Royal Yacht *Britannia* in 1983, Nancy came away convinced that she and the Queen were as alike as two new pins. 'It was not the Queen and first lady but two mothers and wives talking about their lives, mostly our children,' she recalled. Yet it is hard to imagine the Queen swapping heart-warming stories about Prince Andrew or Princess Anne with the angular First Lady: more likely, Mrs Reagan made the running, and the Queen expressed an appropriate interest ('Oh, really?'). It's like throwing a ball against a wall and catching it: the active participant does the catching and the throwing; the job of the wall is to remain so solid and still that the ball can keep bouncing back.

'The Queen, seated next to Bill, wore a sparkling diamond tiara that caught the light as she nodded and laughed at Bill's stories,' Hillary Clinton recalled of their presidential visit to Buckingham Palace.

To some extent, this was both the Queen's talent and purpose: *to radiate.*

6

Had a drink and dressed, then drove off to Buckingham Palace. A sensational evening. The most lovely sight I have ever seen. Everyone looking shiny and happy; something indestructible. Everybody conceivable was there ... The King and Queen were sweet as always. Talked to Philip and Princess Elizabeth, who looked **radiant**.

Noël Coward, 18 November 1947

After many false alarms, there was a hush, then we all cheered as the royal couple walked into our humble dining hall ... the queen looked quietly **radiant** in a kelly-green princess style coat and hat ... I must say the royal couple is most genial and attractive, with a kind of **radiance** which appeals to me ... I stood within a few feet of the handsome wise-cracking Duke, while the Queen **radiated** quietly.

Sylvia Plath on the Royal Visit to Newnham College,
Cambridge, 24 October 1955

And at the Royal Film Performance, I was presented to the **radiant** young Queen. Elizabeth II is Her Most Gracious Majesty indeed ...

Cecil B. DeMille on the 1956 Royal Film Performance
of *The Ten Commandments*

Gerry Wellington told me how struck he was by the Queen's astonishing **radiance** at the opening of Parliament this morning – her lovely teeth, hair and eyes, and that amazing quality of skin. Then add the wonderful voice and the romance, and you have a deeply moving effect.

Harold Nicolson, 4 November 1952

She is rather serious in her manner, and does not smile much; but when she does it is a lovely **radiant** smile.

Cynthia Gladwyn on the Queen's State Visit to Paris,
14 April 1957

She was positively dazzling, the light so soft gave her an incandescent look. Her eyes flashed like crystal, her teeth dazzling, her smile **radiant**.

Cecil Beaton, soirée at Windsor Castle, 11 April 1972

I said hello to Roger Daltrey and had a bit of a chit-chat with Brian May. One of the lads from Status Quo was there … We were having a whale of a time when, suddenly, the Queen appeared at the far end of the room. She is a tiny figure, hardly more than five feet tall, but she has such presence. How can I put it exactly? She just … **radiates** royalty.

Rob Halford, lead vocalist with Judas Priest, writing of a reception for the music business at Buckingham Palace, 2005

The Queen continues to shrink and is now a smiling, diminutive old lady, **radiant** today.

Sir Roy Strong, Westminster Abbey, March 2015

Liz Truss flew to Balmoral to be anointed by the Queen, who is looking **radiant** but very fragile.

Chris Mullin, former Labour minister, 6 September 2022

7

The first biography of Princess Elizabeth appeared in November 1930, when she was four years old.

The Story of
Princess Elizabeth
TOLD WITH THE SANCTION OF HER PARENTS
by ANNE RING
FORMERLY ATTACHED TO
H.R.H. THE DUCHESS OF YORK'S HOUSEHOLD
With many Photogravures

Like so many of her biographies, *The Story of Princess Elizabeth* suggested a Princess touched by divinity.

'She is the World's best known Baby, and what a delightful thought it is that the Baby herself is unconscious of it!' it began. From that moment on, she is as good as gold. 'Sometimes, of course, she cried a little ... but more often she smiled, thus creating the impression, which nothing has subsequently altered, of being an adorable and a very good Baby.'

The Story of Princess Elizabeth included eyewitness accounts from those lucky enough to have glimpsed this extraordinary infant. 'An admirer of Princess Elizabeth who saw her when she was six or seven weeks old has written of the occasion, "We were taken right upstairs to the nursery at the top of the house ... She is a most darling baby, with fine limbs, and I should think perhaps she will be tall, she has big blue eyes and tiny ears set close to her head, and the whitest skin in the world ... Nurse says she is always good."'

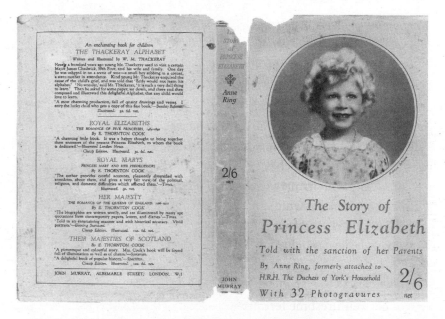

The baby 'grew more beautiful daily, and certainly had no lack of admirers to tell her so. Already Princess Elizabeth was filled with a sense of comfort and well-being and serene courage.' All of this is some time before she has celebrated her first birthday.

When she was just eight months old, the Princess's parents went abroad on a long tour, leaving their baby in the hands of her mother's maid, 'an utterly devoted slave'.

Every afternoon, she would be carried down to see her grandparents, King George V and Queen Mary, 'and the appearance at the door of a very little person in a white gown and fringed sash would be greeted by the Queen's delighted cry of "Here comes the Bambino!"'

Her parents arrived back in Britain six months later, 'richly laden with precious things for the Princess; there were singing canaries and talking parrots, dolls and picture books, carved native models and boxes made of strange woods and curios of all sorts, more indeed than would fill a nursery'. But, thankfully, 'the Princess's Mother is wise; no one knows better than the Duchess of York, whose own childhood was simple yet so happy, that it is neither the number of a child's toys nor their expensiveness which make him happy, and she never allows the Princess to be bewildered with too many toys at once'.

And so it goes on. The four-year-old Princess grows more perfect every day, in every way. 'When Princess Elizabeth's nurse, descending to the Morning Room or the Drawing Room, says in her quiet tones, "I think it is bedtime now, Elizabeth", there are no poutings or protests, just a few last joyous skips and impromptu dance steps, a few last minute laughs at Mummy's delicious bedtime jokes, and then Princess Elizabeth's hand slips into her Nurse's hand, and the two go off gaily together across the deep chestnut pile of the Hall carpet to the accommodating lift, which in two seconds has whisked them up to the familiar dear domain, which is theirs to hold and share.'

Like any child, she loves to play. At her mother's family home, Glamis Castle, she delights in paddling in a burn. 'The Princess, like a wood-elf or a wagtail perched on a grey-green stone and looking up mischievously at her Mother, thrills at the first delicious chill on the soles of her venturesome feet.'

Is she ever naughty? Hardly. On the rare occasion she oversteps the mark, she learns from it. 'Like all children, Princess Elizabeth will sometimes make use of an unexpected phrase or expression she has somewhere overheard. "My goodness!" she remarked one day in the hearing of her Mother, and was at once told that this was not pretty and mustn't be repeated. Princess Elizabeth has therefore since that day carefully guarded her lips against "My goodness!" but, alas, that grown-ups are not all so watchful! It does sometimes occur that Princess Elizabeth hears some grown-up person, who ought to know better, exclaim "My goodness!" then up go her small arms in a gesture of mock amazement, and she presses her palms tightly over her mouth, while her blue eyes are full of roguish laughter.'

The biography of even the most enterprising four-year-old needs bulking up to make it long enough for publication. Anne Ring rises to the challenge with gusto, wrapping hers in layer upon layer of tissuey verbiage. 'Princess Elizabeth on every one of her birthdays received letters from nearly every part of the globe. They are mostly from children like herself, those young admirers, from the small Mamies and Maisies of America writing from Main Streets in obscure home-towns to tell of their dolls and their favourite candies, and to ask hopefully for the Princess's photograph – to youthful British pioneers with Romance astir in their small-boy breasts, who write in large round-hand from the wilds of the Australian Bush, enclosing in their letters the seeds of some queer plant, a flattened sprig of wattle, or the sweet-scented purple-black baronia flower ...'

Like so many biographers of the Royal Family, past and present, she fills pages that might otherwise be blank with clothes, more clothes and yet more clothes: 'Any attempt to chronicle the early life of a Princess would probably be looked upon as hopelessly inadequate without some reference to her clothes. Assuredly, the day will come when Princess Elizabeth will feel what every woman knows, the exquisite thrill of trying on a hat, or of finding a diaphanous butterfly ball gown with its silver shoes, all ready to slip into, on the bed in a firelit bedroom.'

Would *every* woman have known that exquisite thrill? Or were her readers flattered by the author's presumption of their own affluence?

Anne Ring was in fact the pseudonym of Beryl Poignand (1887–1965), who had served as governess to the Princess's mother, Elizabeth Bowes-Lyon, during the First World War.

Described by the Queen Mother's authorised biographer as 'a friend, almost a co-conspirator, throughout Elizabeth's teenage years and an important confidante thereafter', Poignand had been unusually chummy with her bright young charge, and was to remain so for many decades. By the end of 1915, the future Queen Mother, then aged fifteen, had begun to address her governess as 'My Dear Silly Ass', suggesting an unusual level of informality. For everyone else, Elizabeth Bowes-Lyon would maintain her sugary charm, but as a teenager she felt able to sound off to Poignand about the secret frustrations and disappointments in her life.

In 1916, the 16-year-old Elizabeth Bowes-Lyon travelled all the way to Hackney* in East London to sit exams in drawing, English, geogra-

---

* Hackney was the birthplace of, among others, Michael Caine, Alfred Hitchcock, the Kray Brothers, Harold Pinter, Sid Vicious and Barbara Windsor (no relation).

phy and arithmetic. She failed them all. Her response to this setback could almost have been written by her plain-speaking American contemporary Ernest Hemingway. 'All that I say is, <u>DAMN THE EXAM!!</u>' she wrote to Poignand. 'Good heavens! What was the use of toiling down to that – er – place Hackney? None, I tell you none. It makes me <u>boil</u> with rage to think of that vile stuff, tapioca, eaten for – nothing? Oh hell … Yes, I am very disappointed …'

By 1918, she was a young lady, with suitors galore, all of them well connected. 'You are my best friend and adviser,' she wrote to Poignand. In March, she told her that 'As usual I danced the first dance with P.W. [the Prince of Wales], I don't know why but I usually do!' After the First World War, the bubbly young Elizabeth was to receive numerous marriage proposals from soldiers who had been billeted at Glamis, among them a Captain Glass. 'Awful thing happened on Thursday!' she wrote to Poignand. 'C… G… s proposed to me!! Oh Gosh, I couldn't help it, wasn't it awful?' In July 1920, 'I danced with Prince Albert [her future husband, George VI] who I hadn't known before, he is quite a nice youth.'

Three years later, she confided her misgivings about Prince Albert to her old governess. 'I don't seem to be able to like anybody enough to marry them! Isn't it odd?' But Prince Albert would not take no for an answer, and on his third proposal his persistence paid off. Consequently, she was invited to stay at Sandringham. 'It is a bit of a strain staying with one's future in-laws, whoever they are,' she wrote to Poignand, adding swiftly: 'Mine have been all too angelic to me, I must say.'

They were married in 1923, and the Duchess of York, as she then became, gave birth to Princess Elizabeth in 1926. At the start of 1930, she granted permission to her old governess to pen a biography of the little Princess, still only three years old, though she cannily insisted on final approval. The finished product came in at 127 pages, fleshed out with thirty-two photographs. Heaven knows why Beryl Poignand hit upon Anne Ring as her pseudonym, though if you drop one of the 'n's, it becomes an anagram of Earning.

'This seems quite passable in a twaddly way' was the Duchess of York's somewhat sniffy reaction after she finished reading the manuscript on 1 October. '... The only thing that she might take out is a remark at the bottom of page 7 to the effect that I may one day rule this country. That is just too much, and she can easily omit the words, "she may one day rule as Queen". It always irritates me, this assumption that the Prince of Wales will not marry – he is quite young* and it is rude to him in a way too. Otherwise it is all quite innocent ...'

Poignand obediently altered it, concluding her book, 'We all hope that it will be a very long time, indeed, before any successor is called to the very high position so graciously and successfully filled by His Majesty King George the Fifth, who has won the love and honour of the citizens of the Empire all the world over. And so in these pages we leave Princess Elizabeth a sweet and lovable child of four-and-a-half years, standing on the brink of a wonderful future.'

The Queen Mother took no objection to the rest of the manuscript, allowing many flattering passages about herself to stay in, no matter how unctuous:

> to all came the instantaneous conviction that ... she was 'all glorious within' and that her beauty lay not merely in the charm of her face, but had its source in the tender and understanding qualities of her heart.
>
> ... at present Princess Elizabeth leaves the choice of her clothes to her Mother, and who could be better qualified than the Duchess, who in these days of a general sameness in women's dress achieves individuality without ever a touch of the extravagant.

Twenty years later, she was still permitting her old governess to publish fluffy pieces about the Royal Family. 'Darling Philip,' she wrote from Buckingham Palace to her new son-in-law on 15 July 1949, 'Would you be very kind & glance through the enclosed little article, which has been written by old Miss Poignand to go opposite a reproduction of Halliday's portrait of yourself? She occasionally writes little pen portraits for magazines, which helps her to earn small amounts of

---

* He was 36 at the time.

money. She was asked to write this by *Woman's Journal* which has a large circulation. I thought it quite innocuous …'

Oddly enough, just three months before, she had set in motion a bitter, hard-fought campaign against another governess, forbidding her to write a book about the two little Princesses, and taking revenge when she did so.

8

As a student at the Moray House Training College in Edinburgh, Marion Crawford was filled with an almost missionary zeal to make the world a better place. 'I wanted to do something about the misery and unhappiness I saw all round me. I wanted desperately to help. I always had a great sense of vocation, and the feeling I had a job to do in life, and I had quite made up my mind that this was what my job was to be.'

But, as so often happens, she was waylaid by the twists and turns of providence. Her first job involved teaching the four 'very nice' children of Lady Elgin, but she had no intention of making a career of it. At the end of each day, she would walk three miles home to study child psychology, with the intention of becoming a child psychologist.

Before long, she added a short session with Lady Rose Leveson-Gower's daughter Mary to her daily roster. One day in 1933, Lady Rose's sister, the Duchess of York, called by for tea with her husband, the Duke. Lady Rose invited Marion to join them. Marion was immediately struck by the Duchess. 'She had the nicest, easiest, most friendly of manners, and a merry laugh ... Her hands and feet were tiny. My whole impression was of someone small and quite perfect.' The Duke, she noticed, had 'not so much of a stutter in the ordinary sense, as a slight nervous constriction of the throat'.

The Duke and Duchess were, it emerged, looking for a governess for their two little children. The Duke was keen to choose a governess more convivial than the finger-wagging gorgons who had loomed over him as a child. Young, friendly and energetic, Miss Crawford seemed just the ticket, and they offered her the job. Though apprehensive about leaving Scotland for the hurly-burly of London, she agreed to try it for a month, to see if it suited her.

She was 24 when she arrived, just before Princess Elizabeth's seventh birthday; she was to remain with them for another fourteen years, by which time Princess Elizabeth was 21 and Miss Crawford 38. By then, Princess Elizabeth had grown as close to Crawfie as her mother had, thirty years earlier, to Beryl Poignand, and, in much the same way, their friendship allowed her to throw discretion to the winds. 'The officers are charming and we have had great fun with them … There are one or two real smashers, and I bet you'd have a WONDERFUL time if you were here,' Princess Elizabeth wrote to Crawfie on a Royal

voyage to South Africa in February 1947, at the age of 20. It is the kind of letter written by close girlfriends: Crawfie brought out a surprisingly footloose, carefree quality in her, hidden from the rest of the world.

It had been the same when Elizabeth was a child. 'We laughed a great deal and had great fun spitting over a bridge into a stream, trying to hit leaves as they floated by!' the Princesses' contemporary Alathea Fitzalan Howard recorded in her diary. 'Crawfie is such fun.'

Crawfie's memoir of *The Little Princesses* is full of fun and games: together, they play hopscotch and Cowboys and Indians and hide-and-seek; laughter is never far away.

From an early age, Princess Elizabeth's passion – one might almost call it an overriding passion – was for horses. At their very first meeting, in the night nursery, Crawfie found her new charge pretending to drive a carriage and horses, having tied the cords of her dressing gown to the knobs of her bed. 'I mostly go once or twice round the park before I go to sleep, you know,' she explained.

Soon, the Princess would enlist Crawfie as her personal horse, harnessing her with a pair of red reins with bells attached.

'Off we would go, delivering groceries. I would be gentled, patted, given my nosebag, and jerked to a standstill, while Lilibet,* at imaginary houses, delivered imaginary groceries, and held long and intimate conversations with her make-believe customers.

'Sometimes she would whisper to me, "Crawfie, you must pretend to be impatient. Paw the ground a bit." So I would paw.' Once in a while, Lilibet would switch roles, taking the part of the horse, 'prancing around, sidling up to me, nosing in my pockets for sugar, making convincing little whinnying noises'.

Crawfie was in charge of the little Princesses, Elizabeth and Margaret, from 9 a.m. to 6 p.m., and then they would be returned to their nanny. She taught them the usual range of subjects – English, maths, geography, history – but also played with them, read to them

---

* 'She had given herself this name when she found "Elizabeth" rather difficult to get around, and it had stuck to her ever since,' explains Crawfie.

and took them for walks. In many ways, she was their only friend, as they saw few other children, other than those they encountered in Hamilton Gardens, just round the corner from their house, where they were taken to play. 'They would have loved to speak to them and make friends,' recalled Crawfie, 'but this was never encouraged.' They didn't seem to twig that they were being observed. 'So engrossed in their games were the children', Crawfie recalled, 'that they never noticed the faces so often lined up at the railing that gave on to the park, watching them.' This ability to ignore onlookers, whenever necessary, was to prove invaluable training for later life.

From the start, Crawfie found the two little Princesses very different in character: Margaret was bouncy, outgoing, frivolous, tardy, mischievous and imaginative; Elizabeth was calm, shy, conscientious, prompt, considerate and straightforward. Reading her memoir, it soon becomes apparent which of the two girls Crawfie preferred. Margaret is 'highly strung' and 'apt at times to be comically regal', whereas Elizabeth is 'unusually good', 'enchanting', 'immensely interesting' and with 'a reasonableness rare in anyone so very young'.

One was impulsive, the other cautious. Handed spoonfuls of barley sugar by their father, Margaret would wolf down all the pieces in one go, while Lilibet took care to line them up, from smallest to largest, before placing them 'daintily, and methodically' in her mouth: she had already embarked on a lifetime's habit of delayed gratification.

Her need for order was particularly marked; her books would always be in straight lines on the shelf and her clothes and belongings 'immaculately tidy'. The Princesses' miniature cottage ('a present from the people of Wales') contained a range of silver which Elizabeth insisted on wrapping in newspaper 'to prevent it getting tarnished, Crawfie'. She was five years old at the time. Later, during the war years, she 'used to set us a great example by wearing her gas mask every day as required, and by carefully cleaning the eyepiece every evening with the ointment provided'.

Decades later, such a strong urge to tidy and arrange, arrange and tidy, might have been diagnosed as Obsessive–Compulsive Disorder. 'At one time I got quite anxious about Lilibet and her fads. She became almost too methodical and tidy,' noted Crawfie. 'She would hop out of bed several times a night to get her shoes quite straight, her clothes arranged just so.' With her gift for pointed mimicry, her little sister seems to have teased her out of it.

Sometimes, Lilibet refused to join in the fun, especially when pranks were on the cards, like popping sticky sweets into the pockets of equerries. 'Lilibet was always too serious-minded to play practical jokes and never failed to consider what the feelings of the people would be if anything of this sort were to be played on them.'

In her entire memoir, Crawfie recalls just one single act of disobedience from the young Lilibet. Set against all her good behaviour, it is peculiarly startling.

Aged seven or so, young Lilibet is being taught French by 'a certain Mademoiselle', who favours the old-fashioned rote approach, involving lengthy columns of French verbs. Crawfie is playing with little Margaret in the next-door room.

> One day curious sounds emerged from the schoolroom. I went in to see what had happened. I found poor Mademoiselle shattered and transfixed with horror. Lilibet, rebelling all of a sudden, and goaded by boredom to violent measures, had picked up the big ornamental silver inkpot and placed it without any warning upside down on her head. She sat there, with ink trickling down her face and slowly dyeing her golden curls blue. I never really got to the bottom of what had happened. Mademoiselle was past explaining, and had to retire and drink water …

Throughout the rest of Crawfie's memoir, the young Elizabeth is depicted as angelic. The episode of the ink trickling down her hair and face is so out of kilter with the rest of the narrative that it must surely be authentic, or else why put it in?

This was, as far as I can tell, the only time Elizabeth ever did anything quite so transgressive. The rest of her life was measured and obedient and considerate: ninety-six years of concentrated self-control. But that day in the schoolroom she had let fly. One minute, she was hard at work on her French verbs, the next – 'goaded by boredom to violent measures' – the ink was trickling down her face, her curly hair transformed from gold to blue.*

One day, as the three of them – Lilibet and Margaret and Crawfie – were walking past Hyde Park Corner, Lilibet looked with envy at everyone streaming out of the Underground station and said, 'Oh, dear, what fun it must be to ride in those trains.' That evening, Crawfie asked permission from the girls' father to let them ride on the Underground. He readily granted it, just so long as a police detective accompanied them. In the event, the Duchess's lady in waiting, Lady Helen Graham, went along too.

'The little girls sat there very demurely, wide-eyed and enchanted.' At first, nobody recognised them, but according to Crawfie the detective 'looked so very obviously a detective that people began to look round to try to discover what he was detecting. Mercifully, we arrived at Tottenham Court Road and got out before anyone had discovered the reason.'†

From Tottenham Court Road, they walked to the café of the Young Women's Christian Association in Mortimer Street, where, for the first

---

* Five days after the death of his mother, King Charles III visited Belfast. As he began signing the visitors' book in the Royal residence of Hillsborough Castle, he realised he had written the wrong date – 12 September rather than 13 September. This irritated him, and then, as he passed the pen back to his wife, he saw it was leaking. 'Oh, God, I hate—' he began, before Camilla interrupted him, saying that the ink was 'going everywhere'. While the new King furiously wiped his hands with a handkerchief, an aide brought a new pen over to Camilla, who calmly signed the book while the King carried on raging in the background. 'Can't bear this bloody thing! It's what they do every stinking time!'

There was further trouble with pens and ink three days later, when King Charles was sitting at a desk, ready to sign the Accession Proclamation, which formalised his position as monarch of the UK and the Commonwealth. Noticing a silver pen box and inkwell – said to be presents from his two sons – he motioned furiously for them to be removed.

Videos of the two events went viral. 'First day on the job and already he's fed up. LOL,' wrote one viewer. To those with long memories, these two ink-based incidents served as a reminder of the patience his mother had maintained throughout the ninety-six years of her life, with the exception of that one small blip during her French lesson.

† In fact, the news spread fast: the following day, the London *Evening Standard* reported that Princess Margaret had sat next to Mrs Simmons, a tea lady from Muswell Hill.

and last time in their lives, they collected their own trays from a counter and queued to be served. When Lilibet left her teapot behind, a server shouted after her, 'If you want it you must come and fetch it.' They then sat down to enjoy their modest meal, relishing the novelty. 'Tea out of thick cups, other people's bread and butter, tea you paid for with money, these were wonderful treats,' added Crawfie.

But word soon went round that the little Princesses were there, and crowds began to gather. Sensing trouble, Crawfie nipped over to the office of the YWCA and phoned for a car to be sent from the Duke's garage, ready to transport them safely home.

9

Often derided as sentimental by the very same Royal biographers who mine it for information, *The Little Princesses* was nearly lost to history. This was how the Queen Mother began her letter (marked 'Private') to Marion Crawford after her recently retired governess first proposed writing about her two charges in March 1949:

> My Dear Crawfie,
> I am so sorry to have been so long in giving you my view about the questions you asked me, but, you know they were extremely difficult to answer especially as I fear that the answers are still the same as I gave you when you came to see me.
>   I do feel, most definitely, that you should not write and sign articles about the children, as people in positions of confidence must be utterly oyster.

As you can see, the letter begins pleasantly enough, with the use of 'My Dear' and 'Crawfie' and cosy family coinages like 'utterly oyster' instead of the more brutal 'keep your mouth shut or else'.

But, bit by bit, it grows more terse, more dismissive, more threatening, all wrapped in the circumlocutions of *politesse*. It might almost be a monologue delivered by a nameless stranger with an overbearing manner in a play by Harold Pinter:

> If you, the moment you finished teaching Margaret, started writing about her and Lilibet, well, we should never feel confidence in anyone again. I know you understand this, because you have been so

wonderfully discreet all the years you were with us. Also, you would lose all your friends, because such a thing has never been done or even contemplated amongst the people who serve us so loyally, and I do hope that you will put all the American temptations aside very firmly. Having been with us in our family life for so long, you must be prepared to be attacked by journalists to give away private and confidential things, and I know that your good sense & loyal affection will guide you well. I do feel most strongly that you must resist the allure of American money & persistent editors, & say No No No to offers of dollars for articles about something as private & as precious as our family.

But for whatever reason – money? recognition? self-assertion? feelings of neglect? – Marion Crawford, cosy with her new husband in her grace-and-favour cottage in Kensington Palace,* failed to take the hint. In August 1949, she completed a series of extracts from her planned book for *Ladies' Home Journal*, still confident that, as she put it to her editor, 'the Queen will not only agree but also write a preface in her own handwriting'.

Far from it: the Queen Mother was livid, announcing in a letter to Lady Astor, 'Our late & completely trusted governess has gone off her head.' Through her private secretary, she insisted on at least thirteen changes to the text. She particularly objected to the revelation that, having drawn 'Royal Flush' in a game of charades, the Duchess of Kent

---

* When she retired in 1948, Crawfie was given Nottingham Cottage, in the grounds of Kensington Palace, to live in. This address was to gain a measure of fame seventy years later when it became home to the Duke and Duchess of Sussex after their engagement. In their Netflix series *Harry and Meghan* they complained that it had been far too small for their needs. 'Kensington Palace sounds very regal of course it does. It says "palace" in the name,' ventured the Duchess. 'But Nottingham Cottage was so small. Harry would just hit his head constantly in that place because he's so tall.'

'The whole thing was really small on a slight lean with low ceilings,' agreed the Duke.

'It was a chapter in our lives where I don't think anyone could believe what it was actually like behind the scenes,' continued the Duchess.

They went on to reveal that when their new friend Oprah Winfrey had dropped by for tea she had been stunned by its modesty. 'When she came in, she sat down and she said, "No one would ever believe it!"' recalled the Duke ruefully.

had mimed pulling a lavatory chain. Crawfie incorporated these alterations, and having done so, appears to have convinced herself that the manuscript had royal approval. How wrong she was!

The Little Princesses: The Intimate Story of H.R.H. Princess Elizabeth and H.R.H. Princess Margaret by Their Governess appeared the following year. From that moment on, Crawfie became a non-person, evicted from her home, excised from the Royal Christmas card list and, in the words of one courtier, 'shunned by colleagues from top to bottom'. At the very mention of her name, the Royal table would fall silent. The Princesses never spoke to her again. Yet this was the woman who had shared their lives for fourteen years, who had played games with them, taught, cosseted and comforted them, who had seen more of them than their parents, and who had, in a real sense, been their closest friend. Asked about her former governess some thirty years later, Princess Margaret replied with just two words: 'She sneaked.'

Perhaps a woman of Crawfie's intelligence should have expected it. After all, she had been an eyewitness to the fate of the Princesses' Uncle David. In her early years with the little Princesses, the Duke of Windsor, then still the Prince of Wales, had been a constant visitor to 145 Piccadilly, and loved to play with his two little nieces. 'He was very fond of his brother, and he was devoted to Lilibet. He often took part in their after-tea games – Snap, and Happy Families. He gave Lilibet all the A. A. Milne children's books – *Winnie-the-Pooh*, *When We Were Very Young*, and the others,' remembered Crawfie.

But once Mrs Simpson put her head around the door, things changed. 'It was impossible not to notice the change in Uncle David. He had been so youthful and gay. Now he looked distraught, and seemed not to be listening to what was said to him. He made plans with the children, and then forgot them.'

In 1942, when a third brother, the Duke of Kent, was killed in an aeroplane crash, his loss hadn't seemed so out of the ordinary. 'It was the second uncle they had lost completely, for though the first, Uncle David, was not dead, they did not see him any more. The royal conspiracy of silence had closed about him as it did about so many other uncomfortable things. In the Palace and the Castle, his name was never mentioned.'

And now Crawfie, too, had joined the roll call of the unmentionables. 'The Royal Family is quite good at blanking out anything unpleasant or uncomfortable,' Lord Snowdon once observed. In recent years, it is a skill they have had to employ with increasing frequency. 'These days, the names of Harry and Meghan, the Duke and Duchess of Sussex, do not crop up very often in court circles,' observed Gyles Brandreth in 2022. 'When they do, courtiers flinch almost imperceptibly and change the subject – or, if that's not possible, refer to them obliquely as "persons who live overseas". Mention the Sussexes to other members of the royal family … and they simply smile briefly and say, "We wish them all the best" – and nothing else.'

10

The 13-year-old Princess Elizabeth visited London Zoo on 10 May 1939. With her little sister Princess Margaret, she took turns feeding the baby giant panda.

Spotting a photograph of the encounter between the Princesses and the panda in the next day's *Times*, Virginia Woolf found herself reconsidering the deeper purpose of the monarchy. Rooted in an unconscious yearning for art and religion, it provided the British with an escape from 'the drudgery ... of being ourselves'.

'Love of Royalty, or, to give it its crude name, snobbery, is related to love of pageantry which has some connection with love of beauty,' she wrote. '... But perhaps the most profound satisfaction that Royalty provides is that it gives us a Paradise to inhabit, and one much more domestic than that provided by the Church of England. Pile carpets are more palpable than fields of asphodel,* and the music of the Scots Greys more audible than the hymns angels play upon their harps.'

The glories of such a fairy tale should, she felt, be protected from the intrusion of dreary reality. 'Real people live in Buckingham Palace, but always smiling, perfectly dressed, immune, we like to imagine, if not from death and sorrow, still from the humdrum and the pettifogging.' It was 'a consolation to know that such beings exist. If they live, then we too live in them, vicariously.'

The citizens of France were served by their religion, with its processions and images, its candles and incense. 'The Roman Catholic religion provides with this pageantry a substitute for Royalty. It gives the poorest old crone, who has nothing but a bunch of roses to stick in a pot, something to dream about, and, what is equally important, something to do.' But Anglicanism offered no such release. 'It is a black and white indoor affair which makes no appeal to our senses.'

And where did the panda come in? On the same page of *The Times* as the Princess and the panda was a photograph, close to life-size, of a rare caterpillar discovered recently in Kensington. 'How little ... we know of the lives of caterpillars, living mysteriously on the heights of elm trees; urged by instincts that are not ours; immune from worry.'

Woolf detected that the Princess and the Caterpillar had something in common. Might we not switch from studying one to studying the other? 'If a mere caterpillar found in Kensington can cause this thrill and if this thrill is much the same as that which Royalty used to provide when Royalty was barred and beautiful and immune from human weakness, then perhaps Science will do instead ... This

---

* In Greek mythology, the asphodel is associated with death and the underworld; in the world of Harry Potter, it is a key ingredient in the potion known as the Draught of Living Death.

unknown world is after all more beautiful than Buckingham Palace, and its inhabitants will never, in all probability, come down from the tree-top to mate with the Smiths and the Simpsons. If the picture paper would come to our help, we might dream a new dream, acquire a new snobbery ... The camera has an immense power in its eye, if it would only turn that eye in rather a different direction. It might wean us by degrees from the Princess to the panda, and shunt us past religion to pay homage to Science, as some think it a more venerable royal house than the House of Windsor.'

Mrs Woolf's thoughts on royalty were commissioned by Tom Hopkinson for the magazine *Picture Post*, which had been launched a year before. But, after reading her piece, Hopkinson felt nervous about going ahead with its publication. 'If we were a paper for the minority used to speculative thought ... we should certainly use your article,' he wrote to Mrs Woolf on 11 August. 'As it is, I think it would be widely taken as an attack on the Royal family, and on the institution of kingship in this country; and it is an institution in whose name many of our readers may very shortly be obliged to fight.'

By way of compensation, *Picture Post* paid Mrs Woolf the 25 guineas they had promised her.

Seventy-three years later, Hilary Mantel, chronicler of King Henry VIII and his wives, gave a lecture on royalty for the *London Review of Books*, which then published it as an essay. 'One is compelled to look at them: to ask what they are made of, and is their substance the same as ours.' Mantel made no reference to Virginia Woolf's obscure essay, so it was almost certainly coincidental that she then adopted the analogy of the panda. 'Our current royal family doesn't have the difficulties in breeding that pandas do, but pandas and royal persons alike are expensive to conserve and ill-adapted to any modern environment. But aren't they interesting? Aren't they nice to look at? Some people find them endearing; some pity them for their precarious situation; everybody stares at them, and however airy the enclosure they inhabit, it's still a cage.'

For a brief time, Mantel's essay became a tabloid sensation, not for its reference to pandas but for its perceived attack on the then Duchess of Cambridge, Kate Middleton, whom she described as appearing to have been 'designed by a committee and built by craftsmen ... without quirks, without oddities, without the risk of the emergence of character ... precision-made, machine-made'.

The ensuing tabloid hoo-ha – 'Booker prize winner's venomous attack on Kate' ran a headline in the *Daily Mail*, along with a quote from Prime Minister David Cameron condemning Mantel's words as 'completely misguided' and the leader of the opposition calling them 'pretty offensive' – meant that Prince Harry, not a natural reader of the *LRB*, got to hear of Mantel's essay. In his memoir, *Spare*, he says that it argued that 'pandas and royal persons alike are expensive to conserve and ill-adapted to any modern environment. But aren't they interesting? Aren't they nice to look at?'

He was upset, and indeed talked about it with his new South London therapist. In *Spare* he goes over what he told her, describing what he calls Mantel's 'panda crack' as 'uniquely barbarous. We did live in a zoo, but by the same token I knew, as a soldier, that turning people into animals, into non-people is the first step in mistreating them, in destroying them. If even a celebrated intellectual could dismiss us as animals, what hope for the man or woman on the street?'

11

In December 1936, the month that also saw the abdication of King Edward VIII, John Murray published a slim picture book called *Our Princesses and Their Dogs* by Michael Chance, with 'Photographs by Studio Lisa'. It had been published, the blurb announced, with the approval of Their Royal Highnesses the Duke and Duchess of York, who, by the time of publication, were Their Royal Majesties King George VI and Queen Elizabeth.

It is written in the genuflective style still favoured by many of today's Royal 'experts'. 'All the world knows that in their relations with those with whom they come in contact our Princesses reveal a simplicity

worthy of their House, a graciousness that is all their own: which is only another way of saying that had they been commoners they would still stand out from others as children of uncommon charm. But few people realise the marked similarity between the unaffected sincerity that so delightfully characterises these Royal but very human children and the cheerful contentment of their dogs.'

At this point, many of today's readers may be in need of a lie-down. But still the prose gushes forth. 'Accustomed as I am to meeting every kind of dog in the company of all kinds of masters and mistresses, I doubt if I have ever encountered dogs who shared with their owners a quieter or serener companionship. In other words, our Princesses and their dogs are true friends together. Which, indeed, should be the relationship between all children and their pets.

'Because Her Royal Highness the Duchess of York warmly subscribes to this view, it is doubly gratifying that Her Royal Highness should herself have graciously suggested that this book should be dedicated "To All Children Who Love Dogs". No dedication could be simpler, none more impressive.'

In that perilous month for the monarchy, *Our Princesses and Their Dogs* offered a reassuring narrative, portraying carefree Royal pets untroubled by the upsets besetting their human counterparts. A full-page photograph of the 10-year-old Princess Elizabeth holding her corgi Jane legs-up in her arms is captioned, '"It may be an upside-down world" says Jane, "but I wouldn't change places with any Corgi alive."'

Though the text is short – barely 1,500 words – and concentrates on the Princesses' two corgis – 'Gay, active, intelligent and faithful little creatures are Dookie and Jane' – it rapidly grows foggy and hard to follow, particularly when listing all the various dogs belonging to the Royal Family: the three yellow Labradors Mimsy, Stiffy and Scrummy, the Tibetan Lion Dog Choo-Choo ('as Oriental in character as he is in ancestry'), the Golden Retriever Judy and the Cocker Spaniel Ben. 'All these dogs live together on terms of perfect amity,' observes the author. He then congratulates the Princesses for teaching their dogs 'the real meaning of the word happiness'.

'Moreover, just as we humans know that in all the world there are no Royalties so unselfconscious as our own, none so considerate of others, so devoid of artificiality, so rich in human qualities, it may well be that Dookie and Jane, being dogs of sense, instinctively share our knowledge.'

To learn more about the Queen's corgis, I turn to *All the Queen's Corgis* by the prolific and dependable Royal author Penny Junor, who has also published books about Prince William (*The Man Who Will Be King*); Prince Harry (*Brother. Soldier. Son. Husband*); the Duchess of Cornwall (*The Duchess: Camilla Parker Bowles and the Love Affair That Rocked the Crown*); Charles and Diana together (*Portrait of a Marriage*); Princess Diana (*Diana, Princess of Wales*); Prince Charles (*Victim or Villain?*); and the Royal Family as a whole (*The Firm: The Troubled Life of the House of Windsor*).

Of all the tough subjects available to a Royal biographer, the Queen's corgis must surely take the biscuit. It is comparatively easy, even for the layman, to distinguish between, say, William and Harry, or Edward and Andrew, or Diana and Camilla. But how can even the most diligent Royal expert distinguish between Pickles and Tinker, or Dagger and Dipper, or Rufus and Brush?

Fortunately, *All the Queen's Corgis* comes with a handy double-page spread: 'The Line of Succession: Queen Elizabeth II's corgi family tree'. Like all family trees, it starts in an Eden of simplicity:

SUSAN = Rozavel Lucky Strike

These two corgis give birth to Honey and Sugar. Honey then marries, as it were, Rozavel Bailey, and gives birth to Bee, while Sugar gives birth to Sherry and Whisky (father unnamed).

So far, so good; but before long, things start spinning out of control: Bee teams up with Rozavel Beat the Band to produce Buzz, who produces no offspring, and Heather, who gets together with Lees Maldwyn Lancelot to produce Foxy and Tiny. Then Foxy mates with Convista Endeavour and together they produce Mask, Rufus, Cindy and Brush, while Tiny and his partner Pipkin, a dachsund belonging to Princess Margaret, produce Pickles and Tinker.

Brush gives birth to three puppies with Kaytop Marshall – Geordie, Jolly and Sweep. The latter two both get together with the good-time corgi Pipkin (who has already partnered Tiny, producing Pickles and Tinker). Jolly's union with Pipkin produces Chipper and Sweep's produces Piper. By my calculation, this makes Piper and Chipper simultaneously half-siblings and first cousins. Their uncle Geordie then marries Rozavel Crown Princess and they produce Smoky, who—

Whoah! Are you still with me? Trying to remember all the Queen's corgis, in the right order, along with their various partners and relations, is like trying to remember Pi to the nearest twenty decimal points – or, rather, to the nearest eighty-three decimal points, as there are eighty-three corgis (or dorgis – half dachsund, half corgi) in the family tree, and the line from Susan, the Queen's very first corgi, to Willow, who passed away in April 2018, spans a full fourteen generations.

This means that Junor's book soon becomes an impenetrably complex family saga, with little to differentiate one character from another, and three or four random newcomers yolloping in on every page. For example, on page 92 we learn that:

Neither Sherry nor Whisky had litters, but the Queen Mother bred from Sugar's sister, Honey. Honey was mated with Rozavel Bailey in 1956 and produced Bee, who in the fullness of time was mated with another of Thelma Gray's dogs, Rozavel Beat the Band. The Queen Mother did not keep any of that litter but the Queen took two of the puppies, Heather and Buzz. Heather became a mother in 1965 to Foxy and Tiny …

Phew! And so it goes on – 'Foxy and Tiny had litters, from Foxy, the Queen Mother kept Mask, Rufus, Cindy and Brush' – and on – 'the Queen took a pup that she named Shadow. Shadow then produced Myth and Fable, and, in 1984, Myth produced Kelpie, who was a great favourite.' It's the canine equivalent of the Old Testament's 'And

Ezekias begat Manasses; and Manasses begat Amon; and Amon begat Josias; and Josias begat …'

As in the Bible, there are moments of high drama that interrupt the flow of names, as though *Burke's Peerage* were hosting *The Texas Chainsaw Massacre*. Corgis, are, it turns out, an unpredictable, temperamental bunch, one minute cuddly, the next psycho, the Corleones of the dog world. The family's first corgi, Dookie, who first put his head round the door when the Queen was seven, 'turned out to be a bad-tempered little dog by all accounts. He terrorised the household, biting visitors and courtiers alike … In addition to the long list of palace employees who were nipped, he bit the politician Lord Lothian, who bled profusely.'

Dookie did not restrict his aggression to humans: he would happily attack the dining-room chairs at Royal Lodge, the family home in Windsor Great Park. 'There was scarcely a dining chair that didn't bear teeth-marks.'

Susan – i.e. Princess Elizabeth's first corgi of her own (keep up!) – was very nearly as vicious, biting the ankles of 23-year-old Alfred Edge, a Grenadier Guardsman on sentry duty at Buckingham Palace, and Leonard Hubbard, the Royal clock winder. And Susan's daughter Honey followed suit, biting the knee of PC Horlock and the uniformed bottom of John Morrogh-Bernard, an Irish Guards subaltern.

Like the Corleone clan, their disposition towards violence stayed in their genes from one generation to the next. In 1984, Piper, the great-great-great-grand-dorgi of Honey, sank his teeth in several victims, including the Queen Mother and Prince Edward, and was despatched on a one-way trip to Gatcombe, to be overseen by Princess Anne, who has a soft spot for nippers and biters.

Incidentally, in his memoir *A Royal Duty*, the butler Paul Burrell recalls the day in 1977 when the Queen's corgis set upon her younger two sons' inappropriately named corgi Jolly as it ambled along a corridor of Windsor Castle. I suspect that Penny Junor might have judged the scene too nightmarish for her gentle readers. Burrell describes this bloody ambush as being 'like a fox snared by hounds. She was the smallest and weakest, being literally savaged by the others. As I turned

the corner, the poor little thing's stomach had been torn open and there was blood and mess everywhere.' When they attempted to pull them apart, both Burrell and the Queen's page were bitten, and a doctor had to be called. 'It was nothing a tetanus jab and a sticking plaster couldn't mend but Jolly was taken away and underwent emergency surgery. She survived, but only after twenty stitches to her abdomen.'

The Queen Mother's corgis were every bit as edgy. In 1989, her corgi Ranger* attacked the Queen's elderly dorgi Chipper† and, in the words of a neutral observer, 'ripped him to shreds'. Two years later, when the

---

* Great-niece of Piper.

† First cousin of Piper.

Queen attempted to intervene in a set-to between her corgis and her mother's, she was bitten so badly that her left hand required three stitches.

Coincidentally, the way to scare off a belligerent corgi is the same as for a belligerent human being: a blast from the bagpipes. Happily, the Queen always kept a set of bagpipes to hand. 'The pitch of the pipes seems to hurt most dogs' ears,' Jim Motherwell, the Queen's piper from 1997 to 2003, tells Penny Junor. At the sound of the bagpipes, he adds, most corgis stop whatever they are doing and slink away, as though in pain.

Princess Anne's three prettily named bull terriers – Florence, Eglantyne and Dotty – were red in tooth and claw. Arriving at Sandringham on Christmas Eve 2003, Princess Anne made the mistake of ringing the bell, alerting five of the Queen's corgis to hurtle downstairs to offer their own particular welcome. The ensuing scene might have sprung from a movie by Tarantino: 'As it was opened Florence pushed in and savaged Pharos,'* writes Junor. 'The Queen had had a knee operation so had to wait for a lift to take her down, and by the time she arrived at the scene, it was too late: the dogs were locked in mortal combat. Pharos was 13 and no match for the power-ful terrier. She clamped her jaw onto his back leg and shook him like a rag doll. They managed to pull the dogs apart with the help of some footmen but the leg was badly broken in three places and the following day, to the Queen's great distress, he was put to sleep.'

Was Dotty a prey to nominative determinism? On Easter Monday 2002, after a walk with Princess Anne in Windsor Great Park, Dotty spotted two little boys, aged twelve and seven, racing along on their bicycles. She immediately made a break for it. Confronted by this barking bull terrier, both boys fell off their bikes. Princess Anne yelled, but Dotty carried on, biting one boy on the leg and the collar bone and scratching the other on his leg, his back and his arm. Both boys were rushed to hospital 'in a traumatised state', though neither needed stitches.

---

* Tenth-generation descendant of Susan.

The Princess Royal (booked under the downbeat name of Anne Elizabeth Alice Laurence) and her husband, Commodore Tim Laurence, were jointly prosecuted for being in charge of a dog that was dangerously out of control in a public place, though the charge against Laurence was dropped after the Princess admitted sole responsibility.

Appearing as a character witness for Dotty at Slough Crown Court, the dog psychologist Dr Roger Mugford, who had been advising the Queen since 1984, gave his professional assessment of Dotty's temperament and character. She was, he said, a 'totally placid, playful, tolerant dog' who could be trained not to repeat the offence. In written evidence, one character witness described her as 'like a big puppy'. Passing sentence, the district judge reflected that the two little boys had suffered considerably from the incident, so much so that it had put them off dogs entirely. 'It was a very, very unfortunate episode and I can only hope that the children, as time goes by, will become more amenable to dogs,' she said.

She spared Dotty's life but ordered her to undergo special training and to be kept on a lead in all public places. The Princess was fined £500 and ordered to pay £250 compensation to each of the boys. Outside the courtroom, the parents of the victims criticised the leniency of the sentence, arguing that Dotty should have been put down. 'We do not think justice has been done. The dog is still free and is a danger to society.' The Princess left the court with a criminal record.

Two years later, on the day after Boxing Day 2004, Florence bit a 50-year-old maid who was trying to clean Princess Anne's rooms at Sandringham. Once again, Dr Mugford leapt to the defence. Florence was, he maintained, 'just a dog who is feeling a bit out of sorts about something, perhaps pain or old age, and was feeling a bit cranky on the day'.

The Queen's favourite indoor pastime was jigsaws, the bigger the better. Arriving at Sandringham in January 1967 with four other Labour ministers, Richard Crossman found her tackling 'an enormous, incredibly difficult jigsaw'. He noticed that 'while she was standing there talking to the company at large, her fingers were straying and she was quietly fitting in the pieces while apparently not looking round'. Major Colin Burgess, who served as equerry to the Queen Mother in the 1990s, recalled that every Christmas a massive jigsaw puzzle – 'about 10,000 pieces' – was put out on a large table at Sandringham. It was ostensibly for the family and guests, but he reckoned that 60 per cent of the work on it was done by the Queen. 'She loved puzzles. That was her big thing.' The Queen Mother was probably the next most energetic. When Eddie Mirzoeff, the producer and director of the BBC's documentary *Elizabeth R*, visited Sandringham in 1990, he found her bent over a 2,000-piece jigsaw puzzle.

'That looks terribly difficult,' he said.

'It's much more difficult than the one we did yesterday,' came the reply.

Jigsaws appeal to those who like to make order out of chaos. Corgis offer the reverse. They are jigsaw pieces gone haywire: jigsaw pieces with legs. In such a planned and regimented life, a life dictated by order, convention, duty and dignity, was it the randomness of her corgis that so appealed to the Queen? They offered her no respect, no awe, and only the barest shred of obedience. They were haphazard, aggressive, demanding and carefree. They barked when they should have kept quiet, ran about when they should have stayed still and snapped at whoever was to hand, regardless of status. They were four-legged dictators, drunken toddlers, hoodlums on the rampage. They knew nothing of deference or dignity. Yet their lack of a language, or at least an intelligible language, ensured their discretion: no Royal corgi ever published its memoirs or poured out its heart to Oprah Winfrey.

Paul Burrell says that it was a joke among the Palace staff that the things most important to the Queen were horses, dogs, Prince Philip and her children, in that order. 'That is a little unfair,' he adds. 'It is just that she is perhaps *more passionate* about horses and dogs.' One of her prime ministers once asked her how she could tell the difference between her various dogs. Her reply was brusque: 'Do you get your children confused?' Penny Junor quotes Lady Pamela Hicks, the younger daughter of Earl Mountbatten of Burma and a former lady in waiting to the Queen. 'The Queen is a very private person; a loner. She longs to be in a room with nobody else. The dogs, the horses, her husband … She has few friends and if she had to choose between the dogs, the horses and friends, there is no doubt which she would choose.'

Those who knew her would compare her character to that of a regular upper-class English countrywoman: straightforward, understated, matter of fact, down to earth. Yet being followed around by ten corgis at a time would mark out anyone else as deeply eccentric. Prince Philip would grow irritated by the way they kept blocking his path. 'Bloody dogs! Why do you have to have so many?!' he once snapped at the Queen. 'But they're so *collectable*,' she explained.

She would often break one of the key tenets of conventional upper-class behaviour, feeding her corgis titbits from the table – toast at breakfast, scones in the afternoon and whatever the humans were having at lunch and dinner. She also kept a supply of doggy biscuits to hand, ready to feed any corgi that took the trouble to adopt a sufficiently needy expression.

After a convivial lunch at Windsor Castle in 2008, the secretary of state for health, Alan Johnson, mentioned to his Cabinet colleague Paul Murphy how much he had enjoyed the cheese and, in particular, the unusual dark biscuits that had been served with it. Murphy corrected him: 'Those dark biscuits were for the dogs.' According to Major Colin Burgess, the Queen Mother's equerry in the mid-1990s, this was a frequent mistake, in which the Queen and her mother connived: guests would find a couple of these biscuits on their plates 'and you could see them looking round at other guests wondering what the biscuits were for before gingerly picking them up to eat. Suddenly the Queen or Queen Mother would shout, "No, no, no, they're for the dogs." Nearly every guest made this mistake. They thought it was an extra course, albeit a very strange one. The Queen and Queen Mother could easily have avoided this by telling them what the biscuits were for as they handed them out, but their naughty streak got the better of them.'

The corgis encouraged the stuff-and-nonsense side of the Queen's character. She liked to tell people that they were bred as Welsh cattle-herders, and that they were sometimes known as 'heelers' on account of their tendency to nip at the heels of cattle in order to keep them on the move. Her corgis were sometimes referred to as 'a moving carpet', though this was a peculiarly perilous carpet, prone to trip, jostle and bite.

'Human ankles can be a substitute for cattle hooves, as many a royal footman discovered,' observed Andrew Parker Bowles. In any such conflict, the Queen tended to take the corgis' side. A courtier who had just been bitten on the ankle received short shrift. 'Well, what do you expect?' she snapped. 'You've just trodden on his toe. Now, what have you come to see me about?'

In his diaries, the socialist MP Chris Mullin records being informed by an unnamed privy counsellor that he had been despatched to Buckingham Palace in 1973 with paperwork relating to a man sentenced to death for murdering the governor of Bermuda. The convicted man had appealed to the Queen for mercy, and the official advice to her was 'reject'. 'She duly signed away the culprit's life, remarking as she did so, "Fancy appealing to me for mercy. Do you know he even shot the dog?"'

The Queen was equally unforgiving to those who sought to undermine her corgis by stealth. A Palace footman who had suffered a bite tried to exact his revenge by lacing the corgis' dinners with gin. When the Queen found out, this footman was immediately demoted, and never again permitted to work with them.

In her support of dogs over humans, she followed her mother's instincts. Penny Junor records an incident at the Castle of Mey, the Queen Mother's fifteen-bedroom Scottish holiday home, complete with dungeon. As the Queen Mother was ushering her lunch guests into the drawing room for coffee, she spotted a large dog's mess on the carpet. 'Where did that come from?' she asked, adding, 'It wasn't one of my dogs.'

No one knew what to say, so her silver-tongued private secretary, Martin Gilliatt, stepped into the breach: 'Well, if it wasn't one of your dogs, ma'am, it certainly wasn't you, so it must have been me.'

Gazing at photographs of the Queen Mother with her corgis in

1947, Nancy Mitford was struck by a resemblance. 'Corgis *exactly* the same shape as the plucky little Queen,' she wrote to her mother.

Corgis were rebellious in a way that Queen Elizabeth II could never be. Their clamour was her refuge, their indifference her comfort. Unlike humans, they were unimpressed by her majesty. Even her children would have to defer to her, bowing or curtsying, walking behind her and so forth. But the behaviour of the corgis was modified by no such deference: she would follow them into the room, rather than vice versa, and if they felt like barking, bark they did. And she, in turn, released from pleasantries, could bark back at them. When Gordon Brown and his family stayed at Balmoral during his relatively brief time as prime minister, he found the Queen 'a gracious hostess' but noticed she could be petulant towards her dogs. 'She was surrounded by her corgis and the boys were delighted and shocked in equal measure when she told one of her dogs to "shut up".'

Her attachment to her corgis was lifelong and profound, often outlasting her attachment to their human counterparts. When the Queen visited Sheffield, the leader of the City Council, David Blunkett, who was blind, hosted a lunch for her. 'It was strange when twice she asked me if I would like my meat cutting up – strange not because it was not a kind and thoughtful question, but because of the comment she made when I politely declined: "You know, I often do it for the corgis."'

Perhaps, above all, the corgis were a distraction from the constraints of such a formal existence. 'She has used the dogs not just to put others at their ease, but to ease her own discomfort,' observes Junor astutely. '... If there is an awkward lull, she will turn her attention to one of the dogs to fill the silence, or bend down to give them titbits from her plate at the table.'

Visitors often noticed the way her conversation would revolve around the corgis. They were neutral territory, like the weather. In November 1964, the Labour Cabinet minister Richard Crossman noted that for ten minutes 'she talked, as I am told she always does, about her corgis. (Two fat corgis, roughly the same colour as the carpet, were lying at her feet.) She remarked how often people fell over the dogs. I asked what good they were and she said they were Welsh dogs used for rounding up cattle by biting their legs. So we talked about whether cattle stepped on them and I said our Suki, a poodle, was much quicker than a corgi at evading the cows. Then the Queen got on to talking about cows and said how terribly pleased she was when she had entered for the Dairy Show for the first time and won the championship for Jersey cows ...'

The cartoonist Matt Pritchett was invited to lunch at the Palace in 2006. As he waited with his fellow guests for the arrival of the Queen and Prince Philip, he nervously went over what he might say ('I love your early work, I've got all your stamps') but then:

A fanfare of corgi barks could be heard, then footsteps, then the doors opened. And there they were.

For a moment I was speechless, but soon they just got the room talking, puncturing any tension effortlessly, until we were all having a merry time. I suppose that was one of her many gifts: knowing that everybody who met her was, in some way, having an internal meltdown at the experience, so she needed to subtly relax them – and quickly.

The corgis could also provide an escape from talking about anything too painful. David Nott is a consultant surgeon at three London hospitals. Two months a year, he offers his services to victims in war zones: Bosnia, Gaza, Darfur, Afghanistan, Syria. Stationed in Aleppo in 2014, he had been operating in a makeshift hospital, often by torchlight, while bombs exploded around him. Ten days after his return, he was a guest at one of the Queen's regular lunches for eminent people.

'I hear you've just come back from Aleppo?' she began.

Nott's mind raced back to a day when seven children from the same family had been brought to him in the hospital. Their mother was dead. One of the boys had his buttocks blown off; the white blobs over his face were his sister's brains. Nott could not save the boy: all he could do was comfort him and hold his hand while he died. In twenty years of operating, it was the most pitiful sight he had ever seen.

Overcome with emotion, Nott found himself unable to answer the Queen's simple question. 'I could feel my bottom lip quivering. I couldn't say a word. There's no doubt I was suffering from post-traumatic stress.' Instead, he stared long and hard at the wall.

'It wasn't that I didn't want to speak to her. I just couldn't. I could not say anything. So she picked all this up. She said, "Shall I help you?" I thought, how on earth can the Queen help me? Then she started talking about her dogs and asked if I'd like to see them. I said I would. I was trying not to cry, to hold it all together, and suddenly a courtier appeared with the corgis, who went under the table. Then a silver tin with a screw-top lid labelled "Dog biscuits" was brought to the table. The Queen opened it, broke a biscuit in two and gave half to me, and she said, "Why don't we feed the dogs?" We kept feeding them and stroking them for half an hour or so as she chatted and told me all about them. And she did it because she knew I was seriously traumatised. The humanity of what she was doing was unbelievable.'

Her love of her corgis was constant and profound. When one of them died, Lady Pamela Hicks wrote her a brief note of condolence. In return, she received a letter of six pages, listing all the dog's virtues. Penny Junor quotes from a letter the Queen wrote by hand to her local Sandringham vet thanking him for 'the immense amount of trouble you took' before her beloved corgi Susan finally died in January 1959, at the age of fifteen. She had even taken Susan on her honeymoon, writing home to her mother from Birkhall, on the Balmoral estate, 'It is so lovely and peaceful just now – Susan is stretched out before the fire … It is heaven up here.'

'I had always dreaded losing her,' she wrote to the Sandringham vet, 'as I had had her since she was six weeks old but I am so thankful that her suffering was so mercifully short – she was very happily beating for us out shooting on the Friday before!'

Sometimes, her corgis seemed to act not only as companions but also as avatars, behaving as she herself might have done in a life less constrained. In 2003, the Russian president Vladimir Putin undertook a state visit to Britain. At a Palace reception, he was introduced to David Blunkett, who was by now home secretary. Blunkett's guide dog

Sadie greeted the Russian president with a series of aggressive barks. The Queen patted the dog. Blunkett took this for a sign of approval, 'as if to say, "Good dog! *Good* dog!"' He later apologised for Sadie's unseemly behaviour. 'Dogs have interesting instincts, don't they?' replied the Queen, with a knowing look.

12

In the first half of the twentieth century, it was obligatory for men, women and children to stand whenever the National Anthem was played. 'As children if God Save the King was played on the radio, my parents would have stood up, and so would all of us as children, from quite an early age,' recalled Bernard Weatherill, a child of the 1920s.*

At the age of eleven, Princess Elizabeth attended a children's matinee at the Holborn Empire. As she entered, 1,500 children stood up and sang a specially composed children's verse of the National Anthem. The dirge-like song was to follow her everywhere for the rest of her life. Who knows how she felt, silently listening to crowds imploring God to send her victorious, happy and glorious, sometimes at a rate of twice a day? Her invariable response was to look thoughtful but unconcerned, keeping her eyes ahead, as though waiting patiently for a bus.

Only radical elements among the intelligentsia sniffed at the practice of standing to attention while it played. 'It is a strange fact, but it is unquestionably true that almost any English intellectual would feel more ashamed of standing to attention during "God Save the King" than of stealing from a poor box,' observed George Orwell in 1941.

From time to time in the immediate post-war period, there were rumblings against the bellicose second verse. In 1948, a radio listener from Christchurch, New Zealand, put a question to the panel of the

---

* Bernard Weatherill (1920–2007), Speaker of the House of Commons (1983–92). Apprenticed in his youth as a tailor, in later life Lord Weatherill always kept a thimble in his pocket to remind himself of his origins. He is widely regarded as the best of the post-war Speakers.

Brains Trust on the BBC Home Service: 'Some of the sentiments of our National Anthem are out of date. Should it not be rewritten?'

One of the panellists, the conductor Sir Malcolm Sargent, was indignant. 'No!' he said, and went on to quote the second verse:

> O Lord our God arise,
> Scatter his enemies,
> And make them fall.

'That is the verse that everybody hates,' he said.

It goes on:

> Confound their politics
> Frustrate their knavish tricks …
> God save us all.

The point being that if their politics *are* bad, if they *are* against the King, if their tricks *are* knavish, then they *should* be confounded. This verse entirely echoes the spirit of any thinking person who is also religious. There's nothing wrong in the lines as they stand!

But Sargent's fellow panellist Professor C. E. M. Joad was equally adamant in his opposition. 'Well, sir, I would like to say No to that. Part of the verse is stupid and part of it is wicked, and it's a pity to go on perpetrating what is both stupid and wicked.'

Yet Sargent remained intransigent. After conducting a Royal Birthday tribute programme to King George VI in June 1949, he announced to the audience: 'You'll notice that we have sung the complete version of the National Anthem … I confess I had many protests with regard to the second verse … So far as I am concerned and so far as the Royal Choral Society is concerned, we will always wish to ask God's help that the enemies of the King may be scattered and that any knavish tricks they may wish to indulge in may be frustrated!'

Regardless of such niggles, throughout the 1940s and 1950s only the very drunk, the defiantly radical or the fast asleep would remain seated for the National Anthem, which was played at the end (and sometimes also at the beginning) of most public entertainments throughout the Commonwealth. In Australia, the young Thomas Keneally,* brought up in the dairy town of Kempsey, New South Wales, never questioned the practice. 'George VI was much respected. As soon as I started going to the movies, round about the age of five, there he was. And he was our *King*. I just stood up for him at the start of the "pictures" as we called them. Only my grandfather didn't stand up in the pictures. But that was considered an acute embarrassment to the entire family.'

As a Fulbright scholar at Cambridge University in the mid-1950s, Sylvia Plath, from Boston, Massachusetts, conscientiously followed the correct procedure whenever the National Anthem came on. 'We stand at attention to "God Save the Queen" at the end of movies, dances & plays (Once I made the fatal mistake of thinking it was a new dance!) & I must say, I am beginning to feel loyal!' she wrote home in December 1955.

But by the early 1960s the playing of the National Anthem with such frequency was beginning to be questioned. On an episode of radio's *Any Questions* in 1962, Michael Foot MP argued against it being played in theatres and cinemas. He was opposed by Lady Isobel Barnett† and by the extravagantly moustachioed Conservative MP Gerald Nabarro, who insisted that 'it should be played on all public occasions and as frequently as possible'.

In some of the more rebellious parts of the British Isles, the runners were beginning to outnumber the standers. At the end of one particular evening's entertainment in a Glasgow cinema in 1961, only one

---

* Thomas Keneally (b.1935), Australian novelist and playwright, best known for his 'non-fiction novel' *Schindler's Ark*. He was to become the founding chairman of the Australian Republican Movement in 1991.

† Though popularly known as Lady Isobel Barnett, she was, strictly speaking, Isobel, Lady Barnett, as she gained her title when her husband Geoffrey was knighted in 1953. Born in 1918, she died in 1980.

member of the audience remained standing as the National Anthem was played; the rest hotfooted it for last orders in the local pubs or to catch a bus. The newspapers reported that this solitary royalist had then been accidentally locked into the cinema for the night. From across the nation, voices were raised in his support. 'I myself have been jostled, winded and even injured severely by a stiletto heel in the stampede to escape,' wrote G. Atkinson of Islington.

But most Britons remained upstanding for at least another couple of years. The American journalist Michael Braun was at a concert by the Beatles at the Cambridge Regal on 26 November 1963. When the start of the show was signalled by the National Anthem, the audience – most of them teenagers – all rose from their seats and stood to attention. At the entrance of the Beatles, they all screamed, and continued to scream right through to the final chord of 'Twist and Shout'. 'Some girls are now waving handkerchiefs. Others are sitting in a foetal position: back arched, legs folded under, and hands alternately punching their thighs and covering their ears. Most of the boys just keep their hands over their ears.'

The hollering continued after the Beatles had left the stage, but the moment the National Anthem came on, all the girls stopped screaming and stood stock still, as rigid as ramrods, until the final note sounded, at which point they all began screaming just as loudly as before. At that time, this routine – scream, stand still for two minutes, scream again – was so failsafe and predictable that the Beatles would take advantage of it to make a speedy getaway through the stage door and into their waiting Austin Princess. Meanwhile even the most ardent fans remained inside, standing to attention, out of respect for Her Majesty.

But, in under a year, everything began to change. After performing in Leicester in October 1964, the Beatles attempted to execute their old trick but, this time, a group of sixty or seventy fans proved less obedient, rushing out of the auditorium while the National Anthem was playing, and swarming around the Beatles in their car, hammering on the roof and windows, causing their driver to career into another car. Ambushed by fans, the four Beatles were forced to wait for the police to come and set them free, the heralds of a less ordered society now also its hostages.

Despite these outcrops of rebellion, the National Anthem was still being played on occasions great and small in 1968. In the middle-class south, audiences remained loyally upstanding. Going to cinemas and theatres in Dorking and Guildford as a child, I would dutifully stand with the rest of the audience, feeling a little awkward and embarrassed as the familiar drone came through the loudspeakers before and after each film or play.

On a state visit to South America that November, the Queen heard it played by live bands or orchestras on eighteen different occasions, all in the space of a fortnight. No one in human history was ever to hear it more frequently, though she was also the only person in the world barred from joining in.

'Our gran must be the Queen's most loyal viewer' ran a reader's letter to the *Sun* newspaper that year. 'Every Christmas she comes to our house for dinner and to watch the Queen's speech. She always brings a Union Jack, which she drapes on top of the telly. As the National Anthem plays she puts on her best hat and keeps it on until the Queen has finished speaking.' But by then only the most diehard remained standing when the National Anthem came on the television. That year's Christmas edition of the iconoclastic TV comedy *Till Death Us Do Part** opened with the working-class reactionary Alf Garnett standing to attention as it closed the Queen's Christmas address. Meanwhile the rest of his family have already begun tucking into their roast turkey. Alf's radical son-in-law, Mike, tells him to sit down, but he won't hear of it. 'It's a mark of respect, innit?' he retorts. 'It's your national anthem, you great 'airy nelly. You've gotta stand … It's a mark of respect to her, innit? You're meant to stand for royalty, ain't you?'

'Not in front of the television set in your own home, though,' says Mike. 'I mean, that's carrying patriotism a bit far, that is, eh?'

---

* Later adapted in the US as *All in the Family*, with Archie Bunker the Americanised Alf Garnett.

'Listen, you traitorous Scouse git. I've got a bit of respect for Her Majesty, I 'ave. She has to 'ave her Christmas dinner late, 'cos of doin' that speech. She has to go off to the BBC!'

'They'd keep it warm for 'er,' interjects his quietly subversive wife, Else. ''E'd make sure it was kept 'ot for 'er ... They'd put it in the oven for 'er.'

Alf Garnett ignores Else, and continues to rant at his son-in-law. 'And she does that for us every year, she does. And you ain't even got the respect to stand up for the end of it, you socialist Scouse git!'

'Well,' says Else. 'I think it's nice of 'er to come on the telly every year and 'ave a little chat with us. I think everyone appreciates it. I do. But I don't think she expects us all to stand up at the end of it. I mean, not in our own 'omes, she don't.'

'Course she don't,' agrees their daughter, Rita. 'I mean, 'alf the country don't even stand up in the pictures when they play it.'

And so the argument goes on, edgy Christmas entertainment for the programme's millions of viewers.

By the 1970s, the Queen was in her forties, and the old reverence surrounding her theme tune was fast unwinding. At the Isle of Wight Festival in 1970, Jimi Hendrix was overheard asking, 'How does it go

again?' before coming onstage. 'It's so good to be back in England,' he announced when he got there. 'I'd like to start off with a thing that everybody knows out there. You can join and start singing – matter of fact, it'd sound better if you stand up for your country and your brothers and start singing – and if you don't, fuck yer.' He then performed a brief instrumental version – so mangled and strangulated as to be virtually unrecognisable – of 'God Save the Queen', an echo of the radically distorted version of 'The Star-Spangled Banner', which he had played at Woodstock just over a year before.

In 1974, after a national survey, the people of Australia decided to replace 'God Save the Queen' with 'Advance Australia Fair'. But the decision proved controversial. The *Guardian* reported: 'British emigrants are returning from Australia "in record numbers", a London travel agency said yesterday. "Australia's decision to get itself a new national anthem to replace God Save the Queen has apparently proved the final straw for many British families out there," Mr Simon Goodman, a director of Simms of Regent Street, said.'

In 1977, the Sex Pistols chose to greet the Queen's Silver Jubilee by forcing the familiar words 'God Save the Queen' to rhyme first with 'fascist regime', then with 'she ain't no human being' and finally with 'not what she seems'. By now, the National Anthem had come to symbolise the old-fashioned and the fuddy-duddy: theatres and cinemas had long abandoned it, even the grandest of them only bothering to play it if the Queen herself was present.

But, as often happened in the history of the British monarchy, the pendulum swung back, rebellion was subsumed into tradition, and scorn replaced by respect. Thirty-two years later, Brian May, the lead guitarist with the ambiguously named group Queen,* was invited to kick off his namesake's Golden Jubilee 'Party at the Palace' celebrations

---

* Asked why he had wanted his colleagues to change the name of their band from Smile to Queen, their lead singer Freddie Mercury explained, 'It's very regal, obviously, and it sounds splendid. It's a strong name, very universal and immediate. I was certainly aware of the gay connotations, but that was just one facet of it.' Incidentally, the first use of the word 'queen' to denote a male homosexual can be traced to 1924, so it precedes the birth of Her Majesty by two years.

in 2002 by standing on the roof of Buckingham Palace and playing 'God Save the Queen' on his electric guitar to the audience below, most of them having no choice but to stand. His performance was met with thunderous applause.

13

Had Alathea Fitzalan Howard been born a boy, she would eventually have become the Duke of Norfolk, and, as hereditary earl marshal, would have masterminded all the great state occasions. But it was not to be. 'ALAS NO TASSEL' read her mother's blunt telegram to Alathea's grandparents at the baby's birth in 1923.

The passing of the years served only to deepen Alathea's regret. When her brother produced a son in 1956, she confided to her diary, 'I do wish I'd been a boy!'

At the beginning of the Second World War, Alathea, now aged 16, had been sent to live at Cumberland Lodge in Windsor Great Park with her widowed grandfather, Lord Fitzalan, and her maiden aunt, Magdalen.

Fitzalan had been the last viceroy of Ireland, the first Roman Catholic to have held the post since the Reformation. He was exceptionally devout, reciting the rosary at 6.30 every evening. He insisted family members join him; for servants, attendance was preferred but not obligatory. Small wonder that Alathea was drawn to the younger, grander, less pious family next door, in Windsor Castle. 'I can never deny that I love all the honour and ceremony involved in a royal visit … Moreover, in that Castle, with its gilded rooms and red corridors, there is an atmosphere of happy family life that I myself have never known,' she confided to her diary. 'Ironically enough it is in the home of the King and Queen of England that I find more happiness and homeliness than I do here: it is the first lady in the Land who has won my affection before my own mother.'

The Windsors were to become for her a sort of fantasy family, cosier and more friendly than her own, more glamorous than all the others in the land. 'Everyone looked either awful or not suited to the occasion, except the princesses, Sonia* and me,' wrote Alathea after Princess Elizabeth's fourteenth birthday party. 'The whole family are really <u>charming</u>.' Her appreciation was at least partly tinged with ambition. On 20 November 1940, she chastised her mother for being blind to the social opportunities they offered. 'What she would <u>never</u> see is that Lilibet is worth a hundred friends (from the point of view of the usefulness she means) and it doesn't in the <u>least</u> matter her being two years younger ...' Looking through her diary in old age, Alathea would be struck by her own snobbery. 'I have to say that I don't really find myself *sympathique* ... my attitude towards the Royal Family was like that of Louis XIV's courtiers at Marly.'

The young Alathea had scrutinised Princess Elizabeth with a rare intensity, chronicling her virtues and shortcomings in her diary with equal relish. 'A† thinks Lilibet has an enormous chest!' she wrote on 15 March 1941, when the Princess was still only 14. 'It is a great pity as it'll be awful one day.'

She beadily charted what the Princesses wore and what they said, the events to which they had remembered to invite her and those to which – hurtfully – they had forgotten. Her absent mother airily dismissed this preoccupation of hers. 'Daddy told me that Mummy said to him that I ought to be put in a museum, because I'm so old fashioned – he said it as a joke but it hurt me, and I think Mummy is unkind.'

Yearning to be closer to the Princesses, Alathea grew to resent any rivals for their affections, particularly if they were below her on the social scale. 'They really shouldn't do it,' she wrote, after the Royal Family had invited rather too many local children for a concert at Windsor Castle at which Margaret played a dormouse and Elizabeth tap-danced. 'They ought to get up little plays for their own with their friends but not dance <u>with</u> all the evacuees like this.'

---

* Sonia Graham-Hodgson, who lived nearby.

† Annabel Newman, elder daughter of Sir Cecil Newman.

This lonely girl, bored of living with her staid and stuffy grandfather, came to regard the Windsors as her surrogate family, full of joy and laughter. Yet she never quite felt on their wavelength; their sense of humour, in particular, she found a little juvenile. 'They all shrieked with laughter but I'm afraid I could only pretend I thought it funny,' she wrote after joining them in the Castle to watch a Marx Brothers movie in March 1941. Two months later, it happened again. 'They all screamed with laughter, so I had to too,' she wrote, following a showing of *Sailors Three* with Tommy Trinder, 'but I must have an entirely different mentality because I just don't like silly films!'

The Royal Family's preference for knockabout comedy was, for her, their one and only failing. 'The only thing that does bore me about the Royal Family is that they all will tell jokes that they've heard on the wireless, etc. No one else I know is in the least interested in those sort of silly jokes, but then the K and Q and the princesses are v. simple people.'

From an early age, Alathea had set her sights on becoming a lady in waiting to her young friend. She was, she calculated, perfect for the post – 'Lilibet said she thought I was her best friend now, which delighted me. She said that Sonia used to be but she never saw her now.' She embarked on a crablike campaign to achieve her ambition. On 1 November 1941, when the King asked her, in passing, how her secretarial lessons were going, she replied that she hated typing, and then immediately regretted it: might this chance admission have cost her the job she so coveted?

The longer she remained in Windsor, the more determinedly she pursued her goal. One day, she was presented to the King of Greece and came away more convinced than ever of her suitability. 'Since God has ordained for me to sit at my ease with the crowned heads of Europe, surely he must mean me to be great? And must it not then be my duty to seek greatness?'

Like many others, before and since, her proximity to the Royal Family was what kept her going. 'Lilibet … provides the very meaning of my life.' Her happiness was dependent on their approval. In December 1941, she had been thrilled to be asked to the Castle for a performance by George Formby,* but after the show both Princesses left the room without offering a word of goodbye to her, 'only nods and smiles'. Alathea felt a bitter disappointment. 'The idea that they haven't really seen me for weeks doesn't occur to them, still less that I truly do miss them ... I tore up the programme of today's show because I knew it would never hold happy memories for me.'

There were further Ripleyesque moments when, rather than simply serve her younger friend, she wanted to *be* her. 'It is strange how everyone pities her so – I envy her more than I could possibly express to anyone.' Occasionally, her envy was tempered by disapproval. A few weeks later, she noted that Lilibet had grown a little too chubby, and both Princesses had begun to look dowdy. 'Their clothes have deteriorated lately. I can't bear their Aertex shirts ... somehow now they always look frightfully ordinary.'

New responsibilities and appointments accrued to Lilibet, transporting her off into the crusty world of adulthood: on 26 February 1942, her parents appointed her Colonel of the Grenadier Guards. She was not yet 16. Slowly but surely, the lives of Alathea and Elizabeth were moving apart, wrenched by etiquette and protocol. Can one ever really be friends with a princess? On 11 May 1942, Princess Margaret, still only 11, asked her, 'Do you call me Margaret or Princess Margaret? It's no point calling me Princess Margaret if you call Lilibet Lilibet!' Alathea confided this dilemma to her diary. 'I am actually rather worried as to whether I ought to begin calling them "Princess" – it's better to be on the safe side, of course, but it's so difficult beginning.' Three weeks later, the matter was still unresolved. 'Princess M told me

---

* Described in one of his own films as having 'a face like a horse and a row of teeth like a graveyard', George Formby (1904–61) was the highest-paid British film star of the 1930s and 1940s. The contract he signed with Columbia Pictures in 1941 gave him more money than Humphrey Bogart, Errol Flynn and Bette Davis. Formby's speciality was singing risqué songs such as 'With My Little Stick of Blackpool Rock', accompanying himself on his ukulele. He was a particular favourite of the Royal Family: after appearing in the 1938 film *It's in the Air*, he received a letter from King George VI saying that his family had been 'convulsed with laughter'. Decades later, the George Formby Society wrote to the Queen asking if she remembered their goofy idol. 'I still remember all his songs and sing them,' the Queen enthused to her senior correspondence secretary.

today to call her "Margaret" but PE hasn't said <u>anything</u>. So, I'm in rather a mix-up about it!'

In the character of Alathea, there is sometimes a smidgin of Annie Wilkes, the deranged fan in Stephen King's novel *Misery*: she worships Lilibet but is also exasperated by her, turning an unforgiving eye on her imperfections. When Lilibet's uncle the Duke of Kent dies in an aeroplane crash, Alathea writes a suitable letter of condolence, and is then shocked by the clumsiness of Lilibet's reply 'like that of a child of eleven … It gives such a bad impression to outsiders.'

Why couldn't the Princess behave more like a princess? Having watched Lilibet perform in *The Sleeping Beauty*, Alathea huffed to her diary, 'How can PE with her sense of her non-exalted position bear to act in a rowdy variety show? Now, *especially* as she's older, she ought to assume a more regal bearing. As for getting guardsmen in with low comedian jokes, it is beyond my comprehension!' Alathea feared for the long-term future of her unsophisticated young friend. 'I suddenly fell to wondering what fate awaited this girl, who was in character and tastes so much simpler than I. Will she stand out in history as another great Elizabeth, or will she merely be a commonplace puppet in a rapidly degenerating monarchy?'

As with so many friendships between girls, the little sister often got in the way. 'I never seem to be alone with her without PM. It's odd she doesn't mind being accompanied everywhere by her little sister and that she never seems to desire to talk alone with a friend.'

Three months later, she still considered her relationship with Princess Elizabeth less intimate than it might have been. She recognised in the teenage Elizabeth an emotional detachment and social reserve that would later come to define her character. 'PE was sweet today and said it was a pity that they didn't see more of me now (whose fault is that?) but I wish she wasn't so dispassionate – royalty are not always like that. No such things as vows of eternal friendship could ever pass between us – I happen to be part of her surroundings, taken for granted while I am there, but she shows no desire to talk or exchange thoughts and ideas with one of her own age. Her temperament is quite unsuited to forming strong or violent attachments – no doubt this is a blessing in one of her position and she is wholly fitted for being a queen nowadays …'

Lilibet was also, in Alathea's eyes, recklessly egalitarian, going camping with commoners, 'which I thoroughly disapprove of – it's outrageous and undignified and I think the Queen is wrong to allow it … I think democracy is responsible for this, but if it is carried to this pitch, royalty will lose the last remaining prestige that still remains to it. But the modern world is not suited to kings, and if I were one, no doubt I should cause a revolution!'

By now, it was April 1944, with Princess Elizabeth's eighteenth birthday fast approaching. So far, no party invitation had been received. 'Why does Lilibet cause such havoc in my mind? She has promoted by far the greatest pleasure in my life, represented by far the greatest happiness that I have ever known, and in proportion I suppose I must suffer when she appears to fail me for I could never mean to her what she means to me. At the moment I want more than anything else to take part in her eighteenth birthday and it is agony to wait and wait in silence and then perhaps be bitterly disappointed.'

Unfortunately, the longed-for invitation never arrived. 'I must content myself with the honour of having given her a present.' Alathea spent Lilibet's big day reading all about her in the newspapers, acknowledging to herself that she envied not only her nature – 'normal, rational and simple' – but also the contrast between the Princess's home life and her own.

Six days later, she was bucked to receive a thank-you letter – 'a most charming one' – from the Princess, 'ending with best love'.

Though her devotion remained just as constant, she was by now seeing the Princesses just once a week, at their drawing lessons. Then, one day, her newspaper informed her that Princess Margaret was to start new drawing lessons, this time with a professional artist. She imagined the worst: this would be the end of their little get-togethers, the end of their friendship with her. 'I try to understand that PE is now grown-up and has given up her lessons and that PM is now to study seriously with a famous artist … I feel I shall never see them again, that they will forget my existence – they are so busy and so happy; they can't realise my loneliness, or how I love and depend on them.'

Happily, three days later, Crawfie announced that their regular drawing lessons would be continuing. 'I was so pleased to see her again and we had a gay tea. I began calling her Ma'am for the first time!'

On 11 July 1944, Alathea, by now 20 years old, was glancing through *The Times* when she stumbled across an announcement that broke her heart: Lady Mary Palmer, daughter of the Earl of Selborne, had been appointed lady in waiting to Princess Elizabeth. It was a terrible blow: her one great ambition had crumbled to dust.

'The shock to my feelings was great, though I put on a forced cheerfulness all day ... That someone whom until ten days ago PE hardly knew by sight should take the place for which I have yearned for so many years.' She felt excluded and forlorn.

That night, Alathea woke with a start, 'thought at first it wasn't true' and found it impossible to get back to sleep. She sought solace in her Roman Catholic faith. 'I accept it as a trial from God, sent no doubt for my own good, and my implicit faith in him helps me to bear it in a more sanguine manner.' But the wound failed to heal. 'To have one's cherished ambition and dearest wish crushed', she wrote the next day, '... is a blow from which it takes a good deal to recover.'

For many months, she continued to brood on this rejection: through the summer, autumn, winter of 1944, and well into the spring of 1945. Three days before the end of the war in Europe, her wound was given another savage poke with the announcement in the newspapers that Princess Elizabeth had appointed a second lady in waiting, the Hon. Mrs Jean Gibbs. Once again, Alathea had been overlooked.

'I felt mostly annoyance that another quite unknown person, who is herself not even of noble family, should step in but I must accept now the fact they wish for married women, who perhaps are more experienced in the world, and not for her to choose her own friends.'

The war came to an end; Alathea's agony continued, despite her resolve to accept her rejection. 'The one role for which I believed myself fitted God has denied me the happiness of fulfilling.' Why had she been overlooked? 'I cannot decide whether it was my youth, my religion, my lack of title or merely lack of worldly experience which was against me.'

In December, she bumped into the second lady in waiting, Jean Gibbs. 'Try as I would, I could not rid myself of a deep, painful envy of her. It still seems to me unfair that what I longed so passionately for should have been granted to one who never gave it a thought before and who never even knew any of the Royal Family ... now that I have finally admitted defeat it has left a dark blank, which I am seeking desperately and so far vainly to fill by a successful marriage.'

She was not invited to the Queen's Coronation in 1953. Worse, she had to watch as her mother set off for Westminster Abbey, in full regalia. 'Once upon time I too would have been invited but my star waned a long time ago.' After watching the ceremony on television, she went down to the Mall and stood in the crowd as they cheered the new Queen on the Palace balcony, a long way distant.

Alathea Fitzalan Howard was never asked to be a lady in waiting, and never stopped regretting it. In 1982, a year before she turned 60, she wrote in her diary: 'It occurs to me sometimes that my diary would make very dull reading these days, and had I been made lady-in-waiting to The Queen, as at one time seemed to me and to others not only possible but probable, it would one day be really worth reading. Well, *tant pis*, it's a need I can't give up.'

14

On 18 December 1943, Alathea spotted Prince Philip of Greece and Denmark in the audience at the annual Windsor Castle pantomime. 'He seems so suited to PE [Princess Elizabeth] and I kept wondering today whether he is her future husband,' she wrote in her diary. 'I think it is the most desirable event that could possibly happen. She would like it and, though he could not be in love with her, I believe he is not averse to the idea.'

Just over a year later, on 15 February 1945, she wrote: 'PM [Princess Margaret] told me Prince Philip sent PE a photograph of himself for Christmas and she danced round the room with it for joy! She then

said: "I wonder who Lilibet will marry?" Prince Philip certainly seems to consider the possibility and PE would welcome it, I am sure.'

For Princess Elizabeth, it had been love at first sight. On 3 April 1941, just before the Princess's fifteenth birthday, Alathea joined Elizabeth and Margaret in a game of cards before tea time. 'They said something about Philip, so I said, "Who's Philip?" Lilibet said, "He's called Prince Philip of Greece," and then they both burst out laughing. I asked why, knowing quite well! Margaret said, "We can't tell you," but L said, "Yes we can. Can you keep a secret?" Then she said that P was her "boy" ... I biked home feeling very happy and also proud at being let into such a great secret, which I shall never betray.'

'Lilibet told me that Philip, her beau, had been for the weekend and that I must come and see him if he came again!' runs Alathea's diary entry for Thursday, 23 October 1941. Earlier that year, on 21 January, Chips Channon, with his keen ear for gossip, noted in his diary, 'He is to be our Prince Consort, and that is why he is serving in our Navy!!? He is a *charmeur*, but I should deplore such a marriage; he and Princess Elizabeth are too inter-related.' Three years later, on 16 February 1944, he was more supportive: 'I do know that a marriage may well be arranged one day between Princess Elizabeth and Prince Philip of Greece. At least I hope so.'*

Who was he? Like many actors prominent on our national stage, Prince Philip created a convincing character for himself – quizzical, bluff, tetchy, no-nonsense – at an oblique angle to his upbringing, which was far from straightforward.

He was born in Corfu, on the kitchen table of a house called Mon Repos. His family might have been the creation of David Lynch or Charles Addams. His great-uncle George had conducted a long affair with his own uncle, Waldemar. His mother's father had a tattoo of a dragon stretching from his chest to his legs. According to one biogra-

---

* Even in old age, Philip bridled at any mention of Channon and his diary, perhaps because they contradicted his claim that Princess Elizabeth was 'not even remotely' on his radar until the end of the war, and suggested, instead, that his marriage had been more of an arrangement than a romance.

pher, one of his aunts, Marie Bonaparte, 'twice underwent an unusual procedure to alter the position of her clitoris to bring it closer to the point of penile contact'.

In 1930, when he was eight years old, his mother Alice was diagnosed as a paranoid schizophrenic, suffering from 'a neurotic pre-psychotic libidinous condition'. Sigmund Freud himself examined her and proposed reducing her libido through the use of X-rays. But her condition persisted, and she was committed to a sanatorium on Lake Constance.

His father, Prince Andrew of Greece and Denmark, was a sozzled playboy who ended his days in his bedroom at the Hôtel Métropole in Monte Carlo, in the company of a one-time actress who now chose to style herself Comtesse Andrée de La Bigne. When Andrew died of a heart attack in the summer of 1944 at the age of 62, he hadn't set eyes on his 23-year-old son for five years. All that he left to his son were some old trunks containing clothing, a shaving brush, cufflinks and a signet ring. Philip wore that signet ring for the rest of his life.

Prince Philip's sisters made a habit of marrying Nazis. His sister Sophie's husband Christoph was a valued member of the SS, and Sophie herself a member of the Nationalsozialistische Frauenschaft, or Nazi Women's League.* Christoph's brother, Philipp (sic), is widely considered to have been Hitler's second-best friend, after Albert Speer. As the head of Hermann Göring's research office, Christoph was in charge of tapping the Duke and Duchess of Windsor's telephones on their visit to Salzburg in 1937. Philip's sister Cecilie, her husband Georg Donatus and their two children were killed in a plane crash in November 1937. Their funeral was attended by Hermann Göring. Joseph Goebbels and Adolf Hitler both sent their condolences; their coffins were festooned with swastikas.

With his mother channelling psychic messages in her sanatorium – he didn't see her for five years either – the young Philip was largely brought up by his mother's brother, the Marquess of Milford Haven, who had amassed one of the largest collections of pornography in, as it were, private hands, much of it of a sado-masochistic bent ('Lady Gay: Sparkling Tales of Fun and Flagellation'). The Marquess's wife, Nada, was the lover of Gloria Morgan Vanderbilt, and equally offbeat. After winning a Charleston contest in Cannes, she ordered a tub of champagne to soothe her feet; she then charged it to her hosts.

From the age of 11 up to the time of his marriage, Philip was of no fixed abode. Hovering in the foreground throughout his gothic childhood, like the nurse in *Romeo and Juliet*, was his mother's brother, Lord 'Dickie' Mountbatten, whose Olympian talents for social climbing meant he never let the world's highest summit out of his sight: with deft use of all the right ropes, maps, hammers and crampons, he strove to guide the dashing and suitably royal but virtually penniless Philip into marriage with the future Queen Elizabeth II. 'His vanity, though child-like, was monstrous, his ambition unbridled,' wrote his authorised biographer.

---

* After years in the wilderness, Sophie was gradually permitted into the Royal Family's outer circle, becoming godmother to Prince Edward in 1964, and being invited to the Queen and Prince Philip's golden wedding celebrations in 1997. She died in 2001.

Under the guiding hand of Mountbatten, Philip's education seems to have been designed to dispel any lingering whiff of the louche, the fascistic or the bohemian. He first attended Cheam prep school, where pupils were regularly beaten with a cricket bat for misbehaviour. Later in life, Philip looked back on such punishments with approval. 'Children may be indulged at home, but school is expected to be a spartan and disciplined experience in the process of developing into self-controlled, considerate and independent adults,' he wrote in a preface to a history of the school in 1974. He gave a cricket bat to Prince Charles for his first birthday. Some might think this an odd gift for a baby, but, as Philip explained at the time, 'I want him to be a man's man.'

Philip continued his education at Gordonstoun, best known for its cold showers, shorts, early-morning runs and general heartiness; the headmaster regarded the high jump as an effective cure for stammering. Despite its bullish outlook, it had vehemently anti-Nazi credentials: it had been founded in 1934 by a German-Jewish refugee called Kurt Hahn, who was an outspoken opponent of Hitler.

After Gordonstoun, Philip went into the Navy, where he came down hard on any sign of sloppiness. Guided by his Uncle Dickie, in June 1944 he changed his nationality from Greek to British. According to the reliable historian Ben Pimlott, this was all part of a 'considered plan, aimed at remoulding Philip for the requirements of the position both uncle and nephew wished him to hold'. But absolute discretion was essential. Dickie urged his sister – Philip's mother Alice – not to breathe a word of it to King George VI and Queen Elizabeth. 'The best hopes are to let it happen – if it will – without parents interfering,' he advised her in February 1945. 'The young people appear genuinely devoted and I think after the war it is very likely to occur.'

15

Wedding gifts arrived from far and wide, 2,583 in all. Many were extravagant: a home cinema from the Earl and Countess Mountbatten; an Astrakhan racehorse from the Aga Khan; a 175-piece porcelain dinner service from the leader of the Chinese Republic and his wife, President and Madame Chiang Kai-shek; the silver helmet of a Japanese Samurai from the Raja and Ranee of Sarawak; a gold tiara and gold cigarette case bearing the Royal Arms of Ethiopia from His Imperial Majesty Haile Selassie I, King of Kings, Lord of Lords, Elect of God.

Others were less showy, though possibly more handy: a wastepaper basket from Mrs H. G. Cronk; a bathroom sponge from the Revd Robert and Mrs Hyde. There were bed jackets galore and handkerchiefs sufficient for several lifetimes of nose-blowing.

The Royal Family's passion for afternoon tea was reflected in great quantities of teapots and other tea-time paraphernalia. Mr and Mrs Anthony de Rothschild sent a full Sèvres tea service; His Holiness Pope Pius XII a set of twelve Old Dresden two-handled chocolate cups, with covers and saucers. Many of the less well-off sent tea cosies they had knitted themselves.

Bibles, too, were popular, outnumbered only by 148 pairs of nylon stockings from Americans sensitive to Britain's post-war shortage. Most came from individuals, but many from associations or manufacturers: a dozen pairs from the Shilo Ladies' Club of Manitoba; eighteen pairs from the Prestige Hosiery Company of Philadelphia.

Generosity was hard to separate from product placement; manufacturers seized the chance to associate their wares with the year's most glamorous event: a box of silk headscarves arrived, courtesy of Le Panache de France; Messrs Frances, Thornton and Roberts Limited gave two powder puffs. The Directors, Staff and Workpeople of Two-Way Talkie Limited sent a two-way talkie; the Directors and Employees of Messrs Hoover Limited sent a hoover.

Many authors proved equally unabashed. Field Marshal the Viscount Montgomery of Alamein, never a shrinking violet, sent two books he had authored himself, each celebrating one of his own victories: *El Alamein to the River Sangro* and *Normandy to the Baltic*. Colonel Sir James Sleeman sent an autobiographical work, *From Rifle to Camera*, and the children's author Alison Uttley sent a selection of her works featuring Little Grey Rabbit and Sam Pig.

To counter accusations of gluttony in a country where sugar was still rationed, courtiers had a quiet word with some of the more illustrious cake-makers: were they to be so good as to donate a wedding cake, they would be cordially invited to a viewing party in the State Dining Room at Buckingham Palace, in the presence of Their Majesties King George VI and Queen Elizabeth. They needed no encouragement. Messrs Peek, Frean & Co. Limited, Messrs Huntley & Palmer Limited and Messrs W. and R. Jacob (Liverpool) Limited were among those companies credited with baking twelve sumptuous cakes; the tallest was four feet high and took four months to prepare.

Around the world, members of hundreds of different groups and organisations clubbed together to send something special, to reflect their own particular interests. From the Aboriginal Tribes of British Guiana came a Tibisiri hammock and a fan; from the People of Ipswich, a silver cake basket engraved with the Arms of the Borough; from the Welsh Corgi League, a paperweight statuette of a corgi; from the Members of the Finnish–British Society an informative book – *Finland and the Finns* – bound in birchwood.

The Loyal Citizens of the Kalgoorlie and Boulder District of Western Australia sent a pair of bookends made of native wood, and the Girl Scouts of the United States of America gave a crystal paperweight engraved with their badge, along with a Loyal Address bound in red morocco. Going for something rather more offbeat, the Hungarian

Students of the Law at the University of Budapest presented the young couple with a statue of Santa Claus.

Perhaps the most touching gifts were constructed by those with little to spare: a handmade album inset with coloured beads from the Ukrainian Prisoners of War in No. 82 Camp, Fakenham, Norfolk; a two-handled tray and bowl of beaten copper given by the Badly Disabled Men in the Church Army Rehabilitation Centre; a model galleon constructed by a young resident of the Shaftesbury Society Home for Crippled Boys.

A variety of exotic creatures from the animal kingdom laid down their lives for the Royal couple, albeit on an involuntary basis: a black alligator handbag arrived from Lederer de Paris of New York; a crocodile handbag from Bagcraft; a homemade leopard-skin blotting pad from the African community of Northern Rhodesia; a beaver coat from the Hudson's Bay Company. Lieutenant Colonel Donald Cameron, Major Sir John Brook and Other Officers of the Lovat Scouts donated a set of hand-painted deer-horn menu holders. The Queen's devoted friend Alathea Fitzalan Howard gave the bride a dark blue lizard-skin bag.

One or two of the gifts were unusual, to say the least. The president of the United States and Mrs Truman opted for something folksy: a glass vase engraved with a merry-go-round at an American country fair. Osbert Sitwell gave a twelve-yard-long hand-coloured panorama of the Coronation of George IV. From India, Mahatma Gandhi contributed a small tablecloth. He asked the last Viceroy of India, Earl Mountbatten of Burma, to carry it to London, along with this message: 'Dear Lord Mountbatten, This little thing is made out of doubled yarn of my own spinning. The knitting done by a Punjabi girl who was trained by Abha's husband, my grandson. Lady Mountbatten knows Abha. Please give the bride and the bridegroom this with my blessings, with the wish that they would have a long and happy life of service of men. Yours sincerely, M. K. Gandhi.' As luck would have it, Queen Mary mistook the tablecloth for one of Gandhi's celebrated loincloths. 'Such an indelicate object – what a horrible thing!' she protested.

Peculiarly generous was the Steinway grand piano from the Royal Air Force, which arrived with 'a cheque for the Princess Elizabeth's personal use'. But amid all this largesse some other members of the armed services proved reluctant to dip into their pockets for the wealthiest young bride in the world. James Lees-Milne noted in his diary that Simon Mosley, a friend in the Coldstream Guards, had informed him of his comrades' reluctance to stump up. 'Fifty per cent of them had refused to contribute towards a wedding present. The dissentients came to him in a body and, quite pleasantly, gave him their reasons. *One*, they said the Royal Family did nothing for anybody, and *two*, the Royal Family would not contribute towards a present for their weddings.' When Mosley protested that without the Royal Family the Brigade of Guards would cease to exist, they had bluntly replied, 'Good! Let them both cease to exist!'

Two nights before the wedding, a reception was held at St James's Palace for all those – grand, lowly or anywhere in between – who had contributed presents. They entered through a corridor lined with Lady Butler's great paintings of Empire: *Khartoum, 1898: The Funeral Service of General Gordon*; *The Roll-Call, Crimea, 1854*; *The Defence of Rorke's Drift, Zululand, 1879.*

The assembled presents were laid out for all to admire, though those given by members of the Royal Family – among them a pair of Purdey guns from the King, a set of twelve engraved champagne glasses and a fitted picnic case from Princess Margaret, a collection of jewellery, mahogany tables, needlework cushions and silver salvers from Queen Mary – were cordoned off from the rest.

A 264-page book accompanying the exhibition included all the gifts from foreign Royals. Today it reads like a roll call of long-lost monarchies: a pair of silver ewers from the King of Romania; two gold cups dated to around 1500 BC from the King and Queen of the Hellenes; a finely veneered walnut casket mounted with a plaque of Afghan lapis lazuli from the King of Afghanistan; a gold necklace from the King of Egypt; a gold cigarette case with diamond motifs from Queen Marie of Yugoslavia; a silver- and gold-inlaid casket complete with a gold map of England, a ruby marking the position of London, from His Highness the Regent of Iraq; a silver brazier decorated with garlands and cupids' heads from HM King Umberto II of Italy; and from Prince Philip's mother, HRH Princess Andrew of Greece, a portrait of herself by Philip de László, as well as a diamond tiara.

The stuffiness of the crowded rooms at St James's Palace contributed to the collapse of several guests, among them the Duchess of Kent, the donor of a gold dress watch with a picture of St Christopher on the reverse, and the Countess Wavell, who, together with her husband, Field Marshal the Earl Wavell, had given T. E. Lawrence's *Seven Pillars of Wisdom*, bound in red Niger leather, bearing the Princess Elizabeth's cypher in gold.

'The heat was appalling,' complained Chips Channon in his diary. With his exacting eye, he noted 'some fine but many horrible presents', though even he had to admit to being impressed by a wreath of diamond roses from the Nizam of Hyderabad. Best of all, 'My silver-box, ersatz Fabergé, was in a conspicuous position.'*

Missing from this special exhibition were several tons of tinned food, including 500 cases of tinned pineapple sent by the government of Queensland. These had already been distributed to needy widows and pensioners, along with a gracious message from the bride.

---

* Afterwards, Channon entertained Stanisław Mkołajczyk, the former prime minister of Poland, to dinner at his home in Belgrave Square. Mkołajczyk had escaped from Poland just ten days before, and was now predicting the end of European civilisation, as Channon confided in his diary: 'The Russians will attack within three years, he thinks. It will be a bacteriological warfare: England will go down; only America may survive. Sickened and horrified, I drove him home.'

16

It took the King and Queen some time to come round to Prince Philip. The Queen Mother found him 'lacking our kind of sense of humour' and would refer to him privately as 'the Hun', though the Windsors themselves had only recently changed their name from the tell-tale Saxe-Coburg-Gotha in order to avoid that very charge. In those early days, the well-connected Harold Nicolson was told by a courtier that the King and Queen both 'felt he was rough, ill-tempered, uneducated and would probably not be faithful'.

Most of the courtiers took against him, regarding him as an upstart. According to one of Prince Philip's friends, 'it rankled' that they considered him an outsider: after all, like his bride, he was a great-great-grandson of Queen Victoria. On a visit to Windsor Castle soon after his engagement, a courtier began to inform him, with needless pomp, of the history of the building. 'Yes, I know,' he snapped. 'My mother was born here.'

'They were bloody to him,' said John Brabourne, the husband of Mountbatten's eldest daughter. 'They didn't like him, they didn't trust him, and it showed. I think it hurt. But he didn't let it show. He just got on with it.' Getting on with it was to become Philip's guiding principle; he had little time for those who failed to get on with it, whatever it might happen to be.

After the wedding, Philip found his purpose uncertain, and the flummery and flunkery of Buckingham Palace constricting. Privacy was hard to come by: the Queen's dresser, Bobo MacDonald, kept bustling about as though Elizabeth were still single, endlessly popping her head around doors to check that she had everything she needed.

She would even potter in and out of the bathroom when Elizabeth was in the bath, marking her territory, trying to keep Philip at bay.

He was, by nature, a moderniser, impatient to make things more streamlined and up to date. Yet the monarchy prided itself on being slow and old-fashioned. It represented the world of yesterday, serving its subjects by keeping the future at bay.

17

Sir Ralph Glyn (Con. Abingdon) suggested that there might well be places such as Balmoral scattered throughout the Commonwealth to which the Royal Family could go to mix with their subjects.

News Chronicle, 1947

Perhaps one of the most insistent inquiries from overseas has been on where the Royal couple will live after their marriage. The fact that the Princess and her husband will probably have to share Buckingham Palace with their parents has done more than any amount of propaganda to convince the rest of the world that there is a housing shortage in Britain.

Weekly Telegraph, 1947

The Princess and her husband would have preferred their child to be born at their country house, Windlesham Moor, near Sunningdale, but it was felt that a possible heir to the throne should not first see the light in a rented house.

Daily Herald, 1948

The baby Prince is reported to be doing well, and to be a very healthy active boy, who behaves day and night as a Prince might be expected to do.

Nursing Mirror, 1948

I often think what fun it must be to be on the staff at Buckingham Palace. How proud you'd be to think that if it wasn't for you Princess Margaret wouldn't have had that boiled egg.

Woman magazine, 1948

Bristol schoolchildren are to be shown how to cheer and yet remain dignified when Princess Margaret visits the city next month.

Daily Mail, 1949

I was very horrified to see that some of the guests seemed suddenly to forget any manners they had ever learnt and stood on their chairs to watch the Royal party assemble for tea, an inexcusable gesture at any party, but quite unforgivable at a Royal Garden Party.

Tatler, 1949

Princess Margaret seems on the way to becoming a House of Commons 'fan'. The Princess herself declared that the House gives her a chance of seeing human nature 'in the raw' such as she seldom has elsewhere.

Glasgow Bulletin, 1949

Most people are pained and ashamed when they hear news about strikes, etc., announced before news about the Royal Family. I would ask all loyal people to send a post card to the BBC urging them to put Royal news in its proper place.

Letter to the *Yorkshire Post*, 1950

Said Mr Profumo: 'I do not think anything will give the Russians a
better idea of our democratic way of life than having a look at the
Queen on her birthday, surrounded by some of the most valiant
troops in the world.'

Daily Mail, 1952

'My favourite programme', said the Queen Mother, when the
conversation turned to radio, 'is *Mrs Dale's Diary*. I try never to miss
it because it is the only way of knowing what goes on in a middle-class
family.'

Evening News, 1952

Undoubtedly, the real beauty of the garden, which was jointly
constructed by Messrs. William Wood, of Taplow, and the L.C.C., did
most to draw the enormous crowds which swam like dazed but
willing fish into our rapacious net; but other reasons also prevailed –
one of the chief being to smell the roses already smelt by T.R.H.
Prince William of Gloucester and Prince Michael of Kent, and above
all to see the exact spot in which H.M. The Queen sheltered from the
rain which so inconveniently marred her visit.

WVS Bulletin, 1952

I wonder how many other people have noticed that when the names
of our new Royal Family are placed in the following order – Philip,
Elizabeth, Anne, Charles, Edinburgh – they give us the word PEACE.

Letter to *Manchester Evening News*, 1952

'There is an ornament standing in Mrs Lena Atkinson's prefab ... it is the cup used by the Queen Mother when she popped into Mrs Atkinson's for tea yesterday. There is still the faintest trace of lipstick on the cup. 'I haven't washed it,' Mrs Atkinson told me. 'And I don't think I ever shall.'

Daily Mirror, 1953

The danger of the Queen Mother's high-heeled shoes catching in the tram-lines outside Sheffield town hall posed a problem for corporation engineers yesterday. But they soon hit on the solution. They diverted the city's trams for two hours and laid tarmac across the lines.

Sunday Dispatch, 1958

18

My parents were both keen fans of Prince Philip. I remember my mother saying he had 'S.A.', a coy abbreviation, now largely forgotten, of Sex Appeal. They even owned a little hardback book of his sayings called *The Wit of Prince Philip*, published in 1965, halfway through the Swinging Sixties.

I still have their copy. The blurb reads:

Prince Philip has never been afraid to place a Royal foot inside the door of controversy when 'campaigning' for something in which he believes. While effectively walking the traditional tightrope of Royal

neutrality he has, nevertheless, pungently made plain his views on public health, racialism, juvenile delinquency, Anglo-American and East–West relations, the export drive, design, the Monarchy and Constitution ... Even his critics – and there are a few – agree that he is a man who, with wit and wisdom, charm and purpose, has attempted to do a difficult and invaluable job superlatively well, and – by the consensus of world opinion – succeeded.

Flicking through *The Wit of Prince Philip* some sixty years on, I am struck by quite how many after-dinner speeches he agreed to deliver year in, year out. Canadian War Correspondents, the Centenary Dinner of Sheffield Football Club, the National Union of Manufacturers, the Honourable Company of Master Mariners, the Annual Dinner of the Institute of Fuel: he certainly got around.

Even at this distance in time, the book delivers a whiff of cigar smoke, the clink of port glasses, ticklish coughs and appreciative 'hear-hears' and 'hur-hurs':

> *To a City Livery Club Luncheon in October 1948*: 'Just before coming out to lunch today I was asked by my wife where I was going, and I said I was going to the City Livery Club; so she said, "Oh! am I a Liveryman?" and I replied, "No, I'm sorry, you are not; you are only a livery woman."'

> *Visiting a Manchester textile group in July 1965, Prince Philip greeted the chairman of the knitting division*: 'So you're the head knit!'

> *Prince Philip described a party at Lambeth Palace, London residence of the archbishop of Canterbury, as*: 'a surplice of bishops'.

> *In Australia, during a visit to some caves, he was warned to beware of the drips*: 'Oh those! I've run into plenty in my life.'

Some of the examples seem to be not so much witty as blunt:

March 1963: 'The *Daily Express* is a bloody awful newspaper.'

At a luncheon of the Modular Society, December 1962: 'I seem to have got a terrible reputation for telling people what they ought to be doing.'

Asked if he knew the Scilly Isles, off the coast of Cornwall: 'My son – er – owns them.'

The editor divides Prince Philip's bons mots into various different categories: On Foreign Relations, On Travel and Adventure, On the Commonwealth, On Education, etcetera. To some of them are attached brief summaries of the Prince's opinions on a particular topic:

> One of his pet themes in 1958 was Britain's traffic problem. He put forward what he called 'three personal suggestions' for helping the flow of traffic: diesel exhausts directed upwards instead of sideways; roads driven straight through roundabouts to be open on Bank Holidays and other busy periods; and the making of films, like TV shorts, to instruct drivers how to avoid dangers on the fast new motorways.

Prince Philip was in many ways a tweedy saloon-bar philosopher, a combustible keg of forthright and often cranky opinions, robustly delivered. He was driven by instinct to adopt the contrary position: talking to a leading Shakespearian he was insistent that Henry Neville was the true author of the plays. The day after watching Tom Jones at the 1969 Royal Variety Show, he was the lunch guest of the Small Businessmen's Association. When one of their members said that no one could make a fortune in Britain any more, he replied: 'What about Tom Jones? He's made a million and he's a bloody awful singer.'

Occasionally, he had to apologise, or at least to explain himself. On a visit to South America in 1962, he told the president of

Paraguay, General Alfredo Stroessner, who had kept the country under martial law for thirty-five years, that it was 'a pleasant change to be in a country that isn't ruled by its people'. Following a hullaballoo in the British press, the Palace explained that the Prince was referring 'only to minor nuisances in Britain, like the Lord's Day Observance Society'.

But he remained impossible to harness. In June 1981, speaking on the *Jimmy Young Show* on Radio 2, he complained:

> A few years ago everybody was saying we must have more leisure, everybody is working too much. Now that everybody has got so much leisure – it may be involuntary, but they have got it – they are complaining they are unemployed. People do not seem to be able to make up their mind what they want, do they?

The following year, he contributed a list of his fourteen 'Most Ugsome Words' to an obscure magazine called *Logophile*. They were:

1. Nihilism
2. Macho
3. Charismatic
4. Pseudo-
5. Audio-
6. Socio-
7. Upcoming
8. Avant-garde
9. Conurbation
10. Camp
11. Obscene
12. Gay
13. Logophile
14. Imperialism

'They are parasitic words,' he explained. 'They make no sense on their own and don't improve the words to which they are added.' Maybe so; but they also represented progressive attitudes that were not to his taste. He believed in standing on your own two feet. He saw protest as whining and social welfare as a licence for laziness. 'Just at this moment we are suffering a national defeat comparable to any lost military campaign, and, what is more, self-inflicted,' he complained in 1961, adding, 'Gentlemen, I think it is about time we pulled our fingers out.'

In January 1977, the year of the Queen's Silver Jubilee, he was asked by the magazine *Director* for his views on the state of the nation. Britain, he said:

> should not concentrate so heavily on the unfortunate, the underprivileged. A hundred years ago everyone knew what he should do. He should go out, work hard, earn a living, provide for his children, provide for health, provide for old age, leave something solid for his children, accumulate some wealth and some treasures of various kinds. He wanted to be remembered for being a successful person, to contribute to charity, to build up something for the community.
>
> If you want any of these things today, they are all cut off. You need not try to provide for your children, because the state says, 'No, we are better able to educate them' … You need not try to provide for your old age, because you have got to be taxed to provide other social benefits, and in any case there is a national pension scheme. You must not accumulate wealth (well, it is not a question of must not, but it is so arranged that you should not). We have turned the whole thing, in a sense, upside down.

The following year, the young director of the Victoria and Albert Museum, Roy Strong, spoke to him at a dinner at Windsor Castle thrown for Kurt Waldheim,* the then secretary general of the United

---

* Kurt Waldheim (1918–2007), frosty secretary general of the United Nations (1972–81) and president of Austria (1986–92). He had long claimed to have been discharged from the German Army in 1942, but in 1985 it was discovered that he had in fact served in the Army until 1945, rising to the rank of *Oberleutnant*. He was also implicated in war crimes.

Nations. Strong found him 'opinionated, full of the woes of Britain, groaning on about the evils of Capital Gains Tax, VAT, the stifling of patronage, and enunciating all the other reactionary attitudes one rather suspected'.

Tony Blair remembered talking to Prince Philip at a Buckingham Palace reception for a handful of Labour MPs shortly after the New Labour landslide of 1997.

> It was going fine until Prince Philip wandered up to Joan Walley, a very sincere leftish feminist MP.
> 'Hello,' he said, 'where do you represent?'
> 'Stoke,' she said.
> 'Ghastly place, isn't it?' he replied.

The word 'gaffe' clung to him. His supporters argued that, far from being gaffes, they were conversational jump-starts: Philip would say something punchy in the hope of receiving something punchy in return. In the few minutes allotted, this would allow a conversation to leapfrog the usual platitudes of where-have-you-come-from and what-do-you-do into more exciting territory. But others did not see it that way. 'The guy is a bully and the least I had to do with him the better off I personally would be,' said Donald Stovel Macdonald, the high commissioner of Canada to the UK from 1988 to 1991. 'He was rude. One of my colleagues hadn't landed on D-Day, but he had been in one of the reinforcement groups that came up afterwards, and he was wounded almost to death. And he was the host for Prince Philip and Prince Philip made some disparaging comment about the Canadian Armed Forces – and here was a guy who had almost lost his life ... I think the man is an oaf.'

Another Canadian, Hugh Segal, chief of staff to the prime minister Brian Mulroney, recalled the time Prince Philip flew to Canada and stopped off for refuelling at the Canadian Forces Base in Gander:

Our commanding officer was out there with his wife. They were standing at the bottom of the stairs, and down he comes – he's not in a very good mood at all – and the commanding officer says: 'Hello. How was the flight, Sir?' And the Duke says: 'Have you ever flown before?' And the commanding officer says: 'Yes.' And the Duke says: 'Well, it was a lot like that.'

His life could be measured out in gaffes, many of them elevated to some kind of immortality in anthologies of quotations. Here, for instance, is a selection from *Read My Lips: A Treasury of Things Politicians Wish They Hadn't Said* (1996) compiled by Matthew Parris and Phil Mason:

Wasn't it too bad you sent your royal family to the guillotine?

> Prince Philip to the French minister of the interior,
> on the tumultuous reception he and the Queen received
> from Parisian crowds during their visit in 1957

Are you sure you want to go through with this?

> Prince Philip, aside to new prime minister Jomo Kenyatta during
> the Kenya independence ceremony in 1963, inadvertently picked up by
> microphones and broadcast to the watching crowd.

The monarchy exists not for its own benefit, but for that of the country. We don't come here for our health. We can think of better ways of enjoying ourselves.

> Prince Philip, addressing audience in Ottawa in 1969

What a po-faced lot these Dutch are.

> Prince Philip, during motorcade drive on visit to Amsterdam, 1968

Five per cent! Five per cent! You must be out of your minds.

> Prince Philip, on learning the birthrate on a visit
> to the Solomon Islands, 1982

Don't stay here too long or you'll go back with slitty eyes.

> Prince Philip, to British students in Peking, 1986

If a cricketer suddenly decided to go into a school and batter a lot of people to death with a cricket bat – which he could do very easily – are you going to ban cricket bats?

> Prince Philip, responding to a question about
> gun control, 19 December 1996

I don't think a prostitute is more moral than a wife, but they are doing the same thing.

> Prince Philip, 1988

How do you keep the natives off the booze long enough to get them past the test?

> Prince Philip, to a driving instructor during a visit to Oban, 1995

And so it went on. 'You managed not to get eaten, then?' he asked a student who had been trekking in Papua New Guinea. To a student in Budapest he said, 'You can't have been here that long – you haven't got a pot belly.' He asked a blind lady with a guide dog, 'Do you know they have eating-dogs for the anorexic now?'

A little salty, perhaps, but characteristic of a naval officer of his generation, and perhaps intended as ice-breakers, to prompt a bit of banter.

* * *

The Queen's father and grandfather both had quick tempers, and were prone to overstatement. When a Buckingham Palace footman dropped a tray, King George V screamed, 'That's right! Break up the whole bloody Palace!'

The Queen's first cousin Margaret Rhodes once saw King George VI hurling his guns into the heather in a rage at having shot so badly. It may be that the Queen, with her love of her father and grandfather and her respect for tradition, expected the same of her husband. Among the Palace staff, Philip was known for losing it. 'He had a legendary temper, which reduced some valets and pages to tears,' recalled Paul Burrell. 'When someone was found wanting, his volcanic temper erupted and his deep voice became a frightening bellow. Doors slammed and the entire floor seemed to reverberate to his furious parting shots: "You are all bloody idiots!" or "It's all a load of bollocks!" As a former naval officer, he expected his men to cope with his fire, but with his housemaids he was always kind and considerate.'

He was a bull in a china shop, a man holding forth in a role predicated on holding back. 'I can see you've ruined the island' were his first words to Colin Tennant when he disembarked in Mustique from the Royal Yacht *Britannia* in 1977. 'Colin was dashed by the remark,' recalls Tennant's wife Anne. There was an element of Basil Fawlty in him, as there was of Sybil Fawlty in the Queen, one of them ruffling feathers while the other attempted to smooth them. Lord Mountbatten remembered being driven too fast by Prince Philip in Cowdray Park. Sitting alongside her husband, the Queen kept drawing in her breath at particularly nerve-wracking moments. Suddenly, Philip turned to her and snapped, 'If you do that once more I shall put you out of the car!'

She immediately stopped her gasping. Once they had arrived, Mountbatten asked her, 'Why didn't you protest? You were quite right, he was going much too fast.'

'But you heard what he said,' she replied.

'I used to dread sitting next to him,' Margaret Rhodes said of the young Prince Philip. 'He'd be so contradictory. You'd say something just to say something, and he'd jump down your throat. "Why do you say that? What do you mean?" Quite frightening, until you got used to it. I think he's always had that debunking element in him. It was just his way ... He was like that with the Queen. He'd say, "Why the bloody hell? What the bloody hell?" I think she did find it very disconcerting.' His intellectual curiosity, and instinctive iconoclasm, could send him into crackpot territories: in the 1950s, he subscribed to the *Flying Saucer Review*.

But the Queen learned both to tolerate his views and to stand up to his barracking. In 1976, Susan Crosland travelled to America with the Queen and Prince Philip aboard *Britannia*, accompanying her husband, the then foreign secretary Anthony Crosland. 'On one occasion when Philip was sounding off about something, the Queen said to him quite sharply, "Oh, Philip, do shut up. You don't know what you're talking about."' And she would encourage others to stand up to him, too. Mountbatten's daughter Patricia remembered one particularly incendiary dinner party. 'Philip and I had a right old ding-dong about South Africa. It was a terrible argument and the Queen kept encouraging me. "That's right, Patricia," she said. "You go at him, nobody ever goes at him.'"

Sometimes, the Queen was the more crafty one, almost like a mother with an errant son, or, if you will, a handler with her corgi. She was alert to the benefits in distraction. In 2003, Chris Mullin, then a parliamentary under-secretary at the Foreign Office, accompanied the Queen and Prince Philip to the opening of the new British Council offices in Nigeria. He sat alongside them as the head of the British Council read out a little speech.

I am next to the Duke, alongside a group of English women. When Green has finished the Duke remarks loudly, 'Huh, that speech contained more jargon per square inch than any I've heard for a long time.' Then he turned to the women. 'You're teachers, aren't you? Can you tell me what all that meant?'

One of the women, a bit right-on, replies, 'No, sir. We're not actually teachers ...'

'Not teachers? What are you then?'

'Well, sir, we empower people.'

That set him off. 'EMPOWER? Doesn't sound like English to me ...'

By now the Queen, noticing that trouble is brewing, has turned and is pointing vaguely over the balcony. 'Look ...'

The Duke, stopping mid-sentence, retreats instantly to her side, somewhat bemused.

'... at the pottery.'

When they have gone, I go and look. I see no pottery.

The Queen knew how to handle him. One senior Australian Labor Party politician was having tea with the Queen at Buckingham Palace, discussing an important constitutional issue, when he was interrupted. 'The Queen was sitting across from me and Philip was talking to somebody else. And then Philip butted in and said something which was absolutely bloody stupid. The Queen was marvellous the way she handled him: she said in so many words: "You don't know what you're talking about. Let's get on with it." She did it very politely.'

As a father Philip had no suitable role model, so it's perhaps not surprising that his eldest son often felt uneasy in his presence, and, later in life, took his revenge in an act of verbal patricide.

'He was quick to rebuke his son, in public not less than in private, for inconsequential errors,' wrote Jonathan Dimbleby, in a semi-authorised biography based on a series of conversations with Prince Charles. 'Indeed, he often seemed intent not merely on correcting the Prince but even mocking him as well, so that he seemed to be foolish and tongue-tied in front of friends as well as family. To their distress and embarrassment, the small boy was frequently brought to tears by the banter to which he was subjected and to which he could find no retort. On occasion, even his closest friends found the Duke's behaviour inexplicably harsh. One remembers that after a paternal reprimand at lunch, "the tears welled into his eyes with a whole table full of people staying there … And I thought how could you do that?" Another, who both liked and admired the Duke "enormously", observed the "belittling" of the Prince and drew the conclusion that the father thought the son was "a bit of a wimp" … and Charles realised what his father thought, and it hurt him deeply.'

Was he always faithful? Some biographers say yes and some others say no, both with equal certainty. 'Philip … learned to carry on his flirtations and relationships in circles rich and grand enough to provide protection from the paparazzi and the tabloids,' wrote the biographer Sarah Bradford, before totting them all up, in an abstract way: '… The women are always younger than he, usually beautiful and highly aristocratic. They include a princess, a duchess, two or perhaps three countesses and other titled and untitled ladies.' Yet Gyles Brandreth, setting out to 'nail this issue for once and for all', could find no evidence, and calls all these stories 'rumours without foundation'.

Philip's own father had been absent from his childhood, and his mother was far from maternal. Small wonder, then, that he himself subscribed to the stand-on-your-own-two-feet school of parenting. As an old lady, his mother lived in Buckingham Palace dressed as a nun, having invented her own Order. 'Wearing the habit meant that she did not have to worry about clothes or getting her hair done,' explained Philip, matter-of-factly. Throughout his life, he steadfastly refused to analyse his parents, or their effect on his own character. His peppery best-foot-forward persona was entirely a product of his own imagination and willpower; despite the odd blip, it served him well.

19

At 7.30 a.m. on 6 February 1952, an under-valet, James Macdonald, calls in on the King's bedroom at Sandringham with a cup of tea. He draws back the curtains and finds the King dead.

An hour and a quarter later, the King's principal private secretary, Sir Alan Lascelles, telephones his assistant, Edward Ford, in London. Using the code word 'Hyde Park Corner', he asks him to inform the prime minister and Queen Mary.

Arriving at Downing Street around 9 a.m., Ford finds Winston Churchill sitting up in bed, holding a chewed cigar, his paperwork scattered around him. 'I've got bad news, Prime Minister', says Ford. 'The King died this morning. I know nothing more.'

'Bad news? The worst', replies Churchill. Looking down at all his papers, he adds, 'How unimportant these matters seem. Our chief is dead.'

Later, his private secretary, Jock Colville arrives, to find Churchill in tears. 'I had not realised how much the King meant to him. I tried to cheer him up by saying how well he would get on with the new Queen, but all he could say was that he did not know her and that she was only a child.'

At 10.45 a.m., British news agencies are permitted to announce the death of the King.

* * *

On being told that his grandfather was found dead by someone who had taken in his tea, the three-year-old Prince Charles asks: 'Who drank the tea?'

Wearing his barrister's wig and gown in court for the very first time, the 28-year-old Robin Day is listening to his pupil master beginning his opening argument in a case when a court official hands a note to the judge. Mr Justice Harman stands up 'straight as a ramrod', removes his monocle and says: 'Gentlemen, I have an announcement. The King is dead. Long live the Queen! This Court is now adjourned.' The judge then leaves the courtroom, leaving everyone in shock.

'So ended, after ten minutes, my first day as a barrister in court,' recalls Sir Robin Day, by now a renowned political broadcaster, some forty years later. 'We disrobed and went out to the Kardomah café in Fleet Street. Over coffee we chatted. Those ringing words, "Long Live the Queen", had not been heard for over half a century, not since Queen Victoria was on the throne. Now it was Queen Elizabeth. Queen Elizabeth II. Were we at the beginning of a new era?'

On the Conservative benches, Henry 'Chips' Channon wastes little time in being catty about his late Sovereign. 'His death is regrettable; it is a pity it couldn't have been postponed for a while – but it is not a disaster at all,' he confides in his diary. 'He was cross, uninteresting, lightly nervous and often disagreeable. But he could, on occasion, be kind.'

Channon suspects it was the endless party games that took the King to an early grave. 'He rarely worked – it is a myth to believe he did – he wore himself out by fidgeting and doing nothing. For years he has sat up until the early hours of dawn playing foolish games; for years he has not had proper sleep or rest. Guests who have stayed at Balmoral or Windsor have complained of utter exhaustion after only a few days.'

He predicts a colourless reign ahead. 'The strange, slightly "tinny" reign is over and a new era dawns … The new Queen is determined, humourless, serious and will be a success but not loved – after her youth and dignity wear off. The Queen Mother will take a back seat and will gradually decline in importance – she will hate that but will find compensation in doing little as her indolence and general laziness are proverbial.'

Princess Elizabeth and Prince Philip are away in Kenya, on the first leg of a Commonwealth tour that is also scheduled to take them to Australia and New Zealand. At Sagana Lodge near Nairobi – a wedding present from the colonial government – the Royal party has just finished lunch. By an unfortunate oversight, the news has yet to reach them: the telegraph operator confused 'Hyde Park Corner' for the address not the message, so hadn't bothered to forward it. The first member of the Royal party in Kenya to receive the news is Princess Elizabeth's private secretary, Martin Charteris, stationed at a nearby hotel, who hears it on the radio. Charteris immediately telephones Prince Philip's private secretary, Mike Parker, at Sagana Lodge. Parker tunes into the BBC on his wireless, and hears the news for himself. He finds Prince Philip, who is on his bed, reading the newspapers, and tells him that His Majesty has died. Prince Philip says nothing, but breathes heavily, in and out, as though in a state of shock.

When Prince Philip enters her room, the 25-year-old Princess Elizabeth is busy writing to her father, telling him of her adventures at Treetops the day before.

Not long after, Mike Parker spots the young couple on the lawn of Sagana Lodge, away from everyone else. 'They walked slowly up and down the lawn, up and down, up and down, while he talked and talked and talked.'

When they re-enter the Lodge, her lady in waiting Pamela Mountbatten goes up to the new Queen and gives her a hug. Then she thinks, 'That's wrong – she's now Queen,' and drops into a deep curtsy. Already, rules of protocol have begun to distance the Queen from her family and friends.

Martin Charteris arrives at Sagana Lodge and goes to see the new Queen. He finds her sitting at her desk – 'upright, erect, utterly resolved, very composed, absolute master of her fate' – pencil in hand, making notes. He asks what name she wishes to employ as Queen. 'My own name, of course,' she replies.

The press line the road as the Royal party leave Sagana. Martin Charteris has asked them to put their cameras aside, so not a single photograph is taken of the departing mourners. They fly from Nanyuki to Entebbe, from where they will fly home to London. After a while, the Queen leaves her seat and heads for the loo. As she returns to her seat, her face is set, but it is clear to her fellow passengers that she has been crying.

At Entebbe, the new Queen's mourning clothes, packed for this eventuality, are waiting for her, having been re-routed from Mombasa. There isn't a suitable hat, so a telegram is sent asking for one to be delivered to the plane on their arrival in London.

Within an hour of hearing of the King's death, the industrious John Masefield,* who has been Poet Laureate since 1930, is hard at work on a commemorative poem. By the end of the day, he has delivered a twenty-one-line elegy, 'At the Passing of a Beloved Monarch', to *The Times*, ready for the newsstands the following morning:

> What is a Nation's love? No little thing:
> A vast dumb tenderness beyond all price.

In the final two lines, he finds a rhyme for 'May this devotion help them in their grief', as he hopes for:

> A Kingdom grown so worthy of her Chief
> That millions yet unborn shall bless her reign.

---

* Though Poet Laureate for some thirty-seven years, John Masefield (1878–1967) was never confident in his muse: whenever he sent a poem to *The Times*, he always included a stamped addressed envelope, ready for its rejection.

The new Queen arrives at London Airport at 4 p.m. on 7 February. Her flight is met by the prime minister, Winston Churchill, the leader of the opposition, Clement Attlee, and the Duke of Gloucester.*

Upon her arrival at Clarence House, her grandmother, Queen Mary, drives over from Marlborough House to greet her, saying: 'Her old Granny and subject must be the first to kiss her hand'.

That same day, Churchill broadcasts a speech on the BBC. The King's death, he says, 'has stilled the clatter and traffic of twentieth century life in many lands, and made countless millions of human beings pause and look around them.' He praises the late King for 'the simple dignity of his life, his manly virtues, his sense of duty ... his gay charm and happy nature, his example as husband and father in his own family circle, his courage in peace or war'. The King, he says, was sustained by the sincerity of his Christian faith: 'During these last months the King walked with death as if death were a companion, an acquaintance whom he recognized and did not fear.' He points out also that 'Dear to the hearts and homes of all his people is the joy and pride of a united family ... No family in these tumultuous times was happier or loved one another more than the Royal Family around the King.'

At the close of his broadcast, he turns to the future. 'Famous have been the reigns of our Queens ... Now that we have a second Queen Elizabeth, also ascending the Throne in her twenty-sixth year, our thoughts are carried back nearly 400 years to the magnificent figure who presided over and in many ways embodied and inspired the grandeur and genius of the Elizabethan age. Queen Elizabeth the Second, like her predecessor, did not pass her childhood in any certain expectation of the crown. But already we know her well ... I, whose youth was passed in the august, unchallenged and tranquil glories of the

---

* Prince Henry, Duke of Gloucester (1900–74) was the third son of King George V and Queen Mary, and thus the uncle of the Queen. 'He is tall and bulky, and his head is wonderfully Hanoverian, flat at the back and rising to the real pineapple point of William the Fourth,' observed Queen Mary's biographer, James Pope-Hennessy. 'He has protruding Guelph eyes. He is an immensely kind, potentially irritable man, whose chief aim in life is to laugh. This, as is well known, he does in his own manner: an hysterical piglet squeal which becomes uncontrollable ...'

Victorian era, may well feel a thrill in invoking once more the prayer and the anthem, "God Save the Queen!"'

The next day, the Queen's privy counsellors gather at St James's Palace for a formal meeting of the Accession Council. Among them is the severe former chancellor of the Exchequer, the socialist Hugh Dalton. Looking around, he notices 'people one didn't remember were still alive, and some looking quite perky and self-important'. The new Queen enters alone, looking 'very small'. In Dalton's view, 'She does her part well, facing hundreds of old men in black clothes with long faces'. The Queen reads the Declaration of Sovereignty in a 'high-pitched, rather reedy voice'. When she has finished reading it, she adds: 'My heart is too full for me to say more to you today than that I shall always work as my father did.'

News of the death of King George VI affects his subjects in a variety of ways. In Bournemouth, John McGarry writes in his diary of his disappointment at the lack of grieving in his home town. His mother is going ahead with a party. 'Fancy on such a sad day. Go out at 7.30, meet Dorothy. Go out for a stroll on cliffs and have a lovely time … Get back at 9.45 to find everybody having a good time. What disgusting manners.'

Over in the House of Commons the Labour MP Richard Crossman strikes a detached note. Later that day he writes in his diary: 'No one I have met genuinely feels anything about this, except Clem Attlee.'

But is the House of Commons – or at least Crossman's version of it – out of kilter with the country as a whole? A week later, Crossman feels obliged to note that the *Daily Mirror* has 'put on half a million' while the London evening paper the *Star* has 'more than doubled its circulation'. With some reluctance, he concludes that royalty has become 'the one inexhaustible subject'.

The aspirant young novelist John Fowles, just three weeks older than the new Queen, is teaching English at a school on the Greek island of Spetsai when he hears the news. 'Death of King George VI – people keep on coming up to me, and gleefully announcing the sad news. When I came into dinner, all the boys at my table looked at me with a joyful smile, and the prefect said, with a broad grin, "The king of England is died." I think they were faintly surprised I was not in black, and weeping.'

Like Channon, Fowles is steadfastly unmoved by the King's passing. 'This king had no characteristics – a neutral, insipid personality. The modern king is a constitutional nobody; his only chance of being remembered is by his personality.' Nor does he hold much hope for the new Queen: 'this Elizabeth is a prig, a throwback, a second Victoria.'

The free-spirited novelist Rose Macaulay is another sceptic, though less strident. On the day of the King's death she notes that the BBC is broadcasting nothing but the same news, over and over again. 'A friend of mine, dropping into a pub for a drink, heard a woman there say bitterly, "It's bloody murder, that's what it is, having no wireless. That's what drives a woman into the pubs."' The BBC has declared that, during the coming period of national mourning, comedians must abstain from broadcasting jokes in bad taste. 'The comedians must be waiting eagerly for this close time for vulgarity to end … No doubt the public are waiting impatiently too. This solemn announcement was somehow very funny.'

In a bar in Notting Hill Gate, a morose drinker says, 'He's only shit and soil now like anyone else.' Two of his fellow drinkers promptly attack him; for his own safety he is hustled away.

Across the Atlantic, Oscar Hammerstein, the lyricist of one of the Queen's favourite musicals, *South Pacific*, notes that 'The King's death has had a deep effect upon the American people, and there has been more space in the newspapers on this subject than on any other than I can remember for a very long time. The silver lining is, of course, the accession to the throne of a very attractive and intelligent young woman who has it in her to become a great Queen.'

* * *

Lady Diana Cooper, who was eight years old when Queen Victoria died, still remembers 'how funny it was saying "God Save the King" and Nanny saying "Mr Brown will be KC now, not QC"'. And now it is happening all over again: the workmen have already started changing the KCs to QCs on the boards outside Robin Day's chambers.

Two days after the death of the King, Lord Mountbatten boasts to his house guests at Broadlands that the House of Mountbatten now reigns.

The following day, Chips Channon is still at it, declaring the late King 'a dreadful bore'.

Others are more gracious. Amid the thousands of messages of condolence received by the new Queen is a telegram from the flamboyant Spanish surrealist painter Salvador Dalí. 'Do accept testimony of my profound emotion and also my hope and belief that your reign will be a fulfilment of the new renaissance of the mystic values of the world,' he writes airily.

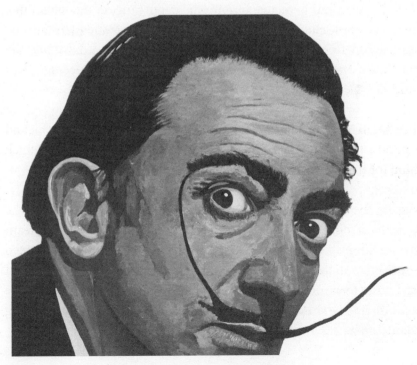

Five days after the death of the King, Rose Macaulay is already fed up with 'this present desert of royal funerals, royal accession proclamations, lauding of the late monarch and the new one, mournful valedictory music and words on the radio ... Most people are by now very tired of it; out of no disrespect to the good king dead or the new queen enthroned, for there is great feeling for both, but the feeling is inflated and blown up out of all proportion by our publicists.'

That same day, the 26-year-old Margaret Thatcher, survivor of two election defeats as the Conservative candidate for Dartford, strikes a feminist note in an article for the *Sunday Graphic*. Under the headline 'Wake Up, Women' she writes: 'If, as many earnestly pray, the accession of Elizabeth II can help to remove the last shreds of prejudice against women aspiring to the highest places, then a new era for women will indeed be at hand.'

A total of 305,800 mourners file past the King's coffin in Westminster Hall. 'Never safer, better guarded lay a sleeping King than this,' the commentator Richard Dimbleby tells his wireless audience in the curious back-to-front phraseology standard on Royal occasions such as this, 'with a golden light to warm his resting place and the muffled tread of his devoted people to keep him company. They come from a mile away in the night, moving pace by pace in hours of waiting, come into the silent majesty of the scene and as silently leave again.'

On the morning of 15 February, Frances Partridge, a junior member of the Bloomsbury Group, is worrying about how to manoeuvre her way through the funeral procession in order to get to lunch in Kensington. She is on a bus heading for Kensington when it stops in Oxford Street. 'My bus decanted me at Selfridges and all at once – like a bucket emptying its contents on me – I saw a horde of human beings advancing towards me. The procession must just have passed as their faces distinctly showed traces of a cathartic experience, like blackboards after a teacher had wiped them.'

* * *

That same morning, Evelyn Waugh writes from his home in Gloucestershire to his old friend Nancy Mitford, in Paris, saying he is feeling 'wretchedly low spirited'. His letter finds him at his most iconoclastic.

'Do your foreign set know that our King is dead? Mr Churchill made a dreadful speech on the TSF.* Triteness only enlivened by gross blunders … I suppose George VI's reign will go into history as the most disastrous my unhappy country has known since Matilda and Stephen. One interesting point stands out. The King died at the moment when Princess Elizabeth first put on a pair of "slacks" – within a matter of minutes anyway.' Waugh clearly believes in a deathly link between incorrect attire and the downfall of monarchs. 'The Duke of Windsor lost his throne by his beret much more than by his adultery,' he observes.

Two youths who refuse to observe the two-minute silence in Fleet Street are set upon by members of the public, and, in the words of one observer, 'nearly lynched'. The youths take refuge in a block of flats and are then shielded by the police from furious monarchists, though a woman manages to wallop one of them with her umbrella.

Exemplifying the British aristocracy's lofty disdain for the *arriviste* Royal Family, Nancy Mitford is as dismissive as Waugh. She writes from Paris to her friend Lady Pamela Berry: 'I fear the whole thing has turned us into a laughing stock, so thoroughly overdone … A military gentleman of my little group, I may tell you, was *rather shocked* at the slovenliness of the procession to Paddington & I hear that your Prime Minister made a wireless pronouncement in doubtful taste, but I expect you were sobbing so loud you couldn't hear it. (Every time *I* tuned into London I got an earful of Elgar.) Have you been to Windsor to have a peep at the dead flowers?'

After posting the letter, she telephones a friend and tells her what she has just written. 'Nobody in London will ever speak to you again,'

---

* *Télégraphie sans fil,* or wireless.

concludes the friend. This makes Nancy Mitford wonder whether she may have gone too far. She then attempts to repair any damage by writing a second letter to Pamela Berry. Like many such letters, it only increases the damage. 'Darling Pam, Perhaps I rather overdid it in my letter of yesterday and if so I am sorry. You know with me, partly I am by nature mischievous & partly I hate hypocrisy & rather hate Kings though I see that with the Empire etc they are perhaps necessary. I feel if we are to have one how *much* nicer to have a young queen than that very dull man ...'

Pamela Berry reacts furiously, accusing Mitford of supporting the restoration of the Duke of Windsor. A little shaken – 'after all one doesn't want to wound people's sacred feelings' – Nancy attempts to explain her point of view, once again, to Pamela. She insists that, though she loves the Duke, his 'extraordinary rapacity' would make him 'totally unsuitable' to be King. 'If we *must* have a chieftain I prefer Queen E whom I regard as entirely perfect in every way.'

The period of mourning has lasted a full ten days. Afterwards, a survey by the BBC finds that 59 per cent of listeners disapprove of the way that programmes were altered, and only 29 per cent approve. 'There are few English who do not say frankly that the time has dragged like a year and who are not relieved that it is over,' reports Mollie Panter-Downes, the London correspondent of the *New Yorker*.

On 18 February, twelve days after the death of her son, Queen Mary sends for the prime minister's private secretary, Jock Colville. She has had a sleepless night, and is in a maelstrom of fury and anxiety. It emerges that Prince Ernst August of Hanover, one of the guests at the Broadlands dinner party ten days ago, has tipped her off about Lord Mountbatten's boast that the House of Mountbatten now reigns. This follows on from a strongly worded memorandum sent by Prince Philip to Downing Street, protesting against a proposed proclamation that the family name should remain Windsor. 'What the devil does that damned fool Edinburgh think that the family name has to do with him?' storms Queen Mary. Colville tells Churchill, who tells his

Cabinet, who unanimously agree that they would never contemplate any such change.*

On 24 February, a beautiful, cloudless day in Spetsai, John Fowles is still in a funk. 'The ludicrous unreality of all the *oraisons funèbres*† and pompous praise for the late King and new Queen. The necrophilous lingering over all the funeral arrangements; the criticism of the ceremony – criticism has become so ingrained a feature of the modern world that nature itself will soon be criticized – and the declarations of devotion. Most silly of all, the parallels with the great Queen Elizabeth. England was a family then, vigorous, but still a hierarchy; people did not mind looking up. Now the world is a hive of individual units; they look levelly; have no family national love for a monarch. If the monarchy remains, it is because the lives of the masses are so colourless that they welcome the chance of any sublimation. And the crown is a psychological anchor, a break – a sea-anchor. It keeps us dragging safely back.'

---

* But Mountbatten was undeterred. Eight years later, he managed to persuade the Macmillan government that the surname of the Royal Family should be 'Mountbatten-Windsor'. 'Here's the story,' he told the great genealogist Hugh Massingberd, having summoned him to his London mews house in early 1979, in order to garner his support for the use of the new family surname on future marriage certificates. 'Princess Elizabeth married my nephew, Prince Philip, in 1947, and had two children, Prince Charles and Princess Anne. Then in 1952 Princess Elizabeth became Queen and so should have begun the reign of the House of Mountbatten on the throne. But that old drunk Churchill, backed up by that crooked swine Beaverbrook, objected to this and forced the Queen to announce that the "House of Windsor" would continue as before. My nephew was furious, as you can imagine. "It makes me into an amoeba," he said, "a bloody amoeba."'

† Funeral orations.

20

Like many parents in the 1930s, Jeannette Charles's mother liked to cut knitting patterns from the pages of magazines, and then knit the garments for her daughter. Often, they were copies of styles recently worn by Princess Elizabeth, who was just a year older.

Every now and then, someone would comment on little Jeannette's resemblance to Princess Elizabeth. As Jeannette grew up, she would regularly be mistaken for her.

'I can remember looking in mirrors as a teenager and seeing a royal likeness gazing back at me, and it was a bit of a giggle to have boys shouting, "Princess Elizabeth!" as I walked home from school.'

In 1946, she and her sister Marie went on their first trip abroad, travelling from Harwich to Hook of Holland. Their ferry docked at 6 a.m., and as the pair of them walked down the gangplank 'something very strange happened: people on the quayside started shouting, cheering, clapping and waving'.

Jeannette looked behind her for the cause of the commotion. 'When I heard someone shout "Princess Elizabeth!" the truth dawned: they were waving and shouting at me.'

Her sister found it terribly funny, but Jeannette felt embarrassed and wished she were invisible. 'I can still remember that awful creeping feeling of shame, as if I had done something wrong, deliberately deceived the waiting crowd.'

As they set foot on dry land a little girl curtsied, and a woman touched her, saying, 'You are the Princess Elizabeth, no?' Jeannette ran as fast as she could to the coach and then huddled in the back. It happened again in Naples, when she found herself surrounded by a gang of teenage boys shouting 'Principessa Elizabetta!'

Jeannette had always dreamt of becoming an actress, and on her return joined local amateur dramatic groups in Wembley. But her looks proved an impediment. 'Every time I came on stage, even if I was dressed in character as, say, a maid, there would be surprised comments from the audience and perhaps a few titters. My resemblance to Princess Elizabeth was wrecking any chance I had of sustaining a successful theatrical illusion.'

Even in the town of Midland, Texas, where she went to work as a nanny, she would be mistaken for the Princess. Her employer considered this an asset, and insisted she serve drinks to his guests. 'In his eyes, it was like having a member of the royal family to wait on them.'

When the Queen visited New York in 1957, the paths of the doppelgängers nearly crossed. Jeannette was sitting in Jack Dempsey's Restaurant in Times Square when a group of people gathered, pressing their noses to the window. 'The crowd got bigger and bigger until eventually it was so huge that, although we hadn't finished our meal, the manager pleaded with us to slip out by a back door to keep his window intact and to disperse the throng which was threatening to jam up the square.'

And so it went on, year after year. When she became a mother, it was no better. At Christmas, Jeannette's young children would jump up and down when the Queen appeared on their television, shouting, 'Look! There's Mummy!'

A lot of people looked a bit like the Queen in those days, and the Queen looked like a lot of people. I myself was one of six children. We were looked after by a nanny called Iris Barker. When I was about five or six years old, I began to spot her everywhere, all the time: on television, in the *Daily Express*, on stamps. It seemed clear to me that Iris was the Queen, or, to put it another way, the Queen was Iris. But how did it work? When she left our house after tea, did she nip up to Buckingham Palace to complete her other tasks? In a quiet moment, I asked my mother if Iris was the Queen. No, she said, she wasn't, but, yes, she did look rather like her.

In 1971, the Queen visited Jeannette's home town of Maldon in Essex. Hearing that she would be passing, Jeannette placed herself on the main road, next to the war memorial. The Royal Rolls hoved into view. 'I was standing right to the edge of the kerb, close enough to the car to have been able to reach out and touch it. The Queen inclined her head, waving gently all the time, glanced in my direction – and froze, staring, hand immobile in the air as our eyes met from a distance of a couple of feet. In fact, the car was so close it almost brushed against me.

'As it moved on, she turned her head to keep me in sight. I stood transfixed. The Queen was looking out of the rear window as the car went up a slight incline. She was still staring after me as the car reached a bend in the road and slid out of sight. I watched her receding, powerless to move. Even when she had gone, I stood staring at the empty road. It was as if I was paralysed.' It was, she thought, like staring into a mirror. 'I started shaking like a jelly, and could feel tears welling up in my eyes. I felt dizzy and sick, and thought I was going to pass out. There are those who believe that everyone has a double somewhere in the world, and who can say? Maybe it's true. What I do know is that when you see your *doppelgänger*, the effect is cataclysmic.' Jeannette went home, sat down and burst into tears.

The following year, she spotted an advertisement in her local newspaper. An artist was offering to paint family portraits for a reasonable sum. Jeannette immediately commissioned one of herself for her husband Ken. Once it was completed, the artist phoned Jeannette to ask if she could submit it to the Royal Academy Summer Exhibition.

To the artist's delight, the painting was accepted for hanging. But a few weeks later she received a call from the Royal Academy saying that it was no longer required. They had taken it to be a portrait of the Queen, but the Palace had informed them that the Queen had never given the artist a sitting. Their rule was never to accept paintings copied from photographs: hence, it was disallowed.

The news of this bizarre mix-up reached the press. The following day, the *Daily Express* ran a photograph of Jeannette beneath the headline, 'No, she's NOT the Queen'. Overnight, she was famous. 'The telephone rang and rang ... People wanted to interview me for local papers, national papers, magazines and radio programmes around the world. I was excited and tearful by turns ... Every time I stepped out of my door, people were waiting to pounce on me, notepads and tape recorders at the ready.'

Taken on by the Ugly Agency, which specialised in models with unusual looks, she proved an immediate success, appearing in television advertisements for cigars and beer. However an advertisement for a London magazine depicting Jeannette as the Queen ('If your home no longer meets your needs, then why not look in the *London Weekly Advertiser*?') was banned by London Underground. 'We feel it is in very bad taste,' explained a spokesman. 'We regard it as insulting to the royal family.'

The ban resulted in further publicity, and more work. In England, Germany, Japan and the Middle East she appeared in advertisements for whisky, silver polish, paper plates and soft tissues. With the supermodel Jerry Hall, she performed in a series of Mexican television commercials advertising Britannia Jeans. She was particularly popular at conferences and awards ceremonies, employed, at one time or another, by American Express, General Electric, Holiday Inn, Mars Bars, Brooke Bond tea, Crown Paint, Mini Metro and companies selling computer software and cavity wall insulation.

Around this time, Jeannette calculated that if she wished to expand her career she should sound more like the Queen. Accordingly, she hired a voice coach, who advised her to tape the Queen's annual Christmas message and treat it as a Linguaphone course. 'I record it, listen to it; record my own version of it, listen to it, record myself again, adjusting my tone where necessary, honing and refining and perfecting as I go.'

She travelled far and wide: to Singapore to address an Asian Advertising Congress, to Germany to film promotional videos for F.U.S. Jeans and McDonald's, to Canada to open a waxworks exhibition, to Switzerland to film a commercial for a chain of fish-and-chip restaurants, alongside lookalikes of, among others, the pope and Joan Collins.

The Sandhurst Military Academy even employed her to stand in for the Queen at a rehearsal for their annual Sovereign's Day Parade. 'I walked around making small talk and shaking hands. What gave me a great fillip was the three rousing cheers the cadets raised for me at the end of my inspection. I loved the feeling of exhilaration it produced which I'm sure Her Majesty must have experienced, too, when she inspected the real parade.'

Her new career catapulted her into showbusiness: she appeared on a chat show with Russell Harty ('so friendly and courteous'), at the Palladium with Dorothy Squires ('so marvellous, a real star') and on a Thames Television magazine programme hosted by Eamonn Andrews ('such fun to talk to … a gorgeous interviewer'). She also became a regular on television comedy shows, working with Freddie Starr, the Goodies, Cilla Black, Dave Allen, Morecambe and Wise, Jim Davidson, Eric Sykes, the Two Ronnies, *Monty Python's Flying Circus* and *Saturday Night Live*. Most of the sketches involved the Queen doing something either humdrum, such as putting her milk bottles out, or outlandish, such as strolling around with a trumpet on her head. Later, she appeared in the Austin Powers film *Goldmember* opposite Michael Caine and Beyoncé, and in *The Naked Gun* opposite Priscilla Presley and Leslie Nielsen. She didn't take to O. J. Simpson. 'He said to me, "Little lady, I earn more in a day than you'll ever earn in a year." And I thought, "You conceited oaf."' By this time lookalikes representing lesser members of the Royal Family – Charles, Diana, Fergie, Andrew – had joined her in the market.

Throughout her career, Jeannette Charles insisted on respecting the dignity of her *doppelgänger*. 'I am a staunch royalist and I would hate to be part of anything that upset or embarrassed our royal family in any way.' For this reason, she refused to be photographed in a saucy calendar as Miss January, wearing fishnet tights and a black corset. She also gave short shrift to Ali G when he asked her to drop her knickers. Nevertheless, her boundaries remained elastic. In one sketch for the

TV series *Q*, Spike Milligan played a tramp hanging around outside Buckingham Palace; Mrs Charles, appearing as the Queen, took a gun from her handbag and shot him.

When filming around Buckingham Palace, she would regularly be taken for the Queen. 'I do believe it's sometimes kinder not to disillusion people, particularly if they are children. I can remember when I myself learned there was no Father Christmas, and it came as an awful shock to me.'

There was a more sinister side to her peculiar job. She once answered her telephone to hear a man saying, 'We're going to kill you.' Horrified, she hung up. It rang again. 'We're going to kill you.' The police advised her to fit an alarm system. Following the kidnap attempt on Princess Anne in 1974, Mrs Charles began to worry that a cheap-skate or short-sighted kidnapper might make off with her rather than her more profitable counterpart. From that point on, wherever she went in public, she took care to be surrounded by others.

It is said that Saddam Hussein employed a number of doubles as decoys, and so does Vladimir Putin. I doubt Jeannette Charles would

ever have been hired by the Secret Services to act as the Queen's decoy. Her dogs, too, would have had trouble passing muster as corgis: they were Rottweilers.

She died in June 2024. Like the Queen, she had lived to the age of 96. Did she ever really look like her? At four foot eleven inches, she was three inches shorter. Her facial features were more exaggerated and coarser: the Queen as she might appear in a bad dream.

21

It's recurring: Kingsley Amis kisses the Queen for a while, and then tells her, 'Come on, let's go off somewhere,' or words to that effect. But she replies, 'Kingsley, I can't' or 'No, Kingsley, we mustn't.' She never lets him to go all the way, though the same cannot be said of Margaret Thatcher.

Joanna Lumley is the Queen's driver. The vehicle is a jeep. The Queen is completely in command, jumping into the seat beside Joanna and telling her which road to take. Both driver and passenger are wearing camouflage gear: they are on some sort of mission. They chat easily, Joanna deferential but not creepy. Joanna is sure that the Queen trusts her, as she has clearly been driving her around for years.

Graham Greene gets together with the Queen on a pretty regular basis. In 1966, there is a muddle about the reception at Buckingham Palace where he is to be made a Companion of Honour. There has been a change of date, and he was away in the Congo when the note arrived. For some reason, his secretary had lied, telling the Palace that he had received no such note.

When Greene turns up at the Palace, he is taken to one side by a state official.

'Tell me the truth,' he says. 'Your secretary lied, didn't she?'

'Yes,' admits Greene. 'I can't imagine why. I was in the Congo.'

They pass by the Queen, who is sitting on her throne. Greene pauses to shake her hand. She gives him a smile. 'Not yet,' she says, 'it would be a breach of protocol.'

Greene realises he has lost his place in the queue.

The official and Greene go into the garden to pass the time. There are a lot of bishops about, and children sitting at tables eating buns and ice cream. After an hour, they go back in. Greene is feeling hungry, and so, clearly, is the Queen, as she has sat herself down at a table with a bun.

Greene is a little put out because she calls him by his original Christian name, Henry, which he has always disliked.

Two years earlier, Greene finds himself, quite by chance, sitting beside the Queen during a service at St George's Chapel, Windsor. The officiating clergyman is preaching an absurd sermon, and Greene is perilously close to bursting into a fit of giggles, and so is the Queen. Thoughtfully, she holds an Order of Service in front of Greene's mouth to hide his grin.

Prince Philip enters. Greene is not at all surprised to see that he is wearing a scoutmaster's uniform, but resents having to surrender his chair to him. Before Greene moves away the Queen confides in him, 'I can't bear the way he smiles.'

A housewife from Leeds bumps into the Queen on a bus and invites her to tea, saying, 'I expect you don't get much chance of an ordinary good cuppa, do you, love?' The Queen arrives at her terraced cottage, knocks on the door and sheepishly confesses, 'I hope you don't mind, I've brought my mother along too.' The housewife then notices the Queen Mother hiding around the corner in gumboots, waiting to be invited in.

On the night of 15 December 1936, Henry 'Chips' Channon finds himself in Paradise. There, to his surprise, is Wallis Simpson sitting on a throne, the Archangel Gabriel at her side. She greets Chips in what he later describes as 'the nasal drawl that is as attractive as it is irritating'.

'You see, Chips, if I couldn't be Queen of England,' she says, 'I've got to be the next best thing, for I'm Queen of Heaven.'

* * *

In 1957, the year Clancy Sigal is granted permission by the Home Office for an indefinite stay in Britain, the Chicago-born writer starts to have regular encounters with Her Majesty. On one occasion, she invites him to tea and tells him she secretly admires his writing. On another, she personally awards him a medal. Virtually every time they happen to meet, Sigal saves the Queen's life from the bullet of a crazed assassin. His encounter with her sister Princess Margaret is more fruity: by chance, they hail the same taxi on a rainy night in Fulham Road and end up at her place, not his.

In 1955, C. S. Lewis, the author of *The Lion, the Witch and the Wardrobe*, is being presented to the Queen. He is halfway through this audience when he finds to his horror that he has forgotten to remove his hat. At that moment, a lady in waiting approaches him from behind 'with the speed of a roller-skater' and snatches it off his head with the words, 'Don't be a fool!'

He leaves the Queen's presence feeling pensive. Walking through the great gallery, he notices a photograph of himself on an occasional table. He reacts by tearing it into pieces, before moving on.

Two or three times a year, the humorist Arthur Marshall breakfasts with the Queen in her Windsor boudoir. 'Only the two of us and everything just as snug as snug. After her All-Bran and prunes, Her Majesty favours for her main dish really rather a *mound* of tinned salmon, while at the "preserve" stage, Robertson's Golden Shred seems especially pleasing to the royal tooth. Conversation flows, and we *roar*! No corgis, and Prince Philip breakfasting in bed.'

During the night of 7 September, the Australian artist Donald Friend finds himself dressed in a rumpled dinner jacket, 'strangled by a collar', just as the Queen is passing by, dressed in 'a vast cloth-of-gold crinoline sewn with seed-pearls, turquoises and alexandrites, tiaraed with diamonds, hung with Mary Stuart's pearls, brooched with diamond sunbursts'.

The Queen's attention is caught by the plump, crumpled figure standing before her.

She upbraids him. 'What is your name? Why are you wearing no Orders?'

'Donald Friend, as it please your Majesty,' he replies. 'I have no Orders, Ma'am.' He sinks to his knees in exhaustion.

'*No Orders?* – this is shocking.' She glares furiously at her trembling ministers and courtiers. They too quail.

'Bring me some Orders. And a sword!'

A quick-thinking gossip columnist finds one in a case of rare weapons hung on the gallery wall between a Ned Kelly painting by Sidney Nolan and a painting of Pirates and Ladies by Norman Lindsay. Meanwhile, ladies in waiting busily pin assorted Orders on Donald Friend.

'Out of my way,' commands the Queen, brandishing the gleaming blade. She graciously dubs him on both shoulders. 'Arise, thou good and trusty Sir Donald.'

She hands a courtier the sword, says, 'Put this thing back where it belongs. I've done my dubbing for the day,' and sweeps away.

When morning comes, and he returns to consciousness, Donald Friend worries that his unnerving nocturnal encounter with his Sovereign reflects 'the dilemma of a mediocrity who took a fancy sometimes to appear among the pompous disguised as a celebrity'. But might it also reflect some deeper guilt? In Freudian terms, is the Queen his super-ego? After his death, his diaries reveal that he preyed on young boys in Bali during the 1960s and 1970s.

In 1965, the novelist and biographer Tim Jeal accompanies the Queen on a visit to the handkerchief department in Harrods. She has promised to buy him a handkerchief, but he is being very difficult, 'rejecting large amounts of handkerchiefs, tossing them disdainfully on the counter'.

The two of them then board the Royal Yacht *Britannia* together. 'I think we were going to be married. I was certainly looking forward to some sort of ceremony, probably a coronation; there was close affection between us.'

* * *

130

Pablo Picasso enjoys regular threesomes with the Queen and Princess Margaret. He often tells his English friend Roland Penrose about these trysts. 'If the English knew what I had done in my dreams with your Royal ladies, they would take me to the Tower of London and chop off my head,' he says.

In the 1970s, the actress Judi Dench and her mother are paid a surprise visit by Prince Philip and Princess Anne. She is mortified to see that the Prince has nothing to sit on other than a large basin filled with straw and strong-smelling manure. But he sits right in it, without so much as a murmur. Judi and her mother are both beside themselves with embarrassment and don't know where to look. Prince Philip seeks to reassure them. 'Don't worry,' he says. 'We take everything in our stride.'

Around the same time, the journalist Anthea Disney is presented to the Queen. They shake hands. They are both wearing leather gloves, and these gloves stick together. They try to disengage, but it proves impossible. They just stand there, looking like fools. 'The Queen was especially perturbed because this sort of thing did not generally happen, and was not on the schedule,' recalls Disney. 'Then she began to laugh. Eventually, we took our hands out of the gloves, and parted company with one glove each, leaving the other pair of gloves still locked together in a handshake, on the floor.'

At a dinner party, Princess Margaret tells the author A. N. Wilson of her frequent nocturnal encounters with her sister, the Queen. They always follow the same pattern. She – Princess Margaret – has done something truly awful, something that transgresses everything she has been brought up to believe, something which has made the Queen angry.

Princess Margaret wakes up in a state of anxiety. She cannot rest until she has heard her sister's voice in her waking life. All she needs is to hear the familiar voice: 'Hello.' 'Hello.' They will then hang up, and the rest of the day can proceed without the black cloud of being 'in disgrace'.

* * *

The slippery American novelist Paul Theroux is sitting with the Queen on a sofa in a room in Buckingham Palace. She is young, and her face is thin, as it is on stamps. 'You seem dreadfully unhappy,' she says. Theroux is in fact miserable, but too shy to admit it.

She wears a stiff dress of green brocade, with a deep cleavage. Her rings sparkle. Using both her hands, she pulls apart the bodice of her gown. 'Her breasts tumbled out,' recalls Theroux, 'and I put my head between them, her nipples cool against my ears.'

'Isn't that better?' asks the Queen.

Theroux sobs between her breasts, unable to reply.

Peter Ling, the creator of two long-running television soap operas, *Compact* and *Crossroads*, takes tea with the Queen two or three times a week for several months. Afterwards, he tells his wife how nice the Queen was, but she finds these tales boring and teases him, so he stops telling her.

Ten years pass. His wife wakes up one morning and says that she, too, has just had tea with the Queen. 'I must say,' she adds, 'I do see what you mean about her ... she really is awfully *nice*, isn't she?'

A well-known writer* is on the lavatory. 'I'm sitting down, thinking it is perfectly safe, and then I find out that the Queen is standing beside me while I am doing it, carrying on a conversation, and I am thinking, "Do you think if I sat fully enough on the seat she wouldn't think it was the lavatory, she'd just think we were in a drawing room or something of that kind?"' He finds himself in this situation over and over again. 'I think the Queen represents God in one's dreams, all-seeing and from whom no secrets are hidden,' he conjectures.

Boris Johnson is prime minister; this is no dream. But one night he dreams that he is late for a meeting with the Queen and the Duke of Edinburgh. The next time he sees her, he tells her about this night-

---

* Who wishes to remain anonymous.

mare. 'Oh yes,' she replies, in a tone that suggests she has heard it all before, probably from other prime ministers. 'Were you naked?'

The author Brian Masters* regularly turns up for dinner at Buckingham Palace. Just as he is sitting down, he realises he has forgotten to put on any clothes. He fumbles to cover himself with a horribly small napkin. The Queen and her well-brought-up family make no allusion to his nakedness, and chat on as though nothing were amiss.

In 1972, Brian Masters writes a book called *Dreams About H.M. The Queen*, in which he collects two or three hundred dreams about her, from all kinds of people. By his estimation a third of the country have dreamt about the Royal Family at one time or another.

'The next time you dream of the Queen, ask yourself how you felt in the dream, how she treated you, how you behaved, what sensation was paramount in your heart when you awoke,' he advises. 'The exercise is far from useless. The Queen will, without knowing it, tell you something about yourself. In addition to all her accomplishments and skills, H.M. the Queen is unofficial private psychiatrist and unapplauded Dutch uncle to a great number of her subjects. She is Queen of the British psyche.'

---

* Biographer of serial killers Rosemary West, Dennis Nilsen and Jeffrey Dahmer.

22

Correct behaviour, and the fear of transgression, lie at the heart of most of our dreams about the Queen. She knows how to behave, and we don't. We dread doing the wrong thing, and showing ourselves up. In Freudian terms, she is our super-ego; in Christian terms, our conscience.

She herself was brought up to abide by a strict code of behaviour. Whenever the little Princess Elizabeth came to say goodnight to her grandfather, King George V, he expected her to walk backwards towards the door, then curtsy and say, 'I trust Your Majesty will sleep well.'

Her grandmother, Queen Mary, was equally strict, adhering to the customs of the Victorian age until her death in 1953. On one country-house visit, she arrived with two dressers, a footman, a page, two chauffeurs, a lady in waiting, a maid for the lady in waiting and a detective. Before her arrival she sent a list of her needs, quite as detailed as any rider sent out by today's rock stars: a chair to be placed outside her bedroom for her page to sit on, fresh barley water placed in her room at two-hourly intervals, six clean towels per day, and so forth.

Queen Mary could be capricious, inventing protocol to suit her changing moods. One of her grandsons, the Duke of Kent,* recalls her behaviour during tennis tournaments at Wimbledon. 'If Queen Mary decided she'd like to go and have a cup of tea, and some chocolate cake, she would rise and the game had to stop … Queen Mary didn't

---

* Prince Edward, Duke of Kent (b.1935), first cousin of the Queen, eldest son of the Kents in the next paragraph.

like sitting in the sun, so if the sun came on to the Royal Box, she would move back a row or two, which also displaced everybody.'

These arbitrary rules could sometimes multiply the embarrassments they had been designed to reduce. Peter Russell, the butler to the Duke and Duchess of Kent in the 1950s, remembered the intricate system initiated whenever Queen Mary and her daughter-in-law wished to pay a visit to the lavatory. 'It was the practice of the Queen or the Queen Mother that if they wanted to use the loo, they informed the Duchess, who in turn told me. I then told the head housemaid, who arranged for a housemaid to stand near the door, holding a hand towel for appearance's sake. The house-keeper would tell me when all was at the ready. I would tell the Duchess who discreetly would inform Her Majesty.'

The Queen Mother, born in the reign of Queen Victoria, cheerfully continued many of her mother-in-law's rules of behaviour. In June 1952, she expressed a wish to visit Sissinghurst, the home of Harold Nicolson and Vita Sackville-West. Luncheon was duly arranged. A

natural bohemian, who liked to wear trousers, Vita was determined to get things right: 'I shall have to put a skirt on.' Nicolson sought advice on royal protocol from Lady Diana Cooper, and relayed it to Vita. 'She sits at the end of the table and I on her *left* hand ... The reason is that when she enters a house it is technically *her* house, and she therefore takes the head of the table.'

Major Colin Burgess served as her equerry from 1994 to 1996. 'People who met the Queen Mother for the first time would sometimes be in a bit of a panic and ask me, "What do I do, what do I do?" I would then explain the few simple rules to follow when in the presence of a member of the Royal Family. I would tell them that at the first instance you had to address her as "Your Majesty" and bow, and if you left the room you should bow again to her before leaving, unless you were going in and out all the time ... Once you had called her "Your Majesty", you would say "ma'am" after that. By the way, "ma'am" is pronounced like "jam"; people who stretch out the middle "a" because they think they are being posh are a source of great amusement to the Royal Family ... Some people came to Clarence House for lunch visibly shaking, they would be so worried. But I would do my best to reassure them; sometimes, I even had to show women how to curtsey properly, and you can only imagine how that must have looked! I would say, "It's really easy. Just remember only to shake hands with her if she offers a hand. Don't speak unless you're spoken to and don't talk over her. That's it really."'

The Queen inherited her parents' adherence to the rules of protocol and tradition, believing that everyone, high and low, felt more secure for knowing where they stood. Printed cards in the guest bedrooms asked guests 'to refrain from offering presents of money to the Servants of Her Majesty's establishment', while adding that monetary gifts were permitted for the acting valets and ladies' maids.

Tipping the Almighty comes with its own set of rules. Before church each Sunday, the Queen's dresser would tightly fold a £5 note into a quarter of its size. She would then press it flat with an iron before giving it to the Queen. When the time came for the collection, the Queen would drop the folded note into the box, with her head to the fore.

When Paul Burrell joined the Buckingham Palace staff as a footman at the end of 1976 he was handed five different uniforms by the deputy sergeant footman: full livery for state occasions, a tailcoat with top hat for semi-state occasions and Royal Ascot, a double-breasted, high-neck tailcoat for the Royal Yacht *Britannia*; a white safari jacket for hot climates; and livery of a black tailcoat, black tie and scarlet waistcoat for everyday wear.

He soon discovered that 'everything about the Royal Family, even private mealtimes, is planned, scripted and orchestrated to perfection'. Every tray had a correct layout plan: 'cup and saucer with handle and spoon pointing towards five o'clock; plates and saucers turned so the royal crests were at twelve o'clock; salt on right, mustard on left with the pepper behind; sugar basin with cubed white sugar, never granulated, and sugar tongs; toast always in a silver toast rack and never on a plate; no more than three balls of butter in the dish'. One of his instructions was that he mustn't look at anyone in the eye, another that the Royal Family does not like to be watched while eating.

He was also instructed in 'Bathroom procedure'. A towel should be draped lengthways over the chair so that when the gentleman sat down he could pull it around him and stand up as if he were wearing a robe. He learned from the Prince of Wales's valets that the prince had more particular requirements, too: 'A silver key, bearing his feathers, was attached to the end of a toothpaste tube like a sardine-tin key and turned to squeeze enough to fit on the brush. His cotton pyjamas had to be ironed each morning.'

Servants aimed for invisibility. 'At Sandringham, maids would dart into a walk-in cupboard under the stairs so as not to be seen when the Queen was coming down the main hall.'

Before setting off from Buckingham Palace for the Christmas season, the Queen made a point of having a word with each member of her household staff. Over a period of two hours, she would stand in the Bow Room, receiving each member of her 300 staff individually, from the most junior to the most senior. She would bid them a Happy Christmas, before giving them each a small present that they had previously selected for themselves from a catalogue. All the women would be obliged to wear white cotton gloves, while the Queen, abandoning her usual gloves, received them with bare hands.

The Household staff were instructed to avoid physical contact with the Queen. This could lead to awkwardness. A former under-butler, Martin Higgins, remembers finding himself dancing with her at the annual Balmoral ball. 'It's all of the royal family, neighbours, estate workers and staff, and it's all about Scottish dancing. So, you're generally changing partners and everything. The first dance was called the Paul Jones, with all the ladies holding hands and dancing in an inner circle in one direction, and all of the chaps holding hands in an outer circle and dancing in the opposite direction. Once the music stops, the person you're facing is your partner. On this occasion, the music stopped and I was facing the Queen. And I thought "oh goodness". She looked at me and I looked at her, and she smiled and came across. And of course this wasn't a Scottish dance, it was a slow quickstep, so you had to put your hand round the Queen, which obviously you shouldn't really be doing. I tried to do that without touching her. When it was all over she said: "Martin, I had asked the orchestra not to play this kind of music. It's so hard to dance to, don't you think?"'

Her father, King George VI, would lose his temper at the sight of a medal misplaced or a button undone. At the wedding of his elder daughter, his eyes focused on a watch chain being worn with uniform by King Peter of Yugoslavia. Regarding the combination as beyond the pale, he told him to remove the watch at once. 'It looks damned silly and damned sloppy.' The Queen inherited his passion for correct dress, though she was less forthright in her slapdowns. When a newly appointed British ambassador attended the customary 'kissing hands' ceremony* at Buckingham Palace in full diplomatic uniform, he forgot

---

* In this ceremony, the appointee kneels on a footstool in front of the Queen, who offers her right hand, palm downward, fingers closed. The appointee extends his right hand, palm upward, takes the Queen's hand and brushes it with his lips. This applies to privy counsellors and government ministers. Ambassadors, governors general and Church officials are excused the kissing. When I was a young author, making my way in the world, I never for one moment imagined that one day I might be driven to write this footnote.

his gloves. Immediately afterwards, the lord chamberlain sent the Foreign Office a note asking if the rules had been changed without his knowledge. 'It was pretty clear that he was writing on the Queen's instructions,' observed a fellow ambassador. 'She does notice things; she's a master of detail.'

It made little difference that the origins of these dress codes were obscure or unknown or contradictory; those bold enough to question them were given short shrift. For some, the emphasis on gloves proved a source of particular consternation. 'I didn't like the feeling I got when I was standing in the receiving line waiting to meet the Queen,' recalled Barbra Streisand, of her appearance at the Royal Film Performance of *Funny Lady* in 1975. 'I struggled with whether I should curtsy or not. After all, she wasn't my queen. And the idea of curtsying to anyone felt demeaning. It reminded me of all those old notions of actors as second-class citizens, who had to enter through the kitchen ... the prince and the showgirl ... and tapped into the obstinate part of me. Then there were all these rules. According to protocol, you're not supposed to speak until the queen speaks to you. And women were required to wear gloves. Huh? That seemed like something out of another era. And if women were required to wear gloves, why not men?'

Before she was presented to the Queen, Streisand's husband bet her a hundred dollars that she would not ask the Queen this very question. On the big day, draped in a lavender cape, Streisand performed 'a kind of curtsy' to the Queen. She then asked her, 'Why do women have to wear white gloves to shake your hand, but not men?'

She thought the Queen looked 'a bit startled' at the question. 'I'll have to think about that one,' she replied. 'I suppose it's tradition.' She then 'smiled graciously' before moving on.

23

Letter dated 27 May 1953 to Queen Elizabeth II:

Clarence House

Darling Angel,

I don't want to bother you when you are so busy, but I must somehow borrow a row of diamonds for the Coronation, & if I don't hear from you I will get hold of one of Granny's – OK?

Your loving Mummy*

---

* A helpful footnote by William Shawcross in *Counting One's Blessings: The Selected Letters of Queen Elizabeth the Queen Mother* informs us that 'From photographs of the Coronation, it seems that the Queen Mother wore three separate necklaces – probably her own Coronation necklace given her by the King in 1937, the Teck collet necklace, which first belonged to George III's daughter Princess Mary, Duchess of Gloucester, and the necklace that Queen Alexandra was given as a wedding present by the City of London in 1863.'

24

An estimated 150 Continental prostitutes will be arriving in the West End in readiness for the Coronation. This is only to be expected: these grand theatrical events affect people in different ways, and the aphrodisiacal power of the monarchy remains a neglected field of study. Back in 1937, Scotland Yard set up an 'Anti-Vice Squad', otherwise known as the 'Clubs Office', charged with cleaning up the capital before the Coronation of King George VI. Records from the criminal courts show a similar crackdown on pimps and prostitutes prior to the Great Exhibition of 1851 and the Coronation of Queen Victoria in 1837.

Liverpool Public Libraries announce the winner in the under-eleven age group for an essay in celebration of the coming event.

This winning essay is by Paul McCartney, age 10 years, 10 months. It begins: 'On the Coronation Day of William the Conqueror, senseless Saxon folk gathered round Westminster Abbey to cheer their Norman king as he walked down the aisle. The Normans thinking this was an insult turned upon the Saxons killing nearly all of them. But on the Coronation of our lovely young queen, Queen Elizabeth II, no rioting nor killing will take place because present day royalty rule with affection rather than force.'

It continues, 'The crowds outside Buckingham Palace will be greater than they have been for any other Coronation, so will the processional route to the Abbey. Preparations are going on all over the world, even in Australia people are preparing to take that long voyage to England. In London, children, for a Coronation treat, are being given a free seat by the roadside. But the London children are not the only lucky children, for youngsters in other parts of Britain are receiving mugs with a portrait of the Queen engraved on the china ... But after all this bother, many people will agree with me that it was well worth it.'

Young Paul is presented with his prize, Geoffrey Trease's *The Seven Queens of England*, by the lord mayor of Liverpool in a ceremony at Picton Hall on 27 May 1952. 'It was my first ever experience of nerves,' he will later recall. 'I was shaking like a jelly.'

Three years younger than the new Queen, the 23-year-old Jacqueline Bouvier travels to England on the SS *United States*. She has been commissioned by the *Washington Times-Herald* to cover the popular response to the Coronation. The trip is to serve a dual purpose: a dashing young senator from Massachusetts by the name of John F. Kennedy has asked her to marry him, and it will give her time to consider his proposal.

Fellow passengers bound for the Coronation include the CBS News anchorman Walter Cronkite and delegations from Colombia, Cuba, the Dominican Republic and Guatemala, accompanied by soldiers in national dress uniforms. Though they have not been invited to the ceremony, the Duke and Duchess of Windsor are also on board. They are on their way to Paris, together with the Duchess's close friend Jimmy Donahue and Donahue's mother Jessie, the Woolworth heiress. 'Passengers stare at the Duke, aware that if he had not abdicated they would not be sailing to the Coronation of his niece,' observes Miss Bouvier.

Described in her byline as 'Girl Reporter', she starts work the moment the ship docks. 'The whole country is concerned with the Coronation, the whole Coronation, and nothing but the Coronation,' she writes. 'Every home one could see through the windows of the boat train between Southampton and London bore a picture of Queen Elizabeth pasted on the outside of the house or in a window. Every building is decorated: great swoops of multi-colored bunting adorn all the big hotels ...' Her piece appears under the headline 'Crowd of Americans Fill Bright and Pretty London'.

* * *

Three days before the Coronation, Jacqueline Bouvier quizzes Norman Waters, a naval steward, one of many thousands of servicemen set to line the Coronation route. 'We've been training standing long periods of time with nothing to eat,' he tells her. 'Some of the lads got taken to the sick bay. Not me, though ... I'm standing there till I drop.' Expectations are high, and joy is in the air. A London taxi driver tells her: 'Everybody's so good natured now. I was telling my missus we should have something like this every year.'

Outside the Dorchester Hotel, she eavesdrops on two upper-class women. 'One woman turned to another and said, "No, darling, let's lunch at Claridge's. That's where all the deposed monarchs are staying."'

At the weekend, the feisty young Labour MP Barbara Castle holds forth on the BBC's *Brains Trust* from Lowestoft. 'Why should we have all this neurotic outburst?' she asks, declaring, 'I hope it is the last Coronation of this kind this country will ever see, utterly unrepresentative as it is of the Britain and the Commonwealth of the ordinary people.'

Aged nine, Robert Lacey, future biographer of the Queen, overhears adults talk of the sacred moment of the anointing. They say the Queen will be under a canopy, shielded from the TV cameras, alone with the archbishop of Canterbury. Young Robert is fascinated by the secrecy and privacy of it all. Will she remove the top of her dress? Will she be anointed on her bare breasts? Later in life, he recognises this as 'a horrific thought for a respectable young boy to have about the Queen of England'. But, then again, when has any nine-year-old boy ever been able to keep his thoughts respectable?

The day before the Coronation, Mary Whitehouse, a 42-year-old mother of three from Wolverhampton, is given the opportunity to air her thoughts on the coming event on the BBC's *Woman's Hour*. She sent her essay to the BBC unsolicited. Upon receiving a telegram saying 'Script accepted. Please contact immediately,' she 'collapsed on the bottom stair, shaking like a leaf'. Her brief talk is called 'A

Housewife's Thoughts on the Eve of the Coronation'. It is her first venture into the world of broadcasting, and reflects the uncompromising moral code for which she will one day be famous.

'The Queen will live to make our nation great, and so must I. While hers may often be in spectacular ways, my own dedication may just be in the caring I put into the tiny details of my everyday life. Yes even in the washing up, in things like seeing that I wash most carefully round the handles of cups and saucepans – in the thought and preparation that goes into the cooking – every tiny eye out of the potatoes and spotless hands to cook with …

'In these small ways, I need to accept fully the responsibility for what my nation is, and for what the world is. The fear, the greed, the hate, which so distress me in the world at large ought to distress me just as much when I see them, in smaller ways, in myself. At least there I can fight it, and in my heart and home I need to build a citadel against these things. During her Coronation service the Queen dedicates herself to the cause of righteousness. Let us do the same.'

During the final rehearsal in the Abbey – the last of twelve across the past fortnight – the young pages are given ceremonial swords. The temptation proves too much for the 13-year-old Andrew Parker Bowles.* 'Everyone drew their swords and started jousting away. The earl marshal sent in the Gold Staff officers to sort us out. We were cuffed around the ears. Nowadays that would be called assault or something.'

Watching this rehearsal, in his commentary box on high, Richard Dimbleby thinks the archbishop of Canterbury is placing the crown on the Queen's head rather too speedily. He thinks he should spend more time on it, milking the moment for all it is worth. Once the rehearsal is over, he approaches the archbishop and suggests he might raise the crown in the air and count 'two, three' before lowering it on to the head of the Queen.

*　*　*

---

* Later to become best known as the former husband of Queen Camilla.

Cecil Beaton arrives for the final rehearsal in a state of fear. He will be very busy on the day itself: not only will he be taking the official photographs of the Royal Family after the ceremony, but he is also charged with sketching the ceremony while it happens.

He is filled with a sense of dread, as though about to attend his own execution. He imagines nightmare scenarios in which he is bullied by the butch military types in attendance. 'What is that bulge in your coat pocket? Indian ink? Do you think Indian ink is allowed in the Abbey? Go on! Move on!'

In the event, his premonitions came to nothing; he is treated with exquisite civility by the two Gold Staff officers who usher him to his place. 'I'd never, in fact, encountered such beautiful manners before. It was as if I'd attained the Heavenly Kingdom ...'

On Coronation Eve, one of the Queen's ladies in waiting says, 'You must be feeling nervous, ma'am.'

'Of course I am,' replies the Queen, 'but I really do think Aureole will win.' Aureole is her horse that is running in the Derby this coming weekend.* Does she really mean it, or is she only joking? Like so many of her remarks, it is probably a bit of both.

That same day, the Honours List is released. Henry 'Chips' Channon MP is disappointed. 'I had a twinge of remorse,' he writes in his diary, 'for I secretly realise that had it not been for various interconnected reasons my name might have been included.' In his diary, he lists these as his divorce, his reluctance to speak in the House of Commons, the 'bitter hostility' felt towards him by Randolph Churchill, and, he adds, obliquely, 'perhaps "rumours"', presumably of his homosexuality. 'Thus I was disappointed unduly.'

George E. Browne, who also goes by the stage name of Young Tiger, secures himself an overnight vantage point at Marble Arch. He was born in Trinidad, and arrived in Britain twelve years ago in 1941, at the age of

---

* Aureole finished second.

21. A talented singer and musician, he joined the chorus of *Show Boat*, and then performed at the Orchid Room, where on one occasion he greeted the Duke of Edinburgh with an impromptu calypso.

Along the six-mile processional route, half a million people are camping out all night. 'Crowds schooled to sit out the Luftwaffe's visits on hard cold stone were not going to be put off by a drop of rain,' notes the *Guardian* music and theatre critic Philip Hope-Wallace.

The night is marked by unseasonably chilly winds. From 4 a.m. on Coronation Day, Tuesday, 2 June 1953, over 20,000 police line the route. People with tickets to the service have been asked to take their places between 6 a.m. and 8 a.m., so they know to expect a long wait: the Queen is not scheduled to enter the Abbey until 11.15 a.m. With the addition of tiered seating the capacity of Westminster Abbey has been raised from 2,000 to 8,000. The extra seats have been specially tested by members of the armed services. For safety's sake, they spent two hours sitting up and down on them. The padding of these chairs is made to exact specifications: 12 per cent cow-tail hair, 12 per cent horse-mane hair, 76 per cent North American grey winter hog. Nothing is left to chance. The statue of Oliver Cromwell at Westminster has been boxed in for the day; the powers-that-be do not want to send out the wrong signals.

The BBC has announced that it will start broadcasting the test card an hour and a quarter before the programme itself begins, allowing viewers time to warm up their sets and adjust their aerials.

Richard Dimbleby has spent the night in his Dutch sailing barge, the *Vabel*, which he has brought from Chichester Harbour and moored on the Thames just above Westminster Bridge. He likes to cut a dash. At 4 a.m., he changes into his morning suit: striped trousers, tailcoat and top hat. At 5.15 a.m., a police launch pulls up alongside to transport him, his wife and their 14-year-old son David to Westminster Pier. As he passes by, people who have camped out all night – quite a few for several nights – cheer him, and he courteously raises his top hat in acknowledgement.

Bidding goodbye to his wife and son, who will be watching the two-mile procession from a shop in Regent Street, Dimbleby enters the Abbey at 5.30 a.m. and takes his seat in his soundproofed commentary box, immediately behind the high altar, ready to broadcast to twenty million viewers, or over half the adult population of Great Britain. He is set to remain there until 2.30 in the afternoon, thus justifying his sobriquet 'Gold Microphone-in-Waiting'. He has his commentary typed out and pasted inside a book, episode by episode, complete with reminders to himself in the margins: *Talk slowly. Start smartly. Wait on actions* and *Wait until Canopy well on way.*

Aware of the cramped space it has been allocated in the Abbey, the BBC has picked its smallest cameramen for the task of filming the ceremony.

At 5 a.m., one of the Queen's six maids of honour, Lady Anne Coke,* is in her uncle's flat in Berkeley Square, having 'ridiculous amounts of make-up' applied to her face. With quantities of blusher and lipstick and 'great dark eyebrows', she emerges from the process thinking she looks like a pantomime dame. Presently, the hairdresser arrives and takes ages curling her hair. Once the procedure is over, Anne takes a look in the mirror. 'Oh my heavens,' she thinks. 'I look like a sheep.'

Margaret, Duchess of Argyll† is in her place by 6 a.m. Her head is topped by a coronet on loan from Clare, Duchess of Sutherland,

---

* Born 1932, the eldest daughter of the 5th Earl of Leicester, Lady Anne Coke married Lord Glenconner, aka Colin Tennant, in 1956, and was appointed lady in waiting to Princess Margaret in 1973.

† Margaret, Duchess of Argyll (1912–93) was born Ethel Margaret Whigham. After affairs with, among others, Prince Aly Khan, Prince George, Duke of Kent and David Niven, she married American businessman Charles Sweeny in 1933. They divorced in 1947. She was then briefly engaged to Joseph Thomas of Lehman Brothers, before becoming the third wife of the 11th Duke of Argyll. Their 1963 divorce case scandalised polite society, after the Duke exhibited a set of Polaroid photographs of his wife naked, save for a pearl necklace, fellating a man whose face was out of shot. To this day, the identity of the headless man remains a source of lively speculation. Leading suspects include Douglas Fairbanks Jr, government minister Duncan Sandys and Sigismund von Braun, the brother of the scientist Wernher von Braun.

'who luckily had two'. She is delighted to find that she has one of the best seats in the Abbey, within a few feet of the Queen. 'We had been advised to come fortified with malted milk tablets, and these I chewed constantly, unaware that the television cameras were upon me. I fear my busy jaw must have been quite a talking point in many homes.'

The Poet Laureate, John Masefield, issues his 'Prayer for a Beginning Reign'. Its tone is antiquated almost to the point of crustiness. The third verse goes:

Grant, KING OF KINGS, All-Merciful, All-Knowing,
That in Her reign Her people may advance
In all fair knowledge of starry sowing
In all arts that rejoice
In beauty of sound of instrument and voice,
In colour and form that leave the soul befriended
In ancient joy, our Land's inheritance
In thought, the quest for guidance never-ended
For Light of THINE to make our living splendid
In service to the Queen who guides our going.

The poem is not appreciated by one and all. 'You would never guess from Masefield's lines, heavy as dumplings, that he had once been a sensitive, talented versifier,' concludes the fiercely anti-monarchist Labour MP Willie Hamilton some decades later. 'Perhaps this threadbare bilge was more symbolic of the occasion than he would have cared to admit.'

Chips Channon takes his seat in the Abbey at 8.25 a.m. Opposite him, the peeresses' benches are gradually filling up: 'the front row of thirteen duchesses was a splendid sight'. He finds the long wait enthralling, giving him plenty of time to study the endless procession of 'distinguished guests, relations, minor royalties' and, finally, the Royal Family.

Cecil Beaton sets off for the Abbey amid heavy sheets of rain, having filled his top hat with sandwiches, Indian ink and bits and pieces for his sketches.

Beaton takes up his place in the rafters, close to the pipes of the great organ. To observe the passing scene, he will have to peer precipitously over the edge of the balcony. On the other hand, it is an excellent vantage point: he can see everyone walking down the nave, as well as most of the activity in front of the high altar. Hungover, and feeling 'nervous, cold and rather sick', he buoys himself up by sucking on barley sugar.

From 7.55 a.m. onwards, a range of grandees, from the lord mayor of London to Mr Malik from the USSR, process towards the Abbey in a spectacular parade involving twenty-nine bands, twenty-seven carriages and 13,000 soldiers representing fifty countries. It is pouring with rain. At 9.15 a.m., the Colonial Rulers set off in four carriages, among them the eye-catching Queen Salote of Tonga, who has ruled her country since 1918. Queen Salote is six foot three inches, weighs twenty stone and is swathed in purple silk; on her head she wears a magnificent plume that waves about in the strong wind. But it often rains in Tonga, so she is used to it. 'She beamed, waved, mopped rain from her face with a handkerchief, beamed again,' reports a correspondent from *Time* magazine. 'The soaked, footsore crowd who had waited interminable hours to see the procession instantly warmed to Queen Salote.'

The premier Baron of England, Lord Mowbray, Segrave and Stourton, whose barony dates back to 1283, is allotted a front-row seat, in front of all the dukes. Before the service, his son walks over to tell him how lucky he is. 'Lucky? *Lucky?*' he replies. 'My dear boy, these upstart dukes were still tilling the fields when we were barons.'

Ever the odd one out, the art connoisseur Douglas Cooper has cultivated a dislike of Queen Elizabeth II that now hovers close to hatred. 'Envy is what his resentment was really about,' his apprentice, John Richardson, observes decades later. 'Douglas felt *he* should be monarch.' Yet, like so many arty types, Cooper is in two minds about the Royal Family: he reacted to the news that the Queen Mother was touring Provençal houses by stating that he had reinforced the gates of his home with barbed wire in order to keep her out, yet at the same time he begged the organiser of her tour to bring her to dine there.

With equal perversity, he has been determined not to miss the big day. Somehow, he has managed to wheedle himself a seat in a stand overlooking the entrance to Westminster Abbey, even though these seats are meant to be restricted to the families of peers.

Yesterday, he contracted a high fever. His temperature still registers 102 degrees, and the weather is cold and wet, but nothing will deter him from attending.

He purposely arrives late, so as to irritate everyone else in the stand. He is wearing an antique fur-lined overcoat with a sumptuous sea-otter collar. His pockets contain a hypochondriac's banquet, crammed with pills and drops and linctuses, as well as a flask of brandy. As he forces his way past the aristocratic families, they are horrified to see a thermometer sticking out of his mouth at a jaunty angle. After him, easing his path with apologies – 'I'm afraid he's not very well' – comes Richardson, his knowing young apprentice.

The pair take their places. Cooper removes the thermometer from his mouth, and peers at it before proclaiming loudly, 'It's come right down, it's only 103 degrees.' He then announces, just as loudly, 'I'm here to bring the woman bad luck. When is her tumbril due?'

Across the country, street parties begin as early as 9.30 a.m. Rationing is still in force, but the prime minister has decreed that every household be permitted an extra pound of sugar. Caterers have been allowed additional fat and sugar for crisps, cakes and toffee apple. Additionally, the Queen has declared an amnesty for wartime deserters, some of whom have been on the run since 1945.

The grandees also include the prime ministers of the Commonwealth: from India, Jawaharlal Nehru, in his silken jacket; from Australia, Robert Menzies ('British to my boot-straps'); and from South Africa, Dr Malan, the pro-Hitler, anti-British, anti-black, anti-brown leader of the Purified National Party.

In the Abbey since 7 a.m., the Countess of Huntingdon* is feeling the cold. 'The peeresses were confined in what was, in effect, a wind tunnel. A draught as strong as those artificial ones so cleverly manufactured in the Underground blew on our backs, and to judge by the temperature, it had come straight from Everest. Our teeth chattered,

---

* The Countess of Huntingdon (1907–94) wrote biographies of a mixed batch of characters – Beatrix Potter, the Brontës and Samuel Johnson – under her maiden name, Margaret Lane. As a journalist, she once interviewed Al Capone.

we quaked inwardly with cold, we wrapped ourselves in our trains and watched our arms turn blue.'

For the next hour or two, Cooper and Richardson watch the grandees arrive: first the ambassadors, politicians, celebrities, court officials and foreign Royal Families, and then members of the British Royal Family.

From his place on high, Beaton enters a state of rhapsody, triggered by so much pomp and opulence. 'The peeresses *en bloc* the most ravishing sight – like a bed of auricula-eyed sweet william – in their dark red velvet and foam-white, dew-spangled with diamonds.' As William Walton's *Orb and Sceptre* blazes out on the organ, he watches the procession of the foreign Royal Families: 'Norway, Greece, Nepal, Japan, Ethiopia, Morocco, Thailand, Peru, the Sultans under Her Majesty's protection, Queen Salote of Tonga, a great big, warm personality. Is Russia here? Then the Princes and Princesses of the royal blood: the mother of the Duke of Edinburgh, a contrast to the grandeur, in the ash-grey draperies of a nun.' Beneath these ecstasies, his eagle eye remains on the lookout for suitable prey. 'Princess Marie Louise, agonizingly old, but still athletic, is obviously very angry with her fatuous lady-in-waiting for making such a balls-up with her train.' Nor does he miss 'all the Peeresses' bald spots, and their surreptitious nipping out of a flask, or arranging of a train' and 'that great old relic, Winston Churchill' as he 'lurches forward on unsteady feet, a fluttering mass of white ribbons at his shoulder and white feathers on the hat in his hand.'

It is a day for dressing up, not least for the 260 grandees taking part in the procession up the aisle. Some of the grandest are wearing two uniforms, one on top of the other. Prince Philip wears the full-dress uniform of an admiral of the fleet beneath the crimson velvet robes of state of a royal duke. The Earl Mountbatten of Burma is draped from head to toe with orders and decorations. 'Prince Dickie was simply magnificent,' notes his mother's elderly maid, Edith Pye. 'Absolutely a Coronation in himself!' Winston Churchill wears his uniform of lord warden of the Cinque Ports beneath his Garter Mantle. The hereditary earl marshal, the 16th Duke of Norfolk, the man responsible for the whole event, is in a scarlet coat embroidered in gold, with white knee breeches and stockings, and carries a gold baton tipped with ebony. The archbishops of York and Canterbury both have their mitres on.

The archbishop of Canterbury shakes the hands of the maids of honour as they wait for the Queen on the steps to the annexe of the Abbey. One of them, Rosie Spencer-Churchill, shakes his hand rather too hard and accidentally snaps the vial of smelling salts she is storing in her long white gloves in case of emergency. The stench is appalling. 'Good heavens!' exclaims the archbishop. 'What have you done?' The maids of honour get the giggles, but the archbishop is unamused, wiping his hands with his handkerchief and striding away.

At 11 a.m., the Queen's golden coach arrives. Her pages step forward to open the doors, and she emerges in her dress of ivory silk. 'Everyone in our stand had risen and was cheering for all their worth,' John Richardson recalls. 'Everyone, that is, except Douglas. He was booing, loud as he could.' Richardson is embarrassed. 'Our immediate neigh-bours looked as if they might lynch us.'

The Queen's maids of honour gather up the silk handles of the train. They make their way through the Great West Door to the annexe. The Queen appears not at all nervous, notes Lady Ann Coke, but 'as calm as she always is'. At 11.15 a.m., she turns to her maids of honour, says, 'Ready, girls?' and sets forth.

As the massed choirs sing Parry's anthem 'I Was Glad', the Queen processes up the main aisle. Chips Channon judges her 'calm and competent and even charming'. She looks 'regal, touching and quite perfect. Prince Philip like a medieval knight!' He thinks the moment 'splendid, so breath-taking in its solemn splendour'.

*   *   *

Cecil Beaton, too finds the scene 'most dramatic and spectacular, at the head of her retinue of white, lily-like ladies, the Queen. Her cheeks are sugar pink: her hair tightly curled around the Victorian diadem of precious stones perched straight on her brow. Her pink hands are folded meekly on the elaborate grandeur of her encrusted skirt; she is still a young girl with a demeanour of simplicity and humility … This girlish figure has enormous dignity; she belongs in this scene of almost Byzantine magnificence.'

Once the Queen has entered the Abbey, those in the outside stands know they will have to wait two and a quarter hours before she emerges. Everyone else remains still and patient, but not Douglas Cooper: he rushes out of the stand, announcing that he must see his doctor.

Cooper bluffs his way into the House of Lords, dragging Richardson behind him. He marches up to the bar and orders a bottle of champagne. Just as the barmaid is about to pop it open, an aged House of Lords servant tells her to stop, snapping: 'Why are you serving these people? They've no right to be here.'

'I thought they were new creations,' says the barmaid.

'Well, they're not.'

At this point, Cooper brandishes his thermometer. 'I'm waiting here to see my doctor, who is in the Abbey.'

'Well, you can't wait here,' says the Lords servant, and throws them out.

'New creations!' fumes Cooper as they exit. 'Fucking flunky!'

Amid all this glory, Beaton sketches away. The archbishops and bishops present the Queen to the east. "'*Vivat! Vivat!*" shout, surprisingly, the boys from Westminster School: trumpets sound to split the roofs and shatter the heart.'

The archbishop says: 'Sirs, I here present unto you Queen Elizabeth, your undoubted Queen, wherefore all you who are come this day to do your homage and service. Are you willing to do the same?' The congregation responds, 'God Save Queen Elizabeth,' and a fanfare of trumpets rings out. The Queen makes a curtsy. Watching the service on television, the Old Etonian man-of-letters James Lees-Milne sees it as 'a gesture on her part of obeisance and yet tremendous majesty – the only occasion she will ever be known to curtsy'.

The Queen takes the Coronation Oath – 'The things which I have here promised, I will perform and keep. So help me God' – and kisses the Bible. The archbishop intones the Prayer of Consecration.

As the choir sings Handel's 'Zadok the Priest', and the Queen walks towards the altar and the throne, her maid of honour Lady Anne Coke begins to feel dizzy. She tries to ignore it, but her vision is fast becoming cloudy. She reaches into her glove and breaks the vial of smelling salts she has there, but it seems to have no effect. She frantically wiggles her toes, all the while thinking, 'I must not faint … I can't faint in front of the entire British Empire.'

Noticing her plight, Black Rod, Lieutenant General Sir Brian Horrocks, puts a discreet arm around her and encourages her to use a pillar to steady herself. He holds her there until she recovers.

The Queen is divested of her crimson robe, her Diadem and Collar of the Garter. She is now dressed only in a simple white shift. Four Knights of the Garter hold a canopy of cloth of gold over her. The Spurs, Sword and Orb are presented, and, on the Queen's fourth finger of the right hand, the Ring.

John Betjeman watches the dean, 'a tall, monkish, medieval-looking man', step forward with the gold ampulla, lower a spoon into it and then wait as the archbishop dips his thumb into the holy oil ready to anoint the Queen. The four-year-old Prince Charles, dressed all in white, is sitting between his grandmother, the Queen Mother, and his aunt, Princess Margaret. He is irritated that the Palace barber has cut his hair too short and plastered his scalp with what he later remembers as 'the most appalling gunge'.

*   *   *

'It is the moment of the anointment, the hallowing,' intones Richard Dimbleby in his commentary box as the canopy is raised above her, 'the moment so old, history can scarcely go deep enough to contain it.'

From up on high, Dimbleby is excelling himself, lending additional grandeur to an event already overflowing with it. He revels in arcane symbolism, regardless of whether it is authentic or invented a week or two ago: he tells of how the Queen's throne is set high on a dais, recalling a time when the early kings sat on a mound of earth to be crowned and were then raised up on the shoulders of the nobles 'so that the people might see them'. The Queen's Robe, he explains, 'may well be descended from the imperial cloaks of the Byzantine Emperors'. The language he employs is simple, but delivered with suitably archaic syntax: 'The ring wherein is set a sapphire'.

'The moment of the Queen's crowning is come,' says Dimbleby.

The archbishop picks up the crown of St Edward, which contains 440 precious and semi-precious stones. Just for today, a small gold star has been added to the front so that the archbishop will know which way round to place it on the Queen's head. The crown is a foot high, and weighs over four and a half pounds. As the archbishop lowers it onto her head, those entitled to coronets put them on, and the 8,000-strong congregation bellow, 'God Save the Queen!'

Perhaps for the first time, but certainly not the last, a television commentator has shaped the event he is there to report. Looking down on the ceremony, Richard Dimbleby notes with pleasure that his advice has been taken: immediately before the crowning, the archbishop raises the crown above the Queen's head, counts 'one – two – three' to himself and then gradually lowers it down upon her head.

Beaton finds the crowning itself 'superbly dramatic: the expression on the small face of the Queen is one of intense expectancy until, with magnificent assurance, the Archbishop thrusts down with speed and forces the crown onto the neat head. At this moment the hoarse shouts

of "God Save the Queen" break out. The peers put on their coronets and caps of State, and the peeresses, with long, gloved arms looking like wishbones, hold up their coronets. A fanfare of trumpets, a blaze of violins, an eruption from the big organ, and the guns are shot off from the Tower down the river.'

Watching the crowning on television at Magdalen College, Oxford, the academic and children's author C. S. Lewis detects a note of tragedy. He is struck by the way the young Queen is overwhelmed by the sacramental side of the ceremony: 'Hence, in the spectators, a feeling of (one hardly knows how to describe it) – awe – pity – pathos – mystery. The pressing of that huge, heavy crown on that small, young head becomes a sort of symbol of the situation of *humanity* itself: humanity called by God to be his vicegerent and high priest on earth, yet feeling so inadequate. As if he said "In my inexorable love I shall lay upon the dust that you are glories and dangers and responsibilities beyond your understanding" … One has missed the whole point unless one feels that we have all been crowned and that coronation is somehow, if splendid, a tragic splendour.'

During the ceremony, the congregants have had plenty of time to study the key players. Lady Diana Cooper finds herself particularly disappointed by Princess Margaret, 'wings clipped by the King's death, not all glorious within, rather dusky and heavy-featured'.

Attending in his robes as the vice-chancellor of Oxford, Maurice Bowra is obliged to remain in Westminster Abbey from 7 o'clock in the morning until 3 o'clock in the afternoon. Last year, he met his new monarch when he paid a visit to Buckingham Palace ('a pretty house') to present the University's Loyal Address on her succession. He considers her a marked improvement on her father:* 'She is rather pretty and much less vulgar to look at than most of her family.'

Today, he enjoys perusing the congregation, in all its splendid variety: 'Nice little Malays in silk clothes with small turbans, a tremendous Fuzzy-Wuzzy with a mop of hair ... and even old dons in scarlet gowns and medals. Everyone dressed up to the nines, but dignified and genuine and not at all Fancy Dress.' He homes in on incongruities, such as duchesses carrying sandwiches in their coronets, and 'Winston wrapped up in the Garter robe like a bath towel, rather unsteady but very old and grand.'

Amid all this splendour – 'the Great Officers of State swished their robes with dignity' – Chips Channon finds his rapacious irritation fed by various socialists who are refusing to play the game. 'From time to time my eyes wandered and I saw Aneurin Bevan in a blue lounge suit, unsuitable as possible.' Nevertheless, the 'pretty little pages' and the 'nodding, chatting, gossiping duchesses' remain beyond reproach, 'although the Archbishop's voice was not as sonorous as that of the

---

* A decade later, Bowra changes his mind, after attending a dinner at Buckingham Palace in honour of the King and Queen of Greece, an event ruined, he thought, by the Queen looking 'sulky' throughout and by the incessant playing of bagpipes. All in all, he considered her 'a bit of a sourpuss'.

wicked old Lang'* and 'the four Garter Knights rather bungled the canopy and were clumsy'. But all in all – 'the Queen simply dressed almost in a shift, and then later resplendent … the red, the gold, the sparkle, the solemnity' – he is in his element.

In America, many viewers are upset at the way their TV networks interrupt the ceremony to screen advertisements from sponsors. The *New York Times* condemns NBC's interruption of its coverage to show a chimpanzee. It was, says its editorial writer, 'utterly disgraceful. No apology can be adequate.'

At 1.40 p.m., the Queen steps down from the Coronation Chair and the choir sings William Walton's *Te Deum*. The composer himself is among the congregation; he has tucked a supply of whisky miniatures into his top hat, to keep himself going.

The Countess of Huntingdon looks on as the Queen, 'stiff, golden and glittering as one of those brocaded waxen figures in a Spanish church', is supported up the steps to the throne following the crowning. 'If ever a woman consciously and visibly dedicated herself to a solemn destiny, this was she.'

'An element of pity and sympathy crept in,' she notes, 'for between the inhuman magnificence of the crown, and the glittering of the vestment-like golden robe, the Queen's face was very young, very human, very tense. The eyes were downcast, the small hands holding rod and sceptre anxiously rigid, the cheeks pale and the mouth grave in its concentration on the huge responsibility of the moment … A kind of sigh of sympathy and satisfaction went up. In beauty, in solemnity, it was a perfect moment.'

On leave from National Service, the 19-year-old Alan Bennett watches the Coronation on television at a friend's house. 'As so often with the

---

* Cosmo Gordon Lang (1864–1945), archbishop of Canterbury from 1928 to 1942. Channon disapproved of Lang for his public condemnation of King Edward VIII for betraying the 'high and sacred trust' of God in pursuit of 'a craving for private happiness'.

central rituals of English life, I was in two minds about it. Yes, the pageantry was moving, the music thrilling, but I was a soldier. I knew there was no pageantry without a great deal of bullying.'

Paul McCartney has been watching the ceremony sitting cross-legged on the floor at the McCartney family home in Liverpool. Their house is the first in the street to have a television. Along with many other Britons, Jim and Mary McCartney started renting theirs with the Coronation in mind. 'H-shaped aerials are sprouting from the rooftops,' noted the *Liverpolitan and Merseyside Digest* back in May. A couple of weeks ago, Mary McCartney asked Paul and his little brother Mike to 'skedaddle' for a couple of hours. Upon their return, a television had appeared in their sitting room. Neither boy had ever seen one before.

There are 2.7 million televisions in the country, but an estimated 20.4 million viewers, so sitting rooms up and down the country are unusually crowded. A popular, friendly couple, Jim and Mary have invited neighbours to join them around the tiny ten-inch screen. 'Mr McCartney realised it was a very important day in our lives and that we should see it,' recalls a neighbouring child. 'He was the loveliest man and he gave us all pop to drink.' Everyone has dressed up for the occasion, including Paul and Mike.

They watch the fuzzy screen for the full seven hours, and then join a party in the middle of their road. Over in the Dingle area of Liverpool, 12-year-old Richy Starkey (Ringo Starr in later life) attends a street party in Admiral Grove in fancy dress. He has come as a Hawaiian girl, topped with a crown of flowers and a garland around his neck. In a photograph taken of the big day, he stands arm in arm with another little boy, who is blacked up in the manner of Al Jolson.

In New York, the young Queen's favourite author, P. G. Wodehouse,* watches the Coronation on a television at his apartment on Park Avenue. He regards the whole event as overlong and lacking any

---

* In 1941, the Royal Librarian reported that the Queen Mother had ordered the 15-year-old Princess Elizabeth eighteen different novels by P. G. Wodehouse.

proper theatricality. 'It needed work and should have been fixed up in New Haven [where Broadway plays were tried out],' he complains to his friend and collaborator Guy Bolton, going on to suggest that it would have benefited from a cut of half an hour and dancing girls to replace the archbishop's reading from the Gospel.

* * *

Setting a pattern that will be a hallmark of the Queen's long reign, those who look at her are prone to see their own outlook reflected back. Patrick Hamilton, bleak chronicler of seedy bars and woebegone bedsits, is horrified by what he sees. 'Only by seeing could you *believe* what has been going on ... the seething, hysterical mobs which have been pouring daily into London to look at the decorations,' he writes to his brother Bruce on Coronation Day. '... I was in all the blitzes during the war, and I stood up to them all with reasonable equanimity. This has really *terrified* me! ... And one is depressed as well as terrified. Nothing is worse for the soul, or can make one feel more *lonely*, than the knowledge that one is going against the masses (mostly Labour-voting, needless to say).'

In his dank boarding house on Harrow-on-the-Hill, the 56-year-old artist and poet David Jones overcomes his distaste for television and walks to a neighbour's house to watch the ceremony on the small screen. He is enthralled, recognising within the spectacle his own imaginative world of myth and mysticism, a world beyond the here-and-now. The young Queen, he thinks, looks 'incredibly beautiful ... of immense dignity and *humility*'. He is impressed by the splendour and historical continuity of it all, but notes also 'something far deeper and more primal and quite ageless' – the monarch as human sacrifice, the 'feeling of the gold-clad victim'. Later, he visits a cinema in order to view a newsreel of the Coronation. Though he will not die for another twenty-one years, this is to be his final visit to a cinema.

The 30-year-old Lucian Freud, an artist with a very different vision, prowls around Clarendon Crescent in Paddington and sketches the grimy slum dwellings decked out in red, white and blue. From a first-floor balcony, he sketches a discarded pram, grotty bunting, waving in the wind like underpants on a washing line, children squatting on steps and a sulky image of the Queen framed by a window.

* * *

In Korea, where war has been waging for the past three years, British troops fire shells containing red, white and blue smoke, by way of celebration.

Down from Oxford, despite tut-tuts from his more radical friends and colleagues, Isaiah Berlin, philosopher and historian, finds a nook for himself in the window of the *Daily Telegraph* office in Piccadilly, affording him a grand view of the procession as it returns from the Abbey.

His family arrived in Britain from Russia over twenty years ago, in 1931. Fêted by his adopted country, he still thinks of himself as an outsider. 'I love England, I have been well treated here, and I cherish many things about English life, but I am a Russian Jew; that is how I was born and that is who I will be at the end of my life.'

As he watches the ceremony on a television in the *Telegraph* office, it fills him with fresh surprise at his adoptive country, particularly the unexpected seriousness of it all. 'The Queen carried the whole thing through with a kind of curious slow trance, wearing the heavy Byzantine robes not at all like an actress on the stage, nor like someone intent and serious, but in a kind of curious religious mist.'

Yet at the heart of the ceremony sits an omission emblematic of national decline. At his Coronation, in 1937, the Queen's father, King George VI, was crowned 'by the Grace of God of the United Kingdom of Great Britain and Northern Ireland and of the British Dominions beyond the Seas, King, defender of the Faith, Emperor of India'. Today, his daughter is crowned 'by the Grace of God of the United Kingdom of Great Britain and Northern Ireland and of Her other Realms and Territories, Queen, Head of the Commonwealth, Defender of the Faith'. The monarch is Emperor no more.

'The fanfares blared, the congregation stood, *Vivat! Vivat!* rang out across the fane: but there was no denying the bathos of this grey title, or hiding the process of retreat that had given birth to it,' observes James Morris many years later. 'No longer was the Queen an Empress, and, in an association of nations in which Hindus and Muslims outnumbered Christians by three to one, she was only debatably a Defender of the Faith.'

Over in Paris, the Boulevard Haussmann is decorated with vast banners. Jean Cocteau, at the age of 62 still at the forefront of the French avant-garde, has been glued to the radio broadcast of the Coronation from 9 a.m. to 6 p.m. Described by Edith Wharton as a man 'to whom every great line of poetry was a sunrise, every sunset the foundation of the Heavenly City', he is enraptured, his imagination liberated by the absence of any picture. 'Impossible not to be moved, excited, amazed by such a belief in the temporal and in the eternal, by that gold talon thrust so deep into our poor earthly globe, by that solid unreality, by rites as strange and inevitable as those of the hive ... I don't think anything analogous can happen anywhere else. Perhaps this is the last time that the world will see such a thing. It began with pages, fairy-tale servants, scarlet cavalcades. It ended with jet squadrons in the sky. And all these centuries whirled around a pumpkin transformed into a coach, in which sat a charming young woman.'

Writing his diary that evening, Cocteau is driven to wonder about the charming young woman, 'sealed in the armour of her ancestors'. What has become of her? 'The queen was changed into a symbol. She will no longer be the same woman tonight. Power of a ceremony. A ceremony, in all its forms, spares humanity its fear of being nothing.' The flamboyant Frenchman's faith in England is restored. 'In order to defeat England, you would have to sink the island itself, and everyone on it would die standing up, like an old admiral.'

Finally, Cocteau's thoughts turn to the sorry figures of 'The Duke and Duchess of Windsor watching the Coronation in front of a little television set, cups and saucers visible in the picture.'

It so happens that the Windsors are elsewhere in Paris, watching the Coronation at the home of the American heiress Margaret Biddle. Only last year, the Duke complained to the Duchess, 'What a

stinking* lot my relations are and you've never seen such a seedy worn-out bunch of old hags most of them have become.' For all his resentment, he continued to daydream about being welcomed to the Abbey for the Coronation of his niece, though by December he had abandoned the idea, following pressure from above. After lunching with the Queen in November, the archbishop of Canterbury concluded that 'it would create a very difficult situation for everybody, and if he had not the wits to see that for himself, then he ought to be told it'. Accordingly, the archbishop had been to see Sir Alan Lascelles, the Queen's private secretary, who, fearing that 'a hint to the Duke that he was not wanted might only incite him to want to come', wrote a strong letter to the Duke's lawyers, insisting that no invitation would be forthcoming.

---

* Oddly enough, the same adjective employed by King Charles III upon experiencing trouble with his fountain pen, some sixty-nine years later.

Buckling under this pressure, the Duke was driven to compose a face-saving statement for the press, explaining that it would be contrary to precedent for any sovereign or former sovereign to attend.

Throughout today's televised ceremony, the Duke keeps up a running commentary, explaining each small detail of the ritual, and pointing out who is who. He tells a fellow guest that the Queen is more suited than a king to the demands of this ancient ceremony in which 'a combination of humility and jewellery play so important a role'. Others in the room find his voice, emerging from the semi-darkness, curiously husky. At times, it is as if he is finding it hard to speak.

After the ceremony, there is a gathering in the Great Hall of Westminster. Princess Margaret approaches her late father's equerry, Group Captain Peter Townsend. 'She looked superb, sparkling, ravishing,' he recalls. As they chat, she brushes a bit of fluff from his RAF uniform. The two of them laugh, and think no more about it. But the gesture does not pass unnoticed by the assembled newsmen, who correctly interpret it as a sign of intimacy.

By the time Cooper and Richardson have returned from playing truant in the House of Lords, the newly crowned Queen is climbing back into her coach. 'The great procession of royal personages in their carriages and the magnificently caparisoned Household Cavalry and the mounted regiments of what was left of the Empire were parading in front of us,' Richardson recalls. 'Douglas did not boo; he stood up and cheered as fervently as a patriotic schoolboy – not the Royal Family but the Bengal Lancers.'

The congregation shuffles out of the Abbey in ordered batches, announced over a loudspeaker. Once outside, Chips Channon finds that it is raining, but 'just as the Gold Coach turned into Parliament Square the sun smiled for a second and I saw the Queen's white gloved hand and great crown and the procession curled up Whitehall'.

He and his son Paul wait for their car, diverted by the sight of 'hundreds of ermined, be-coronetted friends' also waiting. Back home in Belgrave Square, he spares a thought for the uninvited, who took up their positions two days ago in the cold and the rain, 'and sat drenched but fervently loyal for forty-eight hours'. He also spares a thought for poor Lady Carnock, so drunk that she had to be forcibly removed from the Abbey before the ceremony had started.

Andrew Parker Bowles and his fellow pages are escorted to the House of Lords and treated to a feast, 'an amazing spread of food one had never seen before'. It includes bananas, oranges and, of course, Coronation chicken.

Looking down on the returning procession from his perch at the *Telegraph*, Isaiah Berlin relishes the moment when Winston Churchill, 'with huge fat fingers stuck out in a V sign blessing the populace in a gracious manner', suddenly catches sight of his current bête noire, Michael Berry, son of the owner of the *Daily Telegraph*. 'Immediately the happy grin of public jollity was succeeded by a scowl of private recognition, very much as one is suddenly checked in the middle of some public activity by suddenly seeing a quizzical private face glaring at one from some unexpected corner. He withdrew back into his carriage like a snail, took back his hand, growled at his wife, buried his head sulkily in his shoulders, and continued in this fashion for another five minutes, after which he stuck out his head again, the fingers came out and all was radiance once more.'

It has been a disappointing day for 15-year-old Norman Allen, who was hoping to make a tidy sum selling Coronation programmes to the waiting crowds. He began the day with seventy-five programmes, and is ending it with seventy-two. 'It was raining and nobody wanted wet programmes,' he recalls, decades later.

On her return to her house in Marylebone, Queen Salote removes her rain-soaked gown, woven from the bark of a hibiscus tree, enjoys a hot bath and retires to bed. Later, she tells newsmen how much she loves the British weather. 'The public was as wet as I, and we were both enjoying ourselves. Oh, it was marvellous. The greatest day ever.' From now on, wherever she goes in Britain – to cricket at Lord's, to the ballet at Covent Garden, to Edinburgh, Cambridge and Canterbury – she is be cheered to the rafters.

In Soho Street, Glasgow, every lamp post, doorway and windowsill is decorated with bunting and streamers and trestle tables are laden with food and drink. The celebrations carry on way beyond the bedtime of four-year-old Marie Laurie, but she peeks at the scene from her bedroom window, her chin resting on her hands. In the twilight, people sing and dance. Marie's father 'more than a little drunk' spies her at the window. 'Gi' us a song, Marie, hen!' he calls out.

Little Marie sings the hit song 'In a Golden Coach', currently available in three different versions, two of which are gracing the Hit Parade:*

> In a golden coach, there's a heart of gold
> Driving through old London town
> With the sweetest Queen the world's ever seen
> Wearing her golden crown.
> As she drives in state through the palace gate
> Her beauty the whole world will see
> In a golden coach there's a heart of gold
> That belongs to you and me.

Decades later, Marie Laurie, now more familiarly known as Lulu, cites this as her very first public performance.

Preparing to shoot an epilogue for the BBC some hours after the ceremony, Richard Dimbleby surveys the empty Abbey benches from his commentary box and notes 'the melancholy sight of the litter left behind by the peers. It seemed to me amazing that even on this occa-

---

* Other Coronation-based titles include 'Queen Elizabeth Waltz', 'The Queen of Everyone's Heart', 'Britannia Rag', 'A Waltz for the Queen', 'Windsor Waltz' and 'Coronation Rag'.

sion we could not break ourselves of one of our worst national habits. Tiers and tiers of stalls on which the peers had been sitting were covered with sandwich wrappings, sandwiches, morning newspapers, fruit peel, sweets and even a few empty miniature bottles.'

But his final, sonorous, topsy-turvy sentences* overlook these unappealing elements: 'And so this day of days, most memorable, comes to an end, and with it begins a new era, the new Elizabethan age, an age in which the love and faith and hope of all the Commonwealth rest on the slim shoulders of the beautiful queen who has just been crowned. Long may she reign!'

After the ceremony, Cecil Beaton rushes home, swallows 'a fistful of aspirins', changes clothes, sleeps for the better part of an hour, awakes refreshed and beetles off to the Palace, where he is booked to take the official photographs in the Green Drawing Room.

First he photographs family groups: 'The Queen Mother, dimpled and chuckling, with eyes as bright as any of her jewels' – and Margaret, 'with pink and white make-up and a sex twinkle of understanding'. As he photographs the various members of the Royal Family in informal poses, making all the right noises – 'Charming!' 'Divine!' – Prince Philip is seen to bristle.

The Queen, 'cool, smiling, sovereign of the situation', arrives with her maids of honour. He thinks she looks 'extremely minute' under her robes; on this unseasonably cold day, her nose and hands are chilled, her eyes tired. 'Yes, the crown does get rather heavy,' she tells him. St Edward's Crown weighs 4.9 pounds; it has been on her head for nearly three hours.

Prince Philip stands at the side cracking jokes, with a pursed smile. It makes Beaton feel uneasy. 'I believe he doesn't like or approve of me. This is a pity because though I'm not one for "Navy type" jokes, and obviously have nothing in common with him, I admire him enormously.'

---

* They are his legacy: upside-down phraseology is now obligatory at Royal events. 'For the first time through the centre gateway of Admiralty Arch arrives Lady Diana,' said one of the commentators at the 1981 Royal Wedding, a typical piece of Royal commentary, or, to put it another way, of commentary Royal a piece typical.

Lady Anne Coke is conscious of Philip becoming 'frightfully bossy ... telling us where to stand and when to smile'. As a result of this interference, Beaton grows increasingly tetchy. Eventually, he puts down his camera, snaps, 'Sir, if you would like to take the photographs, please do!' and walks away. The Queen looks on in horror, and so does the Queen Mother. Realising he has gone too far, the Duke moves away.

Once it is all over, the Queen leads her family and entourage out on to the Palace balcony. The noise from the cheers of the crowd is so loud that Lady Anne Coke can feel it physically hitting her.

That evening, the famous Ed Murrow,* head of CBS News, travels on a plane back to America, a BOAC Stratocruiser that has been transformed into a flying laboratory and cutting room, the seats ripped out and replaced by film-processing and editing machines; when the plane touches down, the film will be ready for immediate transmission.

In New York, many of the store windows are decorated with models of the crown jewels and photographs of the Queen; in Rockefeller Plaza, 2,000 people an hour have been filing past a giant model of the Coronation coach and horses.

Chips Channon attends a dinner party for 200 at the French embassy. 'Most had come in day clothes as they had been mingling in the streets with the good-humoured crowds.'

He goes to bed elated. The old values have been triumphantly reasserted. 'What a day for England, for aristocracy and the traditional forces of the world. Shall we see the like again?' He himself has now been present at three coronations but he will never see another. His final question of the day is 'Will my Paul be an old man at that of King Charles III?' Paul is at this point 17 years old. A future member of Margaret Thatcher's Cabinet, he is destined to die at the age of 71 in

---

* Edward R. Murrow (1908–65) first came to fame with a series of live radio broadcasts from Europe between 1938 and 1941, among them his vivid reports on the Blitz.

January 2007, a full sixteen years before the Coronation of King Charles III.

Before going to bed, the up-and-coming Labour politician Barbara Castle notes that she is in trouble for the fiercely anti-monarchist views she delivered during a BBC *Brains Trust* recording in Lowestoft. She knows she is swimming against the tide. 'I think there is no doubt this is a minority view, even among the working class.' As she is writing this in her diary, a familiar voice comes on the wireless. 'The Queen's correct & piping girlish voice is enunciating the formulae for dedication; Winston has just introduced her on the radio, exploiting the romantic mood of the moment to its fruitiest uttermost.'

Having left the Abbey at half-past midnight, a full seventeen hours after entering it. Richard Dimbleby enjoys a sound sleep on his barge on the Thames. He is filled with patriotic thoughts. 'Visitors from abroad who were in London on Tuesday were envious of everything they saw, and none more so than the Americans – a race of such vitality but so lacking in tradition – who know that they must wait a thousand years before they can show the world anything so significant or so lovely.'

The following day, the *Manchester Guardian* publishes a cartoon by David Low. Captioned 'Morning After' it portrays middle-aged children in Union Jack nappies and paper crowns crawling amid the debris of a party. The television is on the tilt and the words '£100,000,000 SPREE' spread across the carpet.

Never does a cartoon generate more hate mail, with barely one in ten speaking out in its support.

'Low has reached his nadir,' writes Mr William Bushell from Heald Green, Greater Manchester. 'After a day of heartfelt national rejoicing, of inspiration, and of dedication to a new reign … he dares to produce this morning's sickly, sneering, tawdry cartoon.'

'To say the least it is a joke in bad taste and I feel certain that the "gentlemen" behind the Iron Curtain are rubbing their hands with glee,' writes Mr M. B. Sketchley from Heaton Moor, West Stockport. 'Therefore I suggest Mr Low leave your paper and apply there for a job!'

Perhaps the happiest memories of the Coronation are those of the archbishop of Canterbury, whose sermon the following Sunday is full of it. 'You will, I expect, find it as difficult as I do to give your minds to anything else,' he enthuses. 'Every train of thought or conversation comes back to it. The wonder of it, the unforgettable bearing of the Queen, the overwhelming sense of dedication to God, or worship of God, consecration by God, and communion with God, embracing everyone in the Abbey ... The country and Commonwealth last Tuesday were not far from the Kingdom of Heaven.'

Back in Oxford four days later, Isaiah Berlin philosophises on the power of the Coronation to stir the usually calm English soul. 'Nobody would quite have thought that this sober, unimaginative and essentially prosy country could rise to such a pitch of national excitement over this dark mystical Byzantine ceremony ...'

Soon after arriving back in America, the 'Girl Reporter' Jacqueline Bouvier agrees to marry her dashing young senator from Boston, John F. Kennedy. The ambitious Kennedy family postpone the official announcement for a fortnight, so that it will do nothing to lessen the impact of a profile of John in the *Saturday Evening Post*: 'Jack Kennedy – the Senate's Gay Young Bachelor'.

They marry three months later. In years to come, Jackie Kennedy will look back on her time in London with nostalgia. It was, she tells her stepbrother Hugh Auchincloss, 'the last time I was truly free to be me'.

Having completed his kitchen-sink image of Coronation Day, Lucian Freud decides to give it to Fleur Cowles, the editor of the recently defunct *Flair* magazine, who is in England representing President Eisenhower at the Coronation. He trusts it will repay her for all the money she gave him when he was last in New York. But it backfires.

She dislikes the picture intensely. 'You can have your rotten drawing, in filthy condition,' she writes, in her forthright way, as she returns it to him.

George E. Browne, aka Young Tiger, is so inspired by what he saw from his spot at Marble Arch that he composes a calypso, 'I Was There (At the Coronation)'. He records it with a steel band.

> Her majesty looked really divine
> In her crimson robe, furred with ermine
> The Duke of Edinburgh dignified and neat
> Sat beside her as Admiral of the Fleet.
>
> [Chorus]
> He was there
> At the Coronation
> I was there
> At the Coronation ...
>
> The procession was about 50,000 strong
> It stretched for much more than 6 miles long
> Millions of people, all happily
> Shouting three cheers for her majesty
>
> [Chorus]
> They were there
> At the Coronation
> I was there
> At the Coronation
>
> As I stood looking, rapturously
> A feeling of elation came over me
> I felt what pleasure, such beauty gives
> I shall never forget as long as I live

[Chorus]
I was there
At the Coronation
We were there
At the Coronation
I was there
At the Coronation
Millions there
At the Coronation

Weeks later, in the huge hall of the British Army School in Kuala Lumpur, the seven-year-old Joanna Lumley sports a Coronation medal pinned to her chest as she watches the movie *The Coronation* in full colour. She inks her name on the back of her double-decker wooden pencil box with a sliding top. The box carries a stencil of the new Queen, looking back over her shoulder with a friendly smile.

'I knew then, as I know now, that she would never let me down,' Joanna will reflect, nearly seventy years on.

Vita Sackville-West is 'immensely moved' by the Coronation, so much so that she composes a Coronation poem, which she sends to the *Times Literary Supplement*. Might she have half an eye on succeeding John Masefield as Poet Laureate?

> Madam, how strange to be your Majesty.
> How strange to wake in an ordinary bed
> And, half awake, to think 'Now who am I?'

25

It is 6 June 1953: Coronation Day. We are in the western reaches of Notting Hill, a stone's throw from Ladbroke Grove. On an otherwise cold and drizzly afternoon, the sun has come out, lighting up this tall row of terraced houses, decked out with Union Jacks and bunting.

At the entrance to the street, just out of shot, hangs a large picture of the sovereign, and a banner reading 'Long Live the Queen'. The forty-odd families in the cul-de-sac's twenty houses have raised a mammoth £114 for today's celebrations.

'We want to give the kids the best time of their lives, especially since the bad publicity of this street must have had a terrible effect on their little minds,' one resident tells *The Kensington Post*.

The festivities centre around a long table, draped in a white cloth. Children are sitting around it, some in party hats. The men are in suits and ties, though not hats. The women are in their party dresses, some having added a cardigan to keep out the cold. Those serving the children wear aprons. The little boys, their hair neatly parted, sport V-neck jerseys and shorts.

The photographer must have been at a first-floor window, or perhaps he or she was perched on the roof of a dormer window below. They probably have just made themselves known with a shout or a wave, as over half the partygoers are looking up towards the camera.

No one looks all that cheerful, other than the woman in the centre of the photograph, standing with her arms folded. Perhaps they have just all said 'Cheese!' and are now relaxing. Or perhaps they are preparing to say 'Cheese!' Or perhaps they will never say 'Cheese!':

back then, seventy years ago, there was less of an emphasis on smiling for the camera.

To the right of the table is a pram. The baby hidden by the hood would today be in its early seventies, roughly the same age as Tony Blair or Chaka Khan. The children at the table, tucking into jelly, would be in their late seventies or early eighties.

The terrace is gaily decorated. The house at the far end, No. 10, has two Union Jacks hanging from the second floor, and two strings of bunting attached to the first floor, but no decorations on the ground floor. Directly opposite it, nestled against the wall at the end of the street, is some sort of Punch stall.

We are in Rillington Place. Until three months ago, the ground-floor flat in No. 10 was occupied by John 'Reg' Christie, a clerk with the British Road Services at Shepherd's Bush, but on 20 March he moved out. Four days later, a new tenant was attempting to insert brackets into the wall of Christie's old kitchen only to find it hollow. Peeling back the wallpaper, he found himself staring at a bare human back. In this concealed alcove were the corpses of three women, each strangled with a length of rope. Their discovery was overshadowed in the press by the death of Queen Mary that very same day. Further investigation

uncovered Mrs Christie, not seen since mid-December, dead beneath the floorboards. Three days later, a further two skeletons were found buried in the garden: they had both been there for a decade.

As the body count in Rillington Place rose from three, to four, to six, the two different news stories – the death of Queen Mary and the manhunt for a serial killer – vied for dominance of the front pages.

On the day of Queen Mary's funeral ('Race Against Time to Trap Horror Killer' read the *Daily Mirror* headline), Christie was spotted by a policeman staring at the river near Putney Bridge. Taken into custody, he confessed to the murders of his wife and the three women in the alcove. On 5 June, the day before this photograph was taken, he confessed to the murders of the two women whose skeletons had been found in the back garden.*

It says something for the resilience of the other inhabitants of Rillington Place that they refuse to let these macabre discoveries overshadow their Coronation Day party. George Rogers, the Labour MP for Kensington North, opened the festivities with a speech. 'This street has had some bad publicity lately, but you have made it one of the finest decorated streets in London; certainly I have seen nothing to compare with it'. The fancy dress competition is won by children dressed as, respectively, a king, a television set and a blancmange.

However, the residents are not indifferent to what has happened. Mrs McFadden at No. 5 has already organised a petition calling for the name of their street to be changed. 'Every householder signed it,' reads one report, 'for somehow a violent death in their midst brought a sense of social, communal shame to the more decent folk.' At the end of the year, Rillington Place is renamed Runton Close. Thirty years later, the entire terrace is demolished. Today, a small communal garden stands in the space once occupied by No. 10.

---

* Later that month, Christie was tried, found guilty and sentenced to death for the murder of his wife Ethel. In all, he had probably killed seven women and a baby. He was also responsible for another death: three years earlier, he had given evidence against Timothy Evans, who had been renting the upstairs flat at 10 Rillington Place. Evans was executed for the murder of his wife and child; it now seems probable that the perpetrator was Christie. John Christie was executed at Pentonville on 15 July 1953.

26

A wax effigy of Reg Christie in his shirtsleeves was on display at Madame Tussaud's within an hour of his execution, papering the wall of the secret alcove in his squalid kitchen at Rillington Place.*

Today, he is still there, still busy papering the wall. Yet posterity is a selective master, indifferent to grandeur. While some of the most notorious murderers live on in wax – Dr Crippen, Charles Manson, the Acid Bath Murderer John Haigh and Reg Christie – the Royal Family has been ruthlessly cropped. The Queen Mother, a familiar figure for eighty-odd years at Madame Tussauds since her wedding in 1923, has been excised, and so have other members of the Royal Family who once seemed so solid and permanent: King Edward VII and Queen Alexandra, King George V and Queen Mary, the Duke and Duchess of Windsor, King George VI, Princess Margaret. What hope for today's lesser Royals?

The Queen first appeared as a waxwork in June 1928, at the age of two, sitting on top of two silk cushions, looking upwards, in a frilly white dress with a string of beads around her neck, her hair abundantly curly. Three years later, this waxwork was replaced by one of her in riding boots and leather gloves astride her pony.

As her appearance matured, so did her waxworks: over the course of her life, twenty-four different waxworks of the Queen appeared in the Baker Street Madame Tussauds – on average, a new waxwork once every four years.

---

* Bernard Tussaud, the great-great-grandson of Madame Tussaud, had attended Christie's trial at the Old Bailey, active with his sketchbook and pencils.

The Queen's final waxwork was created for the Madame Tussauds in Blackpool, to coincide with her Platinum Jubilee in 2022. It had taken their team 800 hours to create: 350 hours to sculpt the figure, 187 hours to insert the hair, and 30 hours for the teeth. Fine red silk threads had been used to recreate the veins in the whites of her eyes. Before taking up its place in the museum, her waxwork was paraded in a carriage along the front of the seaside resort, flanked by real-life guards dressed in Royal livery.

Later in 2022, the Panoptikum wax museum in Hamburg, founded in 1879, caused a stir at the unveiling of a new waxwork of the Queen. While demonstrating the waxwork, Dr Susanne Faerber, great-great-granddaughter of the museum's founder, removed the Queen's hat to reveal an entirely bald scalp.

'As we are using real human hair for our waxworks, which is very expensive, some figures which have hats don't have complete hair,' she explained.

Asked by a journalist from the *Daily Mail* whether it was disrespect-ful to display the Queen's bald head, Dr Faerber replied: 'It is a

waxwork, not the real person – this should always be kept in mind. Besides, the position of Her Majesty is in Germany different than the handling of the Royal Family in Great Britain, where the press have to be more sensitive dealing with them.'

In May 2023, I visited the late Queen at Madame Tussauds in Baker Street. It was my first visit since the 1960s, when I had been on a school trip to see the museum's noisy, smoky, unexpectedly arty recreation of the Battle of Trafalgar.

Six decades on, Trafalgar has disappeared, and the waxworks of the most prominent celebrities of my childhood – Bobby Moore, Harold Wilson, Twiggy, David Frost, Vera Lynn, Sandie Shaw, Morecambe and Wise, even the Beatles – have all gone too.

In an old black-and-white photograph of the recently installed 5-year-old Princess Elizabeth from 1931, a varied group of waxwork clerics lurks in the background: bishops, archbishops, cardinals, popes. Nowadays, none of these is present, not even the current pope or the current archbishop of Canterbury. Politicians are also on the wane: the only prime minister I managed to spot was Sir Winston Churchill, outside No. 10, a few feet away from Mrs Pankhurst, the suffragette.

More recent prime ministers – Thatcher, Blair, Cameron, Johnson – are nowhere to be seen. Perhaps they have been melted down, remoulded, squeezed into corsets and turned into the four young women from Little Mix, ready to lounge provocatively in the flashy Awards Night area alongside Ed Sheeran and Lady Gaga.

The only area where you can still find some old familiar faces is the Chamber of Horrors. A comparative newcomer is the serial killer Dennis Nilsen, staring grimly through the bars of his cell. Madame Tussaud herself liked to collect original items, the sicker the better, and today's organisation follows suit. A nondescript shirt and trousers are draped over a hanger, next to a caption reading 'Original shirt and trousers that were worn by Dennis Nilsen serving time in prison for multiple murders'. Also on display is 'Dennis Nilsen's personal TV taken from his house in Cranley Gardens, London, where he committed multiple murders'. Ghouling away at these gruesome exhibits, I was reminded of the time Nilsen's biographer, Brian Masters, visited him in prison: when Masters told him that a man in America had just beaten his record to become the world's most prolific serial killer, Nilsen replied: 'That's showbiz.'

Madame Tussauds takes this macabre joke seriously: serial killers stand just a few yards from the stars of Hollywood and the Royal Family, with little to distinguish between them. In the bizarre world of the waxwork, the act of murder offers the psychopath a charmed route to eternal fame.

Pop singers, on the other hand, come and go. Liam and Noel Gallagher are no more, and Frank Sinatra, Elvis Presley, Mick Jagger, Madonna, Elton John and Michael Jackson have also been boiled down, their places taken by more up-to-the-minute stars like Ariana Grande, Stormzy, Dua Lipa and Miley Cyrus. How long before this batch find themselves thrown into the pot, boiled down and remoulded into other stars, newer, younger, sexier, more popular?

Little over a decade ago, all the Queen's children and their spouses were on display. Nowadays, only King Charles, Queen Camilla and the Prince and Princess of Wales make the grade. Edward and Sophie and Anne and Tim are nowhere to be seen. Princess Diana is all by herself, but relegated, in a dowdy dress, to a naughty corner, along with a discreet plaque for younger visitors unable to remember her: 'Princess Diana 1961–1997. High-profile charity supporter and iconic presence on the world stage, her activism and glamour made her an international icon. Mother to Prince William and Prince Harry.'

And what of Prince Harry? On my visit just before the Coronation of King Charles III, I found him hanging on by his fingers in the Royal section, but standing at a discreet distance from the other four, in his dinner jacket and bowtie. Where was Meghan? Standing alone, in the Awards Party area around the corner, within spitting distance of Kim Kardashian and the Beckhams.

Prince Andrew has left the building. For over half a century, man and boy, he was a permanent resident, but not now. When the time is right, perhaps he will be allowed to return, possibly to his own little niche in the Chamber of Horrors, squeezing into a bath or tucking into a life-size slice of pizza from the Pizza Express in Woking.

The Queen is still on display, alongside Prince Philip, in a separate corner from the others. Their waxworks are no longer separated from the spectators by a red rope. In recent years, Madame Tussauds has become geared towards the selfie generation: everyone is free to rub shoulders with them, mobile phones held high.

Unlike their real-life counterparts, these waxworks are submissive, immobile, acquiescent. Visitors – particularly, I noticed, those from the Indian subcontinent – queue with an air of reverence to pose beside the Queen and Prince Philip, before moving on to athlete Mo Farah or 'award-winning actor and fashion icon' John Boyega.

Reduced to wax, the Queen exists for the needs of the consumer, there to fulfil a fantasy. In the Awards Party section, just past the Royals, when you press a button, up pops a message on a big screen: 'And the winner is … YOU!'

27

The Queen delivered her first Christmas message in 1952. Originally, it was only on radio, but from 1957 it was also televised.

For seventy years, the Christmas broadcast remained remarkably consistent. It was broadcast in Britain at 3 p.m. on Christmas Day, bookended by the National Anthem. There would be a Christmas tree in the background, along with framed photographs of members of the Royal Family, which eagle-eyed observers would treat as indicators of

who was in and who was out; in 2021, the Duke and Duchess of Sussex were nowhere to be seen.

The Queen's accessories changed little over the years. She always wore a watch, pearl earrings and three strings of pearls: only her brooch would vary. Her message too, remained reassuring. Only very occasionally would she make oblique references to shifts in the fortunes of her own family: for instance, in 1992, the year that had seen the end of the marriages of three of her four children and the disastrous fire at Windsor Castle, she said that 'like many other families we have lived through many difficulties this year'.

Her Christmas message always contained references to the Commonwealth. She would talk of the importance of family, send good wishes to those away from home or suffering, and recall the spiritual message of the Christmas story. She would finish by saying, 'Happy Christmas', occasionally adding 'God bless you all'. The broadcast would close with a shot of the Queen's flag floating in the wind, to the background music of 'God Save the Queen'.

Just as predictable were the regular mutterings from the intelligentsia that it had grown predictable, and that it would soon become a thing of the past. 'I think the annual Christmas broadcast of the Sovereign is something that isn't likely to go on very much longer,' the urbane broadcaster Ludovic Kennedy complained in 1969. 'It's, in a way, if one can say so, a sort of Buckingham Palace Party Political Broadcast of the Year and like all party political broadcasts it's apt to be a bit dull.'

On Christmas Day at Sandringham, the Queen herself generally sat in another room while the rest of her family watched her on television.

The following speech is a composite, stitched together from sentences from her Christmas broadcasts over the course of a single decade. The first sentence comes from her first broadcast of the 1960s, the second sentence comes from her second broadcast, and so on, up to 1969. For some, this collage will demonstrate her blandness; for others, her consistency.

1960: I am glad at Christmas time to have this opportunity of speaking directly to all the peoples of the Commonwealth and of sending my good wishes.

1961: It is traditionally the time for family reunions, present-giving, and children's parties.

1962: Surely it is because the family festival is like a firm landmark in the stormy seas of modern life.

1963: We know the reward is peace on earth, good will towards men, but we cannot win it without determination and concerted effort.

1964: I know that life is hard for many.

1965: A festival which we owe to that Family long ago which spent this time in extreme adversity and discomfort.

1966: It is difficult to realise that it was less than fifty years ago that women in Britain were first given the vote, but Parliament was first asked to grant this one hundred years ago.

1967: The future of Canada as a great and prosperous country depends just as much on the will of the present generation to work together.

1968: The British people together have achieved great things in the past and have overcome many dangers, but we cannot make further progress if we resurrect ancient squabbles.

1969: I hope they will all feel the warmth and comfort of companionship and that all of you will enjoy a very happy Christmas with your families and friends.

28

The Queen broadcast her 1953 Christmas message – the second of her reign – from Auckland, New Zealand. She and Prince Philip were in the second month of a six-month tour of the Commonwealth, having left their children behind. 'Of course, we all want our children at Christmas time – for that is the season above all others when each family gathers at its own hearth. I hope that perhaps mine are listening to me now and I am sure that when the time comes they, too, will be great travellers.'

Elsewhere in her message, she spoke of the changing role of the monarchy. 'Some people have expressed the hope that my reign may mark a new Elizabethan age. Frankly I do not myself feel at all like my great Tudor forebear, who was blessed with neither husband nor children, who ruled as a despot, and was never able to leave her native shores.'

This was a striking passage, but that year's message is most keenly remembered for one particular phrase, which came at the start of her second paragraph:

'My husband and I ...'

It was the first time she had ever employed it, but it was to pop up regularly in her speeches over the coming years. Within a decade, it had become the stuff of comedy. At the dawning of the new age of anti-Establishment satire, comedians started to mimic her, opening their impersonations with the phrase 'May hesbnd end Ay'. This served two comic purposes: it would make it clear who they were imitating, and be guaranteed an easy laugh. Before long, 'May hesbend end Ay' had been taken up by every saloon-bar jester, and had become as much a catchphrase of the era as 'Shaken not stirred' or 'See you later, alligator'. More often than not, it is the Queen's only contribution to dictionaries of quotations, whereas her great Tudor forebear generally manage five or six.*

Who wants to be a figure of fun? She stopped using it. From the early Sixties onwards, she and her speechwriters tried to avoid ridicule by changing it to 'Prince Philip and I'. But the phrase had stuck: for the rest of the decade, the jokers simply carried on regardless, parroting the tried-and-tested 'May hesbend end Ay'.

But then, on the occasion of her twenty-fifth wedding anniversary in 1972, the Queen started her address at the Guildhall in London with the words: 'I think everybody really will concede that on this, of all days, I should begin my speech with the words "my husband and I".'

With this, she staked her claim to ownership of the joke, and it paid off: nowadays, it is this, and not the 1953 original, that is now included in dictionaries of modern quotations, and in dictionaries of humorous quotations too. As was so often the case, it was the Queen, and not the comics, who had the last laugh.

---

* The most familiar of which is probably 'I know I have the body of a weak and feeble woman, but I have the heart and stomach of a king …'

29

Her accent changed with the times, just like everyone else's. In her 1953 broadcast, 'had' rhymes with 'bed'; thirty years later, it rhymes with 'bad'. And 'home', which once rhymed with 'tame', now rhymed with 'Rome'. She ended her 1954 broadcast by wishing everyone a 'heppy' New Year, with 'happy' rhyming with 'preppy'; by 1980, it rhymed with 'nappy'.

In 2000, a team of researchers led by Dr Jonathan Harrington of Macquarie University in Sydney studied all the Queen's Christmas broadcasts. They published their findings in the *Journal of the International Phonetic Association*, in an essay breezily titled 'Monophthongal vowel changes in Received Pronunciation: an acoustic analysis of the Queen's Christmas Broadcasts'. They concluded that the Queen had gradually made small, almost imperceptible changes to her accent. Over the years, it had inched closer to the accent 'characteristic of speakers who are younger and/or lower in the social hierarchy'. On the other hand, right to the very end, she continued to say 'orf' for 'off'.

She herself enjoyed mimicry, and slipped into it with ease. Her family were not off-limits. The day after her equestrian granddaughter Zara Phillips collected the 2006 BBC Sports Personality of the Year award, liberally peppering her acceptance speech with the word 'amazing' ('It's just amazing to be here among these people and to win this is absolutely amazing'), the racing trainer Ian Balding telephoned the Queen. Before he finished congratulating her, she chipped in: 'Wasn't it amaaaazing, amaaaazing!'

30

A mimic's guide

Air: Belonging to ourselves. 'Air femleh orphan getheraind the
   tillyvishn'

Ashered evthot: I would have considered. 'Ashered evthot they would
   have knayn by nyar'

Beckwd: Having made less progress. 'Sedly, it's a beckwd country'

Bend: Group of people with a common purpose. 'The Bend of the
   Rahlmirreens'

Bettle: Sustained fight between armed forces. 'The Bettle of Hestings'

Bleck: Opposite of white

Chair up: Become less miserable

Delated: Thrilled

Disgrayable: Unpleasant

Duke um ear orphan?: Question to break the ice

Ears: Affirmative response

Eckshleh: Really

Efrica: The world's second-largest continent

Eggrevating: Causing annoyance

Elaine: By oneself, solitary

Eldfeshnd: Passé, out of date

Endrew: Second son

Enshent: Long ago

Femleh: 'The heppy arrival of air fourth grendchild gev great cause
   for femleh celebrations'

Fessin Etting: Of extreme interest

Flesh: A sudden burst of bright light. 'It was all over in a flesh'

Flip: The Duke of Edinburgh

Fraw lino: To the furthest extent of my knowledge. 'Fraw lino, President Trump will want to lend his helicorpter on the lawn'

Gawn: Departed

Glaibe: The Earth. 'Em gled too to be eble to thenk once again air haists all raind the glaibe'

Gled: Pleased

Greta Tyood: Thankfulness

Hail: Entire

Hairm: The place one lives. 'Ay wish you a heppy Christmas, in your hairms on Christmas Deh'

Haip: Wish. 'Ay haip you awl hev a very heppy Christmas'

Hens: Those parts of a person's arms beyond the wrist. 'Flip is velly good with his hens'

Hesbnd: Male spouse

Het: Item of clothing worn on the head

Hevyew cumfar?: Another question to break the ice

Hosh lair sair: Useful means of signalling understatement: 'He was, hosh lair sair, far from thin'

Innek rurt: Not precisely true. 'The prime minister supplied one with information that proved innek rurt'

Jem: Preservative served at afternoon tea

Kennew medgin?: Beyond belief

Kenny duh: Large country to the north of the USA

Laife: Term of existence. 'To dedicate your laife'

Lake: To appreciate or approve of

Lawst: Mislaid

Maiment: Brief period of time

Maist: Greatest in amount, quantity or degree. 'Maist emusing'

Near: Expression of disagreement. 'Ay could tell he wanted me to say ears, but Ay said a firm near'

Nyar: At the present time. 'Nyar and then'

O.A.C.: Expression of polite interest. 'Your Majesty, this is our latest device to assist us with low-bandwidth double-loop granular scanning.' 'O.A.C.'

Orf: Not orn

Orn: Not orf

Orphan: Frequent

Orstrelia: Island continent in the southern hemisphere

Pet law yet: Royal versifier

Preps: Possibly

Pwoower: The less well-off. 'Richaw pwoower, we mist all shay air concern fruthuz'

Quate: Expression of agreement

Rmate: Distant, far away

Rotherham pressiv: Somewhat admirable

Sairviss: Assistance. 'A laife of sairviss'

Say-say: Neither very good nor very bad

Sand: Something you can hear. 'The sand of distant drums'

Sed: Unhappy

Sephew words: Speak a little. 'Ev bnosked to sephew words'

Spake: Talked. 'Ay spake to the Embesseder'

Stender dzovbe hevyer: Codes of practice. 'In the stadiums, stender dzovbe hevyer hev gretly improved'

Syootibaw: Appropriate. 'Sich a shame Herry didn't merry someone, hosh lair sair, more syootibaw'

Tare curver: Assume control

Thaisands: A great number. 'Ev trevelled menny thaisands of miles'

Thenk: Express gratitude

Thrain: Ceremonial chair or seat

Trevel: To go from one place to another

Urver: Finished or complete; to surmount. 'Hill jest hev to get urver it'

Vair: To a high degree. 'Hair vair yin tresting'

Wall: The whole quantity. 'It tex wall sworts'

Ware flafe: Accustomed pattern of behaviour. 'The jungle fake run around with nothing awn. It's their ware flafe'

Weld: The earth, with all its countries and people. 'We are at the maircy of weld events'

X: Deeds. 'The X of the Apostles'

Yang: Youthful. 'Air yang people nyeed awl the hilp we kin give them'

Yin Tresting: Not as yin tresting as vair yin tresting but more yin tresting than 'O.A.C.'

Zaydeeyek: Imaginary band in the heavens divided into twelve constellations for astrological purposes

31

Even though she met more people than anyone else who ever lived – four million different people over the course of her lifetime, according to former prime minister David Cameron in his eulogy* – the Queen was never a natural conversationalist. Faced with a crowd, she learned to employ a small stock of generalised questions to speed her through each brief encounter: 'How long have you been waiting?' 'Where have you come from?' 'What do you do?' The response would prompt a formulaic reply that had the necessary sheen of specificity – 'Two hours! That's a long time!' 'Oh, Basingstoke?!' 'Really? A carpenter?' Then she would move on to the next stranger, and a similar exchange.

But she could find it hard work to embark on anything longer; finding common ground could be troublesome. On her tour of Canada in 1959, she was shown around a prefabricated home in the new town of Schefferville by its occupant. 'I find it difficult keeping my floors clean, too,' she was heard to comment. As the writer Adam Mars-Jones has pointed out, 'in view of her two hundred-man staff and Household of four hundred, this comes close to the upper limit of size for a little white lie'. On the other hand, what else could she have said? If she replied, truthfully, 'That's never been a worry for me, what with my vast staff and limitless money,' she might have been accused of showing off. Yet she had to say something. Perhaps it was her innate honesty that

---

* According to one survey, the average cold-caller addresses between thirty-five and forty people a day, though most of these conversations are generally very brief (e.g. 'Hello. Can I—?' 'Get lost.'). At this rate, even the most diligent cold-caller would have to work for two or three lifetimes before hoping to overtake the Queen.

proved her conversational undoing. Unlike her mother ('What a wonderful home, oh, I do so envy you!') she found it hard to dissemble.

The Queen Mother might draw a conversation to a close by saying, 'How very kind of you to come and see us!' or 'Well, I'd love to stand here talking all day, but I really must get on!' But nature had denied her daughter the inclination to gush. 'I would far prefer to sit next to her than the Q. Mother,' reflected James Lees-Milne after speaking to the Queen at a Hatchards Authors of the Year party in 1982. 'There is none of that sugary insincerity in the Queen. She is absolutely direct.' Less charming but more scrupulous, she was more like her father, who found it hard to think of anything to say to anyone at any time. 'He is good, he is dull, he is dutiful and good-natured,' wrote Chips Channon, who was none of these. 'He is completely uninteresting, undistinguished and a god-awful bore.'

On a royal tour of South Africa in 1947, the Queen Mother – or Queen Elizabeth, as she was then – asked an ex-serviceman where he had fought in the Second World War.

'Italy,' came the reply.

'Italy,' the Queen Mother repeated to the King.

'Oh, Italy,' said the King.

'Yes, Italy,' repeated the ex-serviceman.

'Um,' replied the King, still lost for words. The Queen Mother then flashed a smile, and the Royal couple moved on.

Duff and Diana Cooper went to lunch with them the following year. Diana's account of the King's conversation makes it sound closer to a litany of grumbles. 'The King's approach is of the whining variety, delivered in a plaintive voice: "We can't get enough to heat the place." "I can't get them to cut the trees in the Mall – can't even see Big Ben now." "I dunno what it is – if one gets hold of a good book someone always takes it before one has finished."' She noted that the King's wife and daughters didn't bother to tune into what he said: 'They don't listen to him much; it's *her* family and household. "All right, Daddy," then a quick turn away and "What did you say, Mummy darling?"'

When it came to conversation, King George VI's younger brother, Prince Henry, Duke of Gloucester, believed that there were few assets more useful than ignorance. On this point, he disagreed with his mother, Queen Mary. 'I remember my mother was furious with me, perfectly furious,' he reminisced to James Pope-Hennessy. 'Before I went out you see she gave me all her books about Australia to read. Well I never read 'em. So she asked me if I had read 'em so I said no I haven't read 'em and I'm not going to read 'em and I'm going to tell you why. She was furious. But I said to her, look here, if I read all about the places I can't ask the damn silly questions you have to ask when you meet all these people because I should know the answers. And I shouldn't have anything to say to them if I didn't ask 'em questions. And if I knew all the answers I wouldn't have anything to ask. She saw what I meant in the end.'

His father – the Queen's grandfather, King George V – was equally tongue-tied, perhaps more so, though he could be spurred to speech by irritation. 'He disapproved of Soviet Russia, painted finger-nails, women who smoked in public, cocktails, frivolous hats, American jazz and the growing habit of going away for weekends,' recalled the Duke of Windsor. This list of the things loathed by the father could double as a list of the things loved by the eldest son, with the possible exception of Soviet Russia.

In his autobiography, the Duke of Windsor offers a grim portrait of his parents' idea of entertaining. During Ascot week, they would invite a dozen or so guests to Windsor Castle. Every evening at 8.30 prompt, the Master of the Household greeted the King and Queen and their children at the door of the Green Drawing Room. After bowing the Master of the Household would back into the room, heralding their arrival to the male guests, who would have arranged themselves in a semi-circle on one side, and the female guests, arranged in a semi-circle on the other. The King, his sons and male members of the Royal Household would be dressed in the Windsor uniform, which consisted of a dark blue tailcoat with scarlet collar and cuffs, a single-breasted white waistcoat and plain black trousers. All the other male guests were expected to wear black tailcoats and knee breeches.

The King would shake hands with the women while the Queen shook hands with the men. Then they would all process into dinner to the sound of 'God Save the King' played by the Guards' string band, sitting in an airless space behind a grille. They continued to play throughout the meal, sweating in their tight tunics.

Dinner, served by liveried footmen, would last no more than an hour, after which the women would curtsy to the King before being led back into the drawing room by the Queen, leaving the King and his male guests to their coffee and port for a maximum of twenty minutes. The King and Queen would then bid all their guests good night; and that was that.

'Nothing was lacking but gaiety,' observed the Duke of Windsor.

Queen Elizabeth II's conversation with outsiders was constitutionally constricted: even if she wanted, she could never be outspoken or abrasive, for fear of causing offence. This gave rise to blandness, which could cause offence in some circles, particularly to those hoping for a bit of cut-and-thrust. 'The Queen confined herself to platitudes on principle, never saying anything of the slightest interest about any subject whatever, let alone about royalty itself,' reflected the historian Piers Brendon. His fellow historian A. N. Wilson was in broad agreement: 'People revered the Crown, but they were not really interested in the Queen for the very simple reason that she is not really interesting.' Nevertheless, he recognised that 'Her uninterestingness is a positive asset.'

Wilson himself had undergone sticky times with royalty. 'There are people who pay money in order to have dinner with royalty. It would be ungracious to say that I would pay money not to do so, but there is almost always, in my experience, an element of the unsatisfactory about the experience. It is not so much that you have to be on good behaviour, as that both you and the royal personage are being put through your paces, rather than being truly yourself. If you want a monarchy to exist, the Royal Family have, by definition, to be different from the rest of us. Yet both they, poor things, and the rest of us wave across a great gulf at one another, and sometimes want to be friends ... A commoner can't easily have a proper conversation with royal people because they are NOT like us, and in the case of the older British royals you cannot be sure that they will understand even quite simple references to contemporary life. (One thinks of Prince Charles, when visiting the White House and offered a tea bag by the waiter, to put in his pot of hot water – "What IS it? I mean, what does one DO with it?") I think that is why so many photographs of royal personages meeting commoners depict everyone having the giggles. It is the brittle banter that you find in hospital wards.'

In the company of the Queen, even the chattiest of chatterboxes might find themselves tongue-tied. 'I find her difficult to talk to. The timing always seems jerky and inopportune,' complained Cecil Beaton. He felt she was 'affable enough but showed no signs of real interest in anything … not one word of conversation'. Her grandfather's pernickety biographer, Harold Nicolson, found her 'dull and surrounded by dull people'. In 1976, at an awkward gathering for those in the 'Media and the Arts', the playwright Tom Stoppard found himself placed next to an elderly lady in waiting. The experience, he confessed, was 'rather stiff': the lady in waiting talked to him about the TV series *Upstairs Downstairs*, complaining that the footman in one of the episodes had worn the wrong livery. Afterwards, his ten-minute conversation with the Queen also proved 'hard work, nice as she was'.

Presented to the Queen after performing in the opening ceremony for the Welsh Assembly in 1999, the 12-year-old 'Voice of an Angel' singer Charlotte Church also found the Queen's conversation lacklustre:

> When she got to me, she said, 'Have you been singing long?' Her handshake was ridiculous, though, as if she was frightened of catching something. Come on, go the whole way! Before I had a chance to say anything more than a mumbled 'Yes', Prince Philip chipped in, 'Elizabeth, don't you know who this young girl is? We listen to her all the time on the radio. It's Charlotte Church.'
>
> She then muttered something inaudible and moved on. To be honest, I felt a bit sorry for her because she looked a little lost to me. It must be so hard thinking of something to say to a line of people that you've never met or know nothing about, with only the briefest bit of information whispered in your ear by an aide. She's probably really nice, but she looks so uncomfortable, as if she's racking her brains for

a sentence, whereas Prince Philip's much more relaxed and funny and just chats about anything.

Charlotte Church was not alone: grown-ups experienced a similar problem. At a private drinks party in 1990, Gyles Brandreth found himself stuck in a corner of the room with the Queen. 'There was no obvious means of escape for either of us, and neither of us could think of anything very interesting to say.' Later that night, he jotted down this transcript of their sticky conversation:

> GB: (getting the ball rolling) Had a busy day, Ma'am?
> HMQ: (with a small sigh) Yes, very.
> GB: At the Palace?
> HMQ: Yes.
> GB: A lot of visitors!
> HMQ: Yes.

(Pause)

> GB: (brightly) The Prime Minister?
> HMQ: Yes.

(Pause)

> GB: He's very nice.
> HMQ: Yes, very.

(Long pause)

> GB: (struggling) The recession's bad.
> HMQ: (looking grave) Yes.
> GB: (trying to jolly things along) I think this must be my third recession.
> HMQ: (nodding) We do seem to get them every few years ... and none of my governments seems to know what to do about them.

(A moment of tinkly laughter from HMQ, a huge guffaw from GB, then total silence)

GB: (suddenly frantic) I've been to Wimbledon today.

HMQ: (brightening briefly) Oh, yes?

GB: (determined) Yes.

HMQ: I've been to Wimbledon, too.

GB: (now we're getting somewhere) Today?

HMQ: No.

GB: (oh well, we tried) No, of course not. (PAUSE) I wasn't at the tennis.

HMQ: No?

GB: No, I was at the theatre. (LONG PAUSE). Have you been to the theatre in Wimbledon?

(Pause)

HMQ: I imagine so.

(Interminable pause)

GB: (a last, desperate attempt) You know, Ma'am, my wife's a vegetarian.

HMQ: (what will she say?) That must be very dull.

GB: (what next?) And one of my daughters is a vegetarian, too.

HMQ: Oh, dear.

The forthright author Rebecca West was invited to lunch at Buckingham Palace in February 1959. Her fellow guests included 'a very boring Australian journalist' and the playwright Terence Rattigan ('who is a pansy'). Over drinks, West came to see that the 32-year-old Queen was a sitting target for bores. 'It was obvious she finds it a little difficult to make conversation,' she reported back to a friend. 'I realised a terrible thing about her life. She asked the Australian journalist, who was being recalled from London to Australia after three years here, how he was going home. He told her, oh, he told her. He was going by air, his wife was going on a boat with the children, he would arrive on such and such a date, his wife would arrive on such a date, the boat she was going on was such and such a boat. The poor child spends her life asking questions *which people answer!*'

Attending a presentation of Australian and New Zealand delegates to the Royal Family in May 1943 the Conservative politician Leo Amery felt a similar sense of pity. He watched as Princess Margaret, then only twelve, struggled to look interested while 'one of the Australian delegates furnished her with all the statistics of sheep in Australia, the bales of wool produced and the pounds of wool in each bale'.

In the presence of the Queen, some were driven to silence, and others – either by nervousness or self-regard, or a combustible mixture of both – to blather. At dinners and receptions, courtiers were expected to cope with some of her more garrulous guests. This gave them a glimpse of what the Queen had to cope with, day in, day out. Her cousin Margaret Rhodes was once, in her words, 'commanded to attend' a state banquet for 150, in honour of the King of Malaysia. Her fellow guests included the archbishop of Canterbury, the prime minister and various members of the Cabinet. 'Well, there I was, amidst all this splendour, sitting next to a man whose firm was supplying a new sewage system to Malaysia. He insisted on passing on every possible detail. It was not a conversation of memorable enjoyment, but of course the food and wine were excellent and to an extent I was able to anaesthetise myself from waste flows and piping in Kuala Lumpur.'

Polite by nature, the Queen adhered to the manners of the day, so it could come as a surprise to her guests to see her dip into her handbag, mid-event, whip out a mirror and lipstick, and set to work on her lips. She would execute this task with single-minded efficiency. She emerged with her lips refreshed, but it also gave her the chance to retreat into a world of her own, to take time off, if only for a few seconds, from the exhausting business of listening to other people talk about themselves.

In many memoirs of the great and the good, the tedium of the Queen's job may be glimpsed between the self-absorbed lines. In *Two Lucky People: The Memoirs of Milton and Rose D. Friedman,* the husband-and-wife free-market economists are invited to a reception on the Royal Yacht *Britannia* when it is moored in San Francisco in 1983:

> David Packard had given the queen a Hewlett-Packard computer and Milton was able to advise her on how she could use it to keep track of her race horses. Prince Philip was very interested in social policy and well informed on the issues we talked about. In this age of democracy, Elizabeth and Philip, like the king and queen of Sweden, were very friendly, unpretentious, attractive people. 'Regal' is not a word that springs to mind to describe their behaviour.

On formal occasions, protocol dictated that any conversation was to be initiated by the Queen, and that it was for the Queen alone to ask any further questions. From the guest's point of view, this made talking to her more like appearing on a quiz show, with a gong sounding in your head each time you overstepped the mark. And sometimes the Queen was lost for words.

At a Royal gala evening at Covent Garden in 1958, Maria Callas took eight curtain calls after performing the mad scene from Bellini's *I puritani*. In the line-up afterwards, the Queen chatted graciously with each artiste in turn, but when she came to Callas she simply smiled and moved on. Over dinner that evening, Callas asked the Queen's first cousin, the opera administrator Lord Harewood, why the Queen had failed to speak to her. He promised to find out, and phoned her the next day. 'I just didn't know what to ask her or say to her,' explained the Queen.*

Was the Queen worried that even the most carefully phrased question might reveal her ignorance of opera, or of Callas's career? After all, she regarded opera with some suspicion: on one of her rare visits to the English National Opera, she mentioned her opera-loving cousin to the general director, Peter Jonas. 'Funny thing about George,' she added. 'In most respects he's perfectly normal.'

She was able to tread conversational water, but few topics excited her. 'Making small talk with the Queen is not easy unless you understand horses and dogs,' reflected Gyles Brandreth. One story, possibly apocryphal, has it that after an hour spent talking to Emperor Hirohito of Japan, she complained to one of her courtiers,

---

* In his slim memoir *Music: A Joy for Life* (1976) the former prime minister Edward Heath relates an occasion on which Malcolm Sargent was trying to persuade Maria Callas to sing at St James's Palace. 'It was not without its incidents. Madame Callas, having agreed to sing, suddenly decided she would not do so unless the Queen were present. Malcolm Sargent's diplomatic skills were exercised to the utmost to persuade her to change her mind, but to no avail. Finally he played his last card. "Do you know, my dear, the Queen Mother is going to be present and that in itself is a very great honour. If the Queen were to come she is, of course, younger than you and a most beautiful woman. People might be tempted to make comparisons."'

'At this,' writes Heath, 'Maria Callas capitulated.'

'That man can talk of nothing but tropical fish'; in turn, the Emperor complained to one of his courtiers, 'That woman can talk of nothing but horses.'

At a special Diamond Jubilee exhibition at Kensington Palace, her biographer Robert Hardman watched the Queen as she viewed a newly remastered film of Queen Victoria's own Diamond Jubilee. Hardman noticed that she was completely absorbed by this extraordinary footage. 'What thoughts might be going through the monarch's mind as she watched Queen Victoria celebrating the anniversary she herself was about to enjoy – the only other monarch in history to have done so? After a few moments, she broke the silence. "That's interesting," she noted. "They had eight horses on the landau."'

She rarely started a conversation with a stranger without knowing that within less than a minute she would have to draw it to an end: anything approaching absorption would play havoc with her timetable. 'The Queen never got engaged in a topic to the extent that she would mind becoming disengaged,' recalled one former minister.

In her public role, she was meant to avoid offering her own opinions; her tongue was officially tied. 'Even those who see her regularly, like her fourteen Prime Ministers with their weekly audiences, do not really know what she thinks about many of the major issues they discuss,' said Alastair Campbell, Tony Blair's former press secretary. Her critics sometimes took her to task for this reticence. 'She has done nothing and said nothing that anybody will remember,' complained the crotchety historian Dr David Starkey* in 2015, when she became the longest-serving monarch in British history. 'She will not give her name to her age. Or, I suspect, to anything else.'

But perhaps that was her aim. Others, more sensitive to nuance than Campbell or Starkey, saw that she could use silence to convey meaning, questions to express opinions, and understatement to signal disapproval. To put it another way, she was able to speak between the

---

* Dr David Starkey (b. 1945), an expert on the Tudors, was once called 'the rudest man in Britain'. Perhaps by way of explanation, he said that 'high malice is almost inherent in the profession of historian'.

lines, making her meaning clear without spelling it out. She was the least rhetorical of public speakers. The statements for which she is remembered are almost all of them understatements, from 'Recollections may vary', after her grandson and his wife had publicly accused members of her family of racist talk, to her appraisal of the bloody relations between Britain and Ireland, delivered in Dublin on her first state visit to Ireland at the age of 82: 'Of course the relationship has not always been straightforward; nor has it been entirely benign.'

She was minimalist and exact, ever anxious to avoid going too far. In the early years of her reign, she had been due to visit Kingston upon Hull, in Yorkshire. One of her private secretaries presented her with a draft of the speech she was to deliver there. It began, 'I am very pleased to be in Kingston today.' She crossed out the word 'very'. 'I will be *pleased* to be in Kingston, but I will not be *very* pleased,' she explained.

Did her taciturn manner conceal a deeper intuition? Investing the 70-year-old author Sybille Bedford with an OBE in 1981, the Queen asked her what she did.

'I am a writer, ma'am.'

'How long have you been writing?'

'All my life.'

'Oh, dear! Oh, well.'

This was the extent of their conversation. In transcript, the Queen's contribution may seem almost comically brusque. But with those last four words she had in fact hit the nail on the head. Throughout her life, Sybille Bedford had found the act of writing close to unbearable. 'I sit before my hostile typewriter and sicken before the abnormal effort,' she once confessed. 'What is this blight I have suffered from all my life that makes trying to write ... such tearing, crushing, defeating agony?'

The Queen's natural reticence could often trigger strange reactions. When the playwright Harold Pinter attended lunch at Buckingham Palace with his wife Lady Antonia Fraser, his fellow playwright Václav Havel, the crime writer P. D. James and one or two others, the master of the pause was driven to fill in one of the Queen's very own pauses with gibberish. 'Do you know, Ma'am,' he said, 'that vegetables were introduced into England very late? Henry VIII never ate a vegetable.'

To which the Queen replied: 'Oh, yes?'

Later that same lunch, Pinter found himself struggling again. As Lady Antonia Fraser remembered it:

> Havel, always a merry fellow, even in the darkest days, started to tease Harold about all the policemen surrounding Buckingham Palace and said something about Harold not really liking our policemen, meaning in Czechoslovakia, in the communist days, not London. The Queen caught the dialogue and leaning forward said to Harold, 'Do you really not like our policemen, Mr Pinter?' Harold, realising his mistake, chose to reply expansively with all the flourish of the actor he once was: 'Your Majesty, I adore policemen.'

'I'm sure they will be relieved to hear it,' replied the Queen, putting an end to the conversation. The Queen gave a little smile, and so of course did Harold.

As in a Pinter play, her seemingly banal phrases were apt to contain a knowing subtext, so coded as to be evident only to those on her wavelength. Julian Spalding, then director of Glasgow Museums, once had to show her round an exhibition of cutting-edge contemporary art:

I'd decided on the way I'd take her round, avoiding, purely selfishly I have to admit, for my own ease of explanation in the event of being asked, the more explicitly referenced sexual parts. Call me a coward but give me a break; I didn't rate the work anyway. I would normally, taking anyone round an exhibition, say a few things to introduce my enthusiasm, but in this instance, I was simply tongue-tied. I knew the Queen wasn't very interested in art, anyway, and in this art nor was I. The Queen, I'm sure, had been informed about my opinion. I hadn't exactly kept quiet in the press. But now I detected an impish twinkle in her eye at my inability to say a word. (I was already beginning, rather to my surprise, to like her.) So, she helped me out.

'Is that an exhibit?' she asked. Her voice took me by surprise. She spoke very fast, with a grating, high-pitched edge to her tone. Her voice was clipped and sharp, totally unlike her public, deliberate, low-tuned drawl. I suddenly sensed I was in the presence of a very different woman and didn't know her at all. Her choice of word was perfect – you get exhibits in exhibitions; they don't have to be works of art. And that's exactly what they were: exhibits, not works of art. I felt more at ease, but still didn't really know what to say ... Every so often she asked, 'Is that an exhibit?' But I realised she wasn't really expecting an answer, so I stayed dumb, just nodding each time, enjoying the game.

Then she asked, at the end of one gallery, 'Is that an exhibit? What's that?' The additional question caught me off my guard. 'It's bunches of grapes cast in lead – I think it's lead,' I looked more closely, 'yes, lead – hung on wires from the ceiling.'

'Thank you for telling me,' she snapped.

Then we turned a corner. 'What's that? Is that an exhibit, too?' she exclaimed, looking at a row of grey filing cabinets with their bottom drawers pulled out into each of which was stuffed a length of rolled up carpet ... I nodded. A further question followed. 'And who's that by?'

'It's by an artist called Melanie Counsell. She got the idea, I think, when she worked in a mental hospital.'

'Her mind was affected, was it?' came the quick-fire retort, as usual ambiguous, but precisely to the point.

The art of indicating what you mean without saying it, which the Queen has honed over years of practice, was displayed beautifully at the official banquet held in the City Chambers after this visit. Her Majesty read her speech from a little rostrum propped for the moment on her table. 'This morning,' she said in her familiar, slow, mannered drawl so unlike the zappy tones I had just enjoyed, 'I visited the McLellan Galleries.' The room erupted into laughter, and continued for some time, breaking into little eddies here and there as people imagined her encounter with these 'exhibits'. The Queen looked round the room, her eyes slightly widening in surprise. She waited for the laughter to die down. Then, without looking down again at her notes – which made me think her next remark was unscripted, a rare occurrence for someone who had learnt for years never to depart from a text – she said in her official slow voice, 'I enjoyed the experience.' The room burst into laughter again, and so did I.

The Beatles' shortest song, just twenty-three seconds from start to end, deals with this reticence. 'Her Majesty's a pretty nice girl,' sang Paul McCartney, 'but she doesn't have a lot to say.' Half a century after he recorded it, McCartney explained: 'It's tongue-in-cheek, treating the queen as if she were just a nice girl and not bothering with the fact that she would become the longest-reigning monarch ever in the UK, or that she was queen of the nation.' He pointed out that 'she doesn't say much – only the annual Queen's Speech at Christmas and the opening of Parliament ... As it turns out, I have had the pleasure of meeting the queen over the years … she came up to officially open the Liverpool Institute for the Performing Arts, which is the performing-arts school I'd helped set up in my old grammar school. She very kindly cut the ribbon. So, when I meet her nowadays, she asks me about that. "How's your school in Liverpool?" And I say, "It's doing rather well, Ma'am."'

As it happens, McCartney performed 'Her Majesty' for Her Majesty at 2002 at the Golden Jubilee 'Party at the Palace'. Afterwards, he was presented to her.

'I don't know how to break this to you,' he remarked later, 'but she didn't have a lot to say.'

32

A knock on the door. It is my son, Edward.

'Hello Edward,' I say, informally.

'Hello Mummy,' he replies.

We shake hands. What's that expression they use these days? That's it. We are a 'close-knit family'.

'Have you come far?' I ask.

'Not really,' he says. 'We don't live all that far away. Though the traffic was quite busy.'

'There are a lot of cars on the roads these days,' I say. 'You sometimes wonder where they are all going!'

'Yes!' he agrees. 'You can't help but wonder,' he says, 'where they are all going!'

'Yes!' I agree.

I saw quite a bit of the Prime Minister during the past year. We have regular meetings. He greatly values my tremendous wealth of wisdom and experience.

It is my duty as Monarch to advise and inform. 'My son pointed out that there was an awful lot of traffic on the roads this morning,' I say.

'That will be the cars,' he says.

'And lorries,' I say.

'Yes. Cars and lorries,' he agrees. Once again, he has been able to draw on my wealth of experience.

'People getting from A to B,' he adds.

'They might be better off walking,' I say, giving it some thought.

'Perhaps the third lane of the motorway could be reserved for pedestrians, with cars and lorries in the first.'

The Prime Minister says that is one idea he has never thought of. He will look into it.

'… which would leave the second lane free for horses and carriages and so forth,' I add.

I ask after his wife. 'And how is Mrs er?'

They do appreciate it when one shows a bit of interest. He says his wife is very well.

'Well, goodbye,' I say, rising from my chair, shaking his hand and leaving the room. This is his signal to depart.

33

Rebecca Hossack is a London art dealer who specialises in Aboriginal art. An Australian by birth, she set up her first gallery in Windmill Street in 1988.

'When I first met the Aboriginal artist Clifford Possum in the creek bed in Alice Springs in 1989, I asked him if he'd like to have a show in London, and his first response was: "Queen".

'And so I said, "Of course, when you come to London, you can meet the Queen." But my main thought was, "Brilliant: this great Aboriginal artist is going to come to London to have an exhibition at my gallery."

'So, several months later, I went to pick him up from Heathrow, and there he was in his cowboy hat. He didn't really speak much English – though he spoke six Aboriginal languages. He was a very clever man. But almost the first thing he said to me was "Queen". Of course I'd forgotten my promise that he could meet the Queen, but I thought, well, we'll just drive him past Buckingham Palace, and that will be enough. So we drove past the palace, and there it was, the flag flying.

'I said, "Clifford, that's where the Queen lives." And he went, "In, go in!" And then I realised he had told everyone in Alice Springs that he was going to London to meet the Queen. (It turned out he'd even been photographed for the front page of the *Alice Springs Advertiser* with the headline "Clifford Flies to London to Meet the Queen".)

'I didn't know what to do. I thought, "What have I done?" I have been yet another white person who has betrayed the trust of the Aboriginal people. I have promised something, and entirely failed to deliver it.

'So I rang up Malcolm Williamson, who was Master of the Queen's Music at the time, and an Australian, and he said, "Well, I'll see if I can get you an invitation to a Royal garden party, but I don't think he can meet her." And I thought, well, perhaps that'll do. I still felt terrible, though.

'That night it was the private view of Clifford's exhibition at my gallery in Fitzrovia. The gallery was crowded with people. It was the first ever major Aboriginal art exhibition in London. It was a hot summer's night, and this distinguished-looking man with a white beard came in. It turned out he was Lord Harewood, and he was with his wife, who was an Australian musician. They'd seen the Aboriginal flag hanging outside the gallery as they'd been walking down Windmill Street, and they'd just popped in. They were amazed and impressed by Clifford's pictures. We had some nice chat, and he asked why I seemed a little distracted. And I said, "I've done something so terrible. Clifford's come to London expecting to meet the Queen, and he can't. I've lied to him, and he's going to lose so much face."

'He didn't say anything to this. But the next morning, the telephone rang at 9 o'clock. It was Lord Harewood. He said, "I've spoken to my cousin, the Queen, and she would be delighted to meet you and Clifford at the Garden Party this afternoon." I nearly dropped to the ground. In my whole life, that was the most extraordinary thing that ever happened. It was a true miracle.

'So we had to go and hire Clifford a top hat and morning suit from Moss Bros. He put paintbrushes in his hat-band, and he wore white tennis-shoes which he painted with a possum dreaming. He was so excited.

'We went to Buckingham Palace and sat in some antechamber, and then we came down the steps into the garden, and all the people were behind ropes on either side; but somehow we were in the middle, and the Queen came up to us.

'It was the most amazing moment. Clifford seemed to rise in stature, with his top hat. He was very dignified. He and the Queen had a conversation. It was extraordinary. I think he was the first Aboriginal to go to Buckingham Palace. He spoke to her and it was quite a long conversation. I was astonished because, with me, it seemed he couldn't really speak much English. But they were actually communicating. She had bush tobacco in her garden, which is called Pituri, and the Aboriginals chew it, and he noticed it and so she and he talked about that. It was miraculous. The Queen maintained her very correct English and Clifford somehow picked up what she was saying, and responded. It was an encounter between two impressive people from very different worlds, conversing across this great divide.

'Afterwards Clifford said to me it was his "Number One Day".'

34

Many – perhaps most – of those who met her came away fretting that they had said too much, or too little, or had been too pushy, outspoken, unforthcoming or loopy. Coming face to face with the most recognisable person in the world drove many into a frenzy of grandiose circumlocution.

In 1969, the Queen asked the newly appointed American ambassador Walter Annenberg where he and his wife were living. He replied: 'We're in the Embassy residence, subject, of course, to some of the discomfiture as a result of a need for, uh, elements of refurbishing and rehabilitation.' Unfortunately, their conversation was being filmed by the BBC, and, nowadays, it is this absurdly prolix sentence, of all those he uttered over the course of his life, for which Annenberg is most commonly remembered.

Some preferred to stay silent. Sitting next to the young Princess Elizabeth at a poetry recital, shortly before her seventeenth birthday, T. S. Eliot chose to say nothing, even though he thought they might have something in common. 'There was no conversation; she didn't say anything, and I thought that perhaps she was getting too old to be addressed first. I wanted to say that I was as bored as she was: but that might not have been quite the right thing.'

But often the presence of Her Majesty could spur even her most self-assured subjects into spouting nonsense. At a Palace reception for British Book Week, the actress Miriam Margolyes was approached by the Queen, 'her handbag clamped like a grenade to her elbow'.

'And what do *you* do?' asked the Queen.

Margolyes felt the gibberish gush forth. 'Instead of saying like any normal person, "Your Majesty, I am an actress who records audio books," I took a deep breath, and declared, "Your Majesty, I am the best reader of stories in the whole world!"

According to Margolyes, the Queen looked back at her, rolled her eyes, sighed, and turned to Margolyes's neighbour. 'And what do *you* do?'

As she was explaining that that she was an academic who was trying to help dyslexic children to read, with a new method involving printing words in different colours, Margolyes chipped in: 'How fascinating! My goodness, I didn't know that!'

At which point, the Queen turned to Margolyes and said sharply, 'Be quiet!', with, in Margolyes's recollection, 'a crisp emphasis on the final "t"'.

'I'm so sorry, Your Majesty, I got carried away with excitement,' replied Margolyes. The Queen then told the semi-circle about a visit she had made to a girls' school in North London that morning, and how important good teachers were.

'But you see, Your Majesty, we are so lucky to be born English and to have English as our first language!' continued Margolyes, before embarking on a long peroration about the joys of reading Keats and Austen in their own language, ending, 'Imagine, for example, Your Majesty, if we had been born *Albanian*!'

A startled look came over the Queen. 'Alarm crossed her face, and she moved away, anxious to put some distance between herself and this clearly crazed woman. Clutching the handbag even more closely, and murmuring, "Yes, yes," vaguely to herself, she disappeared into the throng.'

Did it ever cross the Queen's mind that most of her subjects were deranged? In 1956, Lady Annabel Birley and her husband Mark were at a large reception. As they entered, her old friend Patrick Plunkett, the then Deputy Master of the Queen's Household, grabbed her arm. 'There you are! Come and meet the Queen!'

Lost for something to say, Lady Annabel thought of dogs. 'Ma'am, we have a very small dachsund called Noodle who we love and who is very spoilt and sleeps every night in our bed,' she said. The Queen then turned to her husband Mark who went blank, and repeated, 'Ma'am, we have a very small dachsund called Noodle who is very spoilt and sleeps every night in our bed ...' The Queen, recalled Lady Annabel, 'simply nodded and smiled'.

In December 1968, the 73-year-old Robert Graves, best known as the author of *I, Claudius* and *Goodbye to All That*, travelled from his home in Majorca to receive the Queen's Gold Medal for Poetry. It was, she told him, the first time she had presented the gold medal personally.

'And you've done it beautifully, my dear,' he replied. 'You must do it more often.' He then went on to say that he would refuse anything offered by the prime minister. 'She laughed most sympathetically,' he recalled. Spurred on by her laughter, he informed her that that they were both descended, via King Edward IV, from the Prophet Muhammad, adding that he thought she might care to mention this in her next Christmas broadcast, for the benefit of her Muslim subjects.

In 1965, the four Beatles went to the Palace to receive their MBEs. As teenagers, they had entertained lustful thoughts about the young Princess Elizabeth. 'They were very formative teenage years, and the queen was, sort of, 24, or something, so, to us, she was a babe,' recalled Paul, half a century later. 'We were like, "Phwoar!" There was a certain lustfulness in us teenagers. That's what we used to say in Liverpool: "just look at the heat on her!" So we grew up loving the Queen.'

Perhaps their teenage infatuations clouded their brains, or might it have been the marijuana that John Lennon later claimed they had smoked in the Palace loo before the ceremony? Either way, their conversation with the Queen proved awkward.

'Have you been working hard recently?' the Queen asked.

John's mind went blank. He couldn't think what on earth they had been doing. 'No, we've been having a holiday,' he replied. In fact, they had been recording.

She turned to Paul: 'Have you been together long?'

'Yes, we've been together now for forty years ...' he began, echoing the old music hall song, 'My Old Dutch'.

'... And it don't seem a day too much!' Ringo and Paul chorused together.

The Queen looked nonplussed, evidently not catching the allusion. She asked Ringo. 'You started the group, did you?'

'No,' replied Ringo. 'They did. I joined last.'

'It's a pleasure giving it to you,' she said. And, with that, their audience came to an end.

Afterwards, the four of them posed with their MBEs at a press conference in Brian Epstein's Saville Theatre. 'She was just like a mum to us,' said John. 'She was so warm and sweet. She really put us at our ease.'

Forty year later, at a Palace reception for the British music industry, the Queen had just finished exchanging a few words with the radio presenter Terry Wogan and the rock star Phil Collins. Possibly out of a sense of relief that his ordeal was over, Collins began whistling the theme tune from *Close Encounters of the Third Kind*. The Queen heard it, and turned and smiled. 'What was that?' she asked.

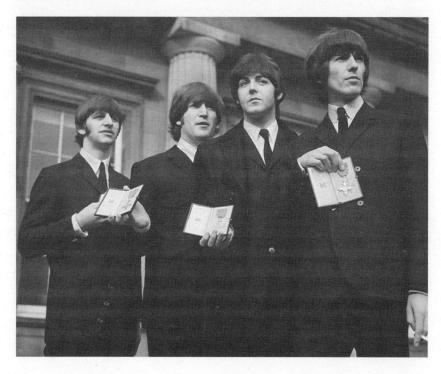

Collins was struck dumb, so Wogan attempted to help him out. 'He was calling ET, ma'am,' he replied ('even as I said it wishing I'd kept my mouth shut').

'Ah,' said the Queen, and moved on.

Collins turned to Wogan. 'Why did I do that?' he said. 'What came over me?'

'The Royal Effect,' said Wogan. 'You say the first thing that comes into your head, and you carry the memory of your foolishness with you to the grave.'

35

The Royal Effect was unavoidable, all-pervasive and timeless. In his work *The Principles of Sociology*, the Victorian philosopher Herbert Spencer* compared the submissive stance adopted by those who greeted royalty with the 'fearful cringing' of primitive people in the presence of superior and possibly hostile powers.

The phenomenon extended well into the twenty-first century and was particularly evident in the theatre. The presence of royalty, designed to add spark to any show, would instead act as a dampener and a distraction.

Cecil Beaton noticed it in 1952 when the young Queen arrived with her mother and Princess Margaret to watch the play *Aren't We All?* by Frederick Lonsdale, for which he had designed the costumes. Throughout the performance, the eyes of half the audience were glued to the Royal Box. The play itself 'received scant attention'.

On 2 May 1968, the Queen visited the Oxford Union to watch a student debate. 'Her Majesty came in to wild applause and happy cheering, Harold Macmillan twinkling at her side,' recorded the perky New College undergraduate Gyles Brandreth in his diary. 'But when the cheering stopped, a sudden chill filled the atmosphere. There was a silence, and a palpable awkwardness, in the hall. There were eight hundred of us there, I suppose, and because of the Queen none of us could be "normal".'

---

* Herbert Spencer (1820–1903) coined the expression 'survival of the fittest'. He was described by Bertrand Russell as 'the single most famous European intellectual in the closing decades of the nineteenth century'.

Deference caused the usual boisterous energy of Oxford Union debates to drain away. 'The debate itself was dismal – dull as ditchwater: so restrained, everyone on best behaviour. It was actually rather a dreadful evening. Once the excitement of seeing the Queen at close quarters had worn off, tedium set in.' As Alan Bennett has the Queen say in his play *A Question of Attribution*: 'The trouble is, whenever I meet someone they're always on their best behaviour. And when one's on one's best behaviour, one isn't always at one's best.'

The Queen attended the long-awaited* opening night of the National Theatre in 1976, causing the theatre's founding director, Peter Hall, to reflect that, despite the Queen's best efforts, or perhaps because of them, 'The presence of royalty nearly always ossifies the public in a theatre.'

On the other side of the footlights, the performers often felt the steam going out of their performances when royalty was present. The following year, as part of her Silver Jubilee celebrations, the Queen attended the filming of an episode of the BBC sitcom *The Good Life*, with the audience and entire floor crew dressed in black tie in her honour. 'It was a very strange atmosphere,' recalled one of the show's stars, Penelope Keith. 'It was nerve-racking. People usually come to have a good time and laugh. But people didn't laugh very much. They were really rather nervous. Most people were waiting to see if the Queen was going to laugh first.'

'To me, a show with royalty present to inhibit the crowd is the opposite of sex,' observed the comedian Bob Monkhouse, veteran of many Royal Variety Performances, '– even when it's good, it's lousy.'

Noël Coward felt the same. In November 1954, he appeared at the London Palladium for a Royal Command Performance in front of Prince Philip, Princess Margaret and the Queen, who was 'looking luminously lovely and ... wearing the largest sapphires I have ever seen'. It was 'a glittering occasion, crammed with stars, all shaking like aspens ... The moment I arrived in the dressing room and found Bob

---

* And how! The idea for a National Theatre had first been mooted 128 years earlier, in 1848.

Hope tight-lipped, Jack Buchanan quivering and Norman Wisdom sweating, I realised that the audience was vile, as it is usually on such regal nights. In the entr'acte Cole and Charles* came round from the front and said it was the worst they had ever encountered and that I was to be prepared for a fate worse than death.' As it turned out, Coward's snappy renditions of his old favourites 'got the whole house cheering'. But, in his view, Bob Hope, who followed him, succumbed to the Royal malaise and 'lost them entirely'.

The chirpy Tommy Steele appeared in the 1957 Royal Variety Show,† the first pop star ever to be so honoured. Backed by the Steelmen, he kicked off with 'Rock with the Caveman', his top-20 hit from the year before. The closing bars were greeted with complete silence from the audience. Next, he performed Elvis Presley's 'Hound Dog', accompanied by Presley-style hip-swivels. More silence. 'Are you ready for the 'and clap?' he asked, in his Cockney accent. No reply. Carrying on regardless, he launched into his number-1 hit, 'Singing the Blues'. At this point, the Queen began to clap her hands politely, to be joined, a few beats later, by the Queen Mother. According to the *Record Mirror*, Prince Philip then 'swayed his body rhythmically'. Following this Royal lead, the previously starchy Palladium audience 'broke out into a crescendo of hand-clapping and cheering which really rocked the house to the rafters'.

Four years later, the Queen attended the cutting-edge satirical revue *Beyond the Fringe* at the Fortune with the future prime minister Sir Alec Douglas-Home. Alan Bennett, one of its four young stars, performed a comic monologue in parodic defence of corporal and capital punishment in which his character vehemently rebutted any suggestion that the thought of either gave him any pleasure. 'On the contrary, they produce no erec— ... no reaction whatsoever.'

---

* Cole Lesley was Coward's secretary and companion, and Charles Russell was at that time his business manager.

† Top of the bill was Mario Lanza. Other performers included Judy Garland, Vera Lynn, the Crazy Gang, Alma Cogan, Tommy Cooper, Winifred Atwell, Gracie Fields, Count Basie and his Orchestra, Norrie Paramor's Big Ben Banjo Band and Arthur Askey.

Usually the line drew roars or laughter, but on that night not a sound came from the audience, which remained similarly mute for the rest of the evening. 'The Queen in the audience killed it stone dead. However well you performed, it would go by in total silence,' recalled Bennett. Peter Cook, the wildest of his co-stars, made things worse by advising Bennett, just before the curtain rose, 'Whatever you do, don't say "fuck".'* Six decades on, Bennett remembers it as 'agony'.

The seasoned comedian Eric Sykes accepted an invitation to perform at Windsor Castle in 1954. He arrived in high spirits. 'In my mind my act was a riot. As a golfer imagines the shape of flight his golf ball will take before he makes a shot, so it was with me and my comedy routine, only in my case I visualised a hole in one.'

The Queen and Royal Family took the front seats, the Castle staff standing in ordered lines behind them. When his moment came, Sykes walked on to the opening bars of 'In a Monastery Garden' performed by Billy Cotton and his Band, and began an old routine in which he imitated bird noises. 'Here was the comedy that I'd imagined would bring the place down ... I was now on my fifth or sixth impression of a bird noise. I'd done a thrush, a blackbird and a robin.' But they were all met by silence. He then imitated a bicycle that hadn't been oiled. 'This didn't get a titter, but I knew that I would get them with my next impression. It was my favourite, the crow. Slapping the back of my neck, I cawed loudly as a crow will inevitably do when you are standing over a putt; and I hopped across the stage, flapping up my coat tails to simulate flight.'

The audience still made no response. At this point, he began to panic. 'Cold sweat was trickling from my armpits. I was up to my waist and sinking rapidly in a swamp of indifference. I was dying a death – oh yes, there were stifled sniggers and hiccups, but these were from behind me. The audience, being the staff of Windsor Castle standing behind the seated royal party, were a frozen tableau, and the less reaction I got the more outrageous became my impressions.'

---

* The Royal darling Noël Coward battled with the same demon. Looking back on a weekend in 1969 with the Queen Mother he recognised 'a tiny pall of "best behaviour" overlaying the proceedings ... It isn't that I have a basic urge to say "fuck" every five minutes, but I'm conscious of a resentment that I couldn't if I wanted to.'

The only people laughing were Billy Cotton and his Band, and they were laughing at him rather than with him. 'But from the audience there was nothing but a perplexed silence.' Aping a peacock with a bad leg, he tottered off the stage.

Afterwards, a colleague passed on to him the Queen's only comment on his performance: 'He doesn't sing very well, does he?'

36

Any theatre in which the Queen was present became an arena for two competing shows on either side of the curtain. Though the show in the auditorium might be poorly lit and lack dialogue and plot, it would still attract more attention than the show on stage.

Whenever she entered a theatre, the eyes of the audience would turn from the stage and remain on her for the rest of the evening. In May 1955, the American writer Leo Lerman attended the first night of *The Firebird* at Sadler's Wells, starring Margot Fonteyn. To his delight, he found himself sitting immediately behind the Queen, the Duke of Edinburgh and Princess Margaret, 'so close that unavoidably my foot sometimes poked the duke's bottom'.

The Royal Family became his focus of attention, the onstage goings-on little more than a distraction. Gazing at the 29-year-old Queen, he judged her 'remarkably like (in face) Queen Victoria at times – sort of that same lowering, reproachful, bad-little-girl look. This in repose, but when she is animated she becomes quite pretty.'

'They are very pleasant together,' Lerman reported back. 'Some parts of *Firebird* amused [the Duke] into comments, across the queen, to the man with Princess M. The queen did some wifely shushing. She applauded everything diligently.' At the end of the performance, he spotted the Duke leaning over and giving the Queen a little kiss.

On 4 May 1968, Cecil Beaton went with Dicky Buckle* to the

---

* Richard Buckle (1916–2001), witty ballet critic and biographer of Nijinsky and Diaghilev. Of Margot Fonteyn, he once said: 'She has perfected the art of answering questions at length and saying absolutely nothing. She would never, even under torture, admit that pink was her favourite colour, for fear of offending orange and mauve.'

Danish Ballet at Sadler's Wells, ready to enjoy 'a good gawk at the Royal Family with the King and Queen of Denmark in the royal box'. Under his pitiless gawking, only Princess Anne passed muster:

> The Queen dignified, very dowdy and not really animated enough, the Queen Mother surprisingly faded, Princess Margaret with an outrageous, enormous Roman matron hair-do, much too important for such a squat little figure. Princess Anne, her hair rather pretty and well dressed and her eyes quite heavily painted. Luckily I did not see the common little Lord Snowdon, who was wearing his hair in a dyed quiff ...

The waspish director of the Victoria and Albert Museum, Roy Strong, was another theatregoer who never let a performance distract him from the Queen, furtively inspecting her for shortcomings. At the opening of the National Theatre in 1976, he chronicled his Sovereign's arrival with a disapproving eye. 'At last the Queen actually turned up in floating apricot chiffon, quite hideous and with her hair another colour.' Also in the audience was Kenneth Tynan, whose eyes kept veering from the eighteenth-century Venetian comedy onstage to the more compelling drama in the seats. 'Larry [Olivier], who was sitting beside the Queen, dropped off to sleep. HRH instantly noticed and directed a beady glare in his direction, fearful lest he should topple forwards into the acting area. The glare lasted for five minutes until Larry, galvanised by some particularly noisy piece of business, returned to wakefulness.'

For Strong, no performance was ever so powerful that it could not be upstaged by Her Majesty. At Glyndebourne in 1984, his wife Julia told him that 'at certain angles' the 58-year-old Queen 'was now an old lady and looked older than her mother now at eighty-four. It is unfortunate that she still dyes her hair rather badly.'

Six years later, at an arts weekend at Royal Lodge, he once again compared and contrasted mother and daughter, observing that the Queen:

wore little jewellery and the inevitable red dress. She forms an enormous contrast with her mother still flirting and playing the Marshalin, loving to dress up and wear her jewels, almost swaying in her dresses, with a curved movement of her body and arrangement of her arms, whereas, in sharp contrast, the Queen's movements are angular and sensible.

Nothing could stop the heads of an audience turning in her direction, and, in some arenas, she distracted the players, too. When Winston Churchill spoke in the House of Commons on 23 January 1948, a time of international crisis, eyes swivelled up from the chamber to the young Princess Elizabeth in the gallery above. Chips Channon studied her for an hour. In his diary entry for that day, he appeared to be unaware of his own hypocrisy in criticising the Princess for paying insufficient attention to the main event:

> The great debate (it means, of course, eventual war or at least 'showdown' with Russia) continues. Winston was up and was impressive and grave. Princess Elizabeth, badly dressed with a hideous hat and a long feather, was in the Speaker's Gallery ... I watched her closely for an hour as I listened to Churchill and to Crossman who was fiery. I thought her dowdy and her attention wandered – was she looking for Philip? – to other galleries even whilst Winston was warning the world!

Churches, too, might have been designed for Royal observation. After an initial show of reluctance to attend church at Badminton in April 1976, James Lees-Milne found himself in the perfect place for a good snoop, alongside his wife, Alvilde:

> What shocks me is that whenever they are here the church is filled to the brim for Sunday morning service ... I did not want to attend today, to be among the gapers. However, A. insisted ... We sat in the middle of the nave close to the Royal Family, so I did have a good stare. All the young princes and princesses, and Mark Phillips, sat in one front pew, and a very pretty lot of children they were. Princess Margaret however looked miserable, trussed up like a brooding hen, pigeon-breasted and discontented. I like the Royal Family to exist, but I don't want to know or be known by them. The Prince of Wales sporting a beastly beard, I hope temporary.

On Christmas Eve that same year, he watched them again in St George's Chapel Windsor:

Had a splendid view of the entire Royal Family, headed by the Queen, passing by the opening on their way down the north aisle to the choir opening. Queen Mother's hat like an apricot cockerel, enormous and unbecoming.

Attending the Christmas Day service in the same place in 1981, he took the opportunity to cast an unfestive eye over the Royal Family:

Queen wearing hideous turquoise blue dress, Prince of Wales with scar on left cheek, Duke of Edinburgh shorter than I had supposed, and lined. Princess Pushy of Kent, as they call her, in hideous hat. Prince Michael's beard a mistake.

Sir Roy Strong was at Westminster Abbey for the inauguration of the General Synod in 2000 when:

the Queen arrived in a hideous bright emerald green coat and a hat shaped like a ziggurat … She is now a cross between Queen Mary, with the same grim countenance when in repose, and Queen Victoria in terms of height. If you catch her eyes they're sharp but with a twinkle, so that's still there.

And again, at the 2001 Commonwealth Day Observance in Westminster Abbey:

Her hair was softer, protruding underneath, but in profile and repose she looked rather disapproving of everything and everyone.

At the Queen Mother's funeral on 9 April 2002:

The Duchess [of Kent] looking deranged, very pale and moving as though under sedation, Princess Michael had her hair all over the place, the Prince bluff and browbeaten … Beatrice and Eugenie like kewpie dolls … The Queen looked composed while the Duke indulged in his usual set of attitudes.

Ten days later, the memorial service for Princess Margaret at Westminster provided him with another bonanza:

> The Royal Family seemed enchanted with all of it, the Queen beaming … Harry, a tall, gangling youth with short, reddish hair who exuded trouble in the making. The Prince [Charles] looked awful, each death seeming to bring his eyes closer together – so close that I began to wonder whether sooner or later he wouldn't become a Cyclops … Afterwards we glimpsed the tough jawline of Camilla Parker Bowles beneath the obligatory bucket-shaped black hat.

But, in time, his thoughts turned to the deceased Princess:

> She was such a capricious, arrogant and thoughtless woman … The common touch she had not.

At the Maundy service in Westminster Abbey on 21 April 2011:

> The Queen was in a horrendous brilliant turquoise outfit with a diamond brooch on her hat and another one on her coat, top left.

Four years later, on 9 March 2015, the Queen was back in the Abbey for another Commonwealth Day Observance. Strong noted how she:

> continues to shrink and is now a smiling, diminutive old lady.

Even in prayer, the Queen found no hiding place. At a service at Holy Trinity, Sloane Street on 20 October 1998, she was kneeling within sight of Gyles Brandreth, who duly noted in his diary: 'I watch the Queen as she prays: she concentrates, her eyes shut tight.'

37

On 2 March 1970, Dirk Bogarde stands in the receiving line at the Warner Cinema in London's West End, anticipating the arrival of the Queen. The occasion is the world premiere of the new Visconti film *Death in Venice*, in which Bogarde plays the doomed composer Gustav von Aschenbach. It is in aid of the charity Venice in Peril.

Next to Bogarde stands the film's director Luchino Visconti and the 15-year-old actor Björn Andrésen, described by Bogarde as 'the perfect Tadzio … an almost mystical beauty'. At the head of the line are the film's porky financiers, dismissed by Bogarde as 'the American Money and their frilly wives'.

The Queen arrives accompanied by Princess Anne, who is dressed, notes the fastidious Bogarde, 'in orange furnishing-fabric and ear-phones'. The Queen says a few words to the Americans, but virtually nothing to the Italian production team, preferring to nod and smile. When she comes to Visconti she looks 'rather fixedly for some moments as if he were a cenotaph: wordless'. Of Bogarde himself, she asks how long the film took to make, one of her tried-and-trusted questions at events such as this. She then moves on with her daughter 'and a small posy' to the auditorium. Visconti watches her depart with a disappointed smile, shrugs and whispers, 'Maladroit', to Bogarde.

Bogarde has attended Royal premieres before; he finds them awkward, for all the usual reasons. 'It is tremendously sad that a Royal Occasion of this kind is inevitably plunged into a doomed kind of silence. No one laughs, dares to speak, cough even. No one can possibly enjoy it, most particularly the Queen herself who, as I know, is much more fun than the glumness of these occasions would lead one to suppose.'

John Julius Norwich,[*] the well-connected chairman of Venice in Peril, sits next to the Queen. The film is slow and melancholy. After only a few minutes, he hears her sigh. And then she sighs again. 'It was a long sigh. I was in agony as the sighs continued throughout the film and I wondered what to say when the lights came up.'

After two hours and ten minutes, the film comes to an end with a lengthy sequence involving the plague-ridden Aschenbach dying in a deck chair, his hair dye running down his face, while Tadzio, in the distance, walks into the sea as the sun goes down, and all to the mournful accompaniment of the Adagettio from Mahler's 5th Symphony.

The End.

The lights come up. The audience is silent, 'not daring to laugh, applaud, or even speak above a church whisper', as Bogarde remembers it. Turning to John Julius Norwich, the Queen flashes a bright smile, and says: 'Well, that was a bit gloomy, wasn't it?'

---

* Aka Viscount Norwich (1929–2018), son of Duff and Lady Diana Cooper, prolific author and occasional TV presenter.

Norwich thinks that she is, in her way, trying to set him at ease. 'She could sense my discomfort.'

Everyone rises as the Royal party walk back down the centre aisle in complete silence.

Immediately afterwards, at a crowded reception at Burlington House, Dirk Bogarde is approached by one of the American financiers, 'busy biting the side of his thumb with ill-suppressed anxiety'. The financier turns to his colleagues.

'You know,' he says, 'what I can't understand is how the Queen of England could bring her daughter to see a movie about an old man chasing a kid's ass.'

38

The two were contemporaries: the Queen born on 26 April 1926, and Norma Jeane Mortenson just over a month later, on 1 June 1926.

But there the similarities conclude: Elizabeth's birth was greeted with worldwide celebrations; Norma Jeane was born at the Los Angeles General Hospital, the outcome of a fling: her father, she was later to discover, was not Mortenson but a work colleague of her mother called Gifford. Her mother couldn't cope: Norma Jeane was looked after by foster parents. 'I thought the people I lived with were my parents. I called them mama and dad,' begins a fragment of autobiography. 'The woman said to me one day, "Don't call me mama. You're old enough to know better. I'm not related to you in any way. You just board here. Your mama's coming to see you tomorrow. You can call *her* mama if you want to."'

Her mother, Gladys, took Norma Jeane back in the summer of 1933, when she was seven. 'She seldom spoke to me except to say, "Don't make so much noise, Norma." She would say this even when I was lying in bed at night and turning the pages of a book. Even the sound of a page turning made her nervous.' The following year, Gladys suffered a mental breakdown. 'My mother … was screaming and laughing. They took her away to the Norwalk Mental Hospital. I knew the name of the hospital in a vague way. It was where my mother's father and grandmother had been taken when they started screaming and laughing.' Diagnosed with paranoid schizophrenia, Gladys spent the rest of her life in and out of mental institutions. In 1935 Norma Jeane was transferred to the Los Angeles Orphans Home.

'I didn't like the world around me because it was kind of grim ... Some of my foster families used to send me to the movies to get me out of the house and there I'd sit all day and way into the night. Up in front, there with the screen so big, a little kid all alone, and I loved it.'

In the summer of 1956, blessed with a glamorous new name, and as famous as can be, Marilyn Monroe arrived in England to shoot *The Prince and the Showgirl* with Laurence Olivier. She brought with her twenty-seven items of luggage and her bespectacled dramatist husband Arthur Miller. For the four months of production, the couple were to rent Parkside House in Englefield Green, which came with twelve bedrooms, half-a-dozen staff and gardens backing on to Windsor Great Park. Marilyn was entranced. 'Compared to California, England seems tiny and quaint with its little toy trains chugging through the miniature countryside ...' she wrote to a friend. 'I am dying to walk bareheaded in the rain. I want to eat real roast beef and Yorkshire pudding ... I want to buy a tweed suit ... I want to ride a bicycle, and I'd like someone to explain the jokes in *Punch* – they don't seem funny to me.'

Marilyn Monroe and her husband – inevitably called 'Mr Monroe' by the popular newspapers, and by an actor on set as 'this tall weird man' – were the closest Hollywood came to royalty. On her first day at Pinewood Studios, Marilyn arrived with a retinue of courtiers, including a hairdresser and make-up man, a secretary, a cook, two publicists, two bodyguards and her intense Stanislavskian acting coach Paula Strasberg, who was clocking up $2,500 a week, plus expenses.*

On 29 October 1956, the couple arrived at the Royal Command Performance at the Empire Cinema, Leicester Square for the premiere

---

* Arthur Miller came to resent Paula Strasberg's domineering ways: 'Marilyn, a natural comedienne, seemed distracted by half-digested, spitballed imagery and pseudo-Stanislavskian parallelisms that left her unable to free her own native joyousness.'

Marilyn Monroe would require multiple takes before getting her lines right, leaving her fellow actors wooden and exhausted. The director of *Some Like It Hot*, Billy Wilder, remembered: 'We spent quite a few takes getting, "It's me, Sugar!" I had signs painted on the door: "IT'S ME. SUGAR." "Action" would come and she would say, "It's Sugar, me!" or even, "Sugar, it's me." I took her to one side after Take 50, and I said, "Don't worry about it." And she said, "Worry about what?"'

of *The Battle of the River Plate*. Taking a day off filming, Marilyn was, in the words of her young assistant Colin Clark, 'in a complete spin' at the prospect of meeting the Queen. Clark noted that she spent much of the day 'curtsying all over the house, and even trying to talk in an English accent, goodness knows why. I suppose that meeting the Queen is a wonderful sign of success for every actor and actress ... More than anything MM wants to feel accepted, and to her the invitation to a great Premiere like this, and shaking hands with Royalty, means that she has been accepted as one of the great actresses of her time. She is no longer just a sex symbol or a calendar girl.'

Unusually for Marilyn, she arrived in good time, well ahead of Her Majesty. In Arthur Miller's recollection, she came 'sewn into a spectacular red velvet dress with a Gay Nineties look that barely allowed her to sit'. It certainly accentuated her curves, leaving much of her famous bosom touched only by the chill autumn air. By contrast, Queen Elizabeth arrived in a black evening gown, long white gloves and a diamond-and-emerald tiara.

The audience made its way into the auditorium to the sound of Nelson Elms on the organ and the orchestra of the Royal Marines School of Music. Meanwhile, an abundance of celebrities – Victor Mature, Brigitte Bardot, Norman Wisdom, Anita Ekberg, Anthony Quayle, Sylvia Syms, Peter Finch, Joan Crawford – was shepherded into line at the top of the stairs, ready to be presented to Her Majesty, with many survivors of the real Battle of the River Plate alongside them.

Marilyn was positioned halfway down the long, long row, between Victor Mature and Anthony Quayle. Like everyone else, she was clearly nervous. Victor Mature later said that he was so frightened that he had no memory of anything the Queen said to him; even the formidable Joan Crawford admitted that she had never been so scared in her life.

Archive film footage shows Marilyn tensing up and growing fidgety when the Queen is still a dozen celebrities away from her, adjusting the skimpy straps of her dress, staring straight ahead, taking deep breaths, sucking on her lips, and stealing quick glances back along the

line at the approaching figure, one of the few women in the world more famous than herself.

'The Queen had arrived in a blasting glare from the diamonds in her tiara, political theatre in the theatre,' recalled Arthur Miller, thirty years later. 'But we were all performing, she with her extended hand and we with our grateful smiles, bows, and curtsies.' In fact, Miller was never in the line, as he had not been invited to join it.

Never one to let an event glide by without grappling with its deeper meaning, Miller calculated that this Royal event was proof that 'the world as theatre is not metaphor but naturalistic description, in this case of ritualized formality regulated at every step of the way by precedent and rehearsal'.*

---

* Nearly thirty years later, having watched President Reagan shaking the hands of celebrities in the Lincoln Center, Miller concluded that Reagan's more easy-going style was 'no less a performance, a relaxed offhand American type of acting as contrasted with the Queen's. She created far more awe – but awe is her line of work, and rather a triumph considering how few operational battleships she has any more.'

Eventually, the moment for the presentation arrived. With no need to consult his discreet little crib-sheet, Mr Reginald Bromhead, president and chairman of the Cinematograph Trade Benevolent Fund, presented Marilyn. The two most chronicled women of the twentieth century shook hands; Marilyn executed a perfect curtsy, the culmination of so much rehearsal.

Film footage suggests that the meeting between the Queen and the Showgirl was too brief for more than a word or two. As Marilyn curtsies, the Queen seems to cast her eyes quickly up and down her famous body, and then they both smile; but these line-ups are speedy affairs, efficient to the point of iciness: within a few seconds the Queen has moved on to the next in line, Anthony Quayle.

Princess Margaret, bringing up the rear, infinitely more attracted to the world of showbusiness than her elder sister, took the greater interest, her lack of height ensuring her head was in alignment with Marilyn's remarkable embonpoint. She asked how her film was going. 'It's going very well,' replied Marilyn, adding, in the Sunday Best language that so often affects those confronted by royalty, 'And it will be with regret that we have to leave in about a fortnight's time.'

By the time Princess Margaret moved on to Anthony Quayle, Marilyn had grown sufficiently skittish to butt in on their conversation. Hearing them talk about her husband's new play, *A View from the Bridge*, she asked the Princess to go and see it. 'The Princess laughed and said she might,' she reported afterwards.

When the film was over, the various famous attendees had been drilled to line up onstage and each to take a bow, one by one. As Marilyn had failed to make the rehearsal, she kept asking Anthony Quayle what to do when her name was called.

As the time came to leave the theatre, she became more relaxed, posing gaily for photographs and talking to reporters. 'Did you find it hard to curtsy?' asked one reporter. 'Not a bit,' she replied, offering him a dainty demonstration.

'The Queen is very warm-hearted,' she added. 'She radiates sweetness. She asked how I liked living in Windsor, and I said, "What?" and she said that as I lived in Englefield Green, near to Windsor, we were neighbours. So I told her that Arthur and I went on bicycle rides in the park.'

The following day, despite rave reviews for her appearance – one headline read 'Marilyn Monroe Captures Britain' – she arrived at the studio very late, and very tired. She appeared distant and remote, having swallowed too many pills.

Four years after their brief encounter, the Queen told a friend that she thought Miss Monroe 'very sweet. But I felt sorry for her, because she was so nervous that she had licked all her lipstick off.'

39

In her *Book of Etiquette* (1972), Dame Barbara Cartland writes: 'When I attend a film premiere I am horrified to see how badly and how clumsily the film stars and the majority of those presented greet Her Majesty.' For those faced with this prospect, she offers this advice:

> A man stands almost to attention and bows his head from the neck only. To bow from the waist is incorrect.
> A woman curtsies as low as possible with her back straight, looking the Queen in the face.

Throughout her life, the Queen adhered to correct form. This included the troublesome business of curtsying, which others in her circle considered roughly a couple of centuries out of date. Staying at Sandringham in February 1949, Lady Gladwyn noted that, after dinner, 'the ladies left the room, I curtseying to the King before we went out. All this ceremony, this curtseying and standing about was, I suppose, the usual polite behaviour in good society in the eighteenth century. We live unceremoniously these days, and manners have so deteriorated, that it was a constant effort to remember it all. I do honestly feel that curtseying is a gesture that has now become obsolete, and its absence would in no way detract from the dignity of the Crown.'

Among the women of the Royal Family, who curtsied to whom was a matter of some complexity. (The males had it easier, bowing to each other simultaneously, with no need to gauge who should go first.) The Queen always took the order of precedence very seriously. In January

1947, the Duke of Devonshire told James Lees-Milne that the 20-year-old Princess Elizabeth made it 'very plain' to her mother that whereas her mother was a commoner 'she, Princess Elizabeth, is of royal blood'. After her Coronation, she expected everyone, including her sister, her mother and her children, to greet her with a bow or a curtsy. Some took it further. A friend of Princess Anne noticed that she would automatically stand up when taking a telephone call from her mother.

Every now and then, something changed, and the rules had to be rejigged. In 2005, Camilla Parker Bowles finally married Prince Charles. Normally, the various Princesses would have been expected to curtsy to the wife of the Prince of Wales but, bearing in mind the rickety circumstances of the marriage, the Queen decided to alter the rules. Accordingly, she charged her private secretary with drawing up a document called 'Precedence of the Royal Family to be Observed at Court'.

It was a complex work of tact and ingenuity. Those Princesses who had been born Royal – that is, Anne, Alexandra, Beatrice, Eugenie – would remain ahead of Camilla, with no need to curtsy to her, while Prince Edward's wife, Sophie, was still obliged to curtsy to her, and to all the others too. The division ran deep in the family between those born Royal and those who merely married Royal. 'I detested Queen Mary,' Princess Margaret said of her own grandmother. 'Of course, she had an inferiority complex. We were Royal and she was not.' Queen Mary had been born a Serene Highness, not a Royal Highness. The difference, invisible to most, was very important to Princess Margaret, who treasured the definite article in 'Her Royal Highness *the* Princess Margaret'. Her grandmother lacked the 'the', so necessarily felt inferior.

In 2012, Prince William married Kate Middleton, and once more the internal logic of the Royal curtsy had to be rejigged. From now on, Kate would be expected to curtsy to Anne and Camilla; in turn Kate would be curtsied to by Beatrice and Eugenie; and all of them would, of course, curtsy to the Queen. If Prince William was absent, Kate would have to curtsy to all the blood Princesses, but if he was with her

she would have to curtsy only to Princess Anne and Princess Alexandra.*

When Meghan Markle married Prince Harry in 2018, she was expected to follow the same set of rules, which meant she would have to curtsy to her new sister-in-law, Kate. Coming from America, she

---

* I found writing this section one of the toughest of all, the writerly equivalent of an SAS assault course for namby-pambies, combining logic, geometry, etiquette and origami, all rolled into one. If any woman who is marrying into the Royal Family at some future date should study it, follow its instructions and fall flat on her face, I can only apologise. Incidentally, ever since Camilla became Queen, every woman in the world must expect to curtsy to her, excluding other Queens and heads of state, but including all Princesses.

had found curtsying a hurdle, ever since her first meeting with the Queen in 2016.

'My grandmother was the first senior member of the family that Meghan met,' Prince Harry explained to the Netflix cameras in 2022. 'She had no idea what it all consisted of, so it was a bit of a shock to the system for her. How do you explain that to people? How do you explain that you bow to your grandmother? And that you will need to curtsy? Especially to an American. That's weird.'

On their way to the Royal Lodge, Prince Harry mentioned to his new girlfriend that she would need to curtsy to his grandmother.

'I didn't know I was going to meet her until moments before,' Meghan recalled. 'He said, "You know how to curtsy, right?" And I just thought it was a joke.

'Now I'm starting to realise, "This is a big deal!" I mean, Americans will understand this … We have medieval times, dinner and tournament. It was like that. It was intense.' From her seated position in front of the Netflix cameras, she dropped a parodic curtsy, with her arms flung absurdly wide: a camp rendition of a gesture that was already pretty camp. As his wife executed her comedic curtsy, Harry looked straight ahead, possibly wishing he was somewhere else.

In his memoir *Spare*, Harry elaborated on this first curtsy, adding details absent from his wife's original account. Apparently, he had asked Meghan if she knew how to curtsy. 'She said she thought so. But she also couldn't tell if I was serious.' As he parked their car in the drive,

Fergie came outside, somewhat aflutter, and said: *Do you know how to curtsy?*

Meg shook her head.

Fergie demonstrated once. Meg imitated her.

There wasn't time for a more advanced tutorial. We couldn't keep Granny waiting.

When Harry and Meghan entered the Queen's sitting room, Princess Eugenie and her boyfriend, later husband, Jack Brooksbank, a 'Tequila Brand Ambassador', were present, and so too was Prince Andrew. Face to face with the Queen, according to Harry, Meghan 'dropped a deep, flawless curtsy'. After a little bit of chat ('we asked about the church service. *Lovely*') the Queen bade them goodbye, and Meghan 'dipped into a curtsy again'.

Over drinks afterwards, 'Everyone complimented Meg on her curtsy. *So good! So deep!*'

40

The Queen had an instinct for ritual; without it, the monarchy would lose its mystery, its magic, its power.

One might imagine an on-the-button public relations adviser, alert to the way the egalitarian wind was blowing, advising her to dispense with the moribund Royal Maundy ritual. Following Christ's instruction (*mandatum*, or maundy) at the Last Supper, every Easter the sovereign goes among beggars to wash their feet and distribute alms. This ceremony was first recorded in the reign of King John (1199–1216). By the seventeenth century, the Stuarts had let it lapse. Their successors then revived it, but in a half-hearted hands-off way, outsourcing it to bishops, who chose to skip the foot-washing and simply dole out a few coins.

King George V made more of an effort, attending in person every once in a while. One year, Princess Elizabeth accompanied her grandfather to the ritual, and she was deeply affected by it. Off her own bat, she decided to become the first monarch in centuries to perform the Royal Maundy ritual in person, every year.

In many ways, it was the stuff of pantomime, the Queen holding the traditional nosegay (to ward off odours), Children of the Maundy processing behind her, Yeomen of the Guard carrying purses of Maundy money on gold dishes held high above their heads, and local pensioners, two for each year of their Sovereign's life, lining up to receive commemorative silver coins, the entire ceremony being overseen by the Lord High Almoner, a bishop specially appointed for the task.

When does ritual become camp, and camp become ritual? Were the president of the United States of America to turn up each year in, say,

Montgomery, Alabama, and deliver tiny purses of coins from gold dishes to a row of the old and needy, this would probably be greeted with outrage or derision. But, in the hands of the Queen, her natural sincerity somehow stopped ritual descending into absurdity. On some level, she meant it. However contrived the ceremonial, she performed it in earnest.

In 1992, one of the elderly Maundy recipients at Chester Cathedral was Mercia Tapsell, a veteran of the Salvation Army. For her, it represented something real and profound. 'It surpassed anything that I ever thought. I didn't ever think that I should be in the cathedral with the Queen and all the dignitaries that were there. And the singing, the organ, the Queen, just everything and everybody – it's really been out of this world. Just to hear "Zadok the Priest", I think, has lifted me to Cloud Nine, because it's something that I love. And to hear that and to have the Queen pass so close to me. And yes, she smiled. She smiled at me.'

41

When monarchy smiles, the world smiles back. Or at least, that is the idea. 'You prefer to be natural?' asks Sir Robert Chiltern in Oscar Wilde's *An Ideal Husband*. 'Sometimes,' replies Mrs Cheveley. 'But it is such a very difficult pose to keep up.'

Throughout her life, the Queen worked hard to keep her smile intact. 'My face is aching with smiling,' she said to Martin Charteris on her tour of Canada in 1951, following complaints in the press that she

was not smiling enough. By that time, a few of her close friends had taken to nicknaming her 'Grinners'. To smile and keep smiling, to make the world feel appreciated, was an important part of her job. It was an action that, like so much human endeavour, hovered somewhere between the true and the false: 'pretending to be me', as Larkin once put it.

Has anyone in history ever smiled more frequently, or for such prolonged periods of time? To sustain a smile takes effort, just as standing on one foot takes effort. 'She does find this constant smiling very exhausting, you know,' her Mistress of the Robes told Gyles Brandreth at the end of a day's tour of the West Country. 'After a day like today, her jaw really aches.'

Being driven at a snail's pace through gleeful crowds on a tour of Australia in 1954, she overheard a bystander complaining that she looked cross. The observation upset her. 'I've the kind of face that if I'm not smiling, I look cross,' she told a helper. 'But I'm not cross. If you try to smile for two hours continuously it gives you a nervous tic. But the moment I stop smiling, somebody will see me and say "Doesn't she look cross?"'*

---

* She faced this criticism throughout her life, even from those who were sometimes obliged to smile in a professional capacity and might have recognised the effort required. On 10 February 1992, the Liberal Democrat leader Paddy Ashdown went to *Don Giovanni* at the Royal Opera House. 'The national anthem, then the Queen came in looking rather grey and grumpy. Why will she never smile?'

42

As we have seen, it was almost as though her conversation were written in disappearing ink. Among monarchs, this was not unusual. In his study of the nineteenth-century monarchy, Roger Fulford notes that 'In most cases the conversations of ordinary mortals with royal persons are of imponderable insipidities. Subjects come away from a chat with their Sovereign with nothing more enduring to repeat to their friends than embroidered examples of their own brilliance or their own gaucheries.'

Frances Donaldson, the biographer of the Queen's uncle King Edward VIII, believed that it sometimes worked the other way round, too. 'When people who have previously believed themselves immune to the attractions of Royalty find themselves in its presence, they are often taken by surprise by the ecstasy of pleasure and appreciation they feel. The easiest way to rationalise this pleasure is to invest the royal personage with qualities that account for it – thus intelligent people can often be found repeating with a radiant expression the most ordinary expressions of humanity, the most moderate examples of the Royal wit.'

Some wondered if she thought the world smelled of fresh paint. Other than the countryside, she rarely came across anything in its natural state. Everything she set eyes on was cleaner, brighter, newer, grander, cheerier, smarter than it had been a few days before. Everything, and everyone, had been spruced up: hair coiffed, walls painted, carpets laid, smiles put in place. 'The automatic flushing system of a "gents" at Totnes Guildhall will be stopped when the Queen visits the town on 27 July – so that the noise does not disturb

249

the Royal party. It has also been suggested that guests should stand in a semi-circle – to hide the entrance,' read a report in the *Sunday Pictorial* in 1962.

Human behaviour altered in her presence. People would beam and simper, as though bidding to reassure her that this was the best of all possible worlds.

'Before the royal arrival, there is a heightened sense of expectation: nervous laughter from those due to be presented, repeated checking of watches, self-conscious straightening of ties, last-minute visits to the loo,' reported Gyles Brandreth, following her on a visit to a hospital in 2001. 'When the royal party appears, a sudden hush descends, the atmosphere a mixture of excitement and awkwardness, interrupted by sudden bursts of laughter. When the Queen says to a hospital orderly, "You work here full time? Really?" for no good reason we all fall about with merriment. In the presence of Her Majesty, nobody behaves naturally. And the moment the royal visit is over, the relief is intense.'

Attending a Royal Garden Party in 1980, the architect Hugh Casson also noticed that no one was behaving naturally. He himself had a special ticket granting him admission to the Royal tent. 'A red ticket, a permissive wave from a gloved hand, a table on which stand twenty toppers, upturned as if waiting to be filled up from a teapot, royal footmen, helpful ushers, introductions. Royalty in close proximity always changes the air and causes behaviour to go into a different gear. Preoccupations with falling crumbs, top heavy teaspoons, the tendency of high heels to sink inexorably and anchor-like into the turf. Beyond the ropes, the guests sit on chairs or stand gazing with frank curiosity at the Queen and us downing eclairs. We behave under such scrutiny like extras in the background of a Drury Lane musical ... feigned conversation interest ... tiny forced laughs ... exaggerated courtesies ... wariness in the face of *mille-feuilles*.'

Her presence could transform a scene in the eyes of those present, blocking out any unpleasantness. After the United Kingdom officially became a member of the European Economic Community on 1 January 1973, Edward Heath, the then prime minister, launched 'Fanfare for Europe', a nationwide celebration that kicked off with a gala night at Covent Garden. In his memoirs, Heath recalled only that his heart was 'full of joy at the recognition that Her Majesty the Queen had given to our country's greatest achievement'. He apparently remembered nothing of the 300 or so anti-EEC protesters gathered outside screaming 'Sieg Heil!'; nor what one onlooker described as 'the look of horrified distaste, quickly suppressed' that crossed the Queen's face when the orchestra sallied forth with a jazzed-up version of the National Anthem.

Like the *Mona Lisa*, the Queen brought out the solipsist in everyone: however many there were in a room, each person felt her eyes catching theirs, her thoughts turning towards them. 'When I get to meet the Queen, I feel about two inches tall, irrelevant,' Sasha Swire, the wife of a junior minister for Northern Ireland, confided to her diary after being presented to the Queen in Belfast on 21 October 2010. 'She fixes her beady eyes on me briefly then swans past, not saying a word.' For Swire, her silence spoke volumes. 'She is telling me I am just a plus-one, not a player or a heroine.'

On the north-east leg of the Queen's Diamond Jubilee tour in 2012, the retired Labour MP Chris Mullin joined a hundred local dignitaries for a lunch in her honour at Durham Castle. 'She was at the next table. I owed my presence to my chairmanship of the regional lottery fund. I caught her staring at me during the national anthem and half-wondered whether someone had tipped her off that she had a walk-on part in my diaries.'

Others attributed psychic powers to her. Early in his time as editor of Rupert Murdoch's *Sunday Times*, Andrew Neil stood in line with other newspaper executives as the Queen arrived to celebrate the 200th anniversary of *The Times*. 'She shook my hand, smiled weakly and quickly moved on. That was before we had written anything to offend the royals but maybe she sensed even then that I was trouble in the making.'

Another editor, Piers Morgan, felt the same sense of rejection when he was invited to a reception at the Palace in 1998 in celebration of the Prince of Wales's fiftieth birthday. First he met, or almost met, the Duke of Edinburgh: 'a defiant disgust radiated from every craggy nostril and he said not a word before turning abruptly to his left and marching off as fast as he'd arrived'. As the Queen walked past, Morgan, never backward in coming forward, collared her and introduced himself:

> She stared at me with a slightly unnerving look.
> 'Oh, yes, how do you do?' she said. 'Are you enjoying the party?' Her eyes bored into me with a mixture of irritation and pity.
> 'Yes, your majesty, it's a marvellous occasion. And very nice of you to honour Prince Charles in such a lovely way.'
> She couldn't have looked less keen on prolonging this encounter if I'd shouted, '*Vive la République*' at her. 'Yes, it's all gone very well, hasn't it?' Silence. An embarrassingly long silence. And then she moved on, unsmiling and ice cold. She has none of the warmth of her mother or son, but is not quite as rude as her husband. As I left, I nipped into the cloakroom and nicked some loo paper. There wasn't a lot left. I reckon I wasn't the first to take a little souvenir home.

Anti-monarchists were keen to lunch with her, but keen also to brag of their resistance to her charms. The prickly Australian novelist Patrick White was invited to lunch on the Royal Yacht *Britannia* when it was docked in Sydney in 1963. 'My first impulse was to take the train somewhere,' he wrote to his cousin Peggy in England, 'but now I think I shall go, to see who else is there (I believe they only have twenty guests), and to watch how the colonial notorieties react. One might use bits of it later on.'

To other friends, he was equally dismissive, though his reluctance went hand in hand with boastfulness. 'I am lunching with the Queen on the yacht this coming Sunday,' he told his friend, the editor Clem Christesen;* '... my publisher says she is probably the first of the Windsors to invite a serious writer to lunch ... It is going to be a strained occasion in any case. I shall have to stop and take something

---

* Clem Christesen, founder and from 1940 to 1974 editor of the quarterly Australian literary magazine *Meanjin*.

at the Newcastle Hotel, but the question is what, and how much? There is a theory that Vodka doesn't leave a smell ...'

White watched from the dock as the Royal party approached, the Queen in blue and Prince Philip 'in a kind of tweedy number the colour of dry cowshit'. He then boarded the yacht 'in fear and trembling', before realising that his fellow guests were even more nervous than he was. After lunch:

> we were led up to Ma'am, who began to discuss with [Admiral] Nicholl the oiling of stabilisers. She is fed up because the stabilisers in *Britannia* are apparently of an old-fashioned variety, which have to be taken out for oiling, while the latest can be oiled in position. After they had been through all this another lady who had been led up, all

coffee lice [sic] and chiffon hat, spoke about the Barrier reef, so I thought I had better put in a word as obviously a word wasn't going to be put to me. I told Ma'am she must make a point of seeing Fraser Island one day, and about the interesting wreck which had taken place there, and of the Nolan paintings which no doubt she had seen. At which she gave a shriek, or as close to a shriek as she could come, and said: 'Ohhh, yurse! The Naked Lehdy! We saw one in Adelaide.' Poor girl, she might loosen up if one took her in hand, but as it is she struck me as being quite without charm, except of a perfectly stereotyped English county kind, and hard as nails under the Little-Thing-in-Blew appearance. I suppose it's just as well that she's tough. One wasn't led up to the Jokey Juke – he approached, and I think he made up his mind early on that he was going to keep well away from anything that might be an intellectual or an artist.*

At the start of 1982, the prickly left-wing British film director Lindsay Anderson was just finishing work on his broad-brushed state-of-the-nation film *Britannia Hospital* – a satire centring on a visit by the Queen Mother to a corrupt hospital – when, quite by chance, he was invited to lunch at the Palace. He accepted at once, but – or, rather, and – emerged bristling, his republicanism reinforced and his self-esteem proudly intact. 'It really was an extraordinary experience – extraordinary in its absolute ordinariness. All the falsely unassuming charm of the English Establishment, masking an arrogance just as stiff as the most extravagant European aristocratic *hauteur*. The

---

* As the years rolled by, White's antipathy towards the Queen grew ever more vehement. In 1982, he called her 'that abominable woman', and six years later he referred to Australia's bicentennial celebrations also as 'abominable'. 'We are hardly ever without a member of the British Royal Family,' he complained to a friend. 'Busloads of school-children waving flags try to make them look popular, but the people in general are apathetic. Betty England opened our new Parliament House, which costs billions and looks like a vast hotel for the new rich.' In his 1981 memoir, *Flaws in the Glass* (nicknamed by some 'Claws in the Arse', owing to its extreme cattiness), he further develops his antipathy, describing the Queen on that occasion as wearing 'her pale-blue-specially-for-the-Colonies dress' and Prince Philip as 'more than ever a Glücksburg bully aping the English in his tweedy hacking jacket'. White once confessed: 'I have to admit to a bitter nature.'

Queen's modest, smiling welcome making not the slightest effort to conceal the fact that she hadn't the slightest idea who one was – and didn't care … I left the Palace extremely glad to have made *Britannia Hospital*.'

Once again, the Queen had acted as a mirror. To his friend Christopher Isherwood, over in California, Anderson complained: 'the English are so touchy and so vulnerable in these days of decline that they react against it more fiercely than ever'.

Those by nature wary of the Queen convinced themselves that she regarded them with an equal suspicion. Class warriors spotted a fellow class warrior, albeit one working for the other side. In 1970, the Queen paid an official visit to Hull soon after the burly trades union official John Prescott was first elected Member of Parliament for Kingston upon Hull. When the Royal Yacht *Britannia* docked in the harbour, all three Hull MPs stood ready to be presented. A bullish republican, Prescott had at first refused to attend, but his local Labour Party insisted he should. He was adamant, though, that he would never, ever bow to royalty.

> So we lined up, with Pauline, a convinced monarchist, doing her curtsy. I was surprised at how small the Queen was, and when it came to my turn, she mumbled something. I couldn't hear what it was, so naturally I bent down. She just smiled. She knew she'd got me. As far as everyone watching was concerned, and the local photographers, it looked as if I was bowing. But I wasn't. She deliberately lowered her voice and caught me out.

As much as her most fervent supporters, her opponents sensed in her the watchfulness of Miss Marple, the psychoanalytical heft of Sigmund Freud. Behind her Royal exterior, all smiles and waves, was she secretly peering deep into the darkest recesses of the human soul? Awarding a CBE to the British film director John Schlesinger in 1970, she experienced a bit of difficulty as she tried to manoeuvre the ribbon around his broad neck. 'Now, Mr Schlesinger, we must try and get this *straight*,' she said. According to his friend Alan Bennett,

Schlesinger came away convinced that the emphasis on the word 'straight' was 'very much hers' and he chose to take it 'as both a coded acknowledgement of his situation and a seal of royal approval'. For Bennett, this showed that Schlesinger 'was so aware of his sexuality that he managed to detect a corresponding awareness in the unlikeliest of places'.

Few behaved in her presence as they would with anybody else. Even her immediate family sensed an invisible barrier, and reacted to it. Whenever she entered a room, things grew sticky. People felt so uneasy that her consequent task was to set them at ease. To this extent, she lived the life of the outcast, to be approached with fear or pity or curiosity or awe but never with indifference. Such is the birthright of the sovereign. It applied to her grandfather just as it applied to her son and would one day apply to her grandson, and to his grandson too. 'When royalty leaves the room,' observed the American socialite Norah Langhorne,* 'it's like getting a seed out of your tooth.'

Of her grandfather King George V's relationship with his own grandmother, Queen Victoria, his biographer Harold Nicolson wrote, 'Even as a child Prince George must have noticed that in her presence those whom he himself feared or venerated became awestruck or diminished. The contrast between her personal homeliness and the majesty by which she was encompassed led him insensibly to look upon the Monarchy as something distinct from ordinary life, as something more ancient and durable than any political or family institution, as something sacramental, mystic and ordained.'

In our own day, Prince Harry admitted to feeling frightened of his grandmother. 'Did she realise that, no matter how much I loved her, I was often nervous in her presence?'

The mere sight of the Queen could spur otherwise stable people to go haywire. When the photographer John Swannell was preparing to photograph her in Buckingham Palace for the Diamond Jubilee, he asked her to stand by a window overlooking the Mall. This would not be possible, she said: she had once posed by that very same window

---

* Mother of the splendid comic monologuist Joyce Grenfell.

and a motorist driving along the Mall had looked up, spotted her and crashed his car.

Those loosely within her milieu, generally at ease in upper-class society, found that her mere presence in a room would turn them into caricatures of themselves. In June 1973, James Lees-Milne was invited to a party at Windsor Castle, 'honoured to be asked, but reluctant to go'. But he went.

'As we walked through the door the Queen was standing in the doorway talking. So we flattened ourselves against the wall. Until she passed on everyone stood stock still.' Lees-Milne remarked to a fellow guest 'how obsequious most people look on talking to royalty, bowing and scraping ingratiatingly. How impossible to be natural. I am sure one must try to be.' But when the party came to an end, he found, to his disgust, that he was falling headlong into that self-same trap. 'When it came to saying goodbye to the Queen at the head of the staircase, all I could murmur was, "It has been the greatest treat, Ma'am." Really, how could I? She smiled wanly.'

People struggled to describe the effect of her presence, and the ancient associations that gave it an otherworldly quality. 'She hovers there in the halfway world of dream,' thought the novelist and poet Ben Okri.

> To watch a line of some of the most powerful people in the world waiting to be introduced to the Queen was to watch something unreal, the visible form of the magnetic power of the moon on the tides.
>
> People struggled to compose themselves before they were to be announced. Animation or sometimes panic came over their features. This could be seen with republicans as much as with royalists. The reason for this was something more than monarchy. It was one of the secret achievements of Queen Elizabeth herself. The source of that achievement is that she was a solid part of the nation's subconscious … The nation drew her into its psyche for shelter and for stability … When men and women of power adjusted their faces, as they waited to be presented to the little old lady who was their queen, who fixed

each one with a piercing and compassionate gaze, we caught a glimpse of the secret of that ancestral spell, the source of one of the longest enchantments in history.

Like a mythical beast glimpsed fleetingly in the jungle, her presence would give her fellow human beings a start, either drawing them in or, almost as often, driving them away.

43

The novelist Hilary Mantel was among authors invited to a Buckingham Palace reception for the book trade. She arrived expecting to see her fellow guests elbowing their way into the path of the Queen, only to discover the opposite. As she entered each room, they would hurry away, 'as if swept by the tide':

> They acted as if they feared excruciating embarrassment should they be caught and obliged to converse. The self-possessed became gauche and the eloquent were struck dumb. The guests studied the walls, the floor, they looked elsewhere except at Her Majesty. They studied exhibits in glass cases and the paintings on the walls, which were of course worth looking at, but they studied them with great intentness, as if their eyes had been glued.

Many of these absconders chose to huddle around a small painting by Vermeer, turning their backs to the room. Mantel joined them. 'We concentrated on it at the expense of the enigma moving among us, smiling with gallant determination.'

But, as the Queen passed by, Mantel swung round. At that moment, predator and prey seemed to swap roles.

> I stared at her. I am ashamed now to say it but I passed my eyes over her as a cannibal views his dinner, my gaze sharp enough to pick the meat off her bones. I felt that such was the force of my devouring curiosity that the party had dematerialised and the walls melted and there were only two of us in the vast room, and such was the hard

power of my stare that Her Majesty turned and looked back at me, as if she had been jabbed in the shoulder; and for a split second her face expressed not anger but hurt bewilderment.

Is this really what happened? Or was Mantel, like so many before her, reading too much into a casual exchange of glances? Was she peering down into the well and catching her own face staring back at her? Did the Queen really feel 'not anger but hurt bewilderment'? Or did she feel nothing at all, because she was simply passing through a crowd of self-conscious odd bods, as she had done so many times before?

Mantel once wrote a novel about a clairvoyant called Alison who believes she can 'see straight through the living to their ambitions and secret sorrows'. In some respects, Alison is a version of Mantel herself. 'In writing about Al, I was looking at perhaps what I might have become in default of education,' she once explained. Childhood experiences of seeing ghosts – or, at least, thinking she was seeing ghosts – had also prepared her for the imaginative life of the historical novelist.

'I am used to "seeing" things that aren't there. Or – to put it in a way more acceptable to me – I am used to seeing things that "aren't there",' she begins her memoir, *Giving Up the Ghost*. Clearly, she saw parallels between the roles of clairvoyant and novelist: both look into people's souls so as to let loose things unspoken.

As Mantel gazed with 'devouring curiosity' at the Queen sweeping by in that crowded room in Buckingham Palace, she divined a transformation.

She looked young: for a moment she had turned back from a figurehead into the young woman she was, before monarchy froze her and made her a thing, a thing which only had meaning when it was exposed, a thing that existed only to be looked at.

Once more, their roles were reversed.

And I felt sorry then. I wanted to apologise. I wanted to say: it's nothing personal, it's monarchy I'm staring at.

Instead, as the Palace servants moved around with their trays of meat on skewers, Mantel stole behind a sofa and sat on the floor, as exhausted as a clairvoyant after a gruelling session with a spirit from the world beyond. 'It was violently interesting,' she concluded of her momentary glimpse of the Queen.

The next time Mantel visited the Palace was to be created Dame Commander of the British Empire, in 2015. Before she set off for the Palace, friends kept asking her: 'Will it be the actual queen, the queen herself?' In these questions, Mantel once again caught a whiff of the supernatural. 'Did they think contact with the anointed hand would change you? Was that what the guests at the palace feared: to be changed by powerful royal magic, without knowing how?'

44

I was in a large, sparsely furnished sitting room when the Queen came in wearing a sparkling silver dress. She was neither friendly nor unfriendly but I couldn't really hear what she was saying. I introduced myself and remembered to sort of bow, but she said I'd got the hand-shake wrong and made me do it again, with a double-fist-pump action. We then sat down, me on a sofa and the Queen on a chair. The BBC sports commentator Clare Balding was suddenly in the room, also sitting down, but we weren't introduced. I looked out of the window, and there were two small castles quite nearby, so I thought we must be in Windsor Castle, though I couldn't remember how I got there.

We went through to another room for lunch. There was a table for six. Clare Balding had already sat down when the table suddenly collapsed on her. She looked as though she'd been knocked out. I lifted the table off her and put my hand on her, to reassure her. The Queen left the room and then came back, followed by workmen anxious to repair the table. The Queen didn't seem especially worried about Clare Balding.

The Queen kept coming in and out. At one point I introduced myself to Clare Balding, saying that we'd been at the same party only a few days before (this was true). She was perfectly friendly. I told her that I was worried I was wearing the wrong clothes for lunch with the Queen – just underpants and a grey woolly jersey.

Suddenly, Prince Charles was there, scrubbing at the pink carpet, applying some sort of liquid to it, trying to repair a stain caused by Clare's fall. He looked cross. I thought I'd go outside for a while, so I went through a stone hallway where there were workmen, and noticed that I now had no shoes on, only socks. When I got out into a court-yard, I stepped in gooey mud, and then re-entered the hallway, trying to stay on tiptoe, so as to keep the mud from getting everywhere. I kept hoping that this was all a dream, as it was so embarrassing getting mud everywhere and being dressed wrong, but at the same time I real-ised that if it was a dream I wouldn't have anything to write about, whereas if it was going on in real life it would be well worth including in this book.

I brushed past Prince Charles and was hoping to introduce myself to him but he obviously thought I was a workman and just gave me a cursory nod. Clare Balding reappeared. I told her I was dressed wrongly for lunch with the Queen. I was now wearing a grey baseball shirt instead of the jersey, but still just underpants with no trousers. I could tell that Clare agreed with me.

45

Royalty creates a fairy-tale landscape, where everything is just as it should be, in the best of all possible worlds. A few days before her father died, Princess Elizabeth was taken on a tour of a brand-new maternity hospital in Nairobi. The day before her arrival, the hospital had been empty, but when she arrived, it was full. The miracle had been stage-managed: over the space of a few hours, exactly the right number of mothers and babies had been rounded up, so that every bed would appear occupied.

Towards the end of that year she was shown around the racing stables of Newmarket. 'The Queen was escorted up a gentle, red-carpeted ramp which, like all the passages and stairwells she used, had been sprayed with scent,' ran a report in the *Daily Express*. '"We did not spray the stables," said a Jockey Club member, "since we were informed that the Queen liked the smell of horses."'

Four years later, getting ready for a visit by the Queen, the towns-folk of Lagos dutifully purchased thousands of hats, having misunderstood an instruction from their government that headgear was to be removed in the presence of royalty.

In 1954, a young advertising copywriter, Theo Aaronson, was work-ing as a waiter in a fashionable new Chelsea restaurant called Au Père de Nico. One evening, just as they were about to close, the owner accepted a last-minute booking. The 24-year-old Princess Margaret, the toast of the town, was set to arrive.

The manager was aghast. The restaurant, which was by now completely empty, was like a morgue. He frantically raked in whatever friends lived nearby and ordered his more presentable-looking waiters to change into their street clothes. By the time the Princess's party arrived, the place was filled with apparently animated diners.

Fortified only by coffee provided by the penny-pinching proprietor, the faux-diners had to pretend to make merry. Two hours later, the Princess left for Kensington Palace with her illusion of a bustling restaurant intact.

Others went to even more extreme lengths to protect members of the Royal Family from the intrusion of reality. 'In all, Princess Anne was in Eastbourne for 66 minutes,' read a report of a brief Royal visit in the *Western Morning News*. 'To make sure the Princess would be able to negotiate the narrow companionways, steep ladders and hatchways in a tight skirt, Lieutenant-Commander Stephen Emberton went through a special rehearsal – in drag.'

46

'The essence of Camp is its love of the unnatural: of artifice and exaggeration,' wrote Susan Sontag in her famous essay. Much of the camp of royalty springs from notions of tradition, ceremony and protocol which, far from being centuries old, are in fact recent constructions. As A. N. Wilson points out in his biography of Queen Victoria, few aristocratic titles go back beyond the seventeenth century, and only one of the English dukedoms, Norfolk, dates to the medieval period: the family that bears this title, the Howards, is descended from harbourmasters.

The veteran BBC Royal commentator David Dimbleby, son of Richard, points out in his memoir that the ceremonial surrounding the annual state opening of Parliament 'does not, despite appearances, date back to the reign of Elizabeth I or beyond. It was the creation of a Royal Commission set up in 1902.'

It is instant history, its meaning lost in the dry ice of its own invention.

> Even the experts on the procedure in the House of Lords differ in
> their explanations of its significance and it is a commentator's
> nightmare to offer an explanation for what is going on. It is simple
> enough to explain that the Queen's crown is brought to Westminster
> in a coach with the Queen's Jeweller in attendance. But who is the
> Queen's Jeweller and what does he do? Woe betide you if you forget to
> point out that the coach is accompanied by two Royal Bargemasters
> who sit at the back of the coach instead of the usual footmen, there
> because the crown used to be brought to Westminster from the Tower

of London by river. Who, what, and why are the Ladies of the Bedchamber? Most mysterious of all, what is the Cap of Maintenance, a scarlet velvet cap fringed with ermine, vulgarly known by the ceremonial experts as the squirrel on a stick. No one knows what it is doing there.

Dimbleby goes on to say that for years the Lord Great Chamberlain had to walk backwards as the Queen walked forwards, 'turning his back on her, I was assured, being lèse-majesté, or contrary to dignity of the sovereign'. But then one year the Lord Great Chamberlain started to walk forwards. No explanation was offered for this about-turn. Dimbleby remains baffled: 'So much for tradition.'

Prince Charles's investiture as Prince of Wales at Caernarfon Castle in 1969 was surely the campest of all these new traditions. He was only the second Prince of Wales ever to embark on such a ceremony: the first was his great-uncle, the future King Edward VIII, in the far-from-distant days of 1911.* The prime minister of the day, Lloyd George, had persuaded King George V that some sort of 'mini-coronation' might ease the fractious relations between the English and the Welsh, and so an ancient ceremony was invented. Lord Snowdon – plain Antony Armstrong-Jones until his marriage to Princess Margaret nine years earlier – was swiftly appointed Constable of Caernarfon Castle and charged with coming up with a suitable ceremony. 'You know about art,' said the Duke of Norfolk, the chairman of the Investiture Committee, 'you get on with it.'

Snowdon designed three thrones of Welsh slate to fit in the castle courtyard. A huge Perspex canopy was supported by steel pikestaffs, to add a touch of authenticity. Specially antiquated coats of arms of expanded polystyrene completed the picture. Residents of Caernarfon were given free paint to spruce up their house fronts in the architect-approved colours of pink, cream and green.

Green was also to the fore in the special costume Snowdon designed

---

* He created his elder son Prince of Wales on 9 September 2022, the day after the Queen's death, but there are still no plans for an investiture.

for himself as the Constable. 'It was dark green, Welsh green, with a very high collar, like an Indian collar,' he told Gyles Brandreth, decades later. 'I know people mocked it at the time, calling me Buttons. In fact, it didn't have any buttons on it at all: it did up with a zip.'

There was precious little camaraderie among the presiding bigwigs. 'The Duke of Norfolk and Snowdon are by now on such bad terms that it is no longer a question of them not speaking to each other, they cannot even bear to look at each other,' noted Lady Gladwyn in her diary. Snowdon had to have his plans approved by the Garter King of Arms. 'You had to call him "Garter",' he recalled. 'His actual name was

Sir Anthony Wagner, so you can imagine our nickname for him. There was a frightful row about the dragons we wanted to put on the banners … Garter wouldn't have it. Garter stood his ground. Eventually I said to him, "Oh, come on, Garter darling, can't you be more elastic?"' All in all, it was as camp as the annual pantomime at the London Palladium, which that year was *Dick Whittington*, starring Tommy Steele in the title role and Billy Dainty as Sarah the Cook.

Well-positioned in the third row of the Investiture was Lady Gladwyn. She greatly enjoyed the processions, while acknowledging their inauthenticity. 'The diplomats opposite me must have been amazed at the fancy dress of some of those partaking. The Druids would have looked far better had not their garments been made of nylon.' She noted, too, an unusual bronze tinge to Snowdon's face: 'I fancy it was made up for television.'

Once it was all over, the Marquess of Anglesey, charged with carrying the Sword of State, told Lady Gladwyn that he had overheard the Queen and the Duke of Edinburgh engaged in a tiff just before the start of the ceremony. 'Probably unnerved by fear of something dreadful happening, she [the Queen] agitatedly remarked that she hoped the text of what she had to say would be on her seat; and Prince Philip (probably cross because he was not in the limelight) answered rudely that he had no idea, and that it was her show not his.'

47

Royal camp is contagious, infecting everyone it touches: family, staff, clergy, grandees. Invited to dinner by the Queen's Chaplain, one young member of the Palace staff found himself welcomed on the doorstep with the words: 'Oh, come in, gorgeous! What's a hunk like you doing out in this miserable weather?' In 1967, before a dinner in the State Dining Room at Buckingham Palace, Guy Hunting, a novice footman, who had previously worked for Noël Coward, was told he would be serving the leader of the Liberal Party, Jeremy Thorpe. 'Not much chance of a mild flirtation with that placement, I thought.'

But he was wrong. In a memoir written decades later, he recalled the dining-room doors opening and the guests flooding in. As Thorpe hovered by his allotted chair, he turned to Hunting and said:

'What a beautiful room! The walls are such an amazing colour!'

'Isn't it wonderful? It's just been completely redecorated and this is the first time it has been used for ages,' I gabbled.

At that he stood back, subjecting me to a searching look.

'Well, I must say your uniform is pretty magnificent too,' he exclaimed. 'I'm going to a fancy dress ball at Edward Montagu's next week and would love to borrow it.'

As everyone took their seats, the two continued to chat, the leader of the Liberal Party insisting that the footman 'must let me know if you need any help'.

In time, they became close friends. 'He relished any snippet I could dredge up about life with the monarch or the Master [Noël Coward], obviously fascinated by both. When he said how much he would like to get to know them better I had to explain that my influence with the former was such that I didn't think I was able to bring them closer together. However, some months later I was able to arrange for him to meet the Master.'

Thanks to this introduction, Coward invited Thorpe to lunch *à deux* in his suite at the Savoy Hotel. 'Gossipy conversation flowed easily between them as they enjoyed their drinks and moved onto a delicious lunch. With the cheese course, however, the Master's mood became darker as he talked of unfulfilled sexual desire and unrequited love.' Coward invited Thorpe to enjoy a glass of Armagnac in his bedroom, only to find 'Jeremy climbing into his overcoat and mumbling about a vote in the House and letters to sign. A chase of sorts ensued, with the younger man dodging between easy chairs and coffee tables until he reached the safety of the door to the suite ... They never met again.'

48

'Why is it that gay men, in very large numbers, are simply obsessed with HM?' asked the author Philip Hensher, himself a gay man, in the year of the Queen's Platinum Jubilee.

> We skip off Fringe-visiting duties at the Edinburgh Festival to go with minute, leisurely scrutiny through the G-plan interiors of the Royal Yacht *Britannia*, berthed at Leith. We have long, detailed, happy dreams in which Her Majesty walks with us as a close, confiding friend with a marvellous brooch. We were first in the queue when Buckingham Palace opened to ordinary tourists. We long for the day when you can go on tours of Balmoral – that sentence on the Balmoral website, 'the Ballroom is the only room available to visitors – all other areas are Her Majesty's private residence', is like a dagger to the disappointed heart.*

He argued that, with certain exceptions, 'the enthusiasm and energy expended by many gay men in wondering about Her Majesty is quite remarkable, and one which has helped define her reign'. Some of this energy is devoted to gossiping about which of the different members of her family are gay, but most 'goes into maintaining that curious tone of mockery and awed deference that Proust captures so well when the

---

* Hensher's heart need be disappointed no more. In April 2024, it was announced that for £100 a ticket forty people a day could tour key rooms at Balmoral, including two dining rooms, the drawing room and the ballroom. Afternoon tea is on offer for an extra £50 per head.

Baron de Charlus comments on the fan that the Queen of Naples forgets at a reception. "Oh how moving … it is all the more touching for being so hideous …'"

In their millions, they discuss her shoes and handbags 'at great, derisive lengths … We love her, we deeply admire her for the most part, and we have decidedly caustic views on her shoes, hats, bags and the Tupperware boxes she apparently uses to preserve her cornflakes at breakfast.'

For Hensher, it all came down to camp,

of which gay men are not the sole possessors, but certainly the primary guardians. Camp is like a flirtation; it means and yet does not mean what it says, like someone testing the possibility of love by stating love in a way that could be withdrawn. In the case of camp, we admire what may be hideous; we are enraptured by what we laugh at; we don't mean what we say, and yet we mean it with all our hearts. Camp is camp because its meanings prove impossible to pin down. Do we, as gay men, identify with the Queen because, like us once, she is not allowed to say what she thinks and feels? Or do we like her because, as Quentin Crisp thought, we are inexhaustibly interested in other people's lives, and of all people's lives, hers is least like ours?

Ceremony, protocol, precedence and ritual: they all allow for ambiguity. They mean both nothing and everything. Their purpose is enshrouded by history; forgotten, invented or reconstituted.

49

In his thank-you letter to the Queen after staying at Balmoral in the summer of 1959, President Eisenhower said that he and his wife were 'delighted about the coming "event", as is everyone in your kingdom'.

That coming event was the birth of the Queen's third child, after a break of ten years. In the week leading up to the great moment, the newspapers featured little else. And why not? After all, this was to be the first baby born to a reigning monarch for over a century.

On 19 February 1960, a crowd of 2,000 gathered outside Buckingham Palace in anticipation. 'I think she'd like to know that we're out here, wishing her well,' said one woman. 'I've got three children myself – boy, girl and another boy. That's why I hope her third's a boy.'

At 4.15 p.m., a servant walked to the Palace railings and pinned up a handwritten notice:

The Queen was safely delivered of a son at 3.30pm today. Her Majesty and the infant Prince are both doing well.

A great cheer rang out.

The new Prince, whose name remained a secret, weighed seven pounds three ounces, and had blue eyes and light brown hair. His birth shunted his elder sister, Princess Anne, to third place in the order of succession.

'OH BOY!' ran the headline in the *Daily Mirror*, which devoted six pages to the story. Gun salutes were fired in Hyde Park, the Tower of London, Windsor Castle and Cardiff Castle. The Black Arrows of the Royal Air Force staged a fly-past of thirty-six Hunter jets. On the Thames, tugs tooted their sirens. The bells of St Paul's Cathedral sounded, as did bells from churches up and down the land.

At her boarding school in the Isle of Wight, 13-year-old Jane Birkin found the news a welcome relief from the grind of French vocab and Latin grammar and the unpleasantness of her dorm where 'everybody is horrid'. 'Queen has a baby boy!' she wrote in her diary. 'Born at 4 o'clock in the afternoon on 19 February! May be called Albert, I hope not. Cheers from the whole school. HURRAY, all over the blackboards is written, "IT'S A BOY IT'S A BOY GARCON".'

There were, though, small pockets of cynicism here and there. 'What a sentimental hold the monarchy has over the middle classes!' observed Harold Nicolson. He added, sniffily: 'All the solicitors, actors and publishers at the Garrick were beaming, as if they had acquired some personal gift.'

It was later announced that the baby was to be named Andrew, after Prince Philip's father, Albert after the Queen's father;* Christian, after Prince Philip's great-grandfather, King Christian IX of Denmark; and Edward, after the Queen's great-grandfather, King Edward VII. His christening was conducted on 8 April by the archbishop of Canterbury. Prince Andrew was dressed in the traditional Royal christening robe of Honiton lace, over a satin petticoat commissioned by Queen Victoria in 1842 for the christening of the future King Edward VII.

Cecil Beaton was engaged to take the first formal photographs in March. The Queen's midwife, Sister Helen Rowe, arrived in the Nash room with the new baby, together with Anne and Charles. 'Oh, well, I suppose we'd better start photographing right away if that would be all right,' said Beaton. The nine-year-old Princess Anne replied, 'Well, I don't think it will be.' According to his biographer, Beaton 'loathed her on sight'.†

The Queen and Prince Philip then entered, and Prince Philip immediately began bossing Beaton about, telling him how to get a good photograph: 'Take it from here. Why not there?'

'I felt as I were being chased in a nightmare when one's legs sink into the mire,' recalled Beaton. 'The family stood to attention. I said something to make them smile, so clicked. I clicked like mad at anything that seemed passable. The baby, thank God, behaved itself and did not cry or spew.'

Beaton noted that the baby's 11-year-old brother, Prince Charles, seemed crushed by the oppressive atmosphere, 'as if awaiting a clout from behind, or for his father to tweak his ear or pull the tuft of hair at

---

* Who switched it to George on his accession.

† Beaton had first come a cropper with Anne within a few weeks of her birth, when the Queen invited him to photograph her. 'Babies are difficult at the best of times and this was one of the worst times because the baby only wanted to be allowed to sleep,' he recalled. '... I was not allowed to take a jack along with me to keep her eyes open, so we had to make bird noises, rattle keys, clap our hands, jump up and down. The more idiotic the performance the more bored the baby. Only a drop of glycerine on the tongue seemed to bring any favourable reaction.'

the crown of his head'. The session ended with Prince Philip saying, 'Surely we've had enough. If he's not got what he wants by now, he's an even worse photographer than I think he is. Ha! Ha!'

The photographs of Andrew and his siblings were made public later in the month. They were widely appreciated, even by those with little interest in royalty or babies. 'Prince Andrew looks a nice baby,' cooed Vita Sackville-West. 'He looks a person already, not like a poached egg, like most new-born babies. And did you notice what a startling resemblance he bears to his grandfather, George VI?'

But these were the last images the public were to see of Prince Andrew for quite some time. For the first sixteen months of his life, Prince Andrew was never seen in public. This led to rumours and speculation. Was there perhaps something not quite right about him?

50

A brief history of royal rumours

1925

Disinclined to have intercourse with her husband, but determined to produce an heir, the then Duchess of York agreed to be artificially inseminated by a trusted doctor. The Duchess is herself the daughter of the family cook, 'an attractive Frenchwoman named Marguérite Rodière'. Lady Colin Campbell, who reveals this news in 2012, adds that the Duke of Windsor once told her that he had seen 'various documents' supporting the claim, and that 'on his deathbed' the Queen Mother's father had confided to his doctor that it was 'absolutely true'. This is why the Duke used to refer to her as 'Cookie'.

1930

Princess Margaret is born deaf and dumb. According to Jessica Mitford, she also has webbed feet. Sixty-two years later, on 30 April 1992, Mitford writes to her friend Maya Angelou confessing, 'I rather loathe the Royals, esp. Princess M. ... When the princesses were little I tried to spread a rumor in London that they'd been born with webbed feet which was why nobody had ever seen them with their shoes off; also, that Princess Lillibet (as Elizabeth was known by an adoring Brit. public) was actually the Monster of Glamis.'

December 1936
Following the abdication of King Edward VIII, many are convinced that his younger brother, the Duke of York, will refuse the throne, out of fraternal loyalty, and that it will pass to the 10-year-old Princess Elizabeth, with her grandmother, Queen Mary, acting as regent. The news is greeted with widespread approval, as the young Princess and her grandmother are the two most popular members of the Royal Family.

April/May 1937
In the run-up to his Coronation on 12 May, King George VI suffers an epileptic fit. The news circulates on the London Stock Exchange, before becoming widespread.

If George VI and Queen Elizabeth fail to give birth to a baby boy, their elder daughter Princess Elizabeth will, in due course, become Queen. But Evelyn Waugh rules out the possibility of another child; he has heard that Queen Elizabeth can only get pregnant if suspended by her legs from a chandelier.

18 February 1957
Time magazine reports a rift between the Queen and Prince Philip. 'Last week the mongering winds were howling louder around Buckingham Palace than they had since the day of Wallis Warfield Simpson and Edward VIII.'

At Buckingham Palace, Commander Colville reacts to these reports by issuing a statement: 'It is quite untrue that there is a rift between the Queen and the Duke.' As so often happens, this denial serves only to lend the story credence. 'London Hushes Royal Rift' runs a headline in America.

11 January 1958
Labour backbencher Wilfred Fienburgh informs his dinner guests that Harold Macmillan's youngest daughter is really the child of his fellow MP Bob Boothby, that Princess Margaret still carries a torch for Peter Townsend, that the Cabinet want the Queen to have another child, and that Prince Philip has a mistress who is a Wren officer.

21 April 1959

Evelyn Waugh writes to Diana Cooper with the news that 'A highly placed official in Tanganyika told me in strict confidence that the Queen's marriage was "on the rocks" because of the Duke of Edinburgh's infatuation with Judy Montagu.'

1972

The Paris news magazine *France Dimanche* calculates that over the past fourteen years the French media have published sixty-three reports of Queen Elizabeth II's abdication, ninety-two reports that she is pregnant, and seventy-seven reports of her forthcoming divorce.

February 1975

Marcia Williams, the moody, long-standing private secretary to the prime minister, Harold Wilson, is furious when Bernard Donoughue, his senior policy adviser, is invited to a reception at Buckingham Palace. Their colleague Joe Haines explains to Donoughue that Marcia nurses a grudge against the Royal Family because she believes her mother to be the illegitimate daughter of King Edward VIII. Apparently, one of the King's officials, named Falkender, took the blame, and that is why, when Marcia was made a baroness, she adopted the name Falkender. The Queen is afraid to invite her to the Palace, regarding her as a rival to the throne.*

March 1976

As Harold Wilson plans his farewell dinner at No. 10, Marcia Williams informs him that the Queen will try to shun her, knowing her to be a direct descendant of her great-grandfather, and thus in competition.

On the evening of 23 March 1976, all the leading figures in Harold Wilson's administration assemble at Downing Street for his farewell

---

* In 2024, her otherwise sympathetic biographer, Linda McDougall, could find no evidence of any sort of familial link between Lady Falkender and the Royal Family. But the suspicion that one is secretly royal is not uncommon: for a description of the quest of Robert Brown, an accountant from Jersey, to assert his identity as the illegitimate child of the Queen's sister, see my book *Ma'am Darling: 99 Glimpses of Princess Margaret*.

dinner, including Marcia Williams. Upon her arrival, the Queen is introduced to everybody by the outgoing prime minister. 'Marcia gave a deep and well-practised curtsy, as only one member of royalty can do to another!' observes the sceptical Donoughue, wielding his exclamation mark as a sword. He notes that other distinguished guests were ferried over to speak to the Queen after dinner, 'but Marcia was not', even though 'she hovered nearby expectantly'. Later Donoughue is told 'over the private office network from the Palace that although the Queen did not mind shaking hands with her at the beginning, she did not see any reason to devote time talking to her'.

17 June 1977
Under the headline 'Charles to Marry Astrid – Official', the *Daily Express* reveals that Prince Charles is all set to marry Princess Marie-Astrid of Luxembourg.

1980–1990
Within psychiatric circles, it is said that the Queen has been treated for depression with electroconvulsive therapy.

1986
Morrissey, the morose and gangly lead singer with the Smiths, has long nursed an intense dislike of the Royal Family. 'Always have done. It's fairy tale nonsense ... money spent on royalty is money burnt. I've never met anyone who supports royalty, and believe me I've searched.'

This year, he gives musical expression to his antipathy. 'The Queen Is Dead' is the title track of the Smiths' third album. In the first verse, Morrissey addresses the Queen as 'Her Very Lowness', and then directs a question at her son: 'Charles, don't you ever crave / To appear on the front of the *Daily Mail*/Dressed in your mother's veil?' Like so many Royal obsessives, his observations suggest a strong autobiographical element. Later in the song he suggests that 'when you are tied to your mother's apron, no one talks about castration'. Coincidentally, Morrissey's own mother is named Elizabeth, and she is often to be found at his concerts.

Morrissey is determined that 'The Queen Is Dead' should go to the top of the charts. A beady monitor of his own sales figures, on a Tuesday morning, he walks from his house in Chelsea's Cadogan Square to the telephone box opposite the Peter Jones department store on the King's Road and rings his record company. The news is disappointing. 'It's number 2. Phil Collins kept us off.'

He is certain that unseen forces have stopped the album going to number 1 because of its title. He sits 'hunched and contorted' in front of a fire for the rest of the day, brooding on an Establishment conspiracy. Later that week, a tabloid newspaper carries the headline 'MORRISSEY SAYS SORRY TO THE QUEEN'. He rings his publicist in a fury, asking, 'Who has the right to print such lies?' His publicist replies, 'All publicity is good publicity.'

Over the years, Morrissey keeps up his tirades against the Queen. 'For a broad historical view of what the Queen is and how she "rules", examine Gaddafi or Mubarak, and see if you can spot any difference,' he advises in 2011.

1989

Swimming with Lord Wyatt,* Lord Weinstock† happens to mention that, before a dinner party he was throwing for the Queen, her staff informed him that she didn't eat shellfish. 'That is probably because of her Jewish ancestry, Prince Albert being the son of his mother and a Jewish music master,' replies Wyatt, with his perpetual air of omniscience.

1991

It is widely rumoured that the Queen will use her annual Christmas broadcast to announce her intention to abdicate on 6 February 1992, the fortieth anniversary of her accession. But when the day comes the Queen speaks only of her hope to serve the nation 'for years to come'.

May 1999

Lyndon LaRouche, the owner and editor of *Executive Intelligence Review*, reveals that Princess Diana was assassinated on the orders of Prince Philip, in consultation with the American vice-president, Al Gore, who is a secret agent for the Royal Family. Apparently, the Princess had discovered that the Royal Family were behind a plan to terrorise the United States into becoming a British colony again, so that the House of Windsor would have a monopoly on the US cocaine market.

2000

Prince Philip is asked by a journalist from the *Independent* newspaper if it is true that he once had a homosexual affair with former French president Giscard d'Estaing, and that Prince Andrew was fathered by another man. He denies both allegations.

---

* Woodrow Wyatt (1918–97), maverick politician, newspaper columnist and socialite, chairman of the Horserace Totalisator Board from 1976 to his death, and the *News of the World*'s 'Voice of Reason'.

† Arnold Weinstock (1924–2002), managing director of the General Electric Company from 1963 to 1996 and successful racehorse owner.

25 August 2002

On the fifth anniversary of the death of his son Dodi and Princess Diana, Mohamed al-Fayed tells the *Observer* that Prince Philip runs Britain and, together with the CIA, was behind the murder of Princess Diana because of the threat she posed to the American arms industry. 'I know that they mummified her body before she came here, taking everything out, because they did not want any evidence of her pregnancy.'

2010

Lyndon LaRouche discovers that the Queen has been writing science fiction under various pseudonyms, aimed at distracting the young. Determined to silence LaRouche, Her Majesty has enlisted MI6 to assassinate him.

17 February 2017

Former TV sports broadcaster David Icke continues to insist that the Queen is a shape-shifting lizard from outer space. She is not alone: other lizards include Kris Kristofferson, Bob Hope, both President Bushes, former prime minister Edward Heath and Boxcar Willie. 'I did not sit in a dark room and come up with this theory nor go looking for it,' says Icke. 'I have travelled and been to fifty countries to research it.'

51

John F. Kennedy first met Princess Elizabeth at a Court Levee at St James's Palace in the autumn of 1938; he was 21 and she was twelve. 'It takes place in the morning and you wear tails. The King stands & you go up and bow. Met Queen Mary and was at tea with the Princess Elizabeth with whom I made a great deal of time. Thursday night – am going to Court in my new silk breeches, which are cut to my crotch tightly and in which I look mighty attractive.'

When they next met, twenty-three years later, he was the president of the United States of America and she was Queen of the United Kingdom. Her crusty prime minister, Harold Macmillan, had origi-nally entertained qualms about the glamorous young president, judging him a 'young, cocky Irishman' and 'a strange character' who showed signs of being 'obstinate, sensitive, ruthless and highly sexed'. But he had soon come round to him; Kennedy had taken to wearing baggier trousers.

In the early months of her husband's presidency, the brittle First Lady, Jackie Kennedy, swung between insecurity and entitlement with little in between. Someone once overheard her saying, 'Oh Jack, I'm sorry for you that I'm such a dud,' and her husband replying, 'I love you as you are.' Was each of them telling only half the truth?

On their European tour in the early summer of 1961, they were both sustained by pharmaceuticals: amphetamines and vitamins for the First Lady, and novocaine and Demerol for the president, who suffered from chronic back problems. Despite it all, Jackie had wowed Paris and Vienna; even the infamously gruff Nikita Khrushchev had ended his dinner with her by promising to send her a puppy.

From Vienna, the Kennedys flew to London to attend the christening of Jackie's niece Christina Radziwill. The British turned out to be rather more guarded in their reception of Jackie, finding her something of a curiosity. 'She is a queer fish,' observed the Duchess of Devonshire. 'Her face is one of the oddest I ever saw. It is put together in a very wild way.'

Dinner at Buckingham Palace involved complex manoeuvrings. Officials had asked the Kennedys who they wanted to be invited. Jackie's modest request had been for invitations to be sent to Princess Margaret and Princess Marina, and also her sister Princess Lee Radziwill and Lee's husband, Prince Stanislaw Radziwill. But Lee was

on her second marriage and Stanislaw was on his third; at that time, Palace protocol excluded divorcees. According to the unreliable Gore Vidal, 'The Palace sent a delicately phrased reply to the effect that *Mr.* and *Mrs.* Radziwill, as divorced people, were not invitable.'

Jackie was upset at this, and complained to her friend, David Ormsby-Gore, the British ambassador in Washington. He tried to explain the rules, but, when she refused to take no for an answer, suggested she get in touch with the US chief of protocol.

Harold Macmillan recorded the ensuing awkwardness in his diary.

> After much hesitation the Queen waived her rule about divorce. Prince and Princess Radzinski [sic] were invited, although they have had two or three partners apiece to date. She was very unwilling to do this, or to put their names in the Court Circular. I think had the Kennedys been staying at the American Embassy, I could have advised the Queen to omit the Radzinskis [sic]. But since the President and Mrs K. were actually staying with the Prince and Princess, it seemed impossible to do so.

So Jackie got her way, but was upset first by the shenanigans and then by the dreariness of the dinner itself, to which neither Princess Margaret nor Princess Marina had been invited. According to Vidal, she complained: 'The Queen had her revenge. No Margaret, no Marina, no one except every Commonwealth minister of agriculture that they could find.' Nor was conversation easy. Jackie confided to Vidal that the Queen had been 'pretty heavy-going'. When the gleeful Vidal mentioned to Princess Margaret what the First Lady had said about her sister, she replied, 'But that's what she's *there for*.'

Throughout, Jackie felt cold-shouldered. 'I think the Queen resented me,' she told Vidal. 'Philip was nice, but nervous. One felt absolutely no relationship between them.' Only once, she added, had the Queen seemed remotely human. When Jackie was telling her how hard it was to be on public view for such long periods of time, 'The Queen looked rather conspiratorial and said, "One gets crafty after a while and learns how to save oneself."'

After dinner, the Queen asked Jackie if she liked paintings, and then took her on a tour of the long gallery. But still they failed to click.

Stopping in front of a Van Dyck, the Queen said, 'That's a good horse.'

To which Jackie replied, 'Yes, that is a good horse.'

And this, if Jackie and/or Gore are to be trusted, was the extent of their contact with one another. The First Lady thought the Queen lacked style. To the blabbermouth Cecil Beaton, she declared that she 'was not impressed by the flowers or the furnishings of the apartments at Buckingham Palace, or by the Queen's dark-blue tulle dress and shoulder straps, or her flat hair-style'.

Others, more charitable, offered rosier accounts. Macmillan considered the evening 'very pleasant', and so did Kennedy's chief of protocol, Angier Biddle Duke: 'It was a delightful evening, very pleasant, very charming, very attractive evening.' But, then again, only the most cack-handed head of protocol would choose to describe an evening at Buckingham Palace as rubbish.

'May I ... say how grateful my wife and I are for the cordial hospitality offered to us by your Majesty and Prince Philip during our visit to London last Monday,' President Kennedy wrote in a note celebrating the Queen's official birthday, a few days later. 'We shall always cherish the memory of that delightful evening.'

Nine months later, in March 1962, Jackie came over on a private visit, and the Queen invited her to lunch à deux.

'I don't think I should say anything about it except how grateful I am and how charming she was,' Jackie told the television cameras, before making good her escape.

52

In 1962, the First Lady allowed cameras into the White House to film *A Tour of the White House with Mrs John F. Kennedy*. Three years later, in one of the Palace's periodic attempts to modernise, the Queen was persuaded to give the go-ahead to something similar.

Royal Palaces was a joint production between BBC and ITV. As a former Surveyor of the King's Pictures and director of the National Gallery, independently wealthy and with a castle of his own, Sir Kenneth Clark* was considered just the man to present it. But, like many grandees, he entertained mixed feelings about the Royal Family, regarding them as a little too bourgeois. 'I have to spend two days at Windsor with the Monarch advising him about his pictures – interminably standing and grinning,' he complained to his friend Edith Wharton back in 1936. 'I found the new King and Queen very pleasant – she just above the average country house type, he just below it.'

At first, the TV production seemed to go swimmingly. The Queen made all the Royal palaces available for filming: Buckingham Palace, Windsor Castle, Holyrood, Hampton Court and the Royal Pavilion in Brighton. Clark devoted fourteen weeks to the project. Nevertheless, he felt uneasy about it, suspecting that his usual approach – patrician, gently ironic – might be at odds with the unstinting adoration expected by the Palace. 'I worry a lot about my *Royal Palaces*,' he complained to his friend Janet Stone. 'Every time I see the people it is clear that what

---

* Later to become known to readers of *Private Eye* as 'Lord Clark of Civilisation'.

they really want is a sort of Arthur Bryant* script, and I can't do it …
it is so much *not* my line.'

Nevertheless, he stood his ground, earning the respect of his peers.
In Cecil Beaton's view he 'brought a greatness to the subject. He did
not give us any of the *Woman's Own* gush about the glorious little lady
of the throne. He talked of kings and queens as real people in history.
He criticised from a very lofty plane some of the works of art in the
palaces and, although giving great credit where it was due, was probably a little condescending about the position of Zoffany and the
specialists in "conversation pieces" in the world of art masterpieces.
But the whole effort was successful, lively and of real interest. And this
is in itself difficult for the Palace, on guard against any digression from
the banal.'

Amid much toing and froing, an early version of the script was
shown to court officials, who immediately demanded the deletion of
the word 'sycophants' to describe the courtiers of King Henry VIII.
Even after 400 years, the Queen's portly ancestor's shaky reputation
required protection.

The Palace wanted to see a copy of the completed script, but Clark
resisted. 'The Lord Chamberlain's office are longing to find fault with
it, and are in a rage because I have refused to submit the script.' But,
later on, when the Queen herself asked to see a rough copy of the
programme, Clark felt unable to say no.

The royal screening took place at Buckingham Palace in October
1966. Clark arrived with his producer and the cameraman. He found
himself outnumbered: the Queen arrived with the Duke of Edinburgh,
Prince Charles, various courtiers and the Lord Chamberlain.

It all went very badly. The sound was not working, so Clark
was obliged to read the text out loud over the film 'while the royal
corgies bit my ankles'. All in all, the screening was, he felt, 'a total
failure'.

---

* Described by the historian Andrew Roberts as 'a supreme toady, fraudulent scholar and
humbug', Sir Arthur Bryant (1899–1985) is remembered for his highly romanticised view of
the past.

The second the lights went up, the Queen rose to her feet with 'a face of iron'. Clark approached her, 'hand outstretched, waiting for congratulations, to be met with an irate: "Did you *have* to be so sarcastic?"'

'Well, Ma'am,' he replied, 'if you didn't like the film, you must admit the photography was good. May I present the photographer?'

But by now the Queen had had enough. According to Clark, she swept out, followed by her embarrassed courtiers. Only Prince Philip remained behind, ready to do battle.

'How do you *know* the people guzzled at the palace banquets?' he snapped.

Clark stood his ground. 'Because half the population was undernourished. Few had good meals. This was an occasion for a tuck-in.'

The only member of the Royal Family who showed an interest was Prince Charles, described by Clark's friend Cecil Beaton as 'a nice, sensitive boy, who would be interested in works of art if his father were not determined to knock "all that sort of rubbish out of him"'.

Clark looked back on the screening with despondency and a touch of anger. 'All did *not* go well when I showed it to the monarch. She was *furious*, and would have liked to stop it, but couldn't find a pretext for doing so – not a single disrespectful word or sentiment (except that Henry VIII was fat!). All she could say was "it's so sarcastic" – which means devoid of the slop and unction to which she is conditioned. She didn't say a word about the photography and wouldn't speak to my poor producer. The courtiers were confused. I had foreseen all this but in a way it's remarkable that my lack of enthusiasm for the monarchy should have oozed through my extremely respectable (and very dull) script.'

Some of his colleagues tried to comfort him; his producer even sent him a letter of commiseration: 'It must have been for you a disheartening and wounding reaction to the film last night: although perhaps one that you had anticipated.' He might have been better advised to remember Benjamin Disraeli's advice to Matthew Arnold: 'Everyone likes flattery; and when you come to Royalty you should lay it on with a trowel.'

53

Philip Larkin's fourteen brushes with royalty

Pussy cat, pussy cat, where have you been?
I've been to London to visit the Queen.

i

Others are more reluctant to visit the Queen, or even have her visit them. In October 1946, Philip Larkin writes home from Leicester. Aged 25, he has just taken up a new job as assistant librarian at the university there. 'The King and Queen are coming to Leicester on Wednesday, but I have no chance of seeing them.' He is unimpressed by them anyway, reminding his parents that King George VI had broken golden key while attempting to open the New Bodley door in a ceremony in Oxford the week before. 'Someone had to shin up & get in a window & let them in from inside. What a paltry business this ceremony racket is!'

ii

His next brush, or near brush, with royalty occurs in Belfast in July 1953. By now sub-librarian at Queen's University, Larkin looks on as the newly crowned Queen Elizabeth II arrives for an official visit. 'Some beefeaters turned up, and a few trumpeters, looking like jockeys in cloth of gold. Afterwards I went and lay down,' he writes to his friend Patsy Strang. The Queen, he adds, 'looked like an ordinary well-dressed rather sunburned girl. She was dressed in a sea green stiff-silky coat, and matching hat. I shouldn't have looked at her twice in the street. She is popularly supposed to have had "a great reception", & I can't offer any evidence to the contrary, so will let it pass.' He closes this letter, downbeat even for him, with the news that he has just purchased a pair of pale green swimming trunks. 'They have a tiny little pocket, I can't quite think for what, money perhaps.'

iii

Four years later, in May 1957 now promoted to university librarian at Hull ('a cloister of mediocrities isolated by the bleak reaches of East Riding') he tells his mother that he has come within a whisker of meeting the Queen and the Duke of Edinburgh. 'I could have got myself presented if my elbows had been sharp enough: at the heel of the hunt they were throwing people at her like fish to a seal ... Ah well, one day I shall meet her as Philip Larkin, & not as the paltry librarian of a piffling university. Or so I like to think!'

On the other hand, he found it 'quite exciting' to observe the Queen close at hand. 'She is quite slim & looks very young still & was wearing a blue coat, white hat, & black bag & shoes. Rather ordinary clothes really.'

iv

By April 1960, he can no longer avoid meeting a Royal. The prospect of the Queen Mother officially opening the new University Library at Hull has begun to haunt him. 'I dream of it at night. The other night I dreamed that I was showing her over not only the Library, but a house that was strange to me though I knew I lived there ... I'm beginning to pray for a broken leg, yellow jack, close arrest. Anything to avoid the disparaging eye of colleagues. "Why did you—?" "Supposing—?" "Surely—?" "Isn't it rather small?" "Isn't this so stiff?" "Why does that make such a noise?" "You don't mean to say your staff—?" "You don't mean to say you let the students—?" "You don't mean to say *you*—?" Oh dear, oh dear, oh dear.'

v

Five years on, Larkin is awarded the Gold Medal for Poetry. His mother is proud. 'You are adding to the honour of the Larkin family and keeping the name before the public as Daddy did before you.' She brings the medal back to her own house for safe keeping. Some consider the design disappointing, including his sister: 'Kitty said she could have done better herself.'

His mother writes Philip a letter, three days later, saying she hopes he thanked the Queen.

'No, I didn't thank the Queen for the medal,' he replies. 'I remembered Dr Johnson's remark "It was not for me to bandy civilities with my sovereign", and simply acknowledged its receipt. I expect she is now thinking "That's the last time I do anything for that man."' He ends his letter home by mentioning that he had narrowly avoided a hedgehog while driving from York to Hull the night before.

vi

With the death of John Masefield in 1967, the post of Poet Laureate falls vacant. 'Well, nobody has offered me the job of being poet laureate yet. I expect there is a subcommittee sitting on it somewhere,' he writes to his mother on 21 May. He thinks and hopes that John Betjeman will get the job – 'he is not only the right *kind* of poet, but a *good* poet ...' However, he has not ruled himself out entirely. 'It would be a tremendous honour to be offered it, but I should be very worried about it. Anyway, I hardly think it's likely ...'

His mother replies saying that his sister considers Philip's poems better than Betjeman's: 'I agree, though, it *would* be rather a worry to you, for you have so little time to write. You are a *very* busy creature, dashing off to London and attending so many meetings and functions.'

As it happens, Cecil Day Lewis is chosen to succeed Masefield as Poet Laureate, a post he holds for four years, until his death in 1972. In turn, he is succeeded by John Betjeman, whose biographer, Bevis Hillier, notes that Larkin is 'thought to have dished his chances by publishing "They fuck you up, your mum and dad", which is "a sentiment unlikely to be endorsed by the Queen".

vii

In April 1973, Larkin receives an invitation to lunch at Buckingham Palace. He enjoys himself, up to a point. 'The Queen was pleasant enough, but I didn't have enough of her to lose my nervousness,' he writes to Judy Egerton. 'Princess Alexandra was jolly in a flirtatious country-house way. The other guests were unknown to me, but I got on well enough with the Keeper of the Royal Stamps.'

He recounts his conversation with Princess Alexandra in greater detail to his friend Ann Thwaite. She had, he says, 'fired questions' at him:

Q: What sort of poems do you write?
A: Gloomy.
Q: Why are they gloomy?
A: Because I'm a gloomy sort of person.
Q: Why are you a gloomy sort of person?

While the guests were being shown one or two of the paintings, he found himself tongue-tied. 'I wished I had your knowledge & cd have said something about the pictures on the wall.' He had watched the corgis 'being fed with nonchalance by HM'. The food was, he thought, 'all right, and *plenty of drink*', though he disapproved of the menu being written in French – 'not what I go to B. Palace for'.

All in all, though, he is pleased to have been invited and takes it as a 'wonderful compliment to me, or to the book, or to poetry, or to Oxford, or to all four, and just what canting Anglophobes say wouldn't happen. Don't you agree?' In a rare fit of munificence, he posts Princess Alexandra a copy of his collection *High Windows*, but she fails to acknowledge it.

viii

After this royal interlude, Larkin returns to the drudgery of Hull. 'I am back in my dull life again, trying to readjust. There is the housing problem to face. I have bought an ironing board, in an effort to wash my own shirts – the laundry is really too awful – it not only doesn't wash shirts, it *adds* dirt …'

He believes that Britain is going from bad to worse, and regards the Queen as a symbol of national decline. 'You can't be more depressed than I about the state of the country,' he writes to his old schoolfriend Colin Gunner in June 1974. 'To my mind it is only a question of time before we are a sort of sub-Ireland, or Italy, with the population scratching a living by sucking up to tourists and the Queen doing two performances a day of Trooping the Colour for coach loads of Middle-Westerners and Russian Moujiks. God, what an end to a great country …'

ix

In 1975, his award of a CBE is announced in the Queen's Birthday Honours. For a full four weeks, he frets about what to wear for the big day. 'I'm beginning to think I ought to buy a new raincoat to go to Buckingham Palace,' he writes on 8 October. A week later, he travels into town to buy one, as 'mine seems to have a great many inexplicable stains on it. I don't want to spoil the Queen's day!' Unfortunately, he spends 'rather a frustrating morning' shopping in Hull, finding that the parking meters require shilling coins, when he doesn't have any to hand. Ten days later, he makes another foray to the shops, but doesn't like any of the raincoats on display. Nevertheless, 'It's a beautiful day here, and I am *almost* glad to be alive! Very rare for me!'

He finally finds what he wants, and arrives promptly at Buckingham Palace in his smart new raincoat on 4 November at 10 a.m. for 10.30 a.m. For an hour and a half, he is made to wait with his fellow CBEs – 'a morning hanging about the palace' – before being marched into an anteroom, 'from which we were fed singly into the Ballroom and the royal presence. I bowed and she lassoed me with a pink silk ribbon from which depended a gold (gold-coloured, anyway) cross with some enamelling.'

The Queen asks him her preferred question for writers: 'Are you still writing?' Larkin replies that he is 'still trying' and 'she grinned very nicely and shook hands & I thankfully retreated'. The man in front of him asks Larkin if the Queen knew he was a writer. 'I said yes, she seemed to. He said rather thoughtfully that she'd asked him what he did! ... So I felt one up, a feeble one, perhaps half one.'

x

Larkin's ruminations on Britain's decline are set to continue for the rest of his life. In 1977, he attempts to write a poem for the Queen's Silver Jubilee, coming up with:

> After Healey's trading figures,
> After Wilson's squalid crew,
> And the rising tide of ****ers –
> What a treat to look at you.

'Shall I add five or six verses to that for you?' he asks his friend Anthony Thwaite, explaining that '"You" in the poem is HM, of course. Perhaps that needs making a bit clearer. "What a treat to turn to you", perhaps. If one does to HM. She hasn't come across with that grace & favour house yet ...'

xi

A year later, inspiration has still not struck. He has been asked by his editor at Faber & Faber, Charles Monteith, to produce a short poem to commemorate the Queen's Silver Jubilee. The completed poem will be inscribed in stone and placed alongside one by Ted Hughes in Queen Square, where Faber has its offices. He takes two stabs at it. The first, the product of 'three nights' thought' goes:

In times when nothing stood
But worsened, or grew strange,
There was one constant good;
She did not change.

'You're welcome to first British chiselling rights in that,' he tells Monteith. 'But please don't print it. I'm sure Ted will do better.' He has, in fact, done rather better himself with a parody of a Ted Hughes poem to the Queen, which he also encloses:

The sky split apart in malice
Stars rattled like pans on a shelf
Crow shat on Buckingham Palace
God pissed Himself.

xii

In 1981, it is announced that his old chum Kingsley Amis is to receive a CBE in the New Year's Honours. 'Gratters on the CBE, old man,' writes Larkin, who goes on to offer advice based on his own experience at the ceremony. 'Start thinking of … what to say when HM says something inaudible under the strains of Gilbert and S, and the general hum of the concourse. Lucky I got it but it was a nasty moment. The wrong answer and you're on your way to the Tower. It's the most terrible godawful waste of *time*, too. A whole morning gone, no drinks, no pisses. Still, fun in a way I suppose.'

He ends his letter to Amis fantasising about his new role as grandee at Hull University. 'Dear Dr Larkin, My friend and I had an argument as to which of us has the biggest breasts and we wondered if you would act as—'.

xiii

For the rest of his life, Larkin's ruminations about the Royal Family revolve largely around Princess Margaret's cleavage. 'Nice photo of Princess Margaret in the *S. Times* this week wearing a La Lollo Waspie, in an article on corsets,' he writes to his friend Robert Conquest on 29

June 1981, exactly a month before the marriage of the Prince and Princess of Wales. 'See what you miss by being abroad!'

In January 1985, three months after the birth of Prince Harry, an event by which he remains resolutely unmoved, he tells the poet Blake Morrison that he has been 'meditating a poem on Princess Margaret, having to knock off first the booze and now the fags – now *that's* the kind of royal poem I could write with feeling. These bloody babies leave me cold.'

xiv

At the end of summer 1985, suffering from inoperable oesophageal cancer ('brush up your shovel and headstone', he advises his biographer Andrew Motion), Philip Larkin hears that he is to be made a Companion of Honour, his investiture scheduled for 25 November. 'I don't know what CH is,' he complains. 'I suspect it is something you hang around your neck. In theory I have to receive it from HM's hands, but I don't see myself doing so.'

He is right. When the time comes, he is too ill to go, and the medal is sent by post. He dies a week later, in the early hours of the morning, at the age of 63, whispering, 'I am going to the inevitable', to the nurse who is holding his hand.

54

Even the steeliest characters could grow overwrought at the prospect of a visit from Her Majesty.

'Daphne is in a bit of a tizzy about it all,' writes Boy Browning, the veteran courtier,* recently retired, of the looming visit by the Queen and Prince Philip to Menabilly, the home he shares with his wife, the novelist Daphne du Maurier. The Royal Yacht is due to dock at Fowey, in Cornwall, and then the Royal couple will be driven to Menabilly for afternoon tea.

Daphne is one of those monarchists who prefers to admire from a distance; she dreads being in the presence of royalty, with all its attendant alterations and embellishments. She hated every minute of the week she was obliged to spend at Balmoral, back in September 1953. 'It was very desperately wain [embarrassing] ... I felt as if I were sitting on the edge of a chair all the time, not sure what I should do, and even though the present royals are young, one can't help remembering their august rank all the time and being nervous about it.'

She enjoyed being out in the fresh air, walking on the Highland moors, but the prospect of the evenings 'in full regalia' would always loom over her. When she had finally completed her week at Balmoral, she felt exhausted. 'Went home and collapsed, feeling deathly tired ... such a relief to be home and not bobbing up and down to royals.'

---

* Lieutenant General Sir Frederick Arthur Montague 'Boy' Browning, GCVO, KBE, CB, DSO (1896–1965), Comptroller and Treasurer to HRH Princess Elizabeth 1948–52; Treasurer to the Duke of Edinburgh 1952–9.

And now, in July 1962, she is going to have to go through the whole rigmarole again, in her role as Lady Browning. Theirs is a marriage of opposites. In retirement, Boy Browning is crotchety and cantankerous, complaining of the cold and fretting needlessly that they don't actually own their home and have 'no legal right to breathe here'. But the prospect of the Royal visit puts a spring in his step. A highly decorated veteran of both world wars,* he plans it like a military operation. Daphne, on the other hand, is filled with apprehension. 'It is the Doom of all time ... It means a commotion, and all her entourage, and policemen and chauffeurs – how *shall* we manage? It has ruined my summer!'

The coming invasion calls to mind her creepy 1952 short story 'The Birds', which, by an eerie coincidence, Alfred Hitchcock has just finished filming in California. She writes to Buckingham Palace to ask whether, on a point of etiquette, she should wear a hat and/or gloves for the occasion. (Perhaps she is overdoing her fretfulness, simply to spite her husband.) A lady in waiting replies that, since it is tea in her own house, neither is required. With one worry out of the way, she is soon on to the next: in general, Daphne favours trousers, and owns only three dresses, none of which now fit her. And what of the general state of the house? She is no housewife, and fears that years of neglect have made the house too sordid for a Royal visit. Mr Burt, their 81-year-old gardener, gets to work, washing down the mantelpiece in the Long Room with Jeyes Fluid. Esther Rowe, her housekeeper, insists that the whole house be 'scrubbed and better scrubbed', regardless of the fact that the Queen will only be entering a single room. And what if Her Majesty needs to spend a penny? Daphne tactfully removes the lewd Cruikshank prints of the Queen's great-great-uncle Prince Frederick, Duke of York† romping with Daphne's great-great-grandmother, Mary Anne Clarke.‡ She also runs around filling twenty-six vases with flowers, before declaring that she is utterly exhausted and can do no more.

---

* He was sometimes called 'the father of the airborne forces'.

† Son of King George III, and subject of the nursery rhyme 'The Grand Old Duke of York'.

‡ And heroine of du Maurier's novel *Mary Anne*.

"It could be the most terrifying motion picture I have ever made!"— *Alfred Hitchcock*

NOTHING YOU HAVE EVER WITNESSED BEFORE HAS PREPARED YOU FOR SUCH SHEER STABBING SHOCK!

ALFRED HITCHCOCK'S "The Birds"

TECHNICOLOR®

Based on Daphne Du Maurier's classic suspense story!

ROD TAYLOR · JESSICA TANDY · SUZANNE PLESHETTE *and introducing* 'TIPPI' HEDREN

Screenplay by EVAN HUNTER · Directed by ALFRED HITCHCOCK

A Fascinating New Personality

But when the big day comes she rises to the occasion. She finds the sight of the Rolls-Royce with its Royal Standard driving slowly up to their front door 'rather splendid', and thinks the young Queen perched inside looks 'stunning'. The hour and a half they spend entertaining her seems to pass in a flash. Afternoon tea is served for fourteen, though sadly the Queen herself is 'not much interested in the enormous spread I had prepared'. The only mishap comes when the 80-year-old Lord Lieutenant of Cornwall, Sir Edward Bolitho, spills his tea, but he comforts himself by making short work of the Cornish splits, thickly spread with jam and clotted cream.

55

There was a hitch in the arrangements about the car in which the Queen and the Duke should drive. Corsican officials found a car they considered splendid enough for the occasion. Then they discovered that the car's owner had been divorced. It was thought that the Queen might be embarrassed over that.

Sunday Express, 1961

At a two roomed cottage near Glamis Castle, a white-haired mother spoke proudly yesterday of a little service she had been able to give the Royal Family. She revealed that 34 years ago she agreed to her baby son taking the birth registration number of 13 so that it should not go to Princess Margaret.

Sunday Express, 1964

A copy of the photograph of bare-chested Prince Charles, taken in his swimming-trunks on Bondi beach, Australia, should be displayed in every British embassy, bank and tourist office overseas, so that the world can see what robust, healthy young men this country breeds today. A future king, alert-looking and stripped to the waist for action, is the sort of go-ahead image that Britain needs abroad.

Letter to the *People* newspaper, 1966

At Grantham, Lincs, tarmac will be laid 120 yards down an unmade road to give the Queen Mother a smooth drive when she opens an old folks' home on Wednesday. Afterwards the £300 surface will be ripped up.

Sunday Mirror, 1967

Prince Charles, aged 18, passed his driving test first bash yesterday. He went through the 45-minute exam at Isleworth, Middlesex, in a special car with a special examiner over a special route. Apart from that it was quite normal.

Daily Sketch, 1967

Did you see the pictures of the Queen travelling on the London Underground? Was it not rather sad that this was her first such journey for 30 years? It shows how much the Royal Family has to sacrifice for duty.

Letter to the *Sunday Express,* 1969

56

The Queen was always alert to any attempt to marginalise the monarchy. In the cold war between republicans and monarchists, she possessed a fierce instinct for survival. 'The thing you must realise about the Royal Family is that they live in a constant state of fear,' someone close to them told me as I was writing this book. In his memoir *Spare*, Prince Harry suggests that the life of the Royal Family is defined by paranoia: 'Fear of the public. Fear of the future. Fear of the day the nation would say: OK shut it down.'

The Queen's contemporary Tony Benn, just a year her senior, was from the radical wing of the Labour Party. To him, the monarchy was fuddy-duddy, and out of place in a modern, forward-looking egalitarian society.

In May 1963, he visited Oxford to deliver an address to the University Labour Club. Most of it was a rehash of a paper on the Labour Party's Election Strategy he had written for the new party leader, Harold Wilson, but he added a few ideas of his own into the mix.

'I added a section on the first things a new Labour Government should do,' Benn recorded in his diary straight after delivering the speech. 'Among these were some "mood changing measures" – like no dinner jackets for Labour Ministers at Buckingham Palace, mini-cars for official business and postage stamps without the Queen's head on them.' Of these three new measures, two concerned the Queen. The last of them was, he reckoned, 'the most popular thing in the speech. Republicanism is on the increase.'

The following year, Labour won the general election and Wilson appointed Benn his new postmaster general. In October 1964, he was sworn in as a privy counsellor. Also present at the ceremony, and equally outraged by its absurdity, was the new minister of housing and local government, Richard Crossman, who thought it a nonsense. 'I don't suppose anything more dull, pretentious or plain silly has ever been invented. There we were, sixteen grown men. For over an hour we were taught how to stand up, how to kneel on one knee on a cushion, how to raise the right hand with the Bible in it, how to advance three paces towards the Queen, how to take the hand and kiss it, how to move back ten paces without falling over the stools – which had been carefully arranged so that you did fall over them. Oh, dear! We did this from 11.10 to 12.15. At 12.15 all of us went out, each to his own car, and we drove to the Palace and there stood about until we entered a great drawing-room. At the other end there was this little woman with a beautiful waist, and she had to stand with her hand on the table for forty minutes while we went through this rigmarole.'

Like many British intellectuals, Crossman strove to distance himself from the monarchy, while simultaneously finding it hard to resist its pull. 'It is the most idiotic flummery,' he confessed to his diary after a meeting of the Privy Council the following year, 'and I must admit that I feel morally superior to my colleagues in despising it … I know my attitude is partly a piece of conscious arrogance – I want to prove to myself that I don't like these things, although I sometimes find myself mildly enjoying them and I even slightly resent myself for refusing ever to attend them.'*

Benn, too, found the rehearsal 'terribly degrading as we were told that we had to kneel on a footstool before the Queen and assent to the Privy Council oath which had a real Mau-Mau quality. Charlie <Pannell> and I chattered during the rehearsal and tried to look as if

---

* Crossman's opposition softened with the years. In a parliamentary debate in 1971, he argued in favour of monarchy 'not because the Monarch is the wealthiest woman in the country but because of the frailty of human nature. We are not all rational. If we were all rational we would all like an elected president. Because we are not rational but emotional creatures, it is good for us to have something we can look up to, to admire and respect, and it is safer to have it impotent.'

we were not taking it too seriously. I'm afraid the officials were profoundly shocked. I made no attempt to conceal my feelings.'

As he was being led into the drawing room by an officer in breeches, spurs, a sword and full Court Dress, Benn took the opportunity to ask the new lord president of the Council whether he really had to go through with the ceremony, 'as I did find the terms of the oath so degrading and distasteful'.

But he conquered his distaste, and was delivered into the Queen's presence. After shaking her hand, he stood in a row with all the other new privy counsellors. 'We then went up to the Queen one after another, kneeling and picking up her hand and kissing it, and then bowing. I did the most miniature bow ever seen and returned to my line.'

Benn left the Palace in a fury, 'boiling with indignation and feeling that this was an attempt to impose tribal magic and personal loyalty on people whose real duty was only to their electors'.*

Postmaster general was a relatively modest post, less grand than its title suggests, but it gave Benn the chance to pursue a covert crusade against the monarchy, an institution he regarded as incompatible with a forward-looking nation. He developed a radical new plan to advance a 'new Britain ... forged in the white-hot heat of technology', a vision his leader, Harold Wilson, had espoused in opposition. Though the monarch's head had been on every stamp since the introduction of the Penny Black in 1840, he was determined to have it removed. Written in earnest, his diaries from this period nevertheless contain all the plottings and pratfalls of an Ealing comedy.

---

* At the other end of the political spectrum, the maverick right-wing Conservative MP Alan Clark felt a similar distaste at his induction into the Privy Council in February 1991. Guided by 'two Palace functionaries – handsome, nicely dressed, middle-aged; both of them with that shallow courtesy, smooth complexion and careful coiffure of the Establishment homosexual', he underwent the ceremony, after which the Queen 'got up from her chair and moved over, *regally*, to initiate a painfully, grotesquely, banal conversation ... Not for the first time I wondered about the Queen. Is she really rather dull and stupid? Or is she thinking, "How do people as dull and stupid as this ever get to be Ministers?" Or is, for her, the whole thing so stale and *déjà vu* after forty years that she'd really rather be going round the stables at Highclere, patting racehorses on the nose?'

On 13 January 1965, Benn ordered his civil servants to submit his revolutionary new proposal to the Stamp Advisory Committee. 'I sold it to them on design grounds – that it would widen the designer's freedom of action.' But the following month, he discovered that his civil servants had failed to submit his proposal for the headless stamp to the Committee. This struck him as a deliberate veto. 'They were just not prepared to do what I told them to do,' he grumbled. He sensed a conspiracy at play. If so, how high up did it go? At every turn, Benn's scheming came to nothing. However stealthily he placed his banana skin on the floor, he was always the one who slipped on it.

On 10 March, he arrived at the Palace with his brand-new stamp designs in a huge black box. Not a single one of them featured the Queen's head. He planned to let the Queen down gently, so began by beating around the bush, going on about how he wanted these stamps to be seen 'in an entirely new context as part of the arts and not just adhesive money labels for postage purposes'. British stamp designers were, he told her, keen to celebrate British composers, landscapes, painters and so forth. '"However," I said, "this raises the whole question of the use of the head on the stamps."' Whereupon 'The Queen frowned and smiled.'

They were both exceptionally polite people: it may have been the only thing they had in common. But politeness goes hand in hand with inscrutability. Confronted by his sovereign's mixed facial messages, Benn bit the bullet. Had she personally overruled the idea of stamps without her head on them? 'The Queen was clearly embarrassed and indicated that she had no personal feeling about them at all. I said I knew she wouldn't and that I knew it was all a misunderstanding.'

Each of them – the monarch and her anti-monarchist postmaster general – was trying to outsmart the other. But who would emerge victorious?

Seizing the initiative, Benn whisked out his new stamp designs, knelt on the floor and laid them out in front of the Queen 'with all the charm I could muster'. Half an hour later, he emerged from the Palace confident that he had won. 'I went back to the House of Commons feeling absolutely on top of the world.' It had been, he told his diary, 'the best day since I took office with almost complete victory on the whole front'.

By the end of his month, he was having intimations that things were not going quite as smoothly as expected. Sir Kenneth Clark, the chairman of the Stamp Advisory Committee, expressed surprise that the Queen had capitulated, adding that, when he was first appointed to the Committee as a young man, the Queen's grandfather, King George V, had told him, 'Never let the sovereign's head come off the stamps', and he had promised that he would not.

'At this stage I expected that he would announce his resignation,' recalled Benn. Instead, Clark suggested that if the sovereign's head remained on regular stamps then the Palace might agree to remove them from commemorative stamps.

Turning the pages of his newspaper on the morning of Saturday, 12 June 1965, Benn read that the Beatles were to be awarded MBEs. He was appalled. This was yet another blow to the republican cause. 'No doubt Harold did this to be popular and I expect it *was* popular – though it may have been unpopular with some people too. The *Daily Mirror*'s headline was "Now They've Got into the Topmost Chart of All". But the plain truth is that the Beatles have done more for the royal family by accepting MBEs than the royal family have done for the Beatles by giving them. Nobody goes to see the Beatles because they've got MBEs but the royal family love the idea that the honours list is popular because it all helps to buttress them and indirectly their influence is used to strengthen all the forces of conservatism in society. I think Harold Wilson makes the most appalling mistake if he thinks that in this way he can buy popularity, for he is ultimately bolstering a force that is an enemy of his political stand.'

This setback served only to fuel Benn's republican verve. His next move was to send Buckingham Palace more designs for headless stamps. Craftily, he picked the Battle of Britain commemorative issues to showcase the headless designs, calculating that this would make objections a good deal more tricky. But, once again, his cunning plan came to nothing: the Queen's private secretary responded by saying that the Queen was 'not too happy' and had rejected them.

To get his own back, Benn gave the go-ahead to their inclusion in a new Post Office exhibition beneath a sign saying 'UNACCEPTED'. 'The real value of this exhibition ... was to get the press – both national and philatelic – accustomed to the idea that very good stamps could be designed without the Queen's head,' he noted.

Throughout that summer, Benn continued his crablike manoeuvres. But by now the Queen had mustered new allies. In October, Benn opened a letter from the prime minister's principal private secretary, stating that, under certain circumstances, the Queen might 'reject the advice of her Ministers'. The letter forbade him to commission any headless stamps or to show any more headless-stamp designs to the press without the prime minister's express permission.

'It looks as if my new stamp policy has been torpedoed,' he reflected. He suspected that the Queen's private secretary, Sir Michael Adeane, had conveyed Her Majesty's displeasure to the prime minister's private secretary, 'who has decided to frighten me off by conveying it to me ... This is exactly how the Palace works. It doesn't want to appear unpopular, yet at the same time it does not want certain things to happen and it uses the threat of controversy to stop any changes from going too far.' Unseen forces were at work. 'Whether or not the Queen cares personally about it, Adeane and all the flunkeys at Buckingham Palace certainly do. Their whole position depends upon maintaining this type of claptrap.'

Benn refused to accept defeat. In November 1965, he took his box of headless stamps directly to Harold Wilson, bypassing the prime minister's watchful private secretary, Derek Mitchell. 'I thought he was a little uneasy to begin with and this was no doubt because Mitchell had told him I was being difficult.' He showed him a selection, and Harold Wilson seemed 'absolutely captivated by them', particularly those involving old railway trains, for which he had a lifelong passion.*

---

* At Oxford University, Wilson had written his thesis on the early days of the railways. In 2012, at the age of 58, his son Giles abandoned his career as a maths teacher to fulfil his childhood ambition of becoming a train driver. He began by driving trains from Waterloo to Guildford and Dorking.

But, all of a sudden, Wilson's tone changed. He said he had spoken to the Queen, and she had made it quite clear that she didn't want her head removed. 'She is a nice woman and you absolutely charmed her into saying yes when she didn't really mean it.'

Benn was nonplussed, seeing it as a betrayal: 'I suspect that Harold more or less invited her to say no.' At this point, Wilson's fiery political secretary Marcia Williams strode in, furious that the Queen should have won the argument. 'She burst out and said that it was a scandal that in modern England the Queen should have any say about anything at all, and why did she choose the stamps, what had it to do with her and couldn't Ministers reach their own decisions.'

Later that day, Harold Wilson returned from his weekly audience with the Queen. 'We spent ten minutes on Rhodesia,' he told Benn, 'and an hour and five minutes on stamps.' Her Majesty, he added, might well be prepared to accept her silhouette in the corner, but 'her head has to appear on everything'.

Benn had been outflanked by the Queen, and he knew it. On New Year's Eve 1965, he reflected on his defeat. 'I think I must put my vendetta with the Palace into cold storage. Whatever my views may be, it is clear that Harold's intentions are that we should be more royal than the Tory Party and he finds the Queen a very useful tool. This may give him a certain short-term advantage and he is exploiting it as hard as he can. I doubt whether he is so foolish as to be taken in by smiles from the Queen and the flunkeys at Buckingham Palace and for that I am grateful. But I am sure that in the long run his attitude simply strengthens the reactionary elements in our society and cannot help those who want to make change. It is obvious that I shall have to abandon my hopes of getting the Queen's head off the stamps.'

Six months later Wilson promoted him to minister of technology. On his visit to the Palace to be sworn in, the Queen appeared quietly triumphant. As they shook hands, she said: 'I'm sure you'll miss your stamps.'

'Yes, indeed I shall,' he replied, 'but I shall never forget your kindness and encouragement.' He noticed that, in response, the Queen gave him 'a rather puzzled smile and I bowed and went out backwards'.

Three days later, he heard that the director general of the Post Office was 'almost delirious with excitement' at his departure, and that his successor as postmaster general had assured the Queen that her head would remain firmly in place. 'This was so depressing,' he reflected. 'I really couldn't bear it.'

In his new role, Benn accompanied the Queen to the opening of the new Post Office Tower in central London the following year. His head was still abuzz with radical new ideas for modernisation. Showing her around the state-of-the-art revolving restaurant at the top, he suggested it would be perfect for state banquets: she could sit in the stationary central part of the Tower, while her guests rotated, giving everyone a

chance to exchange a few words with the Queen every twenty minutes or so.

Decades later, when they were both old and grey, a courtier suggested to the Queen that she might invite Mr Benn to Buckingham Palace, along with a handful of other elder statesmen.

Her response was instant and unequivocal.

'No,' she replied. 'He doesn't like us.'

57

In the middle of the eleventh century, a woman afflicted with sores was taken to the bathroom of King Edward the Confessor. The foremost historian of the period, William of Malmesbury, takes up the story:

> The pious king, dipping his hands into the water and stroking her neck, soon restored her to a happy state of health; the tumours that were filled with worms and corrupt blood bursting and disappearing. But as the sores left wide and disgusting cavities, he ordered her to be supported at the Crown's expense till perfectly cured. Before the seventh morning a beautiful new skin appeared, so that no vestige of the disease could be perceived. A year afterwards, she had twins, which added greatly to the sanctity of Edward.

Belief in the healing power of the monarch was still going strong 600 years later. Even after King Charles I's defeat in the civil war, sick people continued to flock to him in such numbers that the republican Parliament felt it necessary to condemn 'the Superstition of being Touched for the Healing of the King's Evil'.

After the King's beheading in January 1649, handkerchiefs said to have been dipped in his blood were much in demand among the infirm. Eleven years later, with the restoration of the monarchy, his son King Charles II revived the ceremony of the Royal Touch: between May and September of 1660, no fewer than 23,000 sick people queued to be touched by the new King.

'Kings are justly called Gods,' his grandfather, King James I, had once declared, 'because they exercise a manner of resemblance to

Divine power on earth.' This notion was generally taken as a given, even by the foremost scientists of the day: the eminent chemist Robert Boyle (1627–91) was firm in his belief that the Royal Touch was a cure for scrofula. Jeremy Collier (1650–1726), author of the *Ecclesiastical History of Great Britain*, wouldn't hear a word against the healing power of the Royal Touch. 'To dispute the matter of fact is to go to the excesses of scepticism, to deny our senses, and be incredulous even to ridiculousness.'

Like tales of the infant Jesus, narrators of Queen Elizabeth II's childhood portray her as either divinely normal or divinely perfect or quite often both at the same time. Captain Eric Acland, author of *The Princess Elizabeth: Probable Future Ruler of the Greatest Empire in the World*, published in 1937, shortly before her eleventh birthday, presents the little Princess as blessed in thought, word and deed. When her grandfather falls ill in March 1929, she dutifully tends to him, though she is not yet three years old:

> 'I made Grandpa all well, Mummy,' the Princess later told the
> Duchess, and the great doctors were not at all certain that she was not
> right.

In Acland's telling, little Elizabeth is almost divinely gifted. Before her fourth birthday, she resolves to learn the alphabet, ready to recite it to her admiring family. She surpasses herself:

> Not only did the little Princess say the alphabet, but she sang it.

Small wonder, then, that:

> The people of England loved The Princess Elizabeth very dearly. They
> loved her ... because she was such a good, kind little girl.

By the time she was 10 years old, Elizabeth appears to have developed a precocious theological expertise, rather like Jesus in the Temple. An oft-repeated story has it that when a preacher – in some versions, the archbishop of Canterbury – was leaving Glamis Castle – or possibly Buckingham Palace – he promised to send the little Princess a book. She thanked him graciously, but asked him if it could be 'Not about God. I already know everything about him.'

After her uncle's abdication in 1936, Princess Elizabeth received quantities of letters from children in disaster areas, among them Chinese orphans fleeing from the Japanese. Around the world, many credited the little Princess with semi-miraculous powers. And many continued to do so, right up to her death, and possibly beyond it. 'I have a theory', wrote the actress Joanna Lumley in 2021, 'that the abdication of King Edward VIII was like a lightning bolt that struck the young Princess Elizabeth. It ought to have burned her up, but instead, like lightning striking sand and turning it into glass, it transformed her into a fabulous new and different being.'

In many memoirs, otherwise humdrum meetings with the Queen are lit by flashes of divine intervention. In 1983, the Queen returned to Treetops in Kenya, where she had been staying when her father died and she became Queen. In his memoir, the assistant hunter R. J. Prickett recalls showing her around the site, surrounded by warthogs, bushbuck and baboons. Suddenly, he became aware of an old bull buffalo called, aptly enough, Satan, glowering at the Royal party and refusing to move.

Arriving at the old site of Treetops, Prickett saw that Satan had reappeared, and was now just fifty yards away:

> Queen and buffalo stared at each other for a long, long minute. And then a strange thing happened. Satan, who had been resolutely staring at the Queen, suddenly started walking towards us, and just as I was beginning nervously to grip the rifle, he stopped at what was now little more than twenty paces away. Then an even more wondrous thing happened. He started to kneel down facing Her Majesty, with hind-quarters high in the air, and I remember muttering, with suspended breath, 'He's going to lie down.' The next moment he threw himself sideways, still facing us. I know that buffalo always lie that way, but to me that kneeling down was an act of supplication to the

Queen, and maybe his apology for being so rude as to keep her waiting on the salt-lick.

Like all her predecessors since King Henry VIII, the Queen was the Supreme Governor of the Church of England. On the matter of who had chosen her, the Book of Common Prayer was unequivocal:

ALMIGHTY GOD, Whose kingdom is everlasting, and power infinite: Have mercy upon the whole Church, and so rule the heart of thy chosen servant ELIZABETH our Queen and Governor ...

And so, too, was her Poet Laureate, John Masefield, whose poem for her Coronation, 'A Prayer for a Beginning Reign', celebrated her appointment by the Almighty:

Therefore, to THEE, All-glorious, let us pray
For Her, THY Destined, consecrate today
We, then, beseech THEE, Everlasting Power
That This, THY dedicated Soul, may reign
In peace, in wisdom, for her mortal hour
In this beloved Land.

Throughout her life, Princess Margaret remained adamant that her sister had been divinely appointed. 'She is God's representative in this realm,' she insisted to the author A. N. Wilson. Her view was shared by a sizeable minority of her generation. In 1956, some 34 per cent of those questioned believed that the Queen had been chosen by God. Seven years later, the figure had dropped, though only by a fraction, to 30 per cent.

A recent archbishop of Canterbury concurred in this belief. 'While governments come and go, the sovereign remains and holds all in place, not by power – she has none – but as a symbol,' wrote George Carey in a chapter of his autobiography titled 'The Glory of the Crown': 'She is placed there by Almighty God, and held there by the affection and loyalty of her people.'

It can be hard for those with only a vague attachment to the monarchy and/or the Church of England to believe that their otherwise modest and level-headed Queen was earnest in her belief that she had been appointed by God. But she was. 'That God had called her from birth to fulfil her responsibilities as Sovereign was very evidently her conviction, and it was founded on a firm Christian faith ...' says Carey.

Other archbishops of Canterbury have been less convinced of her divine calling. Michael Ramsey* once fell into what he described, in his wry, understated way, as 'quite an argument' with the Queen Mother on the issue. She had referred, in passing, to her daughter as 'head of the Church'. Ramsey considered it his duty to contradict her: 'supreme governor' did not mean the same as 'head'. Conducting a service at St Paul's Cathedral, he was overheard muttering, 'God first', before bowing first to the altar and only then to the Queen.

---

* Archbishop of Canterbury from 1961 to 1974.

58

'Why perpetuate the archaic institution of Poet Laureate?' wrote Anthony Curtis in the *Sunday Telegraph* in May 1967. 'Isn't the death of John Masefield the moment to terminate what has become a charming absurdity? After all, even two days after his death no one is going to pretend that those four and six line verses that he used to contribute so punctiliously on important Royal and State occasions represent a side of his work in which posterity is likely to be the least bit interested.'

Masefield had been Poet Laureate since his appointment by King George V in 1930, the longest tenure since Alfred, Lord Tennyson. His laureateship had seen the deaths of King George V and King George VI, the abdication of King Edward VIII, the Coronation of Queen Elizabeth II and the births of all her four children.

He had been such a conscientious Laureate that the Queen Mother almost considered him part of the Household. 'What a wonderful list of English poets you have collected – and even if a few fall out, it will still be a marvellous gathering,' she wrote to Osbert Sitwell in 1943, after he had sent her plans for a Poetry Reading. 'What about the Poet Laureate? Don't you think he ought to come & read a verse or two of welcome to me, written of course especially for the occasion!'

But Masefield's efforts, though earnest, did not always meet with triumph. Like many Laureates, he found that the demands to create something suitably majestic drove him to sacrifice meaning to rhyme, and to employ the archaic, back-to-front syntax so beloved of commentators. To celebrate the birth of Prince Charles in 1948, he wrote:

May destiny, allotting what befalls
Grant to the newly-born this saving grace
A Guard more sure than ships and fortress-walls
The loyal love and service of a race.

At the start of 1952, he composed two Royal poems in quick succession: the first, 'On the Setting Forth of their Royal Highnesses Princess Elizabeth and the Duke of Edinburgh', issued on 31 January, ended with the lines:

May all the weathers of your way be fair;
And safe returning crown your journey done.

Six days later, King George VI died in his sleep. John Betjeman seemed to be the popular choice to succeed him as the next Laureate, though there were those who disagreed. The prime minister's secretary for appointments, John Hewitt, received many applications from random members of the public. The beat poet Allen Ginsberg wrote to him advancing the claims of Donovan, the hippy singer-songwriter.*

Others weighed in, too. Lord Goodman, chairman of the Arts Council and portly embodiment of the new Sixties Establishment, was determined that Betjeman should not be given the job. 'The songster of tennis lawns and cathedral cloisters does not, it seems to me, make a very suitable incumbent for the poet laureateship of a new and vital world in which we hope we are living,' he wrote to Hewitt. 'An aroma of lavender and faint musk is really not right for an appointment of this kind at this moment. It is much too nostalgic and backward looking.'

Should the Laureate be backward-looking or forward-looking? Should he – or she – embrace tradition, or trumpet modernity? This was the dilemma confronting not only the Laureate but also the

---

* Born Donovan Leitch in 1946, best known for his hits 'Catch the Wind', 'Sunshine Superman' and 'Mellow Yellow', and his 1967 flower-power double-album *A Gift from a Flower to a Garden*.

monarch and her court. Who to pick? If Betjeman was too cosy, others seemed too outlandish.

The chairman of the Poetry Society, Geoffrey Handley-Taylor, advised against Stevie Smith, condemning her as 'unstable' and warning, 'She sang her verses at the recent Festival Hall affair and afterwards tore her bouquet to pieces on the platform.'* He also warned that the fiery Scottish poet Hugh MacDiarmid was 'heavily on the bottle and has rejoined the Communist Party', while Edmund Blunden 'suffered from severe mental lapses and was almost unintelligible at times'. But neither was he keen on Betjeman, considering him 'rather a lightweight who called himself a poetic hack rather than a poet and there was some truth in this'.

On 2 January 1968, the prime minister, Harold Wilson, announced that the job would go to Cecil Day-Lewis.

Though a less fervent royalist than his predecessor, Day-Lewis got down to work with unusual speed. His first official poem was published in the *Daily Mail* just three days later. It made no mention of the monarchy, instead praising the 'I'm Backing Britain' campaign, launched by five typists at a factory in Surbiton. His next poem, 'Hail Teesside!', published on 1 April, also ignored the monarchy, celebrating the unification of six north-eastern towns into a single administrative region.

For reasons of his own, Prince Charles chose to overlook Day-Lewis when it came to commissioning something for his Investiture as Prince of Wales in 1969. Some time before, he had taken a shine to John Betjeman at a dinner party ('I remember thinking what fun he was, how amusing') and collared him before leaving. Betjeman recalled the moment in 'A Ballad of the Investiture 1969', which he published five years later:

---

* Stevie Smith was, however, awarded the Queen's Gold Medal for Poetry in 1969. 'The questions she asked rather kept us on the subject of poetry & I could not help feeling it wasn't absolutely her *very* favourite subject,' she told a friend.

Then, sir, you said what shook me through
So that my courage almost fails:
'I want a poem out of you
On my Investiture in Wales.'
Leaving, you slightly raised your hand –
'And that', you said, 'is a command.'
For years I wondered what to do
And now, at last, I've thought it better
To write a kind of rhyming letter.

The poem deals with the captive nature of royalty:

Earl Marshal leads the victims in.
The Royal Family waits alone.
Now television cameras whirr
Like cats at last induced to purr.

But it also homes in on the historic and the personal:

So we who watch the action done –
A mother to her kneeling son
The Crown of office giving –
Can hardly tell, so rapt our gaze
Whether but seconds pass or days
Or in what age we're living.

You knelt a boy, you rose a man.
And thus your lonelier life began.

But Day-Lewis produced a rousing poem of his own, 'For the Investiture', which was printed in the *Guardian*, alongside a Welsh translation provided by the archdruid of Wales:

May your integrity silence each tongue
That sneers or flatters. May this hour
Reach through its pageantry to the deep reservoir
Whence Britain's heart draws all that is fresh and young.
Over the tuneful land prevails.
One song, one prayer – God Bless the Prince of Wales.

After the death of Day-Lewis in 1972, the names of various poets were bandied about. W. H. Auden attracted much support, though the possibility of his laureateship appalled some of the more reactionary elements. Ross McWhirter, the reactionary co-founder of the *Guinness Book of Records*, warned the Lord Chamberlain of an obscene poem of which Auden was said to be the anonymous author. 'The Platonic Blow', known by some as 'The Gobble Poem', had recently been published in an underground magazine called *Suck*. A celebration of oral sex, it included a fanciful description of the penis as 'a royal column, ineffably solemn and wise'. Might it not embarrass Her Majesty? 'My problem', wrote McWhirter,

> is simply that should this candidate be appointed either in ignorance
> of this or without his first being given a chance to disprove
> authorship, then the subversive underground press are almost certain
> to republish this pornographic 'poem' under the byline 'by the Poet
> Laureate' to the enormous potential embarrassment of Her Majesty's
> Household and of decent-minded citizens.*

He added that he could not 'legally send the offending matter' by post, but was prepared to bring it in person. He was, he said, acting out of 'simple duty'.

The Lord Chamberlain replied that the Poet Laureate was appointed by the monarch on the advice of the prime minister, so McWhirter should contact Sir John Hewitt at Downing Street. When Hewitt came to read the poem, he did so with ever-increasing horror, before

---

* It is now thought that Auden was, indeed, the author.

composing a confidential memo stating that it 'ran to about 30 verses of an utterly revolting character'.

Though Auden himself called the possibility of his appointment 'a load of bosh' which made him 'very cross indeed', he seems to have toyed with the idea, only deciding against it after the death of the Duke of Windsor, just six days later. 'When the Duke died, I thought about what I would write if I had been Poet Laureate. It would have been a difficult task; and my sympathy would have gone out to anyone asked to undertake it … I have no desire for it.' Perhaps to ensure an invitation would not be forthcoming, he added that 'there should be a clear understanding that the Poet Laureate could write on controversial issues, as well as the traditional ones'. Had he been asked to write on the Investiture of the Prince of Wales, he would, he said, have opted to compose 'a poem of thanks' that 'the Prince's unnerving moment when his feet caught in the rigging of his parachute while he was making a jump did not end in disaster'. This, he added, 'would have been much more fun to write'.*

With his eye on the prize, the veteran Forest of Dean poet Leonard Clark wrote a series of letters to Downing Street pointing out the unsuitability of all the other contenders. Vernon Scannell was, he said, 'a charming drunk' who 'could not possibly hold the job down', Philip Larkin 'a shy man [who] might not wear the crown well', and George Barker had 'lived a rather wild life' and 'written too much pornography'. Though Ted Hughes was 'an outstanding poet' he 'is not a well-organised man … It is important to appoint a sound traditional figure and not one of the younger lunatics.'

Other poets, already outsiders, effectively ruled themselves out by parading their radical credentials. 'If I had to write about a public event, I would want to write about the bombing of Hai Phong, which would not be very suitable,' said Stephen Spender.

---

* Had he wished to rule himself out entirely, Auden could have repeated in public a remark he had made in a private conversation in February 1947: 'If that horror Elizabeth marries a commoner, he'll only be prince consort. Why doesn't the United States take over the monarchy and unite with England? England does have important assets. Naturally the longer you wait, the more they will dwindle. At least, you could use it for a summer resort instead of Maine.'

'If Mr Heath is wise enough to offer the post to me, I am crazy enough to accept it,' suggested Adrian Mitchell. 'But I would rather be Ambassador to Chile.' Nor did he advance his cause with his observation that 'Royalty is a neurosis.'

Unbeknown to either of these two poets, they had already been ruled out. 'As you will remember he is the person who put on a vulgar display at Southwark Cathedral when you were there,' Hewitt wrote of Mitchell to the prime minister. The Oxford professor Jon Stallworthy, himself a poet, advised Downing Street that Stephen Spender's reputation 'had not survived the 30s when he was known as one of Auden's lesser satellites'.

In a further note to the prime minister, Hewitt wrote: 'If you are prepared to ignore the younger way-outers like Adrian Mitchell, the down-and-outers like George Barker, the old mandarins of poetry like Sacheverell Sitwell, the poets who live in a twilight world like poor David Gascoyne* and the hard drinkers like Vernon Scannell, the remaining list is stolid but not unimpressive.' John Betjeman was, he cautiously suggested, 'by no means the most eminent English poet, although he may be the best candidate ... at this stage'.

In the event, the prime minister wrote to John Betjeman in early October to say that he was recommending the Queen to appoint him Poet Laureate. On 9 October, his secretary phoned Betjeman in Cornwall to say his appointment had been confirmed. 'I don't think I am very good,' Betjeman told *The Times*, 'and if I thought I was any good I wouldn't be any good.' To a reporter from the *Guardian*, he said that he would write only when moved, and would otherwise 'remain a silent thrush', adding, 'Isn't that a beautiful remark? I just made it up.'

---

* David Gascoyne (1916–2001) was an English surrealist poet, and friend of Salvador Dalí and Max Ernst. In 1969, he became convinced of an imminent apocalypse, which led him to head for Buckingham Palace early in the morning of 29 May, in order to tell the Queen of the plot for world domination by the Scientologists. Outside the Palace gates he was apprehended. 'I immediately found myself in conflict with the earthly powers in the person of a young guardsman.' After a brief struggle, he was placed in a cell, before being driven to the Horton Psychiatric Hospital in Epsom.

He received nearly 6,000 letters congratulating him on his appointment, evidence of his extraordinary popularity. But, as time went by, Betjeman's royal muse was increasingly absent. He was always prone to depression, and the burden of laureateship made him physically ill. 'He was in a really bad state at Christmas, worse than I have ever known him ...' his wife Penelope wrote in a friendly letter to his long-standing companion Lady Elizabeth Cavendish. 'I never thought it would really help his condition to become Poet Laureate: twenty years ago, yes, had Masefield died sooner, but now that he has reached the age of retirement it means that he can NEVER retire and relax completely, but must always have this yoke about his neck. And the correspondence it has involved him in has been enough to finish off anybody.'

Betjeman's daughter Candida felt that, apart from the annual present of wine and the token stipend of £250, 'the job brought nothing but extra work and an enormous feeling that something was expected of him which he couldn't produce. He was utterly uninspired by pomp and circumstance ...'

The first Royal event he was obliged to celebrate lacked any obvious poetry: the marriage of HRH Princess Anne to Captain Mark Phillips in 1973. 'For him, it was like getting blood out of a stone,' recalled Candida.

'I don't think I ever ought to have been made Poet Laureate. I read like a rhyming Marie Corelli,' Betjeman wrote in June 1974 to the prime minister's wife, Mary Wilson, herself a poet, who was now back in Downing Street after the re-election of her husband Harold. He told Philip Larkin that he wanted to give it up. Meanwhile, his doctor became so concerned that he contacted the Keeper of the Privy Purse, a former patient, imploring him to ask the Queen to offer Betjeman comfort. The Queen obliged, telling Betjeman that he really mustn't feel duty-bound to write a poem for every Royal occasion. But Betjeman thought the public expected it of him, and he was always eager to please.

Eventually, he sent his poem for the forthcoming Royal Wedding to the Queen's private secretary, Patrick Plunkett, telling him that 'the lines were composed last night on the Pullman from Manchester to London after four double Scotches slowly consumed … Perhaps in the cold light of tomorrow they will seem unworthy … I have kept horses out of them and I would like to think they are not too much like a Christmas card verse.'

Hundreds of birds in the air
And millions of leaves on the pavement,
And Westminster bells ringing on
To palace and people outside –
And all for the words 'I will'
To love's most willing enslavement.
All of our people rejoice
With venturous bridegroom and bride.

Trumpets blare at the entrance,
Multitudes crane and sway.
Glow, white lily in London,
You are high in our hearts today!

This was the first time Princess Anne had been compared to a lily, and would probably be the last. Betjeman was dejected by the ridicule his poem attracted. 'It was an unhappy squib,' he admitted the following year, 'but I can't think why people were so rude about it.'

59

Exactly two months after the death of Queen Elizabeth II, the Colchester auction house Reeman Dansie held its annual sale of Royal memorabilia. I thought of buying something.

Most of the advertised items were of little interest to me. Lot 34 was a Christmas card showing what the auctioneer described as a 'delightful' photograph of Princess Anne in the 1980s on the Royal Yacht *Britannia*, inscribed 'To you all from Anne'. Its estimate was a comparatively inexpensive £50–£70, so within my reach, but I still couldn't muster any enthusiasm. Other lots included handwritten Christmas cards from George VI and Queen Elizabeth signed 'With our affectionate good wishes for your happiness' (estimate: £80–£120), a 1963 signed print of the *Adoration of the Shepherds* from HM Queen Elizabeth II and HRH The Duke of Edinburgh (£100–£200), a signed 2002 Christmas card 'with twin gilt ciphers, splendid colour photograph of the Royal couple seated in an open landau, signed 'Elizabeth R 2002 Philip' (£100–£150) and a 'hand signed and inscribed 2019 Christmas card with two gilt ciphers to cover, colour photograph of the happy Royal couple driving an MG sports car on their visit to Cuba signed "Much love Charles and Camilla"' (£60–£100).

Presumably thanks to their tragic overtones, Christmas cards from Charles and Diana were expected to sell for five times the amount of those from Charles and Camilla. A 2013 card from 'TRH the Duke and Duchess of Cambridge (now TRH The Prince and Princess of Wales) with envelope' was estimated at £400–£600, suggesting that, even within such a traditional institution as the Royal Family, youth is more popular than age.

In all, about fifty of the lots consisted of Christmas cards from one branch of the Royal Family or another. Visiting the homes of well-connected friends and acquaintances, I have sometimes seen Royal Christmas cards on their mantelpieces. They are easy to spot, as they are always in pride of place, muscling all other cards out of the way. Where a Little Red Robin, a Santa or a Blessed Virgin would normally be, there's a colour photo of one Royal or another.

The auction made it clear that for the descendants of the Royal Family's more needy recipients, an old Royal Christmas card can spell cash in hand. Lot 1, for instance, was an 'extremely rare silver Royal Head chauffeur's cap badge with crowned ERII cypher, provenance: belonged to Mr Leonard Massey RVM,* who worked for Her Late Majesty for over forty years and who was her head chauffeur for many years. Sold with photograph of him driving one of The State Rolls-Royce Phantoms' (£300–£500). Lot 2 was his silver RR lapel badge and leather wallet (£50–£70).

It's hard not to feel sorry for these loyal servants of the Crown who treasure their badges of office and their brief Royal notes of thanks and praise for years on end, only to have them sold by their surviving relatives to the highest bidder when they die. Lots 40, 41, 42, 43 and 44, all estimated at between £100 and £200, consisted of collections of between ten and twelve 'handwritten notes of instruction and praise on producing wonderful meals' from HM Queen Elizabeth the Queen Mother to Her Majesty's cook Miss Irene Anthony RVM 'who worked for The Queen for 45 years'. The auctioneer stated that Lot 42 offered 'a fascinating insight into Her Majesty's liking for lobster, fish and game including a note thanking Rene for a chicken dish and signed by The Queen Mother, Princess Margaret and her two children'. A further twenty-nine lots also once belonged to Miss Irene Anthony RVM, among them 'various gifts including Scottish kilt pin with glass stones in original box supplied by J. Knowles & Co. Ballater, playing cards with crowned ER ciphers, purse lighter and decorative matchbox' (£60–£100).

---

* Royal Victorian Medal.

Other lots were less common and consequently more expensive. Lot 77 was a plaster cast, measuring 24cm, of the left hand of Diana, Princess of Wales wearing her wedding ring, 'believed to be a unique cast of Princess Diana's hand made during her lifetime with her permission and obvious co-operation and therefore of great importance and rarity ... Sold with a letter of provenance from the vendor' (£30,000–£40,000). Lot 114 was 'a very rare and fine 1950s pink satin full-length petticoat made for Her Late Majesty with very fine hand made lacework top with crowned ER ciphers to fringe'. Apparently, it was bought at a charity garden party at Euston Hall, the Suffolk seat of the Duchess of Grafton, lady of the bedchamber, who 'told the buyer that the petticoat was given to her by The Queen after she was finished with it and it had indeed belonged to and had been worn by Her Majesty' (£1,000–£1,500).

Before the auction began, I had been drawn to one of the most offbeat items of all: a memento of Princess Elizabeth's wartime service as a subaltern in the Auxiliary Territorial Service, during which she learned to drive and repair vehicles.* Lot 76, Her Late Majesty Queen Elizabeth II's 'very rare' military provisional driving licence from 1945, 'and related ephemera from her driving instructor in the ATS, the late Miss (Major) Violet Wellesley MBE'. The licence – No. B1232, issued 1 March 1945 – had been filled out in neat longhand – name 'HRH Princess Elizabeth', blue eyes, 5ft 4in high, light brown hair – and was offered with 'charming shots' of the King and Queen visiting the Princess during her time in the ATS. Major Violet Wellesley died in 1971, whereupon 'the unique archive was entrusted to her companion who in turn entrusted it to the vendor'. It was estimated at between £1,000 and £2,000. I thought I might be in with a chance.

It fast became clear that the bidding would easily outpace the auctioneer's estimates. The Christmas cards from Charles and Camilla went for £250 or more, and even the singularly drab Christmas card

---

* In 1968, she told the Labour Cabinet minister Barbara Castle that it had been her first experience of collective activity. '"One had no idea how one compared with other people," she said simply. "And of course there were a lot of mechanical things one had to master." "Did you enjoy it?" I asked. "Oh yes, enormously."'

from Princess Anne, estimated at £50–£70, went for £120. The first bundle of letters from the Queen Mother, congratulating her cook on those wonderful meals, went for £500, or over five times the lower estimate. When the auctioneer came to Lot 76, he declared that it had 'attracted a huge amount of international interest'. My heart sank. Within seconds, the price had whizzed past my self-imposed limit of £1,200 up to £4,200, £4,800, £5,600 … It finally went for £6,800.

Auctions have as odd an effect on the losers as on the winners. The moment you lose, you feel a sense of failure and emptiness, even a loss of self-esteem. You try to comfort yourself by saying, 'But what on earth would I have done with the Queen's driving licence?' After all, you couldn't hang it on a wall. If friends dropped by, you could always pull it out of a drawer and brandish it, but you could only do that once per friend, and I struggled to think of anyone I knew who would be impressed rather than scornful. Or would they have gazed back at me with a pitying look, thinking that, like so many Royal biographers before me, I had succumbed to the Royal disease? Would I soon be sending birthday greetings to Princess Charlotte? Or taking a day return to catch a glimpse of the Princess Royal as she opened a day-care centre in Aylesbury? Or writing an angry letter about Harry and Meghan in capital letters to the editor of the *Sunday Express*?

Losing one bid in an auction also makes you want to win another, even though, before the auction started, the lot in question might have seemed worthless. I found myself hastily flicking through the catalogue in search of something Royal and affordable. Aha! Lot 143: 'The Wedding of HRH Princess Anne to Captain Mark Phillips 1973, piece of Wedding Cake in box and accompanying letter and packaging', £50–£70!

Other items were still selling for way over their estimates. The Queen's petticoat went for £3,000 and even a Christmas card from William and Kate went for £1,400. On the other hand, I reckoned that there wouldn't be much call for a fifty-year-old slice of Princess Anne's wedding cake in a box, particularly as her marriage had ended in divorce and is now remembered only by obsessives. When the auctioneer arrived at Lot 143, he failed to mention any international interest, or even national interest, so I felt I was in with a chance. Bidding started at £46, so I put up my hand for £48, and then it leapt to £50, so I offered £55. My heart was beating fast. At this point, it suddenly hit me that I might be going mad. What would I be doing with a slice of Princess Anne's wedding cake, either in or out of a box? It would be strange, perhaps even perverse, to produce it at a tea party and offer it round, and heaven knows what it looked like now. Even those who might have been impressed with the Queen's driving licence would look down on me for hoarding a morsel of her daughter's stale wedding cake. So I dropped out. The bidding went to £60, then £65, before coming to an abrupt halt. 'Sold at £65!'

To be honest, I regretted it – for an extra £10, it could have been mine! To a very mild extent, I continue to regret it to this day. It would have been a splendid novelty item. At talks to promote this book, I could have produced it from my pocket with a flourish, to admiring oohs and ahhs from the audience. And – who knows? – it might have proved something of an investment, allowing my grandchildren to sell it in fifty years' time for £6,000 as an historical artefact, if the mice hadn't got to it first.

There has long been a market for Royal memorabilia. After completing the execution of King Charles I, the axeman is said to have removed an orange and a handkerchief from the King's pocket and sold them for ten shillings. Two or three years ago, a Ford Escort Ghia once owned by Princess Diana sold for over £50,000. The oddest things attract reverence. Before embarking on a performance at the Royal Festival Hall on 1 July 1999, Nina Simone took a piece of chewing gum out of her mouth and left it on the side of her piano. Twenty years later, that very piece of gum could be viewed on a marble plinth, behind bulletproof glass, at the Royal Danish Library in Copenhagen. In more gum-related auction news, the last piece of gum chewed by Alex Ferguson as manager of Manchester United sold on eBay for £390,000 in 2013.

More recently, the red-and-white 'black sheep' jersey once worn by Princess Diana was sold at auction by Sotheby's New York for $1.14 million, or fourteen times its estimate. So, at the current exchange rate, for the price of Princess Diana's jersey, I could have bought 13,615 portions of Princess Anne's wedding cake.

60

Ted Hughes travelled up to London on Wednesday, 20 November 1974, in order to be first through the door at Moss Bros in Covent Garden on the Thursday morning, ready to receive the Queen's Medal for Poetry later in the day.

He woke to very Hughes-like weather. 'Rain poured down, grates gurgled, gutters clattered, traffic sizzled & we sloshed.' It consequently took him a very long time to find a taxi.

Arriving late at Moss Bros, he was shown through to the hiring department at the back. An Irish assistant presented him with a possible a suit, and then left him to change in a cubicle. The suit proved unsatisfactory. 'Between the bottom of the waistcoat & the top of the pants, I had three inches of white shirt puffing out.'

Hughes imagined himself in front of the Queen, pulling down his trousers to cover his socks, then pulling them up to cover his waist, then pulling his waistcoat down to hide it from above. 'I thought I'll look a right hick.' He then put on his tailcoat, 'and I could see straight-off that I looked totally ridiculous. So there I stood tugging, & twisting, shrinking my legs & shortening my shoulders, when the Irishman came back.'

The assistant offered Hughes more trousers, tails and waistcoats to try on, but the first pair of trousers were too tight and the second were made from 'very thin unpleasant material'. At this point, the Irishman said, 'What's this for? Is it a wedding or something of the sort?'

'Well, as a matter of fact I'm meeting the Queen in about an hour,' replied Hughes.

Suddenly, everything changed. 'He stared at me, he shrank about six inches, his hands began to tremble, his feet got tangled in the odd pairs of pants lying about the floor. Then he tore off my jacket. "Take off those pants," he cried. "All this stuff's rubbish. Let me get you the real thing."'

He reappeared with an armful of fresh suits to try on '& fitted me up, & stroked me, & gazed at me, & picked off invisible grains of moth-dust, then he produced a silver tie, & there I was. I really looked quite presentable.'

Clad in his new morning suit, Hughes caught another taxi to the Grosvenor House Hotel, where he met the Poet Laureate, John Betjeman, who had chaired the committee that had nominated him for the award. 'He's a very sweet man and we … liked each other straight off, so we sat there drinking our drinks, getting "slightly tight" as he put it, and working up to our dash to the Palace.'

Betjeman himself was very nervous on the way there, muttering: 'It's so immense! Such a vast place! Terrifying!'

The policeman at the gate recognised Betjeman and waved them both through. They were welcomed by the deputy Keeper of the Privy Purse, and followed him up some steps along a huge red-carpeted hall, then up several staircases. 'We were overwhelmed by chandeliers, golden panels, giant paintings, lofty ceilings.' Then they were led into a small room which Hughes recognised from the Queen's Christmas message.

The Keeper of the Privy Purse ('jovial fellow') appeared and offered each of the two poets a glass of sherry. He told Hughes that the Queen had been reading his books and had discovered words that she didn't know: she wanted to ask him about them. 'Very good,' replied Hughes. The conversation turned to farming; the Keeper of the Privy Purse said he wished he'd known Hughes was a farmer, as he would have told the Queen. 'She's a great breeder of cattle and horses.'

'I'll tell her,' suggested Betjeman. They were then treated to more sherry, as the Queen's other meetings were running behind schedule.

A very tall young man in a dark blue uniform, 'covered with gold braid & gold ropes & gold tassels', arrived to escort them to their final destination.

The two poets – one short, bald and tubby, the other tall, rugged and lean – were led along a corridor which was, in Hughes's words, 'more palatial than anything I had imagined possible'. They strode past walls encrusted with paintings, and endless display cabinets 'chockfull of jewel boxes, long boxes, short boxes, fat, thin, round, heart-shaped, oval – gold, silver, ivory, studded, agate, jade – anything you can think of. Every two strides, another cabinet full on your left, another on your right, then two strides more & another pair. Everything gleaming & glittering under the chandeliers.'

Up in a lift 'like a miniature palace' – Betjeman pretended to scratch the gold of the lift and wondered if it were 24 carat – and then into a high-ceilinged room with a window looking out over the Palace gardens, 'full of gorgeous furniture, more pictures again, ornaments, every cranny crammed with richness'.

They were joined by 'a sad, tired little lady, the Queen's secretary, Countess of something or other', who informed them that the Queen was just finishing talking to the ambassador to Yemen. After a while the door opened, and a man whispered, 'The Ambassador is now leaving.'

At this point, the equerry gave them both a quick lesson in the etiquette of being presented in a pair. 'Er, I think if you go in side by side, er, and, er, pause at the door and bow, just a small bow—'

'A neck bow,' Betjeman chipped in, tucking in his chin and staring down at the carpet. He was an old hand at it.

'Then you go forward and the Queen will shake your hand. Then you'll sit and when the conversation's over she will ring a tiny bell – don't be alarmed. It simply means, it's over. I'm listening out here, & when I hear that bell, I open the door. The Queen will then say goodbye, may or may not shake your hand, & you will bow, & then turn to the door & at the door face her again and bow once more.'

'A neck bow again,' added Betjeman. They were then treated to more sherry, as the Queen's other meetings were running behind schedule.

They waited their turn in the corridor before being escorted into a large room with a grand piano. 'And there, far away across this great room, was a tiny person whom of course I recognised,' recalled Hughes. 'You know she's small, but this was like meeting Alice in Wonderland,' he told his friend, the poet Craig Raine. He then measured an inch between his finger and his thumb. 'She's *this* big.'

'Nobody else in the room at all. Just her. Then I saw Sir John seemed to have fallen asleep with his chin sunk on his chest, so hastily I sank my chin too, & we presented the Queen with the tops of our heads. Then we stepped in, & she came beaming towards us, & the door closed behind us, as we were alone with the Queen.'

For Hughes, 'she was a complete surprise. I'd imagined her rather tall, rather solemn, rather slow, rather aloof. Not at all. She was tiny ... She had a very lively expression, & spoke so openly & friendly, that I immediately got the idea she liked me as much as I liked her.'

She handed him his medal, 'twice as big as I expected, & very much more beautiful'. Once Hughes had finished marvelling at it, she invited the poets to sit down, giving them a choice of a single chair or the couch opposite. Unfortunately, both of them made for the chair, nearly bumped into each other, realised their mistake and simultaneously settled for the couch.

Like so many people in the presence of the monarch, Hughes was to find it impossible to recall what she talked about, other than 'all sorts of things'. But he did remember her saying she had liked his poem about an otter, 'like a king in hiding'.

Luckily, Hughes had plenty of strange stories up his sleeve about his otter poem, 'so I started to tell her'.

His central memory of its composition was very strange: he had just written the first part – four verses – when his mind had gone blank. Soon, he became aware of a scroll hanging in the air just to his right. On it were verses 'not perfectly distinct but just legible'. He started to copy the words down, starting:

> The hunt's lost him. Pads on mud,
> Among sedges, nostrils a surface bead,
> The otter remains, hours.

Within minutes, he had completed the entire poem, as if in a dream. 'I assumed that Pan* was presenting his version of Otter as a mild hallucination.'

What can the Queen have made of this bizarre poetic manifestation? Quite possibly, nothing at all. She took such things in her stride. Total strangers would often start telling her weird tales of things seen and unseen. It was almost as though she were the boatman to their subconscious.

Hughes was so encouraged by the way she received his tale that he went on to regale her with more. 'She seemed so interested, I told her them all. We quite forgot about Sir John.'

Presently, the Queen brought Betjeman into the conversation by switching the subject to modern architecture and, in particular, the

---

* In Greek mythology, Pan is the god of nature, fertility and the wild.

Hilton Hotel on Park Lane, of which she particularly disapproved, not least because it overlooked the Palace. 'I wish they'd spend as much pulling it down as they spent putting it up,' she commented.

They were chatting away so merrily, and Hughes found her 'so lively and likeable, I was very disappointed when our talk paused, and she reached for her tiny bell. Ting a ling, & the door at the far end of the room opened. We got up. We bowed, & we said goodbye, we began to sidle away – since it's a tradition that you never turn your back on Royalty.' At this point, the Queen noticed his Medal for Poetry sitting on the couch. 'You're forgetting your medal,' she said, giving it to him again. 'I do hope it's real gold.'

Their time was up. 'So smiling & smiling we got to the door, & bowed, & smiled again & alas it was over.'

61

For three years, John Betjeman's celebration of Princess Anne's wedding remained the only royal poem he had composed as Poet Laureate. But then in May 1976 Prince Charles wrote him a letter 'from a creaking, tossing ship in the middle of the English Channel'.

'It would be marvellous if you could find the time to construct one of your masterpieces of scansion for the Queen's Jubilee ... I would be enormously grateful, personally, if you felt able to conjure up your muse ... I am sure you will agree that a Silver Jubilee is something to be remembered with suitable splendour.'

In despair, and already suffering from Parkinson's Disease, Betjeman wrote a postcard back, replying with a simple 'No.' When friends said, 'You can't send him something like that,' he simply replied, 'Well, I did.'

Yet he still felt duty-bound to come up with something. 'He knew how ridiculed many of the previous Laureates had been when they produced official verse,' a friend recalled. 'He'd hate the thought of it and he'd despair: he was going to make a mess of it; it would be rubbished by everyone; and he'd be regarded as the usual disastrous laureate who's a waste of space.'

In the end, Betjeman wrote 'Jubilee Hymn', to be set to music by the Master of the Queen's Music, Malcolm Williamson. 'The commonplace verses I have written for the Jubilee ... are not at all good, just like a Christmas card', he wrote to his wife. 'But they have to be comprehensible to the TUC and natives of Africa ... that's all there is to be said for them.'

From that look of dedication
In those eyes profoundly blue
We know her Coronation
As a sacrament and true.

Prince Charles read it in dismay, thought of asking Betjeman to give it another go, but then decided against. After a performance in the Royal Albert Hall, the splenetic Conservative MP Sir Nicholas Fairbairn condemned it as 'absolutely pathetic ... the most banal, ninth-rate piece of children's verse'. *Private Eye* magazine printed this parody, by Alfred, Lord Betjeperson:

Ding dong, ding dong
Go the bells of London town
Is it really all that long
Since she put on the Crown?

Look at the daffs under the trees
Golden for the jubilee
Their trumpets waving in the breeze
Bring a thrill to you and me

CHORUS:
Dear old Brenda,* don't you love her?
She's the girl for me all right
And what about the Old Queen Mother
She's a nice old stick ... te-tum-te-tum

More forgiving souls sprang to Betjeman's defence, arguing that his words were meant to be sung, not read, and, after all, other Poet Laureates had written far worse. This was true. Consider the little-

---

* In July 1971, *Private Eye*'s 'Grovel' column revealed that the Queen was 'known as Brenda to her immediate staff'. The magazine speedily adopted this nickname for her. In 1975, it emerged that Princess Margaret was Yvonne and Prince Charles was Brian. From 1982 onwards, Princess Diana became Cheryl.

remembered Laurence Eusden (1688–1739) who celebrated King George II with this awkward couplet:

> Thy virtues shine particularly nice,
> Ungloomed with a confinity to vice.

Or Thomas Shadwell (1642–92) who commemorated King William III's recovery after the Battle of the Boyne:

But Heav'n of you took such Peculiar Care
That soon the Royal Breach it did repair.*

Prince Philip penned Betjeman a letter of sympathy. 'Please don't forget that criticism is much easier than creation and the persecution of individuals has always been the pleasure of thick-headed bullies since time immemorial.' But Betjeman was stung by the criticism and wished he had never accepted the post. 'The laureateship seemed to be a ticket to nowhere but anxiety and depression,' recalled his loving daughter Candida.

---

* To these might be added two lines by Alfred Austin, Poet Laureate from 1896 to his death in 1913:

Spring is here! Winter is over!
The cuckoo-flower gets mauver and mauver.

62

One of the only people ever to have been graced with a title longer and grander than the Queen's was His Excellency President for Life Field Marshal Al Jadji Dr Idi Amin, VC, DSO, MC, Member of the Excellent Order of the Source of the Nile, Lord of All the Beasts of the Earth and Fishes of the Sea and Conqueror of the British Empire in Africa and Uganda in Particular.* He was also the King of Scotland, though, like quite a few of his titles, this one was touched by wishful thinking.

Unlike the Queen, Amin had not been born to grandeur. He enrolled in the King's African Rifles, in or around 1946, as a simple cook. His British officers regarded him as reliable and pleasant. His Commanding Officer, Major A. E. D. Mitchell, described him as 'very quiet, well-mannered, respectful and loyal'. Another British officer noted, 'Not much grey matter but a splendid chap to have about.'

By 1952, Amin had risen to the rank of corporal, having made a name for himself in the brutal suppression of the Mau Mau insurrection against British rule in Kenya. 'Idi Amin was … an outstanding individual …' reported Lieutenant Colonel J. K. P Chavasse, 'although he showed a touch of ruthlessness at times'. He added that 'he needed supervision on inter-tribal operations, otherwise he would exceed his instructions and treat suspects with an unnecessary degree of ruthlessness, and, although never proved, outright cruelty …'

---

* Both were rivalled, and possibly beaten, by the Emperor of Ethiopia (1892–1975), who liked to be known by his full title: 'By the Conquering Lion of the Tribe of Judah, His Imperial Majesty Haile Selassie I, King of Kings, Lord of Lords, Elect of God'.

Despite such misgivings, Corporal Amin was given a key role in the preparations for the Queen's visit to Uganda in 1954 and was present when she opened the Owen Falls Dam. A Canadian officer in the King's African Rifles commended him as a 'jolly giant of a man ... a good and willing soldier, pleasant-natured and a lively person to be around. Fun, even.'

He continued to rise through the ranks, and was made a lieutenant in 1961, one of only two Ugandans to become a commissioned officer. When Uganda gained its independence from Britain in 1962, he was promoted to captain, a year later to major, the following year to Commander of the Army, and then in 1970 to Commander of All the Armed Forces.

On 25 January 1971, when the president, Milton Obote, was visiting Singapore for a Commonwealth summit, Idi Amin staged a successful coup and promoted himself to president. Six months later, he announced that he wished to visit Britain for 'for 4 or 5 days' between 8 and 14 July. First, he wished to meet the Queen and the prime minister, then he planned to visit Scotland, in order to swim in the Scottish sea.

The foreign secretary, Sir Alec Douglas-Home, made a show of eagerness, speedily arranging for the president to have dinner with the prime minister and lunch with the Queen, as well as a guided tour ('May we assume that no wives will accompany?') of Edinburgh. Shortly before his arrival in the United Kingdom, Amin added a couple more requests: he wanted a VC10 aircraft on standby, just in case he had to make a speedy return to Uganda, and he would also 'like to buy some brown shoes in Scotland, size 12'.

When Amin was already in the air, the acting British high commissioner in Uganda telegraphed the Foreign Office in London with a memo of 'random thoughts' concerning the visit. Though Amin was 'formerly a heavy drinker, he now seems to be a teetotaller'; 'he likes smoked salmon' and 'At 6ft 6ins and heavily built an ordinary bed is likely to be too small for him'. The wife he would be bringing, Mama Mariam, 'is also tall (I would guess about 5ft 10 ins) and ample. She is handsome and nice. She wants to shop in London.' He added that Amin's brother-in-law and new foreign minister Kibedi 'likes Red

Barrel beer best. He has a wandering eye for a pretty girl and has, possibly significantly, left his wife behind.'

Amin's forthcoming visit had met with widespread approval. The *Daily Telegraph* hailed him as 'a staunch friend of Britain' who 'provides a welcome contrast to those African leaders ... who bring African rule into discredit in their own country'. The Foreign Office offered government ministers a jaunty and largely inaccurate character-sketch of their new visitor: 'Popular and a natural leader of men, but simple and practically illiterate ... As Head of State, he has shown an engaging lack of formality and a disregard for his personal safety. Benevolent but tough. Well-disposed to Britain ... God fearing and deeply religious.'

Amin was greeted at the airport by Lord Mowbray, Segrave and Stourton, a lord in waiting to the Queen. He was then entertained to a formal dinner at Downing Street, hosted by the prime minister, Edward Heath. The following day he was driven to Buckingham Palace for lunch with the Queen.

Theirs was, by any standards, a most peculiar meeting. Emboldened by the intimacy of their meal, Amin took the Queen into his confidence. He was, he told her, planning on going to war: on his return to Uganda, he planned to invade the neighbouring country of Tanzania, in order to establish a 450-mile corridor through to the Indian Ocean.

The Queen was more accustomed to her guests declaring an interest in watercolours or a passion for racing. A declaration of war broke the usual conversational boundaries. In Amin's presence, the Queen remained studiously non-committal, but the moment he left she instructed Palace officials to warn the foreign secretary of his plans; she had always been fond of President Nyerere of Tanzania.

After a trip to Sandhurst, Amin flew in an aircraft of the Queen's Flight to Edinburgh, where he took the salute at the Ceremony of Beating the Retreat. The following day, he enjoyed a shopping expedition in Princes Street, splashing out £700 on a variety of items, including ten pairs of size 12 shoes and fourteen different kilts. In order to accommodate all the president's purchases, a junior official was obliged to forfeit his seat on the private plane back to London.

The following January, the president received a late Christmas card from the Queen. This prompted him to return the compliment by sending her an invitation to attend the forthcoming celebrations for Uganda's tenth anniversary of independence. The Queen replied that she was 'most disappointed' not to be able to come, owing to other commitments. But all was not lost. She still signed it: 'Your Good Friend, Elizabeth R'.

That year, Amin waged what he called an 'economic war', expropriating the property of Asians and Europeans, expelling over 100,000 Ugandan Asians and purging the Ugandan army of Obote supporters. Over the next five years, he massacred lawyers and judges, artists, journalists, students and intellectuals, foreign nationals and religious leaders. Some estimate the total of those murdered at half a million. It later emerged that he kept the severed heads of two or three of his victims in a household refrigerator: he believed their presence would help ward off 'the evil eye'. Around this time, his wife Sarah opened the fridge door to find the head of a former lover staring back at her.

Amin never lost his macabre sense of humour, often targeting the British, who continued to deny him arms and aid. On 14 December 1973, he wrote a letter of mock commiseration to the British prime minister, Edward Heath: 'In the past few months, the people of Uganda have been following with sorrow the alarming economic crisis befalling on Britain. I am today appealing to all the people of Uganda who have all along been traditional friends of the British people to come forward and help their former colonial masters … In this spirit, I have decided to contribute ten thousand Uganda shillings from my savings and I am convinced that many Ugandans will donate generously.' True to his word, the next day he set up a 'Save Britain Fund'.

In January 1974, he informed Heath that 'the people of Kigezi district donated one lorryload of vegetables and wheat. I am now requesting you to send an aircraft to collect this donation urgently before it goes bad.' In February, he volunteered to act as a peacemaker in Northern Ireland, inviting leaders from all sides to Uganda 'where I would discuss with and make suggestions to them as to how to end the fighting'. And so it went on.

In January 1975, he sent a lengthy telegram to the Queen 'as my former Commander in Chief of the King's African Rifles and Head of the Commonwealth of Nations' announcing that, in the wake of Uganda's economic success, 'I have now the time to relax a bit. Consequently, I have decided to spend my economic war honeymoon in England on the 4th August 1975. Your Majesty, it is ardently hoped and expected that you will, through various agencies, arrange for me to see and visit Scotland, Wales and Northern Ireland. I should like to use that chance to talk to these people who are struggling for self-determination and independence for [sic] your political and economic system ...'

He closed his telegram by saying that he was sending this message early 'so that you may have ample time to help you arrange all that is required for my comfortable stay in your country. For example, that there will be, at least, during my stay, a sure and reliable supply of essential commodities because now your economy is ailing in many a field. I look forward to meeting you, your Majesty. Accept, your Majesty, the assurance of my highest esteem.' The telegram was signed 'Al-Hajji General Idi Amin Dada, VC, DSO, MC. President of the Republic of Uganda' with copies to 'Prime Minister Wilson Harold, and Mr Edward Heath, Leader of the Opposition'.

The British high commissioner huffed that 'The telegram does not appear to call for a reply. It is in any case beneath contempt.' The Foreign Office followed suit, advising that 'the message is intemperate in language, its general tenor is insulting, and its content is unacceptable ... there would seem to us to be some advantage in our showing General Amin that his presence here is unwelcome and in making our reply public ... Above all, it is just possible that if no reply is sent, he will turn up at Heathrow on 4 August, with embarrassments that are too hideous to contemplate.' For most of that week, the problem of Amin's telegram and how to respond to it preoccupied the finest minds in Whitehall, Westminster and the Palace. In the end, it was agreed that it was best met by 'a dignified silence'. But Amin was not a man to let bygones be bygones. He saw no dignity in silence. That April, he saw to it that a British schoolmaster called Denis Hills was charged with espionage and sedition, and condemned to death by firing squad. Following an outcry from Britain, Amin announced on the day before the proposed execution that since Her Majesty the Queen was a personal friend, he would consider sparing Hills's life, but only if she first apologised to him on Hills's behalf.

The Queen signed a letter pleading for Hills's life and despatched it to Uganda with his former commanding officer and the head of the King's African Rifles battalion. On arriving in Uganda, they were ushered in to meet Amin in a hut with a very low doorway, which obliged them to bow low to him as they entered. But their efforts proved fruitless: Amin refused their appeal and demanded to see the foreign secretary, James Callaghan, instead.

Callaghan had little choice but to oblige. After 102 days in jail, Hills was finally freed, and flew home with Callaghan.

Goading the Crown became a favourite pastime for Amin. Following the official announcement of the separation of Princess Margaret and Lord Snowdon in February 1976, he issued a public message to Lord Snowdon, noting that the breakdown of his marriage would be 'a lesson to all of us men to be very careful not to marry ladies in very high positions'. The following year, he declared his intention to attend the Commonwealth Heads of Government Meeting in London, which coincided with the Queen's Silver Jubilee celebrations. Whatever his other limitations, he possessed a singular talent for making fools of those who crossed him: his sudden appearance could embarrass the British government, the Queen and the Commonwealth leaders, all in one go.

James Callaghan, who was by now prime minister, had a word with the Commonwealth secretary general, Sonny Ramphal, who flew out to Uganda. On a trip to the Queen Elizabeth game park in the president's own helicopter, Ramphal was informed that this was the very same helicopter out of which Amin's enemies were regularly hurled.

Ramphal tried to persuade Amin that he might embarrass the Queen by appearing at her Silver Jubilee celebrations, but his warning served only as an encouragement. Amin's preferred tactic was to leave everyone guessing, right up to the very end.

63

Scenes from the Silver Jubilee

'Before we start,' says the Labour prime minister, James Callaghan, to his Cabinet on 10 February 1977, 'I would like to mention the Silver Jubilee. The Cabinet ought perhaps to consider a gift to the Queen – a token of some kind.' Before putting the matter out for discussion, Callaghan suggests it should be something practical, something she would really be able to use. Shirley Williams, the education secretary, suggests a saddle. Someone else tells them not to forget that Parliament gave King Charles I a saddle. Everyone laughs.

The radical energy secretary, Tony Benn, says, 'We are a Labour Cabinet, so if we are going to give her something shouldn't it be uniquely Labour?' He then adds, perhaps to defend himself against a charge of zealotry, 'I am not suggesting a leather-bound volume of our Constitution.' At this point the whole Cabinet emits a groan, and Fred Peart, the leader of the House of Lords, puts his head in his hands. 'Let him finish,' says the prime minister.

'Well, I think we should perhaps give her something that comes out of the Labour movement,' continues Benn. 'I have got in my office a vase, given me by the Polish Minister of Mines, carved out of coal by a Polish miner. What about that?'

The Lord Chamberlain's office, which previously turned down a request from Portmeirion Pottery for a licence to produce Jubilee potties, saying they were in 'bad taste', has now given the firm the go-ahead to produce Jubilee 'planters', which are different from potties, as they have two handles rather than just the one.

On 9 March, a new punk band, the Sex Pistols, is signed by A&M Records, after their contract with EMI has been terminated 'in view of the adverse publicity'.

The signing ceremony takes place outside Buckingham Palace. The four members of the band scream abuse at the Royal Family inside. The head of A&M, Derek Green, explains: 'Every band is a risk, but in my opinion the Sex Pistols are less of a risk than most.'

Later, A&M throw a party in their offices to celebrate their signing. The band's bassist Sid Vicious* seizes the opportunity to vomit over Derek Green's desk.

Following further complaints from staff, exactly a week after the signing, the contract between the Sex Pistols and A&M records is terminated. The Sex Pistols are to receive £75,000 compensation, in addition to the £50,000 they have already received from EMI.

On 17 March, the prime minister opens the Cabinet meeting with an announcement. 'I told the Cabinet I would buy a gift for the Queen and I asked her what she would like and she said she would like something she would personally use.' With all due solemnity, he announces that he has chosen a silver coffee pot. They all burst into laughter, thinking that silver coffee pots are not in short supply at the Palace.

The prime minister, a dedicated monarchist, says that his wife Audrey went out and chose it specially. The silver coffee pot is brought into the room and placed on the Cabinet table. It cost £370, so each member of the Cabinet will be obliged to contribute £15.

* * *

---

* Sid Vicious, né John Richie, replaced the original Sex Pistols bassist, Glen Matlock. According to Malcolm McLaren, Matlock was sacked 'because he liked the Beatles', but their lead guitarist, Steve Jones, felt it was because 'he didn't look like a Sex Pistol and he was always washing his feet'.

On 10 May, a month before the Silver Jubilee, Auberon Waugh complains in his diary in *Private Eye* magazine: 'I do wish the Queen would learn how to pronounce the word "Jubilee". Until this shameful year, nobody put the stress on the last syllable. We expect the politicians to get it wrong, and mediamen, and ice-cream salesmen in Blackpool, but we expect the Queen to do her homework.'

Voices of dissent are beginning to be heard in all sorts of unexpected places. On the wall of one of the loos for barristers in the Middle Temple, someone has written: 'Sod the Jubilee. The Ersatz Orgasm of the silent majority.'

Over bottles of Glenlivet, Kingsley Amis and Laurie Lee are judging a *Daily Mail* readers' competition for the best poem about the Silver Jubilee. This is in response to the Poet Laureate's poor offering. As they sort through the entries, Laurie Lee is struck by 'the drowsy evensong drone of the church harmonium' in many of the poems, and the way the Queen is so often portrayed as a vulnerable wife and a suffering mother. 'She has sometimes a look of pain on her face and yet she always carries on with the job. I think people have responded to that,' he adds. This provokes a disobliging grunt from Kingsley Amis. 'Nobody said about George V or VI how tedious it must be to launch a battleship,' he retorts.

On 18 May, the Sex Pistols sign yet another contract, this one with Richard Branson's Virgin Label. Over the past two months, Branson has grown convinced that their notoriety will inject fresh vigour into a label that has become synonymous with drowsy old hippy values. For his part, the Sex Pistols' wily manager, Malcolm McLaren, harbours a dislike of Branson amounting to what his friend and business partner Jamie Reid later describes as 'nigh on complete hatred'. But after their costly fall-outs with EMI and A&M, the Sex Pistols are beginning to realise that no other record company will touch them.

* * *

On 27 May, Virgin Records rush-release the Sex Pistols' single 'God Save the Queen'. On its cover is a photograph of Queen Elizabeth II, but now with a safety pin through her nose and swastikas in her eyes. Over loud and furious backing, Johnny Rotten screams the verse 'God save the Queen, / The fascist regime' and 'God save the Queen, / She ain't no human being' along with the chorus 'No future, / No future, / No future for you'.

The single generates all the reaction Richard Branson has wished for: it is banned by the BBC, the Independent Broadcasting Authority, Boots, Woolworths and W. H. Smith. The packers at the CBS vinyl factory refuse to handle it, but change their minds after being threatened with dismissal. Bernard Brook-Partridge, the Conservative law-and-order spokesman on the Greater London Council, condemns the song as 'absolutely bloody revolting' and the band's activities as 'a deliberate incitement to anti-social behaviour and conduct'.* This feeling is common among all political parties. 'If pop music is going to be used to destroy our established institutions,' the Labour MP Marcus Lipton tells the *Daily Mirror*, 'then it ought to be destroyed first.'

The record's notoriety generates sales, but perhaps not quite so many as its later myth suggests, as it fails to earn a place in the top 40 best-selling singles of the year. It is beaten by songs from, among others, David Soul, the Bee Gees, Wings and Leo Sayer. Many punks interpret this as a deliberate cover-up by the Establishment.

An Italian restaurant in Nottingham is offering red, white and blue spaghetti, in tribute to Her Majesty's Silver Jubilee.

The director of the Victoria and Albert Museum, Roy Strong, spends the weekend before the Silver Jubilee in the country, keeping himself to himself. Meanwhile, 'the village indulged in a turkey lunch, games, watching a coloured TV set up in the village hall, followed by tea and a Jubilee Cake'.

As he writes his diary, he contemplates the Queen's reign. 'One can't help reflecting how enormously the stature of the Queen has increased in the last two or three drear years. Shy, thoughtful, inscrutable, she remains an enigma to me, which I suppose is just as well.'

Like most towns, Wetherby in Yorkshire is swathed in flags. 'It's everywhere,' says a spokesman for the local council. 'Unfortunately, it is being pinched by people for their own decorations – 25 Union Jacks went in the first week.'

On Monday, 6 June, the Queen joins thousands of people in Windsor Great Park, ready to light a 45-foot-high beacon, the first of 102 up and down the country. She is escorted by Major Michael Parker, who

---

* Bernard Brook-Partridge (1927–2018) listed one of his recreations in *Who's Who* as 'being difficult'. A degree of outcry greeted his remark following the death of Sid Vicious in 1979 that 'Most of these groups would be vastly improved by sudden death.'

is in charge of the operation. They are running a bit late, he tells her, so they will have to hurry. Word then reaches him that the flaming torch with which Her Majesty is due to light the beacon has just fizzled out. He realises they will have to play for time. 'Ma'am,' he says, 'would you mind if you were to slow down just a little?'

She smiles. 'Would you please make up your mind?' By this time, the little boy charged with handing her the torch has burst into tears. The fuse fails to catch fire. Parker has a back-up plan: a hidden electrical fuse, operated by a major in the Royal Civil Engineers. Just as the Queen manages to light her fuse, the flame has begun to crawl along the ground, the Major presses his button and the beacon ignites.

'I can't think why you bothered to ask me,' says the Queen.

'Ma'am, I have to say that absolutely everything that could possibly go wrong is going wrong,' says Major Parker.

'Oh, good,' she replies. 'What fun!'

The left-wing *New Statesman* magazine publishes a special anti-Jubilee issue, packed with articles against the Royal Family. An anonymous profile of the Duke of Edinburgh states that 'In his 25 years as consort, there has been no tincture of humility ...' The unnamed author claims that 'British embassies quail at the prospect' of a visit from the Duke, 'the guests harangued, the foreign servants bullied, the hosts taken for granted'. A proper Jubilee, it concludes, 'can't be built around a man who is neither dignified nor efficient'.

Under the heading 'Why They Hate the Queen', the writer James Fenton reveals that a teacher from a North London infant school asked her nine-year-old pupils, who were engaged in Jubilee projects, if they actually liked the Queen. 'Only four out of 24 put up their hands. The rest, when asked to talk about her, exploded with venom. "She's never done an honest day's work in her life," said one. "She's an old faggot," said another.'

Under the heading, 'Doll in the Golden Cage', the writer Mervyn Jones accuses the Queen of being robotic. 'The wave is mechanical, the smile is a response to duty. When she stops to speak to one of her subjects, she utters the correct number of words: no more, no fewer ... One thinks ... of those dolls which are wound up to produce a routine of actions and sounds.'

In the *Daily Telegraph*, Colin Welch accuses the *New Statesman* of 'Caliban-like malignity'. He takes particular issue with Jones, and reminds visitors from overseas that 'The Queen does not drive about at a tremendous speed, like the cruel head of the Russian state, in an opaque and sinister bullet-proof limousine, one of twenty for safety's sake, through streets cleared, fearsomely guarded and overawed. No, you will see her drawn, quite defenceless in her ancient coach, at a snail's pace through cheering millions to give her thanks to God. You will see her afterwards mixing freely with her people. You will see the smiles of welcome, joy and pride on every face.

'You might suppose that she trusts us, and that we love her. And you would be absolutely right.'

At their home in Lyme Regis, the best-selling novelist John Fowles and his wife Elizabeth are suffering from their customary low spirits. 'Eliz depressed, and I too a little,' Fowles records in his diary. He is finding Lyme Regis 'noisier than ever this summer (the accursed power-boats)' and is particularly upset by 'the absurd and Gadarene rush to celebrate the Royal Jubilee, which seems infinitely remote from anything to do with modern Britain and problems – a hope killed, in fact, since the more ancient-patriotic the nation goes, the more it is lying. The monarchy is like the Church of England; five in a hundred are for it, five against, and the rest don't care; can be cozened either way, one suspects, as in so many other matters ...'

Led Zeppelin are performing at Madison Square Garden in New York, on the first night of a week-long engagement that is set to gross over $2 million. Their shows are long: one song 'No Quarter' can take thirty minutes, and one drum solo by John Bonham comes in at just under forty minutes.

Their lead vocalist, Robert Plant, introduces the song 'In My Time of Dying'. 'Tonight is the beginning of Queen Elizabeth the Second's

Silver Jubilee. And that's a heavy one.' Then he pauses, smiles and says, 'So we'll do this for Liz.'

Sir Nicholas Fairbairn MP accepts the challenge to improve on Betjeman's Jubilee hymn:

> Queen Sovereign universal
> Queen my Queen
> Silver Queen, glint of Britain
> Queen woman serene.

His effort is widely considered a disappointment.

On Kensington High Street, Barker's department store has been doing its bit for the Queen. Of its thirty-seven windows, thirty-five exhibit items related to the Jubilee. One window exhorts passers-by to 'Set a Jubilee Dinner Table all in Gold', and another, with a range of furniture, shows how 'Traditional Leather fits into a very Royal Occasion'. Fashion, too, has a Jubilee theme, with a cavalcade of red, white and blue socks woven with the dates '1952–77'. Nor is Jubilee merchandising purely a London phenomenon: in the town of Sutton in Surrey, Shinners Departmental Store is draped with a giant banner bearing the rhyme:

> Oh to be in England
> Now that Spring is here
> Oh to be in Shinners (China and Glass)
> In Jubilee year.

The Regent Street headquarters of Mappin & Webb offers a special silver bowl for £2,500. Elsewhere, you can buy a solid glass coach with eight horses in a bottle (£750), Union Jack underpants and bowler hats, and 600 different Jubilee mugs. It is estimated that 30,000 different products are related to the Silver Jubilee: beers, tea towels, biscuits, napkins, candles, jigsaws, egg timers, thermometers, ashtrays, even

lingerie. Not to be left out, the pornographic magazines *Penthouse*, *Mayfair* and *Forum* all publish special Jubilee editions.

Badges, T-shirts and posters have been printed with the slogans 'Liz Rules OK!' and 'Cool Rule Liz', while others saying 'Sod the Jubilee' and 'Stuff the Jubilee' are targeted at the profitable anti-monarchist market. A new pressure group, the Movement Against a Monarchy, is selling bumper stickers with the slogan 'Rot All Rulers'.

The comedian Kenneth Williams starts Jubilee Day in a downcast frame of mind. He was unmoved by yesterday's street parties: an estimated 2,500 different parties in Merseyside alone.

'Everything seems utterly bleak to me and all these Jubilee celebrations malapropos,' he writes in his diary; 'in a time of economic recession, the Queen should have set an example of austerity: thousands of pounds wasted on processions and bonfires, which could have been used for better purposes.'

* * *

Before the service at St Paul's Cathedral to mark the Queen's Silver Jubilee, rumours abound that President Amin of Uganda is on his way: a Boeing 707 has been sighted above Nice, and now seems to be heading for Britain. Up to this point, a surprise 'coo-eee!' from the Duchess of Windsor was the worst that might have happened: now they are faced with a serial killer popping his head around the Cathedral door.

The Queen and Prince Philip ride in the Gold State Coach from Buckingham Palace to St Paul's for a service of thanksgiving. The procession includes various other members of the Royal Family riding in the Irish State Coach, Queen Alexandra's State Coach and the Glass Coach, accompanied by the Household Cavalry and Yeomen of the Guard. The Prince of Wales rides on horseback in the uniform of the Welsh Guards, of which he is Colonel-in-Chief. They are all cheered by over a million people, many of whom have camped out overnight.

Kenneth Williams and his mother watch the events of the day unfold on television in his spotlessly clean flat. The procession wins him round. 'It was superbly stage-managed and the crowds ecstatically enthusiastic for the Queen. She did a walk-about afterwards, thro' the City to Guildhall and her good-humoured composure and painstaking consideration for the spectators was extraordinarily moving. We opened a bottle of champagne & had lunch, watching the glittering spectacle on television.'

In Lancashire, 10-year-old Michael Pennington, later to become famous as the comedian Johnny Vegas, tells his mother he doesn't want to go as Noddy to their local Silver Jubilee street party in Hayes Street, St Helens. Mrs Pennington threatens to telephone the Queen. ('Never you mind how I got her number.') Michael is determined to go as a Womble, but he is overruled. Other children in the street go as a cat, a nurse, a squaw and a cake.

* * *

Sporting his RAF medals on his old suit, Tony Benn is driven towards St Paul's, along streets packed with people. Despite himself, he enjoys it. 'Crowds and crowds, all waving Union Jacks and cheering. Rather fun, to be honest.'

In the Cathedral, he sits with other members of the Labour Cabinet, though Home Secretary Merlyn Rees is absent: it is his job to deal with President Amin should he put in a surprise appearance. Also present are four former prime ministers: Wilson, Heath, Home and Macmillan.

From his seat five rows back beneath the North Dome, Benn watches the procession of the great and the good: the Gentlemen at Arms, the Beefeaters, the Speaker, the lord chancellor, the choir, the archbishop of Canterbury, the Clerk of the Closet, all the various canons and the Gold Stick in Waiting. After an hour and a quarter, the Royal Family arrive, culminating in the Queen and Prince Philip.

It is, thinks Benn, an extraordinary parade of the British Establishment. His mind turns, as it so often does, to the distribution of power. 'They haven't got much power, since that has been taken over by the bankers and the businessmen, but many of the individuals are also in banking and business. The peers are bankers, or the bankers are made peers. And some of these landowners, the Duchess of Grafton or the Duke of Beaufort, who look quite harmless, are in their own areas still feudal landowners.'

The archbishop of Canterbury, Donald Coggan, delivers a sermon in which he praises the Queen as 'an example of service untiringly done, of duty faithfully fulfilled, and of a home life stable and wonderfully happy'.

Tony Benn is disappointed by the archbishop of Canterbury's sermon. 'Awful ... full of the old reactionary ideas, prayers about the Commonwealth and prosperity, trust in God and so on – awful opium of the people stuff.'

On the way out, he spots the Soviet ambassador, smartly dressed in a top hat and tails.

* * *

At the service itself, the Queen looks out of sorts. Later, over lunch at the Guildhall, Lord Mountbatten asks her why she looked so cross and worried.

The Queen laughs and says, 'I was just thinking how awful it would be if Amin were to gatecrash the party.'

Mountbatten asks her what she would have done.

The Queen nods in the direction of the lord mayor's Pearl Sword.

'I'd have hit him hard over the head with it,' she replies.

Many years later, someone asks her about Idi Amin. 'He was certainly quite a character,' she says, diplomatically.

During her lunch at the Guildhall, the Queen makes a speech. 'When I was twenty-one,' she says, 'I pledged my life to the service of our people. Although that vow was made in my salad days, when I was green in judgement, I do not regret nor retract a word of it.'

On her way back to the Palace, the roar of the crowd is so loud that her coachman can't hear his horses' hooves hitting the pavement.

At 4 p.m., Richard Branson and Malcolm McLaren board a large boat, the *Queen Elizabeth*, along with the Sex Pistols, having first reassured the owner that they are throwing a party for 'some boring German synthesiser band'. Branson and McLaren stand side by side on the upper deck, McLaren in drainpipe trousers and Branson in a hippyish multi-coloured jersey. Before long, they realise they are being shadowed by two police launches.

As night falls on the River Thames at Westminster, the Sex Pistols start performing 'God Save the Queen' and other songs from their limited repertoire at top volume through loudspeakers. They fill the pauses between with noisy curses. Presently, police officers board the boat. After muddled negotiations, they order the band to stop playing and the captain to return the *Queen Elizabeth* to shore.

Once it is docked, more police swarm aboard, to be greeted by shouts of 'Fascist pigs!' from McLaren and Reid. Together with nine others, including McLaren's wife, the fashion designer Vivienne Westwood, they are escorted down the gangplank and straight into waiting police vans. They are then detained overnight in cells at Bow Street and charged with threatening behaviour.

Richard Branson swiftly adopts an ambassadorial role with the police and is not arrested. Instead, he treats his Virgin colleagues to a slap-up dinner in a local Greek restaurant.

That evening, Roy Strong watches Rudolf Nureyev's *Romeo and Juliet*, which he finds 'patchy but not devoid of moments of splendour'. He leaves the Coliseum at 10.45 to find the night sky crackling with fireworks. Then he strolls across Trafalgar Square 'awash with people' and down the Mall, 'where it was surprisingly thinner on the ground'. He considers the gaudy decorations he sees there 'common. Having a cheap Jubilee was one thing but bad taste another.'

Strong stands close to the Palace as a huge crowd assembles. He judges them 'basically middle-class British', though 'educated voices could be heard'. Men in suits pass by with Union Jacks tied to the ends of their umbrellas; every now and then cheering breaks out, and people sing the National Anthem.

'Then came the moment everyone had been waiting for. The vast TV lamps suddenly beamed down. At last the coaches swept by with their postilions in scarlet and their interiors somewhat ludicrously lit up. The surge of emotion and the lump in the throat was almost tangible.'

Cheering, waving and clapping are followed by a lengthy wait. Then, in front of the Palace, the Guards strike up with some military music. At last, the centre window opens, and the Royal Family step on to the balcony. 'The roar below was deafening. The Queen only had to lift her hand a little for a tide of fervour to ripple through the masses looking up. Close to me a group started to sing the national anthem, which was taken up across the tides of humanity. One could not help finding it deeply moving, as indeed was the cry of a Cockney nearby who yelled up to the Queen: "'Ave a good sleep."'

On the BBC, the commentator Tom Fleming is jubilant. 'It's Coronation Night, VE Night, all rolled into one'

* * *

The following morning, Richard Branson pores through all the newspaper reports of the arrest of the Sex Pistols and their manager. 'Fantastic!' he exclaims. He then travels to Bow Street to offer evidence of Malcolm McLaren's good character.

Many years later, he looks back on those giddy days. 'The Sex Pistols were a national event: every shopper up and down the high street, every grandmother, had heard of the Sex Pistols,' he enthuses. '... The Sex Pistols generated more newspaper cuttings than anything else in 1977 apart from the Silver Jubilee itself.'

But their lead singer Johnny Rotten is less enthusiastic. 'I'll tell you honestly,' he tells an interviewer forty years later. 'On the Jubilee boat trip I didn't even know the Jubilee was going on. I just thought it was a party on the Thames. That's about as much interest as I really had.'

The next day, 8 June, Tony Benn and his American wife Caroline attend an evening party at Buckingham Palace. They are ushered in by a uniformed equerry 'bowing and scraping'. Caroline says, 'It's awfully cold in here.' The equerry replies, 'I am afraid the temperature of the boiler is set by those who work here and they wear a heavy uniform of livery and they think it is too hot.'

'Well, that's all right,' replies Caroline, 'because I am all for working conditions being determined by the shop floor. If that's what it is about, then I understand.'

The Benns join the receiving line. When his turn comes to be greeted by the Queen, Benn makes sure he doesn't quite bow; instead, he gives 'an inclination of my head'.

The Benns spend most of the evening talking with foreign statesmen about the iniquities of the International Monetary Fund. However, at one point they chat to Princess Anne about the royal carriages. 'She is interested in everything to do with horses,' notes Benn.

On 10 June, four days after the Jubilee celebration, Roy Strong is invited to a reception at Buckingham Palace for members of the civil service, of which, as director of the Victoria and Albert Museum, he is a part. 'I dreaded it, but there was no way out.'

He finds it 'an odd evening', as he knows members of the Royal Family and the Royal Household rather better than he knows his fellow civil servants. He talks 'at length' to the Duchess of Kent, who tells him that the Queen was 'totally bewildered and overwhelmed by the huge flood of affection directed towards her'.

Princess Margaret makes her way through the assembled civil servants and greets Strong by saying, 'What are you doing here?'

'Don't laugh,' he replies. 'I'm a civil servant.'

In the White Drawing Room, they sit down to chat. Margaret tells him that 'in a fit of pique' her estranged husband Tony has removed lots of furniture from Kensington Palace, including the piano and all the nursery chairs.

They are discussing Nureyev's *Romeo and Juliet* when Princess Margaret catches the eye of her sister, who is about to disappear through a hidden door in the wall, disguised by a console table.

'You're not going, are you?' she yells. The Queen in her tiara replies, 'Yes, I've done all I can. I ask them what they do. They're D.E.S. or T.U.C. or whatever and that's that.' She then turns to Roy Strong. 'It's the first time we've ever had the civil service. I was surprised to see you.'

'Well,' explains Strong. 'I *am* a civil servant!' He goes on to tell her how marvellous the appearance of the Royal Family on the balcony had been. 'I felt somehow that she ought to know.'

Private Eye magazine's 'Great Bores of Today' series, an unforgiving barometer of the spirit of the times, pictures a grotesque middle-aged man in a paper crown eating a sandwich off a paper plate at a trestle table in a Jubilee street party.

The man is saying: '… no I won't hear a word against Her myself I say jolly good luck to Her I wouldn't do Her Job for all the tea in China just imagine it I mean She couldn't do what we're doing now no it's easy for people to knock Her She can't answer back but I wouldn't do Her job for anything I feel sorry for Her I mean just think of it having to smile and wave all the time and open those hospitals not to mention having to listen to lots of boring people going on and on and having to pretend to look interested at some terrible fellow boring on about

something you couldn't care less about no I say good luck to Her she deserves every penny she gets ...'

On Sunday, 19 June, the lead singer of the Sex Pistols, John Lydon, more commonly known as Johnny Rotten, is attacked in Highbury by what he describes as 'a gang of knife-wielding yobs'.

'We love our Queen, you bastard!' they shout. They leave him with two severed tendons in his left hand.

The same afternoon, the group's drummer, Paul Cook, is attacked outside Shepherd's Bush Tube station by six men armed with knives and an iron bar.

* * *

The Silver Jubilee celebrations have left the crotchety film director Lindsay Anderson more republican than ever.

'There will *always* be an England,' he writes in his diary. 'And if we had ever been in any doubt about it, we'd certainly know it now after these endless Jubilee celebrations. Every day there are pictures (on television too, of course) of the Queen walking about, being presented with flowers, driving here and there, and generally personifying the imperturbable genteel spirit of England. In fact the place gets more schizophrenic every day, with this example of unruffled and smiling traditionalism on one page, and on the other, generally facing, strikes and inflation of prices and corruption in the police and violent confliction on the picket lines. Which is the real Britain? I wish I knew!'

* * *

Back home in Herefordshire, Roy Strong and his wife Julia set about digging a new garden in memory of the Silver Jubilee. Their plan is to create a little brick path across it, a sundial in the middle and 'a couple of phoney statues' flanking the entrance to the Rose Garden. 'And all the flowers will be white.'

A month after the Silver Jubilee, on 5 July, the Labour Cabinet forms a semi-circle around a table at Buckingham Palace. In the middle of the table is the silver coffee pot they are planning to present to Her Majesty.

The prime minister, James Callaghan, makes a short speech before the presentation. He tells them that, to mark Queen Victoria's Golden Jubilee in 1887, her prime minister, Lord Salisbury, gave her a portrait of himself. 'But we thought it would be better to give you something useful,' he adds.

Observing that the Queen 'can't say good morning without a script', Tony Benn spots her referring to a piece of paper in her hand before she replies: 'I feel sure the coffee pot will be more useful than a picture.'

Her remark is greeted with polite laughter.

64

How many dinner parties have been destroyed by a blazing row about one aspect or another of the Royal Family? On 23 August 1975, the poet Stephen Spender, his wife Natasha and their daughter Lizzie were enjoying the summer at their house in Provence. That evening, they were having a small dinner party. Their guests were to include the art collector Douglas Cooper (who we last encountered twenty-three years ago, misbehaving himself at the Coronation) and Baron Philippe de Rothschild, who has already warned the Spenders that he considers Cooper a 'terrible man'. Philippe's daughter Philippine and Suzy Delbée-Masurel, the widow of the French interior designer Pierre Delbée, will also be present.

The evening did not go well.

'The first part of the evening was subdued,' Spender wrote in his journal.

> But then the conversation got on to the Royal Family. Douglas declared that he was a republican; all the royals were cretins – the Queen Mother in particular was not even royal but a fat Scottish bourgeois. Lizzie stood up for Prince Charles who had been her fellow house-guest at some weekend party. She said he was modest, witty, friendly and helped with the washing up, etc. D. brushed all this aside saying the P. of W. was a repeat performance of the previous P. of W., Edward VIII, a Nazi. I said they were really hard-working conscientious people and a devoted family. Mme Delbée looked at her plate, too proud to speak out of her personal acquaintance with the Queen Mother who had been our guest. Douglas said – astoundingly

enough – he had passed two hours with the Queen Mother, when, to oblige his friend Charles de Noailles he had shown her his collection. (Mme D. later told Philippe this was quite untrue; it had been carefully arranged that the Queen Mother saw the collection when D. was away.) Douglas was now galloping ahead attacking the royal equerries and everyone who had anything to do with the Royal Family. He moved on to other European royalties and said the only decent and intelligent one – a brilliant man – was Leopold of the Belgians. I asked, 'Do you mean the Leopold who killed a million people in the Belgian Congo, or the Leopold who betrayed his allies in 1940?' D. said that Leopold was quite right to stay with his people in their darkest hour, etc. Philippe asked, 'What about his relations with the Nazis?' D. said they were very limited. Philippe said resoundingly, 'Now we shall speak no more on the subject.' Douglas stopped short. N. introduced a new subject. The temperature sank from fury to cordial mutual dislike.

65

Over the course of her reign, Her Majesty entertained many controversial foreign leaders, including Bashar al-Assad, Mobutu Sese Seko, Robert Mugabe, Idi Amin, Donald Trump, Emperor Hirohito and Vladimir Putin.

She may not have found their company convivial; upon their departure, she may even have voiced a discreet word of disapproval. A few weeks after President Trump's visit, for instance, she confided in one lunch guest that she found him 'very rude': she particularly disliked the way he couldn't stop looking over her shoulder, as though in search of others more interesting. She also believed President Trump 'must

have some sort of arrangement' with his wife Melania, or else why would she have remained married to him?*

But, no matter how unsettling the manners of these disagreeable guests, they represented their countries, and the Queen had no choice but to grin and bear them.

In 1974, President Ceaușescu of Romania put in a request for a state visit. It was an unappealing prospect. Even the Soviets considered Ceaușescu unnecessarily hardline. But in the depths of an economic crisis the Labour government was intent on selling as many aeroplanes as possible.

---

* For his part, Donald Trump was confident he had been her favourite guest ever. 'There are those that say they have never seen the Queen have a better time, a more animated time,' he told Fox News.

When Wilson visited Romania the following year, he raised the question of aeroplane sales. President Ceaușescu seized the chance to repeat his request for a state visit. Rather than sign a contract willy-nilly, he would wait, he said, for a gap in the Queen's diary. He would be pleased to sign, but only during a visit to Britain.

By 1977, Harold Wilson had retired, but the new prime minister, James Callaghan, was every bit as keen to extract a contract from Ceaușescu. Word reached him that Mrs Ceaușescu was hoping for recognition of her 'distinguished work' in the fields of 'polymer science and scientific education': an honorary degree, at the very least, would be most welcome. By chance, Wilson had taken up the chancellorship of Bradford University in retirement, so the Foreign Office sounded him out as to whether he might wangle a degree for Mrs Ceaușescu. He was doubtful: he had been advised that, far from being a distinguished scientist, Mrs Ceaușescu found even the simple act of reading an uphill task and was baffled by basic formulas familiar to most first-year chemistry students. The distinguished scientific works printed under her name had, in fact, been written by others, and remained unread by herself.* The awarding of any honorary degree from Bradford University had to be put to a vote, and Wilson considered it unlikely that, in this particular case, any such vote would be carried.

Recognising the embarrassment of a public rejection, the suave new foreign secretary, Dr David Owen, swiftly abandoned this plan. Instead, he put out feelers to the universities of Heriot-Watt, Sussex and Liverpool, but none of them took the bait. By now, diplomats hoping to smooth the Ceașescus' path were growing twitchy.

'Surely Imperial College could help?' the first secretary of the British embassy in Bucharest asked his opposite number in London: after all, the Ceaușescus' son Valentin had until recently been a student there,

---

* It was published in Britain under the title *Stereospecific Polymerization of Isoprene* by the Pergamon Press, owned by Robert Maxwell, who also published *Nicolae Ceaușescu: Builder of Modern Romania and International Statesman* (1983). 'I believe that she did not even read those works because I very much doubt she had the ability to understand them,' one of those who ghosted her works, Professor Mircea Teodorescu, told the *Guardian* in 2021. He called the misattribution 'a ruthless act of intellectual misappropriation'.

playing goalkeeper for the college football team and graduating with a degree in physics. But Imperial College also refused, and so did the universities of Southampton and York.

Sights were lowered. In the end, the governors of the Polytechnic of Central London stepped forward. In fact, they so relished the chance of being associated with such a high-profile name that they upped their offer to an honorary professorship. And then the president of the Royal Institute of Chemistry went a step further, offering Mrs Ceauşescu the double whammy of an award and a fellowship. She was thrilled to bits.

The state visit was accordingly scheduled for June. But by the middle of March the staff at Buckingham Palace were beginning to feel apprehensive. They had heard from the Romanian ambassador that the president and his wife were planning to travel with an entourage of fifty-five, including ten authorised journalists, four bodyguards and a personal aircrew, all of whom were expecting to stay at the Palace.

Their fears were further fanned by a series of urgent memos and telegrams from the Foreign Office. The British ambassador was painting an unflattering portrait of President Ceauşescu and his wife. 'He is as absolute a dictator as could be found in the world today,' he wrote. He went on to describe Elena Ceauşescu as a 'viper' and their children as 'feckless', before comparing the president's lengthy speeches unfavourably with those of Adolf Hitler.

News also came through of the 'disastrous' behaviour of the Romanian delegation on previous foreign tours. On a visit to Belgium, the president's personal guards had not only acted brutally with the locals but had 'scrambled for places at the dinner table'. The president's head of protocol was, it seemed, notably ill-chosen. He had caused 'considerable offence' on any number of foreign visits. 'He has been known to exercise some physical violence in his efforts to restrain Ambassadors or journalists seeking to approach unnecessarily close to the President.'

A series of memos from the British ambassador set out severe ground rules for the forthcoming visit. The president was, he said, staunchly atheistical and 'will not stand for any religious invocations'.

At a formal dinner in America, Ceauşescu had walked out while grace was being said, returning only when it was over. Nor would he permit any mention of past Eastern European Royal Families. He would also expect to hear boundless praise for his international statesmanship. 'There is no better lubricant and it can be poured on in unlimited quantities,' wrote the ambassador.

Mrs Ceauşescu would doubtless be making her own demands. 'It is important to keep Mrs C happy. Madame likes shopping. She apparently pays, but the payment aspect should be made clear; she gladly accepts anything which is presented.'

By now, President Valéry Giscard d'Estaing of France had alerted the Queen herself to the difficulties involved in giving the Ceauşescus a bed for the night. After their stay in Paris a few months before, the official charged with looking after them had been deeply upset by their manners. 'He came to see me, appalled,' recalled President d'Estaing, 'and said: "It's frightful. The place has been wrecked. They have taken everything away." There were lots of lamps, vases, ashtrays and bathroom fittings. After their departure, the place had been emptied. Everything had been unscrewed. It was as if burglars had moved in for a whole summer.' Ceauşescu's security staff had apparently left nothing to chance, even bashing holes in the walls, on the look-out for hidden wires and bugging devices.

The Queen, ever houseproud, was going to take no chances. She told the Master of the Household to remove any valuable loose items in the Belgian Suite, where the Ceauşescus would be staying. 'They were advised to move the silver brushes from the Palace dressing table or the Romanians would pinch the lot,' recalled Lord Butler, who had served as private secretary to three prime ministers.

With three days to go, the press were growing increasingly hostile to them, causing the foreign secretary to scribble a memo to his private secretary: 'Who agreed to this visit? Did I? If I did, I regret it.'

On 13 June 1978, the Ceauşescus and their entourage flew into Gatwick Airport. They were greeted by the Duke and Duchess of Kent, who then escorted them to the Royal Train for their journey to Victoria Station, where they were greeted by the Queen and Prince

Philip, Prince Charles and Princess Anne, the prime minister, the foreign secretary, the home secretary, the chiefs of the armed forces and a guard of honour from the 1st Battalion, Grenadier Guards. Seven horse-drawn carriages carried them the few hundred yards to Buckingham Palace, President Ceaușescu in the first carriage, sitting next to the Queen.

Their luggage was already waiting for them at the Palace. Fearful that British agents posing as footmen might be planning to place poison or bugging devices in their clothes, President and Mrs Ceaușescu had packed everything in hermetically sealed containers.

After lunch came an exchange of gifts. Sounded out beforehand, President Ceaușescu had asked for a top-of-the-range hunting rifle. Accordingly, the Queen commissioned a rifle with a telescopic sight; it came in a leather case embossed 'NICOLAI CEAUȘESCU' and the cypher 'EⅡR'.

The day before the Ceaușescus' arrival, the British ambassador to Romania dropped round to the Palace to check everything was in order. When he set eyes on the gun case, he was horrified. 'His face fell and he went ashen grey,' recalled the Queen's deputy private secretary,

William Heseltine. 'He said: "You've spelt Nicolai in the Russian way." I could plainly see he thought his head was going to be taken off if it was handed over with this misspelling.' A craftsman from Windsor was duly summoned to the Palace; working through the night, he managed to refashion the offending 'i' into an 'e'.

The president was clearly thrilled with his gun, which was accompanied by his enrolment into the Order of the Bath. Elena Ceauşescu was equally thrilled with a gold brooch. In return, the president and his wife gave the Queen two hand-made rugs.

At the state banquet in the evening, the British contingent dressed in white tie and tails, while the Romanians remained in lounge suits. The Queen made an effort, putting on Queen Alexandra's Russian Fringe Tiara, and her brand-new sash of the Order of Socialist Romania (First Class), which the president had just awarded her. In turn, the president sported the badge of the Knight Grand Cross of the Order of the Bath, which the Queen had just awarded him. 'We wanted to overawe him and make it very clear this was a very special, incredible privilege,' explained Sir Roger du Boulay, vice-marshal of the Diplomatic Corps, many years later. The plan worked. 'He did exactly what he was told to do. We would say: "Now, sir, you need to spend a penny because we don't want you caught short during dinner," and he would.'

Faced with unwelcome guests, the Queen was adept at employing skulduggery to signal, however secretly, her independence. At this particular banquet, she saw to it that, between the pea soup and the 'Selle d'Agneau Windsor', the menu listed 'Paupiettes de Sole Claudine' – a suitably clandestine reminder of her great-great-grandmother, Countess Claudine Rhédey von Kis-Rhéde, whose son was the father of Queen Mary. Back in Romania, any such reference to Romanian/Hungarian royalty would have been treated as a capital offence, but this one passed unnoticed by the president, who was busy boasting of his country's great progress to the Queen, on his left, and then to the Queen Mother, on his right.

But there were no secret protests in the Queen's speech after the banquet. Far from it: she spoke of how 'we have enjoyed excellent co-operation with your country for many years, particularly in the field of aviation', and poured praise on Romania's 'heroic struggle' for independence. 'We in Great Britain today are impressed with the resolved stand you have taken for supporting this independence,' she continued. 'Consequently Romania holds a distinct position and plays a significant part in world affairs. Your personality, Mr President, as a statesman of world-wide repute, experience and influence is widely acknowledged.'

In private, though, she was less effusive. He was, she said, a 'frightful little man'.

The next day, President Ceauşescu granted an interview to the *Guardian*, which duly praised him for his 'immense courage'. The couple were entertained to tea by the Queen Mother, after which Mrs Ceauşescu was driven to the Royal Institute of Chemistry, accompanied by a translator who was secretly a distinguished scientist, and able to correct every mistake as it issued from her mouth. She appeared pleased as Professor Richard Norman praised her for 'work which has the dual merit both of increasing our fundamental understanding of chemical processes and of increasing our effectiveness in exploiting chemistry for the benefit of mankind'. The professor added that he greatly looked forward to working with this 'distinguished expert' in the future.

At the Polytechnic of Central London, Mrs Ceauşescu smiled modestly as further dollops of praise were heaped upon her. The rector made particular mention of 'her renowned Romanian skills in international relationships and diplomacy', while the senior pro-rector praised her as 'a woman of discernment'. After all, 'Did she not discern the calibre of Mr Ceauşescu long before the other Romanians?'

Walking her corgis in the grounds of Buckingham Palace later that same day, the Queen spotted the Ceauşescus looming in the distance. Thinking fast on her feet, she disappeared behind a bush until they had passed by.

'She made it very clear that she intensely disliked having Ceauşescu to stay,' recalled David Owen, decades later. 'He was just a dreadful guest.'

Was it all worth it? At a celebratory lunch with the Ceaușescus at the BAC factory at Filton near Bristol, haggling over the aircraft contract continued until moments before its official signing. The coveted contracts were worth £300 million in all: the Romanians had finally agreed to build eighty-two BAC1-11 passenger aircraft, under licence from the British Aircraft Corporation, and a further 225 Rolls-Royce Spey engines to power them. But, ten years later, only nine of the eighty-two aircraft had seen the light of day. Any remaining hopes that the contract would be honoured were dashed on Christmas Day 1989 when Nicolae and Elena Ceaușescu were apprehended, tried and found guilty of ordering the deaths of 60,000 people and stealing over a billion dollars. They were then placed against a wall and shot dead.

A few months later, the governing board of the Polytechnic of Central London announced that 'as a mark of revulsion' they had now stripped the late Mrs Ceaușescu of her professorship. In turn, the Royal Society of Chemistry, as the Royal Institute of Chemistry had now become, revoked her honorary fellowship, explaining that her behaviour had contravened their code of conduct.

Some time after returning home from their stay in Buckingham Palace, the Ceaușescus had ordered the construction of the biggest palace in the world, Casa Poporului, or the House of the People, in Bucharest. Like so many dictators' homes, it had a hint of Buckingham Palace about it, and was decorated with diamond chandeliers, marble floors and red carpets. One hundred thousand people are said to have taken part in its building; the Ceaușescus failed to live long enough to move in.

66

Most visitors to Buckingham Palace, however unwanted, come bearing invitations; but one of them simply let himself in.

At 6.45 on the morning of 9 July 1982, Michael Fagan, an unemployed decorator, climbed over railings and entered Buckingham Palace through an open window. Reaching a locked door, he climbed back out of the window, shinned up a drainpipe and entered by another window.

In an anteroom to the private apartments, he broke an ashtray into several pieces and kept a shard for himself. At about 7.18 a.m., he entered the Queen's bedroom. It was unguarded: the police sergeant deputed to remain in the corridor overnight had gone off duty at 6 a.m., when the footman and the maid usually took over. But the designated footman was in the gardens, exercising the corgis, and the maid was cleaning another room with the door closed, so as not to disturb Her Majesty. This much is known.

What happened next? There are many accounts, all completely different. Compare and contrast this selection: from *Majesty* by Robert Lacey (2002); *Sovereign: Elizabeth II and the Windsor Dynasty* by Roland Flamini (1991); *Elizabeth: Behind Palace Doors* by Nicholas Davies (2000); *Behind Palace Doors: My Years with the Queen Mother* by Major Colin Burgess (2006); *Elizabeth and Philip: The Untold Story* by Charles Higham and Roy Moseley (1991); *The Crown* (the Netflix drama series), episode 5, season 4; and an interview Michael Fagan himself gave to the *Independent* newspaper in 2012.

The choice is yours. Take your pick.

1. Michael Fagan, aged 31 (Lacey) or 35 (Davies), broke into the Queen's bedroom because:

a) he was in love with her (Lacey)

b) he was suffering from the delusion that he was the son of Rudolf Hess (Davies)

c) he intended to commit suicide in front of her (Burgess)

d) 'I just thought it would be good for you to meet someone normal who can tell it to you, you know, as it is' (*The Crown*)

e) 'I don't know why I did it, something just got into my head' (Fagan interview)

2. The Queen:

a) displayed cool, pointed to the door and said 'Get out' (Lacey)

b) said 'Get out! There is an armed policeman outside this door. What do you want? If it's money—?' (*The Crown*)

c) sat up and asked Fagan who he was and what on earth he was doing in her bedroom (Davies)

d) wasn't scared in the slightest, but thought 'Oh, well, I'll just have to talk to him' (Burgess)

e) 'cannot have failed to feel a sense of terror' while Fagan said, 'I love you, I love you, I love you' (Higham & Moseley)

f) said 'What are you doing here?' (Fagan interview)

3. And then:

a) Fagan asked the Queen for a cigarette, and she replied, 'You see I have none in this room, but I will have some fetched for you' (Flamini)

b) Fagan asked the Queen for a cigarette and she replied, 'No. Filthy habit' (*The Crown*)

c) the Queen asked Fagan if he would like a cigarette, and he said he would (Davies and Higham & Moseley)

4. Fagan went on to tell the Queen:

a) that the Palace security was 'diabolical' (Lacey)

b) about his unhappy family affairs (Flamini)

c) why his father, Rudolf Hess, had flown to Britain in 1941 (Davies)

d) that he had just come to chat, and asked about her children (Burgess)

e) that Mrs Thatcher was 'destroying the country … In this country a president and a head of state cannot coexist. She's put us out of work and she's quietly putting you out of work' (*The Crown*)

f) hardly anything at all; in fact, the two of them barely spoke: 'Nah! She went past me and ran out of the room' (Fagan interview)

5. Finally:

a) the Queen made two calls to the Palace switchboard before a policeman arrived (Lacey)

b) the Queen's heart beat fast as she quietly spoke the word 'policeman' into the phone, and then 'her heart thumping' walked slowly out of the room and told her maid to ring the police. "'Bloody hell, Ma'am," her maid exploded … Elizabeth replied, "Shush, do as I say, and quickly"' (Davies)

c) the Queen and her maid managed to lure Fagan into the pantry, at which point the footman arrived back and 'the Queen had some difficulty keeping away the indignant dogs'. She shouted, 'Oh, come on, get a bloody move on', at the police when they arrived (Flamini)

d) the footman reappeared and kept the trespasser from breaking out (Higham & Moseley)

e) the Queen sympathetically asked Fagan if there was anything else he'd like to say to her, adding, 'I do hope they don't make things too difficult for you, in light of all this … I shall bear in mind what you've said' (*The Crown*)

f) an unarmed footman stood watch until the police arrived. 'The footman came and said, "Cor, fucking hell, mate, you look like you need a drink … He took me to the Queen's pantry … takes a bottle of Famous Grouse from the shelf and pours me a whisky' (Fagan interview)

6. In the aftermath, the Queen:

a) 'lay quietly, shaking nervously' and then 'more than anything ... wanted a bath to somehow wash away the feeling of this man who had sullied her bedroom' (Davies)

b) was angrier than one footman had ever seen her (Lacey)

c) was 'so worn out that she cancelled a visit to Goodwood Races' (Higham & Moseley)

d) went into a state of shock some weeks later and was ordered to rest (Flamini)

e) told Colin Burgess, 'I wasn't scared. The whole thing was so surreal. He just came in, we chatted and then he went without incident, and that was that' (Burgess)

f) took up Fagan's cause with Mrs Thatcher, telling her, 'I don't think he's entirely to blame for his troubles, being a victim of unemployment, which is now more than twice what it was when you came to office just three years ago' (*The Crown*)

67

The Royal Family have long been prey to villains and charlatans. A public association with the monarchy lends dodgy enterprises majesty: with a bow, a handshake and an exchange of pleasantries, rogues are transformed, as if by magic, into philanthropists.

Supporting charities patronised by Her Majesty was the surest method of securing an introduction to her. For instance, in 1984, Robert Maxwell co-sponsored the Christmas production of *The Nutcracker* at the Royal Opera House in aid of the National Society for the Prevention of Cruelty to Children.

'The sheer scale of that event, both in the amount of money raised and in the Christmas magic of its royal first night, surpassed any gala night I had witnessed at Covent Garden,' cooed his wife Elisabeth, chair of the organising committee. 'Perhaps it was the spirit of Christmas that pervaded the opera house or the rare occurrence of the joint presence of the Queen, Prince Philip, the Queen Mother and Princess Margaret. Perhaps it was the continental decoration of the Christmas trees which greeted you in the foyer with their heady scent of spices and cinnamon … Perhaps it was simply the audience's unbelievable elegance in white tie and fabulous beaded ballgowns set off with sparkling jewelry or the magic of the *Nutcracker* story itself. Or perhaps it was the free-flowing champagne, a special gift from a generous champagne producer and guest …'

Or perhaps, one may be tempted to add, it was the respectability conferred on Elizabeth Maxwell and her husband Bob, who even then was playing fast and loose with other people's money.

'Whatever its special quality was, no one present that night will ever forget it.'

Naturally, the Maxwells were rewarded for their munificence with proximity to the Royal Family. 'Bob and I were privileged to sit beside the royal party in the Dress Circle,' Elisabeth boasted in her autobiography *A Mind of My Own*. Her husband sat next to Prince Philip, and, after the interval, next to the Queen Mother. As luck would have it, a combination of the free-flowing champagne and the music made him soporific, and he 'fell asleep as soon as the lights were dimmed'. Betty Maxwell was indignant. 'I was constantly poking him in the ribs to wake him up. I could not let him commit the crime of lèse majesté by falling asleep next to a Queen!'

There was always a price to pay for rubbing shoulders with royalty. 'The joy of attending such fabulous parties was most dearly paid for, as far as I was concerned, by the extreme exertion involved which almost left me too tired to enjoy them … Either too many of the best seats had already been allocated and we couldn't find a pair for one of the most generous sponsors, or tickets would go astray altogether. One irate and fussy woman would threaten never to help again unless she were

presented to the Queen, another resented being right at the end of the presentation line. You could never afford to offend a donor!'

The Maxwells were rewarded for their efforts with an invitation from HRH Princess Margaret to a private dinner at Kensington Palace.

Earlier that year, the 86-year-old Japanese billionaire Ryoichi Sasakawa had announced that his sole remaining ambition in life was to meet the Queen; this was not entirely true, as by then he was also masterminding what he called his 'Nobel Prize Receiving Operation', pumping money into institutions linked to advisers for the Nobel Peace Prize. But meeting the Queen was more easily accomplished than the award of a Nobel Prize: Sasakawa simply asked his British business associate Robert Maxwell to arrange it for him.

Like Maxwell, Sasakawa had a chequered past. Described by one of his more friendly obituarists as 'a monster of egotism, greed, ruthless ambition [and] political deviousness', in 1931 he had assumed leadership of the Patriotic Masses Party, a group of Japanese fascists who dressed in black SS-style uniforms. Already a wealthy man, through a combination of publishing, opium and arms, he had his own private air force: in 1939 he flew in one of his twenty bombers to Rome just to pose for photographs with the Italian Fascist leader, Benito Mussolini.

At the end of the war, he was imprisoned as a war criminal by the Allies, having avoided execution, possibly because of his links with the CIA. On his release three years later, he invested his money in power-boat racing – at that time one of the only legal means of gambling in Japan – and multiplied his fortune a hundredfold. 'I am the world's richest fascist,' he proclaimed.

Like many dodgy plutocrats, Sasakawa craved respectability and now his eyes were fixed on the Nobel Prize. Through his Sasakawa Peace Foundation, he offered handsome bribes to the judges, but, to his great distress, they refused to play ball.

He was, however, able to achieve his final dream. After nimble manoeuvring, Robert Maxwell managed to secure invitations for himself and Sasakawa to a Buckingham Palace Garden Party. Sadly, Maxwell's timing was atrocious: on the very same afternoon as the Garden Party, he had to attend a make-or-break business meeting at the Ritz Hotel with a view to buying Mirror Group Newspapers for upwards of £100 million.

'What are we going to do? He's flown in all the way from Japan specially to meet the Queen. How the fuck are we going to deal with it?' Maxwell asked his dutiful son, Ian.

Ian stared hard at the Garden Party invitation and noticed it had been made out to 'Ian Robert Maxwell', a name which, with a little elasticity, could apply to either father or son. Ian suggested he swap places with his father, taking Sasakawa as his guest. 'It'll never work,' replied Robert, 'they'll know you're not me.' But for the sake of the £100 million deal, he thought it worth a punt.

So on the morning of 9 July 1984 Ryoichi Sasakawa arrived at Buckingham Palace in a vast chauffeur-driven Rolls-Royce Phantom VI, very similar to the Queen's. He emerged from the car in full Japanese formal dress, complete with a long pleated skirt and a kimono jacket.

After scrutinising their invitation, security waved Ian Maxwell and Ryoichi Sasakawa through and out into the gardens. Looking around the Palace lawns at the thousands of partygoers, Ian realised that a presentation was far from inevitable: competition to meet the Queen was clearly intense. 'All I can think is, how the hell am I ever going to get Sasakawa to meet the Queen?'

But opportunity knocked. By chance, the vice-president of the National Society for the Prevention of Cruelty to Children approached Maxwell and asked, 'Is this by any chance Ryoichi Sasakawa?' It turned out that Sasakawa had recently donated £2 million to the charity, and the vice-president wished to repay the debt. Would he perhaps care to meet the charity's patron, Princess Margaret?

Sasakawa spoke not a word of English, but Maxwell eagerly accepted on his behalf.

Years later, Ian Maxwell recapped the events of the afternoon for his father's biographer, John Preston:

We go into the garden and we're told where to stand. After a few minutes Princess Margaret arrives and I'm introduced as Robert Maxwell. I start to tell her that actually I'm Ian Maxwell, Bob's son, but before I can introduce her to Sasakawa, there's this commotion in the background.

The crowd parted and out popped the Queen.

When she sees her, Princess Margaret turns away from us and says, 'Lilibet, come and meet Bob Maxwell's son.'

Seeing the Queen approach, the elderly Japanese crook fell full-square to the ground, while emitting a high-pitched wail. Looking down at the elderly figure spread flat-out before her, the Queen asked, 'What have we here?'

This, replied Ian Maxwell, was Ryoichi Sasakawa, the noted Japanese philanthropist.

The Queen nodded. 'He *can* get up, you know.'

Anxious to build bridges, Maxwell explained that, in Japan, it was customary to lie flat on the ground when presented to a member of the Royal Family. As always, the Queen's instinct was to steer the conversation back on to the straight and narrow.

'How's it going with the *Mirror*?'

'It's up in the air, but I think my father's bid will succeed,' Maxwell replied.

'I do hope so,' said the Queen, and moved on.

Two years later, the Commonwealth Games in Edinburgh were close to collapse. Robert Maxwell rode to the rescue, promising to bail them out with £2 million of his own money. The *Daily Mirror*, of which he was now the owner, led the chorus of praise. Shortly afterwards, Maxwell contacted Ryoichi Sasakawa with a view to persuading him to take care of this new debt. At a press conference on the last day of the Games, Maxwell introduced Sasakawa as 'a former politician who played an important role in the economic revival of his country after the war'. He was also, he added, the man 'who single-handedly funded the eradication of leprosy'. He failed to mention Sasakawa's conviction for war crimes, or his long connection to the opium trade. When it was his turn to speak, Sasakawa made the surprising announcement that he was only 27 years old and would live to be 200. Both estimates proved optimistic: at that point, he was 87 years old: he would die of a heart attack in 1995, at the tender age of 96.

On the last day of the Games, Maxwell's largesse bought him another meeting with the Queen. Ever the showman, he presented her with a gift of coins in a swanky glass display case. 'Permit me to present you, Your Majesty, a token of this great event that I have orchestrated,' he said, in his booming bass voice.

It later emerged that his total contribution to the 1986 Commonwealth Games had been only £250,000. Still glowing from his meeting with the Queen, the ever-generous Mr Sasakawa was happy to cover the £1,750,000 shortfall.

68

Though peace has come to Northern Ireland, walls on Belfast's Shankill Road still carry huge murals of the Queen, many of them stretching the entire length and breadth of a building. Her picture on a wall – usually accompanied by a Union Jack – signals that this is a Protestant Loyalist area.

In 2023, a loyalist from the Shankill Road, John Chambers, explained: 'This is the Shankill Road, the heartland of loyalism, where my heart and soul was forged. Our whole environment was forged by being a Loyalist and a Protestant and hating Catholics. We hated them with a passion, so we did. Looking at it now, it's crazy, but when you're born

in that tribal environment, and your whole life is dominated by the troubles – they were our enemies ... A loyalist is a WASP – White Anglo-Saxon Protestant, basically. We're more British than the British, you know what I mean? Prouder, should I say, than the British to be British. Do you know, they still stand for the Queen? In Northern Ireland, all loyalists in Protestant clubs, at the end of the night, no matter how drunk or wasted or stoned you are, when they play God Save the Queen you have to stand up and salute. If you don't do it, you're going to get a beating or a hiding. They take it very seriously. And I remember, as a child, the BBC every night used to play God Save the Queen at the end of the night and we used to stand up in the house and salute the Queen when they played it. We were that fanatical, we took it that seriously.'

69

At 11.35 a.m. on Thursday, 27 August 1979, seven people set off in a fishing boat from the harbour at Mullaghmore in County Sligo: Lord Mountbatten, his elder daughter Patricia, her husband John Brabourne, their 14-year-old twins Nicholas and Timothy Knatchbull, John's mother, Lady Brabourne, and Paul Maxwell, a 15-year-old boy from Enniskillen who was there to help. They were going to check on some lobster pots. The sun was shining, the sky was blue and the sea was calm.

Mountbatten took the helm. Timothy went on to the roof to act as lookout, ready to point out the lobster pots. Everybody was in a holiday mood.

Unknown to them, they were being observed from the shore.

Paul asked Timothy the time. Timothy looked at his watch and announced in a jokey voice: '11.39 and thirty seconds.' Three of those on board had only six and a half minutes left to live.

At 11.46 a.m., one of the observers pressed a button, detonating five pounds of gelignite hidden beneath the deck. The boat exploded, instantly killing Lord Mountbatten, Paul Maxwell and Nicholas Knatchbull. Lady Brabourne died in hospital. Patricia was not expected to live: her face was subjected to 117 stitches, including twenty in each eye. John had multiple wounds; both his legs were broken.

A couple on a boat nearby pulled Nicholas's twin brother, Timothy, out of the water by his hair. Timothy knew something terrible had happened. He couldn't see or hear. The bomb had perforated his eardrums. He tried to say: 'I'm cold.'

His body had been pierced by shrapnel. By chance, he had been looking to the right when the bomb went off: he was blinded in his right eye, which was already weak, but his left eye remained undamaged. Many of the physical scars he suffered were to be permanent.

The twins were identical: even their mother couldn't always tell them apart. Looking through old photographs of himself and his brother, Timothy still finds it impossible to tell one from the other.

They did everything together, these two boys, and went to the same schools. Their characters, though, were different: Tim was a bit of a show-off; Nicky was neater, more organised and more robust.

Three days after the explosion, lying in bed in Sligo General Hospital,* Timothy was told by Joanna, the elder of their two sisters, that his twin brother had died. 'When you were brought to the hospital you were unconscious. You woke up. Nick never did.'

He had had no inkling of it and found it hard to accept. At any moment, he felt Nicky might walk into the room. He had been in hospital for Nicky's funeral, so had never had the chance to say goodbye. For a time, he toyed with the idea that everyone had conspired to make him think his twin brother was dead. 'I felt he was merely absent and I was still somehow sharing my life with him while he remained out of sight.' But he also knew, logically, that this couldn't be true.

That October, the Queen invited Timothy and his 22-year-old sister Amanda to Balmoral for the weekend. Their flight was diverted, so they landed in Glasgow and had to take a coach through thick fog to Aberdeen, where a chauffeur was waiting to drive them the fifty miles to Balmoral. By now it was very late: the chauffeur explained that everyone at the castle would be asleep, but there would be soup and sandwiches waiting.

'We were planning to shuffle like mice to our rooms, when suddenly we caught sight of the Queen striding down the corridor. She had the air of a mother duck gathering in lost young. Beside her was Prince Charles, Nick's and my godfather. He looked every bit as agitated, yet tender and concerned. As they kissed us hello, it felt wonderful to be

---

* Renamed Sligo University Hospital in 2015.

back. The telegram* Charles had sent me in Sligo came to mind and I concentrated on not becoming tearful. They led us into the drawing room and plied us with the soup and sandwiches.'

It was time for bed. They followed the Queen down the corridor, imagining that she would leave them and head towards her bedroom. Instead, she shepherded them into their bedrooms and started to unpack for them. But Amanda drew the line at this, removing a sweater from the Queen's hands and insisting they would be happier doing it themselves. 'She was in almost unstoppable mothering mode and I loved it. We kissed her good night and then unpacked as we chatted to Charles.'

The next day, wet and windy, they all went out shooting. At lunch, the Queen kept an eye on Timothy. When they had all finished, sensing he was tired, she sent him back to the Castle. Sure enough, he slept all afternoon.

At dinner that night, the Queen placed him beside her. Soon afterwards, she said, 'Timmy, don't you think it's about time for bed?' Thinking about it years later, he recognised these as the words of a stand-in mother. 'I said my goodnights and left for bed with a warm feeling towards the Queen that has stayed with me ever since.'

The next morning, the Queen's doctor arrived to dress the wound on Timothy's right leg. When he asked, 'May I take your boot off?' Timothy thought that perhaps the boots had been intended for outdoor use only. 'Now I wondered whether my mother would disapprove of my wearing them at Balmoral. Suddenly I longed for her.'

At lunch, he was between the Queen and his elder brother Philip, who, together with Prince Edward, had been allowed out of Gordonstoun for the day. 'It felt very cosy and we had a noisy lunch together. It was wonderful to see Philip after some weeks apart. "Do you want more?" I asked after he had finished his pudding. "Well, I

---

* 'It is impossible to find the words to express the numb horror I feel ... at this appalling moment. All I can do is send you my love and boundless sympathy. Your affectionate and devoted godfather Charles'.

wouldn't say no," he replied, camping it up. The Queen giggled. "But would you say yes?" I insisted, and the Queen giggled some more.'

He spoke to the Queen of something that had been on his mind: 'a vague memory of the sound of the bomb. I described it not so much as a noise but a feeling, "percussive" and "tangible". I realised that I was not quite getting my meaning across but found she was a very good listener and drew things out of me that others had not.'

After tea, they went to wave goodbye to Philip and Prince Edward, who had to return to Gordonstoun, where Timothy and Nicky should also have been. 'Just as my mother would, the Queen kept waving until the last moment. My thoughts drifted. I was very pleased not to be going back with them. Without Nick it was going to be a very different experience and I did not feel up to it. The Queen noticed I was looking a little lost and snapped me out of it. With mock force she knocked me with her arm. "Go on," she said, "wave!" I burst into laughter.'

On the Monday, noticing that he had been a bit quiet, the Queen nudged him into conversation. 'Timmy,' she said, 'if you had *Britannia* and could choose anywhere in the world to go, where would you choose?' Thinking it most tactful to pick somewhere beyond the realms of possibility, he said China, and so they started to chat about China.

Prince Philip's form of support was different, but, in its way, just as attuned to the needs of a boy in grief. 'He quietly included me at the heart of the weekend without ever making a fuss. His interest in me was unflashy. By now I was getting used to being spoiled and it was refreshing that he spoke and treated me in exactly the same way as when Nick had been alive. When everything in my life was out of balance, it was good to be about people who were rock solid.'

Decades later, Timothy happened to be talking to someone about how the Queen had looked after him with such care back in 1979. 'Suddenly my eyes filled with tears and I could not say any more.'

Over four decades later he retains vivid memories of her kindness towards him during that dreadful period. Her reserve was sometimes taken for coldness, but he could vouch for her humanity. 'The fact that it was the Queen is of interest to other people, but really it was one woman mothering another woman's child in their hour of need. All my life I have read accounts of the royal family being unloving ... in private, they're the most wonderful, warm, generous family. Anyone who doesn't see that is fooling themselves.'

70

Ted Hughes returned from a cruise on the Nile in November 1984. Sifting through his post, he found a letter from 10 Downing Street marked 'Confidential'. Had he received the prime minister's previous letter? Could he reply, as a matter of urgency?

He then found the earlier letter, which was from Margaret Thatcher. Would he object to his name being put forward to Her Majesty 'for the position of Poet Laureate in Ordinary'?

His first reaction was to assume – correctly, as it turned out – that Philip Larkin had already refused. Over the weekend, he phoned his sister and agent, Olwyn Hughes, who advised him that it would be good for American sales. On the Monday, he telephoned Downing Street with his acceptance.

'The Queen has been pleased to approve that Edward James Hughes be appointed Poet Laureate in Ordinary to Her Majesty in succession to the late Sir John Betjeman,' came the announcement from Buckingham Palace. A press release added that the Poet Laureate was a member of Her Majesty's Household, and that the post carried a salary of £70, complete with a case of wine.*

By and large, his appointment was greeted with enthusiasm. *The Times* noted the contrast between Hughes and his predecessor, John Betjeman, comparing them to a grim young crow and a cuddly old teddy bear. The American press focused more on Hughes's humble origins: the son of a Yorkshire carpenter, he had worked as a night-

---

* A significant dip since the days of the first Laureate, John Dryden, who was awarded £100 a year and a butt of 'the best Canary Wyne' (roughly 126 gallons).

watchman, a gardener and a zoo attendant. To most commentators, he seemed a modern, egalitarian choice.

Yet in one important respect Hughes was a throwback to earlier times, when the Poet Laureates celebrated the monarchy in earnest. Alone among his contemporary poets, he was a passionate and whole-hearted monarchist, to the extent that two years earlier he had written a private poem in celebration of the birth of Prince William ('Sun, moon and all their family stand / Around a new-born babe, in England').

He believed that every nation was in need of a 'sacred myth', which for Britain was its Royal Family. For him, the nation was a wheel 'With a crown at the hub / To keep it whole'. So he took to his laureateship with zest and passion, unencumbered by the awkward mix of embarrassment and weariness that had afflicted so many of his predecessors

Two days after Hughes's appointment as Laureate came Prince Harry's christening. He set to work straightaway. More reluctant Laureates might have viewed the subject matter as unpromising, but not Hughes: he met his tight deadline with 'Rain-Charm for the Duchy', which he subtitled 'A Blessed, Devout Drench for the Christening of His Royal Highness Prince Harry'.

Over ninety lines long, the poem makes no mention of royalty, a christening or even Prince Harry. Instead, it opens on an image of the windscreen of the poet's Volvo 'frosted with dust' after a five-month drought: 1984 had been an exceptionally dry year in the United Kingdom.

> Now the first blobby tears broke painfully.
> Big, sudden thunderdrops. I felt them sploshing like vapoury
> petrol.
> … Then, like taking a great breath, we were under it.
> Thunder gripped and picked up the city.
> Rain didn't so much fall as collapse.
> The pavements danced, like cinders in a riddle.

The poem focuses on baby salmon responding to the rise in the water level, making their way upstream, 'twisting their glints in the suspense'. In notes published later, Hughes spoke of 'their moody behaviour, so unpredictable and mysterious … attuned, with the urgency of survival, to every slightest hint of the weather'. He intended his verses, he said, 'as a fitting splash for the christening of HRH Prince Harry, the Duke of Cornwall's second son'. Given the fate of Prince Harry, it might also be seen as evidence of Hughes's peculiar gift for seeing into the future.

71

The following year, Ted Hughes wrote two poems for the Queen Mother's eighty-fifth birthday.* 'About five days before ... I read that one of her more celebrated ancestors was a scots lord known as the White Lion,' he wrote to a friend. 'It occurred to me that she's the focal point of odd coincidences: her maiden name Lion,† her birth-sign Lion and the fact that she's astrologically very typical, a text book case, in that facially she somehow resembles a Lion ... and her role as bearer of the mythic crown in a collective psychic unity where the totemic symbol of union was the Lion.' In April 1986, he wrote 'A Birthday Masque' to celebrate the Queen's sixtieth birthday. It was an almost impenetrable mash-up of imagery from the Nativity story, the flower world, Taoism, *The Comedy of Errors*, *King Lear*, Welsh mythology, Ancient Egypt, the Sioux Shaman 'Black Elk' and the Islamic Sufi Attar's poem *Conference of the Birds*. But one thing's for sure: it includes words never previously linked to Her Majesty in verse:

---

* Hughes wrote the Queen Mother a long epic poem for her ninetieth birthday, and many more thereafter. 'How fortunate I am to have a friend who is a great poet! Lucky lucky me!' she wrote to him in 1995. He became her frequent guest. 'He had such an amazing mind and was very, very intelligent ...' recalled her equerry, Major Colin Burgess. 'In the evenings, he would read his latest poems. During one of the longer ones, especially once a few glasses of port had been consumed, I would give a sharp cough just towards the end in case anyone had nodded off. By the time Ted looked up from the page, sure enough, everyone was smiling and, above all, awake.'

† In fact, Bowes-Lyon.

Let the first be a Snowdrop, neck bowed
Over her modesty –
Her spermy, fattening gland
Cold under the ground.
She links an arm
With a Foxglove, raggily dressed,
Long-bodied, a rough blood-braid
Of dark nipples.

Those who had previously scorned Betjeman for simplicity and sentimentality now chided Hughes for earnestness and obscurity. Traditionalists considered it unseemly for the Poet Laureate to manacle the Royal Family to his enduring obsession with nature red in tooth and claw. The poet Hilary Corke declared that he found it impossible to read even a few lines of 'A Birthday Masque' 'without emitting several little girlish shrieks of horror'.

But Hughes carried on, regardless. In July of that year he wrote 'The Song of the Honey Bee', a poem 'For the Marriage of His Royal Highness Prince Andrew and Miss Sarah Ferguson':

A helicopter snatched you up.
The pilot, it was me.
The props, like a roulette wheel,
Stopped at felicity.
...
Far from this day, that gives you each
To each as man and wife
That's the dance that makes the honey
Happiness of life.

This poem was not published in book form until 1992, the Queen's *annus horribilis*, when the honey soured, the Yorks separated and photos of the hapless – and topless – Duchess having her toes sucked by her financial adviser were printed on the front pages of newspapers the world over.

72

The Queen, dressed in mauve, is on the balcony at Epsom, peering excitedly through a pair of binoculars as her horse Enharmonic competes in the 1991 Diomed Stakes. Behind her stands her mother, dressed in orange. They are both being filmed for a documentary charting a year in the Queen's life, but the thrill of racing seems to render them impervious.

Though it was the joint 5/1 favourite, Enharmonic, ridden by Steve Cauthen, ends up coming fourth, behind Regal Sabre, Fair Average and Sylva Honda. The Queen is clearly disappointed. Turning away from the race, she looks down at her white gloves. 'Do you know,' she says to her mother. 'I haven't watched through a pair of binoculars for

ages.' She is trying to explain her tears. She wipes her eyes with the back of her gloved hand.

Her mother regards her with a pitying smile. 'Oh dear!' she says, with an aggressive form of sympathy, enclosed in a knowing chuckle.

'Look at it! Pouring with tears!' says the Queen, putting her glasses back on. She offers further explanation: 'I always watch on the television.'

'It's the emotion, perhaps,' says her mother, with another knowing chuckle – 'Hur-hur.' She clearly wishes to contradict her daughter: she wants her to know that she thinks her tears have arisen not from the Surrey wind or from the rub of the binoculars, but from disappointment with her horse.

'No, no, I always watch on television,' the Queen replies, offhandedly. She then realises what her mother has just been implying: that she cared too much about winning and has been the victim of her emotions.

'NO, Mummy!' she protests, her voice rising in exasperation. 'It's if you look into a WIND like that!' She points back to the racecourse. 'It's like looking at a deer!'

The Queen Mother gives another little chuckle as she bustles off. 'Ye-es,' she says, but her 'if-you-insist' tone of voice clearly indicates that by yes she really means no, but doesn't wish to argue.

I have watched this little thirty-two-second clip over and over again, perhaps a dozen times in all. Whenever I do, I feel oddly voyeuristic – strange, given that I've watched countless royal clips over the past two years, with no feelings of intruding. I think it's because, this, alone among so many others, has a feeling of real emotions, and real family dynamics.

At that time, the Queen was 65 and the Queen Mother 90, but this polite little bicker seems as though it might have come from any time in their past sixty years: the Queen, ever the dutiful daughter, determined to be well behaved and no trouble at all, and the Queen Mother, beneath her sugary and deferential exterior, always wanting the last word, always knowing best.

73

No, Mummy! The Queen was usually cautious and mindful: mindful of being on show, mindful of her role as sovereign, mindful of the need to look interested or delighted or a little bit of both. But horse-racing liberated another side of her character; it meant that she could be spontaneous, excitable and competitive.

In no other sphere could she exercise her competitive streak. What would have been the point? Elsewhere, she would always be top dog. By her third birthday, she was on the cover of *Time* magazine. By the age of 25, she had become Her Majesty Queen Elizabeth the Second, by the Grace of God Queen of this Realm and her other Realms and Territories, Head of the Commonwealth, Defender of the Faith. Wherever she went, everyone in the world, her family included, stood up for her, and bowed and curtsied to her. Her subjects asked God to save her, to send her victorious, happy and glorious, long to reign over us. Presidents, prime ministers and pop stars felt nervous in her presence and were anxious to please her. She only had to step out of a car, or appear on a balcony, to be greeted with cheers.

But the world of racing offered her the chance to compete. It also gave her a holiday from her meticulously planned and regimented existence. When she came to open a day-care centre or launch a ship or greet a foreign dignitary, every move she made would have been worked out months in advance: where to go, who to meet, how long to stay. 'A minute of visit requires three hours of planning' was the Palace dictum.

But horse-racing is fast, random and unpredictable. Whatever happens is powered by chance; nothing is preordained. A firm favourite might be pipped at the post; the rank outsider might win. Within a matter of seconds, the accepted order is overturned. It offered her excitement.

Some felt it was her only true passion. 'To my mind she is almost perfect,' Lady Gladwyn, the wife of Britain's ambassador to France, wrote in her diary in April 1957. '... One feels the presence of a very fine character, simple, kind and good; alway anxious to do the right thing; a person who would never let anyone down.' But then Lady Gladwyn went back on herself: 'When I say she was almost perfect, I only mean that I cannot help regretting that she had not got more interesting interests. Apart from horses and racing I could not discover anything that interested her, such as the arts, or gardens, or books ...'

Her passion for racing never waned, right up to her dying day. Only twice was she ever spotted running in public. The first time was in 1954, after her horse Aureole won at Ascot. The correspondent from the *Daily Telegraph* was making his way to the unsaddling enclosure when he was taken aback to see the Queen scooting past. The second was in 1991, when she drew the winner Generous in the Royal Box Derby sweepstake and was filmed running from the television area inside to the front of the box in order to see the finish.

On 4 June 2022, her horse Steal A March was running at Worcester, and the Queen was watching the race on her television at Windsor Castle. 'She began to cheer it on so loudly that the security men rushed in, thinking something terrible was happening,' recalled the horse's trainer, Nicky Henderson. It was her Platinum Jubilee weekend; by then, she was 96 years old.

She could relax in the company of trainers and jockeys, skipping the usual social niceties in order to talk shop. Her ease within the bosom of the racing fraternity gives us a glimpse of another life, another character: the person she might have become had her sister been born a boy, leaving Princess Elizabeth free to pursue a life more her own.

The racing commentator Brough Scott witnessed her cheeriness at a party to celebrate her horse Dunfermline's double victory in the Oaks and the St Leger. 'The Queen was not just in her Palace, this was her element too. She moved from one leathery handshake, from one best Sunday suit to another. Wary weather-beaten faces soon creased into smiles as they relived the golden moments that had brought them all together. There could be no tension because they knew that she knew that those memories had been theirs as much as hers. They knew too that she enjoyed the private moments at the stables every bit as much as the public triumphs at the racetrack ... She talked of the future in that fingers-crossed way that only owner–breeders can.'

'I am not sure Dick thinks that much of the two-year-olds,' she gossiped when her trainer, Major Dick Hern, was out of earshot. 'But you know what he is like.'

Racing allowed her to be carried away, to let her competitive instincts run loose. But it also put her customary restraint in jeopardy. What would she do – what wouldn't she do – to win?

In 1982, she sold her Hern-trained horse Height of Fashion to Sheikh Hamdan Al Maktoum, of the Dubai ruling family, for upwards of a million pounds, an astronomic price at the time. With this money, she bought a private stable at West Ilsley, which she then leased to Major Hern, who also lived in a house she owned. Later that year, Sheikh Hamdan retired Height of Fashion to his stud in Kentucky to be a broodmare.

Two years later, Dick Hern broke his neck in a hunting accident and was paralysed. He managed to continue as a trainer, but then, in the summer of 1988, he suffered a severe heart attack. But he was determined to carry on, so his doughty wife Sheilah wrote to the Queen saying that, though he had undergone major heart surgery, his doctor was confident he would make a good recovery.

The world of racing is chummy, but also strongly competitive; there is no room for the weak. The day before Hern was to undergo a tracheotomy, his wife Sheilah was summoned to an urgent meeting with the Queen's old friend and racing manager, Lord Carnarvon, often known as Porchey,* who told her that, what with one thing and another, her husband was now surplus to needs. 'Dick has been sacked and we have

---

* Carnarvon was called Lord Porchester – hence 'Porchey' – until the death of his father in 1987.

got to get out of the house,' she told the champion jockey Willie Carson that night. This was, Hern thought, 'the worst day of my life'. Years later, Dick Hern said that what had most upset him about Carnarvon's behaviour was that 'when he wanted to tell me I was finished, instead of coming to see me in hospital and looking me in the eye, he summoned my poor wife'.

A week later, the five doctors involved with Hern's recovery convened a meeting. Three of them felt that Hern would be fit enough to continue training, while the other two – both new to his case – were uncertain. Carnarvon seized the opportunity and ordered Sheilah to get her husband to sign a letter stating that 'on the advice of my doctors I have decided to relinquish my Trainer's Licence'.

'Another really nasty day,' Sheilah wrote in her diary, but at that point she didn't realise quite how nasty. Only later did she twig that without a licence her husband's lease on West Ilsley could be automatically terminated. 'I have been set up,' she said.

In desperation, she wrote a letter to the Queen. First, she thanked her for her 'wonderful kindness' in agreeing to let them stay in their home for as long as was necessary, but then adding that his doctors had been amazed at Dick's powers of recovery. 'I know he would very much like to continue to train until his dying day. Sitting in a wheelchair, more or less unable to use his hands, would, I think, drive him dotty.'

But the Queen proved unbudgeable: Hern would no longer train her horses. As word got out, Hern's racing friends rallied round. His fellow trainer Ian Balding warned Carnarvon that the Queen's popularity was in danger of plummeting.

By now on the mend, Hern decided to fight back, and withdrew his request to relinquish his licence, which meant that his lease on the stables at Ilsley could no longer be terminated. That November, he wrote to the Queen asking for a two-year extension as 'I feel that I shall be quite capable of training the horses and it is the work that I love,' and suggesting that, as proof of his fitness for the task, he would undergo a medical examination 'whenever required'.

Again, she turned down the request. Willie Carson felt that this rejection made Hern all the more intent on proving himself up to the job. 'If Dick had been given another two years, he would probably have retired quietly at the end of that period. The refusal put his back up. He is a fighter and very competitive and he became determined to carry on.'

In March 1989, the Palace issued a firm statement. 'The Queen has appointed Mr William Hastings-Bass to take over the West Ilsley stables when Major Hern's lease runs out in November.' Though the rumour of his eviction had been circulating for some time, this was the first official confirmation.

Many in the world of racing condemned this behaviour as uncharitable. Furthermore, Hastings-Bass was Carnarvon's godson and patently not in the same league as Dick Hern. Willie Carson boldly declared it 'a bad decision'. Anger directed at Carnarvon turned, inevitably, on the Queen herself: after all, these two key decisions – to fire her trainer and to evict him from his home – could only have come from above. 'If you don't make some sort of arrangement for Dick Hern,' Ian Balding told Sir Robert Fellowes,* at that time the Queen's deputy private secretary, 'it will be the most unpopular thing the Queen has ever done, and she risks having her horses booed in the winners' enclosure.'

Sensing trouble ahead, Fellowes duly posted Hern a letter. It was headed Windsor Castle, though he insisted he was writing 'in a private capacity'. He spoke of the anguish recent events had caused both the Queen and Lord Carnarvon, but his velvety style only partially concealed the Corleone-ish threat beneath:

> I believe that the sort of stuff being written and said about the West Ilsley lease is bad for racing, bad for the Queen and by extension the country, and not, in fact, in your real interests ... So my conclusion is that you and Sheilah are the only ones who can help matters. Were

---

* Robert Fellowes (b.1941), the son of the Queen's land agent at Sandringham, rose through the ranks of courtiers, from assistant private secretary to the Queen (1977–86), to deputy private secretary (1986–90) and finally to private secretary (1990–9). He accrued suitable titles along the way: he was knighted in 1989 and created a peer in 1999. His full title is currently Lord Fellowes, GCB, GCVO, QSO, PC.

either of you to bring yourselves to tell a respected journalist or two two things, the situation could yet be greatly improved. The two are: (a) that you have always been treated with generosity and consideration by the Queen, and (b) that you respect and understand her decision not to renew your lease. At all events, I do know that, whatever the rights and wrongs of the past months, your health and your future have been the prime considerations for the Queen throughout.

Into this unlikely tale now rides the saviour, in the equally unlikely form of the owner Sheikh Hamdan Al Maktoum. Unlike the Queen, Sheikh Hamdan remained loyal to Dick Hern and bought him new premises outside Lambourn. In May 1989, his horse Nashwan – the offspring of Height of Fashion, the horse he had bought from the Queen – won the 2000 Guineas at Newmarket. Nashwan had been trained by Hern and was ridden by Willie Carson. Victory was sweet. As Carson rode Nashwan into the winners' enclosure, Dick Hern, still confined to a wheelchair, raised his Panama hat in celebration, and the crowd went mad. 'I'd never had a reception like it …' recalled Carson. 'It wasn't just the horse winning the Guineas, it was the situation – Dick Hern being told to leave. There were two sides, people for and people against, and it all came out, coming into that winners' enclosure at Newmarket, where all the people for him just erupted. It was marvellous … I can still hear it in my ears, all the lovely things that were being said, and we got three cheers for Dick Hern from the public, and that doesn't often happen. I could see a tear in that man's eye that day … the tough major. It was a very special day.'

By this time, Hern's rough treatment at the hands of the Queen's racing manager had become common knowledge. 'There were great cheers and a throng surrounding the crippled Dick Hern,' observed Woodrow Wyatt, present in his capacity as chairman of the Tote. 'There was high feeling that the Queen had behaved very badly in not renewing his lease … At lunch in our room I said … "The Queen has done something I thought was impossible. She is turning the Jockey Club and the racing world into republicans."'

Those cheers for Hern and Nashwan were, in Brough Scott's words, 'racing's equivalent of the no-flag moment outside Buckingham Palace before Princess Diana's funeral … an outrage inflamed into near rebellion'. Preparing to file his report of the race for the next day's newspaper, Scott asked 'a leading member of the Establishment' what he should write. 'Go for the jugular,' came the reply.

Soon afterwards, the Palace climbed down, and issued a statement:

> In November 1988, with the knowledge of the officials of the Jockey Club, Her Majesty the Queen made an offer to Major Hern whereby at the end of his present lease, which expires in November of this year, he should share the West Ilsley stables for 1990 with William Hastings-Bass. Although at the time Major Hern felt unable to take up this offer, the Queen has now improved it and Major Hern has gratefully accepted the offer in principle.

This tale has all the ingredients of a fairy tale: magical horse, triumphant underdog, heartless monarch, jubilant populace. How could it have happened? The Queen, usually so loyal, and with such acute antennae for fluctuations in public sentiment, had taken a wrong step. Luckily for her, her henchman attracted most of the ignominy. But, when it came to racing, she was always hands-on; Carnarvon would never have taken those decisions without consulting her.

For the rest of that racing season, the applause remained constant for the Queen Mother, but was notably more muted for her daughter. At Epsom on 7 June, the Queen bore the additional humiliation of watching Nashwan, the progeny of the horse she had sold, trained by the man she had fired, winning the Derby, the one race she had always longed to win. Nashwan went on to win the Eclipse Stakes at Sandown and the King George and Queen Elizabeth Stakes at Ascot. He remains the only horse ever to have won all three races in the same season.

A fortnight later, Woodrow Wyatt attended the polo at Smith's Lawn, always a very social event. For the very first time, he relaxed a little in the presence of the Queen. 'I now find myself almost human talking to the Queen whereas previously I had been tongue tied.' After listening to the Queen's thoughts on the increasing Arab dominance in the world of racing, he went to chat with the Marquess of Tavistock, who said he thought Carnarvon had behaved 'disgracefully' towards Major Hern. 'He said Porchey can do anything with the Queen,' Wyatt confided to his diary that evening. 'When she was very young she was much in love with him and wanted to marry him. But he wouldn't marry her. She then fell in love with Prince Philip. But she still loves Porchester in a way, and, for her, he can do no wrong.'

Others were less gossipy, but no less vehement. Ian Balding described it to Hern's biographer, Peter Willett, as 'the saddest, nastiest, episode in racing history'.

Even the most thorough Royal biographers tend to glide over the episode or to ignore it entirely. Possibly this is because it seems so out of character. They can't see how it fits in with their overall picture of the Queen as measured and loyal and fair. But, then again, all our characters are made up of a variety of warring impulses, and when we give some of them a free rein, they may carry us away.

74

On 15 February 1996, Richard Eyre, the director of the National Theatre* goes to Buckingham Palace, for lunch with the Queen.

His fellow guests include the head of the Fire Service, the chief medical officer and the actress Patricia Routledge, who has recently retired from her role as the snobbish Hyacinth Bucket (pronounced 'Bouquet') in the TV sitcom *Keeping Up Appearances*.†

The guests are chatting to assorted equerries and ladies in waiting when their conversation comes to an abrupt halt. 'In the silence we hear the light tapping of dog paws on parquet.' The corgis enter first, followed by the Queen and Prince Philip.

The Queen, thinks Eyre, is '*exactly*' like Prunella Scales's impersonation of her in Alan Bennett's play *A Question of Attribution* – 'the same mixture of charm, belligerence and bashfulness, and an endearing habit of giggling: an absolutely conventional and very well-briefed upper-class woman'.

Eyre finds himself seated next to her. She asks him about the BBC, and says that the chairman, Marmaduke Hussey, husband of her lady in waiting Lady Susan Hussey, has been placed in a very difficult position over Princess Diana's recent appearance on *Panorama*. 'Frightful thing to do,' she says.

---

* Correctly, though rarely, called the Royal National Theatre.

† 'It was one of what I call my All Walks of Life luncheons,' the Queen tells Sir Anthony Blunt, the Surveyor of the Queen's Pictures and former Soviet spy, in Alan Bennett's play *A Question of Attribution*. 'Today we had the head of the CBI, an Olympic swimmer, a primary school headmistress, a General in the Salvation Army and Glenda Jackson. It was a bit sticky.'

Their conversation moves on to racing and horses (during which she becomes 'very animated') and then to the restoration of historic buildings. Eyre says it is awful that the government are trying to sell off the Naval College at Greenwich. The Queen agrees. 'It all started with Mrs Thatcher,' she says, adding that the government are now selling off the Royal Yacht *Britannia*. 'I feel rather miffed. They're selling it with the contents, and it's my stuff.'

Eyre mentions Harold Macmillan's speech in the House of Lords, in which the stately former prime minister complained that Mrs Thatcher's Tory government was selling off the family silver.

'But of course he didn't have any,' replies the Queen, not quite getting his point. 'It was his wife's – she was a Devonshire.' Eyre replies that he thinks Macmillan was employing a figure of speech.

Their talk turns to theatre and opera. The Queen remembers going to the Royal Opera House at Covent Garden with her mother and sister when it reopened after the war. During Wagner's *Ring*, the giant Norwegian soprano Kirsten Flagstad crushed a tiny tenor, then put a piece of chiffon over her face which kept blowing up because she was out of breath. 'Margaret and I couldn't stop giggling,' says the Queen, 'and Mummy was frightfully cross.' She also remembers seeing some other opera 'in which someone has lost something in a forest'.

'*The Marriage of Figaro*?' suggests Eyre. '*The Magic Flute*?'

'That's it. A flute. Yes, it was hilarious.'

Eyre notices that there is a hook under the table on which she hangs her handbag.

At the cheese course, she takes an oatmeal biscuit out of a silver box and feeds it to her dogs.

After lunch, Prince Philip approaches. He says he stopped going to the theatre in the 1960s: 'All that frightful kitchen-sink stuff.' He wants to know what is coming on at the National Theatre.

'*The Prince's Play*,' replies Eyre. It is an anti-monarchical French play by Victor Hugo. Tactfully, he fails to mention that they have relocated it to Victorian London, and that its villain is now the future King Edward VII: the Queen's great-grandfather is to be seen satisfying his lust on the wives and daughters of courtiers eager for Royal preferment.

Just over a year later, Eyre visits Buckingham Palace again, this time to receive a knighthood. After the run-through, he tells the man who is in charge of the Royal Marines that he likes his uniform, which is very tight and dark blue with a red stripe down the trouser leg. The man looks back at him in an affronted manner, imagining Eyre has been making a pass.

When his turn to be knighted comes, Eyre walks to the front, to musical accompaniment from *My Fair Lady*, and kneels on the little rostrum. His conversation with the Queen is brief but to the point:

HMQ: So you're at the National Theatre?

EYRE: Yes, indeed.

HMQ: How interesting.

75

i

In 2007, the Queen holds a reception at Buckingham Palace for Americans living in London. As she talks to a group of sportsmen, a man barges his way into the gathering.

'Do you play football too?' she asks.

'No. I sell pancake and waffle mix, mostly in the Middle East.'

'How **interesting**, what people will eat,' says the Queen, before moving on.

ii

Visiting the Skypark business centre in Glasgow in July 2021, the Queen says, 'It is a **very interesting** new field. Well done.'

iii

On a video call with scientists and schoolchildren to mark British Science Week in March 2021, the Queen speaks to the co-presenter of *The Sky at Night*, Maggie Aderin-Pocock, who tells her she shares a birthday with Yuri Gagarin, the first man in space.

'I believe, ma'am, that you met him,' she says.

'I did indeed, yes. It was **very interesting** to meet him.'

'What was he like?' asks Aderin-Pocock.

'Russian,' replies the Queen. 'He didn't speak English. But, no, no, he was fascinating.'

iv

In 1938, Richard Baldwyn* lands his first job, in the Harrods toy department. He is tasked with making a model aircraft perform loop-the-loops. One day, the Queen Mother appears with Princess Elizabeth and Princess Margaret. Baldwyn grows flustered and loses control. The plane comes crashing down at their feet.

'How **very interesting**,' says the Queen Mother, and moves on.

v

In 1999, Les Murray arrives at Buckingham Palace to receive the Queen's Gold Medal for Poetry. Brought up on his father's remote dairy farm in New South Wales, Murray used to mind the cattle barefoot, finding warmth in winter by jumping on fresh cowpats. Taunted as 'Fatso' from an early age, he still regards himself as the poet of the misfit. He speaks for 'the aberrant, the original, the wounded'. Active in the Australian Commonwealth Party, he believes that 'Australia will be a great nation, and a power for good in the world, when her head of state is a part-Aboriginal and her prime minister a poor man. Or vice versa.'

Before he is led in to see the Queen, he is briefed by a courtier on the dos and don'ts of correct behaviour. 'Neck bow, not a bow from the waist ... Never begin a conversation ... Address her the first time as Your Majesty and thereafter as Ma'am to rhyme with jam.'

'Mr Les Murray,' announces the courtier, as the double doors burst open. The Queen shakes Murray's hand and hands him a slim leather box. Murray opens it to look inside, and the medal falls to the ground.

Murray picks it up. They sit down. There is a prolonged silence. Unlike those she speaks to, the Queen is untroubled by silence.

'Well,' she says at last. 'Australia.' She pronounces it 'Orstralia'.

---

* Richard Baldwyn (1921–2020) went on to found the budget record label Music for Pleasure. In 1980, he released 'There's No One Quite Like Grandma' by St Winifred's School Choir, which beat Abba, Queen and John Lennon's 'Starting Over' to the top of that year's Christmas top 10. The song had originally been recorded in celebration of the Queen Mother's eightieth birthday.

'Oh, yes, your Majesty,' says Murray, in a great rush. 'Australia's a beautiful place with beautiful cities Perth and Melbourne and Sydney with the Sydney Opera House and beautiful country as well Ayers Rock the Great Barrier Reef and then there are wonderful creatures too the kangaroo of course the Aboriginal people have many different names for the kangaroo and then there's the kookaburra and the echida and the duck-billed platypus which is especially interesting because it has a kind of homing device in its nose that allows it ...'

He rambles on in this vein before coming to an abrupt halt. Then more silence.

'**Very interesting**,' says the Queen. She then presses the bell on her table, signalling for the double doors to be opened, and for Murray to depart.

vi

Letter to *The Times*, 28 November 2022:

Sir, Gyles Brandreth's reflections on the Queen's pragmatic use of English reminded me of an anecdote from my time teaching in 1980's London. A leading teachers' union official was due to meet the Queen. As he queued for the honour an equerry informed him that as soon as Her Majesty said 'How **interesting**' the encounter was over and she would progress to the next person in line. When the Queen eventually reached him, she asked: 'What do you do?' He duly informed her that he was a leading union official. 'How **very, very interesting**,' she replied, and moved on.

Enda Cullen

Armagh

76

I met her once, almost by chance. I was 20 years old, and a friend invited me and a handful of other twenty-somethings to his parents' twenty-fifth wedding anniversary. His parents were titled and unusually wealthy: their Kensington house was by far the smallest they owned, but still came with a fake bookshelf in the sitting room, which led into a ballroom.

This ballroom was where the party was being held. I entered it early with my bunch of friends, all of us more familiar with student events involving beanbags, joss sticks and cider. I imagine we made an effort to smarten up, but we were, for the most part, a scruffy lot. For the first half hour, we huddled in a corner, swiftly holding out our glasses each time a waiter passed by.

I must have been aware that the Queen was there, but I had no thought of meeting her. I felt she was for the real guests, the grown-

In 1970, the eminent paediatrician and psychoanalyst Donald Winnicott wrote his only essay on monarchy. Though in his own words 'not unduly sentimental' about the institution, he took its existence seriously, recognising that 'without the monarchy Great Britain would be quite a different place to live in'.

In 'The Place of the Monarchy', Winnicott suggested that the dream/reality of a monarchy is the surest way of preserving democracy. 'There is … a profound and a great value to the individual in the survival of central things, of which in our country the monarchy is one. Reality becomes more real and the personal impulse of primitive exploration less dangerous.' Moreover, within a democracy 'a monarchy can give rise to a feeling of stability in a country where the political scene is in a state of turmoil, as periodically it should be'.

Winnicott built his considerable reputation on the idea of the

ups. So it came as a surprise when, crossing from one side of the crowded room to the other, I bumped into my friend's father, a very courteous man. 'Ah, Craig,' he said. 'Would you like to be presented?'

So there I was, a second later, shaking hands with the Queen. 'Craig has been writing some amusing articles for *Punch* magazine,' said my host.

'Really? That must be fun,' she replied. I took this as a clear sign that she wanted to know all about *Punch* and *Private Eye* and the difference between the two magazines. I was unstoppable. I told her all about English humour, and Wodehouse and Monty Python and Just William and Marty Feldman, not forgetting Edward Lear and Lewis Carroll. 'How interesting,' she would chip in, every now and then, or sometimes, 'Most amusing,' and these would spur me into new zones, including drama, of which I had until recently been a student, and in particular the theatre of Bertolt Brecht ('Fascinating') and his various theories of comedy and alienation, which I half remembered from the earnest Marxist lecturers who had dominated my old drama department.

'transitional object': an item such as a blanket or a teddy bear which stands in for the mother. This object allows the child to maintain a bond with the mother when she is elsewhere. It thus helps relieve anxiety. As children grow to adulthood, they abandon their blankets and teddy bears, and replace them with more sophisticated transitional objects from the realms of science, religion and culture. These, too, offer security.

For Winnicott, the mental health of each individual exists in the gap between the imagination and reality. 'In psychiatric health, the individual human being does in fact live most of the time in this intermediate area, and the way to study this subject is to let babies teach us by their use of what I call transitional objects, but which could be called their life in Pooh-country, or poetry.'

The monarch was, he thought, just such a transitional object. Those who scorned the monarchy as no more than a sentimental fairy tale were failing to see the point.

'It may be', he wrote, 'that the fairy tale is felt to be an escapist exercise, weakening our resolve to alter bad things in the economy, bad or inadequate housing, the loneliness of old people, the helplessness of the physically handicapped, the

All the while, I kept spying my friends over her left shoulder in the far corner of the room. They were pointing at me and sniggering, but I rose above it. After all, I had to tell Her Majesty about *The Resistible Rise of Arturo Ui* and the various dramatic innovations ('Really? Goodness!') introduced by Brecht. Though I barely knew what I was talking about, and have now forgotten what little I knew, I now think it's possible that, in a funny sort of way, the shadow of Brecht and his theory of alienation was being mirrored in our conversation, if you could call it a conversation. Brecht, I was trying to explain, thought that the play is a representation of reality, and not reality itself. He wanted drama to acknowledge its own artificiality, so that the audience could then see that reality itself was a construct.

I still have vivid memories of our meeting, getting on for half a century ago, when I was young and feckless. I had seen her face every week of my life, perhaps even every day. She was both a person and a symbol, a total stranger yet wholly familiar. And there she was in front of me, expressing an interest ('Yes, I see, hmm, fascinating') in everything I said. Who knows?

discomfort of squalor and poverty, or the tragedy of persecutions based on prejudice. The word "escapist" sums up this attitude, and on these grounds the fairy tale is already damned.' But those whose thoughts ran along these lines were, he thought, ignoring the psychological benefits of a monarchy.

The value of the transitional object is maintained by 'the acceptance of the paradox that links external reality to inner experience'. 'In terms of the baby with a piece of cloth or a teddy-bear essential for security and happiness and symbolic of an ever-available mother … we never make the challenge: did you create this or did you find something already there? … In terms of the monarchy, the man or woman who is on the throne is everyone's dream and yet is a real man or woman with all human characteristics. Only if we are remote from this woman, the Queen, can we afford to dream and to place her in the area of myth.'

'For the millions, and I am one of these millions, this woman is acting my dream for me and at the same time she is a human being whom I might see in her car as I sit waiting in a taxi while she emerges from Buckingham Palace to perform some function which is part of her living

Perhaps for those few minutes I fell under the illusion that I was as familiar to her as she was to me.

As I kept talking, I noticed that, every now and then, she would take a step back. So I would take a step forward, and she would take a step back, and so on. We might have continued like this forever – Ginger Rogers and Fred Astaire – had my friend's father not intervened on her behalf, taking her off to speak to someone else, and leaving me to make my way across the room, and back to reality.

out the role assigned to her by fate, and in which she is maintained by most of us ... While I am cursing because of the delay which means that I shall be late for my appointment, I know that we need the formality, the deference, and the dream-come-true paraphernalia. Quite possibly the woman who is queen is sometimes hating it all too, but we never know, because we have nearly no access to the details of this particular woman's life and person, this being the way to keep up her dream-significance.'

77

Andy Warhol and the Queen were near contemporaries: the Queen was born in Mayfair, London, on 21 April 1926 and Andy Warhol was born in Pittsburgh, Pennsylvania, on 6 August 1928.

I spent a few days shadowing Warhol on his visit to Britain in 1979, and noticed they had other things in common, too. They had both met an inordinate number of people (one out of choice, the other out of duty); both employed a similar stonewall defence in interactions, somehow appearing to participate in conversation without surrendering anything of themselves; both employed generalised enthusiasm in a truncated form. For the Queen, 'How interesting' or 'Really?' was usually sufficient to keep a conversation ticking along; Warhol was also fond of 'interesting', but more often employed its transatlantic equivalent: 'Gee' or 'Gee, that's great.'

For meeting strangers, these non-committal, reflex exclamations were usually more than enough. The job of twentieth-century celebrities was to mirror the expectations of those they encountered.

Warhol and the Queen both preferred to keep their feelings and opinions to themselves. 'She inclines to say less rather than more,' Prince Philip once observed of his wife. Her critics would harp on about her blankness. Polly Toynbee of the *Guardian* once described her as 'the past mistress of nothingness'. Similar observations were often levelled at Warhol, too, though in the bleak world of contemporary art 'nothingness' was often taken for praise.

The Queen took her fame as a given. It was part of her, something she had to live with, like a birthmark. But Warhol, unknown until his early thirties, never stopped hankering for more. 'I want to be as famous as the Queen of England,' he once said.

Warhol's diaries are peppered with references to the Royal Family. 'Checked in at the Savoy ...' reads his entry for Friday, 20 July 1979. 'Sabrina Guinness was at dinner, and she's been going out with Prince Charles a lot, and we think she fucked him.'

He frequently encountered those on its outer fringes, regarding them, with eagerness, as outriders to the main attraction. 'Pingle – the Princess Ingeborg Schleswig-Holstein – came, who works at *Interview* now,' he wrote on his fifty-second birthday, in 1980. 'She's related to Queen Elizabeth.' Three months later, he met the Kents. 'Prince and Princess Michael of Kent arrived and they were really classy,' he said. 'She had on a little hat and a big dress, and she explained that she was pregnant – *she* was friendly to me. She showed me a picture of her eighteen-month-old baby. The prince had on a well-cut suit – the English know how to give you a new body with a suit, putting the stuff in the right places.' Four days later, he welcomed the Kents to his studio. 'I'd painted a background and thought it would dry before anyone got there and that I could roll it up. So I had to spread it out on the floor and then suddenly they arrived and Prince Michael walked right on it, he thought it was floor covering. So Fred asked him to autograph it. And he just signed it "Michael", he didn't use "Prince".'

On his visit to England the year before, Warhol had visited Vivienne Westwood and Malcolm McLaren's punk store on the King's Road, which had recently been renamed Seditionaries.* In the aftermath of punk, it had transformed from a revolutionary Situationist outpost into a pricy tourist destination for punk memorabilia, though Warhol failed to notice the difference. 'We got shirts that were made out of

---

* This shop, at 430 King's Road, had changed its name many times since it first opened in the early Sixties as The 430 Boutique. Its various name changes form a sort of micro-history of fashion trends: Hung On You (1967–9), Mr Freedom (1969–70), Paradise Garage (1970–1). McLaren took it over in 1971, renaming it Let It Rock. In 1973 he changed it to Too Fast to Live, Too Young to Die, then to Sex (1974–6), Seditionaries (1976–80) and finally World's End (1980 to the present day).

Nazi symbols and that you could tie yourself together with,' he enthused. 'And a T-shirt of two cocks pissing on Marilyn Monroe's photograph, saying the word "Piss". Among the retro souvenirs were T-shirts bearing the Queen's head, rendered punk by the addition of the cut-out newspaper headlines 'GOD Save THE QUEEN' and 'SEX PISTOLS' over her eyes and mouth.*

Three years on, Warhol's dealer wrote to the Queen asking for permission to use her portrait in a series of screenprints. Ten days later, he received this letter back:

> Dear Mr Mulder,
> I am commanded by The Queen to
> acknowledge your letter of 6th September
> about Mr. Warhol's plans to paint portraits
> of Their Majesties The Queens of Great
> Britain, Denmark and The Netherlands.
> While The Queen would certainly not wish
> to put any obstacles in Mr. Warhol's way,
> she would not dream of offering any comment
> on this idea.
> > Yours sincerely,
> > W. Heseltine

By 1985, Warhol's screenprints – brightly coloured versions of Grugeon's original 1975 portraits – were ready.

> Dear Mr Mulder,
> I am commanded by The Queen to
> acknowledge your letter of 11 March
> and to thank you for sending the
> photographs of the silkscreen prints by

---

* The original photograph was taken by Peter Grugeon at Windsor Castle in 1975. It was chosen by the Palace to celebrate the Queen's Silver Jubilee in 1977, before being commandeered by the punk designer Jamie Reid for his own subversive purposes.

Andy Warhol which Her Majesty was
most pleased and interested to see.
    Yours sincerely,
    W. Heseltine

Three months later, Warhol rode in Prince Rupert Loewenstein's
Bentley to the opening of his *Reigning Queens* exhibition on West
Broadway and Green Street. He left early, filled with self-loathing. 'I've
hit rock bottom,' he confessed to his diary. 'This show, I have sunk to
the bottom of the gutter. The rock bottom of the skids of the end of the
line. It was like having an opening in somebody's rent-controlled
apartment … It was so low-down and tacky.' He went on to a fashion
show, then to dinner at Mr Chow's with Boy George and Marilyn, both
at the height of their fame. 'And Boy George and Marilyn like me I
think because they can say mean things and then I'm not quick enough
to think of a comeback, so I'm not a threat to them.'

That September, he went to the next opening of *Reigning Queens*,
but only with reluctance. He had still not warmed to these works of his
own. 'I just hate George Mulder for showing here in America. They
were supposed to be only for Europe – nobody here cares about royalty
and it'll just be another bad review.'

Nevertheless, Warhol's personal interest in royalty remained
constant. Few, if any, British artists shared his keen, almost feverish,
fascination with even the most humdrum Royal goings-on. On a trip
to London on 9 July 1986, he noted, 'This is the week in between
Wimbledon and Fergie's marriage, so it was exciting.' And two weeks
later: 'I've been watching this stuff on Fergie and I wonder why doesn't
the Queen Mother get married again.'

He had once taken a fancy to the Queen's second son, but with time
his interest faded. 'Prince Andrew has gotten so ugly, he's looking like
his mother,' he noted in his diary on 11 February 1987. This was to be
one of his last entries: eleven days later, he underwent a routine operation on his gallbladder, and died.

But a quarter of a century after his death, Andy Warhol secured
himself a permanent home in Buckingham Palace. For an undisclosed

sum, the Royal Collection purchased the portrait of the Queen from the *Reigning Queens* portfolio in its expensive 'Royal' edition,* sprinkled with diamond dust, lending it a sparkly effect.

'Warhol has simplified Grugeon's portrait so that all that remains is a mask-like face,' runs the official Royal Collection catalogue entry. 'All character has been removed and we are confronted by a symbol of royal power.'

---

* On 24 November 2022, two months after the death of the Queen, one of these Warhol portraits sold for £954,667, breaking the global record for a Warhol print sold at auction.

78

Another contemporary of the Queen, just six months her senior, was Margaret Thatcher. The 23-year-old Margaret Roberts first set eyes on her future monarch at Newmarket races in 1949. She immediately succumbed to a common delusion. 'SAW PRINCESS ELIZABETH, AND SHE SAW ME!' she wrote in excited capitals in a boyfriend's diary.

Thirteen years later, by now a married woman and the Conservative MP for Finchley, Margaret Thatcher was pleased to be invited to a reception at Buckingham Palace. 'The Queen has a much stronger personality than most people realise and she is certainly not overshadowed by the Duke of Edinburgh,' she told her father in a letter home. As she gazed at the Queen that day, was she, like so many others, unconsciously thinking of herself?

Soon after Mrs Thatcher became leader of the Conservative Party, early in 1975, she had to write a thank-you letter to the Queen for a drinks party at Buckingham Palace. A stickler for matters of protocol and determined not to put a foot wrong, she fretted about how to sign it off. Her diary secretary suggested she simply write a plain, 'Yours sincerely', and this she duly did. But, a day or two later, the Queen's private secretary, Sir Martin Charteris, telephoned, telling the secretary in question ('very sweetly') of her error and of the correct way to do it ('I remain, Your Majesty's most humble and obedient servant'). He then asked her to pass it on to Mrs Thatcher.

Once she became prime minister, Mrs Thatcher would visit the Queen every Tuesday for her weekly audience in Buckingham Palace. These audiences were, says Mrs Thatcher's authorised biographer

Charles Moore, 'rarely productive, because Mrs Thatcher was nervous. The Queen noted the way in which her Prime Minister could never relax in her presence. "Why does she always sit on the edge of her seat?" she asked. The moment she had sat down, she would produce from her bag an agenda from which she launched forth. Far from being, as some docu-dramas and plays have depicted, little speeches in which Mrs Thatcher laid down the law to the Queen, what she said was usually an anodyne recitation of current business.'

The relationship between the two most famous and powerful women in the country was, in the words of the Queen's private secretary, William Heseltine, 'absolutely correct and perhaps not very cosy'. Heseltine felt this might have been at least partly the fault of the Queen, 'for not coming in when Mrs Thatcher drew breath and turning the talk into more of a discussion'. For her part, the Queen seems to have been intrigued by what went on in her prime minister's head.

'Do you think Mrs Thatcher will ever change?' she once asked Lord Carrington, Thatcher's first foreign secretary.

'Oh no, Ma'am,' replied Carrington. 'She would not be Mrs Thatcher if she did.'

How the two women interacted became a topic of speculation.

Susannah Constantine, who had for some time been the girlfriend of Princess Margaret's son, Viscount Linley, once witnessed a tussle over a teapot between the Queen and Mrs Thatcher.

In 1984, at the age of 22, she went to stay at Balmoral. The Thatchers were fellow guests. 'While Denis was actually very relaxed, Thatcher was awkward,' she recalled. In the afternoon, six or seven gathered by the side of the river for tea and sandwiches in a hut 'the size of a suburban front room ... one of them was the prime minister and another the Queen'.

A large teapot, known as Brown Betty, was ready on the table, 'like the Queen herself, unfrivolous, sturdy and practical. Fit for purpose.'

As was her usual practice, the Queen lifted the teapot as Susannah Constantine held out her china cup. 'As if by magic, a redundant Thatcher appeared at her side like a spectre. "Let me do that, Your Majesty."'

Without further ado, Mrs Thatcher put her hand beneath the teapot to take its weight, but 'her offer was met with unexpected resistance from the Queen'. Not knowing what to do, Constantine lowered her cup a little, whereupon Mrs Thatcher 'tightened her fingertips around the base and tried once again to take the pot from its owner, but no … Evidently the Queen had no intention of relinquishing the fat, brown pot. A further, more determined pull from Thatcher was met with an equally resolute hold from Her Majesty.'

Constantine put her cup and saucer back down on the table. 'I didn't imagine the Queen was actually going to *kill* Thatcher … but it was quite tense. Then all of a sudden, without warning, the pot was free: released back to it rightful owner. Thatcher had thrown in the towel.'

Few who witnessed them together could resist gossiping about their peculiar dynamic; any signs of friction were beadily chronicled. For instance, on 10 September 1985, Kenneth Rose* wrote in his diary that the Queen had complained to Lady Trumpington, 'She stays too long and talks too much. She has lived too long among men.'

Gossip like this continued for many years after Mrs Thatcher's fall from power. On 1 June 1997, Rose was Isaiah Berlin's guest at 'a sumptuous tea with delicious smoked-salmon sandwiches … and every sort of chocolate biscuit'. Afterwards, Rose wrote in his diary that Berlin had told him that Mrs Thatcher and the Queen had been at daggers drawn over the Commonwealth:

> Both the Queen and Thatcher came to a gala at Covent Garden,
> but sat in different parts of the house. In the interval the Queen
> let it be known that she did not want to meet Mrs Thatcher – who
> was sent to an upper room for drinks, as was Isaiah. Thatcher

---

* Kenneth Rose (1924–2014), journalist, diarist and biographer of King George V and Lord Curzon, was nicknamed 'the Climbing Rose' and loved to hobnob with royalty. One passage from his journals must suffice as illustration. In 1997, he went to Buckingham Palace to pick up his CBE from the Prince of Wales. 'The Prince beams and says, "Well done, Kenneth." I tell him I am lunching with the Queen Mother afterwards. "Oh good, I shall be calling in to see her just before lunch."'

then said she would like to say goodbye to the Queen, a request that was ignored.

Woodrow Wyatt was another incorrigible gossip, and fierce supporter of Mrs Thatcher. He was also was one of the few people to hold a low opinion of the Queen's character, possibly because he sensed that she could see through him. He would eagerly gather any of her reported slights against his beloved Margaret. On 25 July 1986, he sat next to:

> a largeish, charming woman, Lady Mary Colman. She is a niece of Queen Elizabeth the Queen Mother. She was at Balmoral at a house party on an occasion when Mrs Thatcher had been visiting various things in Scotland ... She said the Queen was horrid to Mrs Thatcher. They were talking about the Falklands and the Queen sharply in a loud voice said, 'I don't agree with you at all,' and Mrs Thatcher went red and looked very uncomfortable. Lady Mary Colman felt that the Queen was trying to put Mrs Thatcher down all the time knowing that she was unaccustomed to the kind of society which is upper class and surrounds the Queen.
>
> Denis Thatcher survives much better in these circumstances than Margaret. He makes jokes and laughs uproariously and is quite oblivious of the Queen's unpleasantness ... The Queen has no feelings. I'd always felt that on the brief occasions I have spoken to her.

That same month, the *Sunday Times* ran the headline 'Queen dismayed by "uncaring" Thatcher'. The accompanying story claimed that the Queen 'believes that the Thatcher government lacks compassion and should be more "caring" towards the less privileged', that as a result of the miners' strike 'long-term damage was being done to the country's social fabric', and that she also had 'misgivings' about Mrs Thatcher's decision to let American bombers use British bases to attack Libya. They differed, too, on the role of the Commonwealth, the Queen supporting its demands for sanctions against the apartheid regime in South Africa, while Mrs Thatcher held out against them.

Following the publication of this story, Sir John Junor,* the veteran editor of the *Sunday Express* and an avid Thatcherite, telephoned Mrs Thatcher, who sounded upset. He told her he was going to demand that the Palace issue a statement saying that there was no truth in the story. Either in her words, or his, or a mixture of both, or neither, she replied: 'Please John, don't do that. The only important thing is the Queen. I don't want to see anything happen that could endanger the monarchy.'

Junor was firmly on the side of Mrs Thatcher. 'I just wondered whether the Queen respected Margaret Thatcher half as much as Margaret Thatcher respected her. Or whether at the root of it all her alleged coolness towards the Prime Minister might be that old problem, feminine jealousy.'

Sure enough, under the direction of the Queen's press secretary, Michael Shea, the Palace was to deny all these claims, saying they were 'entirely without foundation'. It later emerged that it was Shea who had briefed the *Sunday Times* reporter about the story in the first place.

'The very person who had fed us the story was now instructing his office to rubbish it' was how the bullish editor of the *Sunday Times*, Andrew Neil, remembered it. It seemed that Shea had succumbed to a common urge among those on the margins: he wanted to show that he was part of the inner circle. And perhaps, like so many others, he had convinced himself that his thoughts were the Queen's thoughts, and her thoughts were his.

Four months later, Wyatt was driving with Jock Colville, the Queen's former private secretary, Gordon Richardson, governor of the Bank of England, and Arnold Weinstock, managing director of General Electric:

---

* Editor of the *Sunday Express* for thirty-two years, Junor was famous for his strident prejudices. He instructed his staff never to trust a man who smoked a pipe or drank rosé wine, or wore a beard, a hat or suede shoes. He has been described by Max Hastings as 'by common consent one of the most disagreeable men in Britain' and by Peregrine Worsthorne as 'a world-class legendary monster ... a deeply unpleasant, philistine and hypocritical man'. Having once solemnly declared that 'no decent journalist should ever accept a bauble from a politician', he went on to accept a knighthood from Mrs Thatcher.

Arnold said Woodrow knows everything but he won't tell. 'Quite right,' said Jock. He then proceeded to relate to me, after the other two had got out, a recent conversation with the Queen. He asked her whether what the *Sunday Times* and Andrew Neil had put in their paper about her attitude to Mrs Thatcher and the government and sanctions was true. 'Not at all, absolutely wrong,' she had replied. He then asked her what she thought of Mrs Thatcher and she said, 'Jock, you do ask the most impertinent questions,' to which he answered, 'Well, Ma'am, I was your private secretary for some years,' and she laughed and said, 'I get on with her all right but like all Prime Ministers she won't listen.'*

In his autobiography, Neil relayed a private conversation Mrs Thatcher once had with Brian Walden, the MP turned TV inquisitor.

'Does that "Queen vs Thatcher" still rankle?' he enquired.

'Yes, it does, Brian,' she replied firmly. 'It hurt me very badly at the time.'

'But you know it was true,' said Brian. 'The Palace was out to undermine you.'

Thatcher hesitated for a moment, then took off her glasses and pinched her nose, bowed her head and said sadly: 'I know, Brian, I know. The problem is the Queen is the kind of woman who could vote SDP.'†

---

* Like so much gossip, this is a repetition of a repetition of a repetition, given that I am repeating Wyatt who was repeating Colville, who was repeating the Queen. So there is a strong element of Chinese whispers going on. And would the Queen really have said 'I get on with her all right'? It sounds too casual, the linguistic equivalent of Her Majesty suddenly slipping into a T-shirt and trainers. But, given time, gossip transforms into history, and from then on is treated with reverence.

† Formed in 1981 by four senior figures in the Labour Party who believed that their party had swung too far to the left, the Social Democratic Party experienced a speedy rise and even speedier fall before the majority of its members voted to merge with the Liberal Party.

But even after a decade or more as prime minister, Margaret Thatcher's sense of old-fashioned awe in the presence of her monarch never left her. On Christmas Day, she would still make sure that lunch was finished in time to watch the Queen's speech on television. 'She revered both the constitution and the monarch,' recalled her devoted bushy-browed press secretary Sir Bernard Ingham. 'That was manifested in the way she curtsied. I've never seen anyone go so low and I wondered if she'd ever get up. It used to be a bit of a joke – how low will she go this time?'

As her years in Downing Street rolled on, some observers began to notice that Mrs Thatcher was beginning, in a strange, shape-shifting way, to morph into the monarch. Little by little, she took on many of the Queen's most familiar props: her thick-heeled patent-leather shoes, her handbag and, on formal occasions, her regal cloaks and gowns. She even started adopting the royal 'we', employing it in increasingly bizarre ways. 'We are a grandmother,' she told reporters after the birth of her son Mark's baby boy. 'We are in a fortunate position in Britain of being, as it were, the senior person in power,' she announced to an interviewer. And, having visited a block of flats in Moscow: 'We have enjoyed ourselves immensely.'

For her part, the Queen was known to find the Thatchers a little comical in their efforts to please. The Duke of Devonshire told James Lees-Milne that the Queen was 'quite indiscreet' about the Thatchers. 'She said to one of the equerries at the Palace while awaiting them, "Don't make me laugh when Denis bows from the waist."'

After the 1982 Falklands conflict, some felt Mrs Thatcher had usurped the role of the Queen by taking the salute at the victory parade; her visit to the Falklands the following January resembled a royal progress. 'The constant references to "her" troops proclaim that this is a royal visit,' wrote a commentator in *The Times*. In the *Sunday Telegraph*, Peregrine Worsthorne noted that her manner was becoming 'more regal than the Queen's': in key respects a Thatcherite, he worried that her 'new and exalted status' had gone to her head. After national disasters, she would lose no time in visiting the victims. 'In the event of death or serious injury' read a joke badge, popular among her opponents, 'I do not wish to be visited by Margaret Thatcher'. The cartoonists began to depict her, in all her grandeur, riding the Queen's horse for Trooping the Colour.

In the study of dementia, Ribot's Law states that the most recent memories are the first to be lost. Those suffering from the disease may be able to recall events from their childhoods with great clarity, while struggling to remember their own address or the name of the current prime minister.

In 1985, two psychiatrists, Dr Ian Deary and Dr Simon Wessely, reported on a new phenomenon in the *British Medical Journal*. Four of their patients suffering from advanced dementia – unable to remember their own names, or what year it was – were nevertheless able to name Mrs Thatcher as the prime minister. A study of files from 1963 and 1968 revealed one further oddity. In those years, Queen Elizabeth II had been identified with much greater frequency than either of the two prime ministers. But by 1983 'Mrs Thatcher ... was clearly more prominent in our patients' minds than the monarch.'

'We have become a nation with two monarchs,' observed the political commentator (and later novelist) Robert Harris in 1988. '... On her housewife/superstar progress around the world, Margaret Thatcher has steadily become more like the Queen of England than the real thing.' In the *Daily Telegraph*, the satirist Auberon Waugh playfully suggested that the time had come to appoint her Deputy Queen of England.

Some sensed a competitive edge in relations between the two women. During one of her annual diplomatic receptions at the Palace, the Queen noticed that her prime minister, feeling a little faint, had decided to take a seat. 'Oh, look, she's keeled over again,' she observed, coolly.

But if there was friction between them, it vanished with Mrs Thatcher's departure from office. On her way to the Palace to give the Queen notice of her resignation, her long-time driver, Denis Oliver, sought to comfort her, saying, 'Don't worry, Prime Minister, Bob [her personal protection officer] and I will be staying with you when you leave.'

This seemed to catch Mrs Thatcher unawares, and she began to cry. After her audience with the Queen, the tears flowed once more. 'She was deeply upset,' recalled Lord Fellowes; '... when she emerged from her audience, she was in a very distressed state and unable to speak.' She had to be helped down the stairs. Back in Downing Street, 'she went straight upstairs to the flat and ran to the bathroom and she absolutely wept', recalled her personal assistant Cynthia 'Crawfie' Crawford. 'She said: "It's when people are kind to you that you feel it most. The Queen has been so kind to me."'

In 2005, an eightieth-birthday party was thrown for Margaret Thatcher at the Mandarin Oriental Hotel in Knightsbridge. By now, a series of strokes had rendered her mind hazy. As she saw the Queen approaching, she asked, 'Is it all right if I touch her?' She held out her hand as she curtsied, and the Queen took it and steadied her.

'That was unusual for the British, who know you are not supposed to touch the Queen,' observed her former private secretary for foreign affairs, Charles Powell. 'But they were hand in hand, and the Queen led her around the room.'

79

In another dream, I was staying as a guest in Windsor Castle, up the same staircase as the Queen, but one floor down. I was in swimming trunks and a raggedy towelling robe. I knew I should have been dressed more formally, and kept almost bumping into her at every turn. I would spot her and dart up or down narrow stone spiral staircases, like staircases in churches that go up to the bell tower, but these ones led out on to rocky paths, with precipitous falls: Windsor Castle was surrounded by mountains.

Everyone was about to go into the chapel for a formal service. I knew I was meant to attend, but I was still in my towelling robe. I felt I should quickly go and change, but on my way upstairs I saw the Queen coming downstairs towards me, and I thought: I simply don't have the time. So I did my usual trick of leaping into a doorway and down a spiral staircase, and once again found myself out in the countryside, with its rocks and gullies.

Palace staff in livery kept spotting me and coming after me. Eventually, I got back inside the Castle, but couldn't find my way around. By now people had begun coming out of the church service, so I hid from them. I rushed through formal rooms until I entered a sort of dining room cum drawing room, with lots of staff laying tables and so forth: a flurry of activity.

A pleasant Italian butler with a droopy moustache approached me. I told him I was a guest and that I couldn't find my bedroom. He asked me to follow him, and then wanted to know my name. He was about to check it on the guest list when he said, with his Italian accent, 'I a-remember serving you at a-breakfast.' I said that, yes, I had also been wearing my towelling robe then, so he probably remembered me like that.

'Yes,' he said, in a tone of regret, 'I expect you were sorrowful to have a-dressed like a-that.'

80

In 1934, one of Queen Victoria's granddaughters, Marie, Queen of Romania, published her autobiography, *The Story of My Life*.

Virginia Woolf declared that no book published that season was more interesting or more strange. She offered four reasons: 'that she is royal; that she can write; that no royal person has ever been able to write before; and that the consequences may well be extremely serious'.

The Royal Family was, Woolf felt, 'an experiment in the breeding of human nature' and therefore 'of great psychological interest'. For centuries, 'a certain family has been segregated; bred with a care only lavished upon race horses; splendidly housed, clothed and fed; abnormally stimulated in some ways, suppressed in others; worshipped, stared at, and kept shut up, as lions and tigers are kept, in a beautiful brightly lit room behind bars'.

Coincidentally, this accords with Prince Harry's view, expressed almost ninety years later. 'I've seen behind the curtain,' he told the American actor Dax Shepherd on a podcast in 2021, 'I've seen the business model, I know how this operation runs and how it works. I don't want to be part of this. It's a mix of being in *The Truman Show* and being in the zoo.'

Virginia Woolf saw all sorts of dangers in housing a select group of human beings in a zoo. 'The psychological effect upon them must be profound; and the effect upon us is as remarkable … Sane men and women as we are, we cannot rid ourselves of the superstition that there is something miraculous about these people shut up in their cage.'

She believed Queen Marie to be unique among the Royal Families of Europe. Though an indefatigable writer, Queen Victoria had been, in her opinion, a poor observer: 'her poverty stricken words are bruised and battered'. But Queen Marie was a natural writer, with a sharp eye. She noticed things, such as Queen Victoria's teeth ('small, like those of a mouse') and the way she had of shrugging her shoulders when she laughed. She was happy to relay the Queen's failings, such as her extreme nosiness and bossiness, and the way she made her children quail: 'a tremendous, almost a fearful force ... Right into their ripe years her sons and daughters were in great awe of "dearest Mamma"; they avoided discussing her will, and her veto made them tremble. They spoke to her with bated breath, and even when not present she was never mentioned except with lowered voice.'

Marie extended her revelations to her Uncle Bertie (the future King Edward VII) – 'too patronizing, he lorded it too much over everyone, and we were not yet old enough to come under the influence of his charm' – and also to her three cousins who 'made us feel cruelly the inferiority'. She even went for her own parents. Her mother's 'punctuality amounted to a mania ... so severe was she in her training about punctuality that all my life I retained an anxious and almost guilty feeling about time'. And her father was a philistine who hated music and 'had a way of sticking out his underlip in a sort of pout' before losing his temper.

By writing such a detailed memoir, Queen Marie had, said Woolf, escaped the zoo's golden bars. 'She has opened the door of the cage and sauntered out into the street ... She is no longer a royal queen in a cage. She ranges the world, free like any other human being to laugh, to scold, to say what she likes, to be what she is.'

On the other hand, by publishing her autobiography, with all its spiky observations, she had undermined the magic of royalty. 'Royalty is no longer quite royal.' Her Royal relations would no longer be 'mere effigies bowing and smiling, opening bazaars, expressing exalted sentiments and remembering faces always with the same sweet smile'. No: from now on, they would be seen as flesh-and-blood human beings, 'violent and eccentric; charming and ill-tempered; some have bloodshot eyes; others handle flowers with a peculiar tenderness. In short, they are very like ourselves. They live as we do.'

Portraying their human frailties, Queen Marie had jeopardised their mystique. 'What will be the consequences of this familarity ...? Can we go on bowing and curtsying to people who are just like ourselves? Are we not already a little ashamed of the pushing and the staring now that we know ... that one at least of the animals can talk? We begin to wish that the Zoo should be abolished; that the royal animals should be given the run of some wider pasturage – a Royal Whipsnade?'

81

From mystery to celebrity in 13 steps

i

Summer 1898. The 26-year-old Max Beerbohm, wit, dandy, essayist and caricaturist, is holidaying at Cowes on the Isle of Wight. Across the harbour, the royal yacht, the *Osborne*, is anchored; the Prince of Wales, soon to be King Edward VII, is on board. Max can't take his eyes off the yacht, and he is not alone: all day long, other tourists are similarly transfixed, peering at it through their telescopes. They can see nothing of the Prince, but who cares? 'The strongest lens reveals no glimpse of His Royal Highness, but no one seems to despair ... To me there is something strangely impressive in this sense of a great unseen presence, a something not ourselves which yet directs and controls the hearts of us at all hours ... Never was so absolute an obsession.'

ii

1910. King George V and Queen Mary are known to harbour a deep suspicion of those whom others regard as 'interesting'. The worldly Margot Asquith, wife of the prime minister, makes a note of the various types of people the King and Queen strive to avoid. 'To them, clever men are "prigs"; clever women "too advanced"; liberals are "socialist"; the uninteresting "pleasant"; the interesting "intriguers" and the dreamer "mad".' In no particular order, the King dislikes novelty, dining out, the French language ('effeminate'), women who smoke, women who paint their fingernails, authors ('people who write books ought to be shut up'), short dresses, modern dance and foreign travel ('don't care about going abroad, never did').

After speaking to the Comptroller and Treasurer in Queen Mary's Household, Lord Claud Hamilton, Queen Mary's authorised biographer, James Pope-Hennessy, writes a not dissimilar note:

> The lives led by King George and Queen Mary were inconceivably *dull*. There was a function every three months or so, otherwise they just lived in Buckingham Palace; every Sunday they would go out together without a lady or gentleman and motor to Coppins to call on Princess Victoria.

Under the heading 'Shyness' he adds:

> She was incapable of making conversation. Lord Claud often watched her at, e.g. a military dinner when she was the only woman, amongst distinguished generals etc.; after dinner she would just stand there 'cleaning her teeth with her tongue' and saying nothing.

And under 'Food and Drink':

> The King and Queen liked food, but always the same thing repeated. At Buckingham Palace she seldom if indeed ever saw the chef: she would cross off or add items in the daily menu book. When going to Sandringham the menu had to go down days in advance. In 16 years at M.H. [Marlborough House] she *never* saw the chef once.

When he comes to write the biography, Pope Hennessy points out the isolation of the King and Queen:

> The comparative seclusion in which King George V and Queen Mary were living in the nineteen-twenties contrasted strangely with the contemporaneous revival of social life in London and with the wild jazzy tone of that post-war decade. An absolute quiet reigned within Buckingham Palace …

The King, he adds, had:

> little use for metropolitan or social amusements.

while Queen Mary:

> never cared for 'Society', since she deprecated gossip and detested small-talk.

iii

Shortly after Queen Mary's death in March 1953, James Lees-Milne is sitting in a corner of Brooks's Club, eavesdropping on the late Queen's equerry, Sir John Coke. He listens with interest to Sir John telling a fellow member that Queen Mary was the last of her kind.

> He said she never altered her mind once it had been made up; that she had never been known to be late once in her life; that now she was gone there was no member of the Royal family to keep the rest of them up to the mark, no one now to prevent the Queen from having meals with people like Douglas Fairbanks, from motoring in a jeep without wearing a hat, etc.

Douglas Fairbanks was world-famous back then; nowadays he may be in need of a footnote.*

iv

Three months after this conversation in Brooks's Club, Queen Elizabeth II is crowned. By inclination and upbringing, she, too, favours dignity and reticence over glamour and celebrity. But the world is moving on. Hatless motoring fast becomes the norm, and film

---

* And this proves it. Douglas Fairbanks (1883–1939) was an actor, producer and playboy. 'His greatest legacy was in identifying modern celebrity,' writes David Thomson in his *New Biographical Dictionary of Film*. 'He was *so* famous; no one had been known in this way before Doug, Mary [Pickford] and Charlie [Chaplin] stumbled on stardom. And Doug was the most casual about it.'

stars and royalty start to mix on an equal footing. The screens rise, and in comes the daylight, turning what had once seemed like magic into something closer to conjuring.

v

It is 1955. The on–off romance between Princess Margaret and her much older, divorced suitor, Group Captain Peter Townsend, is back in the news. The little daughter of a family with whom the Princess and the Group Captain have been staying tells a journalist that she saw the couple sifting through all the Sunday newspapers for reports and photographs of themselves 'and they just loved them'.

Royalty, once so aloof and standoffish, is now sipping thirstily at the fount of publicity. 'This sort of thing is expected of Rita Hayworth,' notes the acerbic commentator Malcolm Muggeridge* of the couple's avid interest in their own newscuttings, 'but the application of film-star techniques is liable to have, in the long run, disastrous consequences.' He goes on to worry that the British monarchy might 'peter out in pure fantasy ... It is like the king in chess. If he ventures into the middle of the board, the game is lost. He has to be kept in the background and ringed round with pieces more powerful than himself. Indeed, in a sense it could be said that popularity is fatal to monarchy.' After all, he adds, the Russian monarchy was never so popular or treated to such adulation as in 1914. 'Yet when, a few years later, the Tsar and his family were cruelly shot down in a cellar, no one seemed to care much.'

vi

In a bid to keep the monarchy up to date, the Queen allows BBC cameras to film her and her family in public and private moments over the course of a year. Some warn against the project. 'You're killing the

---

* Malcolm Muggeridge (1903–90) was an editor, writer, TV personality and instinctive contrarian. 'It often seemed that in every direction he turned, Mr Muggeridge saw folly and absurdity,' wrote his obituarist in the *New York Times*. 'He observed that much of life was theater "and cheap melodrama at that", and he insisted that he "never greatly cared for the world or felt particularly at home in it".'

monarchy, you know, with this film you're making,' David Attenborough tells the film's director, Richard Cawston. He sees the danger in anthropological terms. 'The whole institution depends on mystique and the tribal chief in his hut. If any member of the tribe ever sees inside the hut, then the whole system of the tribal chiefdom is damaged and the tribe eventually disintegrates.'

Screened in June 1969, *Royal Family* shows the Queen and her family shopping for sweets, decorating a Christmas tree, barbecuing, watching the television and indulging in quite humdrum conversations. Watched by 38 million in the UK and 380 million around the world, it proves more popular than the screening of the moon landing the same year.

It meets with a mixed reception. 'We've seen the Queen in the past as a figurehead. We have now seen her in this film as both a beautiful and a humorous woman,' says broadcaster Ludovic Kennedy. The critic

Milton Shulman is not so sure. Now that the public have been invited into the drawing room, he warns, 'they are soon going to want to peer into the bedroom'. Kenneth Rose agrees, though in slightly different terms. 'The sight of Prince Philip cooking sausages meant that after that people would want to see the dining room, the sitting room, then everything except the loo.' By offering this much more intimate glimpse of the private family, had they merely whetted the public appetite for more?

Within the Royal Family, Princess Anne believed it to have been 'a rotten idea … the last thing you needed was greater access'. The Queen, who had given the go-ahead to the whole project, ended by having second thoughts. By showing them as human beings, it had also shown they were no more than human beings. The copyright in the film was owned by the Crown; since 1977, permission to show it again has been denied.

vii

In February 1981, the Queen books Elton John to provide the entertainment for Prince Andrew's twenty-first birthday party at Windsor Castle. It is just under thirty years since James Pope-Hennessy overheard Sir John Coke saying that the death of Queen Mary spelt trouble ahead.

By now, Elton John is a firm Royal favourite. His lyricist, Bernie Taupin, often comes along to his Command Performances, though he remains wary of such concerts, where one might find 'satiated nobility reclining free of charge inches away from a pop megastar'.

Elton, though, is happy to exchange his music for a bit of grandeur. 'His generosity was hijacked by the Crown and channelled into securing his services as an in-house jukebox,' Taupin later recalls. '… Elton John became the musical brandy and cigars for a motley group of blue bloods and upper-crust insiders …' But Taupin is careful to keep his doubts to himself. 'Apart from the possible suggestion that Elton refrain from playing "The King Must Die" or standing on the piano to proclaim "Are you ready to rock, you royal motherfuckers!" I remained on the sidelines, a mere tagalong …'

Elton's performance is preceded by a discotheque in the ballroom. Her Majesty is keen to keep noise to a minimum, the singer later recalls, so 'the disco was turned down about as low as you could get without switching it off altogether. You could literally hear your feet moving around on the floor over the music.'

As Elvis Presley's 'Hound Dog' starts playing, Princess Anne asks Elton for a dance:

> Well, I say dance: I ended up just awkwardly shuffling from foot to foot, trying to make as little noise as I could so that I didn't drown out the music. If you strained your ears and concentrated hard, you could just about make out that the DJ had segued from Elvis into 'Rock Around the Clock'. Then the Queen appeared, carrying her handbag. She walked over to us and asked if she could join us. So now I was trying to dance as inaudibly as possible with Princess Anne and the Queen – still holding her handbag – while what appeared to be the world's quietest disco played Bill Haley … Here I was, desperately trying to act normal, while the world around me appeared to have gone completely mad.

Presently, Lady Diana Spencer – engaged to the Prince of Wales – enters the ballroom and is introduced to Elton John. 'We immediately clicked. We ended up pretending to dance the Charleston while hooting at the disco's feebleness. She was fabulous company, the best dinner party guest, incredibly indiscreet, a real gossip: you could ask her anything and she'd tell you.'

Though the walls of the room in which the performance takes place have been covered in psychedelic lighting, Taupin finds it 'musty and drab'. Yet the two worlds, pop and royal, do have excess in common. Taupin recognises the Queen's cousin Lord Lichfield, a photographer well known for his appearances on TV quizzes and chat shows. While Elton is playing 'Your Song', Lichfield keels over and crashes to the ground 'in an intoxicated stupor. Not a head turned and no attention was paid to this unfortunate interruption. It was as if it was a standard procedure, something expected and simply a repetitive occurrence.'

Taupin is impressed by how very smoothly this upset is dealt with. 'The Queen simply turned her head slightly, said, "Lichfield's gorn again," and in came the clean-up crew. Four footmen, powdered wigs and all, trundled down the aisle, picked up the unconscious earl, and whisked him out as if under a cloak of invisibility.'

viii

Four years later, the notion of the Royals as a TV soap opera has become commonplace. 'There's the serene-but-horse-playing old mum, the good-but-troubled older son, his fairy princess, the randy young brother, the sad sister, the glamorous-but-grasping social climber, and so on,' notes the American expatriate Clancy Sigal, on the occasion of the Queen's sixtieth birthday. '... I'm not sure that my fellow Americans make that big a distinction between *Dallas, Dynasty* and the Royal Family. As tourists, they flock to Buckingham palace as to a London version of Southfork.' For him, the Royal Family are 'something between sacrificial victims in the traditional religious sense and Hollywood super-stars who are victims of the very publicity that sustains them'. But he admires the Queen's 'impeccable' sense of stage-craft. 'She is producer, director and main star of the royal pageant, a kind of repertory classic which, in between jubilees and royal weddings, has to work hard to hold its audience. The Queen's unthreat-ening dowdiness is a calculated, even inspired, masterstroke of theatricality: the ordinary made majestic, mystical.'

ix

At the beginning of 1987, a few weeks after resigning from the Royal Marines, Prince Edward approaches his mother. He has had a bright idea: a slapstick charity tournament along the lines of television's long-running *It's a Knockout*, but with members of the Royal Family taking part.

The Queen's antennae are sensitive to any threat to the dignity of the monarchy. She doesn't like the sound of it. 'She was against it, but one of her faults is that she can't say no,' one of her friends told her biographer Ben Pimlott.

Prince Philip, too, is firmly opposed. It is, he says, 'unwise and unwelcome'. Aren't there better ways to raise money for charity? 'Why doesn't Edward let the TV people get on with it and just turn up to accept the cheques? He's making us look foolish.'

The Queen's private secretary, Sir William Heseltine, also cautions against the idea, but Prince Edward digs his heels in and the Queen reluctantly grants her approval, though only on condition that members of her family remain aloof from the general buffoonery. Prince Edward finally agrees that they will act as non-participating team captains, above the hurly-burly. 'The games will be different from the old *It's a Knockout*,' he promises at the opening press conference. 'We've deliberately kept a sense of decorum.'

'Both the BBC and John Broome [the owner of the Alton Towers Theme Park] positively drooled at the idea of members of the Royal Family actually leading these teams,' recalls Prince Edward, in his upbeat introduction to *Knockout: The Grand Charity Tournament: A Behind-the-Scenes Look at the Event of the Year*. The title of that book is perhaps an exaggeration: other Events of the Year included a general election, the 'Black Monday' crash of the financial markets and the signing of the US–Soviet Missile Treaty,

Prince Edward's recruitment of a diverse group of celebrities demonstrates the continuing pulling-power of the Royal Family. They include the singers Sheena Easton, Meatloaf, Kiri Te Kanawa, Tom Jones and Chris de Burgh, the comedians John Cleese, Michael Palin, Pamela Stephenson, Mel Smith and Griff Rhys Jones, the actors John Travolta, Christopher Reeve, Jenny Agutter and George Lazenby, and the sportsmen Gary Lineker and Steve Cram. Inevitably, one or two have fallen by the wayside. He had been hoping to recruit a round-the-world yachtsman called Peter Blake, but wires got crossed, and on the big day quite another Peter Blake turns up, this one a little-known actor/singer, famous for a week or two back in September 1977 when he scraped into the top 40 with a single called 'Lipsmackin' Rock 'n' Roll'.

Rehearsals are brief and fraught. The players are kitted out in Tudor gear for their grand entrance, and in a variety of fancy dress thereafter. In an early game, one team dresses as pantomime cooks and the others as onions, potatoes and leeks: the cooks then have to catch the vegetables, remove their skins and toss them into a vast cookery pot. As so often happens with party games, some take it more seriously than others. At one point, the Duchess of York complains that her team is out of shape. 'It's ridiculous. I've got Mel Smith in my potato and you've got Steve Cram in your onion,' she is overheard snapping at Prince Edward.

The referee is the chirpy TV conjuror Paul Daniels, and the chief commentator, chuckling with mirthless laughter, is the plummy-voiced Stuart Hall, later to receive a lengthy custodial sentence for sexual offences against minors. The warm-up acts are the goofy comedian Bernie Clifton, best known for trotting around on a toy ostrich, and rustic songsters the Wurzels, who reached the top of the charts with their novelty single 'I've Got a Brand New Combine Harvester' back in 1976.

The show begins with the cry 'Hear ye hear ye hear ye! Lord Knock of Alton will now open the games!' The former chorister Aled Jones then reads from an outsized scroll, dressed as a page boy. Rowan Atkinson, in the guise of Blackadder, enters with Barbara Windsor as his Queen, both waving their right hands with mock regality. He then delivers an opening speech which comes perilously close to parodying a speech by the mother of the organiser.

> My Lords, Ladies and Gentlemen – and lowly ranks of rather grubby but enthusiastic rabble! Myself and the fair Lady Knock bid you a warm welcome to the Grand Knockout tournament! On this day by noble decree we call forth the mighty from this and many lands to

compete in games whose grandeur, glory and overwhelming silliness will be forever remembered! For the entertainment of us all, let you fall repeatedly on your bottoms this day!

At this point, the four teams come marching in, led by their Royal team-leaders in fancy silk cloaks. 'I would like you to bid welcome to the four teams led by four members of our gracious royal family – His Royal Highness the great and young Duke of York marching his troops to the top of the hill and wherever else he can …' announces Rowan Atkinson, 'and her Royal Highness, the fair Duchess of York …'

The Duchess strides in, pumping the air with her right arm, her mouth opening and shutting at random, as though operating separately from her brain. Atkinson continues his satirical, pseudo-monarchic introductions: 'His Royal Highness the tantalisingly eligible Prince Edward! … And Her Royal Highness the fair Princess Royal, spurring on her champions!'

Stuart Hall, in mauve silk tunic and fancy feathered hat, interviews each team leader. First he points his microphone at the Duke of York.

'Your motley crew, sir – can you describe them in a few words?'

'We are excellent. Fighting fit. Raring to go!' The Duke brandishes a toy panda. 'And we have the most amazing mascot which nobody else has got – called the panda – to support us on our way!'

Hall asks the Duchess of York about the ace cards she is holding for her team, the Blue Bandits.

'Well, we don't have any cards because basically we're the best! We're the best Blue Bandits there are! Hip! Hip! Hooray!'

Prince Edward himself, dressed all in gold, removes his fancy Tudor hat with a flourish. He is clearly charged up. 'What are we going for? Gold! Gold! Gold!'

In her role as Queen, Barbara Windsor, best known for her saucy, flirtatious performances in the *Carry On* films, says: 'It gives me great pleasure on this day of days which, with a bit of luck, will lead to a night of nights, to open this grand *tournée*. The games will commence with a dropping of this favour [holds up hankerchief] given me by the bold Sir Lancelot, he who …' – at this point a cannon fires before it is meant to – '… loves nothing more than the roar of the crowd and the smell of the liniment!'

The first game, 'Call Out the Guards', involves the celebrities attaching cannons to ropes while dressed in roly-poly guards' costumes. They also wear helmets, so viewers find it hard to tell who they are. In most of the other games, the costumes are all-in-one, rendering the celebrities anonymous. Was that John Travolta who just fell over, or might it have been Dame Kiri? Might that be Dr Henry Kissinger dressed as a tomato? Is the Ice Cream Sundae the Queen Mother?

After 'Call Out the Guards', Hall approaches a row of four judges, sheepish-looking men who turn out to be real-life dukes. Asked for a comment, the Duke of Westminster says only: 'That game didn't go as per rehearsal, did it?'

Next in line comes the Duke of Gloucester. 'Are you looking forward to it, sir?'

'Yes, indeed …'

'Ha ha ha ha ha ha!'

And so to the Duke of Roxburgh. 'And your attitudes to our games, Guy?'

'I'm delighted the red team won the first game, so things are going well.'

'You're supposed to be unbiased! Ha ha ha ha ha!'

'Well, I am.'

'He is unbiased, but he wants them to win! Ha ha ha ha ha! And finally, welcome, please, the Duke of Abercorn. Good afternoon, sir.'

'Good afternoon.'

'Are you looking forward to this?'

'Very much indeed. But I'm already sulking because my team's come second.'

'So you've got four biased team judges! Ha ha ha!'

The next round, 'King of the Castle', requires four contestants, clad in wobbly, twelve-foot-high King costumes, to barge each other over. The Duke of York approaches Stuart Hall in high dudgeon. 'I protest! The starter started it without us being ready! And you were standing in front of one of the greens! So we would like to re-run that race!'

By now, it has evidently dawned on Hall and the audience that the Duke's fury is real. Paul Daniels, as referee, refuses to uphold his protest, saying the false start made no difference. 'Did you notice that the one that wasn't ready was actually first down the field?'

Stuart Hall puts on a pained smile, as if willing it to be a joke. But then up pops the Duchess of York: 'We support his protest here!'

'And I suspect you'll find the crowd will support our protest too!' says the Duke. He turns to address the audience. 'Right then, who says we should have a re-run?'

'No!' says Daniels, visibly cross.

'Yes!' says the Duke.

'Do the ayes have it?' asks Hall. He receives a signal from the producers. 'The judges say no re-run! Who said Knockout was all fun and games? Ha ha ha ha ha! It's real this, isn't it?'

'You see the problem here,' says Daniels. 'Some people believe this is real. There'll be no re-runs or anything like that. It was fair and square. They had enough time to get ready.' This contretemps is broadcast as it happened.

After the show, Prince Edward bounces into the clammy press tent, where journalists have been cooped up, without food and drink, forced to watch the entire contest on a TV screen, so as to stop them from pestering the celebrities.

The Prince is delighted by the way it has gone. 'There are an awful lot of people, a tremendous number of people, that I have to thank, apart from Alton Towers, and ultimately I really have to thank the contestants, who have given of their time and their energy and their humour to I think put on one of the best fun afternoons I have ever had and am ever likely to have and I hope that they enjoyed themselves. From what I can gather, they've had a great time, and I know the captains have enjoyed themselves. I only hope that you've enjoyed yourselves. Have you?'

The assembled journalists greet his question with a stony silence. The Prince is visibly peeved.

'Well, thanks for sounding so bloody enthusiastic! What have you been doing in here all night? Have you been watching it? What did you think of it?'

More silence, followed by embarrassed laughter.

'Thanks.'

Prince Edward takes no further questions. Instead, he makes for the exit, petulantly muttering: 'One of these days, you lot are going to have to learn some manners.'

For the first time that day, the journalists look overjoyed. At last, they have their story! Newspaper headlines the following day include 'His Royal Helpless' (*Daily Mirror*), 'It's a Walkout' (*Daily Mail*) and 'Prince of Wails' (*Guardian*). An ITN/Marplan poll at the end of the year finds Prince Edward the least popular member of the Royal Family.

The contestants themselves have mixed memories of the event. Cliff Richard, a member of Princess Anne's team, was kitted out as a leek. 'It was all for charity, but still I think they should never have done it – as I am sure they realised afterwards. It was in the eighties, at a time when they were being told they were out of touch with the world, and I suspect that this was some ill-conceived way of trying to address that problem. At the end it dissolved into a royal bun-fight. I wish someone had said, "Your Majesty, this is not a good idea."'

Meatloaf recalls a contretemps with the Duke of York. 'Fergie wasn't exactly flirting with me, but she was paying attention to me, and I think Andrew got a little – I could be wrong, I'm just reading into this – I think he got a little jealous ... Anyway, he tried to push me in the water. He tried to push me in the moat. So I turned around and I grabbed him and he goes, "You can't touch me. I'm royal." I said, "Well you try to push me in the moat, Jack, I don't give a shit who you are, you're goin' in the moat."'

In *My Story*, the first of her numerous memoirs,* the Duchess of York remembers it as a pivotal episode in the ongoing drama of her

---

* They include *Reinventing Yourself with the Duchess of York* (2001), *What I Know Now: Simple Lessons Learned the Hard Way* (2010) and *Finding Sarah: A Duchess's Journey to Find Herself* (2011). *My Story* was published in 1997.

life. At her marriage to the Duke the year before, she had won over the general public with her healthy sense of fun. But *The Grand Knockout* changed all this. 'My first crime in the decorum department occurred in 1987, when everyone still adored me. It seemed just good family manners to participate, and Andrew and Anne agreed to go on as well. Everybody said it was OK. When Charles and Diana declined the invitation, I remember feeling miffed. I thought they were being most unsportsmanlike, not supporting the Family as we should.' She felt unfairly singled out for vilification. 'I might have mugged and cheered more freely than the rest, being such a fun-loving sort ... Why should I be singled out as coarse and vulgar? What of Edward and Anne and Andrew, whose lead I was following? Why should I be blamed?'

In his semi-authorised biography of Prince Charles, Jonathan Dimbleby describes the event as the 'nadir' for the Royal Family, adding that the Duke and Duchess of York, Princess Anne and Prince Edward 'made fools of themselves in the most vulgar "show" then available on the BBC'. Similarly, in his scholarly biography of the Queen, Professor Ben Pimlott pinpoints it as 'a critical moment in the altering image of British royalty'. Part of the problem, he reckons, was the confusion of roles. 'It was unclear why the royals should lead teams of people who, in general, were famous because of their achievements, rather than their rank; and attempts by the royals to behave like celebrities and be witty fell flat. People who liked to see the Royal Family being natural changed their minds ... In a way, the *Grand Knockout* tournament was the *reductio ad absurdum* of a process that had begun with [the TV documentary] *Royal Family*. The Monarchy had started by trying to make itself less remote. It had sought to come to terms with modern informality, and to display its own off-duty character. In *Knockout* it did so – with appalling, regrettable frankness. If this was what royalty was really like, what was there to look up to?' The whole show was, he concludes, 'excruciating ... and made the public stunningly aware that a sense of decorum was not an automatic quality in the Royal Family'.

A few weeks afterwards, Prince Edward throws a party for the sponsors, fundraisers and celebrities in Buckingham Palace. In the course of the evening, the Duchess of York sits on the throne and performs a mock investiture on Pamela Stephenson. Later, Meatloaf, Prince Edward and the boxer Barry McGuigan sing 'Lady in Red', accompanied by Chris de Burgh on piano. The cast from the hit musical *Cats* then perform a medley of songs from the show.

'I left the party at 2 a.m., by which time it was really rocking,' recalls Toyah Willcox. 'One couldn't help wondering if the Queen was being kept awake by the racket.'

x

By the 1990s, Princess Diana has become a regular guest at Elton John's house near Windsor. One evening, Elton throws a dinner party for the head of the Disney corporation and his wife. He asks them if there is anyone they want to meet and they straightaway say Princess Diana. 'So we invited her, and George Michael, Richard Curtis and his wife Emma Freud, Richard Gere and Sylvester Stallone ...'

The Douglas Fairbankses of their day, Richard Gere and Sylvester Stallone have both set their sights on Princess Diana, who is now separated from the Prince of Wales. The two stars end up in a corridor, squaring up for a fistfight over her. According to Elton John, Stallone stormed off home after dinner:

> 'I never would have come', he snapped, as David and I showed him to the door, 'if I'd known Prince fuckin' Charming was gonna be here.' Then he added: 'If I'd wanted her, I would've taken her!'

xi

Some time later, on a bright summer's day, Bernie Taupin is staying with Sir Elton, as he now is, when the Queen Mother drops by for tea. Taupin talks to the Queen Mother about baseball, 'of which she seemed unnervingly knowledgeable'. The two get along famously. 'If you imagined this wasn't the matriarch of the British Empire, she could easily be your quirky old granny, a fact made more so by her lipstick-smudged teeth and chipped nail polish.'

After tea, the Queen Mother asks Taupin to walk in the garden with her. Together they go, arm in arm. From one spot in the garden, they can see Windsor Castle in the distance, with its flag raised.

'Oh look, Mr Taupin,' says the Queen Mother. 'My daughter's at home.'

xii

'Princess Margaret looks regally around, cigarette in place, holding a large Scotch,' the actress Joan Collins writes in her diary on 12 June 1997, after attending a party at Claridge's. 'She's basically saying to everybody, "Come and worship at my shrine." But it's 1997, folks, and nobody ain't worshipping at any old royal shrine. Granted we all get up and do a bit of a curtsy, but the bowing and scraping doesn't work any more ...'

xiii

Celebrities attending the wedding of Prince Harry and Meghan Markle at St George's Chapel, Windsor, on 19 May 2018 include the footballer David Beckham and his wife, former Spice Girl Victoria, the actors James Corden, Carey Mulligan, Idris Elba and Tom Hardy, the singers Sir Elton John and Joss Stone, the tennis player Serena Williams, the singer James Blunt, the rugby player Jonny Wilkinson and the talk-show host Oprah Winfrey, who has never met the groom, but once met the bride, two months ago.

Finding herself sitting next to George Clooney and his wife Amal at the wedding, Prince Harry's godmother (and Princess Diana's old flat-mate) Carolyn Bartholomew turns to them and asks how they know Harry and Meghan. 'We don't' comes the reply. The Clooneys later deny ever saying this.

* * *

Across this past half-century or more, Britain has changed, and so too has the monarchy. The time is long past since Queen Mary expressed horror at the idea of motoring hatless or entertaining people like Douglas Fairbanks. The social barriers have burst, and the line between celebrity and royalty has grown thinner with each passing day. The essential difference between the Queen and most of the rest of her family is that the Queen never confused being famous with being interesting. She survived the peculiar ordeal of her life by shielding herself in duty. She did the right thing by never doing the wrong thing, and while most of the younger members of the cast were bent on performing their high-kicks and cartwheels, she was careful to retain her dignity, and to sit it out, centre stage.

The Queen's children and grandchildren and their husbands and wives found the lure of celebrity irresistible: they appeared on chat shows, published misery memoirs and children's books, employed PRs to make them better known and better loved, fronted mid-morning television programmes, took part in TV confessionals, delivered opinions, penned children's books, sneaked on one another to gossip columnists, posed for *Hello!* magazine photoshoots and aspired to emulate the celebrities they struggled to cultivate; anything but be thought dull.

82

1992: *Annus horribilis*

February

The Queen visits Australia for the 150th celebrations of Sydney City Council. Paul Keating, the Labour prime minister, whose party has pledged to make Australia a republic by the year 2001, makes a welcoming speech, though some regard it as quite the opposite. In the past, Australian prime ministers have stressed their country's links with Britain, but Keating prefers to stress Australia's links with countries closer to home. Over the past decade, the country has rid itself of its constitutional links with Britain, other than with the Crown itself. 'God Save the Queen' has been replaced as the National Anthem by 'Advance Australia Fair'.

Instead of concentrating its attention on the Queen, the Australian press turns its gaze towards the disintegrating marriages of her children.

During a trip to India by the Prince and Princess of Wales, the Princess poses for photographers sitting by herself in front of the Taj Mahal, looking suitably forlorn. 'Diana Alone' reads one headline.

March

On the sixth anniversary of the Duke and Duchess of York's engagement, Buckingham Palace announces that 'In view of the media speculation which the Queen finds especially undesirable during the general election campaign, Her Majesty is issuing the following statement:

'Last week, lawyers acting for the Duchess of York initiated discussions about a formal separation for the Duke and Duchess.

'These discussions are not yet completed and nothing will be said until they are.

'The Queen hopes that the media will spare the Duke and Duchess of York and their children any intrusion.'

The media fail to follow her request. Under the headline 'Sarah and Andrew: the story of a dead love', *France-Soir* reveals that she is dogged by troubles caused by 'the amorous fiascos of her turbulent family'. Spain's *El Mundo* reveals that 'Prince Andrew lost his nerve recently, during a dinner at Sunninghill ... When the name of Steve Wyatt* was mentioned, the Prince abandoned the dining room, slamming the door behind him.' In Germany, the headline of *Bild* reads 'Fergie and Andy Finished'. *USA Today* reports that the Duchess, 'a tempestuous, controversial redhead', is 'walking out on her naval officer husband'. *Il Messaggero* in Rome quotes the Duchess as saying, 'Instead of staying with me, he prefers his helicopter.'

April
Princess Anne and Captain Mark Phillips finalise their divorce. The Duchess of York leaves her family home, Sunninghill Park.

June
The *Sunday Times* begins its serialisation of *Diana: Her True Story* by Andrew Morton with the headline 'DIANA DRIVEN TO FIVE SUICIDE BIDS BY "UNCARING" CHARLES' and the subheading 'Marriage Collapse Led to Illness; Princess Says She Will Not Be Queen'.

The book claims that the Princess of Wales deliberately threw herself down the stairs at Sandringham, that she slashed her wrists with a razor blade, that she suffered from bulimia, and that, for a large part of their marriage, the Prince of Wales continued a relationship with his old girlfriend, Camilla Parker Bowles. The Royal Family is portrayed as emotionally cold and distant.

---

* Texan oilman with whom the Duchess of York had been photographed cavorting.

Reading the extract over breakfast in Highgrove, the Prince of Wales is left in no doubt that the Princess is the principal source. 'I could hear my wife talking as I read those words,' he tells a friend. Rare in newspaper kiss-and-tells, the snitch still lives in the same house as the snitchee. He goes upstairs and confronts her. She leaves for London.

The following morning, the *Daily Mirror*'s headline is 'I Have Not Co-operated With This Book in Any Way'. A *Mirror* photographer had asked Diana if she had co-operated with Morton, and her reply was unequivocal: 'Absolutely not.'

On ITN News, Andrew Morton fulfils his promise to the Princess, denying that she helped him in any way. The Princess herself insists to the Queen's private secretary, Sir Robert Fellowes, who is also her brother-in-law, that she has had nothing to do with it. Fellowes relays her denial to Lord McGregor, the chairman of the Press Complaints Commission, who in turn condemns the media for this 'odious exhibition of journalists dabbling their fingers in the stuff of other people's souls'.

Princess Diana instructs her private secretary, Patrick Jephson, to issue a strong briefing note to the press denying that she gave access or otherwise cooperated in the production of the book 'for either the text or the photographs or in any other way'.

On 15 June, the Princess of Wales is summoned to a meeting at Windsor Castle with the Queen, Prince Philip and Prince Charles. According to Diana's confidant, James Colthurst, who records his subsequent conversation with her in his diary, Diana is 'shaken rigid' by the meeting. Prince Philip – 'angry, raging and unpleasant' – accuses her of lying to them all about colluding with Morton. She denies it. Charles stays silent. The Princess bursts into tears. Philip asks Charles to explain what is upsetting her. 'What? And read it all in the newspapers tomorrow? No thank you,' he replies.

Prince Philip tells the Princess he has tape recordings of her phone discussions with the *Sunday Times* about serial rights. If she doesn't believe him, he will make them available.

The Princess agrees to have another meeting with her husband and his parents the following day, but she fails to turn up.

At Royal Ascot that same week, Princess Diana is cold-shouldered in the Royal Box and sits at the back by herself. No longer invited to join the Royal Family, the Duchess of York pops up in the crowd, hand in hand with her two little daughters, waving theatrically as the Queen's carriage passes by.

Prince Philip and Princess Diana enter into a correspondence, which is, to some extent, conciliatory: a number of his lengthy letters end 'With fondest love – Pa'. In one, he writes, 'Charles was silly to risk everything for a man in his position. We never dreamed he might feel like leaving you for her. I cannot imagine anyone in their right mind leaving you for Camilla. Such a prospect never entered our heads.' Princess Diana shows these letters to her butler Paul Burrell, who later includes choice extracts from them in his own bestselling memoir, *A Royal Duty*.

Among many other retailers, both Tesco and Harrods refuse to stock *Diana: Her True Story*. The consequent publicity serves only to fuel interest. *Diana: Her True Story* sells a million copies in its first week of publication. By the end of the year, the book will have sold four and a half million copies worldwide.

Presenting the French philosopher Jacques Derrida, often referred to as the father of deconstruction theory, with an honorary degree at Cambridge University, Prince Philip is overheard muttering that his own family seems to be deconstructing.

When the Queen attends the official opening of the refurbished Leicester Square, barely a mile from Buckingham Palace, she is heckled by an onlooker: 'Pay your taxes, you scum!'

July

An opinion poll commissioned by the conservative *Daily Telegraph* suggests that only a quarter of the British population still agree with the statement: 'The monarchy is something to be proud of.'

August

On 20 August, under the headline 'FERGIE'S STOLEN KISSES', the *Daily Mirror* publishes photographs of the Duchess of York lying topless by a swimming pool outside Saint-Tropez while her 'financial adviser', John Bryan, kisses her toes.

'Fergie … has once again made our Royal Family look a laughing stock in front of the world …' reads the accompanying report. '… If the Royal Family is to survive beyond the Queen's reign, it cannot afford another scandal like this.'

By 8 a.m., the report and the saucy photographs that accompany it are proving so popular that the *Daily Mirror*'s publisher orders a further 400,000 copies to be printed.

By chance, the Duchess of York is staying at Balmoral when the newspaper appears. At 9.30 on the morning of publication, she goes to see the Queen. 'The Queen was furious … her anger wounded me to the core,' she will recall in *My Story*. 'There was something special between us, and maybe that was what moved me to mount some feeble defence, instead of just slinking out of her room.

'"Don't you think it's a bit weird that it keeps having to be *me* that gets caught?" I said. "Don't you think it's time someone asked, 'Why is it always her?' I can't be *that* idiotic."'

At dinner that evening, she is conscious that everyone is staring at her. 'I knew they must be seeing me topless, or being nuzzled by a bald American. The courtiers eyed me sneakily, discreetly. The butlers and footmen gaped, and I felt naked in their sight … I felt disgust in that dining room and a queasy fascination, as if they were looking at a burn victim.' Despite all this, the Duchess continues her family holiday at Balmoral for another three days.

The day the Duchess finally leaves Balmoral, the *Sun* newspaper publishes the transcript of a telephone conversation between the Princess of Wales and a car salesman boyfriend, James Gilbey. It was apparently recorded by a radio ham on New Year's Eve 1989; Diana was alone in her bedroom at Sandringham, and Gilbey was sitting in a car parked in the Oxfordshire countryside, en route to a dinner party.

Throughout the transcript, Gilbey refers to the Princess as 'Squidgy' or 'Squidge'. The Princess tells him that her marriage is 'torture' and that the Royal Family have distanced themselves from her because they are jealous of her popularity with the public. 'The distancing will be because I go out and – I hate the word – conquer the world.' She also talks of the way the Queen Mother looks at her: 'It's not hatred, it's sort of interest and pity.' She tells Gilbey of her problems at family meals. 'I was very bad at lunch and I nearly started blubbing. I just felt really sad and empty and thought, "Bloody hell, after all I've done for this fucking family."'

Diana believes she has special powers of empathy. 'I understand people's suffering,' she tells Gilbey. 'It's not only AIDS, it's anyone who suffers. I can smell them a mile away.' The tape also includes a strong suggestion of a sexual relationship between the two of them – enough to jeopardise her claims to be the entirely innocent partner in the breakdown of her marriage.

> DIANA: I don't want to get pregnant.
> JAMES: Darling, that's not going to happen. All right?
> DIANA: (laughs) Yeah.
> JAMES: Don't think like that. It's not going to happen, darling, you won't get pregnant.

The *Sun* makes the original tape available on a premium-rate phone line at the cost of 39p a minute. For a total of £11.70, members of the public can listen to every word.

September

Opinion polls suggest that 80 per cent of the British public think the Queen should no longer be exempt from income tax. The matter has been discussed within the Royal Household since the beginning of the year, but is only now becoming an issue.

November

Under the headlines 'Charles's Secret Bedtime Phone Call' and 'Charles and the Tape Recording of Love', the *Daily Mirror* runs a two-part series called 'Camilla Confidential'. It features the transcript of a phone conversation between the Prince of Wales and Mrs Parker Bowles recorded three years earlier.* The tone and content are overtly sexual, a Windsor version of Serge Gainsbourg and Jane Birkin's breathy 1969 Anglo-French chart-topper 'Je t'aime … moi non plus'.†

> CAMILLA: You're awfully good at feeling your way along.
> CHARLES: Oh, stop! I want to feel my way along you, all over you and up and down you and in and out.
> CAMILLA: Oh.
> CHARLES: Particularly in and out.
> CAMILLA: That's just what I need at the moment.

A week later, at 11.15 a.m. on 20 November, in Windsor Castle a restorer's spotlight sets fire to a curtain in Queen Victoria's private chapel. The ensuing conflagration, visible from miles away, rages for the next fifteen hours, all but destroying nine state apartments and a hundred rooms. Resident at the Castle, Prince Andrew strides up and down, attempting to take control of the rescue effort. He tells the press his mother is 'shocked and devastated'. The Queen is spotted, too, in a raincoat and wellington boots, peering despondently at the firemen as they fight the flames.

---

* How did the recordings emerge? Who made them? Though initially thought to be the product of casual eavesdropping by two local radio hams, they seem more likely to have been leaks of telephone taps by 'the intelligence community'. Like the rest of the public, many figures in the secret services took one side or the other in the great Charles vs Diana strife, and acted accordingly. There is strong evidence that the original recordings were retransmitted at least six times, in the expectation that they would be picked up by the amateurs.

† The lyrics of 'Je t'aime … moi non plus' are remarkably similar. Sadly, the Gainsbourg estate has refused to let me quote them here, presumably on the grounds that it would sully the clean-cut image of Serge Gainsbourg to be associated with the Royal couple. However, those wishing to compare and contrast Serge and Jane to Charles and Camilla may listen to the banned song on YouTube and Spotify.

Four days later, the Queen delivers a speech at the Guildhall. It lacks her customary blend of optimism and reassurance. It includes one unusually memorable passage, delivered in a croaky voice that serves to highlight the uncharacteristic note of dejection.

'Nineteen-ninety-two is not a year on which I shall look back with undiluted pleasure. In the words of one of my more sympathetic correspondents, it has turned out to be an *annus horribilis*.' She then calls for greater understanding from her subjects. 'No institution – city, monarchy, whatever – should expect to be free from the scrutiny of those who give it their loyalty and support, not to mention those who don't. But we are all part of the same fabric of our national society and that scrutiny, by one part of another, can be just as effective if it is made with a touch of gentleness, good humour and understanding.'

Some elements of the popular press greet her speech with little of the gentleness she requested. The *Sun*'s headline is: 'One's Bum Year'.

Two days later, on 26 November, the prime minister announces that, from now on, the Queen and the Prince of Wales will pay tax on their private incomes, and the annual Civil List payment of £900,000 to five other members of the Royal Family will be coming to an end. He adds that the suggestion came in the summer from the monarch herself. But her critics are unappeased. 'HM THE TAX DODGER' reads the headline in the next day's *Daily Mirror*.

December

The heritage secretary announces that, as Windsor Castle was uninsured, the cost of repairs – estimated at between £20 million and £40 million – will be borne by the taxpayer. His announcement is greeted with outrage, even from traditionally conservative quarters. 'While the castle stands it is theirs. But when it burns down, it is ours,' complains Janet Daley in *The Times*. The *Daily Mail* publishes a front-page editorial headed, 'Why the Queen must listen'. Its tone is bullish. 'Why should the populace, many of whom have had to make huge sacrifices during the bitter recession, have to pay the total bill for Windsor Castle, when the Queen, who pays no taxes, contributes next to nothing?'

On 9 December, Buckingham Palace announces the separation of the Prince and Princess of Wales.

Looking back on the year in a speedily published book, *The Rise and Fall of the House of Windsor*, the author A. N. Wilson observes, 'One does not have to be of a very vindictive temperament to savour the essentially comic misfortunes of a talentless and, it has to be said at the outset, largely charmless family who, by the accidents of birth and marriage, happen to be the custodians of the British monarchical system. It is they who have chosen to behave like characters in a Feydeau farce, and they cannot be surprised when the audience laugh … I believe that the Royal Family are in desperate trouble.'

Towards the end of the month, the satirist Auberon Waugh concludes: 'We are no longer a fit country to have a monarchy, being eaten up with rancour, hatred, aggression and envy … The Windsors have served this country well … they should be allowed to return to Germany with dignity and decorum, the plaudits of a grateful people ringing in their ears, and leave Princess Monster behind on her own to

receive the cheers of her adulatory fans, Madonna-like, until they grow bored and decide to tear her to pieces.'

In her Christmas message, recorded in advance, the Queen is conciliatory and thankful. 'Like many other families, we have lived through some difficult days this year. The prayers, understanding and sympathy given to us by so many of you, in good times and bad, have lent us great support and encouragement. It has touched me deeply that much of this has come from those of you who have troubles of your own.'

The *Sun* gets hold of a copy and publishes the text two days before it is broadcast. The Queen, described by a spokesman as 'very, very distressed' by their action, sues the newspaper for breach of copyright. The proprietor of the *Sun*, Rupert Murdoch, agrees to pay all the legal costs, and to donate £200,000 to charity.

83

For such a symbol of ease, for most of its working life the Royal Yacht *Britannia* was an unlikely source of conflict: between government and opposition, between different Cabinet ministers, and between the Queen and her prime ministers.

One day in 1962, the urbane first lord of the Admiralty, Lord Carrington, received a phone call from the Queen's private secretary, Michael Adeane, who said 'in a bleak voice' that the Queen wanted to see him at Buckingham Palace in half an hour.

Carrington duly hurried to Buckingham Palace. According to him, the Queen did not ask him to sit down, but simply pointed to a report in that morning's *Daily Express*. It said that, barely a decade after *Britannia* was first launched, the Royal Yacht was to be refitted at an 'astronomical' cost.

Sensing that the Queen was rattled, he explained to her that *Britannia* had been badly constructed, and the embarrassment and inconvenience of a breakdown mid-voyage were best avoided.

The Queen came straight to the point: 'And who pays?'

Feeling on firmer ground, Carrington explained that the cost would of course be met by the government rather than the Royal Family.

'I see,' observed the Queen bluntly. 'You pay and I get the blame.'

A few years later, in 1968, Adeane wrote to the prime minister, Harold Wilson, on the Queen's behalf. The Queen and Prince Philip had been considering 'some tangible savings' which 'might be able to help the country during its present economic difficulties'. In this spirit, 'The Queen hopes that you and the Secretary of State for Defence may feel free to consider the future of the Royal Yacht.'

On the face of it, she appeared to be suggesting that she could forgo her yacht for the good of the country. Was she calling the prime minister's bluff? If so, it worked. Wilson and his inner circle had already decided against scrapping *Britannia*, fearful that such a move might signal to the world that Britain was on the skids. How could they now explain that a socialist government wanted to hang on to this floating symbol of extravagance when the Queen herself was willing to abandon it? They decided that the Queen's offer must remain secret.

Conservative decisions are often more conveniently taken by socialist governments, and vice versa. Harold Wilson always tried to avoid any public debate about royal finances, for fear of alienating that part of the electorate he hoped to win over.

Twenty-four years later, *Britannia* was still struggling on. The prime minister, John Major, had decided to scrap it, while delaying the decision over whether or not to commission a replacement. This top-secret decision was given the Wodehousian codename Project Celery, a cack-handed acronym for 'Cost-Effective Elegant Royal Yacht'.

Major's bluff, no-nonsense, beer-and-jazz chancellor of the Exchequer, Kenneth Clarke, was firmly opposed. 'I adamantly refused ... to contemplate spending £60 million of public money on anything as nineteenth century as a royal yacht at a time when we were cutting back on public spending. I thought that the public reaction would be very negative, and difficult to manage ... I was also unpersuaded that the yacht made any practical difference to our export performance, which was the only serious argument of any practical kind used in its favour.

'I was led to understand that the Queen was quite distressed by the prospect of our failure to provide this facility for her and her family. I am a great enthusiast for the Queen, and as monarchist as most other British politicians. However, I differ in one respect. Most politicians are so in awe of the royal family that expressions of displeasure from the Palace about issues bearing directly on the family can usually produce quite significant policy shifts.'

But the rest of the Cabinet thought differently, and Clarke's opposition to *Britannia* was to sink in a sea of political calculation. 'Eventually, faced with the distress of my colleagues and their eager belief that recommissioning the yacht would arouse an electorally advantageous patriotic fervour, I gave way.' In January 1997, the defence secretary, Michael Portillo, announced that the government would be spending £50 million on a replacement. Confident that it would muster popular support, the Conservatives included this pledge in the party's 1997 election manifesto.

Labour's shadow chancellor, Gordon Brown, the son of the Revd John Ebenezer Brown, was, by nature, a thrifty Scottish Calvinist. He could see little point in a Royal Yacht, other than as a training vessel for sea cadets. He reckoned that the public were against it, too. Whenever the ditching of the Royal Yacht was mentioned at election rallies, 'nothing got a bigger cheer' according to his Labour colleague Geoffrey Robinson. This was borne out by pollsters: an ICM survey for the *Guardian* found a 3 to 1 majority in favour of scrapping it.

Labour – or New Labour as it had restyled itself – won the May 1997 general election by a landslide. But, like the Conservatives before them, the party leaders continued to bicker over the future of *Britannia*. Gordon Brown's spin-doctor, Charlie Whelan, decided to test public response to a scheme that was 'third way' and involved a modish linking of the public and private sectors. Accordingly, Sunday newspapers were briefed that *Britannia* might have a refit financed by private companies, which would then be allowed to use it whenever the Royal Family didn't need it.

But the briefing flopped: journalists imagined commercial logos plastered all over *Britannia*, and viewed the proposals as yet another example of Blairite contempt for tradition. In Gordon Brown's words, the story 'spiralled out of control': Blair was upset he had not been informed of the scheme, and his fixer, Peter Mandelson, was equally upset that the idea had not been attributed to him and his 'close friend' the Prince of Wales. At the same time, those in the know calculated that the real cost of building a replacement would now be close to £100 million.

Charged with coming to a decision, Geoffrey Robinson, newly appointed as the paymaster general, tried to calculate the economic benefits. '*Britannia*'s log book made very sad reading. In the seven years to 1997 the yacht had been used for only sixty-three days to promote British exports and attract inward investment – just nine days on average per annum! Over the same period its longest uses were two fifteen-day trips comprising Cowes week and the royal family's holiday sailing round the Western Isles. In the last two years of *Britannia*'s life, the Queen used the yacht on only five nights on foreign trips.' He also doubted that private companies would want to hire *Britannia* for six months of the year at a cost of £70,000 per day. But still they dithered. 'The project was left on a discordant note as the House went into recess,' Robinson recalled.

The Queen and other members of her family embarked on their final voyage up to Balmoral on *Britannia* at the beginning of August 1997. On the way, they anchored by the Isle of Mingulay, where the Queen went for a walk by herself and called by unexpectedly on one of the island's only inhabitants, an artist called Julie Brook, with a bunch of flowers she had picked herself. 'We began to chat as if we had always known one another. She looked so happy being here, very straightforward – there was no formality. We chatted away. I told her about the island, the cliffs, the shepherds. She delighted in the kittens and played with them ... and then she told me that this was her last year on the Royal yacht (because it's old), "So next year we might have to hire something – awful."'

After stopping for lunch at the Castle of Mey on 16 August, the Queen exchanged ship-to-shore verses with the Queen Mother, as was their custom. The Queen Mother's private secretary, Martin Leslie, usually a dab hand at such verses, was away, so a message was sent asking the Poet Laureate, Ted Hughes, to come up with some lines. This is what he wrote, though it is not known how much of it was relayed to *Britannia*:

Farewell, to you *Britannia*, once more,
So many summers you have blessed this shore
And blessed the Castle of Mey.
This summer let us say
Heartier farewells than ever before
As you go on your way.

You go, but you go deeper than ever
Into our hearts this year
With all our memories of you, so happy and dear.
Whichever course your Captain takes, you steer
Into this haven of all our hearts, and forever
You shall be anchored here.

In reply to her mother, the Queen sent a verse of her own:

Oh what a heavenly day,
Happy glorious and gay
Delicious food from the land
Peas shelled by majestic hand
Fruit, ice cream from foreign lands
Was it India or Pakistan?

Yet, despite the Queen's fears, Tony Blair's New Labour government was still dithering over the future of the Royal Yacht. Which way would they go? The only book Blair had ever published – a selection of his speeches and essays called *New Britain: My Vision of a Young Country* – displayed a disdain for the ways of the past. 'We live in new age but in an old country ... I want us to be a young country again.' Within its 338 pages, its author included not a single mention of the Queen or the Royal Family. It was as though they didn't exist. Might the dynamic new young prime minister feel they represented the old, outdated way of doing things?

84

As a senior civil servant, George Walden was principal private secretary to the foreign secretary, serving first Dr David Owen and then Lord Carrington. For three years, he accompanied the foreign secretary whenever he travelled on the Royal Yacht *Britannia*. 'In protocol terms I was as lowly as they come: on a list of twenty-one members of the Royal Household I came last, way down there after the Mistress of the Robes and the Lady in Waiting.'

Following visits on *Britannia* to Germany, Denmark, Morocco, Italy, Tunisia and the Gulf States, he decided to write down a list of dos and don'ts.* In the end, he says, 'it turned out to be all don'ts':

1. Do not refer to the Royal Yacht as a ship.

2. Do not make an oik of yourself by running your own bath. With their keen sense of proprieties the flunkies know better than you when you need a bath, and will turn up to run it for you, uninvited and at the most inappropriate moment. When this happens do not say testily, 'I will do it myself', since that could imply a) that you rarely take baths; b) that you are not used to having them run for you; c) that you are a republican as well as an oik.

---

* Repeated here in abbreviated form.

3. Do not scorn dress protocol. Remember that there are people who give their lives to these things. Never overdress at breakfast or underdress at dinner. To make sure you get it right make the effort to master the code of dress in the Royal programme:

UI: Ceremonial Day Uniform with decorations and medals
RN NO. 4: Monkey Jacket with swords and medals
WT: White Tie
LS: Lounge Suit
MS: Morning Suit
DJ: Dinner Jacket
(T): The Queen wears a tiara
DECS: Decorations

Resign yourself to the fact that much of the time on board is spent changing clothes. The maximum I counted was five times a day.

4. When it is your turn to dine next to the Queen when the Royal Yacht is at sea (given your lowly place in the pecking order they only get round to you on exceptionally long journeys) do not clam up, be rigid or frigid. Do not think yourself a lackey or toady for harbouring positive thoughts about Her Majesty. It is true what they say of her: behind the dutiful demeanour lies a strong sense of irony and a genuine wit. Do not, however, seek to match the wit, since it will never sound as good in your mouth as it does in hers. Also because your jokes will invariably be at someone else's expense. If there is anyone in need of criticism, that will be done by Her Majesty, and not by you.

5. Never again question the cost or utility of the Royal Yacht. In the Gulf it was boarded by several hundred businessmen, sheikhs and emirs and other influential persons in a single evening: a couple of hundred for drinks before dinner, a privileged twenty or so for dinner with the Queen, and a further couple of hundred at yet another reception after dinner and display of music on the quayside, provided

by bandsmen on the accompanying frigate. The question is not so much whether royalty earn their living. It is how long shall we be able to get people who are prepared to do it.

6. Never attempt substantive conversation with the highly distinguished person you meet, except the Queen, who has a serious streak. Since you can't talk to her all the time, do not let the endless banter or the light conversation of courtiers get you down. Behave as if you were a character in Evelyn Waugh rather than in Kafka, even though by the end of the voyage that is how you may feel.

7. Never turn down a drink, unless it is of local manufacture. Snatch as much as you can get of everything French. Do not overdo the stupendous breakfasts because there will be little to do at the ceremonial lunches and banquets that will fill your day except eat. Drink as much as you can to drown the boredom. Alcohol is also good for the glazed-eye expression which passes for high politics on such occasions.

8. Never display human emotions, such as impatience or surprise, e.g. when you are driven over oriental carpets to a feast in tents in the middle of a Saudi desert, or when King Hassan of Morocco keeps you (and more importantly the Queen) waiting because of fear of assassination. In general, remember the needs of security, though do not allow the sight of so many people with guns to inflate your self-importance. Being number twenty-one in the Royal Household, while impressive to your mother, does not make you a prime target for assassination.

9. Never ask yourself what royal travel is meant to achieve. Its results are like micro-organisms: imposing when blown up in newspapers or magazines, but invisible to the naked eye. On the other hand, do not sneer at the notion of promoting goodwill between nations. Your experience of diplomacy shows how little of it there is about.

10. Above all remember that royalty are normal people, who smile, make jokes and like to enjoy themselves. Behave normally yourself, but not to the point of smiling too much or making too many jokes. Too much smiling will make you appear a congenital idiot or a subservient buffoon, which royalty do not like to have around them. Too many jokes will invite too few laughs, not because the jokes are not funny but because they are royal. The element of incongruity, vital to humour, will be lacking.

11. In brief, be respectful but not glum (an infallible sign of the Roundhead or Republican), courteous but not over-deferential (a sign of low self-esteem), natural but not too natural (you are with royalty, my friend, and never forget it).

85

In the port of Leith, to the north of Edinburgh, you go into Ocean Terminal, a vast, glassy, shopping centre, packed with all the usual multichain stores – H&M, Frankie and Benny's, Nando's, Superdry, Vision Express – then up an escalator, ready to enter the final resting place of the Royal Yacht *Britannia*, which is now a 'visitor attraction' and party venue.

A hundred yards along the shiny floor you are invited to:

Step into the State Apartments and see where celebrities and world leaders, from Nelson Mandela to Sir Winston Churchill, were entertained by Queen Elizabeth and the Royal Family. Snap a family photo trying on the sailors' uniforms in the Crew's Quarters as you discover where 220 Royal Yachtsmen worked and relaxed. Stop by the NAAFI to sample the delicious fudge, made on board, and look into the gleaming Engine Room. Remember to spot the corgis hiding in the Cuddly Corgi Treasure Hunt!

Through the entrance, you walk past glass cases containing old uniforms, helmets, boots and gloves of the *Britannia*'s Royal Marine Band, past photographs of the crew straining away in tug-of-war competitions and sunning themselves on deck, past the rum pump and the measures 'used to dispense the daily "tot" on *Britannia*', past Prince Philip's double-breasted uniform, donated by the Queen in March 2022.

Many of the photographs in Leith are cloaked in the melancholy of time past. Princess Diana, grinning with joy, arms outstretched, greets her two little boys as they board *Britannia* in 1991. Diana is dead, Harry in exile. Of the three, only William remains in place.

Other photos show the Royal Family hobnobbing with the yacht's crew: 'The Queen and Duke of Edinburgh help make the Christmas Pudding.' In one of them, the Queen is clutching a glass, laughing with four beefy young men, two in drag: 'The Queen chats to some of the Yotties in the Concert Party.' High Camp hovers in the air. Even a photograph labelled 'HM the Queen Mother viewing Catch of the Day' is campy: the Queen Mother in a flamboyant hat and smart coat looks on in delight as what must be a fish but looks like a moist human limb is pulled out of a bag.

I once read an account by a former Palace footman of a two-week Royal trip to Reykjavik in the 1960s. His time on board *Britannia* was, he wrote, 'something of an eye-opener. It was the first time I had been confined in a world that was unutterably masculine, rubbing shoulders each day with friendly, handsome men in a sexy uniform. At first I put it down to wishful thinking, but I soon accepted that there really was a sexual undercurrent where some of the "Yotties" were concerned. This feeling was also confirmed by some of the Palace old hands. During that particular voyage one or two of my workmates retired early to their cabins, armed with quantities of cheap booze, ready to receive naval visitors. Although I was much too gauche and shy to do the same, I have to admit that a taste for men in uniform had been acquired.'

Our tour starts at the front of the yacht. 'From here you can look down onto the Royal bridge, directly below,' says the reassuring Scotsman on the audio commentary. '… The curved teak windbreak was a later feature, added for modesty's sake, to prevent sea breezes lifting Royal skirts.'

I loiter on the top deck, hearing that the anchors each weigh three tons and so forth, when all I really want to do is take a peek inside the Royal cabins.

'You are now on the Shelter deck, and located here is the senior officers' accommodation … On your left is the Admiral's suite, comprising of day cabin and bedroom. As befits his standing, this is the most spacious and comfortable accommodation outside the Royal apartments …'

A table in the Admiral's suite is set for a solitary breakfast, with a Full English – baked beans, tomato, sausage, black pudding, bacon, brown sauce and fried egg – all recreated in unappealing plastic. Alongside it is a fading old copy of the *Guardian*, an unlikely choice of breakfast accompaniment for any admiral.

'When the Royal Family was on board, the Admiral would always dine with them. But when there were no Royal passengers, the Admiral would dine alone, in the day cabin, allowing his fellow officers the chance to unwind away from the boss.'

Aboard *Britannia*, time off was as regimented as time on. Everyone seems to agree that it was not only the Queen's favourite way to travel, but also her favourite place to relax. '*Britannia* was the nearest the Queen has ever had to her "own" home,' writes Robert Hardman in his biography *Queen of the World*. 'All the other palaces and castles were inherited … It was in *Britannia* that the Queen and Duke of Edinburgh could experiment with their own ideas and choose everything, from the light fittings to the carpet.' If the interior decoration of *Britannia* is a projection of the Queen's own interior, then it shows a conservative character, practical and pragmatic, modest, unfussy, straightforward, someone happy to be free of the distractions of history, the complications of art, the need to be thought stylish or interesting. Were it a house, not a ship, *Britannia* would be a functional mid-twentieth-century family home with all the mod cons, or a four-star Trusthouse Forte hotel, reliable and predictable.

In 1990, when she appointed Rear Admiral Sandy Woodward Flag Officer Royal Yachts – the rather lowering job title given to the Captain of *Britannia* – the Queen took him aside. 'People who know us at all know that Buckingham Palace is the office, Windsor Castle is for weekends and the occasional state thing and Sandringham and Balmoral are for holidays,' she told him. 'Well, they aren't what I would call holidays. For example, there are ninety people coming to stay with us at Balmoral this summer. The only holiday I get every year is from Portsmouth the long way round to Aberdeen on the

Royal Yacht, when I can get up when I like and wear what I like and be completely free.'

Yet when one hears of the Royal Family on holiday aboard *Britannia*, dining with the Admiral, and the Admiral dining separately from the commissioned officers, and the non-commissioned officers dining separately from the petty officers, and so on, all the way down to the lowliest rating, it begins to seem like a very rigid form of freedom.

'The Yacht offered the one thing the Queen craved – a spot of normality,' writes Hardman. Obviously, normality comes in all shapes and sizes, but this was a peculiar version of normality, normality as imagined by someone who had never experienced it: a middle-class Surrey home, done up like a hotel, then dropped in the middle of the ocean, with 240 staff in the basement, all with express instructions to keep the illusion of normality intact.

'On your left, you can see the Admiral's bathroom and sleeping cabin. The bathroom contains one of the few baths in this, the working part of the ship. From here, you can look through to the Admiral's sleeping cabin with its row of sycamore-veneer wardrobes. These held

his immaculate uniforms into which he had to change, often up to twelve times a day, depending on his duties.'

Twelve times a day! That's once an hour, on the hour, every hour, from 7am to 7pm, a feverish frenzy of fancy dress. Even on holiday, the Queen, too, was a whirling dervish of the wardrobe, changing clothes throughout the day. And her family would all follow suit, regardless of whether or not she was present. A distinguished actor invited by Prince Charles to a weekend house party at Sandringham told me it reminded him of appearing in pantomime, with the guests obliged to follow Charles in all his quick-change routines, throughout the day. You'd even be expected to slip into something new for afternoon tea, before changing again for dinner.

The yacht, the guide informs us, is divided into two halves. 'Forward of the main mast, the area from which you have just come, is the working part of *Britannia*, where the 20 officers and 220 crew lived, in fairly cramped conditions. In the other direction are the living quarters of the Royal Family and the forty-five members of the Royal Household who assisted the Queen on state visits. As you continue along this deck, you will notice that the windows here are higher than anywhere else on the yacht. This is because these windows look into the Queen and the Duke of Edinburgh's bedrooms. By placing them at this height above the deck any accidental glimpses into the Royal bedrooms could be prevented.'

This was a rarefied kind of privacy, privacy forever in jeopardy, privacy under constant siege from those employed to preserve it.

'You are now standing on the Verandah deck, part of the Royal Quarters of the yacht. It was here that the Royal Family could relax in privacy, sunbathing or enjoying games of quoits or deck hockey on this, the largest deck on *Britannia*. Prince Philip would occasionally set up his easel here and indulge in the Royal pastime of painting.'

Painting benefits from stability: even the calmest sea would produce lollops galore. But Prince Philip was no Pollockian experimentalist, letting random sploshes of paint splatter his canvases. It is hard to believe his measured watercolours benefited from the lurches of the ocean waves.

On the other hand, the Queen welcomed a choppy sea. In 1976, en route to Philadelphia to celebrate the bicentenary of the American Declaration of Independence, *Britannia* ran into Force 9 gales, two days out of Bermuda. The then foreign secretary, Tony Crosland, and his American wife Susan had sailed with them from Britain. Susan recalled how the Queen relished the storm:

> The Queen rose to say goodnight, resting one hand against the handle of the open sliding door which at that moment began sliding shut, *Britannia* having failed to take a breathing space before heaving again. The Queen gripped the handle, pressed her back to the door and moved with it as it slid slowly shut, her chiffon scarf flying in the opposite direction. 'Wheeeee,' said the Queen. *Britannia* shuddered, reeled again. The chiffon scarf flew the other way. 'Wheeeee,' said the Queen. *Britannia* hesitated before the next heave. 'Goodnight,' said the Queen, slipping through the door, Prince Philip half a pace behind her.

The next day, the Queen's guests gathered in the drawing room before lunch.

> 'I have never *seen* so many grey and grim faces round a dinner table,' said the Queen. She paused. 'Philip was not at all well.' She paused. She giggled. I'd forgotten that her Consort is an Admiral of the Fleet.

The decks, the guide inform us, are made of two-inch-thick teak. The junior yachtsmen had the task of scrubbing them down daily to keep them in pristine condition. So that the Royal Family was not disturbed, all work near the Royal apartments was carried out in silence, and completed by eight o'clock in the morning.

Page 12 of the *Official Souvenir Guidebook* carries a large colour photograph of the Queen in her pearl earrings and diamond necklace at *Britannia*'s dining table, beaming away. Alongside, picked out in large letters, is a quote from her:

'This is where I can truly relax.'

Elsewhere in Britain, the class system was breaking down and fragmenting. But here on board the Royal Yacht *Britannia* everyone knew their place, from top to bottom. Inevitably, the rules of interaction were intricate and paradoxical: for example, the sailors would remove their caps near the Royal quarters, as this meant they could be regarded as out of uniform with no need to salute, thus sparing the Royal Family the bother of saluting in return.

We walk through to the Sun Lounge, furnished with bamboo chairs brought back from Hong Kong by Prince Philip in 1959. A selection of board games – Scrabble, Monopoly, Cluedo – sits in one corner; in another, a photograph of Princess Margaret in her prime. A concealed cupboard in the wall opens on to a dinky little drinks cabinet, complete with champagne, gin and Dubonnet. 'This beautiful teak-lined room was one of the Queen's favourite spaces on *Britannia*. It was a true family room, and offered privacy from the rest of the ship.'

There is an Escher-like quality to this ceaseless quest for privacy: with anywhere in the world free to choose from, you end up on a residence 412 feet long, 55 feet wide and 40 feet deep, locked in on all sides by the sea. You then fill it with 240 uniformed strangers, all of them tasked with ensuring your seclusion.

We arrive at what, for most people, must be the focus of their trip to Leith: the principal Royal bedrooms. 'The first window you come to looks into Her Majesty the Queen's bedroom.' Sure enough, there it is: a pleasant, single-bedded room, just big enough for a small desk, a couple of chairs and a dressing table. It wouldn't look out of place in a Travelodge.

A fellow tourist says it's astonishing that the Queen would ever have tolerated a large floor-length window looking through to her bedroom. Someone else points out that window was created later, to give the tourists a chance to gawp.

The next window looks on to Prince Philip's bedroom: the two suites have an interconnecting door. 'The Duke of Edinburgh's

bedroom reflected the Duke's personal taste, and has a more masculine look,' says the guide. 'His pillow cases are the same size as the
Queen's but, on his specific request, do not have the lace borders. Like
all the single beds on the ship, the Queen and the Duke's beds are
standard three-foot models.'

We stare at the beds, the thoughts of even the Queen's most loyal
subjects straying unwanted into forbidden territory. Their bathrooms
and lavatories are kept from public view, the curiosity they promote
being judged too weird to be satisfied.

In the Duke's bedroom there is a group photograph of the Royal
Family on board *Britannia*. Charles carries baby Harry in his arms,
and Diana is holding hands with William, who is in shorts and Start-
Rite sandals. To the left, Princess Margaret has a cardigan draped over
her shoulders. Just behind her is Prince Andrew, looking young and
wholesome: he will not marry Sarah Ferguson until the following year.
In slacks and a red-and-white striped matelot shirt, the Queen has
never looked so casual. More carefree times; but perhaps the past is
always more carefree, unburdened by the knowledge of what is to
come.

'For an official state visit,' says the guide, 'up to five tons of luggage would be brought on board. This included the Queen's clothes, accessories and jewellery, under the watchful eye of Her Majesty's dresser. If either the Queen or the Duke of Edinburgh required anything at any time of the day or night they could simply press a button next to their bed. This would summon a Royal steward to attend to their needs. Now move across the vestibule to the honeymoon suite.'

Aha! Now you're talking! 'This is the only room on *Britannia* with a double bed, brought on board at the request of Prince Charles when he honeymooned on the yacht with Princess Diana.' We all peer through the window at the small double bed, lost in our thoughts about this doomed Royal coupling.

According to Diana, their honeymoon on *Britannia* was a grim, joyless, loveless affair, like something out of an overwrought Victorian melodrama. Charles arrived on honeymoon with seven books by his creepy mentor Sir Laurens van der Post.* 'Diana dashes about chatting up all the sailors and the cooks in the galley, etc, while I remain hermit-like on the verandah deck, sunk with pure joy into one of Laurens van der Post's books,' he wrote to a friend on the second day of their cruise. Happy Holidays!

Diana was less enamoured by the works of van der Post. 'He read them and we had to analyse them over lunch every day,' she complained to Andrew Morton. Seclusion was not just out of the question but, on the part of the groom, actively avoided. 'We had to entertain all the top people on *Britannia* every night, so there was never any time on our own. Found that very difficult to accept,' recalled Diana. The honey-

---

* Sir Laurens van der Post (1906–96), author of *The Lost World of the Kalahari* and many other works, was a godfather to Prince William and a spiritual guru to Prince Charles. After van der Post's death, it was discovered that he had fathered a secret child after an illicit affair with a 14-year-old girl. Described by his biographer as 'a compulsive fantasist', he never lived among the Kalahari Bushmen, as he had claimed, but once spent a fortnight with them; nor did he discover their paintings of the Tsodilo Hills, as he also claimed: they had been well known to Europeans for nearly half a century. His friendship with Carl Jung was also disputed, as was his account of his own wartime heroism in a Japanese prison camp. Asked the cause of his death, a doctor who had known him replied, 'He was weary of sustaining so many lies.'

mooners dined in formal attire with the ship's senior officers, while the Royal Marine band played in an adjoining area.

As if this were not enough, the virgin bride couldn't stop visiting the ship's kitchens, rummaging around the fridges for ice cream and snacks and wolfing them down. 'By then the bulimia was appalling, absolutely appalling. It was rife, four times a day on the yacht. Anything I could find I would gobble up and be sick two minutes later – very tired. So, of course, that slightly got the mood swings going in the sense that one minute one would be happy, next blubbing one's eyes out. I remember crying my eyes out on our honeymoon. I was so tired, for all the wrong reasons totally.'

Prince Charles's account was very different. 'All I can say is that marriage is very jolly,' he wrote to the same friend, 'and it's also extremely nice being together in *Britannia*.'

We go down to the next deck, into the officers' Anteroom, 'strictly off-limits to the rest of the crew … With the bar as its focus, the Anteroom was where the Officers could relax after the tension and discipline of being "front of house" in the eyes of the Royal Family and a watching world,' reads the guidebook. 'Drinks, listening to the radio, Yacht quizzes and some very boisterous games assisted the unwinding process.'

Everyone on board, from high to low, seems to have been on a fruitless quest for privacy: the Royal Family trying to avoid the eyes of the crew, who in turn tried to avoid the eyes of the Royal Family. It was a round-the-clock game of hide-and-seek.

Relaxation was a strenuous affair in these confined surroundings. In the Anteroom, the officers would play 'Wombat Tennis', batting a stuffed toy wombat into the fan on the ceiling and then from one side to the other 'with a great deal of noisy encouragement'.

Every now and then, these carefree games would come to a halt, and best behaviour resumed. 'Beside the light-hearted fun and banter, the Anteroom did take on a more dignified atmosphere when the Officers entertained The Queen and the Duke of Edinburgh, or other members of the Royal Family, for dinner or a drinks party.' That sentence almost cracks under its own starchiness. The Anteroom is decorated with pictures of the Royal Family. 'The Queen and Prince Philip's portraits always took pride of place above the fire.'

Next door, the Officers' Wardroom is where 'the *Britannia*'s 20 Officers would assemble to dine and relax in an atmosphere steeped in tradition'. It sounds as relaxing as a keelhaul: dressed in their 'traditional uniform of a white shirt, black trousers, cummerbund and patent leather shoes', the officers would gather in the Anteroom for pre-dinner drinks. They would then take it in turns to say grace 'delivered in rhyme, with a healthy dose of irreverence'. At dinner, 'for that touch of flair, the Royal Marines' Band when not on royal duty would provide musical accompaniment'; towards the end of the meal 'the officers would stand to drink the loyal toast to Her Majesty the Queen and the Royal Marines Band would play the national anthem. On *Britannia*, the loyal toast was always taken standing, as an extra mark of respect to the Queen. Finally, to round off an altogether stylish evening, the youngest unheard officer would be invited to entertain his colleagues with an amusing after-dinner speech.'

To this day, the walls are decorated with photographs of the Royal Family, 'many of them signed'. In common with the rest of the yacht, images of Princess Margaret are all over the place. 'Second from the left is a wedding portrait of Princess Margaret and Antony Armstrong-Jones taken in 1960 by the photographer Cecil Beaton.' Did this one remain in pride of place even after their marriage went sour? Beaton nursed a deep and bitter resentment of his upstart rival. 'Not even a good photographer!' he exclaimed on first being told the news of their engagement. He then lay awake for three nights in a row, attempting to analyse his own vexation, concluding 'that nothing so momentous as this would ever happen in my life, that all my excitement and interests paled in comparison'. At the Palace reception before the wedding, Beaton gazed at the groom with something close to loathing: 'The man of her choice looked extremely nondescript, biscuit-complexioned, ratty and untidy.' But he recognised that his job as official photographer was to make his loathed rival glow. 'The fact that this man is of little standing, that he is in no way romantic ... makes no matter, for he is the man the Princess has fallen in love with, and so all must be made perfect in the eyes of the world.'

Six decades on, this signed photograph still decorates the Officers' Wardroom: the glamorous young couple in their wedding clothes, made perfect for the world. The photographer and both his subjects now lie dead and buried. How many tourists below the age of fifty could even put a name to them? I once asked my son, then a teenager, if he could name the Queen's four children. He named Charles and Anne quite quickly, and then, after a little prompting, managed Andrew too. 'And there's one more ...' I said. He thought for a long time, and then took a stab: 'Steve?'

Another photo features the Princess Royal and her second husband, the shadowy Tim Laurence, who holds a bull terrier, which glares mercilessly at the camera. Whatever happened to her first husband, Captain Mark Phillips? The Royal Train moves on; figures who were once major players are overtaken by others, younger and more vivid, until they in turn become marginal, and then, as if by magic, vanish.

We shuffle through various kitchens and pantries, among them the Silver Pantry ('with the *Britannia*'s exacting standards, every single item had to be polished daily') and on to 'the largest and grandest room on the Royal Yacht *Britannia* – the State Dining Room'. It is certainly large for a boat, but still looks a bit of a squeeze, its chairs and tables and table settings all hugger-mugger, a gentrified canteen. Around the edge is a variety of bric-à-brac picked up by the Queen on her state visits: a wooden carving of a shark from the Pitcairn Islands, a carved wooden tortoise from the Galapagos, plenty of fancy swords and daggers.

'Here the Queen and the Duke of Edinburgh entertained their guests in spectacular style. Through these doors have walked some of the world's most powerful figures to accept the world's ultimate honour – an invitation to dine at the table of Her Majesty the Queen. Sir Winston Churchill, Rajiv Gandhi, Nelson Mandela, Bill Clinton, Boris Yeltsin, Ronald Reagan and Margaret Thatcher: all have taken their place in history aboard this Royal Yacht.'

Geometry joined forces with gastronomy. 'It took three hours to set the 56 places for a state banquet when the position of every knife, fork and spoon was meticulously measured with a ruler.

'The carpet could also be rolled back to expose a wooden dance floor beneath, though the last time this was used was for Princess Anne's 21st birthday celebrations.' This particular party took place well over half a century ago, on 15 August 1971; 'Get It On' by T. Rex was top of the charts, with the New Seekers' 'Never Ending Song of Love' at number 2.

Like all the clocks on board, the clock in the State Dining Room is set to one minute past three 'as a permanent reminder of the last time Her Majesty stepped off the yacht'. Nowadays, the Royal Yacht is available for 'exclusive evening events and those who are entertained on board still experience the same meticulous attention to detail and famed *Britannia* standards of service'. A website for the corporate hire of *Britannia* offers 'White-gloved Butler service' and 'a red carpet entrance … piped aboard via the Royal Brow'.

'Hire Her Majesty the Queen's former floating palace and experience an event of a lifetime,' suggests the website. 'Where kings, queens, presidents and prime ministers once dined, your event becomes part of a timeline of historic moments experienced aboard *Britannia* … The majestic State Dining Room was where Her Majesty Queen Elizabeth II entertained world leaders, political figures and famous faces. With its white panelled walls adorned with gifts received during state visits, it represents the ultimate lavish event space on board.'

We drift through to the reception room, 'where the royal family and their guests would gather for drinks before lunch or dinner … The Queen was keen that *Britannia* should have the feel of country house comfort rather than anything too formal or ostentatious. Indeed, the initial design scheme for the royal apartments was rejected by the Queen as being too elaborate and fussy …' With their chintz armchairs, white walls and grey carpeting, the two rooms are unfussy to the point of blandness: solid, utilitarian and dependable, as though the Queen herself had been transformed into soft furnishings.

The rest of *Britannia* goes down, down, deeper and down, both figuratively and symbolically, the social hierarchy of the nation represented in one great ship, from the Warrant Officers' and Chief Petty Officers' Mess, down to the Petty Officers' and Royal Marines Sergeants' Mess ('an invitation to drink here was highly sought after by members of the Royal Household staff'), further down through the petty officers' bunks, which fold up into seats, and the Royal Marines Barracks, in which twenty-six bandsmen were stacked into three tiers of bunks in a windowless room the size of the Queen's suite.

In every country they visited, the Marines would be required to play the National Anthem and a selection of popular classics after any state banquet. 'A faultless performance was always demanded and the Royal Marines rehearsed daily. But on a ship where silence was golden this could present a bit of a challenge. Daily rehearsals usually took place as far away from the royal quarters as possible.'

The sick bay, the mail room and the laundry ('a careful schedule ensured that the Royal Family's washing happened on different days to that of the officers and yachtsmen') are all deep below decks. As in a dystopian fiction by H. G. Wells, the deeper down you go, the further away from the light, the more people are squeezed in, until you get to the Engine Room at the very bottom, staffed by eighty engineers, with eight on duty at any one time.

You exit through the Souvenir Shop, stocked with Queen Elizabeth II Memorial Tea Towels, Corgi cuddly toys, handbags and keyrings, rubber ducks in the smart navy-blue uniform of an admiral, *Britannia* Playing Cards, *Britannia* Greetings Cards, *Britannia* Pens, *Britannia* Navy Velour Golf Towels, *Britannia* Captains' Hats, *Britannia* Gold and Silver Ship's Spoons, *Britannia* Travel Card Holders, *Britannia* Leather Luggage Tags, *Britannia* Leather Bookmarks, Queen Elizabeth II Tote Bags and Queen Elizabeth II Fridge Magnets.

86

Sunday, 31 August 1997

The Queen is woken around 1 a.m. to be told that Princess Diana has died in a car crash in Paris. She advises Prince Charles not to wake his sons, but to tell them in the morning. 'We must get the radios out of their rooms,' she adds.

Around the same, BBC Two broadcasts the news that the Princess of Wales is reported to have been in a car crash. It is understood, they say, that she suffered only minor injuries.

By 4 a.m., the prime minister, Tony Blair, and his press secretary, Alastair Campbell, have been informed that the Princess has died. For the next few hours, conference calls go back and forth between the Palace and Downing Street. Blair will be expected to make a public statement. Campbell and Blair go 'round and round in circles about what he should say, and also how'. They don't want it to look tacky.

ITV broadcasts rolling news about the car crash in Paris, but closes it down at 4.20 a.m., under the impression there is nothing more to say. But fate proves them wrong. Twenty minutes later, at 4.40 a.m., they announce the death of Princess Diana.

From this point on, all news presenters wear black ties, and so do the weather forecasters. The scheduled programmes on BBC One are replaced by rolling news.

At 5.45 a.m., Piers Morgan, the editor of the *Daily Mirror*, arrives at his office. He is shown a screen full of photographs of Princess Diana lying dead in the back of the car wreck. There is a trickle of blood running from her lip but otherwise no sign of injury. He stares at the screen for a couple of minutes, just saying 'fuck me' over and over again. 'I had never seen more sensational news images.'

Despite himself, he realises they can never be made public. He runs to the phone and calls the boss of the agency that has sent them. Later, he claims to have said: 'Listen, mate, Diana's possibly been killed by the bloody paparazzi and you are trying to flog me pictures of her still warm corpse. Think about it, for fuck's sake.'

Just before 7 a.m., Prince Charles tells his two sons that their mother has been in a car crash. As Harry remembers it, his father says, 'There were complications. Mummy was quite badly injured and taken to hospital, darling boy.'

'Hospital?'

'Yes. With a head injury.' He says he's afraid she didn't make it. Twenty-five years later, Prince Harry remembers that his father didn't hug him, but said, 'It's going to be OK', as he touched his knee.

At Downing Street, Blair tells Campbell that he's been working on his statement. Campbell advises him that it is 'fine to be emotional, and to call her the People's Princess ... talk about the good she did, how people are feeling'. Blair keeps saying to Campbell, 'I can't really believe this has happened. People will be in a state of real shock. There will be grief that you would not get for anyone else.' He adds that he somehow knew her life would end like this, well before her time.

Going down for breakfast, Campbell sees the news on the television, and starts to cry.

Michael Palin is in his bathroom, getting ready for a run, when he turns on the radio at 8.50 a.m. The fashion designer Jeff Banks is talking about 'someone who has clearly passed away – a woman, a Royal, someone of style'. Palin guesses it must be the Queen Mother and feels cheesed off that her death will overshadow the premiere of his new TV travel show. But then he hears 'the quite paralysing news' that Princess Diana has been killed in a car crash.

'I can't move for a moment. Half dressed, I stand by the basin, staring down at the radio as if it might have developed some technical fault. The words coming out couldn't surely refer to real life.' Should he go ahead with his run? 'I decide to go, of course, but hope there won't be too many people I know, because in a way I feel embarrassed to have heard what I've heard.' He runs on Parliament Hill. People are walking their dogs as though nothing has happened. 'Perhaps, I think, they don't know what I know.'

Around 9.30 a.m., in my home town of Aldeburgh, on the Suffolk coast, I bump into our elderly neighbour Peter Shand Kydd as he emerges from the newsagent. Peter is Princess Diana's stepfather – her mother left her father for him. He is a very lovable figure: iconoclastic, world-weary, darkly humorous. He always reminds me of Babar's dad. I see that he is wearing a black tie. I hesitate, not quite knowing what to say. 'What do you expect to happen if you get a lift from a driver supplied by Mohamed Fayed?' he says, unexpectedly.

At 11.30 a.m., the Royal Family, all in black, except for Prince Charles, who is in a kilt, arrive at Crathie Kirk, just up the hill from Balmoral. As they walk past the gathering of silent bystanders, Prince William and Prince Harry keep their eyes on the ground. Why did the Queen encourage them to face the public on this awful morning? Later, Tony Blair will reflect that:

> The point is: the Queen is a genuine, not an artificial person, by which I mean there is no artifice in how she approaches things. While her absolute preoccupation was protecting the boys, it was to protect them first and foremost as princes. There would have been no question of them not going to church that day, hours after their mother had died. It was their duty as princes.

The principal conflict in the days to come will be between emotion and restraint, natural behaviour vs Royal behaviour.

The service itself proceeds as usual, starting with the news that the recent Open Day raised £2,100 for church funds, and there will be a musical event in the parish later in the week.

The Royal Chaplain remembers 'all those whose lives are darkened by tragedy and grief, who need now more than human comfort and service'. But this is the only allusion to the death of the Princess: her name is never mentioned. The 100-strong congregation ends the service with a rendition of 'God Save the Queen'.

After the service, Prince Harry asks, 'Are you sure Mummy's really dead?'

Before noon, Tony Blair speaks to the cameras outside a church in his constituency. 'We are today a nation, in Britain, in a state of shock, in mourning, in grief that is so deeply painful for us ... She was the People's Princess, and that's how she'll stay, how she will remain in our hearts and in our memories forever.' Watching him on television, Alastair Campbell thinks he has come over well. 'It was a very power-ful piece of communication. The People's Princess was easily the strongest line and the people in the studio afterwards were clearly impressed, and felt he really had caught the mood.'

Prince Charles is adamant that he should go to Paris and accom-pany the late Princess back. But some old-school courtiers argue that a plane from the Queen's Flight should not be used, since, at the time of her death, Diana was not, strictly speaking, a Royal personage.

Monday, 1 September 1997

The Prince of Wales travels on the Queen's Flight from Aberdeen to Paris, accompanied by Diana's two sisters, in order to bring back the Princess's corpse. A few minutes before 7 p.m., RAF BAe 146 arrives at RAF Northolt, with the coffin of the Princess of Wales in the passenger cabin, within sight of her two sisters and her former husband.

The Prince and his former sisters-in-law then wait on the tarmac with the prime minister and other grandees. The coffin bearers from the Queen's Colour Squadron march up to the aircraft. At the stroke of 7 p.m., the hatch opens and the coffin is borne out. In death as in life, the air is filled with the click-click-click of press cameras.

The Princess's sisters, Jane and Sarah, then curtsy to the Prince of Wales, who kisses each of them in turn. The sisters depart in the Royal Daimler: another car is chock-a-block with bouquets.

For a minute or two, the Prince of Wales shares a few words with the grandees before disappearing back inside the plane, which then sets off for Balmoral. 'He's going back to the boys,' explains his spokesman.

Later that evening, Tony Blair tells Alastair Campbell that their job is to make sure the funeral is not 'a classic Establishment event, but a different kind of funeral that unites the country around her personality'.

During this coming week, anything considered remotely 'disrespectful' is taken off air by the BBC. Radio One's Sunday-evening chart show is cancelled, for the first time ever, and songs referring to car crashes, Paris, death, princesses or foreign holidays are forbidden. The small number of pop songs that sound vaguely like hymns – Robbie Williams's 'Angels', John Lennon's 'Imagine' – are played over and over again. Embarrassed by the title of her new album, *Impossible Princess*, Kylie Minogue delays its release.

No hospital drama is to be broadcast on television, nor any film featuring a car crash. A holiday programme drops an item about taking the Orient Express to Paris.

Newspapers which last week criticised Diana for living it up in the South of France with her fancy-man are now proclaiming her a saint who thought only of others. Only last Wednesday, the *Daily Mail*'s star columnist, Lynda Lee Potter, wrote:

> The sight of a paunchy playboy groping a scantily dressed Diana must appal and humiliate Prince William. As the mother of two young sons, she ought to have more decorum and sense.

But today Lee-Potter executes what is known in Fleet Street as a 'reverse ferret' and praises the dead Princess:

> Throughout their childhood she gave her sons endless loving cuddles … She adored her children.

In the US, the *National Enquirer* issues the following statement: 'We apologise for the Princess Diana page-one headline DI GOES SEX MAD, which is still on the stands at some locations. It is currently being replaced with a special 72-page tribute issue: A FAREWELL TO THE PRINCESS WE ALL LOVED.'

Tuesday, 2 September 1997
Private Eye magazine satirises Fleet Street's speedy change of heart:

> The late Princess Diana: An Apology. In recent weeks (not to mention the last ten years) we at the *Daily Gnome*, in common with all other newspapers, may have inadvertently conveyed the impression that the late Princess of Wales was in some way a neurotic, irresponsible and manipulative troublemaker who had repeatedly meddled in political matters that did not concern her and personally embarrassed Her Majesty the Queen by her Mediterranean love-romps ... We now realise as of Sunday morning that the Princess of Hearts was in fact the most saintly woman who has ever lived, who, with her charitable activities, brought hope and succour to hundreds of millions of people all over the world. We would like to express our sincere and deepest hypocrisy to all our readers on this tragic day and hope and pray that they will carry on buying our paper notwithstanding.

Members of the public queue along the Mall to sign a special Book of Condolence at St James's Palace. Before long, many more Books of Condolence are introduced, to ease the congestion. Some people take fifteen minutes to complete their comments. Others write the single word: 'Why?' For Alan Bennett, this 'suggests a certain cosmic awareness', besides having the merit of brevity'.

The newspapers are clamouring for the Queen to put her grief on display. 'Where is our Queen? Where is her flag?' asks the *Sun*. 'Show us you care,' demands the *Express*. 'Your people are suffering. Speak to us, Ma'am,' pleads the *Mirror*.

Sales of the *Daily Mirror* are up an extra 800,000 from last week. 'There has never been anything like this,' reports an excited Piers Morgan.

Over at the *Evening Standard*, the editor asks his top columnists to offer their tributes to Princess Diana. No slave to sentimentality, the newspaper's art critic, Brian Sewell, writes a piece saying that he can 'feel no grief for ... a promiscuous playgirl who died in a foreign lover's arms in a Paris underpass'. Perusing it, the editor is aghast. 'I can't print this. They'll break your windows and poison your dogs.'

The Princess of Wales's brother, Charles Spencer, has been asked to deliver the funeral address. The archbishop of Canterbury, George Carey, thinks it a great mistake: he believes that only clergy and lay readers should preach at funeral services. But Westminster Abbey lies beyond his jurisdiction, so he phones Earl Spencer and offers his assistance, 'urging him to bring out the Christian message of hope and life evermore in God'. The Earl listens politely, but leaves Carey with the impression that he has already worked out what he wants to say.

Wednesday, 3 September 1997
The archbishop of Canterbury sends the dean of Westminster a draft list of prayers for the funeral service. He is 'taken aback' by the 'intense bitterness' that exists between the two families: the Spencers do not want any mention of the Royal Family in the prayers, and the Royal Family insist that the phrase 'People's Princess' be removed. 'The strain', says the archbishop, is 'affecting everybody'.

A lady in waiting phones the archbishop from Buckingham Palace, dismayed by the barrage of attacks on the Queen. 'Could you do something?' He refuses, on the grounds that any public statement he might make in her defence 'could add fuel to the fire'. Instead, he encourages parishes to lay on special services over the weekend, with special prayers for the Royal Family.

* * *

Michael Palin is phoned by a woman from the *Daily Mail*. 'We're asking famous celebrities [sic] where they were when they heard the news about Diana,' she says. He tells her he was in the bathroom.

'Were you in the bath?' she asks tentatively.

I can only be honest. 'No, I was halfway between the basin and the door.'

This is becoming wonderfully surreal. But she's not giving up. She's under orders, clearly.

'And what did you do when you heard, ring friends? Switch on the television?'

'I went running.' Also the truth.

'What were you thinking about when you were running?'

I couldn't take any more of this and gave a quick, probably rather clipped summary of my feelings and the call ended. Frightening. Maybe I'll hear from the Compassion Police if I don't conform to the required State of Grief.

The Queen's deputy private secretary, Sir Robin Janvrin, phones Alastair Campbell. They put the issue of lowering the flag to Her Majesty, he says, but she feels it would be too big a break with tradition.

Already, there is jockeying for invitations to the funeral. Peter Mandelson calls Campbell from America, saying he wishes to attend the funeral 'as a personal friend'. At the *Daily Mirror*, Piers Morgan receives his *ex officio* invitation.

Thursday, 4 September 1997
Still chronicling this strange week, Alan Bennett notes that the BBC News chose to zoom in on a card on the great mass of flowers outside Kensington Palace. It says: 'God created a blonde angel and called her Diana.' He is unmoved.

'It purports to be from a child, though whether one is supposed to be touched by it or (as is my inclination) to throw up isn't plain ...

HMQ to address the nation tomorrow. I'm only surprised Her Majesty hasn't had to submit to a phone-in.'

Two elderly Czech ladies are caught pilfering teddy bears from the piles that have been left in the parks as tributes to the late Princess. They will later be sentenced to a month in prison, reduced on appeal to a couple of nights.

Members of the public give chase to a Sardinian tourist they have spotted stealing another teddy bear. Emerging from court, the Sardinian is punched in the face by a 43-year-old man who explains, 'I did it for Britain.'

Campbell thinks the public mood against the Royal Family is becoming 'dangerous and unpleasant'; the press are 'fuelling a general feeling that the Royals were not responding or even caring'. Tony Blair himself describes it as 'menacing'. Campbell has a conference call with the Lord Chamberlain, Robin Janvrin and the Duke of Edinburgh; the Duke, he thinks, sounds 'old and frail and … clearly nervous'. The Duke says that they will now be coming to London, and that the Queen will broadcast a message. Campbell suggests it should be 'more conversational than the usual Christmas broadcast'.

Alastair Campbell listens in as Tony Blair has a telephone conversation with the Queen:

> It was the first time I'd heard him one on one with the Queen and he really did the Ma'am stuff pretty well, but was also clear and firm too. He said the thing was Diana was a personality who made people feel they knew her when they didn't, so there were many people out there feeling loss and wanting to blame. As he told her, it was unfair that it was being directed at the Queen and the family … He said he felt she had to show that she was vulnerable and they were really feeling it. He said 'I really do feel for you. There can be nothing more miserable than feeling as you do and having your motives questioned.'

Piers Morgan is phoned by Earl Spencer. 'Hello, Mr Morgan, I am ringing on behalf of my mother to ask all tabloid editors not to attend the funeral service.' Morgan senses the rage in his voice; he agrees not to come.

Friday, 5 September 1997

Mother Teresa dies in Calcutta. 'Normally she would get on every front page and have huge pullout tributes to her inside,' notes Morgan. 'But today she was an afterthought, tucked away on page 21.'

Outside Buckingham Palace, a handwritten notice reads: 'Your Majesty, Please Look and Learn.' Amid this popular clamour for them to put their grief on display, the veteran crime-writer P. D. James sympathises with the Queen and her family. 'It seems outrageous that the bereaved should be expected to come down to London publicly to collude in what is increasingly seen as a self-indulgent, almost neurotic display of emotionalism.'

Gyles Brandreth agrees. 'It's completely out of hand. The world has lost the plot,' he writes in his diary. 'The issue of the hour appears to be the Buckingham Palace flagpole. As anyone who knows anything knows, the flagpole is traditionally bare except when the sovereign is in residence when the Royal Standard is flown. And the Royal Standard is never flown at half mast, even on the death of a sovereign. But the tabloids are having none of that – they are baying for blood. Actually they are baying for tears. "Show us you care, Ma'am!" Well, the Queen doesn't cry – and certainly not in public – but she has bowed to public opinion and the union flag is now flying over Buckingham Palace at half mast.'

Princes William and Harry walk up and down outside Kensington Palace, greeting the crowds, shaking their hands, 'as if we were running for office', remembers Harry. They make him uncomfortable and unsettled. '... I disliked how those hands felt. More, I hated how they made me feel. Guilty. Why were all these people crying when I wasn't – and hadn't? ... I remember consoling several folks who were prostrate, overcome, as if they knew Mummy, but also thinking: You didn't, though. You act as if you did ... *but you didn't know her.*'

Thousands spend the night in the Mall, and in Kensington Gardens, where there are an estimated 10,000 candlelit shrines to the late Princess. Outside Westminster Abbey, one man tells a reporter from the *Guardian* that he has left his father in hospital to be there, and is praying his condition does not deteriorate.

In the afternoon, the Queen arrives at Buckingham Palace, dressed all in black. 'We were not confident that when the Queen got out of the car, she would not be hissed and jeered,' recalls one former courtier. But their fears prove unfounded: her arrival is greeted by applause. She walks among the crowds in silence, 'on mournabout,' as Alan Bennett puts it. From out of nowhere, an 11-year-old girl hands her five red roses.

'Would you like me to place them for you?' asks the Queen.

'No, Your Majesty,' the little girl replies. 'They are for you.'

Around her, the crowd begins to clap.

'I remember thinking, "Gosh, it's all right,"' recalls an aide.

According to another aide, it is only after she has arrived in London that the Queen fully comprehends the extent and intensity of public feeling. 'At Balmoral, she hadn't taken it in … All the remarks and people hugging each other, sobbing – the whole nation seemed to have gone bananas. The Queen and Prince Philip felt utterly bewildered.'

On a Radio 4 phone-in, a male listener confesses to being more upset by the death of the Princess of Wales than by the death of his own wife.

On Talk Radio, Dr David Starkey, the iconoclastic historian once dubbed 'the rudest man in Britain', rounds on a caller, questioning the authenticity of his grief. 'Why should you care? I can't see why we should think better of someone when they're dead than when they're alive.'

BBC Radio 4's *Feedback* programme, due to be broadcast today, is shelved. A spokesman says this will give listeners extra time to reflect on the BBC's coverage as a whole. But some suspect it is because 98 per cent of correspondents have complained that the BBC has been overdoing it.

The country still seems to be divided between the lachrymose and the dry-eyed, each side distrusting the other. The veteran cricket commentator Brian Johnston describes it as 'a Latin-American carnival of grief. Where is this – Argentina?' The newly elected MP (and former BBC foreign correspondent) Martin Bell agrees that such open grieving for a public figure is alien to the British, but, unlike Johnston, he welcomes it. 'I have seen revolutions in other countries, but never before in my own ... We surprised the press. We surprised each other. We surprised ourselves. We shed our trivial and selfish cares. We felt as one people and mourned as one people, as if for a loved one in our own closest family – which in a sense she was.'

All the major chain stores and supermarkets in the country have closed all day for the funeral. Signs in the windows of sex shops in London's Soho announce that they will be closing as 'a mark of respect'.

At 6.00 p.m., the Queen speaks to the nation, live on television, from the Chinese Dining Room at Buckingham Palace. Over her shoulders, viewers can see the mourners at the gates.

> Since last Sunday's dreadful news we have seen, throughout Britain and around the world, an overwhelming expression of sadness at Diana's death.
>
> We have all been trying in our different ways to cope. It is not easy to express a sense of loss, since the initial shock is often succeeded by a mixture of other feelings: disbelief, incomprehension, anger – and concern for those who remain. We have all felt those emotions in these last few days. So what I say to you now, as your Queen and as a grandmother, I say from my heart.
>
> First, I want to pay tribute to Diana myself. She was an exceptional and gifted human being. In good times and bad, she never lost her capacity to smile and laugh, nor to inspire others with her warmth and kindness. I admired and respected her – for her energy and commitment to others, and especially for her devotion to her two boys. This week at Balmoral, we have all been trying to help William and Harry come to terms with the devastating loss that they and the rest of us have suffered.
>
> No one who knew Diana will ever forget her. Millions of others who never met her, but felt they knew her, will remember her. I for

one believe there are lessons to be drawn from her life and from the extraordinary and moving reaction to her death. I share in your determination to cherish her memory ...

I hope that tomorrow we can all, wherever we are, join in expressing our grief at Diana's loss, and gratitude for her all-too-short life. It is a chance to show to the whole world the British nation united in grief and respect.

May those who died rest in peace and may we, each and every one of us, thank God for someone who made many, many people happy.

Watching the broadcast, Alastair Campbell is glad to see the Queen following his suggestion to include his phrase 'as a grandmother'.

But the playwright Alan Bennett remains unmoved. 'HMQ gives an unconvincing broadcast,' he writes in his diary, '"unconvincing" not because one doesn't believe that her sentiments are genuine (as to that there's no way of telling) but because she's not a good actress, indeed not an actress at all. What she should have been directed to do is to throw in a few pauses and seem to be searching for her words; then the speech would have been hailed as moving and heartfelt. As it is she reels her message off as she always does. That is the difference between Princess Diana and the Queen: one could act, the other can't.'

The comedian Linda Smith is similarly sceptical. She thinks the Queen looked like 'a battered hostage paraded in front of the cameras to explain how well she was being treated'. The maverick Tory MP Alan Clark, who has long considered the Royal Family infra dig, considers the Queen's words 'utterly without warmth and affection'. Furthermore, he finds it 'pleasing to note the discomfiture of "the Royals" as they struggle to cope with this great outpouring of love for someone they were trying (and succeeded) to destroy – from jealousy and incomprehension'.

Among the intellectuals, Martin Amis is altogether more support- ive. 'It was an extraordinary performance: she gave a near-pathological populace what it wanted, while remaining true to her own self ... She didn't sell her integrity to the yearnings of the many.' An instant Gallup poll suggests that Amis is echoing the general mood: two-thirds have reacted favourably to the speech, with just 19 per cent reacting unfavourably.

When the BBC journalist John Humphrys goes to a concert at the Royal Albert Hall, he finds that the advertised programme has been changed; the symphony he was expecting to hear has been switched for Fauré's Requiem. The conductor asks the audience not to applaud at the end 'as a mark of respect'. Humphrys is incensed. 'How could applauding a group of fine musicians be disrespectful to anyone?'

After supper, Alan Bennett ventures down to the Mall to see what is happening. He finds it 'full of people not particularly silent, no mood at all, really, just walking up and down as if coming away from an event, though it's also like a huge *passeggiata*. People crowd to the walls and hedges, where there are flowers and little candlelit shrines; flowers fixed to trees, poems, painted messages; a Union Jack and teddy bears (which always bode ill) … the populousness of it, as well as the random milling about, make me think that this is perhaps what India is like.'

Suddenly, he spots something bizarre: a fox. 'It is just out of the light, slinking by with its head turned towards the parade of people passing … Besides us only one woman notices it, but that's probably just as well: such is the hysteria and general silliness it might have been hailed as the reincarnation of Princess Diana, another beautiful vixen, with whom lots of parallels suggest themselves.'

Saturday, 6 September 1997

At 4.30 on the morning of the funeral, Earl Spencer wakes up and sets to work on his eulogy. 'I just sat at my desk and I had finished it by 6 o'clock. That was it. I didn't change anything … I was just speaking as a brother to a sister and on behalf of a sister.'

Over a million people line the funeral route, from Kensington Palace to Hyde Park Corner, down Constitution Hill to Buckingham Palace and on to Westminster Abbey. All week, the horses pulling the gun carriage have had flowers thrown at them as they train for their coming ordeal. Amid all the pomp and ceremony, the coffin itself, draped with the Royal Standard, carries a single word – 'Mummy' – written by Prince Harry on a card attached to a wreath of white flowers.

The Queen and other members of the Royal Family gather by the gates of Buckingham Palace. As the funeral cortège passes, the Queen is seen to give a brief bow of her head; Princess Margaret's head remains defiantly upright.

Walking with his uncle, his brother, his father and his grandfather behind his mother's coffin from St James's Palace to the Abbey, the 12-year-old Prince Harry is clenching his fists. A quarter of a century later, he will remember, beyond everything else, the sounds: 'the clinking bridles and clopping hooves of the six sweaty brown horses, the squeaking wheels of the gun carriage'. The rest is silence. 'The only hint that we were marching through a canyon of humanity was the occasional wail.'

The Abbey is filled with mourners from far and wide: royalty and politicians, of course, but also many from the worlds of fashion, pop and showbusiness. Elton John and George Michael arrive at the Abbey together. 'The place was full of people I knew,' recalls Elton John. 'Donatella Versace was there, David Frost, Tom Cruise and Nicole Kidman, Tom Hanks and Rita Wilson.'*

The congregation stands and sings the National Anthem. The two main television channels have started their broadcasts with different objectives. For ITN, its coverage should be 'authoritative but people-based', while the BBC sets out to treat theirs with the solemnity of any other state funeral. In the words of the BBC's chief commentator, David Dimbleby, 'When it came to the service ITN therefore concentrated on the film stars and the celebrities; the BBC on its usual elegant slow pans down the stained-glass windows.'

But tradition is outmanoeuvred by modernity. Producers watching and comparing both channels at the BBC headquarters send urgent instructions to the director in the Abbey: they want to see more of the starry congregation. The cameras duly become more promiscuous.

---

* Other celebrities present at the funeral included Sting, Shirley Bassey, Clive James and Stephen Spielberg.

Diana's astrologer, Debbie Frank, can be spotted sitting next to the TV personality Michael Barrymore.

Earl Spencer takes to the pulpit. He describes his late sister as somebody 'with a natural nobility, who was classless and who proved in the last year that she needed no royal title to generate her particular brand of royal magic'. He pledges 'that we, your blood family, will do all we can to continue the imaginative way in which you were steering these two exceptional young men so that their souls are not simply immersed by duty and tradition, but can sing openly as you planned'.

Once the Earl has finished his address, the stony silence in the Abbey is broken by the sound of applause from the crowd outside. This prompts the congregation inside to follow suit.

Elton John walks to the piano, to sing 'Candle in the Wind'. In 1973, the song was all about Marilyn Monroe,* but over the past few days the lyrics have been jigged around – 'Goodbye, Norma Jean' becoming 'Goodbye, England's Rose' – so that it is now a tribute to the late Princess. He worries that he will forget to look at the teleprompter and start singing the original lyrics instead. 'You'd have a hard time bluffing your way out of singing about Marilyn Monroe being found dead in the nude, or about how your feelings were more than sexual, at a state funeral, in front of a global audience of two billion people ...' But he completes the song without putting his foot in it.

Before the end of the service, the archbishop of Canterbury leads the congregation in the Lord's Prayer.

Afterwards, Elton John is driven straight to Townhouse Studios in Shepherd's Bush, where the Beatles' old producer George Martin is to oversee the recording of his new version of 'Candle in the Wind'.

* * *

---

* In his autobiography, Elton John's lyricist, Bernie Taupin, reveals that he originally wrote 'Candle in the Wind' as a tribute to Montgomery Clift, 'simply because he was more appealing to me'. But 'after some consideration' he had swapped Clift for Monroe, because she was 'more iconically recognizable' and 'more sympathetic in the minds of the masses'.

Though by nature a traditionalist, P. D. James judges the funeral service a success, and Elton John's song appropriate: 'this, after all, was the world in which the Princess was most at home'. On the other hand, she considers Earl Spencer's attack on the Royal Family 'unnecessary and misguided: the wrong words at the wrong time in the wrong place ... I wonder if those sad, mascara-laden eyes will droop in reproach forever over the House of Windsor, or whether this media-fuelled emotion will burn itself out as quickly as it has arisen.' A few months later, on a book-promotion tour in America, interviewers ask her, 'Why wouldn't the Queen grieve?' P. D. James wants to say that, if she had been the Queen, 'My grieving, though sincere, would not have been excessive.' Instead, 'I said that not everyone showed grief by pinning teddy bears and flowers to the railings of public parks.'

The hearse sets off for Althorp, the seat of the Spencer family for over 500 years, surrounded by seven motorcyclists, with an estimated 300,000 people lining the last seven miles. The hearse is showered with flowers along the way until, according to one onlooker, it looks like 'a battered Easter bonnet'. The driver can be seen shifting from side to side in his seat as he tries to peer through the flowers.

The Princess has a private burial on a little island on the lake in the grounds of Althorp. As the coffin descends, Prince Harry is overcome. 'My body convulsed and my chin fell and I began to sob uncontrollably into my hands. I felt ashamed of violating the family ethos, but I couldn't hold it in any longer.'

Elsewhere in Britain, some feel that things have gone too far. 'Am I alone in thinking that the country has momentarily taken leave of its senses?' asks the columnist A. N. Wilson.

The novelist Hilary Mantel thinks that the mass mourning, though kitsch, 'testified to the struggle for self-expression of individuals who were spiritually and imaginatively deprived, who released their own suppressed sorrow in grieving for a woman they did not know'.

Across the country, councils will have to clear up an estimated 15,000 tons of dead flowers, most of them wrapped in polythene. The

Institute of Psychiatry reports a significant increase in suicides among women.

Elton John's new version of 'Candle in the Wind' sells 1.5 million in the UK in its first week, and reaches number 1 in the charts in virtually every country in the world, including the US, Japan, Iceland, Spain, Hungary and Zimbabwe. Before the year is out, it has become the best-selling single in the UK and America since the charts began.*

In Suffolk, a friend's five-year-old daughter asks, 'What was Princess Di called before she died?'

In the weeks after the death of the Princess, the Royal Family are now commonly seen as cold and out of touch. The future of the Royal Yacht *Britannia*, so long in the balance, is now decided. 'A new royal yacht, a refurbishment of *Britannia* or whatever, did not seem to fit the post-Diana atmosphere,' recalls the paymaster general, Geoffrey Robinson. '... I told Gordon† that we should let the project drop. He agreed at once. I telephoned the MoD. They responded with unrecognizable alacrity that that had been their view all along, as I knew. When I phoned him, Sir Robert Fellowes said the Palace felt the same way.'

Robinson formally drops the project in the middle of September, just in time for New Labour's annual party conference in Brighton.

Had Diana survived, so too might the Royal Yacht *Britannia*.

---

* As a result of the single's success, footage of Princess Diana's funeral was repeated week after week on BBC TV's *Top of the Pops*. This made Elton John uneasy. 'It felt as if people were somehow wallowing in her death, like the mourning of her had got out of hand and they were refusing to move on. It seemed unhealthy to me – morbid and unnatural.'

† The then chancellor of the Exchequer, later prime minister, Gordon Brown.

87

Embarrassment is an emotion often unleashed during encounters with royalty. It can give birth to blushing, breathlessness, dizziness, shaking, stumbling, stammering, amnesia and incontinence both verbal and physical; but only very rarely to babies.

In many ways the personification of smart casual, Tony Blair nevertheless felt ill at ease in Royal company. A former public schoolboy, former lead singer with Ugly Rumours and, from 1997, prime minister, he suspected that he did not live up to their expectations, that he had somehow transgressed.

> I always felt that they preferred political leaders of two types: either those who were of them – or at least fully subscribed to their general outlook – or the 'authentic' Labour people, the sort they used to read about, who spoke with an accent and who fitted their view of how such people should be. People like me were a bit nouveau riche, a bit arriviste, a bit confusing and a bit suspect.

His wife Cherie was similarly discomfited, her progressive, egalitarian views out of kilter with the archaic protocols of monarchy. But for as long as they remained in No. 10 the pair of them were duty-bound to stay at Balmoral once a year.

In 1998, when they first stayed at Balmoral together, Cherie noticed two bells beside their bed, one marked 'Valet', the other marked 'Maid'.

The maid who was allocated to me that first year was very young, and kept curtsying and insisted on 'my lady'-ing me. 'Please don't call me my lady,' I implored, but this only flustered her more.

Cherie was also 'extremely disconcerted' to find, on her return to their bedroom, that everything she had brought with her had been unpacked and put in its right place.

> Not only my clothes, but the entire contents of my distinctly ancient toilet bag with its range of unmentionables.

This was to be an intrusion she would never forget; as we shall see, it would change her life. The following day, she found herself engaged in another titular to-and-fro, this time with Princess Anne.

> At one point that first year Princess Anne came over and said something which included 'Mrs Blair'.
> 'Oh. Please call me Cherie,' I said.
> 'I'd rather not,' she replied. 'It's not the way I've been brought up.'
> 'What a shame,' I said.
> My relationship with the Queen's only daughter went rapidly downhill and never recovered.

Though a senior member of a profession steeped in protocol – a Queen's Counsel, no less! – Cherie felt out of her depth at Balmoral:

> I never really got the hang of the protocol business in terms of what you called people and how you greeted them. Diana I called Diana. Charles I called Charles, and in fact would always kiss him, though I'm not convinced he really liked it. The Queen, however, was always Ma'am.
> I would watch other people go through the rigmarole. That first weekend, Sophie Rhys-Jones was still clearly finding her feet with the protocol. Charles came in, she'd bob; Princess Anne came in, she'd

bob. I decided I'd limit my bobbing to the Queen and the Queen Mother and leave it at that.*

In their autobiographies, both Tony and Cherie portray themselves as gauche outsiders, representatives of modern, easy-going, open-necked Cool Britannia, forced, against their wills, to travel back in time to a crustier, more hidebound era.

'I have to say', recalled Tony,

I found the experience of visiting and spending the weekend a vivid combination of the intriguing, the surreal and the utterly freaky. The whole culture of it was totally alien of course, not that the royals weren't very welcoming. but I never did 'country house' or 'stately home' weekends and had a bit of a horror of the notion. The walls are hung with Landseer pictures of stags, scenes of hunting and of course Queen Victoria's Mr Brown. There are footmen – in fact, very nice guys, but still footmen.

Totally alien, surreal, utterly freaky: the post-hippy language is at odds with the grandiloquence of court talk. 'A surreal end to a surreal week' is the disc-jockeyish way Tony Blair summed up his first, brief visit to Balmoral, for a sombre lunch the day after the funeral of Princess Diana.

At their first full stay, the following year, the Blairs were discombobulated by both too much pomp and too little. In his autobiography, Tony Blair presents their time there in terms of a Brian Rix farce, starring himself as the gauche young lead:

---

* Received opinion suggests that Cherie Blair baulked at curtsying to the Queen. In his diaries, Alastair Campbell observes that, on Millennium Eve, 'Cherie even curtsied to the Queen, a bit of a first I think, but it didn't seem to do much good.' In the *Spectator* magazine of 8 April 2006, the Royal biographer Sarah Bradford quoted the Queen herself as saying, 'I can almost feel Mrs Blair's knees stiffening when I come into the room.' However, Mrs Blair denies showing any such reluctance. 'The idea that I refused to curtsy, either then or later, is a complete load of rubbish,' she protested in her 2008 autobiography, *Speaking for Myself*. In the absence of CCTV footage of their various meetings, the jury must remain out on this delicate matter.

When I arrived for the first time on that Sunday, the valet – yes, you got your own valet – asked me if he could fold my clothes and generally iron the underpants and that type of thing, and so disconcerted me that when he then asked me if he could 'draw the bath', I lost the thread completely and actually thought for a moment he wanted to sketch the damn thing. Using the bathroom on the other side of the corridor was a singular act of courage, sneaking open the bedroom door, glancing right and left and then making for it at speed.

Nor did they know what to make of the topsy-turvy tradition of the annual Balmoral D-I-Y barbecue:

> TONY: They do the washing-up. You think I'm joking, but I'm not. They put the gloves on and stick their hands in the sink. You sit there having eaten, the Queen asks if you've finished, she stacks the plates and goes off to the sink.
> CHERIE: The highlight of the visit was undoubtedly the barbecue, though it was not remotely what I'd expected. The barbecue itself was an amazing design and I was so impressed that I asked where it came from. The answer was unexpected to say the least: Prince Philip had designed it himself, and in fact he very kindly gave us one.

Remembering her own previous blushes at the previous year's unprompted dispersal of the 'unmentionables' from her washing bag, on Cherie's second stay at Balmoral in 1999 she took precautions – or, rather, took some precautions, but not others:

> This year I had been a little more circumspect, and had not packed my contraceptive equipment, out of sheer embarrassment.

The repercussions of this decision were lasting:

As usual up there, it had been bitterly cold, and what with one thing and another … But then, I thought, I can't be. I'm too old. It must be the menopause.

But no: her initial instinct proved correct. Nine months later, she gave birth to Leo, the first baby born to the wife of a sitting prime minister in 150 years, living testament to the positive effects of embarrassment.

88

The monarch traditionally has the right 'to be consulted, to advise and to warn'. But not to opine: the Queen took care to keep her opinions to herself, or at least to couch them as questions.

In the days of the Cameron government, she approached the then Chancellor of the Exchequer, George Osborne, at a state dinner and put a question to him: 'The Chief of the Defence Staff is unable to answer my question. He told me to speak to the Defence Secretary, and the Defence Secretary told me to come and speak to you. So I am asking you: you are not going to close the Highland Bagpipe School of the British Army, are you?'

It was an opinion – or maybe a command – framed as a question. Everybody knew that the Queen loved the sound of bagpipes, especially in the morning.

Osborne reacted with deference. 'I was, like, "Of course not, Your Majesty." The next day I got in to the Treasury and I said, "Is there a bagpipe school? And for God's sake tell me we are not closing it down."'

The Treasury team agreed to look into the matter. Before long, they reported back that the Redford Barracks in Edinburgh was home to the Army School of Bagpipe Music and Highland Drumming, and the government were, indeed, planning to make some cuts to it.

'Well, we are not any more,' replied the chancellor.

89

In my next dream, I was in a car with a group of friends. We stopped unexpectedly at a large house in Norfolk and went in. There was a daytime party going on, with a merry atmosphere. I spoke to Anne Glenconner, who told me I had written a horrid book about Princess Margaret.* I tried to defend myself, but then used some excuse to move on. In another room was the Queen, aged about 60, in very good form, relaxed in a cardigan. We started chatting. It was as if we were old friends. At one point, I told her that I thought there were going to be some party games.

She said: 'I do hope not.'

I said: 'Don't you like party games?'

She said, still smiling: 'No, I do not.'

I said: 'Not even Scrabble?'

She said: 'No – I can't ever get them in the hole.'

I was baffled for a while by this comment, but then it came to me. 'Are you sure you don't mean snooker?'

'Yes, that IS what I meant!' she replied and roared with laughter.

* She had said this in real life, too, though not to me. Interviewed by Hadley Freeman for the *Guardian*, she referred to 'that horrible book, we won't mention the name of the person who wrote it. I don't know why people want to rot her like that.' Asked by Hadley Freeman if she was alluding to Craig Brown, she said nothing but 'gave a pained, terse nod'.

90

Lady Glenconner emerges from her memoir *Lady in Waiting* as an agreeable character, and I suppose it's to her credit that she disapproved of my book about her late mistress. After all, we came at Princess Margaret from different angles. As lady in waiting to Princess Margaret, her key task was to calm those upset by her mistress's cavalier manner, and to tolerate behaviour others found intolerable. 'I learned to do quite a lot of this diplomacy,' she writes, 'being clear and trying to be reasonable if I thought Princess Margaret was doing the wrong thing, helping to pacify her when she felt upset, or smooth ruffled feathers of friends or visitors who felt they'd been mistreated.'

Marriage to her impossible husband, Colin Tennant, provided the perfect training for attending to the needs of Princess Margaret. 'I used the same methods of gentle persuasion I'd learned with Colin. Life with him had also taught me to pick my battles carefully, and not get worked up.'

Yet, for all her overt loyalty, her own book is full of stories that portray Princess Margaret in an unsympathetic light. A friend taking the Princess to the theatre in New York says how much the cast is looking forward to meeting her afterwards. 'I don't want to meet them,' snaps Princess Margaret, 'and I'm not going to.' When Colin Tennant offers her the gift of a plot of land on Mustique, she replies, 'And does it come with a house?' Inspecting the proposed site, which is marked out with wooden stakes, she pulls up the stakes while his back is turned and makes it bigger.

'What are you doing, Ma'am?' asked Colin.

'Well, I think I ought to have a bit more land,' was her reply.

'What do you need more land for?' retorted Colin.

'Gatehouses for my protection officers,' declared Princess Margaret.

And that was what she got.

'She WAS royal, so it wasn't surprising she had "royal moments",' explains Lady Glenconner. These moments include Princess Margaret declaring, 'You can't possibly have a picnic without your butler'; expecting a bowl of fresh water and plenty of clean towels to be placed on the beach each time she went for a swim, as she dislikes the feeling of sand between her toes; telling her chauffeur to drive headlong at the pet cats of her enemy and Kensington Palace neighbour Princess Michael of Kent and instructing her lady in waiting ('Go, Anne, get them!') to turn the hose on those same cats; and presenting her ladies in waiting with Christmas gifts of handbags 'that had clearly been given to her and rejected after she had used them a few times'.

Princess Margaret gave one of her ladies in waiting a loo brush for Christmas, declaring, 'I noticed you didn't have one of these when I came to stay.' This lady in waiting was, says Glenconner, 'rather upset by the gesture': she had in fact taken care to tidy her loo brush away, so as not to offend the Princess.

Glenconner notes that Margaret's 'defiant streak extended to her sister, despite her being the Queen'. She tells one story that is particularly revealing. Margaret is ailing, having suffered one or two strokes, and her eyesight is deteriorating. The best of friends, Lady Glenconner visits her every day and reads to her, 'but not without her stopping me and questioning my pronunciation, which she was always correcting. This was a habit of hers.' One day, the Queen drops by for tea. Tactfully, Lady Glenconner retreats to a neighbouring room while the Queen joins Princess Margaret in the bedroom.

Quite soon after she had gone in, she reappeared.

'Oh, Ma'am, is everything all right?' I asked.

'No, it isn't,' the Queen replied. 'Margaret is listening to *The Archers* and every time I try to say something she just says, "Shhh!"'

This story bears out something one of the Queen Mother's closest friends once said of the Queen: 'Regardless of how rude Princess Margaret is to her, she never says anything. That is her policy ... She is a very decent person, but she won't intervene with anyone.'*

Since the publication of Lady Glenconner's memoir in 2019, two further autobiographical works have appeared, both offering eyewitness accounts of Princess Margaret's way of doing things.

Half a century or more after the heavily censored diaries of Chips Channon first appeared in 1967, they were republished in a far longer, unexpurgated edition: by now almost all of their victims were dead and buried, so long past upsetting. At the time of their original publication, Princess Margaret was 37 years old, and in her prime. Apart from one diary entry, written when she was 18 years old – 'Already she is a public character and I wonder what will happen to her? I feel that she will become unpopular as already there is a Marie Antoinette aroma about her' – this original edition omitted anything that might have offended her. It is only much more recently, with Simon Heffer's far more complicated edition, that the full extent of Channon's dislike of Princess Margaret has come to light.

Diary entries that formerly contained no mention of Princess Margaret's presence at this or that event now locate her, kicking and screaming, centre stage. At Ascot in 1953, we find her looking 'dull and dowdy and cross'; a month later, we hear of her 'rudeness and sulky manners'. In March 1954, 'Princess Margaret ... is becoming a bore, a problem and unpopular.' Two months later, she is 'becoming

---

* According to one of the younger members of the Royal Family, the Queen tolerated Princess Margaret's behaviour because she felt a strong sense of guilt about her, as the fortunate often do towards their less fortunate siblings.

cheap and declassée, unpopular and a bore'. Arriving late at a party, 'she was maddening the whole evening, bantering jokes and making fun of people'. At the beginning of June 1954, 'now known variously as "Maggot", "Princess Midget", "Lilliput" and "Her Royal Lowness"', she is involved in an amateur production of a play called *The Frog.* 'She is obsessed by the production, attends all the rehearsals and bullies everybody,' Channon observes, adding, perhaps superfluously, 'she is beginning to get on my nerves'. On 15 June, 'The Clarence House brat is becoming impossible', the next day she is 'increasingly impossible' and a month later, on 24 July 1954, 'increasingly unpopular'.

And so it goes on. By 1955, Princess Margaret's on–off romance with Peter Townsend had become the talk of the town. 'Upper class, and certainly London society, are amused and indifferent, probably rather pro. Also, they are enjoying the little digs: at the royal family who for too long have been on a pedestal … suddenly the royal family realise that they are not quite so invulnerable, so idolised as they perhaps thought … Princess Margaret is not an endearing character.'

Just four months after the appearance of this final volume of the unexpurgated Channon diaries, Princess Margaret came in for another blasting, this time from an unexpected source: her great-nephew, Prince Harry. Ghostwritten by a noted American misery memoirist, his autobiography *Spare*, published in January 2023, is a peculiar amalgam of American gush and British ice.

'I didn't know Princess Margaret, whom I called Aunt Margo,' writes Prince Harry, and/or his ghostwriter. 'She was my great-aunt, yes, we shared 12.5 per cent of our DNA, we spent the bigger holidays together, and yet she was almost a total stranger. Like most Britons, I mainly knew *of* her. I was conversant with the general contours of her sad life.' Like many passages in *Spare*, this one doesn't sound like its ostensible author. 'Conversant with the general contours of her sad life' sounds to me how an American ghostwriter would imagine an upper-class Englishman might speak.

Though Prince Harry fails to mention it, his Aunt Margo had been on non-speaks with his mother, Princess Diana, ever since the publication of her memoir *Diana: Her True Story.* The two Princesses were next-door neighbours in Kensington Palace, which had made blanking each other all the more tricky. 'Poor Lilibet and Charles have done everything they can to get rid of the wretched girl,' Margaret told a friend, 'but she just won't go.' After Diana's death in 1997, Margaret, alone among the Royal Family, had insisted that Diana should not be allowed to rest in a Royal Chapel nor be honoured with a Royal funeral.

'Growing up, I felt nothing for her, except a bit of pity and a lot of jumpiness,' recalls Prince Harry. 'She could kill a houseplant with one scowl. Mostly, whenever she was around, I kept my distance.'

He remembers one particular Christmas at Sandringham. All the members of the family had gathered to open their presents on Christmas Eve, 'a German tradition that survived the anglicizing of the family surname from Saxe-Coburg-Gotha to Windsor'. Harry decided to open the smallest present first. The tag says 'From Aunt Margo'. He tore off the wrapping to uncover a biro.

I said: *Oh. A biro. Wow.*
She said: *Yes. A biro.*
I said: *Thank you so much.*

Princess Margaret points out that the biro had a tiny rubber fish wrapped around it. Prince Harry's disappointment is unassuaged.

I told myself: That is cold-blooded.

He fails to mention that his family members traditionally impose a £5 spending limit on their Christmas gifts to each other.

As he grew older, it struck him, he continues, that he and his Aunt Margo should have been friends, as they had so much in common. 'Two spares. Her relationship with Granny wasn't an *exact* analogue of mine with Willy, but pretty close. The simmering rivalry, the intense competition (driven largely by the older sibling), it all looked familiar.'

By any standards, this is an odd interpretation of the relationship between Margaret and her sister. In her memoir *The Little Princesses*, their governess Marion Crawford briefly describes the 'entirely healthy manner' in which the siblings argued about toys from time to time. 'Neither was above taking a whack at her adversary, if roused, and Lilibet was quick with her left hook! Margaret was more of a close-in fighter, known to bite on occasions. More than once have I been shown a hand bearing the royal teeth marks.' Their fights were started, she says, by hats. 'They hated hats. This put them in a bad humour, and they would snap one another's elastic to shrill cries of "You brute! You beast!" "Margaret always wants what I want" was the common complaint.'

But Crawfie was describing the sisters as they were at the time of their grandfather's death, in 1936, when Margaret was only five and Lilibet nine. There are no reports of smouldering resentments as they grew older. For all her adult restlessness, for all her tiresome behaviour, Margaret always remained supportive of her elder sister, never hankering after her position or her responsibilities. In fact the only suggestion of 'simmering rivalry' and 'intense competition (driven largely by the older sibling)' comes in episode 8 of the first series of the Netflix drama *The Crown*. The writer Peter Morgan invented an offbeat plotline in which Princess Margaret steps into her sister's shoes while the Queen is away on a Commonwealth tour. This never happened. Princess Margaret proves a much less stuffy head of state, delivering a zippy speech at a reception for British ambassadors, who all laugh uproariously at her easy-going wit and bonhomie. This never happened either. Princess Margaret endears herself to miners. Nor did this. She is reprimanded for upstaging her sister by Winston Churchill, who thereby averts a constitutional crisis. Nor this: in fact, the entire storyline is invented.

In another scene, Lord Snowdon talks with Princess Margaret in an aeroplane.

> SNOWDON: Elder sister, younger sister: number one and number two.
>
> MARGARET: Who's number one?
>
> SNOWDON: You, of course – a natural number one whose tragedy it is to have been born number two.

MARGARET: (puffing on a cigarette) This is my burden. She knows
 it, too.
SNOWDON: Yes, I think she does. That's her burden.

This conversation also never happened, but it is, as far as I am aware, the only source for the idea of 'simmering rivalry' and 'intense competition (driven largely by the older sibling)' between the two of them. This suggests that Harry's understanding of the relationship between his grandmother and his Great-Aunt Margot comes not from real life, but from watching actors playing them on *The Crown*.

91

Alan Bennett tells the story of the left-wing playwrights John Osborne,* Harold Pinter and David Hare running into each other at a Buckingham Palace reception. 'All are said to have blamed their attendance on the curiosity of their wives, the wives, with more sense, probably not feeling it necessary to blame anyone at all.'

British artists and intellectuals often felt uncomfortable hobnobbing with royalty, but they found it hard to resist. Offered honours, many thought it seemly to prevaricate. They would then accept, but not without a show of reluctance. Not all, though. 'Perhaps I am unfortunate in my friends or in the corrupt metropolitan circles in which I move,' observed their fellow playwright Alan Bennett, 'but it's seldom I come across someone who has accepted a knighthood and done so with genuine pride and pleasure, still less anyone agreeing that it was well deserved. Nobody ever says that this is just what they have always wanted.'

Bennett himself was offered a CBE 'for services to literature' in the Queen's Birthday Honours of 1988. He had no hesitation in refusing, as it had come from Mrs Thatcher, 'and I didn't want anything from that particular handbag'. His only regret was that he had planned to refuse with a joke, but couldn't think of one.

Eight years later, he was offered a knighthood. 'Admittedly it was quite a thin year so there may have been some scraping of the barrel.' Once again, he couldn't think of a suitable joke to accompany his refusal. 'The nearest I got to humour was to think, quite genuinely, that

* In 1957, Osborne described royalty as 'the gold filling in a mouthful of decay'.

being a knight would be like wearing a suit every day of one's life. This didn't seem quite funny enough, though, so I just said No, thank you.'*

Towards the end of 2003, the *Sunday Times* published a leaked list of almost 300 people who had declined an honour between 1951 and 1999. One or two, like Francis Bacon, had made no secret of their refusal. Asked in old age why he had never accepted a knighthood or Order of Merit, he replied, 'Oh, I couldn't. So *ageing!*'

Alan Bennett was among those on the list of refuseniks, so found himself in the awkward position of being quizzed about it. In this looking-glass world, his explanations were taken for boasts. 'To have accepted an honour without fuss would seem less self-regarding than to turn it down then boast about it,' he later reflected. '… Self-regard, though, is boundless, and, lest it be thought that this refusal has much to do with modesty, when the list of those who had turned down honours was leaked in the newspapers I cared enough to note (I hope wryly) how obscurely placed I was on the list and that sometimes I wasn't mentioned at all.'

'And they still flock like seagulls round a municipal rubbish tip' was the uncompromising way the fiercely anti-monarchist Labour MP Willie Hamilton once described the British appetite for honours.

But every seagull swooped down with an excuse to hand. Isaiah Berlin accepted his knighthood in 1957 to give pleasure to his mother. The Marxist historian Eric Hobsbawm accepted his Companion of Honour in 1997 because his mother would have wanted him to, and, after all, a CH was 'for the awkward squad'.

On 10 May 1983, the left-wing poet Stephen Spender received a letter from the office of the prime minister, Margaret Thatcher. She was recommending him for a knighthood. Spender cast his mind back to 1926. At the age of seventeen, he was crossing the Channel when he

---

* Richard Eyre remembered Bennett quoting Virginia Woolf saying she had been brought up not to accept gifts from strangers, but Bennett himself has no recollection of this 'or of knowing that Virginia Woolf said anything of the sort. (It's a bit pert for her, I would have thought.)'

bumped into the poet Henry Newbolt.* 'He was very kind to a seasick schoolboy and we discussed poets we admired. He mentioned the name of some poet – I forget who – and I said, "Well, I can't like the work of a poet who has a title."' This was, reflected Spender, 'a gaffe with the power to raise a ghost': Newbolt had been knighted by King George V a decade earlier.

Spender accepted his knighthood ('both for myself and for Natasha'), but not without misgivings. 'There comes a time when one craves for recognition – not to be always at the mercy of spite, malice, contempt – and perhaps even the just dismissal – of one's rivals,' he confessed to his diary. 'I feel pegged up in some way, given a shot in the arm. I've always felt some saving angel does guard me from the worst – sometimes thinking it a good sometimes a bad angel. Probably it's an in-between angel. Many of those I respect have refused honours, and that they have done so is their supreme honour.'†

* * *

---

* Sir Henry Newbolt (1862–1938), poet now best remembered for his poem 'Vitaï Lampada' with its lines 'There's a breathless hush in the Close to-night' and 'Play up! Play up! and play the game!'

† Over the years, the list of those refusing knighthoods has included the economist Amartya Sen, the novelists John Galsworthy, Aldous Huxley, Patrick White and Graham Greene, the novelist and playwright J. B. Priestley, the Arabist T. E. Lawrence, the rock star David Bowie, the poet Benjamin Zephaniah, the physicist Stephen Hawking, the composer Ralph Vaughan Williams, the artists Patrick Heron, Augustus John, John Piper, Frank Auerbach and David Hockney, the jazz musician and broadcaster Humphrey Lyttelton, the film director Danny Boyle, the actors Peter O'Toole, Albert Finney, Robert Morley and (three times over) Paul Scofield, the playwrights Alan Bennett and Harold Pinter, the sculptor Henry Moore, the director of the British Museum Neil MacGregor and the artist L. S. Lowry, who is said to hold the record for most honours declined, having turned down a knighthood, a CBE, an OBE and, twice, a CH. The novelist and playwright Michael Frayn declined a knighthood and said, modestly, that he had done so for reasons of modesty. 'I like the name "Michael Frayn"; it's a nice little name to run around with. I've spent 70 years getting used to it and I don't want to change it now.' A. J. P. Taylor was one of many who were suspicious of the honours system. 'The Establishment draws its recruits from outside as soon as they are ready to conform to its standards and become respectable,' he once said. 'There is nothing more agreeable in life than to make peace with the Establishment – and nothing so corrupting.' Rudyard Kipling declined a knighthood twice. His wife explained that he felt he could 'do his work better without it'.

Towards the end of 1991, an envelope marked 'Secret' arrived through the post for the actor Dirk Bogarde. It contained the offer of a knighthood. Could he tick the appropriate box 'Yes' or 'No', and send the form back to 10 Downing Street as soon as possible? Bogarde ticked the box marked 'No'.

He claimed to have then received 'a gentle, but firm, reprimand from a very pleasant Scots lady somewhere in No. 10. Did I realize, she said kindly, that I was behaving with the greatest discourtesy to the Prime Minister [John Major]? This was his first Honours List, the first of his term. It was also, she added sweetly, insulting to HM the Queen.'

It was, Bogarde told her, 'the last thing I wanted'. He had been born Derek Jules Gaspard Ulric Niven van den Bogaerde, which was burden enough. 'It had taken me almost fifty years to get my name clear of English prejudice ... and sticking "Sir" before it would cause great ridicule. It didn't fit. *Please* accept my ticked box?'

The pleasant Scots lady heard him out 'with enormous patience' and then asked him to send her a signed photograph 'preferably in colour'. She gave him until 9 a.m. the following Monday to make up his mind, adding, 'Knighthoods don't grow on trees, you know.'

Bogarde spent 'a fairly miserable weekend' mulling it over. 'No one to turn to, and I then got into a mild panic and thought that perhaps, when the list was submitted to her, the Queen, or someone else, would grab a biro and cry "Oh! God! *Not him!*" and strike him off. 'That would be a terrible humiliation, but I consoled myself glumly that only I, the Queen, the Prime Minister and the pleasant Scots lady at No. 10 would know. I could nurse my wounded ego alone.'

It was not until hours before the deadline, late on the Sunday night – 'rather relaxed on my Scotch – well, not exactly relaxed: clear-headed' – that Bogarde finally plucked up his courage and 'ticked the wretched box for "Yes"'. Like Hobsbawm and Berlin before him, he told himself that he was doing it for a dead parent. 'I thought of Pa, frankly: his huge pleasure at Sandhurst when I marched up the steps as a new little officer wearing his old Sam Browne ... And thought that he might, wherever he was, be very much more amused by my appearance in the Throne Room at Buckingham Palace. So for him, no other reason, I ticked my acceptance.'

When the big day came, Bogarde felt much more confident. He climbed the great staircase, past a large sign to the right stating simply 'Final Lavatory for Gentlemen' ('Quite enough to cause me, of all people, to flood'). After the Queen had knighted him, he 'limped away to selections from *High Society* clutching in my hand my insignia with the pride of a child who had won first prize in the egg-and-spoon race'.

The novelist E. M. Forster was similarly delighted by his award. He had refused a knighthood some years before, complaining to friends that it simply wasn't good enough for him, but at the end of 1952 he readily accepted the offer of a Companionship of Honour.

He was invested by the Queen the following February. 'I was alone with her for about ten minutes – she was quite an ickle thing, very straight and charming, stood with her back to a huge fire, gave me a very handsome decoration in a case ... and we talked about this and that very pleasantly. She shook hands to start and to finish, and I threw in some bows, and occasionally threw in Your Majesty or Ma'am. She was much better at chat than I was.'

The Queen told Forster how sad it was that he had not published a book for some time: fair comment, really, as his last novel, *A Passage to India*, had first been published nearly thirty years before. He politely corrected her: a collection of his essays, *Two Cheers for Democracy*, had been published in 1951. But he did not hold this oversight against her. 'I liked her very much indeed. Finally she rang a buzzer in the mantel piece and I retired.' As he left the long, gold room, he glanced back. 'She looked tiny at the end of it, dressed in blue.' On the other side of the door stood an equerry, ready to escort him back through the Palace. Forster brandished his new insignia and, in high spirits, exclaimed, 'Well, I got my little toy.' His remark met with a frosty silence, though this did nothing to dampen his spirits. Back home in Cambridge, he told a friend that if the Queen had been a boy, he would have fallen in love with her.

Others actively plotted for the highest honours, and turned furious when offered anything less. When Maurice Bowra was knighted in

1951, his friend Evelyn Waugh was filled with envy. In return for a knighthood he would, he said, go on his knees to the prime minister, lick his boots and lie in the mud outside Downing Street. Yet he was always wrongfooting himself, undermining his campaign with rudeness. Invited to lunch at Buckingham Palace, he refused: 'Said I was too deaf to obey. Real reason snobbery.' On another occasion, a kindly lady in waiting invited him to lunch with the Queen Mother. But it all went wrong. When the Queen Mother raised her glass and said, 'Oh, Mr Waugh, champagne! *Isn't* this a luxury?', Waugh frowned contemptuously. 'A luxury? *Really*, ma'am?'

In 1959, Waugh refused a CBE. 'I think it very WRONG that politicians should treat writers as second grade civil servants,' he complained to Nancy Mitford, adding, 'Osbert Sitwell opened the breach by accepting this degrading decoration.'

Close to his death in 1966, but no closer to a knighthood, he wrote to Graham Greene. He now regretted his own snootiness and his compulsion to bite the hand that might otherwise have fed him. 'Some years back I refused the CBE (not good enough, I thought) and am now ashamed. A sin against courtesy is a sin against charity.'

When Angus Wilson was knighted in 1980, his fellow novelist William Golding wrote to congratulate him: 'It shines like a candle in all the dark wastes of unworthy awards!' But Golding, still best known for his 1954 novel *Lord of the Flies*, was a competitive man, and secretly envious. 'I have got myself behind in that race,' he confessed to his journal. Why, he asked himself, had he been overlooked? Was it because he had always turned down invitations to Royal Garden Parties, or because he had been 'very terse with the twit of a photographer who married Princess Margaret'? Lord Snowdon had made the grave mistake, some years before, of telling Golding how very much he admired *Lord of the Rings*.

Golding badgered his publisher, Charles Monteith, to smooth his path towards a knighthood. Monteith dutifully wrote to the secretary of state for industry, who replied that he had forwarded his letter to the minister for the arts, 'so he may follow it up as he sees fit'.

Golding also asked Matthew Evans, the new chairman of Faber & Faber, to lobby on his behalf, and gave him a nudge from time to time. 'Are you Kultivating my K?' he asked on a postcard. A week later, Evans had a word with the secretary of state for education, who in turn had a word with the Cabinet secretary. It had been a long and busy process, but in 1988 Golding finally received his knighthood. When the news arrived, he reacted with an unabashed joy rarely found in his sombre novels.

Golding was invested on 27 July 1988. As the Queen adjusted the ribbon around his neck 'with the occasional maternal tuck', she asked him her usual question for elderly authors: 'Are you still writing?'

'Yes, ma'am.'

'Good.'

This response, felt Golding, exhibited 'a degree of critical insight'.

One of his first acts afterwards was to change his and his wife's names on their passports to Sir William and Lady Golding. As a student at Oxford, he had once been labelled 'Not quite a gentleman', and it still rankled. But now he could rejoice at the deference he received from hotel managers and head waiters. In his private journal, he jotted down Jane Austen's remark in *Pride and Prejudice* concerning the elevation of William Lucas, formerly in trade, to the knighthood: 'The distinction had perhaps been felt too strongly.' Golding sympathised with Lucas: 'I even find in myself the merest inclination to *strut*.'

Later, he repaid the Queen by accepting her invitation to a Garden Party at Buckingham Palace, where Sir William and Lady Golding spent time admiring her herbaceous border. 'I have to declare, though, disloyal as it may seem, our pink mallow is better than Her Majesty's.'

For some authors, the inclination to strut was so keen that it became almost a compulsion. The imperious poet Edith Sitwell found that a damehood was, in the words of her biographer, 'a constant source of pleasure and of satisfaction'. Yet it also seemed to exacerbate her feelings of insecurity. When she next went to America, a reporter asked her, 'Why do you call yourself "Dame" Edith?'

'*I* don't call myself that,' she retorted. 'The Queen does.'

In the months leading up her investiture, Sitwell chastised those who failed to employ her title. When someone introduced her as 'Doctor Sitwell', she corrected him: 'Actually, I'm Dame-ing this year.' After the ceremony, she became even grander, and less gracious. When an aspirant author sent her a manuscript to read, addressing her as Dr Sitwell, she replied:

> Dear Sir,
> *Dame* Edith Sitwell (that is how she should be addressed, not as Dr
> Sitwell) … has made it abundantly clear, over and over again in
> broadcast after broadcast, book after book, article after article, that
> any unsolicited manuscript sent to her is an intrusion into her
> working time, and that under no circumstances whatever will she
> read it.

Some authors were not so easily satisfied. In 1954, the Queen invested Somerset Maugham as a Companion of Honour. Soon afterwards, he dined with George 'Dadie' Rylands and Arthur Marshall. When they offered their congratulations, he snapped, 'But don't you see what the CH means for somebody like me? It means very well done … *but!*'

Maugham felt he deserved the superior Order of Merit. Two years earlier, on a visit to his old school, King's Canterbury, he confided to the headmaster, Canon Shirley, 'I will tell you my two secret wishes – I have never revealed them to any other living person.' First, he wanted his ashes to be buried in the precincts of the Cathedral. Second, 'I think I ought to have the OM. I don't want anything else – I would refuse anything like a knighthood. But they gave Hardy the OM and I think I am the greatest living writer of English, and they ought to give it to me.'

Others in the world of arts accepted their honours with innocent delight. The composer William Walton burst into tears upon opening the letter offering him an OM: 'To think that the Queen actually knows I am alive!' The veteran pop singer Cliff Richard was similarly over-joyed. 'If you were to ask me which of all the days in the fifty years has been the most thrilling, I would have to say it was the one in May 1995 when a letter from 10 Downing Street arrived at my home in Weybridge. The Prime Minister, it said, intended recommending me to the Queen for a knighthood in the Queen's Birthday Honours.' At first, he couldn't believe what he was seeing. Then he wondered if it was a joke. And then 'I laughed and laughed and laughed. I couldn't stop. I was so happy … Would I accept it? What a question. Paper burned with the speed at which I put my pen to it: "Yes please!" I was so thrilled and actually very emotional; just knowing that the Queen along with the Prime Minister and thousands of members of the British public had thought me worthy of this honour … I had to pinch myself; it truly was the most exciting thing that's ever happened to me, and such a boost for my self-esteem.'

When the big day came, Cliff's sisters Donna, Jacqui and Joan accompanied him to the Palace. The four of them were all in tears, and he found himself unable to speak. 'I was so choked up … I couldn't get anything out; it was like the whole of my throat had closed up … I was just terrified I was going to fall off the kneeler, particularly because I'd been warned that some people had.' A courtier had told him that some older women curtsied so deeply that their knees locked and they were unable to get up again.

The sublime contralto Kathleen Ferrier received her offer towards the end of 1952. Just eighteen months before, at the age of 39, she had been diagnosed with breast cancer; since then, her days had been divided between hospital and concert hall. Despite all this, she was, she declared, 'happy as a lark, especially as two weeks ago – can you keep a dead secret until New Year's Day? – I had a letter from the Prime Minister asking if I would be willing to receive the honour – Commander of the British Empire – if the Queen sanctioned it?'

Her response was immediate, with none of the shilly-shallying of Hobsbawm, Spender or Bogarde. 'Can a duck quack? I can't believe it can be true, because these honours usually come after 90 years singing or some such, so perhaps it won't come off – but won't it be exciting, looking at the honours list on New Year's morning, eh? Private and confidential, darling!' When the time came for her investiture, she was too ill to get to the Palace. Instead, a friend brought the award to her bed in University College Hospital. Kathleen Ferrier CBE died there on 8 October 1953, at the age of 41.

92

On 31 December 1999, Sir Ian McKellen threw a sit-down dinner party for forty friends at his home on the Thames, with the plan to watch the Queen pass by on her way to the New Year's Eve celebrations at the brand-new Millennium Dome, further down the river in Greenwich.

As he watched the unprepossessing modern vessel chugging past, he was bitterly disappointed. 'She was on City Cruisers! If she hadn't been wearing lime green, one wouldn't have noticed!' He had imagined something far more regal. 'We wanted proper people rowing her up. I wanted her to do the job superbly.'

What one biographer rated as one of the least enjoyable New Year's Eves of the Queen's reign was to begin in chaos and end in a whimper. As a result of an electrical fault, several thousand special guests had already been obliged to queue for hours at Stratford East Underground station before being admitted to the Dome.

The rest of the evening proceeded in this stop–start fashion. The prime minister, Tony Blair, was escorted from the Play Zone to the VIP centre to present the Queen with a special millennium medal. 'Apart from the Queen, who at least managed the odd smile, the others looked very pissed off to be there,' recalled Alastair Campbell. 'TB worked away at them, trying to charm them into the mood, but [Princess] Anne was like granite.'

While this was happening, a coded bomb warning prompted the police to evacuate the Body Zone, which had been built immediately above the southbound lane of the Blackwall Tunnel. Should they call the entire event off? The commissioner of the Metropolitan Police decided that it was a hoax, and so the faltering celebrations continued.

The archbishop of Canterbury, George Carey, known by some of his cattier fellow clerics as 'Mr Blobby', recited the Lord's Prayer. This was followed by a rendition of the Beatles' 'All You Need is Love' and a jazzed-up version of the National Anthem.

Tony Blair, who had, earlier in the year, promised 'the greatest show on earth', felt a keen sense of disappointment. The sense of dread he experienced at the beginning of the evening proved prescient. 'I don't know what Prince Philip thought of it all, but I shouldn't imagine it's printable,' he recalled, ten years later. 'I suspect Her Majesty would have used different language but with the same sentiment.'

Blair sat next to the Queen and Prince Philip. In the freezing cold, they watched what Roy Strong, viewing the event on television at home, described as 'a dumbed-down television spectacular, the world of pop stars and superficial glitz with the intellectual content of a cheap box of Christmas crackers'. The event ended with an acrobatic spectacle, condemned by another viewer, A. N. Wilson, as 'a strange mixture of the boring and tawdry'. Prince Philip, who had not, up to then, looked even slightly interested, suddenly lit up, leaning over and saying to Blair, 'Well, that is remarkable – you know they're doing that without safety harnesses?' Blair craned his head upwards.

Then an appalling thought struck me, and chilled me to the innards … I swear I knew what was going to happen. I felt like someone in one of those sixth-sense movies who can see the future: from sixty feet up, one of the performers was going to fall in the middle of a somersault, hurtle down and flatten the Queen. I could see it all. 'QUEEN KILLED BY TRAPEZE ARTIST AT DOME'. 'BRITAIN'S MILLENNIUM CELEBRATIONS MARRED'. 'BLAIR ADMITS NOT ALL HAS GONE TO PLAN'. Britain's millennium would indeed be famous; I would go down in history forever.

I kid you not, I joke about it now but at 11.30 p.m. on New Year's Eve 1999, I was absolutely convinced. I have never been more relieved than when it all stopped.

At the stroke of midnight, the VIPs in the front row crossed their arms and tried to link hands with those on either side of them. Though it looked more or less spontaneous, this gesture was in fact the product of extensive negotiations between the Palace, which favoured formality, and No. 10, which preferred chumminess. In the end, the Queen stared straight ahead, looking a little grumpy. She was so far away from Tony Blair on her left and Prince Philip on her right that if she had crossed her arms and held their hands she might have been mistaken for an inmate in a straitjacket, which, in many ways, was what she was. Instead, she just held their hands without crossing her arms and remained tight-lipped while everyone else sang 'Auld Lang Syne'.

The evening's entertainment was pitiful in comparison to the pomp and glory that had attended her great-great-grandparents' visit to the Great Exhibition in Hyde Park on 1 May 1851. 'This day is one of the greatest & most glorious days of our lives,' Queen Victoria wrote in her diary of her visit there with Prince Albert.

> before we neared the Crystal Palace, the sun shone & gleamed upon the gigantic edifice, upon which the flags of every nation were flying. We drove up Rotten Roe [sic] & got out of our carriages at the entrance in that side … The tremendous cheering, the joy expressed in every face, the vastness of the building, with all its decorations & exhibits, the sound of the organ … all this was indeed moving, & a day to live forever. God bless my dearest Albert, & my dear Country which has shown itself so great today.

A century and a half later, the Queen and Prince Philip were visibly disappointed by their nation's markedly less sure-footed celebration of its own era. 'It was pretty clear', observed Alastair Campbell, 'that they would rather be sitting under their travel rugs at Balmoral.'

93

In 1999, Gyles Brandreth attended the annual dinner of the Royal Society of Portrait Painters. He was there in a professional capacity, booked to entertain the members with an amusing after-dinner speech. 'Not an easy acoustic,' he recorded in his diary, 'but they laughed. I like them: they know they're a bit old-fashioned, they know the National Portrait Gallery doesn't rate them, but they keep going. Looking out at them as I spoke, I felt I was watching a slightly faded print of a 1950s English comedy.'

At one moment that evening, Brandreth got into conversation with Sir Robert Fellowes. 'He let slip that he has persuaded the Queen to sit for Lucian Freud. "His usual pose?" I asked. Sir Robert became suddenly alarmed. "This is absolutely confidential," he murmured. But he is clearly excited – and understandably. I think he reckons it could be *the* portrait of the reign. "If she's starkers," said Andrew Festing,* "it certainly will be."'

Word of the pairing travelled fast. Three days later, the Royal biographer and high-society gossip Kenneth Rose noted in his journal, 'One most interesting piece of news. The Queen is being painted by Lucian Freud, at the suggestion of Robert Fellowes. The sittings take

---

* President of the Royal Society of Portrait Painters, 2002–8, and son of Field Marshal Sir Francis Festing. He painted several official portraits of the Queen, among them a group portrait of *Her Majesty Queen Elizabeth II and her Family and Other Crowned Heads of Europe* to commemorate her fiftieth wedding anniversary. After his accession, King Charles had the group painting removed from the drawing room at Sandringham. 'He didn't like it. It was an unwelcome reminder of one of the worst years of his life,' a source told the *Daily Mail*.

place in the studio at the corner of St James's Palace. How extraordinarily daring of the Queen.'

Daring, indeed: though in most other respects a militant non-conformist, Freud was always eager to enact bourgeois society's idea of the artist as shameless bohemian: pugnacious, demonic, priapic. Earlier in the decade, he had been approached to paint Princess Diana's portrait, but his lawyer, Lord Goodman, had put his foot down. 'I wouldn't leave her in the room with Lucian,' he insisted.

A small canvas by Freud once caught the eye of Prince Charles, who then wrote to him asking if he might consider swapping it for 'one of my rotten old watercolours'. A curator at the National Gallery asked Freud how he was going to respond. 'Tell him to fuck off, of course,' came the reply. The idea of this exchange of paintings – in purely financial terms, the equivalent of exchanging £2,000 for £2,000,000 – struck him as outlandish. 'Such a cheek,' he complained to their mutual friend Andrew Parker Bowles. 'It was almost like theft.'

In the Queen's 1983 Birthday Honours, Lucian Freud had been made a Companion of Honour.* Lord Goodman recommended he accept it: after all, the medal was worth £2,000 and came with a nice ribbon. 'Good people have it. Besides, you get to see the Queen.'

The Queen duly presented Freud with his award in a private audience. He felt that she was nervous and shy in his presence, and the conversation failed to flow, except once, when she asked, 'Does stamina mean you're good?' and he replied, 'It can mean you're pig-headed.'

Ten years later, in the spring of 1993, Freud was mentioned as a possible candidate for the next, and highest, rung of the ladder, the Order of Merit.† Asked by the Palace for his suggestions, Sir Isaiah Berlin indulged in the Olympian cud-chewing he so relished.

'It is a sad condition for our country to be in, that there should be no novelist, poet, even painter (even Freud), historian, classical scholar

---

* Motto: 'In action faithful and in honour clear'.

† The Order of Merit is restricted to twenty-four individuals 'of exceptional distinction in the arts, learning, sciences and other areas such as public service'. Appointments are in the sovereign's personal gift.

of such shining quality as to even begin to seem obvious, he wrote back to the courtier Edward Adeane.

Adeane had provided him with a handy list of possibilities, three of whom Berlin readily supported. 'I agree about S. Runciman, H. Casson and John Gielgud.' He was equally sure of Sir Norman Foster ('the best architect we have'). But other candidates proved more troublesome. Though Sir Kenneth Dover was 'probably the best classicist we have ... I don't think he is either well known enough or, indeed, quite grand enough.' The former home secretary Roy Jenkins 'is not quite of the stature, in my view, friend of mine though he is, but it would be perfectly well received'. The playwright Harold Pinter 'is the most distinguished living British dramatist, without a doubt, and of very, very considerable gifts. It might be thought that someone of his passionate left-wing views – not that he is anywhere near Communism or anything politically disreputable – might refuse, but I don't think he would.'

The extraordinary success of Professor Stephen Hawking's *A Brief History of Time* had, paradoxically, damaged Hawking's chances. In academic terms, its popularity lurked suspiciously close to the border of vulgarity. 'I used to urge him on you, you remember, year by year ... But as a result of his book, which serious scientists do not in fact think much of, and all the publicity and hoo-ha, perhaps he has rather forfeited it.' The avant-garde theatre director Peter Brook, though 'a genius', was also 'in general not quite right'.

Berlin felt that others fell at the final fence. 'There is our old friend Trevor-Roper: he is the best British historian now writing, and writes like an angel; but he hasn't produced a major work, and I fear that when he is dead his reputation will somewhat, though not steeply, decline.'

As for Lucian Freud, his habits left much to be desired. 'He is not a good character, far from it. He is a gifted painter, but in my view not quite up to the Bacon standard ... There would be some shock if this was done for him, because his private life is regarded as too disreputable by most of those who know – even like – him.'

But later that year, in spite of Berlin's misgivings, Freud was admitted to the Order of Merit. He was presented to the Queen in the shadow of two large paintings by Guardi. 'Don't you find it hard to get in the mood?' the Queen asked him, while swaying on her feet. 'Did Guardi have to get in the mood?'

'No,' replied Freud, 'Guardi had assistants.'

Newly installed members of the Order of Merit are expected to donate portraits of themselves to the Palace. Towards the end of his audience with the Queen, Freud suggested he might donate a self-portrait. But despite several reminders he failed to come up with the goods. This toing and froing went on for some years. Finally, it was agreed that an etching would be acceptable. 'I lunched with Fellowes again and he said, "She was very struck by your print, she really was,"' boasted Freud, which suggests that even the most fervent bohemian can be prey to a monarch's flattery.

Yet his OM afforded Freud only limited satisfaction. A natural icon-oclast, he felt no affinity with one or two of his fellow members. 'Mother Teresa is one. Not someone to sit next to at lunch.'* Defying protocol, he failed to turn up to the lunch for OMs. 'E.H. Gombrich asked Isaiah [Berlin] why wasn't I there; was I ill or something? Apparently, it's a command attendance.'

The Surveyor of the Queen's Pictures had first approached him in 1988 with the suggestion that he paint Her Majesty's portrait. Freud discussed the matter with Robert Fellowes when their paths crossed ('I'd seen him dancing around in Annabel's').

At first, Freud was adamant that the Queen should come to him, rather than vice versa. To Freud's surprise, Fellowes was agreeable. 'I said, "I live very high up." "That wouldn't be a difficulty." "I mind about my privacy; I wouldn't want attention to arise." "I think we can manage that."' It was only when Freud demanded unlimited sittings that Fellowes put his foot down: in the past Freud had kept models posing for the same portrait for years on end. Nevertheless, when the project eventually got going, in May 2000, it was the Queen who had won all

---

* Freud could be picky when it came to people. At different times, he declared the philosopher A. J. Ayer 'ridiculous', Ian Fleming 'ghastly, phoney, depressing, snobbish', the travel writer Patrick Leigh Fermor 'a ghastly spiv' and the psychoanalyst Melanie Klein 'a ridiculous-looking woman in a hat'.

the most important arguments: their sessions would take place in St James's Palace, and though Freud would get more sittings than most, their association would not be limitless. 'Don't mention how many sittings as the others only get two or three,' he was told. In the end, he managed to extract fifteen sittings from her.

The canvas was tiny – at nine and a quarter inches by six, little bigger than a postcard. He carried it in a shoebox to the makeshift studio in St James's Palace. As the proposed painting was to be a close-up of her face, Freud insisted on standing only a matter of inches from her, almost as though he were her dentist. In the early sittings, two or three security guards remained in the studio with them, keeping their eyes on the diamond and pearl diadem, familiar to the world from postage stamps and banknotes. Always at odds with authority, Freud found these guards distracting; eventually, the Queen instructed them to stay outside. Once they were out of earshot, she mentioned to Freud that she had first met one of them on a friend's estate in Scotland in peculiar circumstances. A wounded cock pheasant had flown out of a hedge straight at her, knocking her down and covering her coat in its blood. Imagining she had been shot, the protection officer leapt on her and started giving her mouth-to-mouth resuscitation. 'We got to know each other rather well,' the Queen continued, in her dry and understated manner. With its visceral mixture of sex, violence, blood, guts and high society, this tale might have been tailor-made for Lucian Freud.

As a sitter, the Queen had always been chatty: she found the process of posing relaxing, a break from her normal routine. Freud, too, was naturally talkative. 'Lucian had a whale of a time with the Queen. They talked about racing and horses,' said his friend Clarissa Eden. But after a while the Queen realised that, as she put it, 'when he talks he stops painting', so she tried to rein in their conversation. 'We must stop talking,' she said. 'We must get on with the portrait.'

When he finally completed the portrait, over a year after embarking on it, Freud decided to make it a personal gift from him to the Queen. 'Duke Ellington gave her some music once. I like that. But mine is the first for which she's sat which has been given to her.'

One Thursday morning, he took the finished canvas to Buckingham Palace and waited in the private apartments, surrounded by various Canaletto townscapes of London and a Gainsborough portrait. 'At first there were a lot of dogs rolling over – corgis. There was nobody else there.'

The Queen asked him where exactly they should look at it. Freud placed it on a yellow chair. It showed her with her mouth and chin scrunched up, doing what had become known in the Palace as her 'Miss Piggy' face. It was far from flattering, but Freud was satisfied with her muted response. 'Very nice of you to do this; I've very much enjoyed watching you mix your colours,' she told him, with her customary tact. This was good enough for Freud: 'She didn't say what she thought of it but seemed very pleased.'

Freud told her that the whole process had been as challenging as a polar expedition, adding, flirtatiously, 'If you were a professional model, you'd be in demand.'

Possibly flattered, she replied, 'You must excuse my hair because it's been sprayed, as we've been rehearsing the Christmas speech.'

The painting was unveiled to the press four days before Christmas. It was not a huge success. The *Sun* placed it on its front page, along with the headline, 'It's a Travesty Your Majesty'. The *Times* thought Freud had given his sovereign 'a six o'clock shadow'.

'It makes her look like one of her corgis who has suffered a stroke,' said Robin Simon, editor of the *British Art Journal*. 'It is a huge error for Lucian Freud. He has gone a portrait too far. The two sides of the painting are like two different portraits. He has just lost it.'

In France, *L'Express* declared it '*peu flatteur*', or 'hardly flattering', something of an understatement, given that it made her look like an all-in wrestler. The Queen later confessed to friends that she didn't like it at all.

Some noticed certain similarities between the facial features of the Queen and those of Lucian Freud in his late self-portraits. While Freud was staring hard at the Queen had he, like so many before him, simply been confronted by an image of himself staring back?

Two years after completing his tiny portrait of the Queen, Lucian Freud began work on a full-length portrait of Brigadier Andrew Parker Bowles,* the former husband of Camilla. When Parker Bowles mentioned to Prince Philip that he was all set to pose for a painting by Freud, the Prince was taken aback. 'What on earth do you want to go and do that for?'

Some time later, the Queen was being shown around an art gallery that had a series of Lucian Freud nudes on display, blotchy, run-down, out of shape, sprawled any-old-how across old mattresses.† Sensing that the paparazzi were angling to take pictures of her against this fleshy, blue-veined background, she moved swiftly away.

'Haven't you been painted by Lucian Freud, ma'am?' asked her host.

'Yes,' she replied. Then, lowering her voice: 'But not like that.'

---

* In 2015, *The Brigadier* sold at Christie's, New York for $34.89 million.

† It shows the peculiarity of the art market that, from the 1980s onwards, it became incumbent on billionaires to acquire a Lucian Freud, along with a private jet, an island and a 500-foot yacht. An enterprising dealer might have sold all four together, as part of some sort of package deal. In the old days, these tycoons would have settled for a Monet of lilies or a Van Gogh of sunflowers. But now prestige and fashion obliged them to purchase something more cutting-edge. In May 2008, the Russian oligarch Roman Abramovich bought Freud's *Benefits Supervisor Sleeping*, a naked portrait of Sue Tilley, an obese Job Centre supervisor, uncomfortably sprawled over a couch. It is unlikely Mr Abramovich would ever have allowed the real Ms Tilley into his drawing room, particularly in such a state of undress. Nevertheless, he was happy to spend £17.2 million on this image of her.

94

Monday

A hectic week. After church, Mr Lucien Freud, who is a painter, arrives to paint my portrait.

I ask if he likes corgis. He tells me that he does.

Good, I say. I ask him if he has been painting long.

He tells me he has.

How interesting, I say. A lovely hobby.

I might have asked him if he would be most awfully kind and paint over the crack on the bathroom ceiling, but I forgot.

They tell me he knows how to charge, so perhaps we got off lightly! Freud. Not a name you hear all that often.

Tuesday

In the evening, Edward and his wife arrive. We all shake hands.

She has fair hair.

'Hello mummy,' he says. 'We were just passing so we thought we'd "drop by" and say hello.'

I say hello.

'Hello,' says his wife.

'You remember Sophie, of course,' says Edward.

'Of course,' I say, making her feel 'at home'. 'Have you come far?'

She says she hasn't come all that far: they live quite near Windsor.

She starts stroking a corgi. 'That's Pipkin,' I say. 'He's a lovely lovely boy, aren't you, Pipkin? Yes, you are – you're a lovely, lovely, lovely boy! Who's a lovely boy, then?' Pipkin loves a little chat. I suppose we all do, really, when you think about it.

I turn to Edward. 'Have you had a busy day?' I ask him. 'Have you come far?'

Philip comes into the room. 'You know Sophie, of course,' I say.

At this time of year, as the days start to grow shorter, it is nice to keep in touch with one's family.

Wednesday

I receive my Prime Minister. He informs me of his plans for revitalising the 'National Health Service' and modernising the railway system.

'This is all very interesting,' I say.

'Thank you,' he says.

'You've obviously put a tremendous amount of thought into it,' I say.

'Yes,' he says.

'Railways are still very popular,' I tell him. 'They are particularly useful if people want to get from A to B and for one reason or another they don't have their driver.'

'You've hit the nail on the head,' he says.

After fifty years as their monarch, I have a wealth of knowledge and experience to offer my Prime Ministers.

'And hospitals form a vitally important part of the health of the nation,' I inform him, adding, 'Though important as hospitals are, they wouldn't be effective without doctors and nurses. Not to mention patients.'

I politely convey that our meeting is at an end by holding out my hand and saying, 'Have you got far to go?'

My Prime Ministers appreciate the sense of continuity that only a monarch can give them.

As he leaves, I notice that one of his shoelaces is undone.

I tell Philip about it in the evening. He roars with laughter. He reminds me of the priceless occasion on which the Bishop of Norwich fell flat on his face and broke his ankle while taking the service at Sandringham. It's a great favourite of ours!

Thursday

A reception at Buckingham Palace for leaders of the Commonwealth, many of them in colourful national dress.

'May I present the President of Somalia, ma'am,' says my Foreign Secretary.

'And where are you from?' I ask him.

'Somalia, ma'am,' he replies, with a deep bow.

'Very convenient,' I say, encouragingly. 'Though possibly on the warm side.'

It is conversations such as these, conducted between friends in the family of nations, that constantly give one hope for a better world ahead of us.

In the evening, my son, His Royal Highness the Prince of Wales, turns up. 'I was just passing by so I thought I'd say hello,' he says.

'Have you been waiting long?' I reply, setting him at his ease. 'Have you done this sort of thing before? Keep you busy, do they?'

95

It is 1 March 2005. A reception for the music business is being held in Buckingham Palace. Four rock gods – Brian May, Jimmy Page, Eric Clapton, Jeff Beck – are standing in line. They look tense and sheepish, schoolboys outside the headmaster's door. They exchange nervous whispers.

They are dressed in smart black suits and sober ties; they all look as if they have had their hair cut for the occasion. Identity badges are pinned to their jacket lapels.

The Queen enters through the door behind them, to their left. She heads for the first in line, Brian May.

AIDE: Some guitarists you may recognise ...

It soon becomes clear that she doesn't. But she beams, and holds out her hand. Brian May shakes it. He has clearly planned what he is going to say.

BRIAN MAY: Very pleased to meet you. I have an apology to make for making so much noise on your roof.
HMQ: Oh, it was YOU on the roof.
BRIAN MAY: It was me.

She looks down at the floor, in search of something to add.

HMQ: Yes. Hmmm. I assume it was quite ... quite alarming up there.
BRIAN MAY: The only alarming thing was how big a fool I could make of myself if it was wrong. I wasn't worried about falling off.

She looks down again. Jimmy Page holds out his hand and introduces himself.

JIMMY PAGE: I'm Jimmy Page.
HMQ: Are you also ...

She hesitates, not quite knowing what it is he does.

JIMMY PAGE: (helping her out) I'm a guitarist as well, yes. Mm-hmm.
HMQ: A guitarist ... Well, I think every aspect of music is represented here this evening. Which is quite fun.
BRIAN MAY: Fantastic, yeah. (Making an effort to fill the silence) Jimmy's a hero of mine. Led Zeppelin was ... a model ...

At this point, perhaps it crosses his mind that, for all their fame, the Queen may draw a blank at Led Zeppelin.

HMQ: Oh, well, that's nice.

She moves along the line.

ERIC CLAPTON: Eric Clapton.
HMQ: Nice to see you.

She shakes Eric Clapton's hand, says nothing, and then shakes Jeff Beck's hand.
Jeff Beck also says nothing.

HMQ: You've all been playing for … quite a long time?
ERIC CLAPTON: About … God! … Forty years.
HMQ: Is it really?
ERIC CLAPTON: We're all a bit long in the tooth.

A few nervous chuckles.

ERIC CLAPTON: And we're all from Surrey.
HMQ: Really. Oh.
ERIC CLAPTON: We all moved through the same band.
HMQ: Very nice to see you.

The Queen moves on.

96

'I can hardly believe it, but up there in the Palace, the Queen of England is expecting me!'

It is 3 June 2005. Rolf Harris, regularly described as a 'popular all-round family entertainer', is addressing a BBC camera outside Buckingham Palace.

'I've painted hundreds of portraits in my time but this one is going to be very special! I'm so excited! It's a tremendous privilege! This is my second visit to the Palace! A few days ago, I came to prepare everything for the sittings, and I even chose an outfit for the Queen to wear!'

Four years the Queen's junior, four months Princess Margaret's senior, Harris was born in Bassendean, a suburb of Perth in Western Australia, his parents having emigrated from Cardiff in Wales. He is well known for his boundless energy and enthusiasm.

'The Queen's been painted over 120 times by some magnificent artists, and of course there are countless unofficial portraits – even ones made from postage stamps and jelly beans! In fact, the Queen's face is the most reproduced face in history – on coins, banknotes and on at least 180 billion stamps!'

He is painting the portrait for the Queen's eightieth birthday. Uniquely, her two sittings for him are being filmed by the BBC.

'What a fantastic opportunity for me to meet the Queen and paint her portrait!' he says, as he sets up his easel in the Yellow Drawing Room of the Palace. '… I know what I want to do! I want to do an impressionist painting which conveys the real personality of the real person, rather than a formal state-occasion-type portrait! Whether I can do it to my satisfaction or not, who knows?!!'

He has positioned the Queen's armchair within spitting distance of his easel. 'The size that I see will be the size that I paint. Makes it so much easier!

'I can't actually believe I'm doing it! I thought I'd be much more nervous than this, but I'm a little apprehensive and very excited, and the Queen will be arriving any minute now – so wish me luck!'

The room falls silent as he awaits the arrival of the Queen. He starts whistling under his breath, as if blowing into an invisible didgeridoo.

The door opens, and in comes the Queen. 'Good afternoon!'

'Your Majesty!' Harris executes a low bow. 'Lovely to meet you!'

He ushers her in. 'We've got a wonderful seat lined up here which you probably know very well!'

'I think I've sat in it before.' Her Majesty appears non-committal, perhaps even slightly wary.

She sits down and crumples her mouth. For a second, she looks just like her Lucian Freud portrait.

'You're OK with the smell of turpentine, I hope!'

'Well, we'll tell, won't we, soon!' She raises her eyebrows, and chuckles. 'I'd've thought it was all right!'

Harris starts covering the canvas with blue paint. 'I hope this canvas isn't TOO close!' he says in voice-over. 'Imagine if I sloshed paint all over the Queen!'

While he continues to slosh, he tries to break the ice.

'You missed a very good Changing of the Guard.'

'I know, because it's dull in the afternoons. You get all the fun of the music and everything going on here in the mornings.'

'There was a great bang! They fired a gun in the middle of the day which frightened the wits out of all of us!'

'Do you know why it was?'

'No.'

She pauses, ready for the punchline: 'Nor did I!'

Harris laughs, perhaps a little too enthusiastically, given the standard of the joke.

'I had to look it up,' she says.

'And?'

'Coronation Day!'

'Ah!'

'It was a long time ago.'

'I was there!' says Harris. 'I was there on that morning.'

The Queen beams.

Harris thinks back fifty-two years. 'I was sitting out in Hyde Park with a blanket round me and the accordion, playing songs all night, waiting for you to come along in the golden coach! It was wonderful!'

'Very cold and wet, I seem to remember.'

'It was a bit … a bit … drear,' says Harris. 'If you could just look at me for a second.'

He spreads some mauve paint over the canvas, and talks some more.

'This takes me back a little bit to 1946, and I was a member of an art class in Western Australia and – er – the exhibition was to be opened by Sir James Mitchell, who was the governor of Western Australia. So my mother, with an eye to the main chance, got me to paint a portrait of him from a newspaper article …'

The Queen has begun to look a touch bored.

'… and then when he was opening it and he got to his portrait my mother leapt upon him and said, "My son would like to paint you in the flesh!"'

The Queen smiles anxiously. Much of her life has been spent smiling at strangers as they burble on.

'… And I was over the side there, dying of embarrassment, and he said, "Have the boy contact my secretary!" So I then had to pluck up the courage and ring the secretary and he said to me, "Sir James can give you an hour from ten to eleven," so I got there about half past ten and I hung around until twenty to eleven and I thought better to be early than late, so I went in and Sir James had been waiting for forty minutes and he said, "You must learn to be more punctual, young man!"'

But the anecdote is not over yet. It comes with an explanation.

'I thought he meant an hour from ten-to-eleven and of course he meant an hour, from ten to eleven! So of course I was too nervous to explain why I'd been late, but, oh gosh, that was awful! Talk about embarrassing! I was sixteen, so you can imagine how nervous I was!'

'Silly secretary,' mutters the Queen, with a slight sniff. She gazes out of the window. There is a brief silence. 'Do you go back? I mean, do you keep in touch?'

'Not as much as I'd like to. I was there last year for the whole month of January and it was so hot. You forget how hot it is! And I'm so unused to that heat.'

'I think I've been hotter in Sydney than I've been anywhere.'

'But then you can go to Sydney in mid-summer and it's pelting with rain. You never know.'

'You go to Canada and you get wet. Every time there's forty thousand people to see you get wet.' She then corrects herself. 'Or they get wet. I think they said in Saskatchewan they only get fourteen inches a year. It all seemed to dump itself on us in one day!'

In voice-over, Harris says to the viewers: 'I can't believe I'm talking to the Queen about the weather! I need to focus on what I'm doing here!'

He dabs with his brush.

'What's the sort of *plan* for your picture? Is it, er—?' ventures the Queen.

'Trying not to do a formal, state-occasion-type painting, but something to *capture the real you*,' says Harris.

The Queen nods, but doesn't smile. *Capturing the real you?* Alarm bells!

In voice-over, Harris offers his view on how it's all going. '... The Queen's so relaxed,' he says. 'That'll make it much easier for me to *capture her real personality*.'

But is she relaxed? And what is her real personality? Who can tell? She certainly doesn't seem particularly tense. Nor does she seem remotely bothered by the presence of the BBC crew, crouching discreetly behind the cameras. On the other hand, she seems much more on-guard than off-guard, as any of us might were we to be confronted by Rolf Harris and his paintbrushes.

Harris makes nervy, breathy, sucking noises: fwoo-fwoo-fwoo.

'I hear my mother in myself when I'm concentrating,' he informs Her Majesty. 'I'm forever going fwoo-fwoo-fwoo. She used to do that all the time.'

'Did she?'

'Especially when she was annoyed. She would go – fwoo-fwoo-fwoo.' Harris supplements the sound effect by drumming the fingers of one hand on the wrist of the other. 'She would do that sort of tuneless whistle! And you'd think "Uh-oh"!'

The Queen smiles sympathetically, like a psychotherapist. 'You knew something was wrong.'

In her eighty years, how many conversations like this has she had? Cyril Connolly once remarked of the pitfalls of celebrity: 'It's you they want to meet. But it's themselves they want to talk about.' The Queen was, in this way, the consummate celebrity. Her profession was meeting people. She avoided speaking about herself: she simply listened and prompted, her role being to let us rattle on about ourselves.

'Yeah, get out into the road, quick, because you'd done something which has annoyed mum!'

Is Harris thinking of his mother because he's looking at the Queen? In dreams, the Queen often substitutes for the mother-figure, ready to approve or chastise.

Perhaps sensing that he has gone on too much about his childhood, Harris attempts to open up the conversation.

'Do you find portraits a terrible chore?'

'No, not really, it's quite nice,' replies the Queen. 'Usually one just sits and – er – people can't get at you because ...' – she looks down at her lap – '... one is busy doing nothing.'

She looks upwards, and smiles.

Harris asks her what she thinks of all her portraits.

'The only trouble is you see yourself ageing in front of you.'

'Does that upset you?'

'Nah!' She pronounces it 'Nah!' rather than 'No'.

'Not really?'

'I'm used to it now.'

A pause.

'Do you get a lot of joy from your grandchildren?'

She nods. 'Hmm.' But says no more. Has he crossed a line?

In the voice-over, Harris says: 'I've been so busy chatting, I haven't got nearly as far as I'd hoped – and I'm almost out of time!'

Wrapping up, he asks the Queen: 'Do you find you're anxious to see what's being done, or just leave it alone?'

The Queen says nothing.

Harris answers for her: 'Just stay out of it! Ha! Ha! Ha!'

'Well, I might take a look as I go out.'

Harris says he will do some more work on it at home, ready for the next sitting in ten days' time. 'Would I be able to take some photographs of you?'

'Yes, do!'

Bringing out his camera, he launches into yet another anecdote, this one about toppling over on the stairs and – 'boomf!' – breaking his camera. 'I thought, aw, lovely camera! But I've stuck it together and it still works!'

'It's all covered in sticking plaster!' observes the Queen, with a frown.

'Imagine you're thrilled to pieces to see me!' enthuses Harris, snapping away. 'That's really good! I'll show you that and see if you're happy with that!'

He shows her the photos on the little camera screen.

The Queen says, 'Mm. That looks all right.' She seems unconcerned.

On her way out, she looks at the painting for the first time.

'That's very speedy!'

'Well, it's a start. It's not you.'

'Hm. It's very clever.'

'Thank you so much for today.'

'Yes, all right. It'll be in about ten days' time.'

'Okay. Thank you.'

'Bye.'

'Thank you very much indeed. Lovely. Thank you.'

Once the Queen has left the room, Harris lets out a long breath and speaks to the camera.

'Hee! Hee! Wasn't she *lovely*?'

* * *

Back home, in his studio by the Thames, Harris works hard at the painting, rising at 5 a.m., but something is still not quite right. 'I've been concentrating on the teeth,' he tells the viewers, 'and I've got some sort of a *sneer* there.' He dabs at the Queen's upper lip.

So that he can continue his painting in the absence of the Queen, the Palace have agreed to deliver her dress to him. 'I just feel *so privileged*. The Queen has been kind enough to let me borrow the *actual dress* that she was wearing on the day of the sitting.'

It so happens that the Palace has to reschedule the second sitting, as the Queen has gone down with a cold. But a few weeks later Harris is back, ushering the Queen to her chair, like a chummy dentist.

'Would you care to take your place? I hope you're feeling much better than you were?'

'I'm not, I'm afraid. I think the day out to sea didn't do me any good at all. The doctor just says it'll get better. They're horrible things. If they attack your throat you can't do much.'

'Dear oh dear.'

'I hope I can help her to relax,' says Harris in voice-over. He then launches into one of his long anecdotes, this one about visiting Wales a couple of weeks ago and the organiser of the event taking him upstairs. 'There was a painting by my grandfather of your grandfather – King George V reviewing the troops in the '14–18 war. It sent shivers up my spine!'

The Queen seems less excited than Harris, but affects an interest.

'You didn't know it was there?'

'I didn't, no.'

Harris carries on painting.

'Do you remember your very first portrait sitting?' he asks her.

'Yes. László,* she replies. 'Horrid he was. Hm.'

---

* Born Fülöp Laub in Budapest, Philip de László (1869–1937) became a naturalised Briton in 1914. His subjects included Emperor Franz Joseph, President Calvin Coolidge, Lord Curzon, Emperor Wilhelm II, President Theodore Roosevelt, King George VI, Elinor Glyn, Vita Sackville-West and King Edward VII. In 1900, he painted the 90-year-old Pope Leo XIII. Thus the same man who painted Pope Leo XIII, who was born in 1810, also painted the Queen, who died in 2022: a leap across time of 212 years.

As far as I know, this is the first time Her Majesty has ever called anyone 'horrid' in public, and it will also be the last.

'Was he?' asks Harris.

'Yes.' Again, she pulls her Lucian Freud face. 'Well, he was one of those people who wanted you to sit permanently looking at him.'*

The conversation moves on to the Queen's corgis.

'At the last sitting,' says Harris. 'I was going to suggest the possibility of bringing the corgis in. But whether they would have been able to be still … I don't know what they're like.'

'Oh no, they'd sit still. One of them would.'

'Are they easy to train?'

'Oh yes, they're heelers – you know, cattle dogs. They bite. They chase people. Depends who they chase, though. The sentries used to have a bad time.'

'Did they chase them?'

'The present lot don't. But they did, yes. I think if someone stamps and threatens you with a big stick when you go past, then it's rather a natural reaction for a dog.'

Harris makes doggy noises – 'Rargh! Rargh! Rargh!' – almost 'Rolf! Rolf! Rolf!' – then draws the conversation back to the subject of himself.

'I've got two huge dogs at home. Standard poodle and Weimaraner.'

'Oh really?'

'Any sound – woo! woo! woo! – they're out there, barking at the gate. Gosh, in my time on *Animal Hospital*, there were so many animals that we saw misbehaving in the waiting room. But, then again, of course, we saw cases of animal neglect and cruelty to animals that you just couldn't believe … We had a lady with 125 cats and dogs, all living throughout the flat everywhere, and just—'

---

* De László himself had much happier memories of their sitting, which took place in 1933, when she was seven years old. He described her as 'a most intelligent and beautiful little girl' who showed 'no sign of shyness' and 'made some very amusing remarks'. He spoke of how, at the end of one sitting, the little Princess had said confidentially, 'I'm going to tell you something, Mr de László, that will surprise you … I paint too, and I'm a very good painter. I'll bring some of my work next time and show you.' However, at their next sitting she was 'very sleepy and restless', having just come from Queen Mary's birthday lunch. This may account for her impatience with the man who was painting her portrait.

'Never going out?'

'Going on the carpets. It was just appalling. So upsetting. So powerfully upsetting.'

Things have taken a downturn. Harris goes quiet and concentrates on the canvas. Attempting to resurrect their conversation, the Queen says:

'I suppose it still goes on.'

'Oh, yes.'

'Some people go on holiday and leave their children behind.'

'Yes.' Harris whistles – fwoo! fwoo! fwoo! – under his breath. 'Do you have a particular style of painting that you like?'

'Well, I suppose landscape is quite nice,' replies the owner of the largest art collection in the world. 'I went to the Stubbs exhibition yesterday. Which was lovely.'

They talk about Stubbs's habit of dissecting horse carcasses in his studio.

'They said the place stank to high heaven!' says Harris. 'You know, it was just appalling! But what an artist!'

After a while, their session comes to an end, and the Queen stands up. On her way out, she takes a look at the painting.

'I think that works very nice. Friendly, anyway.'

'That was my main aim.'

'Well, it's very clever, I think.'

'Thank you.'

'Rather fun. Well, thank you very much. I hope it's a great success.'

At its unveiling in December 2005, Rolf Harris's portrait of the Queen receives a lukewarm reception from the critics. The *Daily Mail* says it depicts the Queen as a 'gurning granny'. The *Daily Telegraph* describes it as representing a nadir of Royal portraiture, with the Queen 'grinning like the monkey on top of a barrel organ'. But the public take a different view, voting it the second-best portrait of all time. The painting then goes on display at the Queen's Gallery in Buckingham Palace for six months. A year after the sitting, Harris is appointed Commander of the Most Excellent Order of the British Empire (CBE).

In 2012, he performs his most famous song, 'Two Little Boys', outside Buckingham Palace at the Queen's Diamond Jubilee Concert. That same year, his portrait of the Queen is displayed in a major retrospective of his paintings at the Walker Gallery in Liverpool. The show, titled *Rolf Harris: Can You Tell What It Is Yet?*, achieves record attendances.

The following year, Rolf Harris is arrested and charged with twelve counts of indecent assault on four teenage girls between 1968 and 1986. In June 2014, he is sentenced to five years and nine months in prison.

On 17 June 2015, the *London Gazette* carries this announcement:

The Queen has directed that the appointment of Rolf Harris to be a Commander of the Civil Division of the Most Excellent Order of the British Empire ... shall be cancelled and annulled and that his name shall be erased from the register of the said Order.

He joins a small and infamous band of people who have had their honours cancelled, among them Robert Mugabe, whose honorary knighthood was revoked in 2008, Nicolae Ceaușescu, whose honorary knighthood was revoked in 1989, the day before his execution, and Benito Mussolini, who was stripped of his honorary Knight Grand Cross in 1940, having recently declared war on the United Kingdom.

The whereabouts of Rolf Harris's portrait of the Queen remains unknown. Both the BBC and the Royal Collection deny owning it or even having seen it in the past few years.

97

At the dawn of the twenty-first century, there was much talk of the Queen abdicating: she was elderly; she had reigned for well over half a century; the Prince of Wales should be given his turn. Such talk unsettled Sir Max Hastings, historian and journalist, former editor of the *Daily Telegraph*. He had great respect for the Queen, and feared that her eldest son lacked her self-discipline and was too self-pitying to be a successful king. Were the Queen to abdicate, the future of the monarchy could be in jeopardy.

Hastings aired his forebodings to a Palace courtier.

'Some of your lot don't understand,' came the reply. 'She *likes* being Queen.'

98

The Queen once told the French president, François Hollande, that as a young girl she dreamt of being an actress.

In a way, suggested Hollande, she had achieved her ambition.

'Yes,' she replied. 'But always the same role.'

The role of monarch is inherently theatrical; wherever you go in public, whatever you do, the audience is always there, ready to be surprised or reassured or charmed or disappointed. The monarch must play the one and only role she was born to play. She must act an idealised version of herself, smilier than she would normally be, more curious, more delighted, more concerned.

Noël Coward and Gertrude Lawrence were once sitting together in a theatre, watching the Queen Mother enter the Royal Box.

'What an entrance!' said Lawrence.

'What a *part*!' said Coward.

The Queen Mother's biographer Hugo Vickers recognised her inherent theatricality. 'Her engagements, whether private or public, were like performances,' he noted, adding, 'Privately, there was less going on, since between these performances she rested.' Her ability to give an audience what they wanted seems to have been innate. From her earliest days, newspaper reports of her public appearances read more like reviews of a brilliant performance. 'She smiled her way into the hearts of the people … her kindly glances, the sweetness of her manner, her whole attitude of gracious charm have won for her a love which must last as long as those who have seen her shall live,' ran an editorial in the Kingston *Daily Gleaner* when she visited Jamaica in 1927.

Her elder daughter was both more reserved in public and more herself in private. If she was playing a part, she did so with restraint, leaving her audience aware that, for all the smiling and the waving and the small talk, there was another character, shyer, less forthcoming, sheltering within. But did this mean she was acting? There were times when the suggestion bewildered her. In 1990, while they were chatting about the press, she complained to the BBC executive Will Wyatt, 'Did you see what Anne Robinson said yesterday? "I have never liked Queen Elizabeth, she's just an actress." Why say that now, after all this time?' Wyatt recalled her looking genuinely puzzled.

After the death of her mother in 2002, the Queen grew more carefree, as though relieved of the burden of her mother's judgement. She relaxed into her role and had more fun. Ten years on, at the age of 86, she readily agreed to perform a version of herself – or a version of a version of herself – in a short James Bond film commissioned for the opening of the London Olympics. Lord Janvrin, her private secretary from 1999 to 2007, doubted she would have gone ahead with the idea had her mother been alive, 'simply because she would have felt her mother wouldn't have approved – that it would have been a bit undignified'. When the idea was first put to her, she leapt at it. Before her deputy private secretary, Edward Young, finished telling her what she would have to do, she interrupted him. 'I know – and then I jump out of the helicopter?'

Back in 1977, the year of the Silver Jubilee, the new James Bond film, *The Spy Who Loved Me*, had opened with Bond escaping from a baddy by skiing off the edge of a mountain. As luck would have it, he had remembered to wear a parachute, which opened to reveal a Union Jack. 'All over the world, instead of howling and throwing stones at the Union Jack, they were bursting into spontaneous applause,' observed the movie's screenwriter, Christopher Wood.

Working on the opening ceremony for the 2012 Olympics, the director Danny Boyle remembered this opening sequence from thirty-five years before. His co-writer Frank Cottrell-Boyce thought it worth replicating. 'Apparently, all you need to do to get people to love our flag is attach it to a national icon and drop them from a great height,' he observed.

Boyle visited the Palace for a meeting with Edward Young and the Queen's dresser, Angela Kelly. At this point, he was only after their advice on what a lookalike Queen might wear to greet James Bond. But to Boyle's surprise Kelly said she thought the Queen might prefer to play herself, and asked them to wait a few minutes. 'I remember the look of shock on Danny's face that I would be asking Her Majesty straight away, but there's no point in waiting around with these things. If she said no, that would be the end of it. I ran upstairs and luckily the Queen was free so I asked her if she would be prepared to do a surprise performance for the Olympics opening ceremony. She was very amused by the idea and agreed immediately. I asked then if she would like a speaking part. Without hesitation, Her Majesty replied, "Of course I must say something. After all, he is coming to rescue me."

'I asked whether she would like to say, "Good evening, James" or "Good evening, Mr Bond," and she chose the latter, knowing the Bond films. Within minutes, I was back in Edward's office delivering the good news to Danny. I think he almost fell off his chair when I said that the Queen's only stipulation was that she could deliver the iconic line, "Good evening, Mr Bond."'*

On the day itself, says Boyle, the Queen 'was a one-take wonder'. She had a keen sense of drama, and knew how to keep an audience on tenterhooks. 'It was her idea that she should be finishing a letter before she spoke.' Like most visitors to the Palace, he was impressed, too, by her consideration towards her staff. 'She wanted her staff to have a day out with a movie star. Daniel came, and he's a movie star! He's James Bond!' When the Queen posed beside him for a still photograph it was clearly as much for her satisfaction as for his. 'She was very, very keen

---

* Some say Kelly has exaggerated her role, and that she had nothing to do with the original request. 'It was Young who asked, while they were at Balmoral,' concludes Valentine Low, in his book *Courtiers*. Low does, however, credit Kelly with persuading the Queen to say 'Good evening, Mr Bond', though he maintains that this happened on the day itself, rather than in advance.

and insistent that her staff did as well. I liked that about her very much. You thought, yeah, that's decent, looking after them like that.'

The film was premiered at the Olympic opening ceremony on 27 July 2012, and viewed by the largest global audience in the history of British television. James Bond arrives at Buckingham Palace in a black taxi, runs up red-carpeted stairs and is greeted ('Evening, sir') by the Queen's real-life Page of the Backstairs, Paul Whybrew, and a couple of equally authentic Royal corgis.

Bond is escorted into the Queen's study. 'Mr Bond, Your Majesty,' says Whybrew. The familiar figure at the desk, her back towards him, fails to look up. Bond stands in silence, looking a little impatient as he waits for her to finish writing a letter. As a clock chimes, he clears his throat to alert her to his presence. The figure at the desk turns around, stands up and says, 'Good evening, Mr Bond.'

Frank Cottrell-Boyce isolates this moment, the great reveal, as key to the film. 'Moments like this happen incrementally. Part of their power is surprise. When we are surprised our prejudices and opinions evaporate for a moment and we're briefly open-hearted. Surprise is the nemesis of cynicism. One of the most common reactions to that

moment was "I never felt patriotic before." Maybe you felt something like patriotism – some love for the best of this place – but didn't know how to articulate it without condoning the worst.'

'Good evening, Your Majesty,' says Bond, or, rather, Daniel Craig playing Bond. The actor had braved car chases, bullets, knives, punch-ups, explosions, defenestrations and any number of fights to the death, but he later admitted to 'shaking with nerves' in her presence.

Without another word, the Queen leads Bond out of her study, along a corridor and downstairs into the Palace gardens; together, they board a helicopter.

To the tune from *The Dam Busters*, their helicopter swoops over the Mall, where cheering crowds are waving Union Jacks, over Trafalgar Square and the Palace of Westminster, past Parliament Square, where the statue of Winston Churchill comes to life, smiling and waving his walking stick, on past the Millennium Wheel, St Paul's Cathedral and Tower Bridge, ending up hovering above the Olympic Stadium in East London. Bond slides open the door of the helicopter, looks down and, to live gasps from the stadium, the Queen leaps out.

As the familiar twangy James Bond theme tune plays, her parachute opens out into a Union Jack. Seconds later, the Queen – the real Queen – enters the stadium in her peach dress to a standing ovation, also real.

Sebastian Coe, the 2012 London Olympics chairman, was sitting next to Prince Charles, with Princes William and Harry behind them. 'When the sequence began, the Prince of Wales looked at me and laughed a bit nervously. When he realised it really was his mother up there on the screen with James Bond, he shook his head in total amazement. And when she appeared to jump from the helicopter, the two princes behind us started shouting, "Go, Granny, go!"'

99

This was to be one of the most striking images of the Queen's reign. Invariably she was photographed encircled by family, or heads of state, or crowds, or courtiers, or soldiers, but here she sits all alone, her face obscured by a covid mask. It is a picture that tells of grief, of lockdown, but, above all, of solitude. She had first met Prince Philip eighty-two years earlier, in 1939, when she was 13 years old and he was 18. It had been love at first sight, she told a friend. Now she was on her own.

Prince Philip died on 9 April 2021, two months short of his hundredth birthday. His death certificate said that he died of 'old age'. He had made detailed, no-nonsense plans for the aftermath: no lying in state, no funeral eulogy, his coffin to be borne on a Land Rover, customised by himself over the years for this very purpose.

He might well have applauded the further paring-back prompted by lockdown measures, such as the mourners in St George's Chapel being reduced from 600 to 30, leaving room for precious few beyond family. 'Best to keep the riff-raff out,' he might have chuckled, in his eternal hope of provoking a response. The choir was restricted to four; communal singing was at that moment against the law.

The Queen, wearing a black mask with white trim specially designed by her dresser Angela Kelly, was escorted to her socially distanced seat in the Quire of St George's Chapel by the dean of Windsor. As she sat down, she placed her black handbag on the empty seat beside her. 'The wartime spirit which nurtured her during her crucial adolescent years in Windsor defined her stoical character, and it was somehow appropriate that when Prince Philip went to his Eternal Reward, it happened during lock-down – the closest thing you could imagine to the wartime of ration books, the liturgical equivalent of powdered eggs,' observed A. N. Wilson. 'Everyone was moved by the sight of her sitting alone in the stalls of St George's Chapel as the choir sang the Russian Kontakion for the Departed to her husband's coffin. But it was also fitting.'

Figures showed that Prince Philip's funeral had been watched by 13.6 million British viewers, or 82 per cent of the available audience. Combined with TV news and press coverage, almost everyone in Britain will have seen this poignant image of the Queen in her isolation.

Nine months later, it emerged that the staff at 10 Downing St had held two different parties on the eve of Prince Philip's funeral. The second party had been attended by roughly thirty staff, who drank and danced through to the early hours of the morning. The *Daily Telegraph* reported that these partygoers had bought alcohol in a nearby supermarket and transported it back in a suitcase, to avoid prying eyes. Over the course of the night, wine had been spilled on the Downing Street carpets and, in the garden, the prime minister's little son's swing had been broken.

Though Boris Johnson had attended neither of these parties, the news came to symbolise the carefree hypocrisy of his administration: the rules they devised for others they saw no need to follow themselves. Just as the Queen, alone in her mask at her husband's funeral, became a symbol of duty and respect for the common law, so this revelry symbolised the opposite.

'We're waiting for the Prime Minister to look into his heart and soul and decide whether or not he has a scrap of human decency in him, because if he does, he will resign,' thundered Emily Thornberry, a senior member of the opposition. 'How the hell can he possibly expect to go before Her Majesty again at a weekly audience and be able to look her in the eye and pretend that everything is all right – because everything is not all right. The one thing he should be saying to Her Majesty is "I am profoundly sorry and I resign." That's what he should do.'

Cornered by reporters while visiting a hospital, the normally buoyant prime minister hung his head low.

'Was having to apologise to the Queen about those parties the night before she laid her husband of over seventy years to rest – was that a moment of shame for you?' asked Beth Rigby, the political editor of Sky News. '... Do you think you can recover from this? You might be able to survive, but can you recover? You're polling is terrible, the public think you should go, your MPs are in revolt – six of them have publicly said you should resign?'

'I understand people's feelings and I understand why people feel as strongly as they do about this issue, and I repeat my apologies for what happened and I'm heartily, heartily sorry for misjudgements that were made in No. 10.' Some commentators thought he was close to tears; others, less forgiving, considered it all an act.

On 9 June 2022, following the mass resignation of fifty members of his government, Boris Johnson announced that he would resign as prime minister. The collective memory of what had become known, inevitably, as 'Partygate' – the contrast between the Queen in her restraint and the prime minister in his excess – had contributed to his downfall. For one last time, she had come to embody Rebecca West's at times fanciful dictum: 'The Royal Family is ourselves behaving better.'

100

A family life in statements

9 August 2019

A Statement from Buckingham Palace

It is emphatically denied that The Duke of York [Prince Andrew] had any form of sexual contact or relationship with Virginia Roberts [Giuffre]. Any claim to the contrary is false and without foundation.

19 August 2019

A Statement from Buckingham Palace

The Duke of York has been appalled by the recent reports of Jeffrey Epstein's alleged crimes. His Royal Highness deplores the exploitation of any human being and the suggestion he would condone, participate or encourage any such behaviour is abhorrent.

24 August 2019

A Statement from His Royal Highness The Duke of York

It is apparent to me since the suicide of Mr. Epstein that there has been an immense amount of media speculation about so much in his life. This is particularly the case in relation to my former association or friendship with Mr. Epstein. Therefore I am eager to clarify the facts to avoid further speculation.

I met Mr. Epstein in 1999. During the time I knew him, I saw him infrequently and probably no more than only once or twice a year. I have stayed in a number of his residences. At no stage during the limited time I spent with him did I see, witness or suspect any behaviour of the sort that subsequently led to his arrest and conviction.

I have said previously that it was a mistake and an error to see him after his release in 2010 and I can only reiterate my regret that I was mistaken to think that what I thought I knew of him was evidently not the real person, given what we now know. I have tremendous sympathy for all those affected by his actions and behaviour.

His suicide has left many unanswered questions and I acknowledge and sympathise with everyone who has been affected and wants some form of closure. This is a difficult time for everyone involved and I am at a loss to be able to understand or explain Mr. Epstein's lifestyle. I deplore the exploitation of any human being and would not condone, participate in, or encourage any such behaviour.

20 November 2019
A Statement by His Royal Highness The Duke of York The Royal Family
@RoyalFamily
It has become clear to me over the last few days that the circumstances relating to my former association with Jeffrey Epstein has [sic] become a major disruption to my family's work and the valuable work going on in the many organisations and charities that I am proud to support.

Therefore, I have asked Her Majesty if I may step back from public duties for the foreseeable future, and she has given her permission.

I continue to unequivocally regret my ill-judged association with Jeffrey Epstein. His suicide has left many unanswered questions, particularly for his victims, and I deeply sympathise with everyone who has been affected and wants some form of closure. I can only hope that, in time, they will be able to rebuild their lives.

Of course, I am willing to help any appropriate law enforcement agency with their investigations, if required.

6.34 p.m., 8 January 2020
A personal message from the Duke and Duchess of Sussex
After many months of reflection and internal discussions, we have chosen to make a transition this year in starting to carve out a progressive new role within this institution.

We intend to step back as "senior" members of the Royal Family and work to become financially independent, while continuing to fully support Her Majesty The Queen.

It is with your encouragement, particularly over the last few years, that we feel prepared to make this adjustment.

We now plan to balance our time between the United Kingdom and North America, continuing to honour our duty to the Queen, the Commonwealth and our patronages.

This geographic balance will enable us to raise our son with an appreciation for the royal tradition into which he was born, while also providing our family with the space to focus on the next chapter, including the launch of our new charitable entity.

We look forward to sharing the full details of this exciting next step in due course, as we continue to collaborate with Her Majesty The Queen, the Prince of Wales, the Duke of Cambridge and all relevant parties.

Until then, please accept our deepest thanks for your continued support.

6.49 p.m., 8 January 2020
Royal Communications: Statement on discussions with the Duke and Duchess of Sussex
Discussions with The Duke and Duchess of Sussex are at an early stage. We understand their desire to take a different approach, but these are complicated issues that will take time to work through.

13 January 2020
Statement from HM the Queen
My family and I are entirely supportive of Harry and Meghan's desire to create a new life as a young family. Although we would have

preferred them to remain full-time working Members of the Royal Family, we respect and understand their wish to live a more independent life as a family while remaining a valued part of my family … These are complex matters for my family to resolve, and there is some more work to be done, but I have asked for final decisions to be reached in the coming days.

18 January 2020

Statement from HM the Queen

Following many months of conversations and more recent discussions, I am pleased that together we have found a constructive and supportive way forward for my grandson and his family.

Harry, Meghan and Archie will always be much loved members of my family.

I recognise the challenges they have experienced as a result of intense scrutiny over the last two years and support their wish for a more independent life.

I want to thank them for all their dedicated work across this country, the Commonwealth and beyond, and am particularly proud of how Meghan has so quickly become one of the family.

It is my whole family's hope that today's agreement allows them to start building a happy and peaceful new life.

18 January 2020

Statement from Buckingham Palace

The Duke and Duchess of Sussex are grateful to Her Majesty and the Royal Family for their ongoing support as they embark on the next chapter of their lives.

As agreed in this new arrangement, they understand that they are required to step back from royal duties, including official military appointments. They will no longer receive public funds for royal duties.

With The Queen's blessing, the Sussexes will continue to maintain their private patronages and associations. While they can no longer formally represent The Queen, the Sussexes have made clear that everything they do will continue to uphold the values of Her Majesty.

The Sussexes will not use their HRH titles as they are no longer working members of the Royal Family.

The Duke and Duchess of Sussex have shared their wish to repay Sovereign Grant expenditure for the refurbishment of Frogmore Cottage, which will remain their UK family home.

Buckingham Palace does not comment on the details of security arrangements. There are well established independent processes to determine the need for publicly funded security.

This new model will take effect in the spring of 2020.

22 February 2020
Statement issued by a spokesman for the Duke and Duchess of Sussex
While the duke and duchess are focused on plans to establish a new non-profit organisation, given the specific UK government rules surrounding use of the word royal, it has been therefore agreed that their non-profit organisation, when it is announced this spring, will not be named Sussex Royal Foundation.

While there is not any jurisdiction by the monarchy or Cabinet Office over the use of the word 'Royal' overseas, The Duke and Duchess of Sussex do not intend to use 'SussexRoyal' in any territory (either within the UK or otherwise) when the transition occurs post-spring 2020. Therefore the trademark applications that were filed as protective measures, acting on advice from and following the same model for The Royal Foundation of the Duke and Duchess of Cambridge, have been removed.

19 February 2021
Buckingham Palace statement on The Duke and Duchess of Sussex
The Duke and Duchess of Sussex have confirmed to Her Majesty The Queen that they will not be returning as working members of The Royal Family.

Following conversations with The Duke, The Queen has written confirming that in stepping away from the work of The Royal Family it is not possible to continue with the responsibilities and duties that come with a life of public service. The honorary military appointments and Royal patronages held by The Duke and Duchess will therefore be returned to Her Majesty, before being redistributed among working members of The Royal Family.

While all are saddened by their decision, The Duke and Duchess remain much loved members of the family.

Notes to editors:
Following The Duke and Duchess of Sussex's decision to step away last year as working members of The Royal Family, a 12-month review was agreed.

A decision has now been made after conversations between The Duke of Sussex and Members of The Royal Family.

The military, Commonwealth and Charitable associations which will revert to The Queen are:

The Royal Marines, RAF Honington, Royal Navy Small Ships and Diving.

The Queen's Commonwealth Trust, The Rugby Football Union, The Rugby Football League, The Royal National Theatre and The Association of Commonwealth Universities.

19 February 2021
A spokesperson for The Duke and Duchess of issued this statement:
As evidenced by their work over the past year, the Duke and Duchess of Sussex remain committed to their duty and service to the UK and around the world, and have offered their continued support to the organisations they have represented regardless of official role. We can all live a life of service. Service is universal.

Tuesday, 9 March 2021

ROYAL COMMUNICATIONS
THE FOLLOWING STATEMENT IS ISSUED BY BUCKINGHAM
PALACE ON BEHALF OF HER MAJESTY THE QUEEN
The whole family is saddened to learn the full extent of how challenging the last few years have been for Harry and Meghan.

The issues raised, particularly that of race, are concerning. Whilst some recollections may vary, they are taken very seriously and will be addressed by the family privately.

Harry, Meghan and Archie will always be much loved family members.

30 March 2021
@ SussexRoyal
As we all find the part to play in this global shift and changing of habits, we are focusing this new chapter to understand how we can best contribute. While you may not see us here, the work continues. Thank you to this community – for the support, the inspiration, and the shared commitment to the good in the world. We look forward to reconnecting with you soon. You've been great!

13 January 2022
A statement from Buckingham Palace regarding The Duke of York
With The Queen's approval and agreement, The Duke of York's military affiliations and Royal patronages have been returned to The Queen.

The Duke of York will continue not to undertake any public duties and is defending this case as a private citizen.

101

In the final year of her life, the Queen agreed to act herself once more, this time playing stooge to a bear from Peru.

A Buckingham Palace footman carries a silver tray with a teapot and two teacups through various grand rooms before placing it on a table.

PADDINGTON BEAR: Thank you for having me. I do hope you have a lovely Jubilee.

HMQ: Tea?

PADDINGTON: Oh, yes please! (drinks it direct from the spout)

The Queen looks a little bemused. The footman clears his throat, disapprovingly, and nods for Paddington to desist.

PADDINGTON: Oh, terribly sorry!

Paddington stands on his chair and reaches out to pour the remaining few drops into the Queen's teapot.

HMQ: Never mind!

Paddington's chair slips, causing the teapot to fly out of his paws into the air. Struggling to catch it, he places a paw in the chocolate eclairs. A dollop of cream lands on the footman's cheek.

PADDINGTON: Oh dear. Perhaps you would like a marmalade
    sandwich? I always keep one for emergencies.
HMQ: So do I – I keep mine in here.

*With a broad smile, she pulls a ready-sliced marmalade sandwich from
her handbag.*

PADDINGTON: Oh!
HMQ: For later!

*The footman looks out of window at the live crowds cheering in the
Mall.*

FOOTMAN: The party is about to start, Your Majesty.
PADDINGTON: (removing his cap, then putting it back on) Happy
    Jubilee, Ma'am. And … thank you. For everything.
HMQ: (smiling) That's very kind.

*Beyond the Palace gates, the Corps of Drums from the Band of Her
Majesty's Royal Marines play the opening beats of 'We Will Rock You'.
The Queen starts tapping out the beat on her teacup with a teaspoon,
and Paddington follows suit. Queen – the rock group, not the sovereign
– take over. Neither Her Majesty nor Paddington join in with the words.*

You got blood on your face, you big disgrace
Waving your banner all over the place …
Somebody better put you back in your place.

At the age of 96, the Queen drew unanimous praise for her performance. 'Wasn't she good? I mean really, *really* good?' reckoned Dame
Judi Dench. 'Her timing was perfect. Every look, every line was just
right. It was completely on the money – none of it overstated. Just
wonderful.'

Frank Cottrell-Boyce, who helped script it, was also impressed. 'She
did it brilliantly and with evident enjoyment. And it wasn't easy.

Paddington's not really there, so it's technically an amazing performance and a brilliantly timed comic performance.' He pointed out that the Queen had been given many more lines than in her James Bond debut, ten years previously, 'partly because it was a lot cheaper to film her than to film Paddington'.

For Cottrell-Boyce, a devout Roman Catholic, the short film had particular significance. 'Paddington is an evacuee, a refugee, one-time prisoner, pretty much every category of need that is mentioned in Matthew 25.* Here, he is being welcomed with tea and good manners. This is a strong statement of a set of values that are not contested in the corridors of power. To have them exemplified so joyfully at such a moment meant something ... The most emotional moment in that encounter with Paddington is when the bear says, "Thank you, Ma'am. For everything." People will ask, "What everything?" Well, make your own list. But I'm thankful for the way she used the peculiar power of

---

* 'For I was an hungred, and ye gave me meat: I was thirsty, and ye gave me drink: I was a stranger, and ye took me in: naked, and ye clothed me: I was sick, and ye visited me: I was in prison, and ye came unto me.'

her archaic role to allow us to glimpse, however fleetingly, that we share something good and we need to defend that.'

Once again, the borders between the authentic and the artificial were blurred – so successfully, in this case, that conspiracy theorists began suggesting that the real Queen had never taken part in it, and that the Establishment had simply created a deepfake Queen, to be inserted later. Cottrell-Boyce still finds this baffling: 'No one seemed to question the reality of Paddington Bear.'

It later emerged that the Queen had experienced trouble with one particular line. Simon Farnaby, the actor who played her footman, recalls: 'There was a bit where Paddington says, "I keep my sandwiches in my hat. I keep it for emergencies." She goes, "So do I. I keep mine in here," and she has a handbag. At first, the Queen's tone was quite harsh. The director would come in and say, "Ma'am, could you just be a bit gentler?' And she'd be so sweet and she'd go: "I'm sorry, yes, of course." He'd go: "Like you're talking to your grandchildren." She'd say: "Oh, of course. I'm so sorry." I was saying to him: "Just give up, just stop, we're not going to get it." And he said: "No, I think just a couple more."'

The Queen was getting tired, but she eventually got the line right, and, according to Farnaby, 'Everyone was relieved. It was OK in the end. It was really sweet and really lovely.'

102

Once it was all over, Farnaby congratulated the Queen on her performance: 'I said, "Ma'am, that was fantastic." She went: "Oh, thank you." And I went: "You're a very good actress." And she said: "Well of course, I do it all the time." I went: "Ooh, you mean like playing the part of the Queen?" And she said: "I beg your pardon?" And then I lost all my confidence. I thought she was giving me the scoop, like it's a part, a role. And I went: "I mean like it's a role, isn't it, the Queen, and you play it?" And she said: "You know I *am* the Queen? Paddington's not real, they're actors, but I *am* the Queen."'

103

Tuesday, 6 September 2022

Her fourteenth prime minister, Boris Johnson, visits the Queen at Balmoral in order to tender his resignation. Usually this is done at Buckingham Palace, but 'mobility problems' are given as the reason that the Queen has decided to remain at Balmoral.

The Queen stands to greet him. They talk about the political situation, and laugh and joke. Johnson finds her 'full of characteristic humour and wisdom'. Their meeting overruns.

When Johnson has left, the Queen is told that Liz Truss's arrival at Aberdeen airport has been delayed due to fog. She seizes the opportunity to phone her racehorse trainer Clive Cox. She wants to hear what he thinks the chances are of her two-year-old filly Love Affairs winning the 3.05 race at Goodwood that afternoon. Cox finds the Queen 'as sharp as a tack'.

12.05 p.m.: While the Queen is waiting for the arrival of her new prime minister, a local Press Association photographer, Jane Barlow, takes photographs of her. On the wall behind the Queen is a painting of Queen Victoria at Balmoral, sitting side-saddle on her horse, which is being held by her manservant John Brown. The Queen is carrying a walking stick in her left hand; her trusty handbag is draped over the same arm. The pair of them pass the time talking about the weather, and how dark it is: it has been a morning of heavy rain and thunderstorms. Barlow thinks the Queen is looking much more frail than she did earlier in the summer. But she seems in good spirits: 'I got a lot of smiles from her.'

12.10 p.m.: Liz Truss is escorted into the drawing room at Balmoral. She curtsies to the Queen in front of a roaring fire. Jane Barlow takes photographs of the two of them together. These are the last photographs of the Queen that will ever be taken. In the days to come, they will be closely studied by those looking retrospectively for portents of death; on social media, some spot that the back of her right hand has turned dark grey, or even black.

During their twenty-minute conversation, the Queen warns Liz Truss that being prime minister can be 'incredibly ageing'. She also offers her two words of advice: 'pace yourself'.

The Queen's latest prime minister was born on 26 July 1975, when the Queen was 49 years old. That same year, 'Bye Bye Baby' by the Bay City Rollers was the biggest-selling British record, Margaret Thatcher became leader of the Conservative Party, Lord Lucan went missing, the British people voted to stay in the Common Market and Martin Amis published his second novel, *Dead Babies*. The Queen's first prime minister, Winston Churchill, had been born just over a century earlier, in 1874. That same year, Giuseppe Verdi premiered his Requiem, Benjamin Disraeli became prime minister for the second time, the

Tichborne Claimant was sentenced to fourteen years' hard labour, the Factory Act brought an end to the employment of children under the age of 10 in textile factories, and Thomas Hardy published *Far from the Madding Crowd*.

When he resigned in 1955, at the age of 80, Churchill had toasted the young Queen: 'Never have the august duties which fall upon the British monarch been discharged with more devotion than in the brilliant opening to your Majesty's reign. We thank God for the gift he has bestowed upon us and vow ourselves anew to the sacred cause and wise and kindly way of life of which your Majesty is the young, gleaming champion.'

The Queen and her new prime minister talk briefly, before Truss's husband Hugh is ushered in. The three of them exchange pleasantries. The Queen bids goodbye to Truss, saying, 'We'll meet again.'

Buckingham Palace releases a statement. 'The Queen received in audience The Right Honourable Elizabeth Truss MP today and requested her to form a new administration. Ms Truss accepted Her Majesty's offer and kissed hands upon her appointment as Prime Minister and First Lord of the Treasury.'

In a short ceremony – the last she will ever perform – the Queen enrols her outgoing communications secretary, Donal McCabe, as a Member of the Royal Victorian Order.

In the afternoon, the Queen's horse, Love Affairs, wins the Fillies' Nursery Handicap at Goodwood by one and a half lengths. Over pre-dinner drinks that evening, the Queen is in good spirits, talking about the various prime ministers she has known; but then she says she is going upstairs, and will have dinner alone.

Wednesday, 7 September 2022
Following a terrorist atrocity in Saskatchewan, in which ten people have been stabbed to death and a further nineteen injured, the Queen sends a message.

I would like to extend my condolences to those who have lost loved ones in the attacks that occurred this past weekend in Saskatchewan. My thoughts and prayers are with those recovering from injuries, and grieving such horrific losses. I mourn with all Canadians at this tragic time. Elizabeth R.

It is to be her last public statement.

She tells her staff that she will remain in bed for the day. Princess Anne, who is staying at Balmoral, sends for the local GP, Dr Douglas Glass. After his visit, the Queen declares that she still plans to attend the meeting of the Privy Council by video-link in the evening.

At roughly the same time, Prince Charles, staying 150 miles away at Dumfries House in Ayrshire, records a message congratulating the cast and crew of *Emmerdale* on the fiftieth anniversary of the TV soap opera.

At the last minute, the evening's scheduled meeting of the Privy Council is cancelled. 'After a full day yesterday, Her Majesty has this afternoon accepted doctors' advice to rest', reads a statement from Buckingham Palace.

Prince Charles decides to cancel the next day's appointments and head for Balmoral in the morning.

That night, the new team at Downing Street are discreetly advised to keep black ties in their desks over the coming days.

Thursday, 8 September 2022

8 a.m.: Princess Anne, who is already staying at Balmoral, is worried, and passes on her concerns to her elder brother.

9.00 a.m.: The new prime minister, Liz Truss, is in the Cabinet Room of 10 Downing Street, going through the announcement of an energy support plan she is due to make to the House of Commons. The Cabinet secretary, Simon Case, asks to see her alone. He tells her that the Queen is ailing. 'It is a matter of hours, not days.' Truss asks for a selection of black dresses to be fetched from her home in Greenwich.

9.30 a.m.: Prince Charles flies with his wife Camilla in the Queen's helicopter from Dumfries House to Birkhall, their home on the Balmoral estate. During the hour-long flight, he reads his briefing papers on Operation London Bridge, the prearranged codename for the death of his mother. With him in the helicopter is his private secretary, Sir Clive Alderton, who half expects to find the Queen standing at the door of Balmoral ready to ask her son and heir, 'What on earth do you think you are doing?'

After they have touched down at Birkhall, the Prince drives them in a Land Rover to Balmoral. Charles and Camilla spend an hour at the Queen's bedside. Her doctor, Douglas Glass, reports that she is stable, but weak: the consensus is that she has a day or two, rather than an hour or two.

11.09 a.m.: Newspapers are aware that things are amiss. At the *Daily Mail*, the editor decides to prepare two versions of the next day's newspaper in parallel: a normal eighty-page edition and another edition of 120 pages, expanded to include commemorative features, photographs and tributes.

12.12 p.m.: While the prime minister, Liz Truss, is listening to the leader of the opposition, Sir Keir Starmer, deliver his response to the government's statement on the cost-of-living crisis, her colleague Nadhim Zahawi passes her a note: the Palace is about to release further news.

A similar note is passed to Starmer's deputy, Angela Rayner, on the opposition benches. It reads: 'The Queen is unwell and Keir needs to leave the chamber as soon as possible to be briefed.' Rayner recognises the urgency of the situation – 'you don't get a note saying the Queen is unwell if she's got a bit of a cough' – but does not want to distract Starmer mid-flow. Only when she sees the Speaker, Sir Lindsay Hoyle, gesticulating towards her does she realise that she should interrupt Starmer regardless.

Around this time, Prince Charles phones Prince Harry, who is in London with his wife for an award ceremony. The number comes up on Harry's mobile phone as 'Unknown'. His father tells him 'Granny's health has taken a turn.' Harry immediately texts his brother William asking whether he and Kate are flying up to Scotland. 'If so, when? And how?' There is no response. Harry and Megan investigate the various flight options.

12.32 p.m.: A rare 'media advisory' message from the Palace to newsrooms signals that something is wrong. 'Following further evaluation this morning, the Queen's doctors are concerned for Her Majesty's health and have recommended she remain under medical supervision. The Queen remains comfortable and at Balmoral.'

12.39 p.m.: The BBC interrupts its programme *Bargain Hunt* to deliver the statement from Buckingham Palace. The controller then reschedules its programmes, regular afternoon shows making way for rolling news, largely concerned with the various members of the Royal Family making their way towards Balmoral.

The BBC's senior news presenter, Huw Edwards, is on his way to a hairdresser in central London. His mobile telephone was stolen last night, so he is unaware of the crisis, or that the BBC are trying to get hold of him.

On social media, word spreads that the Queen is dying, or perhaps even dead: no one is quite sure.

At her home in Spitalfields, the feminist author Jeanette Winterson changes into black and awaits the official announcement. 'As an adopted person, she has been the one and only stable female in my life. Her Beaton portrait hung over our coal fire above the brass flying ducks. When Mrs Winterson was at her most volatile, taking my dad's service revolver out of the duster and fiddling with the bullets embedded in a tin of Pledge, I looked to the Queen for help. She was better than Jesus because she was alive, as well as possessing special powers. Our family stood for the national anthem. We listened to the Queen's speech standing up, and I do still, on the radio, on Christmas Day.'

12.50 p.m.: Buckingham Palace announces that the Queen's sons Andrew and Edward, her grandson William and her daughter-in-law Sophie are all on their way to Balmoral.

1.00 p.m.: Huw Edwards arrives at his hairdresser, where he is passed a message from his son: 'Get to work immediately.'

1.52 p.m.: Harry and Meghan issue a statement that they will both be flying to Scotland and will therefore be unable to attend a charity event in London.

By now, Huw Edwards has arrived at the BBC. He appears on screen, wearing a black suit and very dark blue tie.

2.15 p.m.: Prince Charles calls Harry and asks him not to bring Meghan to Balmoral. Harry finds the reason given 'nonsensical and disrespectful'. Charles stammers an apology, explaining that he doesn't want too many people around and that none of the wives are coming: Kate is remaining in London. 'Then that's all you needed to say,' replies Harry.

2.39 p.m.: Prince William, Prince Edward and his wife Sophie and Prince Andrew set off from RAF Northolt in an RAF jet. At Luton Airport, Prince Harry manages to charter a private Cessna jet for himself.

Beside the Queen's bed, the Revd Kenneth MacKenzie, minister at Crathie church and chaplain to the Queen, reads to her from her Bible.

Shortly after 3.00 p.m., Dr Glass is called to the Queen's bedside from the small surgery at Balmoral, where he has based himself for the day. Around the same time, Princess Anne calls Prince Charles, who is out in the grounds of Birkhall picking mushrooms, and tells him to come immediately. He and the Duchess of Cornwall drive to Balmoral.

By the time Dr Glass arrives at her bedside, the Queen has stopped breathing. Glass emerges from the bedroom and tells Sir Edward Young the sad news. Young makes a note. 'Dougie in at 3.25. Very peaceful. In her sleep. Slipped away. Old age. Death has to be registered in Scotland. Agree 3.10 p.m. She wouldn't have been aware of anything. No pain.'

Sir Edward phones Prince Charles in his Land Rover. He asks him to pull his car over. His first words – 'Your Majesty' – are enough.

Princess Anne is visibly upset. On the spur of the moment, a senior member of staff offers her a hug. 'That is the last time that is going to happen,' she says.

Sir Edward greets the new King and Queen at the front entrance of Balmoral. The King puts a hand on his shoulder and says, 'I know how much you'll miss her and how loyal you were to her.'

Protocol takes precedence. Sir Edward asks the new King under what name he wishes to reign. He then requests his permission to call the prime minister.

King Charles needs to tell Prince William. He calls the switchboard, so that they can put him in touch. Suddenly realising that, as his mother's death has not yet been made public, he cannot announce himself to the operator as king, he says simply, 'It's me.'

It will be over three hours before the news of the Queen's death is officially announced. Later, the death certificate will give her fore-names: Elizabeth Alexandra Mary; her surname: Windsor; her occupation: 'Her Majesty the Queen'; and the cause of her death: 'Old age'.

3.50 p.m.: Prince William and the other Royals land at Aberdeen airport.

4.30 p.m.: In her Downing Street flat, the prime minister, Liz Truss, is working with her aides on the speech she will have to deliver after the Queen's death has been announced. They are all unhappy with the first draft, written by civil servants. In the words of one of her aides it had been written 'in about 1960'. A team at Buckingham Palace are busy ringing round those who need to know: Downing Street, Lambeth Palace, the chief of the defence staff, the prime ministers and high commissioners of the fourteen other countries of which the Queen was head of state, and so on. Throughout the afternoon, TV news channels have had their cameras focused on the gates of Balmoral and the rain-soaked trees surrounding them. With little to see or report beyond speculation, the commentators feel obliged to keep talking.

5.06 p.m.: Prince Andrew, Prince Edward and the Countess of Wessex arrive in a Land Rover driven by Prince William. Talking over a shot of their arrival, the veteran BBC Royal Correspondent Nicholas Witchell says: 'I would say that in the absence of hard facts, the images are now telling the story. The Wessexes in the back of that vehicle: I thought they looked very sombre. Every individual must look at that photograph and draw their own conclusions. Let's leave it at that.'

Witchell then returns to the uneasy mix of solemnity and gossip. 'Which members of the Royal Family are on their way, and which are not? This isn't a moment for Meghan to be there with the other close family. Why has she stayed behind? Undoubtedly people will speculate about that,' he says, swiftly adding, 'But this is not the moment.'

5.30 p.m.: After some delay, Prince Harry's plane takes off from Luton Airport.

6.15 p.m.: Undertakers at the funeral company of William Purves are alerted. Over the past few years, they have taken part in a number of rehearsals for this moment, just in case the Queen were to die in Scotland. Royal protocol remains all-encompassing, even, or perhaps especially, in death: they have swapped their usual silver Mercedes hearse for a black one.

6.30 p.m.: On the BBC, the newscaster Huw Edwards, in a black tie, is saying, 'We are expecting the news from Balmoral that she's having – er – treatment, or that indeed they are unable to help Her Majesty any more.' At this point, his producer speaks into his earpiece: 'The announcement is here. Take your time. Speak when you are ready. Don't rush.'

Edwards looks to the camera and says, 'A few moments ago, Buckingham Palace announced the death of Her Majesty Queen Elizabeth II. The Palace has just issued this statement. It says the Queen died peacefully at Balmoral this afternoon. The King and the Queen Consort will remain at Balmoral this evening and will return to London tomorrow. Within the past few minutes, Buckingham Palace has announced the death of Her Majesty Queen Elizabeth II. To recap on the statement, the Queen died peacefully at Balmoral this after-noon. The King, that is Charles, and the Queen Consort will remain at Balmoral this evening and will return to London tomorrow.' He can then be heard to gulp softly.

The screen is filled with an official portrait of the young Queen Elizabeth II while the National Anthem plays.

In the pouring rain, the Union flag at Buckingham Palace is lowered to half-mast.

Later, a survey by YouGov discovers that 44 per cent of adult Britons shed a tear at the news of the Queen's death: 55 per cent of all women, and 32 per cent of all men.

The American writer A. M. Holmes, another adopted child, texts Jeanette Winterson: 'We're orphans now.'

6.40 p.m.: As his plane approaches Aberdeen airport, Prince Harry receives a text from Meghan: 'Call me the moment you get this.' He looks at the BBC website and realises he is too late.

7.07 p.m.: The prime minister, Liz Truss, dressed all in black, delivers a tribute to the late Queen from a podium outside the front door of 10 Downing Street:

> We are all devastated by the news we have just heard from Balmoral. The death of Her Majesty the Queen is a huge shock to the nation and to the world. Queen Elizabeth was the rock on which modern Britain was built. Our country has grown and flourished under her reign. Britain is the great country it is today because of her … Through thick and thin, Queen Elizabeth II provided us with the stability and strength that we needed. She was the very spirit of Great Britain – and that spirit will endure … She has been a personal inspiration to me and to many Britons … with the passing of the second Elizabethan age, we usher in a new era in the magnificent history of our great country. Exactly as Her Majesty would have wished – by saying the words: 'God save the King.'

Almost immediately, the prime minister's effort comes under attack. 'It's as if Year 8 had been asked to give a presentation on the Queen using Wikipedia,' complains one of Truss' critics.

7.52 p.m.: Prince Harry arrives at Balmoral. He is greeted by Princess Anne, who hugs him and tells him that the others have gone to Birkhall. She asks him if he wants to see Granny.

She leads him upstairs to the Queen's bedroom. He braces himself and enters. He finds the room dimly lit. 'I moved ahead uncertainly, and there she was. I stood, frozen, staring. I stared and stared. It was difficult, but I kept on, thinking how I'd regretted not seeing my mother at the end.'

He whispers to her that he hopes she is happy, that he hopes she is with Grandpa. He tells her that he is in awe of the way she carried out her duties to the last. We know this because he includes it in his memoir, *Spare*, published four months later.

8.15 p.m.: Harry has dinner with some of the other members of his family at Balmoral, though his father, stepmother and brother remain at Birkhall. Towards the end of the meal, he steels himself for the usual bagpipes, but there is nothing but an eerie silence.

The new King releases a statement.

> The death of my beloved Mother, Her Majesty the Queen, is a moment of the greatest sadness for me and all members of my family. We mourn profoundly the passing of a cherished Sovereign and a much loved Mother. I know her loss will be deeply felt throughout the country, the Realms and the Commonwealth, and by countless people around the world.

By the end of the day, the Liberal Democrats have cancelled their party conference, the trades unions have cancelled their planned walkouts for postal and rail workers, the Bank of England has postponed its decision on interest rates, the Last Night of the Proms is called off for the first time since the war and Fortnum & Mason, the Piccadilly store favoured by the Royal Family, has blacked out its windows and stopped its famous clock.

The drivers of London's black cabs gather in the Mall for an impromptu parade. 'Liz is a London girl. She's one of ours,' explains cabbie Michael Ackerman.

A diverse range of celebrities express their grief via social media. J. K. Rowling says that some might find an outpouring of British shock and grief 'quaint or odd', but 'millions felt affection and respect for the woman who uncomplainingly filled her constitutional role for 70 years. Most British people have never known another monarch, so she's been a thread winding through all our lives. She did her duty by the country right up until her dying hours, and became an enduring, positive symbol of Britain all over the world. She's earned her rest.'

'I had the honor of meeting and performing for Queen Elizabeth II on my trip to London in 1977,' tweets Dolly Parton. 'She carried herself with grace and strength her entire life. May she Rest in Peace. My thoughts are with her family at this time.'

Stephen Fry tweets: 'Oh dear. Oh my. Oh heavens. Bless my soul. Oh lor. Heck. I don't know why I'm sobbing. Silly really. Oh dear.'

Paddington Bear tweets: 'Thank you Ma'am, for everything.'

Helen Mirren, who played the title role in the film *The Queen* tweets: 'I am proud to be an Elizabethan. We mourn a woman, who, with or without the crown, was the epitome of nobility.'

Over in America, the English presenter of *The Late Late Show* James Corden wears a black suit and a black tie. He introduces that evening's show with none of his usual wisecracks. He talks about the Queen in a reverential tone, his voice close to cracking.

'Good evening. We of course heard the news today that Queen Elizabeth had passed away aged ninety-six. I, like the rest of the world, am so sad tonight, but also so thankful and grateful to the Queen for the most incredible service and leadership that she has shown during all of our lifetimes.'

He speaks of how she had reigned through fourteen presidents and fifteen prime ministers. 'We viewed her as immortal ... She was universally adored. She represented good in this world, living a life of honour, a life dedicated to service, dedicated to bettering the lives of others. It's always felt as if she was there for all of us ... She didn't need us to hear her opinions. She never gave an interview. She never posted on social media. It was never, for her, about her own PR. And maybe that's why she was as beloved and respected by a president as she was by the guy who lives down the street, and she would treat both of them equally, too. It didn't matter who you were – she was there for you.'

He continues in this vein for three and a half minutes, before ending, 'Queen Elizabeth was unique, her life's work never to be repeated. Every person in the United Kingdom and many across the globe will remember today. They'll remember where they were when they heard the news that will change our country forever. We will always celebrate her life, remember what she stood for. And we will always be thankful for her sacrifice. We'll be right back, everybody.'

And, with that, the programme cuts to an ad break.

In Washington, President Biden orders all flags on US government buildings to be flown at half-mast until her funeral. In Paris, the lights of the Eiffel Tower are dimmed. Around the world, key landmarks are illuminated with giant images of the Queen: the sails of the Sydney Opera House, the Old City wall in Jerusalem, the Brandenburg Gate in Berlin, the statue of Christ the Redeemer in Rio de Janeiro. In New York, the Empire State Building is lit up in silver and purple, and the Stock Exchange falls silent.

Sarah Kremvs, a librarian, leaves her home in Wisconsin to catch a flight to London to pay her respects. 'I had always told my employer that I would leave if the Queen passed away, so I booked my tickets and told them I would be going. Hopefully I have a job when I get back.'

Friday, 9 September 2022

After a sleepless night, Prince Harry leaves Balmoral at daybreak, having still not encountered either his father or his brother.

The newspapers cover little else. The headline of the *Daily Mail* is 'Our hearts are broken'. Its first eighty-three pages are devoted to the news. The *Guardian*, normally the least monarchist, fills its first nineteen pages with the news, and then breaks for six pages of other goings-on in the world, before resuming its Royal coverage for a further twenty-two pages. Its fourteen-page obituary of the Queen is headed, 'A life of duty and service'. It ends: 'By the end of her reign, Britain's people had vastly changed in outlook and circumstances. Despite all the monarchy's vicissitudes, however, Queen Elizabeth II, a figure from another age, who was stiff and formal and not noticeably particularly warm and empathetic, had won and retained the affection, loyalty and support of the overwhelming majority of the British public, who respected her for her diligence and sense of duty.' The prime minister's flagship energy announcement does not appear until page 84.

Statistics abound. Nine out of ten living human beings were born during the Queen's reign; she conferred 404,500 honours, sent 45,000 Christmas cards, hosted 1.5 million people at garden parties, received 3.75 million items of correspondence and was the patron of 5,999 charities, organisations and military regiments.

The crowd of mourners around Buckingham Palace has grown so large that police have instituted a one-way system.

Beneath a large love heart is the message, written in a child's hand: 'We want you back our Queen.'

The statistics keep coming. The Queen met more world leaders than anyone else in history; visited 117 different countries and travelled at least 1.3 million miles. It is fitting, then, that tributes have poured in from all around the world. France's President Macron says: 'She was one with her nation: she embodied a people, a territory, and a shared will. And stability: above the fluctuations and upheaval of politics, she represented an eternity.

'She held a special status in France and a special place in the hearts of the French people. No foreign sovereign has climbed the stairs of the Élysée Palace more often than she ... The Queen of sixteen kingdoms loved France, which loved her back. This evening, the people of the United Kingdom and their Commonwealth are mourning the Queen. The people of France join them in their grief. She who stood with the giants of the twentieth century on the path of history has now left to join them ...'

A card from the Queen is delivered to Gwendolyn Hoare at her home in Manningtree, Essex, congratulating her on her hundredth birthday.

'I send you my congratulations, and best wishes to you on such a special occasion. Elizabeth Regina,' reads the card.

During her lifetime, the Queen is estimated to have sent 307,000 hundredth-birthday messages. Gwendolyn Hoare may well be the last recipient. She has been speaking about receiving such a message 'for decades'. After the announcement of the Queen's death, she was no longer expecting one.

'It makes me quite tearful,' she says. 'I am a royalist, old-fashioned. What an honour! I very much admired the Queen and all she did. So when she went, it was a sad moment, but she didn't go before she sent me this. I wasn't sure that I would get it but I was thrilled when I did. Aren't I honoured? Aren't I lucky?'

In the House of Commons, Liz Truss describes the late Queen as 'one of the greatest leaders the world has ever known'.

Her predecessor, Boris Johnson, tells the House that a few months ago the BBC asked him to pre-record a memorial tribute to the Queen and to talk about her in the past tense. 'I am afraid I simply choked up and I couldn't go on. I am really not easily moved to tears, but I was so overcome with sadness that I had to ask them to go away.'

He continues: 'And I know that today there are countless people in this country and around the world who have experienced the same sudden excess of unexpected emotion. And I think millions of us are trying to understand why we are feeling this deep and personal and almost familial sense of loss. Perhaps it is partly that she has always been there: a changeless human reference point in British life. The person who – all the surveys say – appears most often in our dreams, so unvarying in her Pole Star radiance that we have perhaps been lulled into thinking she might in some way be eternal – but we are coming to understand in her death the full magnitude of what she did for us all.'

He dubs her Elizabeth the Great. 'And when I call her that – Elizabeth the Great – I should add one final quality: her humility. Her single-bar-electric-fire, Tupperware-using refusal to be grand, unlike us politicians with our outriders and our armour-plated convoys. I can tell you as a direct witness she drove herself in her own car, with no detectives and no bodyguard, bouncing at alarming speed over the Scottish landscape, to the total amazement of the ramblers and tourists we encountered.'

The leader of the opposition, Keir Starmer, talks of the Queen's 'special, personal relationship with us all … Covid closed the front doors of every home in the country, it made all our lives smaller and more remote … At the time we were most alone, at a time we had been driven apart, she held the nation close, in a way no one else could have done.'

At 2 p.m., King Charles III circulates among the crowd at the gates of Buckingham Palace. There are cries of 'God Save the King!' One member of the public, Vicky Binley, from Rutland, kisses his hand and says 'Thank you.' King Charles replies: 'I've been dreading this day. I've been dreading this.'

At his local church, the 73-year-old Michael Fagan, who entered the Queen's bedroom, uninvited, forty years ago, lights a candle in her memory.

Johnny Rotten, now known as John Lydon, tweets, 'Rest in Peace Queen Elizabeth II. Send her victorious.' He accompanies his message with the Silver Jubilee portrait of the Queen; this time, it is free of safety pins or graffiti.

Other former rock 'n' roll rebels also pay tribute. 'For my whole life Her Majesty, Queen Elizabeth II has always been there,' tweets Mick Jagger. 'In my childhood I can recall watching her wedding highlights on TV. I remember her as a beautiful young lady, to the much beloved grandmother of the nation. My deepest sympathies are with the Royal family.'

Heavy-metal stars pay their respects. 'Iron Maiden are saddened to learn of the passing of Her Majesty, Queen Elizabeth II – a British institution and global inspiration for more than 70 years. God Bless you Ma'am.'

'I mourn with my country the passing of our greatest Queen,' tweets Ozzy Osbourne of Black Sabbath. 'With a heavy heart I say it is devastating the thought of England without Queen Elizabeth II.'

Elton John posts: 'Along with the rest of the nation, I am deeply saddened to hear the news of Her Majesty Queen Elizabeth's passing. She was an inspiring presence to be around and led the country through some of our greatest and darkest moments with grace, decency and a genuine caring warmth. Queen Elizabeth has been a huge part of my life from childhood to this day, and I will miss her dearly.'

Paul McCartney tweets: 'God bless Queen Elizabeth II. May she rest in peace. Long live The King.'

Liam Gallagher, former leader singer with Oasis, tweets a single word: 'Gutted.'

The registrar at the Royal College of Psychiatrists, Dr Trudi Seneviratne, notes that people might 'feel shocked, anxious, or fearful about changes they don't feel prepared for, or experience deep feelings of loss and sadness'.

Linda Magistris, chief executive of the Good Grief Trust, says that her organisation has been 'inundated' with messages 'from people who are really surprised by the way they feel … It has really affected people quite profoundly across all ages, really all generations.'

A dissenting note to this great outpouring of grief is struck by an article in the *New York Times* by Maya Jasanoff, Coolidge professor of history at Harvard University. Under the heading 'Mourn the Queen, not her Empire', Jasanoff argues that 'The Queen helped obscure a bloody history of decolonisation whose proportions and legacies have yet to be adequately acknowledged. We should not romanticise her era.'

At Balmoral, a footman delivers the Queen's red box, full of official documents, to Sir Edward Young, who unlocks it. Inside, he finds a sealed letter to her eldest son and a private letter to himself. Sensing her destiny, the Queen had planned ahead. The box also contains a list of candidates to fill the six vacancies for the twenty-four holders of the Order of Merit. At work to the end, the Queen had been through the notes and ticked her choices.

At 6 p.m., King Charles III addresses the nation on television. Tears are visible in his eyes.

'I speak to you today with feelings of profound sorrow. Throughout her life, Her Majesty The Queen – my beloved Mother – was an inspiration and example to me and to all my family, and we owe her the most heartfelt debt any family can owe to their mother; for her love, affection, guidance, understanding and example.

'Queen Elizabeth's was a life well lived; a promise with destiny kept and she is mourned most deeply in her passing …

'In 1947, on her twenty-first birthday, she pledged in a broadcast from Cape Town to the Commonwealth to devote her life, whether it be short or long, to the service of her peoples. That was more than a promise: it was a profound personal commitment which defined her whole life. She made sacrifices for duty. Her dedication and devotion as Sovereign never wavered, through times of change and progress, through times of joy and celebration, and through times of sadness and loss.

'… The affection, admiration and respect she inspired became the hallmark of her reign. And, as every member of my family can testify, she combined these qualities with warmth, humour and an unerring ability always to see the best in people. I pay tribute to my Mother's memory and I honour her life of service. I know that her death brings great sadness to so many of you and I share that sense of loss, beyond measure, with you all.

'… As The Queen herself did with such unswerving devotion, I too now solemnly pledge myself, throughout the remaining time God grants me, to uphold the constitutional principles at the heart of our nation …

'In a little over a week's time we will come together as a nation, as a Commonwealth and indeed a global community, to lay my beloved mother to rest. In our sorrow, let us remember and draw strength from the light of her example. On behalf of all my family, I can only offer the most sincere and heartfelt thanks for your condolences and support. They mean more to me than I can ever possibly express. And to my darling Mama, as you begin your last great journey to join my dear late Papa, I want simply to say this: thank you.

'Thank you for your love and devotion to our family and to the family of nations you have served so diligently all these years. May "flights of Angels sing thee to thy rest".'

Saturday, 10 September 2022

Among the mass of floral tributes left in Green Park and St James's Park hundreds of Paddington Bear cuddly toys are visible, as well as teapots and marmalade sandwiches. Walking through Green Park, Charles Moore, former editor of the *Daily Telegraph*, imagines what it would be like to be a visitor who has not heard the news. 'Why, I might have asked myself, is everyone so upset about the death of a small bear with a red hat?'

Sunday, 11 September 2022

The Queen's coffin is borne away from Balmoral on the shoulders of six gamekeepers. This oak coffin was constructed over thirty years ago;

it is lined with lead, and has special fittings on its surface to allow pieces from the Crown jewels to be placed upon it. While a bagpipe plays, the Queen's staff weep as they line up to honour her.

The hearse sets off on its route to Edinburgh, followed by Princess Anne and her husband in the State Bentley. For the entire six-hour journey, people line the roads, sometimes ten deep. Overhead cameras follow their progress through the glens, towns and villages of Scotland. Princess Anne is moved by the way farmers have cleaned their tractors before lining them up along the route, and have plaited their ponies' manes.

Six hours later, the hearse arrives in the Scottish capital. Driving along Edinburgh's Royal Mile it comes to a halt at St Giles' Cathedral, ready for tomorrow's service of thanksgiving. The hundreds who line the Royal Mile include a scattering of republicans. A 22-year-old protester holds up a sign that says 'Fuck imperialism, abolish the monarchy'. The police charge her with a breach of the peace.

Memories of the late Queen abound. In a letter to *The Times*, Mike Hattersley from Milnthorpe in Cumbria recalls the day in 1954 when his mother took him, aged seven, and his brother, aged nine, to witness the Queen's arrival at Bradford Town Hall. They had been too small to spot more than the passing roof of her Rolls-Royce and burst into tears. Their mother then took them to see the Queen departing from Manningham station, but once again they couldn't get anywhere near, so shed more tears. Finally, she rushed them along a street or two and down an alley, helping them up a wall and telling them to watch and wait.

'After the music and cheering at the station died down, half a mile to our right the royal train drew towards us. Behind a glass carriage door stood our Queen and Prince Philip. They had thrown off their coats, and stood together looking out, with their arms round each other. No doubt they were glad their official duties were over, but when they saw two little boys on the wall they came alive, really waving – just for us. That wasn't duty, it was love.'

* * *

Recalling the Queen's encounter with Paddington Bear, just three months ago, the co-writer of that little film, Frank Cottrell-Boyce, senses something valedictory in their tea together: 'A woman waving a happy goodbye to her grandchildren and great-grandchildren, an image of love and a happy death.'

Her death will, he thinks, change the nature of our subconscious. '... It used to be said that millions of people had dreams in which they had tea with the Queen. Now even our dream life is going to have to change.'

The souvenir market is enjoying a boom. On eBay a single teabag is described as 'extremely rare ... It was used by Queen Elizabeth II Regina Britannia and smuggled out of Windsor Castle by the special exterminator who was called in to help her majesty cope with the great London roach infestations of the 1990s.' This rare teabag comes with a certificate of authenticity issued by the Institute of Excellence in Certificates of Authenticity, saying it 'has determined beyond any doubt that the following statements are absolutely true: This is a teabag.'

It sells for $12,000.

Monday, 12 September 2022

3.20 p.m.: The Queen's coffin, draped in the Royal Standard of Scotland and a wreath of roses, white heather and wild flowers, is borne into St Giles' Cathedral in Edinburgh by eight soldiers of the Royal Regiment of Scotland. Walking behind the coffin, Prince Andrew is heckled by a young man in the crowd, 'Andrew!' he screams. 'You're a sick old man!' The police immediately arrest him and charge him with breaching the peace, leading to protests that the right to freedom of speech is being infringed.

The Queen's coffin is laid on the wooden catafalque in the centre of the nave; the 500-year-old Crown of Scotland is placed upon it.

7.45 p.m.: For ten minutes, the late Queen's four children stand in silent vigil around her coffin.

Even at this time of grief, correct dress remains paramount. 'The

Duke of York's humiliation at being stripped of his royal duties was laid bare yesterday when he was the only one of the Queen's children not dressed in military uniform as they followed her coffin,' reports *The Times*. 'The Falklands war veteran has been barred from wearing his navy uniform because he was in effect sacked as a "working" member of the royal family after he was disgraced over his relationship with the paedophile financier Jeffrey Epstein ... The ruling is believed to have been imposed by the King, who is determined that Andrew be not allowed to return as a working royal.'

At the same time, Prince Harry has reportedly been told not to wear his military honours at any ceremonial events, as he is no longer a working member of the Royal Family.

Simon Armitage, the Queen's seventh Poet Laureate, releases an eighteen-line acrostic, 'Floral Tribute', in which the first letters of each line combine to spell her name – 'ELIZABETH' – twice over. 'The country loaded its whole self into your slender hands / Hands that can rest, now, relieved of a century's weight,' read the last two lines of the first verse.

Tuesday, 13 September 2022

7 p.m.: The Queen's coffin arrives at RAF Northolt in a vast RAF C-17 Globemaster, accompanied by Princess Anne. Nearly six million people attempt to follow its path on the internet, causing the aircraft-tracking website Flightradar24 to crash.

The coffin is loaded into a new state hearse. Designed in consultation with the Queen, it sports large windows and a glass roof: in death, as in life, Her Majesty's visibility is paramount. As darkness falls, her coffin is lit by bulbs inside the hearse. For most of the fifteen-mile journey to Buckingham Palace, silent crowds stand in the rain by the side of the road.

At 8 p.m., the hearse passes Lancaster Gate at Hyde Park to cheers and applause. Among those in the crowd is Sarah Kremvs, the errant librarian from Wisconsin.

Sheltering beneath an umbrella outside Buckingham Palace, Gyles Brandreth tells the Queen's goddaughter, India Hicks, how strange it is that such a naturally shy person had, by a quirk of fate, to live her life in public. 'Even now, when she is dead.'

Some choose to honour the memory of the Queen in unconventional ways. At a salon in High Wycombe, Graham Wilson, a 54-year-old construction worker, spends £1,400 on having his left thigh tattooed with two overlapping images of the Queen, one at her Coronation and the other in old age. 'She's iconic and I just wanted to pay homage to her,' he explains. 'When I was watching the news I just knew suddenly it was what I wanted to do. Beth, the tattooist, had a cancellation so it was meant to be.'

Graham's wife Michelle is delighted by the result. 'It's outstanding work. This is going to be his showpiece tattoo. The Queen deserves all the credit she's getting and so much more. She was the rock of Britain. We could spend a fortune on a picture but what are the odds of it being lost or broken? This will be with him all the time and wherever he goes.'

Lady Antonia Fraser, a lifelong monarchist, is inspired to mark the Queen's passing by penning a poem, 'The Corgi's Lament'. 'When a gentle slap / Discouraged my yap / I knew it was her,' says her corgi narrator, who adds that he'll miss her shoes 'Shining and strong / Her dogs, her dears / She calmed our fears / We knew from those shoes / That we can't bear to lose / *She was our Queen.*'

Up and down the country, the skies are abundant with celestial homages.

'Multiple rainbows seemed to spontaneously appear in the skies over the United Kingdom,' reports *Newsweek*.

In the *Daily Telegraph*, Bryony Gordon notes that 'A lone seagull let out a cry as it glided past the Royal Standard, flying at half mast.' Quentin Letts of *The Times* reports that 'At Windsor, the skies opened. The heavens themselves were weeping.'

In Telford, reports the *Independent*, 'A golden cloud in the shape of the Queen's head was spotted in the sky just moments after her death was announced. British mother Leanne Bethell captured photos of the striking formation above the A4169 on Thursday.'

The sea, too, comes alive with tributes.

The *Daily Mail* reports that 'An incredible photograph of a 150-foot wave during a storm in Sunderland shows a remarkable resemblance to the late Queen Elizabeth II.'

An amateur photographer, Ian Sproat, takes a shot of the vast wave as it crashes against the Roker Pier and Lighthouse. 'The shape of the wave forms the silhouette of Her Majesty's face and part of her crown,' reports the *Sun* excitedly. The electrician tells the newspaper: 'I was absolutely gobsmacked when I saw the photo.' For the *Sun*, the coincidence is 'made even more poignant by her daughter Princess Anne's lifelong love of lighthouses'.

Others catch sight of a cloud over Wembley that looks a bit like the young Princess Elizabeth riding her horse. 'Eki Eguae, 37, spotted the cloud on his way back from the shops near his home,' reports the *Daily Mail*.

Some days later, a hummingbird flies into Prince Harry's home in Santa Barbara, and won't leave. A friend tells the Prince that it could well be a sign. Harry reflects that some cultures see hummingbirds as spirits. 'Aztecs call them reincarnated warriors ... So, naturally, when this hummingbird arrived and swooped around our kitchen, and flitted through the sacred airspace we called Lili Land, where we've set the baby's playpen with all her toys and stuffed animals, I thought hopefully, greedily, foolishly: Is our house a detour – or a destination?'

The Prince scoops the hummingbird from the ceiling with his son Archie's fishing net and carries it outside. 'With cupped palms I set the hummingbird gently on a wall in the sun. *Goodbye, my friend.*' But it just remains there, motionless. 'Come on, come on. You're free. *Fly away.* And then, against all odds, and all expectations, that wonderful, magical little creature bestirred itself, and did just that.'

* * *

All Premier League and English Football League games are postponed, and so too all rugby, boxing, cycling, golf and horse-racing events.

At a primary school in West London, a class of six-year-olds is informed that Guinea Pig Awareness Week has been postponed as a mark of respect to HM the Queen.

Organisations react to the news of the Queen's death in different ways. The phrase 'mark of respect' becomes hard to avoid. Respect is marked in all sorts of unexpected ways. The supermarket chain Morrisons turns down the volume of the beeps from its tills. Sadly, this confuses some shoppers, who think that the tills have broken. 'I was standing in the queue for self-service for what felt like an eternity as everyone in front of me struggled,' complains one irate shopper. '… It wasn't until it was my turn that I found out they had turned off the beep. One of the assistants came over so I said, "I think people are struggling as the beep is turned off." She said, "Did you not know we are in a period of national mourning? We have turned off all beeps as a sign of respect," as if I was meant to know this.'

Norwich Council puts a notice on a bike rack saying it is closed for the official period of mourning.

'Due to the passing of Her Majesty Queen Elizabeth II,' reads a sign on the door of the Duke of York pub in York, 'in a mark of respect, we will not be operating Happy Hour.'

The Sheffield & District Fair Play League issues a strong statement. 'It has been brought to our attention that, despite our clearly informing all clubs that football matches this weekend should be cancelled as a mark of respect for the passing of Her Majesty the Queen, two teams within our League have chosen to play a friendly match anyway. The SDFPL Management Team would like to put on record that we absolutely do not condone this disrespectful and despicable behaviour.'

* * *

On Twitter, Nintendo announces that 'As a mark of respect during this period of national mourning, we will not livestream tomorrow's Nintendo Direct.'

Most of the big chain stores – Sainsbury's, Tesco, Ikea, Poundland, W. H. Smith – will be closing for the day of the funeral.

Center Parcs decide to close for twenty-four hours from 10 a.m. 'as a mark of respect'. When holidaying families complain at being turfed out for a night, the company reverses its decision, but insists that many of its facilities must remain closed.

'New episodes of Archetypes will be paused during the official mourning period for Her Majesty The Queen Elizabeth II,' comes the message on the Spotify page for the Duchess of Sussex's *Archetypes* podcast. However, the first three episodes, featuring interviews with tennis player Serena Williams, singer Mariah Carey and actress Mindy Kaling will remain available.

British Cycling, the sport's national governing body, issues a statement recommending that cyclists dismount from their bikes during the funeral 'as a mark of respect'.

The cast and crew of the Netflix drama series *The Crown* are in Barcelona, which has been transformed into Paris, with fake French road signs and shop fronts. The news of the death of the Queen reaches them just as they are preparing to film the death of Princess Diana. Filming is to be suspended 'as a mark of respect'.

Others take the opportunity to combine grieving with marketing.

A round-robin email from Ilkley Brewery in Yorkshire reads: 'To mark the passing of Queen Elizabeth II, and in recognition of her 70 years of service, we're discounting bottles from our seasonal and specials range by 30% so that they are priced at 70% of their normal price. Offer runs until midnight on the day of the funeral. Shop now using code Queen70.'

The Cornwall Hamper Store announces: 'All of our thoughts the last few days have been with Her Majesty the Queen, and the Royal family. So in commemoration of her Majesty Queen Elizabeth, we thought it would only be right to bring back The Cornish Queen Tea & The Royal Seal Box. These will only be available for a limited amount of time.' Their website offers two hampers, one for £22.99 and the other, 'embossed with the Royal Seal of Approval', for £29.99.

On WhatsApp, drug dealers mark the Queen's passing in their own special way. 'Are you feeling upset or feeling down with the sad news about the Queen's death? Then don't hesitate to contact me, I'm about till 1am!' writes one dealer, while another makes a generous offer: 'In Tribute To The Queen Who Was 96 Years Old At Her Time Of Passing, I Will Reduce The Price Of IG Bolivian Flake to £96 Tomorrow And Saturday Guys!'

Meanwhile, a financial-planning firm, Rockwealth, posts this message: 'Elizabeth II is the only head of state most of us have known. It's perfectly natural that her passing should cause us to feel so sad, and to reflect on our own lives and, of course, our own mortality. But perhaps we should go further and say, "Why not use this time of sadness as an opportunity to define our life's purpose?" For us, as a financial planning firm, this is undoubtedly the most important question of all.'

Songs about the late monarch enjoy a remarkable rise in popularity. In America, Billboard reports that sales of the Smiths' 1986 song 'The Queen is Dead' rose 1,687 per cent from 6,000 to 114,000, and the Sex Pistols' 'God Save the Queen' went up 650 per cent from 11,000 to 81,000.

The former Sex Pistol John Lydon criticises members of his old band for trying to cash in on the Queen's death. 'In John's view, the timing for endorsing any Sex Pistols requests for commercial gain in connection with "God Save the Queen" in particular is distasteful and disrespectful to the Queen and her family at this moment in time,' tweets his fastidious spokesperson.

104

On Wednesday, 14 September, the Queen's coffin, draped in the Royal Standard, is carried on a gun carriage pulled by horses from the King's Troop Royal Horse Artillery from Buckingham Palace to Westminster Hall. On top of the coffin sits the Imperial State Crown – the same crown she wore for the first time during the procession back to the Palace after her Coronation. Marching in front of the coffin, the bands of the Scots Guards and Grenadier Guards play Beethoven's funeral marches. The Queen's children and grandchildren follow on foot. Tens of thousands of people line the route, standing in silence as they hear the sound of the marching drums drawing closer and closer. As the procession passes by, many hold their mobile phones high in the air, straining to capture this moment in history.

The coffin is carried into Westminster Hall. It is placed on the catafalque in the centre, a towering candle at each corner while the choir sings Psalm 139.

A short service is led by the archbishop of Canterbury. Once it is over, the first members of the public are admitted. Silence rules. The coffin itself is very small, but dominant. The mourners processing past it are strikingly various, defying any sociological categorisation into gender, class, age or ethnicity. Some stop briefly to salute or bow or curtsy. Others genuflect or make the sign of the cross. They are united in dignity, and perhaps also in an intangible sense of the profundity of the occasion. Standing alone in front of the coffin, each one of them seems to be confronting not just the death of a monarch but death itself.

105

By Saturday, the queue of mourners stretches five miles. Their expected wait is twenty-four hours. Among those queuing is 85-year-old Norman Allen, whom we last encountered as a 15-year-old, struggling to sell damp programmes at the Queen's Coronation.

It's something of a paradox. Although the late Queen took part in any number of activities during her long and varied life, she never queued. Nevertheless, it seems a fitting expression of respect: queuing has long been a passion of the British. 'An Englishman, even if he is alone, forms an orderly queue of one,' noted the Hungarian humorist George Mikes, shortly after arriving in London in 1938. The queue of mourners soon becomes a centre of attention: it has its own Twitter feed, Instagram account and YouTube channel. 'You British are world expert queuers,' says Francisco Pinto, a gardener from Chile, who has himself joined the queue.

After queueing for fifty-three hours, ever since 11.30 a.m. on Monday, Vanessa Nanthakumarian is the first member of the public to be admitted to Westminster Hall.

'It was an emotional experience. I was fighting back tears as I approached the coffin and I managed to dignify myself. I wanted to do something so I said prayers for the Queen, thanked her for her great service and wished her peace and rest.'

Three behind her is Delroy Morrison, a carpenter from Wembley. 'I paused for a moment, doffed my hat to my Queen and said, "Thank you, you have done a good job right up to the very end."'

Many are in tears. Their thoughts about the Queen mix with memories of others they have lost. Grace Gothard from Mitcham in Surrey has also been queueing since Monday morning. 'It reminded me of my own mother. May the Queen rest in peace.'

Ann Corrigan from Swindon says, 'I think everyone felt like she was part of your family. I liked the way she united the country. It didn't matter about your party politics or religion, she respected and cared for us all.'

Tenth in line is Monica Farag, a woman in her sixties. As she leaves the Hall, a white feather floats to the ground in front of her. 'As I got out there, the bird just dropped this feather for me. It is from the Queen.'

Nigel O'Leary, aged 47, has medals pinned to his coat. 'Bosnia, Kosovo, Iraq and two tours of Afghanistan. I wanted to pay my respects to the Queen. She's been my boss for thirty-odd years.'

The queue is so remarkable that it has attracted 'crowd psychologists' from universities all over the country: St Andrews, Dundee, Edinburgh, Keele and Sussex. Professor Stephen Reicher from the school of psychology and neuroscience at the University of St Andrews says that the ordeal is essential to the mourning. 'Hardship is part of why they take part, to demonstrate commitment. It's precisely because it is hard that it is meaningful. That sense of "The Queen showed service for seventy years, I can show commitment for seven hours."' He is struck by the sense of solidarity among those queueing. 'When you have a shared identity, strangers cease to be "other" and become part of your extended self. You see more intimacy, increased co-operation and trust and respect.'

Some of the crowd are deeply Royalist, he says, while for others the death of the Queen mirrors a loss in their own family: they are mourning 'through the Queen rather than for the Queen'. Many want to be part of history. 'It confers a little bit of immortality. Families across the generations can say: "We were there."' He finds studying mourners much easier than studying rioters. 'One problem when studying a riot is it's hard to ask people to "put that down for a moment so I can interview you".'

106

Three days after the death of the Queen, Prince Harry issues a personal statement on Archewell, 'the official website of the Duke and Duchess of Sussex':

> Granny, while this final parting brings us great sadness, I am forever grateful for all of our first meetings – from my earliest childhood memories with you, to meeting you for the first time as my Commander-in-Chief, to the first moment you met my darling wife and hugged your beloved great-grandchildren.

On the eve of the Queen's funeral, Prince Andrew issues his own tribute, which is circulated by his public relations adviser:

Dear Mummy, Mother, Your Majesty, three in one,
Your Majesty, it has been an honour and privilege to serve you.

Mother of the nation, your devotion and personal service to our nation is unique and singular; your people show their love and respect in so many different ways and I know you are looking on, honouring their respect.

Mummy, your love for a son, your compassion, your care, your confidence I will treasure forever. I have found your knowledge and wisdom infinite, with no boundary or containment. I will miss your thoughts, advice and humour.

As our book of experience closes, another opens, and I will forever hold you close to my heart with my deepest love and gratitude and I will tread gladly into the next with you as my guide. God save the King.

Alongside this curious eulogy, Prince Andrew issues a photograph taken by Cecil Beaton in 1960. It shows the Queen holding him as a baby, her cheek resting on his innocent little head.

107

There has been considerable jostling for seats in Westminster Abbey. For some, an invitation is a status symbol. When Sir Gavin Williamson MP, PC, a recent secretary of state for education, is excluded, he grows embittered. He texts the government chief whip, Wendy Morton: 'Think very poor how PC's who aren't favoured have been excluded from the funeral. Very poor and sends a very clear message.' Subsequent angry texts pour out of his phone like acid. 'It is very clear how you are going to treat a number of us which is very stupid and you are showing fuck all interest in pulling things together ...' he writes again to Morton. 'Also this shows exactly how you have rigged it is is [sic] disgusting you are using her death to punish people who are just supportive, absolutely disgusting ... let's see how many more times you fuck us all over. There is a price for everything.'*

The state funeral is watched on television by 37.5 million people in the UK and over 4 billion elsewhere, or roughly half the people on the planet. This sets a new world record. Among the 2,000 mourners packed into the Abbey are 200 heads of state, foreign royals and overseas dignitaries, among them the president of the USA, the prime ministers of Canada and Australia, the president of France, the president of Germany, the president of Kenya and the president of South Korea, as well as the Emperor and Empress of Japan, and the Kings of

---

* As it turned out, the price was Williamson's job: two months later, after these texts were made public, he was obliged to resign from the Cabinet, which he had only recently rejoined.

Sweden, Jordan, Bhutan, Belgium, Norway, Spain, the Netherlands and Denmark. It is the country's largest gathering of foreign dignitaries since the funeral of Sir Winston Churchill in 1965.

According to someone in the Foreign Office, organising the seating plan has been 'a complete nightmare': the fifty-six countries of the Commonwealth have to be given precedence, and various leaders, such as the president of Israel and the prime minister of Palestine, need to be kept apart, as do the current King of Spain, Felipe VI, and his father, Juan Carlos, the former King.

The Abbey's tenor bell tolls ninety-six times, one for each year of the Queen's life.

The coffin is carried on the state gun carriage of the Royal Navy, the same carriage used at the funeral of Queen Victoria and at the funerals of every monarch since. On top of the coffin rests a wreath of pink and yellow and deep burgundy flowers picked from Buckingham Palace, Clarence House and Highgrove. A sprig of myrtle – ancient symbol of a happy marriage – comes from a plant grown from a sprig in Princess Elizabeth's wedding bouquet seventy-five years ago.

'She was joyful,' says the archbishop of Canterbury, 'present to so many, touching a multitude of lives.' He recalls the Queen's declaration on her twenty-first birthday to dedicate her whole life to service. 'Rarely has such a promise been so well kept. Few leaders received the outpouring of love we have seen.'

The Queen chose the hymns herself: 'The Day Thou Gavest, Lord, Is Ended', 'The Lord Is My Shepherd, I Shall Not Want' (which had also been sung at her wedding) and 'Love Divine, All Loves Excelling'. The liturgy comes from the Book of Common Prayer. The lessons are from the New Testament: 1 Corinthians ('Now is Christ risen from the dead') and John 14 ('Let not your heart be troubled').

The service ends with the Last Post sounded by the state trumpeters of the Household Cavalry, followed by two minutes' silence. Outside, the crowds, watching the service on giant screens, fall so silent that the caw of a crow can be heard overhead. Then, inside the Abbey, the sovereign's piper plays a traditional lament. As the lament nears its final bars, he turns and walks away, the sound of his pipes fading into the distance.

The coffin is raised onto the state gun carriage. The sunlight catches the jewels of the Imperial State Crown sitting on top of it.

'Funeral procession, by the centre, slow march!' orders the garrison sergeant major. By the end of the day, an estimated one million people will have seen the Queen's coffin pass.

The procession to Wellington Arch is led by Canadian Mounties, followed by representatives of the George Cross foundations from Malta, the Royal Ulster Constabulary and the National Health Service, among them May Parsons, who administered the very first Covid-19 vaccine in 2020. More than 3,000 military are taking part, their steps scored by the band of the Household Cavalry.

A total of 142 ratings and six officers of the Royal Navy are involved in pulling the state gun carriage or marching behind it.

The Queen's coffin travels past places familiar from her annual schedule: the Cenotaph, where she would lay a wreath each November; Horse Guards Parade, where she would attend Trooping the Colour each June.

At Buckingham Palace, the staff line up outside to bid her farewell.

Tens of thousands of mourners, many of whom have camped out to secure their places, know that the procession is approaching when they hear the sound of the marching drums drawing closer and closer.

At Wellington Arch, eight young pallbearers raise the coffin and place it in the hearse, ready for the journey to Windsor.

The hearse arrives in Windsor Great Park strewn with roses, sunflowers and carnations thrown by mourners lining the route from London. As it progresses slowly up the Long Walk, the Band of the Grenadier Guards plays Beethoven's funeral marches, alternating with the Massed Pipes and Drums playing a selection of pieces, including 'The Skye Boat Song'.

'I was holding it back and gulping,' Teresa Purchase, aged 67, tells a reporter from *The Times*. 'Seeing all the horses come through, and then all the regiments and to see the hearse, that gets to you. I was once a waitress at a dinner the Queen was attending. She was so human, she is your monarch but she is so human as well. It's that human side of her, she was just lovely.'

Terry Pendry, the Queen's head groom, stands on the roadside of the Long Walk holding the Queen's black Fell pony, Emma, one of the Queen's headscarves draped over her saddle. As the Queen's coffin comes into view, Emma is seen to lift her foot. Some think they see Emma bowing slightly as the hearse passes.

At Windsor Castle, the Royal Family process once more behind the hearse. The Queen's two corgis, Muick and Sandy, look on.

In St George's Chapel, the choir sings Psalm 121 while pallbearers from the Grenadier Guards carry the coffin up the nave. It is then laid on a catafalque covered in purple velvet in the quire where King Charles I and King Henry VIII are buried.

After the Russian Orthodox hymn 'Kontakion of the Departed', a reading from Revelation, and more music and prayers, all but one chosen by the Queen, the Crown Jeweller, Bargemaster and Sergeant at Arms remove the instruments of state the Queen received at her Coronation and place them on the altar.

The King himself places the camp colour of the Queen's Company, 1st Battalion Grenadier Guards, on the coffin. In a dramatic moment, the Queen's eighth Lord Chamberlain – Lord Parker of Minsmere, a former head of MI5 – breaks his wand of office to mark his duty's end. The two broken halves are placed on the coffin, to be buried with her. As she witnesses the Sceptre, Orb and Imperial State Crown being removed from the top of the coffin, Princess Anne feels an unexpected emotion: 'I rather weirdly felt a sense of relief – that somehow it's finished.'

The dean of Windsor says, 'Go forth upon thy journey from this world, O Christian soul,' and the Queen's coffin begins its slow, discreet descent into the Royal Vault. The time is 4.50 p.m.

The service closes with the Garter King of Arms reading out the long list of the Queen's British titles:

Thus it hath pleased Almighty God to take out of this transitory life unto His Divine Mercy the late Most High, Most Mighty, and Most Excellent Monarch, Elizabeth the Second, by the Grace of God of the United Kingdom of Great Britain and Northern Ireland and of Her other Realms and Territories Queen, Head of the Commonwealth, Defender of the Faith and Sovereign of the Most Noble Order of the Garter.

Pipe Major James Banks draws a mournful lament from his bagpipes, and walks out of the chapel and towards the Deanery, the sound fading as he goes.

Two and a half hours later, at 7.30 p.m., the Queen's coffin is retrieved from the vault, together with the coffin of Prince Philip, and they are both moved to a memorial side-chapel. There they will rest together, alongside the Queen's parents, King George VI and the Queen Mother, and the ashes of her younger sister, Princess Margaret, whose body was cremated twenty years ago, without ceremony, at the Slough crematorium, three and half miles away.

108

In America, the satirical online newspaper *The Onion* steadfastly refuses to be caught in the wave of mass emotion:

Following Queen Elizabeth II's funeral and her people's farewell to their longest-serving monarch, sources confirmed Monday that England had begun exiting its somber mourning period in order to resume its regular joyless normalcy. When Elizabeth passed on Sept. 8, English citizens reportedly paused their dismal everyday lives and entered a gloomy grieving period from which they were only now starting to emerge, becoming dour and wretched once again. According to reports, the melancholic mood brought on by the monarch's death had begun to lift, and a new period of ordinary melancholy had descended on the country's 56 million people as they went about their colourless existence with the same sadness they'd always known and felt deep in their bones. Having shed their funereal black clothing and donned once more their traditional dreary wardrobes, residents told reporters they were finally moving past the grim, cheerless conversations about what the queen had meant to England and were back to discussing their customary topics of dispiriting tedium. The English vowed to … return to the generally demoralizing experience of living in a country racked by constant cold and rain. Members of the British media announced they would be concluding their deeply stupid coverage of the queen's passing and returning to their regularly scheduled deeply stupid programming.

109

What became of those two remaining corgis, Muick* and Sandy?

The Duke and Duchess of York took them in. In the spring of the following year, the Duchess appeared on many media outlets, promoting her second romantic novel for Mills and Boon, *A Most Intriguing Lady*.

'The corgis are very nice and very polite and well trained,' she told *Hello!* magazine on 5 March. 'I am their favourite but everybody always says it's just because I feed them gravy bones. I love everything about them and I spoil them the most.'

Perhaps sensing that more people wanted to know about the Queen's dogs than about her new book, she multiplied her references to Muick and Sandy with each successive interview.

On BBC's *The One Show* on 27 March 2023, she told the presenters that the corgis acted as a reminder of the 'values' dear to the late Queen.

'One thing I really love when I'm with them actually, because I really think about HM and I just really think about the value system that she supported in this country, and I remember she used to say, "Sarah, there needs to be more kindness in the world, which would disarm malice." We should stop to remember those words with respect and affection for a great leader, who has now passed it to another great leader in her son.'

Many found it hard to imagine the Queen speaking these empty truisms, even to someone as receptive to them as her former daughter-

---

* Pronounced Mick, since you asked.

in-law. But dogs and the dead have this in common: they are powerless to correct those who affect to speak on their behalf.

The Duchess's rambling mix of doggy talk and baby talk continued apace. 'When I look at them, I think "yes, come on". And I think – so important for the whole country to unite and uphold the values that for seventy-two years the monarch gave us all, really … Because they're national treasures I'm terrified when they go out running. They chase everything. Straight into trees, bang! Like that! I go "no, no, no, the nation loves you, stop, stop, stop chasing the squirrels".'

For each new interview, she managed to conjure up fresh revelations about Sandy and Muick. To Rylan Clark on BBC Radio 2 on 2 April, she 'opened up' about them, reporting that, after a period of mourning, they were doing 'really well. They're great, they're really happy, and their tails have gone up now, so I think they are over their grief.' Two days later, to the website Royal Central, she added that the corgis were 'so sweet. I think they have been trained by her to be so gentle. When you take a little digestive biscuit and break it like she used to with her little hands … she must have put a little biccie in front of them, and they gently take it.'

On the TV programme *Loose Women* on 5 April, she returned once more to the corgis, and with yet another fresh detail. 'I went to a dog whisperer and said, "Now tell me about grief." And he said, "Just at night just make sure they have their own space." Yeah, so I do. Because I think they were grieving … their little tails went down. And I wanted them to have waggy tails.'

And so it continued. In the *Sunday Times* on 8 April, she said that 'the corgis can sense the late Queen's presence at Royal Lodge … Her dogs, Muick and Sandy, whom we've adopted, often do bark at nothing, which makes me think that Queen Elizabeth is passing by and laughing. I'm not being weird.'

110

Among those who also died in 2022 were Pope Benedict XVI, Olivia Newton-John, Sidney Poitier, Angela Lansbury, Jerry Lee Lewis, Robbie Coltrane, Mikhail Gorbachev, Pele, Vivienne Westwood, Lester Piggott, Jean-Luc Godard and Hilary Mantel. Of these, only two – Jerry Lee Lewis and Jean-Luc Godard – had never met the Queen.

111

Back in the spring of 1977, after morning service in the church at Badminton, the Queen mentioned to Alvilde Lees-Milne that she planned to open Sandringham to the public in the summer: 'Mummy is simply furious with me for opening it.' Alvilde advised her to cover any fabrics with polythene. 'Visitors touch everything.'

By 2023, Sandringham is as much a tourist destination as Legoland or Chessington World of Adventures. 'With a variety of things to see and do throughout the year, Sandringham offers opportunities to relax and unwind and give a fascinating insight into the heritage of The Royal Family,' reads the message of welcome on its website. 'We have a variety of facilities and a prestigious shop at Sandringham, with seasonal food and Sandringham-inspired gifts. Whether you're rounding off a family day, looking for a souvenir, or enjoying a holiday in the area, choose from a range of options in our restaurant, cafés and shop.'

Wisely, the website avoids mentioning James Pope-Hennessy's assessment of Sandringham after he visited it in 1956:

It is a preposterous, long, brick-and-stone building ... tremendously vulgar and emphatically, almost defiantly hideous and gloomy ... To sum up: this is a hideous house with a horrible atmosphere in parts, in others no atmosphere at all. It was like a visit to the morgue; and everywhere were their faces, painted, drawn or photographed: few pictures not directly relating to themselves.

No mention, either, of the little church at Sandringham, which, plastered with plaques and memorials to the Royal Family, he considered a monument to their self-absorption:

> not, as the books say, like an ordinary country church in the least, but more like the private chapel of a family of ailing megalomaniacs: the shrine of a clique.

At lunchtime on a sunny Friday in October, I join a group of ten outside the Sandringham Visitor Centre, ready to embark on 'A Very Special Exclusive Access Tour', having paid my £85 in advance.

> Begin the tour aboard one of our electric buggies taking in key areas and giving insight into the 60 acre Gardens, before heading further to view the private Walled Garden, not normally open to visitors.
>
> Enjoy all eight downstairs rooms in the House used by the Royal Family at Christmas, encounter the beautiful collections of porcelain, jade, rose quartz, silver Russian gilt and bronzes, family portraits and photographs and Victorian and Edwardian decor that was the epitome of style in 1870.

Our guide asks us where we are all from. Two are from Lincoln, four from Norfolk, two from Maine, and I am from Suffolk. All eyes turn to the young woman next to me.

'And where are you from?'

'Tokyo in Japan.'

'Oh, you've come a long way then!'

We climb into two electric buggies, five in each, plus a guide apiece. They take us through the garden. We stop at the gravestones of three of the Queen's early corgis: Susan, Sugar and Heather.

'Our Jack Russell died last year. It was in the autumn,' recalls one of the ladies from Norfolk.

Our guide points out new trees and shrubs. Some are experiencing a bit of trouble. For a neat man from Lincoln with a sweater draped over his shoulders they call to mind troublesome trees and shrubs of his own. When the guide points to trees given to the Queen for her Silver Jubilee, only three of which survived, he tut-tuts in sympathy. 'We bought our property six years ago from what one might call an over-enthusiastic gardener. She'd planted sixty acer trees far too close together – and they've been giving us trouble ever since, I kid you not!'

Throughout the tour, one or two of my fellow Exclusive Access visitors take pride in comparing the ups and downs in the life of the Royal Family at Sandringham to the ups and downs in their own homes and families. This is how we relate to the Royal Family: we like to recognise our own lives in theirs, just as we recognise human faces in clouds or smoke.

Our electric buggies pull up in the main courtyard, close to a placard advertising a Bank Holiday concert in the Sandringham grounds. Fifty years ago, it would have been the Band of the Royal Marines or a tasteful son et lumière. Now it's 'The Who with Orchestra Plus Richard Ashcroft + The Lightning Seeds', but it serves a similar purpose. Pete Townshend appears on the poster in moody dark glasses. He is four years older than the King, but still bashing angrily away on his guitar, rebellion now absorbed into heritage.

Our little group gathers by the front door. I think this must be where Princess Anne's bull terrier savaged the Queen's corgi in their fight to the death (see p. 53), but refrain from mentioning it.

'We'll split you into two groups,' says the first guide. 'A six and a four is perfectly all right. Don't worry! You can stay with your friends! Just one housekeeping matter. Strictly no photography inside the house, and, of course, your phones are all on silent. That reminds me of that lovely story about our late Queen – you tell it.' She turns to her fellow guide.

'No, you go ahead!'

'Well, it's a lovely story. Someone's phone goes off, and the Queen turns to her and says, "Oh, do take it – *it might be someone important!*"'

We chuckle appreciatively, though most of us must surely have heard it countless times.*

'We will be locking you in. Don't be alarmed! It IS exclusive, it's not open to the public today, so we don't want somebody just walking in.'

In the hallway, we are given a brief history of the estate – Royal since 1862, bought by Queen Victoria for her eldest son, and so forth.

'I hope you weren't expecting it to look like Buckingham Palace because it's the opposite, really – very informal, very relaxed. A country retreat is probably the best way to describe it. It's not a museum. We'll be looking round the family's private sitting rooms. The King wants you to see them as they are when he uses them. Basically, you're seeing the house as it is, apart from the protection to the rugs and of course the red rope barriers, which will be put in the loft or wherever. That's where we all put our stuff, isn't it?!!'

We nod and give knowing smiles. Yes, they're just like us. 'You should see some of the things in our attic!' chips in the man with the

---

* It seems to have been one of the Queen's stock jokes. Variations of it pop up in many reminiscences. For instance, in 2022 her close friend Prue Penn recalled, 'We gave a dinner for her and the Duke of Edinburgh in our house in London. I had a carefully thought-out table which I forgot to take with me into the dining room and got into a serious muddle over the placing of our guests. Her Majesty took over and in no time at all had made a very good job of it. She sat down and said: "Lucky you weren't giving an important dinner party."'

sweater over his shoulders. 'I tell my wife we should get rid of it all, but will she listen?!'

'As you see, there's a homely feel the moment you step into the house. There's no big entrance hall, no sweeping staircase.'

Ah! The staircase! When Diana spoke into Andrew Morton's tape recorder she remembered staying at Sandringham at the end of 1981, pregnant with William:

> I threw myself down the stairs. Charles said I was crying wolf and I said I felt so desperate and I was crying my eyes out and he said: 'I'm not going to listen. You're always doing this to me. I'm going riding now.' So I threw myself down the stairs. The Queen comes out, absolutely horrified, shaking – she was so frightened. I knew I wasn't going to lose the baby; quite bruised around the stomach. Charles went out riding and when he came back, you know, it was just dismissal, total dismissal. He just carried on out of the door.

Again, best not to mention it. But how long before this gothic tale becomes a mainstay of the guided tour? Visitors to Hampton Court are told all about King Henry VIII's marital mishaps. Will our guide in the year 2123 take us on a special detour to tell us all about the day Princess Diana, the great-great-grandmother of the present monarch, hurled herself down these stairs? Will a plaque to the left of the staircase bear Princess Diana's description of the tumble in her own words?

Personal tragedy becomes public drama and then tourist attraction. Events that occurred fifty years ago have already become part of this cycle. Towards the end of our tour, we are taken around the Royal garages, home to various grand Royal cars – King George V's Daimler Double-Six, the Queen's Rolls-Royce Phantom V, and so on. One of them is a 1969 Austin Princess Vanden Plas Limousine, painted in Royal claret. The printed notice alongside it says:

In March 1974, this vehicle was returning Her Royal Highness Princess Anne and Captain Mark Phillips to Buckingham Palace.

The Royal couple escaped an apparent kidnap attempt along Pall Mall when their chauffeur-driven limousine was forced to halt by another car which blocked their route.

A man appeared from a white Ford Escort and fired six shots. The Princess's bodyguard, James Beaton, fired at the man before he was wounded and the chauffeur, Alex Callender, one of Queen Elizabeth II's senior drivers, was also injured.

Her Royal Highness Princess Anne, while shocked by the incident, was unharmed.

People take smiley photographs of themselves next to the Austin Princess, and then we all move on.

In the Sandringham hallway, our guide points out King Edward VII's weighing scales, close to the front door. He used to make his guests sit on them, before and after their visits, 'and if they put on weight, he took it as a compliment that they had so enjoyed his hospitality'.

'Does anyone use them today?' asks the lady from Maine. Most of our group want to hear about the present Royal Family rather than their ancestors.

'I wouldn't be surprised if after a few drinks someone says "let's get on the weighing scales", but frankly I don't know. But I rather hope they do!' says our guide. By chance, I have recently been reading Lady Gladwyn's diaries. When she was a guest at Sandringham in February 1949, Tommy Lascelles took her to this very spot and showed her the old Edwardian album containing the weights of all the guests. Lascelles pointed out the name of the Duke of Clarence, the alcoholic elder brother of King George V, who had been due to marry Queen Mary when he died unexpectedly. Lascelles mentioned that once when the Duke stayed at Sandringham his valet was asked when his master would require breakfast. 'His Royal Highness is always sick at eleven,' came the reply. But such unsavoury stories, reflecting ill on the Royal

Family, aren't mentioned by the guides, and probably won't be permitted for another 200 years.

She takes us through to where the current Royal Family take their morning coffee. 'So then they can sit here and decide what they're doing for the rest of the day, and then, at the far end of the room, after dinner, they perhaps watch television, and there's music systems here also, or jigsaw puzzles, or whatever we all do in our sitting rooms, that's what the family do here. They're just a normal family, when all is said and done! The only difference to our own sitting rooms is the minstrel's gallery – unless you're going to tell me you've got a minstrel's gallery?! Perhaps it should be your next project!'

'Don't tempt fate!' chips in the man with the sweater. 'It's only a couple of years since we built our new conservatory and very handy it is too!'

'With each new monarch, you'll notice subtle changes,' says our guide. 'Each time His Majesty comes, one or two new objects appear – sometimes quite ordinary things, like the coasters with his cypher on, or those cushions, or that Moon Jar. Various bits and bobs.' We stare intently at the coasters and the large porcelain vase in the corner. I find myself thinking how odd it is that, with so much else on his plate, the new King can still find time to worry about personalising his coasters. And why personalise a coaster at all? If I were told that Donald Trump or Kim Kardashian or Julian Fellowes had personalised their coasters, I would think it a vulgar sign of egotism. Is the new King with his personalised coasters any different? Or is it all part of ancient Palace protocol?

'And just over there, you may notice the photograph of Her Late Majesty's visit to the house in the spring of last year. Wearing her famous smile.'

We go through to other rooms, and our attention is drawn to the portraits of Queen Alexandra's Danish family, the chandeliers ('very delicate job to clean') and Queen Mary's needlework cushions ('all her own work').

We look out of the window at ten gardeners toiling away on another of the King's new projects, a revived topiary garden. Or not so revived: it is dead, or dying. 'It's had a few difficulties, as you can probably tell.'

We go to look at the spot where the largest of the Royal Christmas trees is always placed. 'The family will gather in here on Christmas Eve and in the German tradition—' Our guide pauses, as though worried about getting into deep water. 'That's a tradition from the – er – ancestors – they'll actually unwrap their presents on Christmas Eve. And of course they do have a busy schedule on Christmas Day, what with their walk to the church, so they get presents out of the way on Christmas Eve. And there's a very strict spending limit on them!'

Again, this is greeted by a ripple of knowing laughter.

'Do you know the story, perhaps? If you buy an expensive gift, it's frowned upon, because, after all, what would you buy members of the Royal Family? Seemingly, they don't want for much at all – and *unfortunately* some of the newer members of the Royal Family have fallen foul of that rule! But just to give you an idea, the spend limit is ridiculously low, I don't know what the current limit is – but probably five pounds would be the *absolute maximum*, so you've got to think of something quirky or perhaps a little bit cheeky, or something you've made yourself – a jar of chutney or a jar of jam. Those sort of things are really appreciated. To give you an idea of some of the jokey presents – and I'm not sure I should be saying this! – an inflatable toilet seat perhaps, or a grow-your-own-girlfriend kit!! These are things we know have been given in the past – and I'm not going to reveal who gave them or who received them! Or a whoopee cushion is another one!!! So, rather childish presents! But that's what they enjoy receiving.'

'Now, I mentioned that Queen Mary liked collecting things.' My ears perk up. I have often heard tell of Queen Mary's kleptomania. 'When she was at Sandringham, she used to love going over to King's Lynn to have a look around some of the antique shops there, always with an eye for a bargain – and she drove a very hard bargain, we understand! Rumour has it she used to beat the price down to the point where if the shopkeepers noticed her limousine pulling up, they might be tempted to pull the shutters down and turn the lights off!'

I peer intently at a picture that sits on a side-table in the drawing room, a flash photo of King George VI and his family staring bleakly at the camera, rigid and unsmiling. It could almost be the work of

Diane Arbus. 'I noticed you're taking a keen interest in this photo-graph. It's Christmas 1951. You know who's who, yes? That's Queen Mary, of course, and that's Princess Margaret, and Princess Anne next to her brother there.

'Afternoon tea is served in here at four o'clock. His Majesty likes to look out at the topiary garden.' We all stare through the window at the scrubby little yellow and brown bushes in their various states of decay. 'As I say, you can't do these things overnight. It's a long-term thing. It's silly trying to rush it. The weather's so unpredictable ... Charles certainly has a different style of gardening to ... to ...' – she clearly doesn't want to sow division – '... to what it has been in previous years. It's a much wilder sort of feel, it's becoming clear, nothing formal as such. No straight lines.'

A panelled screen features photographs of the many famous people who have stayed at Sandringham. 'Queen Alexandra had a camera, and she would photograph her guests, or ask them to bring portraits.' I take a close look and find Mark Twain, Émile Zola and Henrik Ibsen among them, unlikely visitors all. Whoever next? Sigmund Freud? Vladimir Ilyich Lenin? Kim Kardashian? 'Did those three *really* stay at Sandringham?' I ask the guide. Even as I ask it, I realise I sound like a troublemaker. 'They must have done,' she informs me pleasantly, 'or they wouldn't be there.'

We walk through to the next room. 'This is the only dining room, so all family meals are served here including, of course, the Christmas lunch. The room will always be lit very softly – no overhead lighting, just candles and pelmet lights. So a very comfortable dining area.'

With a change of monarch comes a change of diet. On a sideboard, the 'King's Menu' is now on display. A year ago, the main dish would have been something straightforward like lamb cutlets or beef stew. Now, it is vegetarian, and progressive: 'Green Vegetable Omelette Stuffed with Broad Beans, Peas and Courgettes and Covered in a Basil and Brie Cream Sauce'.

We move on, nodding our heads appreciatively, through a series of rooms decorated with swords, guns (ninety-eight in all), tapestries, pictures of horses, enamel, china, silver and family portraits. Along the way I spot a sketch of a shooting party: to one side stands Prince Andrew, carrying a gun. It's the only picture of him that I have spotted on our tour. Will it still be here in a year's time?

We drift into the ballroom, filled with watercolours on special display. 'All His Majesty's own work. It's the first time they've been gathered together from the different houses around the country.'

At the entrance, a notice carries this quote from King Charles III: 'The great thing about painting, I find, is that it transports me into another dimension which quite literally refreshes parts of the soul which other activities can't reach.'

We drift among the King's careful watercolours of landscapes and buildings. I think of his offer to swap one of them with an original by Lucian Freud. The second guide notices me taking an interest and comes over. 'Not a bad artist,' she says. 'Some of them are typical washy watercolours, but then some are of architecture, and others have got some lovely skies. It's almost as though there are three different artists going on.'

I tell her that some of the buildings are a bit wonky, which is why I prefer the landscapes. 'I think I do too. I love this one in the snow. He doesn't sketch first, and he does them very quickly.'

Our tour of the interior has come to an end. We are taken outside to see the new topiary, in its sorry state. 'It's box blight, caused by a moth. It just destroys the foliage. But you can cut it out and treat it and eventually it does come back.' The American couple sympathise: box blight afflicts their hedges, back home in Maine.

We see an old avenue of trees, still going strong. 'Years ago, when Edward and Alexandra were entertaining, the ladies could parade up and down with their beautiful dresses on in the hot weather and get the shade from the trees.' At the end of the avenue sits what Pope-Hennessy described as 'A giant Chinese god, not exactly a Buddha, with a lascivious smirk on its face (rather the face of Khrushchev)'.

It was, the guide tells us, a gift to King Edward VII. 'It was acquired by a gentleman by the name of Admiral Keppel. That name might ring a bell with you. He was the husband of Alice Keppel who was the, er, lady friend of the Prince of Wales.'

'When you say "lady friend" ...' says the American woman.

'Let's just say he was a bit of a ladies' man.' I sense that the guide feels she has strayed, once again, into deep water. 'And here we have a shaded area, where you can sit out and have lunch.'

'We have a lovely shaded area in our garden,' says the man with the sweater.

We take a look at more topiary, and at the gardeners who are struggling to revive it. 'Very much a work in progress, this. It was all nicely planted but then came the very very hot weather a week later and burnt it. Shall we make a move, then?'

We walk round the huge walled garden and end up in the car museum. How quickly the present becomes the past, and innovations turn into antiques! We peer into the Rolls-Royce used by the Queen for forty years and carried to Russia on the Royal Yacht *Britannia* for her state visit in 1992. A notice tells us that 'The removable rear roof section exposed an inner Perspex lining that afforded spectators a clearer view of the Royal passengers.'

The museum also contains more humble, more touching items, such as King George V's bicycle and the picnic carriage designed by Prince Philip to be pulled behind a car. It's a slightly nerdy contraption full of cupboards and slots and little drawers that push in and pull out. Prince Philip was very proud of it, but barely a week ago a regular at these picnics of theirs was telling me how grim they were. Everyone had to form a queue, and the Queen would dish out 'disgusting 1950s school food' from the picnic carriage 'like a dinner lady'.

At the end of our tour, I visit the Sandringham Gift Shop, stacked with upmarket branded produce, from Sandringham Cream Fudge to Sandringham Celebration Gin, 'distilled with myrtle, persimmon and other botanicals, celebrating many aspects of royal life'. There are Sandringham tennis balls and Sandringham mint humbugs, Sandringham beer and Sandringham cider, Bumpa the Sandringham Bear 'lovingly made by hand in Shropshire' and a Sandringham picnic blanket. Four gold-plated Sandringham spoons cost £40; a Sandringham wooden spoon costs £4.99. Something to suit all pockets! A Sandringham cuddly toy corgi is selling for £14.99 and a

Sandringham tweed cap for £59.99. I keep an eye out for a King Charles III exploding pen, but fail to find one.

A year on from the death of the Queen, products bearing her likeness have been relegated to the lower shelves, among them a handful of children's books. One of them, *Queen Elizabeth*, was written and published within a month of her death. It is the ninety-sixth in a series called 'Little People, BIG DREAMS' whose previous subjects include Frida Kahlo, Rosa Parks, Billie Jean King, RuPaul, Greta Thunberg, Andy Warhol and Yoko Ono. 'I look for people who have never given up on their dreams,' explained the series creator, Maria Isabel Sánchez Vegara, in an interview.

Elizabeth was, it emerges, 'a little girl with a huge sense of duty'. She 'loved dogs and horses and dreamed of living on a farm'. But one day 'she heard chants on the streets. Her Uncle Edward had given up the crown, which meant her father would become king and she would be heiress to the throne.'

Her father died and so 'overnight, the young princess became queen of kingdoms all over the world, from England to faraway South Africa. It was exhausting!' But at least being queen gave Elizabeth the chance 'to meet unforgettable people who had made the world a better place'. An illustration shows her shaking hands with a plump Marilyn Monroe. Stephen Hawking, the Beatles, Elton John, Nelson Mandela, Malala Yousafzai are all in the background, along with Jane Goodall cradling a chimpanzee.

She became a beacon for progressive values. 'No matter how much everything changed around her, Elizabeth tried to stay up to date. She started a new tradition of walking through the crowds to say hello, and she signed a law that gave girls the same right as boys to inherit the throne.' That particular page is illustrated with a picture of the Queen shaking hands with a little black girl while onlookers wave little Union flags. A black man puts a hand on the shoulder of a boy with glasses who, in turn, holds hands with a disabled girl in a wheelchair.

The last page features a picture of Queen Elizabeth in her crown waving away on the balcony of Buckingham Palace, just across the river from Big Ben. A multiracial crowd waves back. 'After 70 long years of putting her duty first, little Lilibet became the most admired and longest-reigning queen in the world. Maybe it wasn't her childhood dream, but she was the queen that her people dreamed of.'

There are fewer adult biographies of the Queen on display. The official guidebook with her photograph on the cover is, I am informed, 'no longer available' though delivery of the new guidebook, presumably with the King on its cover, has been delayed. By and large, books about King Charles III are displayed more prominently than those about his late mother. Most of the biographies of the King on display offer strikingly rosy accounts of his life so far. One children's picture book scoots through nine turbulent years in just two sentences, skating over significant events:

> In August 1996, the 15-year marriage of Charles and Diana ended in divorce. Almost ten years later, on February 10, 2005, Prince Charles and Camilla Parker Bowles announced their engagement, and married later that year on April 9, 2005.

These children's books portray the King as a beacon of enlightened and popular causes. One sports an illustration of him with the England women's football team. Another shows 'Charles the Eco-King': a drawing of His Majesty pruning a tree while a little black boy and a little white girl look on in delight. The neighbouring text explains that:

> The King has always loved the natural world, from farming his food at home to speaking out to protect the whole planet.

A third book reassures readers that our new King will soon establish a position at the centre of our national life:

> Everyone knows the Queen's portrait because it is on every banknote, coin and stamp in the country! The King's portrait will be just as famous one day.

Elsewhere in the shop – 'EXCLUSIVE to Sandringham and for a limited time only' – is a:

> 20-piece limited edition WATERCOLOUR SET … Everything needed to recreate the iconic watercolour of Sandringham House painted by HM King Charles III.

This watercolour set, containing twelve tubes of paint, a pad of paper, a pencil and a ceramic palette is on sale for £159.99. Alongside it, a limited-edition lithograph of the Castle of Mey, 'based on an original watercolour' by King Charles III and 'individually numbered and signed by the artist', is offered at £2,950, with 'only 100 copies available'.

The Queen is dead; long live the King!

112

The closing words of Princess Elizabeth's first radio broadcast, delivered live on the BBC's Children's Hour *on 13 October 1940 to British children evacuated to New Zealand, Canada and the United States:*

'We know, every one of us, that in the end all will be well; for God will care for us and give us victory and peace. And when peace comes, remember it will be for us, the children of today, to make the world of tomorrow a better and happier place.

'My sister is by my side and we are both going to say goodnight to you.

'Come on, Margaret.

'Goodnight, children.

'Goodnight, and good luck to you all.'

SOURCES

Reading too many books about the Queen and the Royal Family, one after another, is like wading through candy floss: you emerge pink and queasy, but also undernourished.

Nevertheless, there are some nutritious exceptions. Of biographies of the Queen, the most reliable and informative are *The Queen: Elizabeth II and the Monarchy* by Ben Pimlott; *Queen of Our Times: The Life of Elizabeth II* and *Queen of the World*, both by Robert Hardman; *Elizabeth the Queen* by Sally Bedell Smith; and *Queen Elizabeth II: An Oral History* by Deborah Hart Strober and Gerald S. Strober. The most entertaining is *Philip and Elizabeth* by Gyles Brandreth. Others include *Queen Elizabeth II: Her Life in Our Times* by Sarah Bradford; *Majesty* by Robert Lacey; *The Ultimate Family* by John Pearson; *The Diamond Queen* by Andrew Marr; *Elizabeth II* by Douglas Hurd and *Elizabeth: An Intimate Portrait* by Gyles Brandreth. I should also mention three illuminating TV documentaries: *Royal Family*, directed by Richard Cawston (1969); *Elizabeth R: A Year in the Life of the Queen*, directed by Edward Mirzoeff (1992) and, most recently, *Elizabeth: A Portrait in Part(s)*, directed by Roger Michell (2022).

There are precious few books about the Queen's childhood: Royal authors were less nosy in those days. The oft-derided *The Little Princesses: The Intimate Story of H.R.H. Princess Elizabeth and H.R.H. Princess Margaret* by Marion Crawford is by far the most informative. I can also recommend the touching and unexpectedly edgy *The Windsor Diaries* by the Princesses' childhood friend Alathea Fitzalan Howard.

If it's royal treacle you're after, few come treaclier than *The Story of Princess Elizabeth* by Anne Ring, and *Princess Elizabeth: Probable Future Ruler of the Greatest Empire in the World* by Captain Eric Acland.

Memoirs by members of the Royal Family vary from the reassuringly dull *A Royal Life* by HRH The Duke of Kent and Hugo Vickers to the unnervingly sensational *Diana: Her True Story – In Her Own Words* by Andrew Morton. Sarah, Duchess of York keeps churning them out: those with a taste for her peculiar mix of self-pity and self-worship may well enjoy *My Story* and *Finding Sarah: A Duchess's Journey to Find Herself*. Also inhabiting this ghostwritten Royal misery-memoir niche is *Spare* by Prince Harry, which, for all its bleak revelations, sounds nothing like him at all. Harry's great-great-uncle and -aunt, the Duke and Duchess of Windsor, were, like him, in a strange sort of exile when they collaborated with their ghostwriters on, respectively, *A King's Story* and *The Heart Has Its Reasons*.

At the other end of the happiness scale, forcefully buoyant, comes *Counting One's Blessings: The Selected Letters of Queen Elizabeth the Queen Mother* edited by William Shawcross. Biographies of relatively recent royals – some sparky, some stuffy, most a bit of both – include *Mountbatten: The Official Biography* by Philip Ziegler; *The Mountbattens* by Andrew Lownie; *The Prince of Wales: A Biography* by Jonathan Dimbleby; *Young Prince Philip* by Philip Eade; *The Duke: A Portrait of Prince Philip* by Tim Heald; *Edward VIII* by Frances Donaldson; *King Edward VIII* by Philip Ziegler; *Alice: Princess Andrew of Greece* by Hugo Vickers; *The Queen Mother* by Hugo Vickers; *Queen Elizabeth the Queen Mother: The Official Biography* by William Shawcross; *Charles and Camilla* by Gyles Brandreth; *Finding Freedom: Harry and Meghan and the Making of a Modern Royal Family* by Omid Scobie and Carolyn Durand; *Meghan: A Hollywood Princess* by Andrew Morton; *Revenge: Meghan, Harry and the War Between the Windsors* by Tom Bower; *The Diary of Princess Pushy's Sister: A Memoir* by Samantha Markle; *Snowdon: The Biography* by Anne de Courcy; and my own *Ma'am Darling: 99 Glimpses of Princess Margaret*.

Biographies of royals more distant from our own time include: *King George VI: His Life and Reign* by John Wheeler-Bennett; *King George VI* by Sarah Bradford; *Hanover to Windsor* by Roger Fulford; *George V: Never a Dull Moment* by Jane Ridley; *King George V* by Kenneth Rose; *King George V* by Harold Nicolson; *Queen Victoria* by A. N. Wilson; *Behind Closed Doors: The Tragic Untold Story of the Duchess of Windsor* by Hugo Vickers; and *Queen Mary* by James Pope-Hennessy. *Behind the Throne: A Domestic History of the Royal Household* by Adrian Tinniswood is full of good things.

Memoirs from below stairs are generally pooh-poohed, but I see no reason to regard them as any less reliable than memoirs from above stairs. The Queen invariably emerges very well from books written by her staff; some of her children, less so. I have picked up revealing snippets from *A Royal Duty* by Paul Burrell; *Behind Palace Doors: My Years with the Queen Mother* by Major Colin Burgess; *Backstairs Billy: The Life of William Tallon* by Tom Quinn; *Adventures of a Gentleman's Gentleman* by Guy Hunting; *Courting Disaster* by Malcolm J. Barker; *The Other Side of the Coin: The Queen, the Dresser and the Wardrobe* by Angela Kelly; *Royal Secrets: The View from Downstairs* by Stephen Barry; and *The Housekeeper's Diary* by Wendy Berry.

A new section in the ever increasing Royal library has been created by the memoirs of former ladies in waiting. *The Final Curtsey: A Royal Memoir by the Queen's Cousin*, Margaret Rhodes, is a relic from a more stoical age, as are *Lady in Waiting* by Anne Glenconner and its follow-up *Whatever Next?* Valentine Low's authoritative *Courtiers: The Hidden Power Behind the Crown* offers fascinating insights into the backstage world of the Royal Family. *The Servants* by Lucy Lethbridge contains good stories about the grandeur of the monarchy in days gone by, and *Norman Hartnell: The Biography* by Michael Pick is a welcome addition to the library of Royal campery.

Diaries and letters tend to be less cautious and more carefree than memoirs and biographies. They certainly give a welcome buzz to research. I have found these ones particularly useful: *Writing Home* by Alan Bennett; *Untold Stories* by Alan Bennett; *The Diaries of James Lees-Milne*, various volumes; *Roy Strong Diaries 1967–1987*; *Scenes* and Apparitions: The Roy Strong Diaries 1988–2003; Types and Shadows: The Roy Strong Diaries 2004–2015; Diary by Hugh Casson; A View from the Foothills: The Diaries of Chris Mullin; Didn't You Use to Be Chris Mullin? Diaries 2010–2022; The Diaries of Harold Nicolson; The Diaries of Virginia Woolf; The Strenuous Years: 1948–66 by Cecil Beaton; The Restless Years 1955–63 by Cecil Beaton; The Unexpurgated Beaton introduced by Hugo Vickers; Beaton in the Sixties: More Unexpurgated Diaries introduced by Hugo Vickers; Malice in Wonderland: My Adventures in the World of Cecil Beaton by Hugo Vickers; Henry 'Chips' Channon: The Diaries, volumes 1, 2 and 3 edited by Simon Heffer; Diaries and Letters of Harold Nicolson, volumes 1, 2 and 3; National Service: Diary of a Decade at the National Theatre by Richard Eyre; The Journals of Woodrow Wyatt, volumes 1 and 2 edited by Sarah Curtis; Who's In, Who's Out: The Journals of Kenneth Rose, volume 1: 1944–1979 edited by D. R. Thorpe; Who Loses, Who Wins: The Journals of Kenneth Rose, volume 2: 1979–2014 edited by D. R. Thorpe; The Alastair Campbell Diaries; Frances Partridge Diaries 1939–1972; John Fowles: The Journals, volumes 1 and 2 edited by Charles Drazin; The Fringes of Power: Downing Street Diaries 1939–1945 by John Colville; The Political Diary of Hugh Dalton 1918–40, 1945–60 edited by Ben Pimlott; The Barbara Castle Diaries 1964–1976 by Barbara Castle; The Peter Hall Diaries; Empire at Bay: The Leo Amery Diaries 1929–1945; The Diaries of Cynthia Gladwyn edited by Miles Jebb; The Paddy Ashdown Diaries, volume 1: 1988–1997; Munkey Diaries 1957–1982 by Jane Birkin; Peter Hall's Diaries; The Diaries of Kenneth Tynan edited by John Lahr; The Andy Warhol Diaries edited by Pat Hackett; Travelling to Work: Diaries 1988–98 by Michael Palin; The Letters of Evelyn Waugh edited by Mark Amory; Mr Wu & Mrs Stitch: The Letters of Evelyn Waugh & Diana Cooper edited by Artemis Cooper; Darling Monster: The Letters of Lady Diana Cooper to Her Son John Julius Norwich 1939–1952; The Letters of Oscar Hammerstein II compiled and edited by Mark Eden Horowitz; Letters to a Friend 1950–1952 by Rose Macaulay; Selected Letters of William Empson edited by John Haffenden; The Mitfords: Letters Between Six Sisters edited by Charlotte Mosley; In Tearing Haste: Letters Between Deborah

Devonshire and Patrick Leigh Fermor edited by Charlotte Mosley; and *Decca: The Letters of Jessica Mitford* edited by Peter Y. Sussman.

One of the themes of this book is the mysterious effect of the Queen on the subconscious lives of her subjects, my own among them. Brian Masters's *Dreams About H.M. The Queen and Other Members of the Royal Family* first alerted me to the bizarre encounters we have with Her Majesty when we nod off. Since then, I have had fun uncovering dreams in diaries and memoirs, among them *The Private Diaries of Alison Uttley*; 'Marmalade Ma'am?' from *Girls Will Be Girls* by Arthur Marshall; 'The Queen's Touch' by Paul Theroux, *New Yorker*, 10 March 1986; *A Queen for All Seasons* by Joanna Lumley; *Experience* by Martin Amis; *Selected Letters of Philip Larkin 1940–1985* edited by Anthony Thwaite; *The Diaries of Donald Friend*, volume 4 edited by Paul Hetherington; *A World of My Own* by Graham Greene; *Getting Personal* by Brian Masters; 'America's Favourite Soap' by Clancy Sigal in *The Queen Observed* edited by Trevor Grove; *Collected Letters of C. S. Lewis*, volume 3 edited by Walter Hopper; *The Elizabethan Renaissance* by A. L. Rowse; and an article by Boris Johnson in the *Daily Mail*, 2 September 2023.

There have been surprisingly few explorations of the psychology of the monarchy, but I'm glad to have unearthed 'The Psychology of Constitutional Monarchy' by Freud's disciple and biographer Ernest Jones in the *New Statesman* magazine in 1936, and the essay 'The Place of the Monarchy' in *Home Is Where We Start From* by the admirable Donald Winnicott. Other pieces of writing exploring the curious effects of monarchy on the national psyche include *Surfing the Zeitgeist* by Gilbert Adair; 'For Queens and Country', an essay by Philip Hensher in *Perspective* magazine; *The Essays of Virginia Woolf*, volume 6: *1933 to 1941* edited by Stuart N. Clarke; *The Principles of Sociology* by Herbert Spencer; *The Interpretation of Cultures* by Clifford Geertz; 'The Context, Performance and Meaning of Ritual: The British Monarchy and the Invention of Tradition 1820–1977' by David Cannadine in *The Invention of Tradition* edited by Eric Hobsbawm and Terence Ranger; 'At Cowes' by Max Beerbohm from *Max Beerbohm Caricatures* edited by J. John Hall; 'Some Words on Royalty' by Max

Beerbohm from *The Prince of Minor Writers: The Selected Essays of Max Beerbohm* edited by Philip Lopate; 'The Princess Myth' by Hilary Mantel from *A Memoir of My Former Self* edited by Nicholas Pearson; 'The Queen and I' from *Tread Softly for You Tread on My Jokes* by Malcolm Muggeridge; and 'Does England Really Need a Queen?' by Malcolm Muggeridge in *Saturday Evening Post*, 19 October 1957; and *Crown and People* by Philip Ziegler. Though not directly concerned with royalty, Susan Sontag's 'Notes on "Camp"' from *Against Interpretation and Other Essays* carries many pleasing overlaps.

A fair proportion of the more serious books about the monarchy are against it. I found the writings of the republican Labour MP Willie Hamilton so entertaining that I wrote far too much about him, and then had to scale it back. Nevertheless, I recommend his two books *Blood on the Walls* and *My Queen and I*; also the winningly abrasive *The Enchanted Glass: Britain and Its Monarchy* by Tom Nairn; *The Monarchy* by Christopher Hitchens; *And What Do You Do?* by Norman Baker; and *Sailing Close to the Wind* by Dennis Skinner.

Personal encounters with the Queen, often bizarre and unexpected, lie at the heart of my *Voyage Around the Queen* and may be further explored in: *Patrick White: A Life* by David Marr; *Patrick White: Letters* edited by David Marr; *Flaws in the Glass: A Self-Portrait* by Patrick White; *Patrick White Speaks* by Patrick White; *Patricia Highsmith: Her Diaries and Notebooks* edited by Anna von Planta; *The Diaries of Lindsay Anderson* edited by Paul Sutton; Lindsay Anderson: letter to Gavin Lambert, 3 January 1982, from *The Diaries of Lindsay Anderson* edited by Paul Sutton; *Diary of an MP's Wife* by Sasha Swire; *Full Disclosure* by Andrew Neil; *Prezza* by John Prescott; *Ten Years to Save the West* by Liz Truss; *Beyond Black* by Hilary Mantel; *Giving Up the Ghost* by Hilary Mantel; 'Royal Bodies' by Hilary Mantel from *Mantel Pieces*; *Becoming* by Michelle Obama; *Living History* by Hillary Rodham Clinton; *Experience* by Martin Amis; *A Journey* by Tony Blair; *Tony Crosland* by Susan Crosland; *Reflections on Her Majesty* by Alan Bennett, BBC Radio 4; *Something Sensational to Read on the Train: The Gyles Brandreth Diaries*; *Crying with Laughter* by Bob Monkhouse; *If I Don't Write It, Nobody Else Will* by Eric Sykes;

Penelope Keith speaking on BBC Radio 4's *The Reunion*; *Know the Truth: A Memoir* by George Carey; *My Story* by Marilyn Monroe; *Timebends* by Arthur Miller; *When Marilyn Met the Queen: Marilyn Monroe's Life in England* by Michelle Morgan; *The Marilyn Monroe Video Archives*; *The Genius and the Goddess* by Jeffrey Meyers; *Rolling Stone* magazine; *The Prince, the Showgirl and Me* by Colin Clark; *Keep Smiling* by Charlotte Church; *Reflections on Her Majesty* by Antonia Fraser, BBC Radio 4; article by Alastair Campbell, *Daily Telegraph*, 5 April 2020; *Art Exposed* by Julian Spalding; *Maria Callas: Diaries of a Friendship* by Robert Sutherland; *Music: A Joy for Life* by Edward Heath; obituary of the Earl of Harewood by Tom Sutcliffe, *Guardian*, 11 July 2011; *The Lyrics* by Paul McCartney; *Royal Subjects* by Theo Aronson; *Is It Me?* by Terry Wogan; *This Much Is True* by Miriam Margolyes; *Annabel: An Unconventional Life* by Annabel Birley; *Dear Robert, Dear Spike: The Graves–Milligan Correspondence* edited by Pauline Scudamore; *Daphne du Maurier* by Margaret Forster; Daphne du Maurier's *Letters from Menabilly: Portrait of a Friendship* edited by Oriel Malet; *Palimpsest: A Memoir* by Gore Vidal; *America's Queen: The Life of Jacqueline Kennedy Onassis* by Sarah Bradford; *Kenneth Clark: Life, Art and Civilisation* by James Stourton; *E. M. Forster: A Life* by P. N. Furbank; *Selected Letters of E. M. Forster*, volume 2: *1921–70* edited by Mary Lago and P. N. Furbank; *The Oxford Book of Literary Anecdotes* edited by John Gross; *Façades: Edith, Osbert and Sacheverell Sitwell* by John Pearson; *The Selected Letters of William Walton* edited by Malcolm Hayes; *Cliff: My Life, My Way* by Cliff Richard; *Willie: The Life of W. Somerset Maugham* by Robert Calder; *Angus Wilson: A Biography* by Margaret Drabble; *William Golding: The Man Who Wrote Lord of the Flies* by John Carey; *Klever Kaff: Letters and Diaries of Kathleen Ferrier* edited by Christopher Fifield; *Cleared for Take-Off* and *An Orderly Man*, both by Dirk Bogarde; *New Selected Journals of Stephen Spender 1939–1995* edited by Lara Feigel and John Sutherland with Natasha Spender; *Eric Hobsbawm: A Life in History* by Richard J. Evans; *Ready for Absolutely Nothing* by Susannah Constantine; *My Name Is Barbra* by Barbra Streisand; *Vita: The Life of V. Sackville-West* by Victoria Glendinning; *Paul McCartney: The Biography* by Philip

Norman; *John* by Cynthia Lennon; *The Beatles Anthology*; *The Beatles Day by Day*; *The Beatles Bible*; *The Beatles, Lennon and Me* by Pete Shotton; *Brief Lives* by Alan Watkins; *Idi Amin: The Story of Africa's Icon of Evil* by Mark Leopold; *Kiss the Hand You Cannot Bite: The Rise and Fall of the Ceaușescus* by Edward Behr; 'When the Ceausescus came to tea' by Robin Ashenden, *Spectator*, 17 September 2022; 'A moral issue to correct: the long tail of Elena Ceaușescu's fraudulent scientific work' by Melissa Davey, *Guardian*, 22 December 2021; *Making an Exhibition of Myself: The Autobiography of Peter Hall*; *Olivier: The Authorised Biography* by Terry Coleman; *Selected Letters of Rebecca West* edited by Bonnie Kime Scott; *The Grand Surprise: The Journals of Leo Lerman*; *Fall: The Mystery of Robert Maxwell* by John Preston; *A Mind of My Own: My Life with Robert Maxwell* by Elisabeth Maxwell; obituary of Ryoichi Sasakawa, *Independent*, 19 July 1995; obituary of Ryoichi Sasakawa, *New York Times*, 20 July 1995; *Philip de László: His Life and Art* by Duff Hart-Davis; *The Queen by Rolf*, first broadcast on the BBC One, 1 January 2006; 'Queen Becomes a Subject for Rolf', *The Times*, 20 December 2005; *The Lives of Lucian Freud: Fame* by William Feaver; *Breakfast with Lucian* by Geordie Greig; Isaiah Berlin's *Affirming: Letters 1975–1997* edited by Henry Hardy and Mark Pottle; *Speaking for Myself* by Cherie Blair; *Me* by Elton John; *Scattershot: Life, Music, Elton and Me* by Bernie Taupin; 'Germaine Greer: I'm like my Nazi mother', *Daily Express*, 12 October 2010; 'A meditation' by Ben Okri, *Guardian*, 9 September 2022; 'A life-long friendship: the Elizabeth I knew' by Prue Penn, *Spectator*, 17 September 2022.

To list my sources for every single chapter would be too tedious for the general reader, but I am going to make exceptions for one or two chapters in particular. For my chapter on the corgis I was reliant on Penny Junor's appropriately dogged research in *All the Queen's Corgis: The Story of Elizabeth II & Her Most Faithful Companions*. I also discovered corgi reminiscences on BBC News, 21 November 2002; the *Guardian*, 22 November 2002; the *Independent*, 4 January 2004; David Nott on *Desert Island Discs*, BBC Radio 4, 10 June 2016; Andrew Parker Bowles's 'Diary', *Spectator*, 17 September 2022; *The Blunkett*

Tapes by David Blunkett; *Our Princesses and Their Dogs* by Michael Chance; 'How I drew Queen Elizabeth throughout her life' by Matt Pritchett, *Daily Telegraph*, 12 September 2022; and *Love from Nancy: The Letters of Nancy Mitford* edited by Charlotte Mosley. My chapter about the Duke and Duchess of York's inheritance of the late Queen's corgis was aided by close studies of *Hello!* magazine, 5 March 2023; BBC Radio 2, 2 April 2023; *Daily Telegraph*, 6 October 2022; *Sunday Times*, 8 April 2023; *Loose Women*, 5 April 2023; and *Royal Central*, 4 April 2023.

For the chapter on Tony Benn and his headless stamps, I enjoyed reading *Out of the Wilderness: Diaries 1963–67* by Tony Benn; *Who's In, Who's Out: The Journals of Kenneth Rose*, volume 1: *1944–1979* edited by D. R. Thorpe; *Downing Street Diary: With Harold Wilson in No. 10* by Bernard Donoughue; *The Alan Clark Diaries*; *The Backbench Diaries of Richard Crossman* and *The Diaries of a Cabinet Minister* by Richard Crossman edited by Janet Morgan; the introduction by Anthony Howard to his condensed edition of *The Crossman Diaries*; Hansard; and *Marcia Williams: The Life and Times of Baroness Falkender* by Linda McDougall.

The chapters on the Queen's forays into show business, first with James Bond and later with Paddington Bear, were greatly helped by an article by Frank Cottrell-Boyce in the *Observer*, 11 September 2022; a *Radio Times* interview with Danny Boyle, 27 April 2013; 'How Paddington acting role came naturally to the Queen' by Valentine Low in *The Times*, 21 October 2023; and 'Late Queen's surprising reply on why she was good at acting' by Victoria Ward in the *Daily Telegraph*, 21 October 2023.

My lengthy chapter on the Queen's Coronation was drawn from a wide range of eyewitness accounts and other sources, including *Villains' Paradise: Britain's Underworld from the Spivs to the Krays* by Donald Thomas; *A Most Dangerous Woman?* by Mary Whitehouse; *The Lives of Lucian Freud: Youth* by William Feaver; *The Sorcerer's Apprentice* by John Richardson; *Through a Glass Darkly: The Life of Patrick Hamilton* by Nigel Jones; *The Collected Letters of C. S. Lewis*, volume 2 edited by Walter Hooper; *Maurice Bowra: A Life* by Leslie

Mitchell; *P. G. Wodehouse: A Life in Letters* edited by Sophie Ratcliffe; Isaiah Berlin's *Enlightening: Letters 1946–1960* edited by Henry Hardy and Jennifer Holmes; *David Jones: Engraver, Soldier, Painter, Poet* by Thomas Dilworth; *Past Tense* by Jean Cocteau; *Time and Chance: An Autobiography* by Peter Townsend; *Cecil Beaton: The Authorized Biography* by Hugo Vickers; *A Queen for All Seasons* by Joanna Lumley; *The BBC: A People's History* by David Hendy; *Keep Talking: A Broadcasting Life* by David Dimbleby; *Farewell the Trumpets: An Imperial Retreat* by James Morris; *Richard Dimbleby, Broadcaster* edited by Leonard Miall; 'This England', *New Statesman*, 14 February 1953; 'The Queen is Crowned' by Margaret Lane (Countess of Huntingdon), *New Statesman*, 6 June 1953; *Coronation: The Crowning of Elizabeth II* by Hugo Vickers; 'Great Britain: Smiling in the Rain', *Time* magazine, 29 June 1953; interview with Cecil Beaton's two assistants at the Coronation, Ray Harwood and John Drysdale, *The Times*, 14 January 2012; *America's Queen: The Life of Jacqueline Kennedy Onassis* by Sarah Bradford; 'Just a face in the crowd at the 1953 Coronation ... Jackie O, the roving reporter', *Mail on Sunday*, 16 April 2023; *How We Celebrate the Coronation: Designs for a New Reign* by the Royal Fine Art Commission Trust; *Forget Not* by Margaret, Duchess of Argyll; article by Jonathan Mayo, *Daily Mail*, 28 May 2022; 'How the Queen's Coronation cartoon provoked a royal outrage', article in the *Guardian*, 1 June 2012; and, of course, the *Channon Diaries* and the *Beaton Diaries*.

The similarly panoramic though rather briefer chapter on the Silver Jubilee was taken from these sources: *When Giants Walked the Earth: A Biography of Led Zeppelin* by Mick Wall; *The Reunion: Silver Jubilee* on BBC Radio 4; *Laurie Lee: The Well-Loved Stranger* by Valerie Grove; *Conflicts of Interest: Diaries 1977–80* by Tony Benn; *The Kenneth Williams Diaries* and *Letters*, both edited by Russell Davies; *Illustrated London News* Silver Jubilee Edition; *The Diaries of Auberon Waugh: A Turbulent Decade 1976–1985*; *The Great British Dream Factory* by Dominic Sandbrook; *Private Eye*, 10 June 1977; *The Diaries* by Lindsay Anderson; *Sex Pistols: Live on Boat Trip, Queen's Jubilee 1977*, parts 1 and 2 (YouTube); *Punk Rock: An Oral History* by John Robb; *The Life &*

Times of Malcolm McLaren: The Biography by Paul Gorman; *Seventies* by Howard Sounes; *Richard Branson: The Inside Story* by Mick Brown; *Losing My Virginity: The Autobiography* by Richard Branson; *Becoming Johnny Vegas* by Johnny Vegas; *New Statesman* Jubilee Issue; *The Odd Thing About the Colonel & Other Pieces* by Colin Welch.

The contradictory reports about Michael Fagan's visit to the Queen's bedroom are to be found in *Majesty* by Robert Lacey; *Sovereign: Elizabeth II and the Windsor Dynasty* by Roland Flamini; *Elizabeth: Behind Palace Doors* by Nicholas Davies; *Behind Palace Doors: My Years with the Queen Mother* by Major Colin Burgess; *Elizabeth and Philip: The Untold Story* by Charles Higham and Roy Moseley; *The Crown* (Netflix drama series), episode 5, season 4; and interview with Michael Fagan by Emily Dugan, *Independent*, 19 February 2012. The Report by Scotland Yard on the 9 July 1982 security breach at Buckingham Palace offered me background information.

I had long been a PhD student of the event that pedants know as *Knockout: The Grand Charity Tournament* but which is generally referred to as *It's a Royal Knockout*. To make sure I wasn't dreaming, I checked *Knockout: The Grand Charity Tournament: A Behind-the-Scenes Look at the Event of the Year* with an Introduction by HRH The Prince Edward; *Knockout: The Grand Charity Tournament* (YouTube); *My Autobiography* by Paul Daniels; *My Story* by Sarah, Duchess of York; *My Life, My Way* by Cliff Richard; *The Dreamer: An Autobiography* by Cliff Richard; *Living Out Loud* by Toyah Willcox; interview with Meatloaf by Tim Dowling, *Guardian*, 5 May 2003; and *It's a Royal Knockout: The Untold Story* (Channel 5).

The chapter detailing the Queen's *annus horribilis* benefited from: *Shadows of a Princess* by P. D. Jephson; *Diana: Story of a Princess* by Tim Clayton and Phil Craig; *The Times Bedside Book 2* edited by Philip Howard; *The Diana Chronicles* by Tina Brown; *A Classless Society: Britain in the 1990s* by Alwyn M. Turner; Auberon Waugh's columns in the *Oldie* magazine, December 1992, January 1993; www.Royal.uk/annus-horribilis-speech; Christmas Broadcast 1992 transcript from www.royal.uk; as well as *A Royal Duty* by Paul Burrell and *Finding Sarah* by the Duchess of York, to which I have already alluded.

For my chapter on Anne Frank and her family, I read *Anne Frank: The Diary of a Young Girl: The Definitive Edition* edited by Otto H. Frank and Mirjam Pressler; and *Anne Frank: The Book, the Life, the Afterlife* by Francine Prose. I also watched 'Queen visits Germany's Bergen-Belsen concentration camp site', BBC News, 26 June 2015. For the chapter on the IRA atrocity in Co. Sligo on 27 August 1979, I read Timothy Knatchbull's memoir *From a Clear Blue Sky* and interviews with him by Lesley White in the *Sunday Times*, 23 August 2009, and Frances Hardy in the *Daily Mail*, 6 August 2010.

The often vexed lives of those poets who place themselves in the service of Royalty are well covered in: *John Betjeman: Letters*, volumes 1 and 2 edited and introduced by Candida Lycett Green; *John Betjeman: New Fame, New Love* and *John Betjeman: The Bonus of Laughter*, both by Bevis Hillier; *Betjeman* by A. N. Wilson; *Collected Poems* by John Betjeman; *Harvest Bells: New and Uncollected Poems* by John Betjeman; *Rain-Charm for the Duchy and other Laureate Poems* by Ted Hughes; *Letters of Ted Hughes* edited by Christopher Reid; *More Dynamite: Essays 1990–2012* by Craig Raine; *Poets by Appointment: Britain's Laureates* by Nick Russel; *Poetry Corner: Collected Verses from Thirty Years of Private Eye*; *Sleeping on Islands: A Life in Poetry* by Andrew Motion; *Me Again: Uncollected Writings of Stevie Smith*; *The Letters of T. S. Eliot to Emily Hale* edited by John Haffenden; *Night Thoughts: The Surreal Life of the Poet David Gascoyne* by Robert Fraser; *Selected Letters of Philip Larkin 1940–1985* edited by Anthony Thwaite; *Philip Larkin: Letters to Monica* edited by Anthony Thwaite; *Philip Larkin: Letters Home 1936–1977* edited by James Booth; *Having Larkin to Stay* by Ann Thwaite; Les Murray obituary, *Daily Telegraph*, 30 April 2019; Les Murray obituary by Michael Schmidt, *Guardian*, 1 May 2019; and Les Murray obituary, *The Times*, 3 June 2019. I also read the Manifesto of the Australian Commonwealth Party for the 1972 federal election.

I scoured a great many newspapers and magazines for details of the death of the Queen, her lying in state and her funeral. Particularly valuable were: *Elizabeth: An Intimate Portrait* by Gyles Brandreth; *Queen of Our Times* by Robert Hardman; *Charles III: New King, New*

Court: The Inside Story by Robert Hardman; *The Times*, 13 September 2022; *Spectator*, 17 September 2022; *Daily Mirror*, 15 September 2022; *Guardian* letters, 15 September 2022; *Private Eye*, 23 September 2022; Robert Hardman, *Daily Mail*, 15 September 2022; Christina Lamb, *Sunday Times*, 18 September 2022; Kaya Burgess, *The Times*, 17 September 2022; Neil Johnson, David Brown and Charlotte Wace, *The Times*, 16 September 2022; and 'England Exits Somber Mourning Period to Resume Joyless Normalcy' in the American satirical magazine the *Onion*, 26 September 2022.

For background to the post-war era and a wealth of telling details, I turned to the masterly series of books by two wonderfully alert historians: David Kynaston's *Austerity Britain 1945–51, Family Britain 1951–57, Modernity Britain 1957–59, Modernity Britain: A Shake of the Dice 1959–62, On the Cusp: Days of '62* and *A Northern Wind: Britain 1962–65*; and Dominic Sandbrook's *Never Had It So Good: A History of Britain from Suez to the Beatles, White Heat: A History of Britain in the Swinging Sixties, State of Emergency: Britain 1970–1974, Seasons in the Sun: Britain 1974–1979* and *Who Dares Wins: Britain 1979–1982*. Also: *Our Times* and *After the Victorians*, both by A. N. Wilson; *The Fifties* by Peter Vansittart; *The Beatles All These Years*, volume 1: *Tune In* by Mark Lewisohn; *Eminent Elizabethans* by Piers Brendon; *Armchair Nation* by Joe Moran; *All In It Together* by Alwyn M. Turner; *Strange Days Indeed: The Golden Age of Paranoia* by Francis Wheen; *Letters from London 1990–1995* by Julian Barnes; *International Gossip: A History of High Society 1970–1980* by Andrew Barrow; and *The Reign: Life in Elizabeth's Britain, Part 1: The Way It Was 1952–79* by Matthew Engel.

Finally, a broad variety of miscellaneous books and articles have been invaluable to my kaleidoscopic or scattergun approach. These include: *By Royal Command* by Bill Pertwee; *Voices Out of the Air: The Royal Christmas Broadcasts 1932–1981* introduced by Tom Fleming; *Treetops: Story of a World Famous Hotel* by R. J. Prickett; *Royal Bodies: Writing about the Windsors from the* London Review of Books; *The Queen & I: The Life of a Lookalike* by Jeannette Charles; 'I'm Elizabeth ... the second!', interview with Jeannette Charles by Jane Fryer, *Daily*

Mail, 28 May 2022; 'I've been a Queen lookalike for 50 years', *Guardian*, 27 May 2022; *Marriage of Her Royal Highness The Princess Elizabeth and Lieutenant Philip Mountbatten R.N.: List of Wedding Gifts*; 'Now, about that passport …', interview by Tim Adams with Mohamed Fayed, *Observer*, 25 August 2002; *To Tread on Royal Toes* by Ray Bellisario; *The Wit of Prince Philip* compiled by Peter Butler; *The Shameful Life of Salvador Dalí* by Ian Gibson; *Grand Inquisitor* by Robin Day; *Margaret Thatcher: The Authorized Biography*, volumes 1, 2 and 3 by Charles Moore; *Margaret Thatcher*, volume 2: *The Iron Lady* by John Campbell; *Full Disclosure* by Andrew Neil; *Listening for a Midnight Tram: The Memoirs of John Junor*; *Lord's Ladies and Gentlemen: 100 Legends of the 20th Century* by Graham Lord; Charles Moore column, *Spectator*, 21/28 December 1985; *The Oxford Book of Royal Anecdotes* edited by Elizabeth Longford; *The Rise and Fall of the House of Windsor* by A. N. Wilson; 'All the Queen's Men: The Monarch and Her Ministers' by Alan Watkins in *The Queen Observed* edited by Trevor Grove; *Debrett's Correct Form*; *The New Biographical Dictionary of Film* by David Thomson; *England, Your England* by George Orwell; *Madame Tussaud's Chamber of Horrors* by Pauline Chapman; *The Peep Show* by Kate Summerscale; 'Rillington Place: What John Christie's residential burial ground looks like now', report in the *Independent*, 24 November 2016; *William Empson*, Vol II: *Against the Christians* by John Haffenden; *Indirect Journey: An Autobiography* by Harold Hobson; *Sybille Bedford: An Appetite for Life* by Selina Hastings; *Two Lucky People: The Memoirs of Milton and Rose D. Friedman*; *Vanderbilt: The Rise and Fall of an American Dynasty* by Anderson Cooper and Katherine Howe; *Michael Ramsey: A Life* by Owen Chadwick; *Gimson's Kings and Queens* by Andrew Gimson; *A Lonely Business: A Self-Portrait of James Pope-Hennessy* edited by Peter Quennell; *Read My Lips: A Treasury of Things Politicians Wish They Hadn't Said* by Matthew Parris and Phil Mason; *20th Century Words* by John Ayto; *The Book of Common Prayer*; *The Book of Human Emotions* by Tiffany Watt Smith; *Lantern Lecture* by Adam Mars-Jones; *Confessions: A Life of Failed Promises* by A. N. Wilson; *The Powerful and the Damned* by Lionel Barber; *The Lost Diaries* edited by Craig Brown; *This Is Craig*

Brown by Craig Brown; various collections of 'This England' columns from the *New Statesman*; *20th Century Anecdotes* compiled by Frank S. Pepper; *Point to Point Navigation* by Gore Vidal; 'The Curious Rules Behind Royal Women and Curtsying' by Sophia Money-Coutts, *Daily Telegraph*, 18 October 2022; *Days of Majesty* by Simon Welfare and Alastair Bruce; *Barbara Cartland's Book of Etiquette*; *The Collector* by John Fowles; *Debrett's Book of the Royal Engagement* by Jean Goodman and David Williamson; *The Rough Guide to Conspiracy Theories* by James McConnachie and Robin Tudge; 'The Queen's Speech, the Queen's Heart', essay by Martin Amis in the *New Yorker*, May 2002; Royalty, Fine Art and Antiques sale, Tuesday 8 November 2022 Catalogue, Reeman Dansie Auctioneers; *Nina Simone's Gum* by Warren Ellis; *George Lyttelton's Commonplace Book*; *Once Upon a Time in Northern Ireland*, episode 2 (BBC Two); *The Unconventional Minister* by Geoffrey Robinson; *Kind of Blue* by Kenneth Clarke; *Storyteller: The Many Lives of Laurens van der Post* by J. D. F. Jones; 'Master Storyteller or Master Deceiver?' by Dinitia Smith, *New York Times*, 3 August 2002; *The Royal Yacht Britannia Official Souvenir Guidebook*; *The Royal Yacht Britannia Official Audioguide*; *Lucky George: Memoirs of an Anti-Politician* by George Walden; *London Millennium Celebration with Queen Elizabeth*, hosted by Peter Jennings on ABC (YouTube); Sarah Bradford, *Spectator*, 8 April 2006; *The Quest for Queen Mary* by James Pope-Hennessy edited by Hugo Vickers; *Private Eye's Starbores* illustrated by Michael Heath; *The Palace Papers* by Tina Brown; *Dick Hern: The Authorised Biography* by Peter Willett; *Of Horses and Heroes* by Brough Scott; *Daydream Believer* by Hugh Massingberd; *Diana's Mourning: A People's History* by James Thomas; and *Queen Elizabeth* by Maria Isabel Sánchez Vegara. Enough!

ACKNOWLEDGEMENTS

Thanks to: Louise Haines, who edited it, Nicholas Pearson, who commissioned it, Peter James, who copy-edited it, Katy Archer, who put it all together, Naomi Mantin, who publicised it, Ola Galewicz, who designed the cover, Cecily Engle, who sealed the deal, Jonathan Galassi, who edited the US edition, and Emma Chichester Clark, who drew the endpiece. Thanks also to: Victoria Pullen, Zoe Shine, Sarah Davis, Oliver Rowse, Nicola Shulman, Frances Spragge, Martin Higgins, Hector Browne, Mary and Johnny James and all at The Aldeburgh Bookshop, the staff of the London Library, Dan Franklin, Rebecca Hossack, Matthew Sturgis, Craig Raine, A.N. Wilson, Olivia Marsden, Matt Clacher, Paul Erdpresser, Chris Gurney, Graham Holmes, Hugo Vickers, D.J. Taylor, Julie Brook, Mark Cousins, Georgina Brown, Frances Wilson, Bill Keegan, the late Olinda Adeane, Brough Scott, Jamie Reid, Malise Ruthven, Paul Keegan, and all those who shared their stories with me but who, for one reason or another, preferred to stay in the shadows. Above all, thanks to my wife Frances, without whose constant encouragement I could never have written it. This book is dedicated to her, and to our family: Tallulah and Tom, Silas and Sarah, Rosie, Bram and Iris, as well as to our next grandchild, due a few weeks before publication.

ILLUSTRATION CREDITS

125: Jeannette Charles and her extended 'royal family', parkerphotography/Alamy Stock Photo

135: Queen Mary, Carpenter/ Central Press/Getty Images

148: Margaret, Duchess of Argyll, Baron/Hulton Archive/Getty Images

157: The coronation, Trinity Mirror/Mirrorpix/Alamy Stock Photo

161: Ringo Starr at a street party

165: The Duke and Duchess of Windsor watch the coronation from Paris, PA Images/Alamy Stock Photo

174: Waving from the balcony at Buckingham Palace, Keystone/ Hulton Archive/Getty Images

177: Rillington Place, TopFoto

180: 'Bald' waxwork of the Queen, dpa picture alliance/Alamy Stock Photo

183: Selfies with Her Majesty, author's own image

184: The Queen delivering the first Christmas message broadcast on television, Royal Collection Trust/© His Majesty King Charles III, 2024

202: The Queen applies her lipstick, David Levenson/Getty Images

206: Harold Pinter, Don Smith/ Radio Times/Getty Images

218: The Beatles with their MBEs, PA Images/Alamy Stock Photo

226: Cecil Beaton, © Hulton-Deutsch Collection/CORBIS/ Getty Images

231: *Death in Venice*, Everett Collection Inc/Alamy Stock Photo

237: The Queen meets Marilyn Monroe, PA Images/Alamy Stock Photo

242: Curtsies, Max Mumby/Indigo/ Getty Images

247: A smiling queen, Daily Mirror/Mirrorpix/Getty Images

253: Patrick White, Fairfax Media/ Getty Images

268: The investiture of the Prince of Wales, Keystone Press/Alamy Stock Photo

274: Newspapers, Paul Popper/ Popperfoto/Getty Images

277: The Royal Family with baby Prince Andrew, © Cecil Beaton/ Victoria and Albert Museum, London

282: Morrissey, Neil H Kitson/ Redferns/Getty Images

286: Jackie Kennedy visits England, Keystone Press/Alamy Stock Photo

288: Jackie Kennedy and the Queen, Bettmann/Getty Images

303: *The Birds*, Universal History Archive/UIG/Getty images

313: Tony Benn and the Queen, Jim Gray/Keystone/Getty Images

335: John Betjeman, Stuart William MacGladrie/Fairfax Media/ Getty Images

342: Philip Larkin at John Betjeman's funeral, Daily Express/Hulton Archive/Getty Images

353: 'God Save the Queen', The Sex Pistols, M&N/Alamy Stock Photo

358: Kenneth Williams, Jeremy Grayson/Radio Times/Getty Images

365: 'Great Bores of Today' cartoon, taken from *Private Eye: The 60 Yearbook*. Used with kind permission of Ian Hislop

366: Silver Jubilee celebrations, Chronicle/Alamy Stock Photo

369: Douglas Cooper, Robert DOISNEAU/Gamma-Rapho/Getty Images

370: Putin and the Queen, © Pool Photograph/Corbis/Corbis/Getty Images

371: Trump and the Queen, WPA Pool/Getty Images

375: Ceaucescu and the Queen, Central Press/Getty Images

384: Robert Maxwell with the Queen, Bettmann/Getty Images

389: A mural of the Queen on Shankhill Road, Ian M Butterfield (Ireland)/Alamy Stock Photo

401: At the races, Anwar Hussein/Getty Images

410: The Queen and Lord Porchester at the races, Daily Mirror/Mirrorpix/Getty Images

416: Les Murray meets the Queen, Fiona Hanson/Alamy Stock Photo

433: Margaret Thatcher and the Queen, PA Photos/TopFoto

446: *Royal Family* documentary, Hulton Archive/Getty Images

450: The Duke and Duchess of Kent, Princess Anne and Prince Edward at 'It's a Royal Knockout', taken from *Knockout: The Grand Charity Tournament* (Harper Collins, 1987)

452: A vegetable race, taken from *Knockout: The Grand Charity Tournament*

469: *Annus Horribilis*, PA Images/Alamy Stock Photo

483: The Queen on *Britannia*, Lichfield Archive/Getty Images

487: The Queen's sitting room on *Britannia*, Keystone/Hulton Archive/Getty Images

544: Lucien Freud painting the Queen, Private collection © David Dawson. All rights reserved 2024/Bridgeman Images

549: The Queen shaking hands, Fiona Hanson/Tim Graham Picture Library/Getty Images

561: Rolf Harris with his portrait of the Queen, Chris Jackson/Getty Images

567: James Bond and the Queen, Lars Baron/Getty Images

568: 'The Queen' jumps from a helicopter during the opening ceremony of the Olympic Games in London, 2012, STAFF/AFP/Getty Images

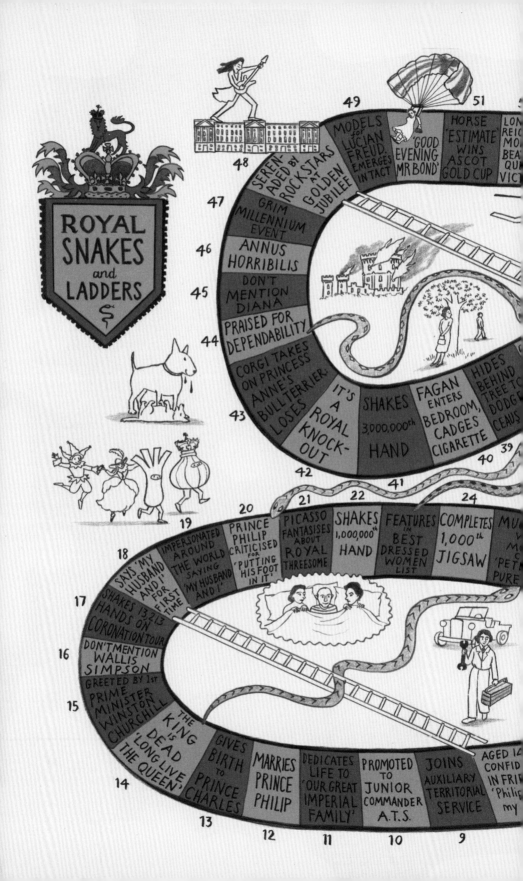